CLYMER® MANUALS

HONDA
VTX1300 SERIES • 2003-2009

WHAT'S IN YOUR TOOLBOX?

Copyright ©2010 Penton Business Media, Inc.

FIRST EDITION
First Printing May, 2010
Second Printing June, 2013

Printed in U.S.A.

CLYMER and colophon are registered trademarks of Penton Business Media, Inc.

ISBN-10: 1-59969-339-9

ISBN-13: 978-1-59969-339-2

Library of Congress: 2010925871

AUTHOR: Ron Wright.

TECHNICAL PHOTOGRAPHY: Ron Wright. Special thanks to Stewart Johnson and Ishwarpreet Brar for shop assistance and parts/technical expert Gabe Ortiz at Clawson Motorsports, Fresno, CA.

TECHNICAL ILLUSTRATIONS: Steve Amos.

WIRING DIAGRAMS: Bob Meyer.

EDITOR: Steve Thomas.

PRODUCTION: Kendra Lueckert.

TOOLS AND EQUIPMENT: K & L Supply Co. at www.klsupply.com.

COVER: Mark Clifford Photography at www.markclifford.com. Motorcycle courtesy of Bert's Mega Mall at bertsmegamall.com, Covina, CA.

All rights reserved. Reproduction or use, without express permission, of editorial or pictorial content, in any manner, is prohibited. No patent liability is assumed with respect to the use of the information contained herein. While every precaution has been taken in the preparation of this book, the publisher assumes no responsibility for errors or omissions. Neither is any liability assumed for damages resulting from use of the information contained herein. Publication of the servicing information in this manual does not imply approval of the manufacturers of the products covered.

All instructions and diagrams have been checked for accuracy and ease of application; however, success and safety in working with tools depend to a great extent upon individual accuracy, skill and caution. For this reason, the publishers are not able to guarantee the result of any procedure contained herein. Nor can they assume responsibility for any damage to property or injury to persons occasioned from the procedures. Persons engaging in the procedure do so entirely at their own risk.

Chapter One
General Information

Chapter Two
Troubleshooting

Chapter Three
Lubrication, Maintenance and Tune-up

Chapter Four
Engine Top End

Chapter Five
Engine Lower End

Chapter Six
Clutch and External Shift Mechanism

Chapter Seven
Transmission and Internal Shift Mechanism

Chapter Eight
Fuel and Emission Control Systems

Chapter Nine
Electrical System

Chapter Ten
Cooling System

Chapter Eleven
Wheels and Tires

Chapter Twelve
Front Suspension and Steering

Chapter Thirteen
Rear Suspension

Chapter Fourteen
Brakes

Chapter Fifteen
Body and Exhaust System

Index

Wiring Diagrams

Associate Publisher James Grooms

EDITORIAL
Content Director
James Grooms

Editor
Steven Thomas

Associate Editor
Rick Arens

Authors
Ed Scott
Ron Wright
Michael Morlan
George Parise
Jay Bogart

Illustrators
Bob Meyer
Steve Amos
Errol McCarthy
Mitzi McCarthy

MARKETING
Marketing Manager
Steven Thomas

SALES
Sales Manager–Powersport/Marine/I&T
Matt Tusken

CUSTOMER SERVICE
Customer Service Manager
Terri Cannon

Customer Service Representatives
Becky Bigham
Dinah Bunnell
April LeBlond
Sherry Rudkin

PRODUCTION
Director of Production
Dylan Goodwin

Group Production Manager
Greg Araujo

Project Managers
Darin Watson
Adriane Wineinger

Production Editor
Ashley Bally

Associate Production Editor
Samantha Collins

P.O. Box 12901, Overland Park, KS 66282-2901 • 800-262-1954 • 913-967-1719

More information available at *clymer.com*

CONTENTS

QUICK REFERENCE DATA IX

CHAPTER ONE
GENERAL INFORMATION 1
    Manual organization
    Warnings, cautions and notes
    Safety
    Serial numbers and information labels
    Fasteners
    Shop supplies
    Tools
    Measuring tools
    Electrical system fundamentals
    Service methods
    Storage
    Specifications

CHAPTER TWO
TROUBLESHOOTING 30
    Starting the engine
    Engine will not start
    Poor engine performance
    Fuel system
    Engine
    Engine lubrication
    Cylinder leakdown test
    Clutch
    Gearshift linkage
    Transmission
    Electrical testing
    Final drive
    Front suspension and steering
    Brake system

CHAPTER THREE
LUBRICATION, MAINTENANCE AND TUNE-UP 50

- Tune-up
- Engine rotation
- Air filter
- Crankcase breather inspection
- Engine compression test
- Spark plugs
- Ignition timing
- Valve clearance
- Idle speed adjustment
- Fuel system hose inspection
- Fuel filter
- Throttle cable
- Clutch cable and clutch lever
- Engine oil and filter
- Engine oil pressure check
- Cooling system
- Pulse secondary air supply system
- Evaporative emission control system
- Battery
- Final drive oil
- Tires and wheels
- Steering bearings
- Front suspension
- Rear suspension
- Brakes
- Headlight
- Sidestand and ignition cut-off switch test
- Front fork oil
- Fastener inspection
- Specifications

CHAPTER FOUR
ENGINE TOP END 79

- Cylinder head covers and rocker arms
- Camshafts
- Cam chain tensioner and cam chain
- Cylinder head
- Valves and valve components
- Cylinder
- Piston and piston rings
- Cylinder stud
- Specifications

CHAPTER FIVE
ENGINE LOWER END 116

- Servicing engine in frame
- Engine
- Crankcase
- Crankcase seal and bearing
- Crankshaft
- Connecting rods
- Balancer shafts
- Oil pump
- Output gear
- Engine break-in
- Specifications

CHAPTER SIX
CLUTCH AND EXTERNAL SHIFT MECHANISM 148

- Right crankcase cover
- Clutch
- Clutch release assembly
- Primary drive and driven gears and oil pump chain and sprockets
- External shift mechanism
- Clutch cable
- Specifications

CHAPTER SEVEN
TRANSMISSION AND INTERNAL SHIFT MECHANISM 168

- Transmission
- Internal shift mechanism
- Specifications

CHAPTER EIGHT
FUEL AND EMISSION CONTROL SYSTEMS 177

Fuel system differences
Fuel tank
Fuel valve
Air filter housing
Carburetor
Intake manifold
Pilot screw adjustment (idle drop procedure)
High altitude adjustment

Throttle cable
Choke cable
Fuel pump and fuel filter
Crankcase breather system
Pulse secondary air supply system
Evaporative emission control system
Specifications

CHAPTER NINE
ELECTRICAL SYSTEM. 211

Electrical component replacement
Electrical connectors
Battery
Battery box
Charging system
Stator coil, ignition pulse generator
  and left crankcase cover
Flywheel, starter clutch and starter
  drive gears
Ignition system testing
Ignition coils
Ignition pulse generator
Ignition control module (ICM)
Throttle position sensor (TPS)
Starter system troubleshooting
Starter
Starter relay switch
Clutch diode
Lighting system
Meter assembly

Vehicle speed sensor (VSS)
Coolant temperature indicator and engine
  coolant temperature (ECT) sensor
Fan switch
Oil pressure switch and oil pressure indicator
Neutral switch
Sidestand switch
Clutch switch
Front brake light switch
Rear brake light switch
Ignition switch
Handlebar switch
Switch continuity test
Turn signal relay
Fuel cutoff relay
Horn
Fuses
Wiring diagrams
Specifications

CHAPTER TEN
COOLING SYSTEM. 265

Cooling system
Radiator
Cooling fan
Coolant reserve tank

Thermostat
Thermostat housing
Water pump
Specifications

CHAPTER ELEVEN
WHEELS AND TIRES. 275

Motorcycle lift
Front wheel
Rear wheel
Front and rear hubs
Driven flange

Wheel service
Tires
Wheel balance
Specifications

CHAPTER TWELVE
FRONT SUSPENSION AND STEERING 298
Handlebar
Handlebar grips
Front fork
Steering head and stem
Steering bearing preload check
Steering head bearing race
Steering stem bearing race
Specifications

CHAPTER THIRTEEN
REAR SUSPENSION 322
Shock absorber
Swing arm
Final drive unit and drive shaft
Final drive unit overhaul
Ring and pinion gear measurements
Specifications

CHAPTER FOURTEEN
BRAKES 349
Brake service
Brake bleeding
Brake fluid draining and flushing
Brake pads
Brake caliper
Front master cylinder
Rear master cylinder and brake pedal
Brake hose and brake pipe
Brake disc
Specifications

CHAPTER FIFTEEN
BODY AND EXHAUST SYSTEM 377
Seat
Side covers
Cylinder head shroud
Cylinder head fin cover
Left crankcase rear cover
Steering side cover
Front fender
Rear fender
Rider footrests
Sidestand
Windshield
Backrest and saddlebags
Exhaust system
Specifications

INDEX 392

WIRING DIAGRAMS 399

QUICK REFERENCE DATA

MOTORCYCLE INFORMATION

MODEL: _____ YEAR: _____

VIN NUMBER: _____

ENGINE SERIAL NUMBER: _____

CARBURETOR IDENTIFICATION NUMBER OR I.D. MARK: _____

IGNITION KEY NUMBER: _____

COLOR LABEL NUMBER: _____

TIRE INFLATION PRESSURE AND TREAD DEPTH*

	Front kPa (psi)	Rear kPa (psi)
Tire pressure		
Up to 90 kg (200 lb.) load	225 (33)	225 (33)
Maximum weight capacity	225 (33)	250 (36)
Tread depth (minimum)	1.5 mm (0.06)	2.0 mm (0.08 in.)

*Specifications are for original equipment tires. Aftermarket tires may have different specifications.

RECOMMENDED LUBRICANTS AND FUEL

Brake fluid	DOT 4 brake fluid
Cooling system	
Type	Honda HP Coolant or equivalent[1]
Standard concentration	50:50 mixture coolant and purified water
Engine oil	
Classification	
JASCO T 903	MA
API	SG or higher[2]
Viscosity	SAE 10W-30
Final drive gear oil	Hypoid gear oil, SAE 80
Fork oil	Pro Honda Suspension Fluid SS-8 or equivalent 10 wt fork oil
Fuel	Unleaded gasoline with a pump octane number of 86 or higher

1. Coolant must not contain silicate inhibitors as they can cause premature wear to the water pump seals. Refer to text for further information.
2. API SG or higher classified oils not specified as ENERGY CONSERVING can be used. Refer to Chapter One for additional information.

ENGINE OIL CAPACITY

	Liters	qt.
Engine oil change only	3.5	3.7
Engine oil and filter change	3.7	3.9
Engine disassembly	4.3	4.5

COOLANT CAPACITY

	Liters	qt.
Radiator and engine	2.7	2.9
Reserve tank	0.95	1.0

FINAL DRIVE OIL CAPACITY

	mL	oz.
After overhaul	150	5.1
Oil change	120	4.1

MAINTENANCE TORQUE SPECIFICATIONS

	N•m	in.-lb.	ft.-lb.
Air filter cover screw	4	35	–
Coolant drain bolt	13	115	–
Engine oil drain bolts*	30	–	22
Engine oil filter	26	–	19
Exhaust valve adjustment cover*	15	–	11
Final drive oil drain bolt*	20	–	15
Final drive oil fill cap	12	106	–
Front master cylinder reservoir cover screw	1.5	13	–
Rear brake reservoir cover mounting bolt	10	88	–
Spark plug	14	–	10
Spoke nipples	4.2	37	–
Timing hole cap*	18	–	13
Timing hole cap cover Allen bolt	10	88	–
Valve adjust screw locknut	22	–	16

*Refer to text for additional information.

CHAPTER ONE

GENERAL INFORMATION

This detailed and comprehensive manual covers the Honda VTX1300 models from 2003-2009. The text provides complete information on maintenance, tune-up, repair and overhaul. Hundreds of photos and drawings guide the reader through every job. All procedures are in step-by-step format and designed for the reader who may be working on the motorcycle for the first time.

MANUAL ORGANIZATION

A shop manual is a reference tool and, as in all Clymer manuals, the chapters are thumb-tabbed for easy reference. Important items are indexed at the end of the manual. Frequently used specifications and capacities from individual chapters are summarized in the *Quick Reference Data* at the front of the manual.

During some of the procedures there will be references to headings in other chapters or sections of the manual. When a specific heading is called out in a step it is *italicized* as it appears in the manual. If a sub-heading is indicated as being "in this section" it is located within the same main heading. For example, the sub-heading *Handling Gasoline Safely* is located within the main heading *SAFETY*.

This chapter provides general information on shop safety, tool use, service fundamentals and shop supplies. **Tables 1-7** at the end of the chapter provide general motorcycle, mechanical and shop information.

Chapter Two provides methods for quick and accurate diagnoses of problems. Troubleshooting procedures present typical symptoms and logical methods to pinpoint and repair a problem.

Chapter Three explains all routine maintenance.

Subsequent chapters describe specific systems, such as engine, clutch, gearbox, transmission shafts, fuel system, exhaust system, drive system, suspension, brakes and body components.

Specification tables, when applicable, are located at the end of each chapter.

WARNINGS, CAUTIONS AND NOTES

The terms WARNING, CAUTION and NOTE have specific meanings in this manual.

A WARNING emphasizes areas where injury or even death could result from negligence. Mechanical damage may also occur. WARNINGS are to be taken seriously.

A CAUTION emphasizes areas where equipment damage could result. Disregarding a CAUTION could cause permanent mechanical damage, though injury is unlikely.

A NOTE provides additional information to make a step or procedure easier or clearer. Disregarding a NOTE could cause inconvenience, but would not cause equipment damage or injury.

CHAPTER ONE

SAFETY

Refer to the following guidelines and practice common sense to safely work on the motorcycle:

1. Do not operate the motorcycle in an enclosed area. The exhaust gases contain carbon monoxide, an odorless, colorless and tasteless poisonous gas. Carbon monoxide levels build quickly in small enclosed areas and can cause unconsciousness and death in a short time. Make sure the work area is properly ventilated, or operate the motorcycle outside.
2. *Never* use gasoline or any flammable liquid to clean parts. Refer to *Handling Gasoline Safely* and *Cleaning Parts* in this section.
3. *Never* smoke or use a torch in the vicinity of flammable liquids, such as gasoline or cleaning solvent.
4. Do not remove the radiator cap or cooling system hose while the engine is hot. The cooling system is pressurized and the high temperature coolant may cause injury.
5. Dispose of and store coolant in a safe manner. Do not allow children or pets access to open containers of coolant. Animals are attracted to antifreeze.
6. Avoid contact with engine oil and other chemicals. Most are known carcinogens. Wash your hands thoroughly after coming in contact with engine oil. If possible, wear a pair of disposable gloves.
7. If welding or brazing on the motorcycle, remove the fuel tank and shocks to a safe distance at least 50 ft. (15 m) away.
8. Use the correct types and sizes of tools to avoid damaging fasteners.
9. Keep tools clean and in good condition. Replace or repair worn or damaged equipment.
10. When loosening a tight fastener, be guided by what would happen if the tool slips.
11. When replacing fasteners, make sure the new fasteners are the same size and strength as the originals.
12. Keep the work area clean and organized.
13. Wear eye protection *any time* the safety of your eyes is in question. This includes procedures involving drilling, grinding, hammering, compressed air and chemicals.
14. Wear the correct clothing for the job. Tie up or cover long hair so it can not catch in moving equipment.
15. Do not carry sharp tools in clothing pockets.
16. Always have an approved fire extinguisher available. Make sure it is rated for gasoline (Class B) and electrical (Class C) fires.
17. Do not use compressed air to clean clothes, the motorcycle or the work area. Debris may be blown into the eyes or skin. *Never* direct compressed air at anyone. Do not allow children to use or play with any compressed air equipment.

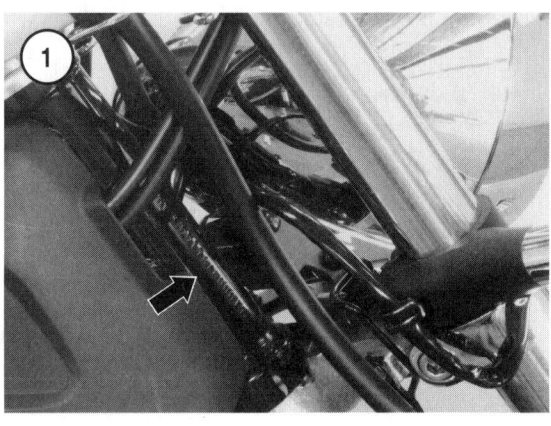

18. When using compressed air to dry rotating parts, hold the part so it cannot rotate. Do not allow the force of the air to spin the part. The air jet is capable of rotating parts at extreme speeds. The part may be damaged or disintegrate, causing serious injury.
19. Do not inhale the dust created by brake pad and clutch wear. These particles may contain asbestos. In addition, some types of insulating materials and gaskets may contain asbestos. Inhaling asbestos particles is hazardous to health.
20. Never work on the motorcycle while someone is working under it.
21. When placing the motorcycle on a stand or overhead lift, make sure it is secure before walking away.

Handling Gasoline Safely

Gasoline is a volatile flammable liquid and is one of the most dangerous items in the shop. Because gasoline is used so often, many people forget that it is hazardous. Only use gasoline as fuel for gasoline internal combustion engines. Keep in mind when working on a motorcycle, gasoline is always present in the fuel tank, fuel line and carburetor. To avoid an accident when working around the fuel system, carefully observe the following precautions:

1. *Never* use gasoline to clean parts. Refer to *Cleaning Parts* in this section.
2. When working on the fuel system, work outside or in a well-ventilated area.
3. Do not add fuel to the fuel tank or service the fuel system while the motorcycle is near open flames, sparks or where someone is smoking. Gasoline vapor is heavier than air, collects in low areas and is more easily ignited than liquid gasoline.
4. Allow the engine to cool completely before working on any fuel system component.
5. Do not store gasoline in glass containers. If the glass breaks, an explosion or fire may occur.

GENERAL INFORMATION

6. Immediately wipe up spilled gasoline with rags. Store the rags in a metal container with a lid until they can be properly disposed, or place them outside in a safe place for the fuel to evaporate.
7. Do not pour water onto a gasoline fire. Water spreads the fire and makes it more difficult to put out. Use a class B, BC or ABC fire extinguisher to extinguish the fire.
8. Always turn off the engine before refueling. Do not spill fuel onto the engine or exhaust system. Do not overfill the fuel tank. Leave an air space at the top of the tank to allow room for the fuel to expand due to temperature fluctuations.

Cleaning Parts

Cleaning parts is one of the more tedious and difficult service jobs performed in the home garage. Many types of chemical cleaners and solvents are available for shop use. Most are poisonous and extremely flammable. To prevent chemical exposure, vapor buildup, fire and injury, observe each product's warning label and note the following:
1. Read and observe the entire product label before using any chemical. Always know what type of chemical is being used and whether it is poisonous and/or flammable.
2. Do not use more than one type of cleaning solvent at a time. If mixing chemicals is required, measure the proper amounts according to the manufacturer.
3. Work in a well-ventilated area.
4. Wear chemical-resistant gloves.
5. Wear safety glasses.
6. Wear a vapor respirator if the instructions call for it.
7. Wash hands and arms thoroughly after cleaning parts.
8. Keep chemicals away from children and pets, especially coolant. Animals are attracted to antifreeze.
9. Thoroughly clean all oil, grease and cleaner residue from any part that must be heated.
10. Use a nylon brush when cleaning parts. Metal brushes may cause a spark.
11. When using a parts washer, only use the solvent recommended by the manufacturer. Make sure the parts washer is equipped with a metal lid that will lower in case of fire.

Warning Labels

Most manufacturers attach information and warning labels to the motorcycle. These labels contain instructions that are important to safety when operating, servicing, transporting and storing the motorcycle. Refer to the owner's manual for the description and location of labels. Order replacement labels from the manufacturer if they are missing or damaged.

SERIAL NUMBERS AND INFORMATION LABELS

Serial numbers are located on the frame, engine and carburetor. Record these numbers in the *Quick Reference Data* section in the front of the manual. Have these numbers available when ordering parts.

The vehicle identification label (VIN) is located on the right side of the steering head (**Figure 1**).

The engine serial number is stamped on the left side of the crankcase (A, **Figure 2**).

The safety certification label is attached on the front, left side frame tube (**Figure 3**).

The carburetor identification number is stamped on the throttle position sensor side of the carburetor body (**Figure 4**).

The color label is attached to the left middle frame tube (B, **Figure 2**). Always refer to this number when ordering painted parts.

Labels for tire pressure, emission control, paint code, dealership service and other miscellaneous data are located under the seat on the rear fender and on various other places on the motorcycle.

FASTENERS

> *WARNING*
> *Do not install fasteners with a strength classification lower than what was originally installed by the manufacturer. Doing so may cause equipment failure and/or damage.*

Proper fastener selection and installation is important to ensure the motorcycle operates as designed and can be serviced efficiently. The choice of original equipment fasteners is not arrived at by chance. Make sure replacement fasteners meet the requirements.

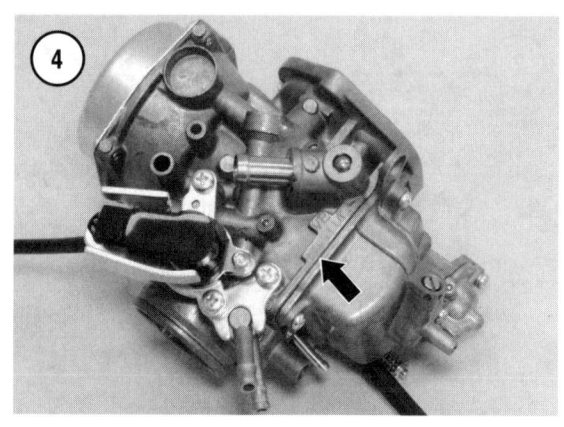

Threaded Fasteners

Threaded fasteners secure most of the components on the motorcycle. Most are tightened by turning them clockwise (right-hand threads). If the normal rotation of the component being tightened would loosen the fastener, it may have left-hand threads. If a left-hand threaded fastener is used, it is noted in the text.

Two dimensions are required to match the thread size of the fastener: the number of threads in a given distance and the outside diameter of the threads.

Two systems are currently used to specify threaded fastener dimensions: the U.S. Standard system and the metric system. Pay particular attention when working with unidentified fasteners; mismatching thread types can damage threads.

To ensure the fastener threads are not mismatched or cross-threaded, start all fasteners by hand. If a fastener is difficult to start or turn, determine the cause before tightening with a wrench.

Match fasteners by their length (L, **Figure 5**), diameter (D) and distance between thread crests (pitch, T). A typical metric bolt may be identified by the numbers, 8—1.25 × 130. This indicates the bolt has a diameter of 8 mm, the distance between thread crests is 1.25 mm and the length is 130 mm. Always measure bolt length as shown in L, **Figure 5** to avoid installing replacements of the wrong lengths.

If a number is located on the top of a metric fastener (**Figure 5**), this indicates the strength. The higher the number, the stronger the fastener. Typically, unnumbered fasteners are the weakest.

Many screws, bolts and studs are combined with nuts to secure particular components. To indicate the size of a nut, manufacturers specify the internal diameter and thread pitch.

The measurement across two flats on a nut or bolt indicates the wrench size.

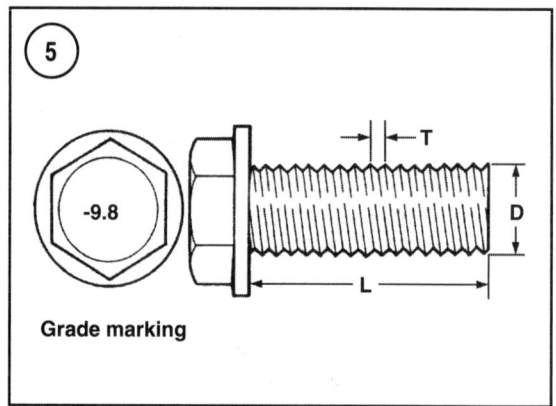

Grade marking

Torque Specifications

The materials used in the manufacture of the motorcycle may be subjected to uneven stresses if fasteners are not installed and tightened correctly. Improperly installed fasteners or ones that worked loose can cause extensive damage. It is essential to use an accurate torque wrench, as described in *Tools* in this chapter, with the torque specifications in this manual.

Specifications for torque are provided in Newton-meters (N•m), foot-pounds (ft.-lb.) and inch-pounds (in.-lb.). Refer to **Table 7** for general torque recommendations. To use **Table 7**, first determine the size of the fastener as described in *Threaded Fasteners* in this section. Torque specifications for specific components are at the end of the appropriate chapters. Torque wrenches are covered in *Tools* in this chapter.

Self-Locking Fasteners

Several types of bolts, screws and nuts incorporate a system that creates interference between the two fasteners. Interference is achieved in various ways. The most common types used are those with a nylon insert nut and those with a dry adhesive coating on the threads of a bolt.

GENERAL INFORMATION

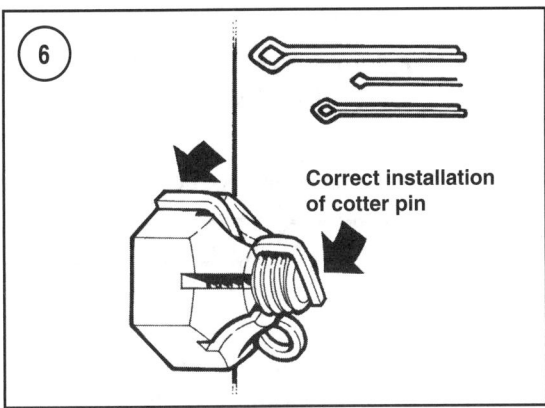

Correct installation of cotter pin

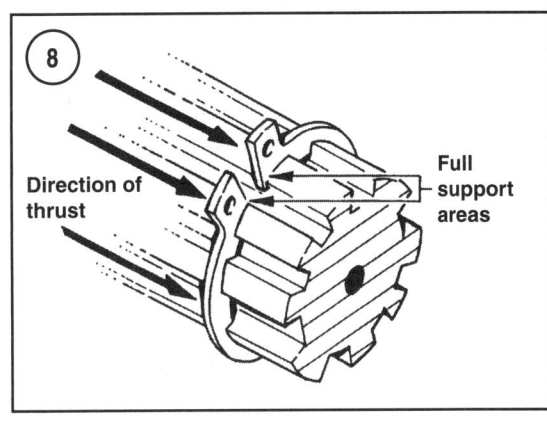

Direction of thrust — **Full support areas**

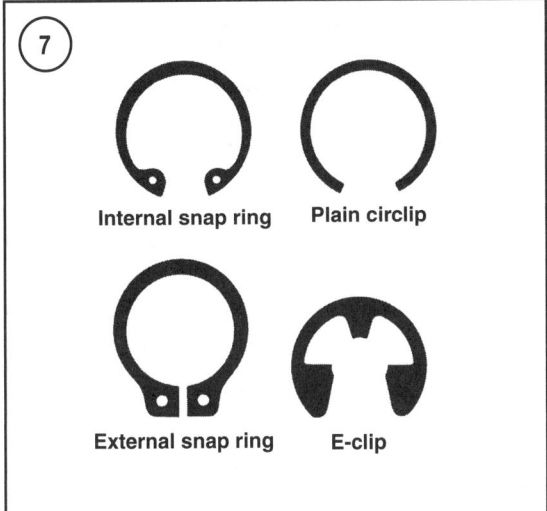

Internal snap ring — Plain circlip
External snap ring — E-clip

Self-locking fasteners offer greater holding strength than standard fasteners, which improves their resistance to vibration. Self-locking fasteners cannot be reused. The materials used to form the lock become distorted after the initial installation and removal. Do not replace self-locking fasteners with standard fasteners.

Some original equipment fasteners are equipped with a threadlocking compound preapplied to the fastener threads. When replacing these fasteners, do not apply a separate threadlocking compound. When it is necessary to reuse one of these fasteners, completely remove all threadlocking compound residue from the threads. Then apply the threadlocking compound specified in the text.

Washers

The two basic types of washers are flat washers and lockwashers. Flat washers are simple discs with a hole to fit a screw or bolt. Lockwashers are used to prevent a fastener from working loose. Washers can be used as spacers and seals or to help distribute fastener load and prevent the fastener from damaging the component.

As with fasteners, when replacing washers make sure the replacements meet the original specifications.

Cotter Pins

A cotter pin is a split metal pin inserted into a hole or slot to prevent a fastener from loosening. In certain applications, such as the rear axle, the fastener must be secured in this way. For these applications, a cotter pin and castellated (slotted) nut is used.

To use a cotter pin, first make sure the diameter is correct for the hole in the fastener. After correctly tightening the fastener and aligning the holes, insert the cotter pin through the hole and bend the ends over the fastener (**Figure 6**). Unless instructed to do so, never loosen a tightened fastener to align the holes. If the holes do not align, tighten the fastener just enough to achieve alignment.

Cotter pins are available in various diameters and lengths. Measure length from the bottom of the head to the tip of the shortest pin.

Snap Rings and E-clips

Snap rings (**Figure 7**) are circular-shaped metal retaining clips. They are required to secure parts and gears in place on parts such as shafts, pins or rods. External type snap rings are used to retain items on shafts. Internal type snap rings secure parts within housing bores. In some applications, in addition to securing the component(s), snap rings of varying thicknesses also determine endplay. These are usually called selective snap rings.

The two basic types of snap rings are machined and stamped snap rings. Machined snap rings (**Figure 8**) can be installed in either direction because both faces have sharp edges. Stamped snap rings (**Figure 9**) are manufactured with a sharp edge and round edge.

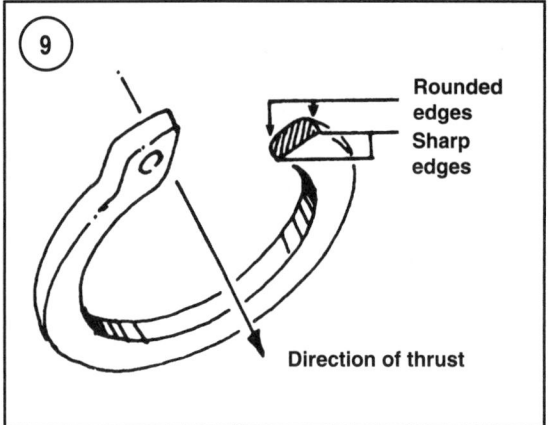

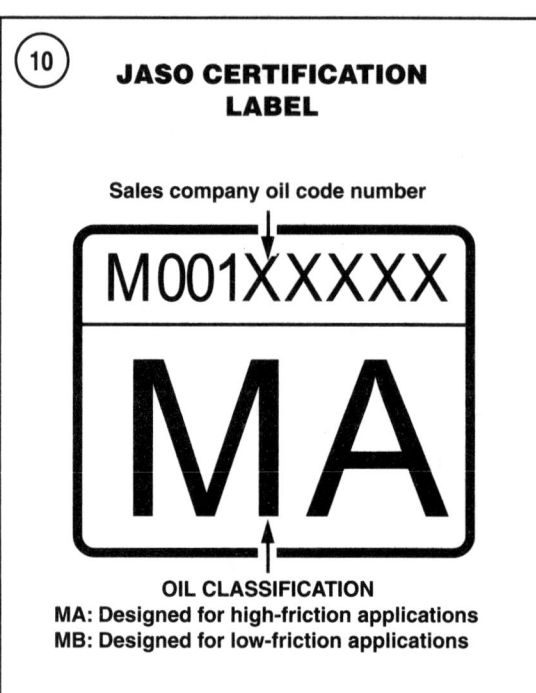

When installing a stamped snap ring in a thrust application, install the sharp edge facing away from the part producing the thrust.

E-clips are used when it is not practical to use a snap ring. Remove E-clips with a flat blade screwdriver by prying between the shaft and E-clip. To install an E-clip, center it over the shaft groove and push or tap it into place.

Observe the following when installing snap rings:
1. Remove and install snap rings with snap ring pliers. Refer to *Tools* in this chapter.
2. In some applications, it may be necessary to replace snap rings after removing them.
3. Compress or expand snap rings only enough to install them. If overly expanded, they lose their retaining ability.
4. After installing a snap ring, make sure it seats completely.
5. Wear eye protection when removing and installing snap rings.

SHOP SUPPLIES

The following section describes the types of shop supplies most often required. Read the product label and follow the manufacturer's recommendations.

Lubricants and Fluids

Engine oils

Engine oil for use in a four-stroke motorcycle engine use is classified by three standards: the Japanese Automobile Standards Organization (JASO) T 903 certification standard, the American Petroleum Institute (API) service classification, the Society of Automotive Engineers (SAE) viscosity index.

The JASO certification specifies the oil has passed requirements specified by Japanese motorcycle manufacturers. The JASO certification label (**Figure 10**) identifies which of the two separate classifications the oil meets. It also includes a registration number to indicate that the oil has passed all JASO certification standards for use in four-stroke motorcycle engines.

Two letters (**Figure 11**) are used to indicate the API service classification. A number or sequence of numbers and letter (10W-40 [**Figure 11**]) identify the oil's SAE viscosity rating. The API service classification and the SAE viscosity index are not indications of oil quality.

Viscosity is an indication of the oil's thickness. Thin oils have a lower number while thick oils have a higher number. Engine oils fall into the 5- to 50-weight range for single-grade oils.

Most manufacturers recommend multi-grade oil. These oils perform efficiently across a wide range of operating conditions. A W after the first number indicates that the oil is a multi-grade type and it shows the low-temperature viscosity.

Always use oil with a classification recommended by the manufacturer. Using oil with a different classification can cause engine damage. Do not use oil with oil additives or oil with graphite or molybdenum additives. Do not use vegetable, non-detergent or castor-based racing oils.

Use a motorcycle oil with a JASCO classification of MA or an API oil with an SG or higher classification that does not specify it as ENERGY CONSERVING (**Figure 11**). Use SAE 10W-30 oil for cool and warm climates and a heavier viscosity oil (10W-40) in hot climates.

GENERAL INFORMATION

API SERVICE SYMBOL

Oil classification → API SERVICE SJ / SAE 10W-40 / ENERGY CONSERVING

When ENERGY CONSERVING is listed in this part of the label, the oil has demonstrated energy-conserving properties in standard tests. Do not use ENERGY CONSERVING classified oil in motorcycle engines. Instead, look for this API service symbol.

API SERVICE SJ / SAE 10W-40 ← Oil viscosity

Greases

Grease is lubricating oil with thickening agents added to it. The National Lubricating Grease Institute (NLGI) grades grease. Grades range from No. 000 to No. 6, with No. 6 being the thickest. Typical multipurpose grease is NLGI No. 2. For specific applications, manufacturers may recommend a water-resistant type grease or one with an additive, such as molybdenum disulfide (MoS2).

Brake fluid

WARNING
Never use mineral-based (petroleum) oil in the brake system. Mineral oil causes rubber parts to swell and break apart, which could cause brake failure.

Brake fluid is the hydraulic fluid used to transmit hydraulic pressure (force) to the wheel brakes. The Department of Transportation (DOT) brake fluid classification is displayed on the fluid container. The models covered in this manual require DOT 4 brake fluid.

Each type of brake fluid has its own definite properties. Do not intermix different types of brake fluid; this may cause brake system failure. DOT 5 silicone brake fluid is not compatible with other brake fluids or in systems for which it was not designed. Mixing DOT 5 fluid with other fluids may cause brake system failure. When adding brake fluid, *only* use fresh DOT 4 brake fluid from a sealed container.

Brake fluid damages any plastic, painted or plated surface it contacts. Use extreme care when working with brake fluid, and remove any spills immediately with soap and water.

Hydraulic brake systems require clean and moisture free brake fluid. Never reuse brake fluid. Keep containers and reservoirs properly sealed.

Coolant

Coolant is a mixture of water and antifreeze used to dissipate engine heat. Ethylene glycol is the most common form of antifreeze used. Check the motorcycle manufacturer's recommendations (Chapter Three) when selecting antifreeze. Most require one specifically designed for use in aluminum engines. These types of antifreeze have additives that inhibit corrosion.

Only mix distilled water with antifreeze. Impurities in tap water may damage internal cooling system passages.

Final drive gear oil

Gear oil is a thick oil specially formulated for final drive units. Always use gear oil with a classification and viscosity recommended by the manufacturer (Chapter Three). Do not use engine oil or transmission oil recommended for two-stroke engines or automobiles.

Cleaners, Degreasers and Solvents

Many chemicals are available to remove oil, grease and other residue from the motorcycle. Before using cleaning solvents, consider their uses and disposal methods, particularly if they are not water-soluble. Local ordinances may require special procedures for the disposal of many types of cleaning chemicals. Refer to *Safety* and *Cleaning Parts* in this chapter for more information on their uses.

Use brake parts cleaner to clean brake system components when contact with petroleum-based products will damage seals. Brake parts cleaner leaves no residue. Use electrical contact cleaner to clean electrical connections and components without leaving any residue. Carburetor cleaner is used to remove fuel deposits and varnish from fuel system components. Use this cleaner carefully; it may damage finishes.

Generally, degreasers are strong cleaners used to remove heavy accumulations of grease from engine and frame components.

Most solvents are designed to be used with a parts washing cabinet for individual component cleaning. For safety, use only nonflammable or high flash point solvents.

Gasket Sealant

Sealants are used in combination with a gasket or seal or occasionally alone. Follow the manufacturer's recommendation when using sealants. Use extreme care when choosing a sealant different from the type originally recommended. Choose sealants based on their resistance to heat, various fluids and their sealing capabilities.

One of the most common sealants is RTV, or room temperature vulcanizing, sealant. This sealant cures at room temperature over a specific time period. This allows the repositioning of components without damaging gaskets.

Moisture in the air causes the RTV sealant to cure. Always install the tube cap as soon as possible after applying RTV sealant. RTV sealant has a limited shelf life and will not cure properly if the shelf life has expired. Keep partial tubes sealed and discard them if they have surpassed the expiration date. If there is no expiration date on a sealant tube, use a permanent marker and write the date on the tube when it is first opened. Manufacturers usually specify a shelf life of one year after a container is opened, though it is recommended to contact the sealant manufacturer to confirm shelf life.

Removing RTV sealant

RTV sealant is used on many engine gasket surfaces. When cleaning parts after disassembly, a razor blade or gasket scraper is required to remove the silicone residue that cannot be pulled off by hand from the gasket surfaces. To avoid damaging gasket surfaces, use a silicone gasket remover (Permatex Silicone Stripper or equivalent) to help soften the residue before scraping.

Applying RTV sealant

Clean all old sealer residue from the mating surfaces. Then inspect the mating surfaces for damage. Remove all sealer material from blind threaded holes; it can cause inaccurate bolt torque. Spray the mating surfaces with aerosol parts cleaner, and then wipe with a lint-free cloth. Because gasket surfaces must be dry and oil-free for the sealant to adhere, be thorough when cleaning and drying the parts.

Apply RTV sealant in a continuous bead 2-3 mm (0.08-0.12 in.) thick. Circle all the fastener holes unless otherwise specified. Do not allow any sealant to enter these holes. Assemble and tighten the fasteners to the specified torque within the time frame recommended by the RTV sealant manufacturer.

Gasket Remover

Aerosol gasket remover can help remove stubborn gaskets. This product can speed up the removal process and prevent damage to the mating surface that may be caused by using a scraping tool. Most of these types of products are very caustic. Follow the gasket remover manufacturer's instructions for use.

Threadlocking Compound

CAUTION
Threadlocking compounds are anaerobic and will damage most plastic parts and surfaces. Use caution when using these products in areas where plastic components are located.

Threadlocking compounds are available in various strengths, temperatures and repair applications. The compound, when applied to fastener threads and allowed to dry, becomes solid filler between the threads. This makes it difficult for the fastener to work loose from vibration or heat expansion and contraction. Some threadlocking compounds also provide a seal against fluid leaks.

Before applying threadlocking compound, remove any old compound from all thread areas and clean

GENERAL INFORMATION

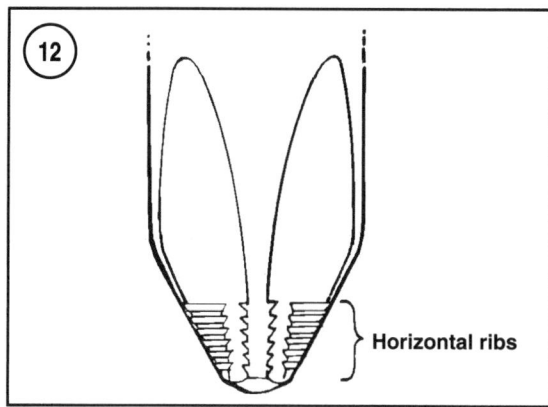

Horizontal ribs

them with aerosol parts cleaner. Use the compound sparingly. Excess fluid can run into adjoining parts.

TOOLS

Most of the procedures in this manual can be carried out with hand tools and test equipment familiar to the home mechanic. Always use the correct tools for the job. Keep tools organized and clean and store them in a tool chest with related tools organized together.

Quality tools are essential. The best are constructed of high-strength alloy steel. These tools are light, easy-to-use and resistant to wear. Their working surfaces are devoid of sharp edges and the tools are carefully polished. They have an easy-to-clean finish and are comfortable to use. Quality tools are a good investment.

When purchasing tools to perform the procedures covered in this manual, consider the tool's potential frequency of use. If a tool kit is just now being started, consider purchasing a tool set from a quality tool supplier. These sets are available in many tool combinations and offer substantial savings when compared to individually purchased tools. As work experience grows and tasks become more complicated, specialized tools can be added.

Some of the procedures in this manual specify special tools. In most cases, the tool is illustrated in use. Well-equipped mechanics may be able to substitute similar tools or fabricate a suitable replacement. However, in some cases, the specialized equipment or expertise may make it impractical for the home mechanic to attempt the procedure. When necessary, such operations are identified in the text with the recommendation to have a dealership or specialist perform the task. It may be less expensive to have a professional perform these jobs, especially when considering the cost of the equipment.

The manufacturer's part number is provided for many of the tools mentioned in this manual. These part numbers are correct at the time of original publication. The publisher cannot guarantee the part number will be correct to the tool's availability in the future.

Screwdrivers

The two basic types of screwdrivers are the slotted tip (flat blade) and the Phillips tip. These are available in sets that often include an assortment of tip sizes and shaft lengths.

As with all tools, use the correct screwdriver. Make sure the size of the tip conforms to the size and shape of the fastener. Use them only for driving screws. Never use a screwdriver for prying or chiseling. Repair or replace worn or damaged screwdrivers. A worn tip may damage the fastener, making it difficult to remove.

Phillips-head screws are often damaged by incorrectly fitting screwdrivers. Quality Phillips screwdrivers are manufactured with their crosshead tip machined to Phillips Screw Company specifications. Poor quality or damaged Phillips screwdrivers can back out and round over the screw head (camout). Compounding the problem of using poor quality screwdrivers are Phillips-head screws made from weak or soft materials and screws initially installed with air tools.

An effective screwdriver for Phillips screws is the ACR Phillips II screwdriver. Horizontal anti-camout ribs (ACR) on the driving faces or flutes of the screwdriver's tip (**Figure 12**) improve the driving-to-fastener grip. While designed for ACR Phillips II screws, ACR Philips II screwdrivers also work well on all common Phillips screws. ACR screwdrivers in different tip sizes and interchangeable bits to fit screwdriver bit holders are available.

Another way to prevent camout and increase the grip of a Phillips screwdriver is to apply valve grinding compound or Permatex Screw & Socket Gripper onto the screwdriver tip. After loosening/tightening the screw, clean the screw recess.

Wrenches

Open-end, box-end and combination wrenches (**Figure 13**) are available in a variety of types and sizes.

The number stamped on the wrench refers to the distance between the work areas. This size must match the size of the fastener head.

The box-end wrench is an excellent tool because it grips the fastener on all sides. This reduces the chance of the tool slipping. The box-end wrench is designed with either a 6- or 12-point opening. For stubborn or damaged fasteners, the 6-point provides superior holding ability by contacting the fastener across a wider area at all six edges. For general use, the 12-point works well. It allows the wrench to be removed and reinstalled without moving the handle over such a wide arc.

An open-end wrench is fast and works best in areas with limited overhead access. It contacts the fastener at only two points, and is subject to slipping under heavy force or if the tool or fastener is worn. A box-end wrench is preferred in most instances, especially when breaking loose and applying the final tightness to a fastener.

The combination wrench has a box-end on one end, and an open-end on the other. This combination makes it a convenient tool.

Adjustable Wrenches

An adjustable wrench (**Figure 14**) can fit nearly any nut or bolt head that has clear access around its entire perimeter.

However, adjustable wrenches contact the fastener at only two points, which makes them more subject to slipping off the fastener. One jaw is adjustable and may loosen, which increases this possibility. Make certain the solid jaw is the one transmitting the force.

However, adjustable wrenches are typically used to prevent a large nut or bolt from turning while the other end is being loosened or tightened with a box-end or socket wrench.

Socket Wrenches, Ratchets and Handles

WARNING
Do not use hand sockets with air or impact tools; they may shatter and cause injury. Always wear eye protection when using impact or air tools.

Sockets that attach to a ratchet handle (**Figure 15**) are available with 6-point (A, **Figure 16**) or 12-point (B, **Figure 16**) openings and different drive sizes. The drive size indicates the size of the square hole that accepts the ratchet handle. The number stamped on the socket is the size of the work area and must match the fastener head.

As with wrenches, a 6-point socket provides superior-holding ability, while a 12-point socket needs to be moved only half as far to reposition it on the fastener.

Sockets are designated for either hand or impact use. Impact sockets are made of a thicker material for more durability. Compare the size and wall thick-

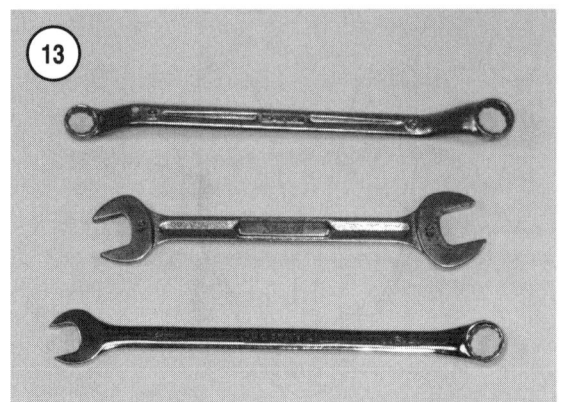

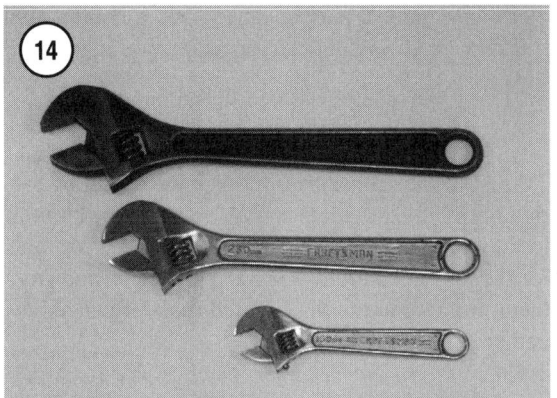

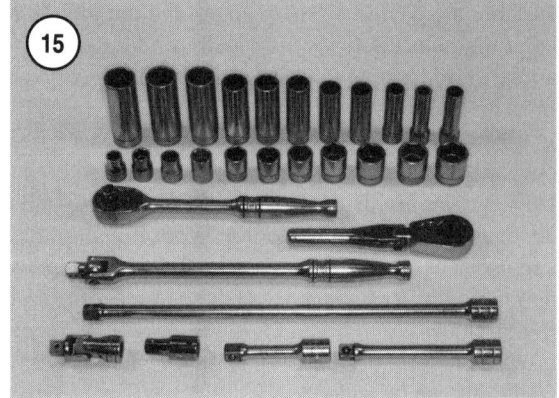

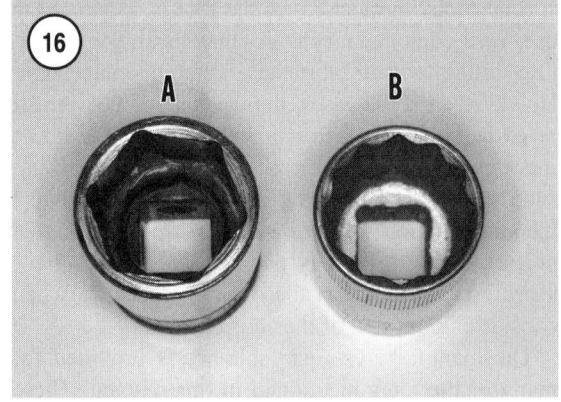

GENERAL INFORMATION

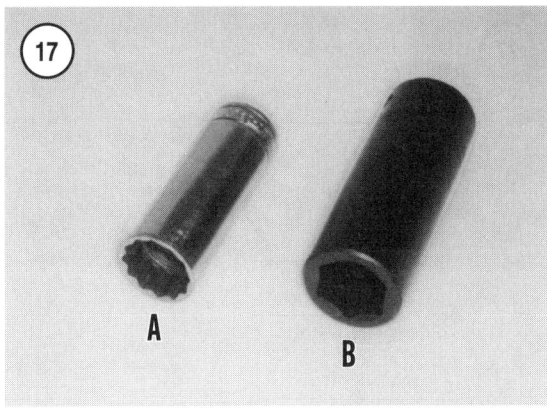

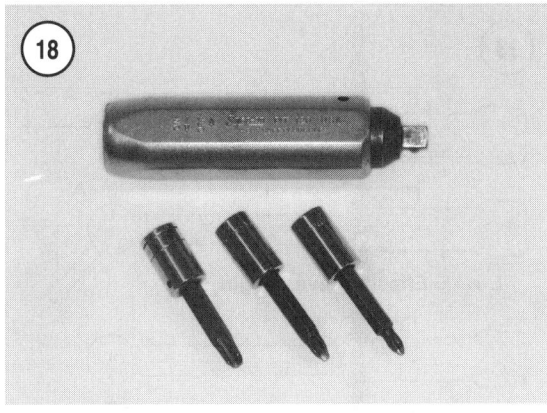

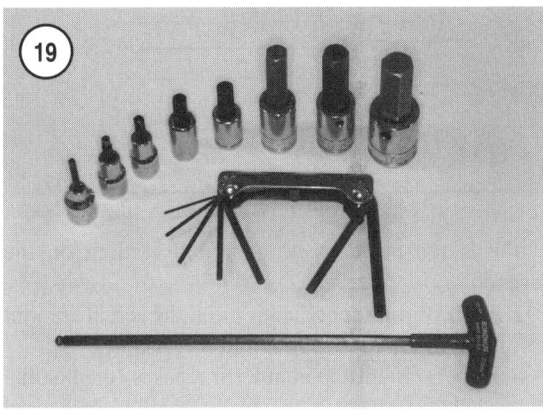

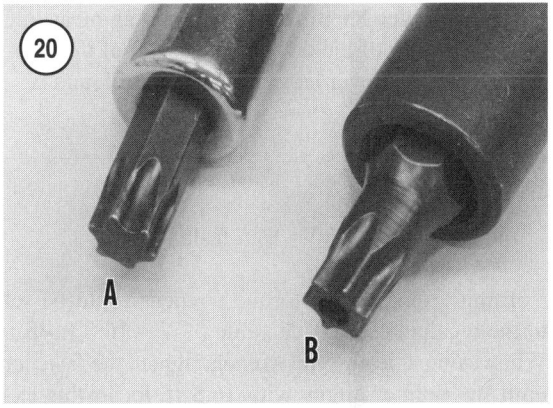

ness of a 19-mm hand socket (A, **Figure 17**) and the 19-mm impact socket (B). Use impact sockets when using an impact driver or air tool. Use hand sockets with hand-driven attachments.

Various handles are available for sockets. The speed handle is used for fast operation. Flexible ratchet heads in varying lengths allow the socket to be turned with varying force and at odd angles. Extension bars allow the socket setup to reach difficult areas. The ratchet is the most versatile. It allows the user to install or remove the nut without removing the socket.

Sockets combined with any number of drivers make them undoubtedly the fastest, safest and most convenient tool for fastener removal and installation.

Impact Driver

WARNING
Do not use hand sockets with air or impact tools because they may shatter and cause injury. Always wear eye protection when using impact or air tools.

An impact driver provides extra force for removing fasteners by converting the impact of a hammer into a turning motion. This makes it possible to remove stubborn fasteners without damaging them. Impact drivers and interchangeable bits (**Figure 18**) are available from most tool suppliers. When using a socket with an impact driver, make sure the socket is designed for impact use. Refer to *Socket Wrenches, Ratchets and Handles* in this section.

Allen Wrenches

Allen, or setscrew wrenches (**Figure 19**), are used on fasteners with hexagonal recesses in the fastener head. These wrenches are available in a L-shaped bar, socket and T-handle types. Allen bolts are sometimes called socket bolts.

Torx Fasteners

A Torx fastener head is a 6-point star-shaped pattern. Torx fasteners are identified with a T and a number indicating their drive size: T25, for example. Torx drivers are available in L-shaped bars, sockets (A, **Figure 20**) and T-handles. Tamper-resistant Torx fasteners are also used and have a round shaft in the center of the fastener head. Tamper-resistance Torx fasteners require a Torx bit with a hole in the center of the bit (B, **Figure 20**) to accommodate the fastener shaft.

CHAPTER ONE

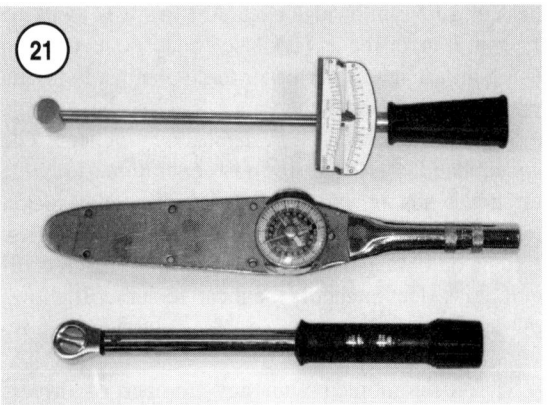

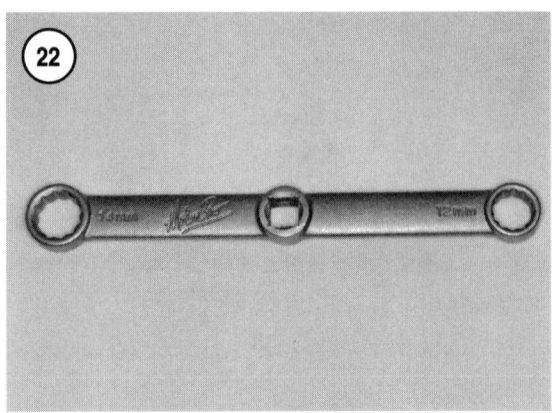

Torque Wrenches

A torque wrench (**Figure 21**) is used with a socket, torque adapter or similar extension to tighten a fastener to a measured torque. Torque wrenches come in several drive sizes (1/4, 3/8, 1/2 and 3/4 inch) and utilize various methods of reading the torque value. The drive size indicates the size of the square drive that accepts the socket, adapter or extension. Common methods of reading the torque value are the reflecting beam, the dial indicator and the audible click. When choosing a torque wrench, consider the torque range, drive size and accuracy. The torque specifications in this manual provide an indication of the range required. A torque wrench is a precision tool that must be properly cared for in order to remain accurate. Store torque wrenches in cases or separate padded drawers within a toolbox. Follow the manufacturer's instructions for their care and calibration.

Torque Adapters

Torque adapters (**Figure 22**), or extensions, extend or reduce the reach of a torque wrench. Specific adapters are required to perform some of the procedures in this manual. These are available from the motorcycle manufacturer or fabricated to suit a specific purpose.

If a torque adapter changes the effective lever length, the torque reading on the wrench will not equal the actual torque applied to the fastener. It is necessary to recalibrate the torque setting on the wrench to compensate for the change of lever length. When a torque adapter is used at a right angle to the drive head, calibration is not required because the lever length has not changed.

To recalculate a torque reading when using a torque adapter, use the following formula, and refer to **Figure 23**.

$$TW = \frac{TA \times L}{L + A}$$

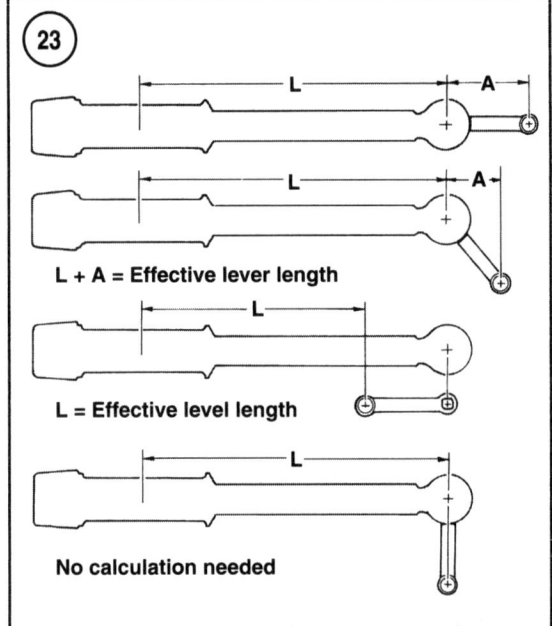

TW is the torque setting or dial reading on the wrench.

TA is the torque specification and the actual amount of torque that will be applied to the fastener.

A is the amount the adapter increases (or in some cases reduces) the effective lever length as measured along the centerline of the torque wrench.

L is the lever length of the wrench as measured from the center of the drive to the center of the grip.

The effective lever length is the sum of L and A.
Example:
TA = 20 ft.-lb.
A = 3 in.
L = 14 in.

$$TW = \frac{20 \times 14}{14 + 3} = \frac{280}{17} = 16.5 \text{ ft.-lb.}$$

In this example, the torque wrench would be set to the recalculated torque value (TW = 16.5 ft.-lb.). When using a beam-type wrench, tighten the fastener until the pointer aligns with 16.5 ft.-lb. In this ex-

GENERAL INFORMATION

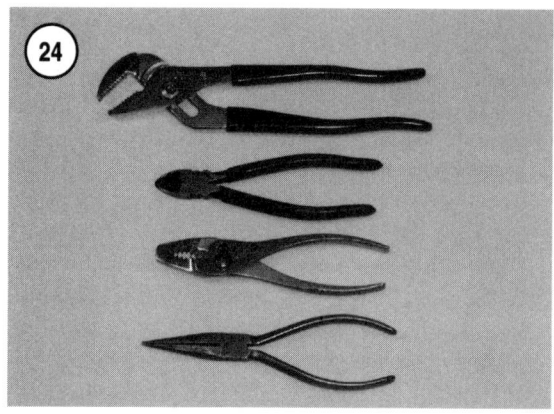

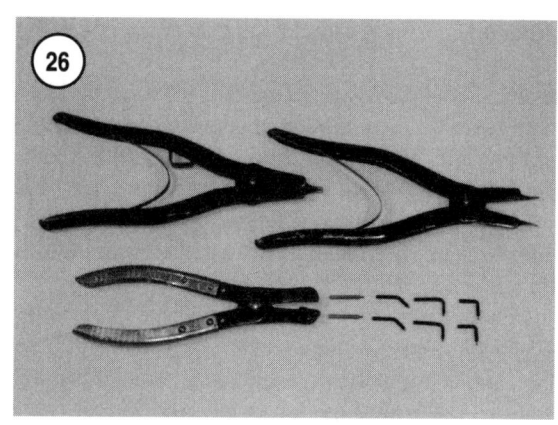

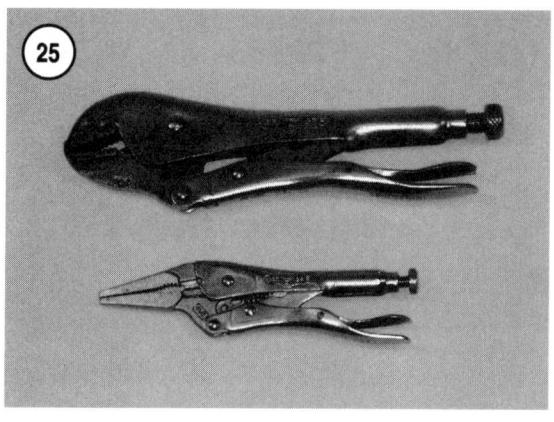

ample, although the torque wrench is pre set to 16.5 ft.-lb., the actual torque is 20 ft.-lb.

Pliers

Pliers come in a wide range of types and sizes. Pliers are useful for holding, cutting, bending, and crimping. Do not use them to turn fasteners unless they are designed to do so. **Figure 24** and **Figure 25** show several types of pliers. Each design has a specialized function. Slip-joint pliers are general-purpose pliers used for gripping and bending. Diagonal cutting pliers are needed to cut wire and can be used to remove cotter pins. Needlenose pliers are used to hold or bend small objects. Locking pliers (**Figure 25**), sometimes called Vise Grips, hold objects tightly. They have many uses ranging from holding two parts together, to gripping the end of a broken stud. Use caution when using locking pliers; the sharp jaws will damage the objects they hold.

Snap Ring Pliers

WARNING
Snap rings can slip and fly off when removing and installing them. In ad-
dition, the snap ring pliers tips may break. Always wear eye protection when using snap ring pliers.

Snap ring pliers are specialized pliers with tips that fit into the ends of snap rings to remove and install them.

Snap ring pliers (**Figure 26**) are available with a fixed action (either internal or external) or are convertible (one tool works on both internal and external snap rings). They may have fixed tips or interchangeable ones of various sizes and angles. For general use, select convertible type pliers with interchangeable tips.

Hammers

WARNING
Always wear eye protection when using hammers. Make sure the hammer face is in good condition and the handle is not cracked. Select the correct hammer for the job and make sure to strike the object squarely. Do not use the handle or the side of the hammer to strike an object.

Various types of hammers are available to fit a number of applications. A ball-peen hammer is used to strike another tool, such as a punch or chisel. Soft-faced hammers are required when a metal object must be struck without damaging it. Never use a metal-faced hammer on engine and suspension components; damage will occur in most cases.

Ignition Grounding Tool

Some test procedures in this manual require turning the engine over without starting it. Do not remove the spark plug cap(s) and crank the engine without grounding the plug cap(s). Doing so will damage the ignition system.

An effective way to ground the system is to fabricate the tool shown in **Figure 27** from a No. 6 screw, two washers and a length of wire with an alligator clip soldered on one end. To use the tool, insert it into the spark plug cap and attach the alligator clip to a known engine ground. A separate grounding tool is required for each spark plug cap.

This tool is safer than a spark plug or spark tester because there is no spark firing across the end of the plug/tester to potentially ignite fuel vapor spraying from an open spark plug hole or leaking fuel component.

MEASURING TOOLS

The ability to accurately measure components is essential to successfully service many components. Equipment is manufactured to close tolerances, and obtaining consistently accurate measurements is essential.

Each type of measuring instrument is designed to measure a dimension with a certain degree of accuracy and within a certain range. When selecting the measuring tool, make sure it is applicable to the task.

As with all tools, measuring tools provide the best results if cared for properly. Improper use can damage the tool and cause inaccurate results. If any measurement is questionable, verify the measurement using another tool. A standard gauge is usually provided with measuring tools to check accuracy and calibrate the tool if necessary.

Accurate measurements are only possible if the mechanic possesses a feel for using the tool. Heavy-handed use of measuring tools produces less accurate results. Hold the tool gently by the fingertips so the point at which the tool contacts the object is easily felt. This feel for the equipment will produce more accurate measurements and reduce the risk of damaging the tool or component. Refer to the following sections for specific measuring tools.

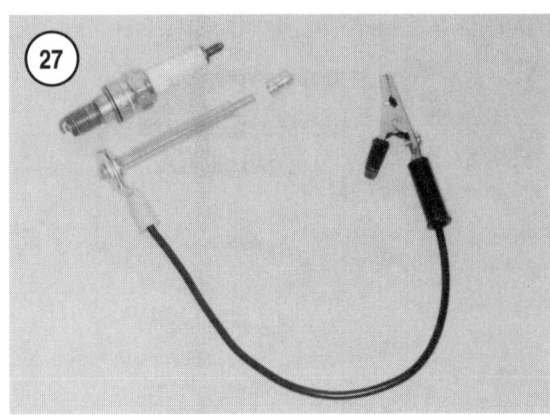

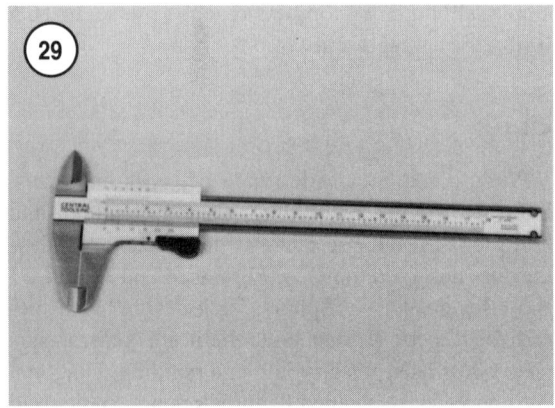

Feeler Gauge

The feeler, or thickness gauge (**Figure 28**), is used for measuring the distance between two surfaces.

A feeler gauge set consists of an assortment of steel strips of graduated thicknesses. Each blade is marked with its thickness. Blades can be of various lengths and angles for different procedures.

A common use for a feeler gauge is to measure valve clearance. Wire (round) type gauges are used to measure spark plug gap.

Calipers

Calipers (**Figure 29**) are excellent tools for obtaining inside, outside and depth measurements. Although not as precise as a micrometer, they allow reasonable precision, typically to within 0.05 mm (0.001 in.). Most calipers have a range up to 150 mm (6 in.).

Calipers are available in dial, vernier or digital versions. Dial calipers have a dial readout that provides convenient reading. Vernier calipers have marked scales that must be compared to determine the measurement. The digital caliper uses a LCD to show the measurement.

GENERAL INFORMATION

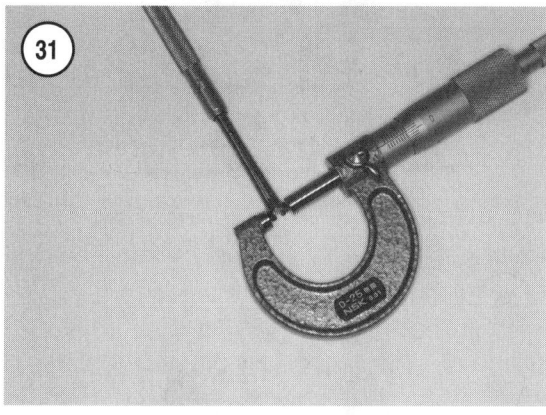

ing 10 mm and 0.50 mm is a measurement of 10.50 mm.

Micrometers

A micrometer (**Figure 31**) is an instrument designed for linear measurement using the decimal divisions of the inch or meter. While there are many types and styles of micrometers, most of the procedures in this manual call for an outside micrometer. The outside micrometer is used to measure the outside diameter of cylindrical forms and the thicknesses of materials.

A micrometer's size indicates the minimum and maximum size of a part that it can measure. The usual sizes are 0-25 mm (0-1 in.), 25-50 mm (1-2 in.), 50-75 mm (2-3 in.) and 75-100 mm (3-4 in.).

Micrometers that cover a wider range of measurements are available. These use a large frame with interchangeable anvils of various lengths. This type of micrometer offers a cost savings; however, its overall size may make it less convenient.

Adjustment

Before using a micrometer, check its adjustment as follows:
1. Clean the anvil and spindle faces.
2A. To check a 0-1 in. or 0-25 mm micrometer:
   a. Turn the thimble until the spindle contacts the anvil. If the micrometer has a ratchet stop, use it to ensure the proper amount of pressure is applied.
   b. If the adjustment is correct, the 0 mark on the thimble will align exactly with the 0 mark on the sleeve line. If the marks do not align, the micrometer is out of adjustment.
   c. Follow the manufacturer's instructions to adjust the micrometer.
2B. To check a micrometer larger than 1 in. or 25 mm, use the standard gauge supplied by the manufacturer. A standard gauge is a steel block, disc or rod that is machined to an exact size.
   a. Place the standard gauge between the spindle and anvil and measure its outside diameter or length. If the micrometer has a ratchet stop, use it to ensure the proper amount of pressure is applied.
   b. If the adjustment is correct, the 0 mark on the thimble will align exactly with the 0 mark on the sleeve line. If the marks do not align, the micrometer is out of adjustment.
   c. Follow the manufacturer's instructions to adjust the micrometer.

Properly maintain the measuring surfaces of the caliper. There must not be any dirt or burrs between the tool and the object being measured. Never force the caliper closed around an object; close the caliper around the highest point so it can be removed with a slight drag. Some calipers require calibration. Always refer to the manufacturer's instructions when using a new or unfamiliar caliper.

To read a vernier caliper refer to **Figure 30**. The fixed scale is marked in 1 mm increments. Ten individual lines on the fixed scale equal 1 cm. The moveable scale is marked in 0.05 mm (hundredth) increments. To obtain a reading, establish the first number by the location of the 0 line on the moveable scale in relation to the first line to the left on the fixed scale. In this example, the number is 10 mm. To determine the next number, note which of the lines on the movable scale align with a mark on the fixed scale. A number of lines will seem close, but only one will align exactly. In this case, 0.50 mm is the reading to add to the first number. The result of add-

Care

Micrometers are precision instruments. They must be used and maintained with great care. Note the following:
1. Store micrometers in protective cases or separate padded drawers in a toolbox.
2. When in storage, make sure the spindle and anvil faces do not contact each other or another object. If they do, temperature changes and corrosion may damage the contact faces.
3. Do not clean a micrometer with compressed air. Dirt forced into the tool causes wear.
4. Lubricate micrometers to prevent corrosion.

Reading

When reading a micrometer, numbers are taken from different scales and added together.

For accurate results, properly maintain the measuring surfaces of the micrometer. There cannot be any dirt or burrs between the tool and the measured object. Never force the micrometer closed around an object. Close the micrometer around the highest point so it can be removed with a slight drag.

The standard metric micrometer is accurate to one one-hundredth of a millimeter (0.01 mm). The sleeve line is graduated in millimeter and half millimeter increments. The marks on the upper half of the sleeve line equal 1.00 mm. Each fifth mark above the sleeve line is identified with a number. The number sequence depends on the size of the micrometer. A 0-25 mm micrometer, for example, will have sleeve marks numbered 0 through 25 in 5 mm increments. This numbering sequence continues with larger micrometers. On all metric micrometers, each mark on the lower half of the sleeve equals 0.50 mm.

The tapered end of the thimble has 50 lines marked around it. Each mark equals 0.01 mm. One complete turn of the thimble aligns its 0 mark with the first line on the lower half of the sleeve line, or 0.50 mm.

When reading a metric micrometer, add the number of millimeters and half-millimeters on the sleeve line to the number of one one-hundredth millimeters on the thimble. Perform the following steps while referring to **Figure 32**.
1. Read the upper half of the sleeve line and count the number of lines visible. Each upper line equals 1 mm.
2. See if the half-millimeter line is visible on the lower sleeve line. If so, add 0.50 mm to the reading in Step 1.
3. Read the thimble mark that aligns with the sleeve line. Each thimble mark equals 0.01 mm.
4. If a thimble mark does not align exactly with the sleeve line, estimate the amount between the lines.

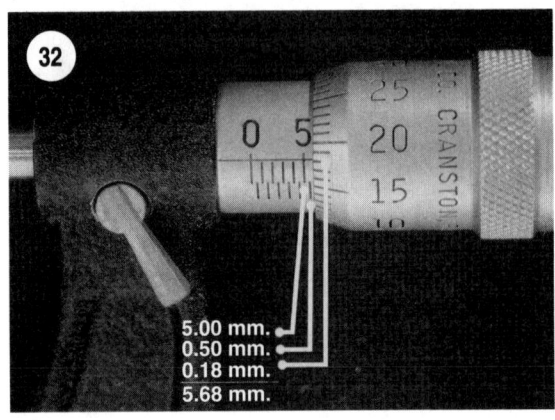

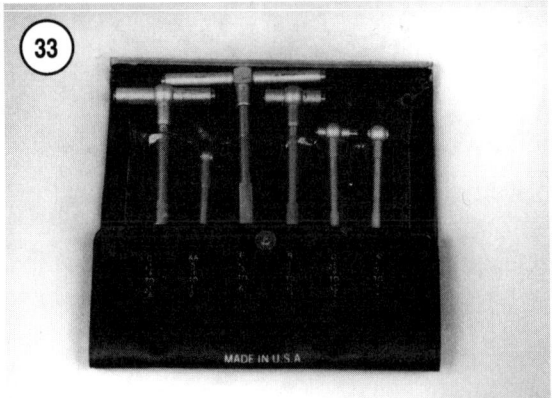

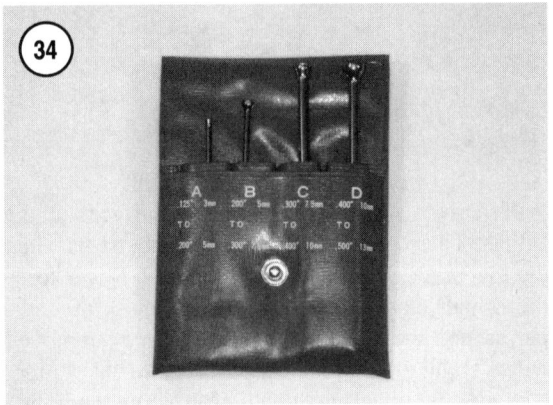

For accurate readings in two-thousandths of a millimeter (0.002 mm), use a metric vernier micrometer.
5. Add the readings from Steps 1-4.

Telescoping and Small Hole Gauges

Use telescoping gauges (**Figure 33**) and small hole gauges (**Figure 34**) to measure bores. Neither gauge has a scale for direct readings. An outside micrometer must be used to determine the reading.

To use a telescoping gauge, select the correct size gauge for the bore. Compress the moveable post and carefully insert the gauge into the bore. Carefully

GENERAL INFORMATION

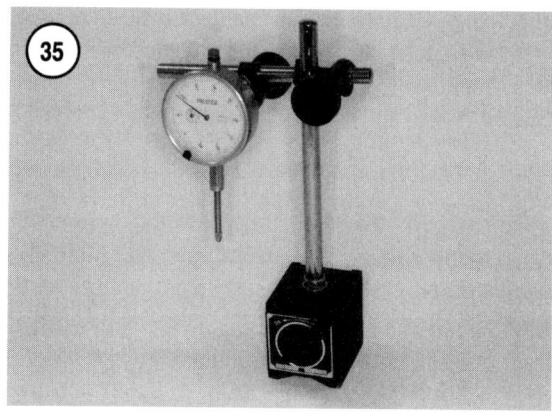

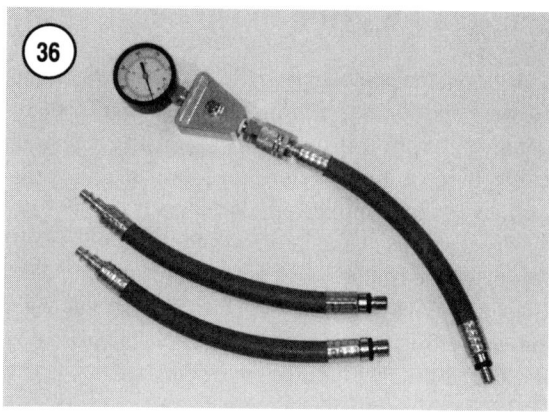

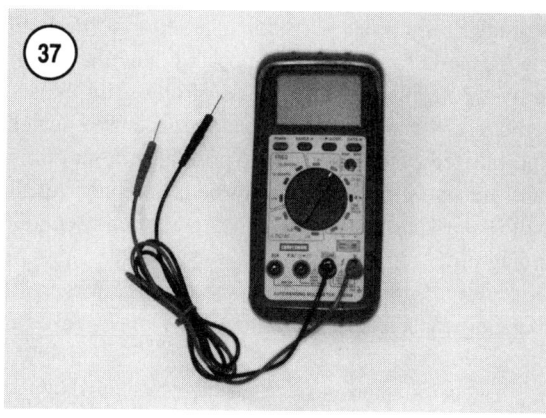

Small hole gauges are typically used to measure valve guides.

Dial Indicator

A dial indicator (**Figure 35**) is a gauge with a dial face and needle used to measure variations in dimensions and movements. Measuring brake rotor runout is a typical use for a dial indicator.

Dial indicators are available in various ranges and graduations and with three types of mounting bases: magnetic, clamp or screw-in stud.

Cylinder Bore Gauge

A cylinder bore gauge is similar to a dial indicator. These typically consist of a dial indicator, handle and different length adapters (anvils) to fit the gauge to various bore sizes. The bore gauge is used to measure bore size, taper and out-of-round. When using a bore gauge, follow the manufacturer's instructions.

Compression Gauge

A compression gauge (**Figure 36**) measures combustion chamber (cylinder) pressure, usually in psi or kg/cm^2. The gauge adapter is either inserted and held in place or screwed into the spark plug hole to obtain the reading. Disable the engine so it will not start and hold the throttle in the wide-open position when performing a compression test. An engine that does not have adequate compression cannot be properly tuned. Refer to Chapter Three.

Multimeter

A multimeter (**Figure 37**) is an essential tool for electrical system diagnosis. The voltage function indicates the voltage applied or available to various electrical components. The ohmmeter function tests circuits for continuity, or lack of continuity, and measures the resistance of a circuit.

Some manufacturers' specifications for electrical components are based on results using a specific test meter. Results may vary if using a meter not recommend by the manufacturer. Such requirements are noted when applicable.

Ohmmeter (analog) calibration

Each time an analog ohmmeter is used or the scale is changed, the ohmmeter must be calibrated.

Digital ohmmeters do not require calibration.

1. Make sure the meter battery is in good condition.

move the gauge in the bore to make sure it is centered. Tighten the knurled end of the gauge to hold the moveable post in position. Remove the gauge and measure the length of the posts. Telescoping gauges are typically used to measure cylinder bores.

To use a small hole gauge, select the correct size gauge for the bore. Carefully insert the gauge into the bore. Tighten the knurled end of the gauge to carefully expand the gauge fingers to the limit within the bore. Do not overtighten the gauge; there is no built-in release. Excessive tightening can damage the bore surface and tool. Remove the gauge and measure the outside dimension with a micrometer (**Figure 31**).

2. Make sure the meter probes are in good condition.
3. Touch the two probes together and observe the needle location on the ohms scale. The needle must align with the 0 mark to obtain accurate measurements.
4. If necessary, rotate the meter ohms adjust knob until the needle and 0 mark align.

ELECTRICAL SYSTEM FUNDAMENTALS

A thorough study of the many types of electrical systems used in today's motorcycles is beyond the scope of this manual. However, a basic understanding of voltage, resistance and amperage is necessary to perform diagnostic tests.

Refer to Chapter Two for troubleshooting.

Voltage

Voltage is the electrical potential or pressure in an electrical circuit and is expressed in volts. The more pressure (voltage) in a circuit, the more work can be performed.

Direct current (DC) voltage means the electricity flows in one direction. All circuits powered by a battery are DC circuits.

Alternating current (AC) means the electricity flows in one direction momentarily and then switches to the opposite direction. Alternator output is an example of AC voltage. This voltage must be changed or rectified to direct current to operate in a battery powered system.

Resistance

Resistance is the opposition to the flow of electricity within a circuit or component and is measured in ohms. Resistance causes a reduction in available current and voltage.

Resistance is measured in an inactive circuit with an ohmmeter. The ohmmeter sends a small amount of current into the circuit and measures how difficult it is to push the current through the circuit.

An ohmmeter, although useful, is not always a good indicator of a circuit's actual ability under operating conditions. This is due to the low voltage (6-9 volts) that the meter uses to test the circuit. The voltage in an ignition coil secondary winding can be several thousand volts. Such high voltage can cause the coil to malfunction, even though it tests acceptable during a resistance test.

Resistance generally increases with temperature. Perform all testing with the component or circuit at room temperature. Resistance tests performed at high temperatures may indicate false resistance readings and cause the unnecessary replacement of a component.

Amperage

Amperage is the unit of measure for the amount of current within a circuit. Current is the actual flow of electricity. The higher the current, the more work can be performed up to a given point. If the current flow exceeds the circuit or component capacity, the system will be damaged.

SERVICE METHODS

Many of the procedures in this manual are straightforward and can be performed by anyone reasonably competent with tools. However, consider previous experience carefully before performing any operation involving complicated procedures.

1. Front, in this manual, refers to the front of the motorcycle. The front of any component is the end closest to the front of the motorcycle. The left and right sides refer to the position of the parts as viewed by the rider sitting on the seat facing forward.
2. When servicing the motorcycle, secure it in a safe manner.
3. Label all similar parts for location and mark all mating parts for position. If possible, photograph or draw the number and thickness of any shim as it is removed. Identify parts by placing them in sealed and labeled plastic bags. It is possible for carefully laid out parts to become disturbed, making it difficult to reassemble the components correctly without a diagram.
4. Label disconnected wires and connectors with masking tape and a marking pen. Do not rely on memory alone.
5. Protect finished surfaces from physical damage or corrosion. Keep gasoline and other chemicals off painted surfaces.
6. Use penetrating oil on frozen or tight bolts. Avoid using heat where possible. Heat can warp, melt or affect the temper of parts. Heat also damages the finish of paint and plastics. Refer to *Heating Components* in this section.
7. When a part is a press fit or requires a special tool for removal, the information or type of tool is identified in the text. Otherwise, if a part is difficult to remove or install, determine the cause before proceeding.
8. To prevent objects or debris from falling into the engine, cover all openings.

GENERAL INFORMATION

9. Read each procedure thoroughly and compare the figures to the actual components before starting the procedure. Perform the procedure in sequence.

10. Recommendations are occasionally made to refer service to a dealership or specialist. In these cases, the work can be performed more economically by the specialist than by the home mechanic.

11. The term *replace* means to discard a defective part and replace it with a new part. *Overhaul* means to remove, disassemble, inspect, measure, repair and/or replace parts as required to recondition an assembly.

12. Some operations require the use of a hydraulic press. If a press is not available, have these operations performed by a shop equipped with the necessary equipment. Do not use makeshift equipment that may damage the motorcycle.

13. Do not direct high-pressure water at steering bearings, carburetor hoses, wheel bearings, suspension and electrical components. The water forces the grease out of the bearings and could damage the seals.

14. Repairs are much faster and easier if the motorcycle is clean before starting work. Degrease the motorcycle with a commercial degreaser; follow the directions on the container for the best results. Clean all parts with cleaning solvent. Refer to *Cleaning Parts* in *Safety* in this chapter.

15. If special tools are required, have them available before starting the procedure. When special tools are required, they will be described at the beginning of the procedure.

16. Make sure all shims and washers are reinstalled in the same location and position.

17. Whenever rotating parts contact a stationary part, look for a shim or washer.

18. Use new gaskets if there is any doubt about the condition of old ones.

19. If self-locking fasteners are used, replace them. Do not install standard fasteners in place of self-locking ones.

20. Use grease to hold small parts in place if they tend to fall out during assembly. Do not apply grease to electrical or brake components.

Heating Components

WARNING
Wear protective gloves to prevent burns and injury when heating parts.

CAUTION
Do not use a welding torch when heating parts. A welding torch applies excessive heat to a small area very quickly, which can damage parts.

A heat gun or propane torch is required to disassemble, assemble, remove and install many parts and components in this manual. Read the safety and operating information supplied by the manufacturer of the heat gun or propane torch while also noting the following:

1. The work area should be clean and dry. Remove all combustible components and materials from the work area. Wipe up all grease, oil and other fluids from parts. Check for leaking or damaged fuel system components. Repair or remove these parts before beginning work.

2. Never use a flame near the battery, fuel tank, fuel lines or other flammable materials.

3. When using a heat gun, remember that the temperature can be in excess of 540° C (1000° F).

4. Have a fire extinguisher near the job.

5. Always wear protective goggles and gloves when heating parts.

6. Before heating a part installed on the motorcycle, check areas around the part and those hidden that could be damaged or possibly ignite. Do not heat surfaces than can be damaged by heat. Shield materials near the part or area to be heated. For example, cables and wiring harnesses.

7. Before heating a part, read the entire procedure to make sure the required tools are available. This allows quick work while the part is at its optimum temperature.

8. The amount of heat recommended to remove or install a part is typically listed in the procedure. However, before heating parts without a specific recommendation, consider the possible effects. To avoid damaging a part, monitor the temperature with heat sticks or an infrared thermometer, if possible. Another way, though not as accurate, is to place tiny drops of water on the part. When the water starts to sizzle, the part is hot enough. Keep the heat in motion to prevent overheating.

Removing Frozen Fasteners

If a fastener cannot be removed, several methods may be used to loosen it. First, liberally apply penetrating oil, and let it penetrate for 10-15 minutes. Rap the fastener several times with a small hammer. Do not hit it hard enough to cause damage. Reapply the penetrating oil if necessary.

For frozen screws, apply penetrating oil as described, and then insert a screwdriver in the slot and rap the top of the screwdriver with a hammer. This loosens the rust so the screw can be removed in the normal way. If the screw head is too damaged to use

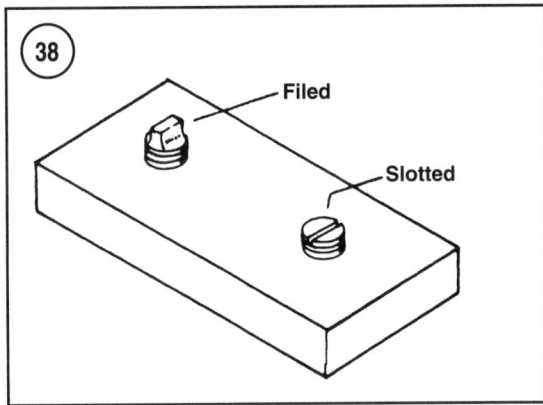

this method, grip the head with locking pliers and twist it out.

If heat is required, refer to *Heating Components* in this section.

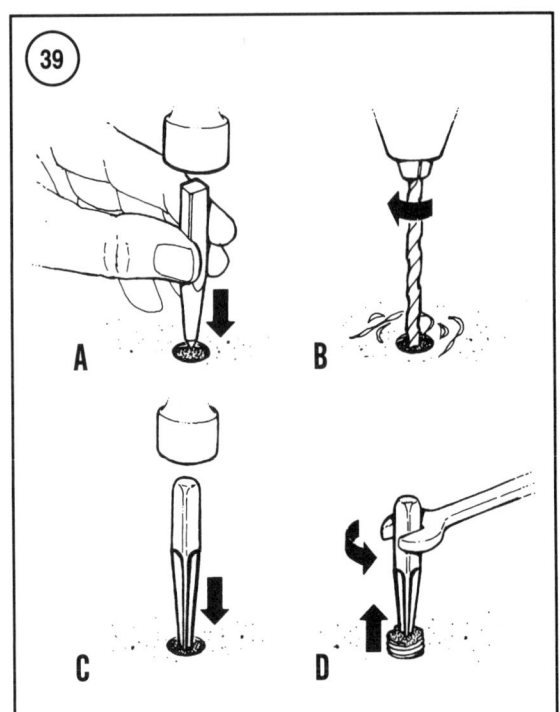

Removing Broken Fasteners

If the head breaks off a screw or bolt, several methods are available for removing the remaining portion. If a large portion of the remainder projects out, try gripping it with locking pliers. If the projecting portion is too small, file it to fit a wrench or cut a slot in it to fit a screwdriver (**Figure 38**).

If the head breaks off flush, use a screw extractor. To do this, center punch the exact center of the screw or bolt (A, **Figure 39**), and then drill a small hole in the screw (B) and tap the extractor into the hole (C). Back the screw out with a wrench on the extractor (D, **Figure 39**).

Repairing Damaged Threads

Occasionally, threads are stripped through carelessness or impact damage. Often the threads can be repaired by running a tap (for internal threads on nuts) or die (for external threads on bolts) through the threads (**Figure 40**). To clean or repair spark plug threads, use a spark plug tap.

If an internal thread is damaged, it may be necessary to install a Helicoil or some other type of thread insert. Follow the manufacturer's instructions when installing its insert.

If it is necessary to drill and tap a hole, refer to **Table 5** for metric tap and drill sizes.

Stud Removal/Installation

A stud removal tool (**Figure 41**) is available from most tool suppliers. This tool makes the removal and installation of studs easier. If one is not available and the threads on the stud are not damaged, thread two

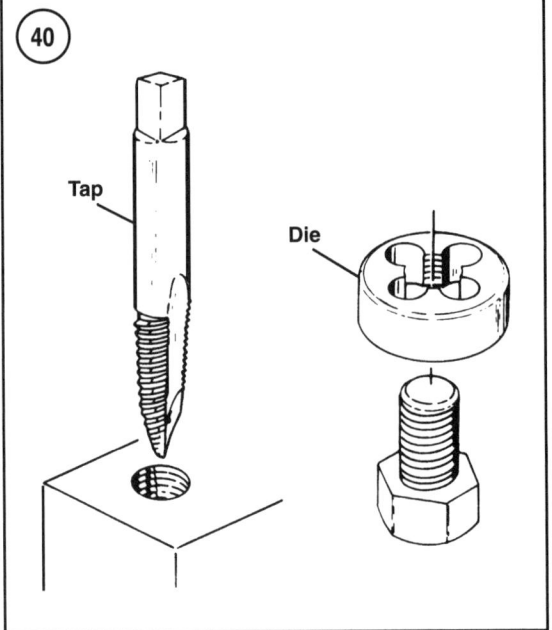

nuts onto the stud and tighten them against each other. Remove the stud by turning the lower nut.
1. Measure the height of the stud above the surface.
2. Thread the stud removal tool onto the stud and tighten it, or thread two nuts onto the stud.
3. Remove the stud by turning the stud remover or the lower nut.
4. Remove any threadlocking compound from the threaded hole. Clean the threads with an aerosol parts cleaner.

GENERAL INFORMATION

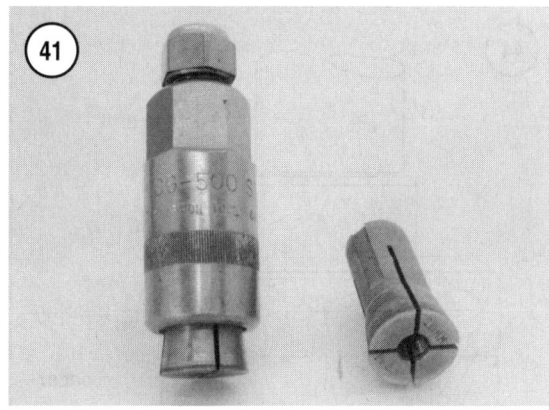

41

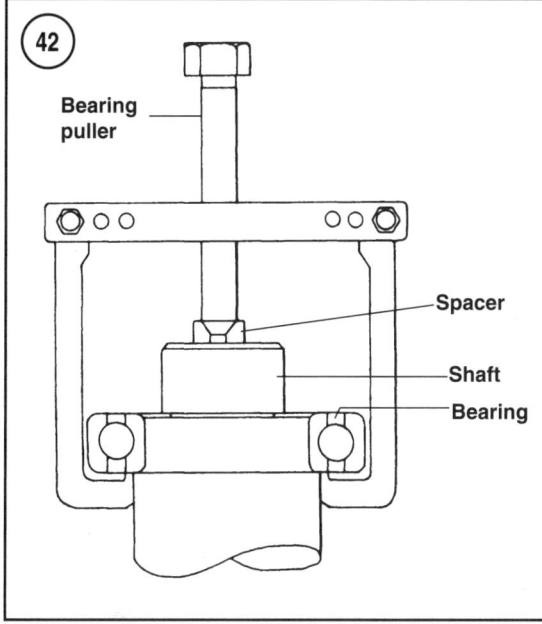

42

Bearing puller
Spacer
Shaft
Bearing

5. Install the stud removal tool onto the new stud, or thread two nuts onto the stud.
6. Apply threadlocking compound to the threads of the stud.
7. Install the stud and tighten with the stud removal tool or the top nut.
8. Install the stud to the height noted in Step 1 or its torque specification.
9. Remove the stud removal tool or the two nuts.

Removing Hoses

When removing stubborn hoses, do not exert excessive force on the hose or fitting. Remove the hose clamp and carefully insert a small screwdriver or similar blunt nose tool between the fitting and hose. Apply a spray lubricant under the hose and carefully twist the hose off the fitting. Clean the fitting of any corrosion or rubber hose material with a wire brush. Clean the inside of the hose thoroughly. Do not use any lubricant when installing the hose (new or old). The lubricant may allow the hose to come off the fitting, even with the clamp secure.

Bearings

Bearings are precision parts, they must be maintained with proper lubrication and maintenance. If a bearing is damaged, replace it immediately. When installing a new bearing, make sure to prevent damaging it. Bearing replacement procedures are included in the individual chapters where applicable; however, use the following sections as a guideline.

Unless otherwise specified, install bearings with the manufacturer's mark or number facing outward.

Removal

While bearings are normally removed only when damaged, there may be times when it is necessary to remove a bearing that is in good condition. However, improper bearing removal will damage the bearing and maybe the shaft or case half. Note the following when removing bearings:
1. Before removing the bearings, note the following:
   a. Refer to the bearing replacement procedure in the appropriate chapter for any special instructions.
   b. Remove any seals that interfere with bearing removal. Refer to *Seal Removal/Installation* in this section.
   c. When removing more than one bearing, identify the bearings before removing them. Refer to the bearing manufacturer's numbers on the bearing.
   d. Note and record the direction in which the bearing numbers face for proper installation.
   e. Remove any set plates or bearing retainers before removing the bearings.
2. When using a puller to remove a bearing from a shaft, make sure the shaft is not damaged. Always place a piece of metal between the end of the shaft and the puller screw. In addition, place the puller arms next to the inner bearing race. Refer to **Figure 42**.
3. When using a hammer to remove a bearing from a shaft, do not strike the hammer directly against the shaft. Instead, use a brass or aluminum rod between the hammer and shaft (**Figure 43**) and make sure to support both bearing races with wooden blocks as shown.
4. The ideal method of bearing removal is with a hydraulic press. Note the following when using a press:

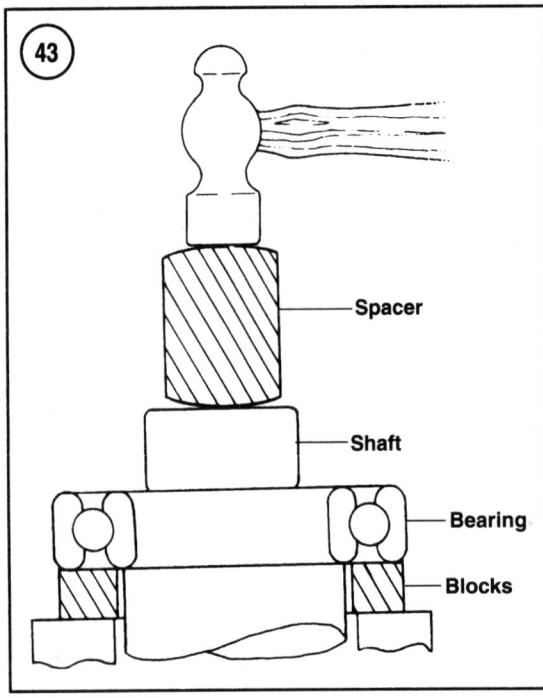

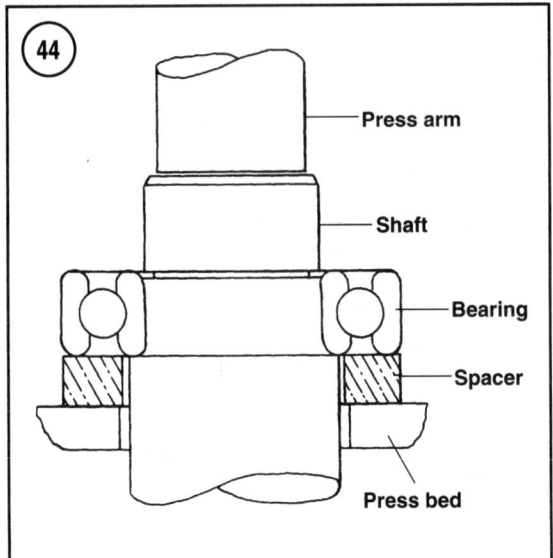

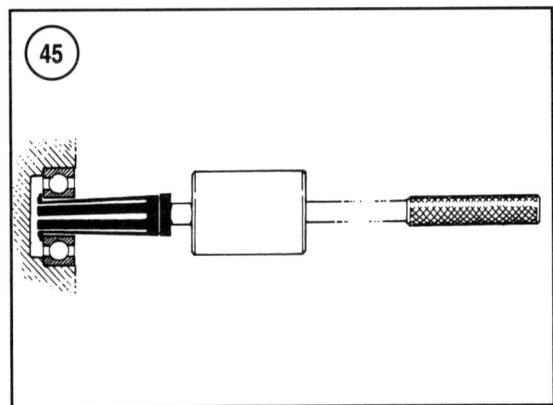

a. Always support the inner and outer bearing races with a suitable size wooden or aluminum ring (**Figure 44**). If only the outer race is supported, pressure applied against the balls and/or the inner race will damage them.
b. Always make sure the press arm (**Figure 44**) aligns with the center of the shaft. If the arm is not centered, it may damage the bearing and/or shaft.
c. The moment the shaft is free of the bearing, it will drop to the floor. Secure or hold the shaft to prevent it from falling.
d. When removing bearings from a housing, support the housing with 4 × 4 in. wooden blocks to prevent damage to gasket surfaces.

5. Use a blind bearing puller to remove bearings installed in blind holes (**Figure 45**).

Installation

1. When installing a bearing in a housing, apply pressure to the *outer* bearing race (**Figure 46**). When installing a bearing on a shaft, apply pressure to the *inner* bearing race (**Figure 47**).
2. When installing a bearing as described in Step 1, a driver is required. Never strike the bearing directly with a hammer or the bearing will be damaged. When installing a bearing, use a piece of pipe or a driver with a diameter that matches the bearing race. **Figure 48** shows the correct way to use a driver and hammer to install a bearing on a shaft.
3. Step 1 describes how to install a bearing in a housing or over a shaft. However, when installing a bearing over a shaft and into the housing at the *same time*, a tight fit will be required for both outer and inner bearing races. In this situation, install a spacer underneath the driver tool so pressure is applied evenly across both races. Refer to **Figure 49**. If the outer race is not supported, the balls push against the outer bearing race and damage it.

Interference fit

1. Follow this procedure when installing a bearing over a shaft. When a tight fit is required, the bearing inside diameter will be smaller than the shaft. In this case, driving the bearing on the shaft using normal methods may cause bearing damage. Instead, heat the bearing before installation. Note the following:
   a. Secure the shaft so it is ready for bearing installation.
   b. Clean all residues from the bearing surface of the shaft. Remove burrs with a file.

GENERAL INFORMATION

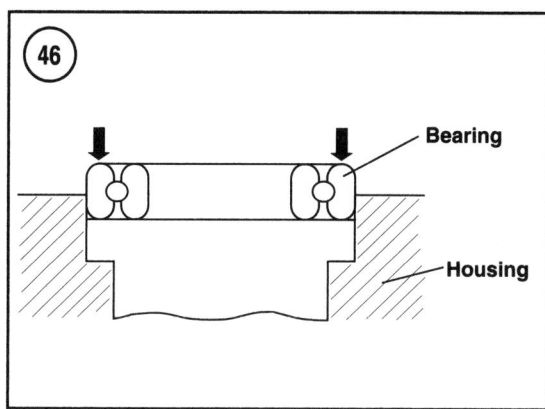

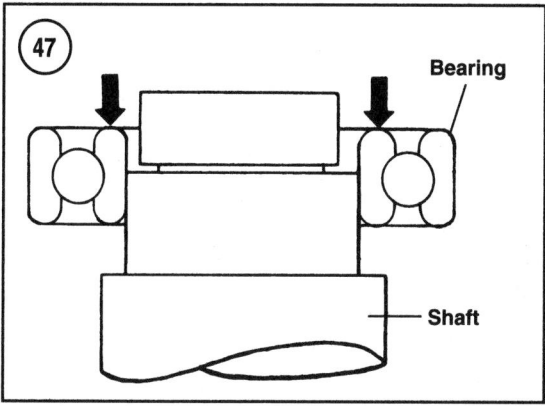

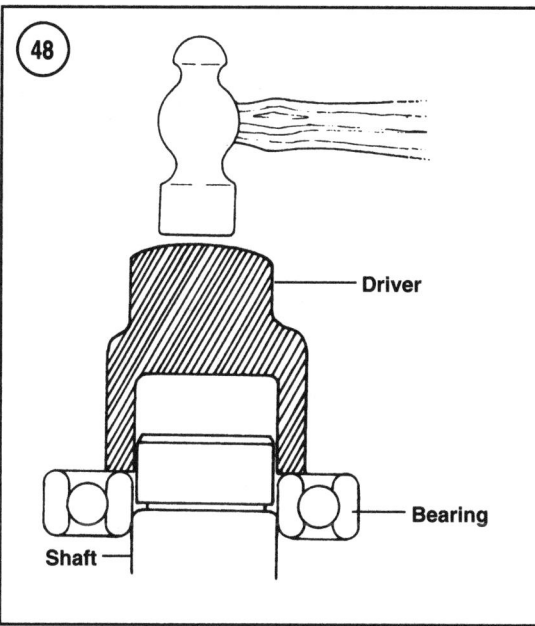

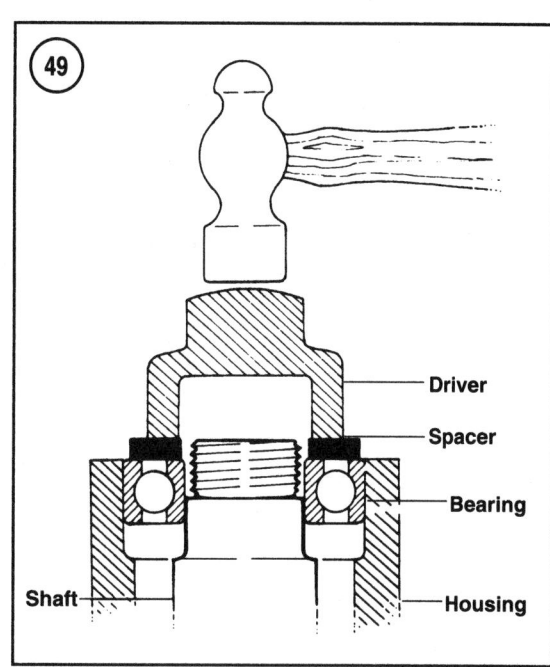

it in the pot. Hang the bearing in the pot so it does not touch the bottom or sides of the pot.

e. Turn the heat on and monitor the thermometer. When the oil temperature rises to approximately 120° C (248° F), remove the bearing from the pot and quickly install it. If necessary, place a socket on the inner bearing race and tap the bearing into place. As the bearing chills, it tightens on the shaft, so installation must be done quickly. Make sure the bearing is installed completely.

2. Follow this step when installing a bearing in a housing. Bearings are generally installed in a housing with a slight interference fit. Driving the bearing into the housing using normal methods may damage the housing or cause bearing damage. Instead, heat the housing before the bearing is installed. Note the following:

a. Before heating the housing in this procedure, wash the housing thoroughly with detergent and water. Rinse and rewash the housing as required to remove all oil and chemicals.

b. Heat the housing to approximately 100° C (212° F) with a heat gun or on a hot plate. Monitor temperature with an infrared thermometer, heat sticks or place tiny drops of water on the housing; if they sizzle and evaporate immediately, the temperature is correct. Heat only one housing at a time.

c. If a hot plate is used, remove the housing and place it on wooden blocks.

d. Hold the housing with the bearing side down and tap the bearing out with a suitable size

c. Fill a suitable pot or beaker with clean mineral oil. Place a thermometer rated above 120° C (248° F) in the oil. Support the thermometer so it does not rest on the bottom or side of the pot.

d. Remove the bearing from its wrapper and secure it with a piece of heavy wire bent to hold

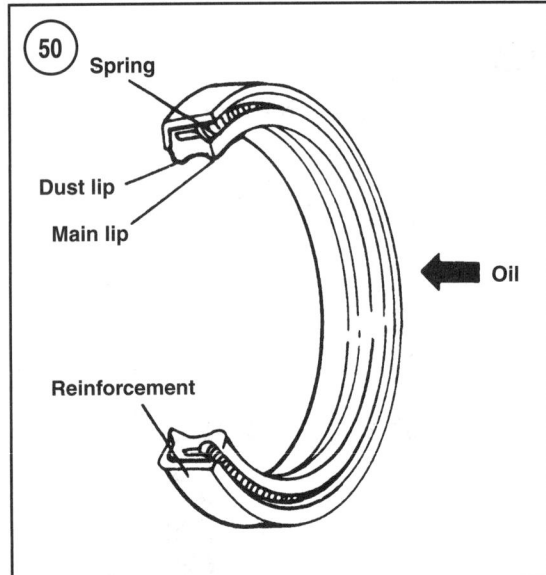

socket and extension. Repeat for all bearings in the housing.

e. Before heating the bearing housing, place the new bearing in a freezer, if possible. Chilling a bearing slightly reduces its outside diameter while the heated bearing housing assembly is slightly larger due to heat expansion. This makes bearing installation easier.

f. While the housing is still hot, install the new bearing(s) into the housing. Install the bearings by hand, if possible. If necessary, lightly tap the bearing(s) into the housing with a socket placed on the outer bearing race (**Figure 46**). Do not install bearings by driving on the inner-bearing race. Install the bearing(s) until it seats completely.

Seal Removal/Installation

Seals (**Figure 50**) are used to contain oil, coolant, grease or combustion gases in a housing or shaft. Improper removal of a seal can damage the housing or shaft. Improper installation of the seal can damage the seal.

1. Prying is generally the easiest and most effective method of removing a seal from the housing. However, always place a rag under the pry tool (**Figure 51**) to prevent damage to the housing.
2. Before installing a typical rubber seal, pack waterproof grease in the seal lips.
3. In most cases, install seals with the manufacturer's numbers or marks face out.
4. Install seals either by hand or with tools. Center the seal in its bore and attempt to install it by hand. If necessary, install the seal with a socket or bearing driver placed on the outside of the seal as shown in **Figure 52**. Drive the seal squarely into the housing until it is flush with its mounting bore. Never install a seal by hitting against the top of the seal with a hammer.

STORAGE

Several months of non-use can cause a general deterioration of the motorcycle. This is especially true in areas of extreme temperature variations. This deterioration can be minimized with careful preparation for storage. A properly stored motorcycle is much easier to return to service.

Storage Area Selection

When selecting a storage area, consider the following:

1. The storage area must be dry. A heated area is best, but not necessary. It should be insulated to minimize extreme temperature variations.
2. If the building has large window areas, mask them to keep sunlight off the motorcycle.
3. Avoid storage areas close to saltwater.
4. Consider the area's risk of fire, theft or vandalism. Check with your insurer regarding motorcycle coverage while in storage.

Preparing the Motorcycle for Storage

The amount of preparation a motorcycle should undergo before storage depends on the expected length of non-use, storage area conditions and personal preference. Consider the following list the minimum requirement:
1. Wash the motorcycle thoroughly. Make sure all dirt, mud and road debris are removed.
2. Start the engine and allow it to reach operating temperature. Drain the engine oil regardless of the riding time since the last service. Fill the engine with the recommended type and quantity of oil.
3. Fill the fuel tank completely.
4. Remove one spark plug from each cylinder head. Ground the spark plug caps to the engine. Refer to *Ignition Ground Tool* in *Tools* this chapter. Pour a teaspoon (15-20 ml) of engine oil into each cylinder. Place a rag over the openings and crank the engine to distribute the oil. Reinstall the spark plugs.
5. Remove the battery. Store it in a cool, dry location. Charge the battery once a month. Refer to *Battery* in Chapter Nine for service.
6. Cover the exhaust and intake openings.
7. Apply a protective substance to the plastic and rubber components, including the tires. Make sure to follow the manufacturer's instructions for each type of product being used.
8. Rotate the tires periodically to prevent a flat spot from developing and damaging the tire.
9. Cover the motorcycle with old bed sheets or something similar. Do not cover it with any plastic material that will trap moisture.

Returning the Motorcycle to Service

The amount of service required when returning a motorcycle to service after storage depends on the length of non-use and storage conditions. In addition to performing the reverse of the above procedure, make sure the brakes, clutch, throttle and engine stop switch work properly before operating the motorcycle. Refer to Chapter Three and evaluate the maintenance and lubrication schedule to determine which areas require service.

Table 1 GENERAL MOTORCYCLE DIMENSIONS

	mm	in.
Footpeg height		
VTX1300C models	275	10.8
All other models	270	10.6
Ground clearance		
VTX1300C models	125	4.9
All other models	130	5.1
Overall height		
VTX1300C models	1110	43.7
All other models	1125	44.3
Overall length		
VTX1300C models	2400	94.5
All other models	2575	101.4
Overall width		
VTX1300C models	920	36.2
All other models	960	37.8
Seat height		
VTX1300C models	690	27.2
All other models	685	27.0
Wheelbase		
VTX1300C models	1665	65.6
All other models	1670	65.7

Table 2 MOTORCYCLE WEIGHT SPECIFICATIONS

	kg	lb.
Curb weight		
VTX1300C models		
49-state and Canada		
2004-2006 models	310	683
2007 models	311	686
2008-on models	308	679
California		
2004-2006 models	312	688
2007 models	313	690
2008-on models	311	686
VTX1300R models		
49-state and Canada		
2005-2006 models	321	708
2007 models	322	710
2008-on models	319	703
California		
2005-2006 models	323	712
2007 models	324	714
2008-on models	322	710
VTX1300S models		
49-state and Canada		
2003-2006 models	318	701
2007 models	319	703
California		
2003-2006 models	320	705
2007 models	321	708
VTX1300T models		
49-state and Canada		
2008-on models	319	703
California		
2008-on models	322	710
Maximum weight capacity		
VTX1300C models		
49-state and Canada	182	401
California	186	410
All other models		
49-state and Canada	183	403
California	187	412

Table 3 CONVERSION FORMULAS

Multiply:	By:	To get the equivalent of:
Length		
Inches	25.4	Millimeter
Inches	2.54	Centimeter
Miles	1.609	Kilometer
Feet	0.3048	Meter
Millimeter	0.03937	Inches
Centimeter	0.3937	Inches
Kilometer	0.6214	Mile
Meter	3.281	Feet
Fluid volume		
U.S. quarts	0.9463	Liters
U.S. gallons	3.785	Liters
U.S. ounces	29.573529	Milliliters
Liters	0.2641721	U.S. gallons
Liters	1.0566882	U.S. quarts
Liters	33.814023	U.S. ounces
Milliliters	0.033814	U.S. ounces
Milliliters	1.0	Cubic centimeters
Milliliters	0.001	Liters

(continued)

Table 3 CONVERSION FORMULAS (continued)

Multiply:	By:	To get the equivalent of:
Pressure		
Pounds per square inch	0.070307	Kilograms per square centimeter
Kilograms per square centimeter	14.223343	Pounds per square inch
Kilopascals	0.1450	Pounds per square inch
Pounds per square inch	6.895	Kilopascals
Speed		
Miles per hour	1.609344	Kilometers per hour
Kilometers per hour	0.6213712	Miles per hour
Temperature		
Fahrenheit	(°F – 32) × 0.556	Centigrade
Centigrade	(°C × 1.8) + 32	Fahrenheit
Torque		
Foot-pounds	1.3558	Newton-meters
Foot-pounds	0.138255	Meters-kilograms
Inch-pounds	0.11299	Newton-meters
Newton-meters	0.7375622	Foot-pounds
Newton-meters	8.8507	Inch-pounds
Meters-kilograms	7.2330139	Foot-pounds
Volume		
Cubic inches	16.387064	Cubic centimeters
Cubic centimeters	0.0610237	Cubic inches
Weight		
Ounces	28.3495	Grams
Pounds	0.4535924	Kilograms
Grams	0.035274	Ounces
Kilograms	2.2046224	Pounds

Table 4 TECHNICAL ABBREVIATIONS

ABDC	After bottom dead center
ATDC	After top dead center
BBDC	Before bottom dead center
BDC	Bottom dead center
BTDC	Before top dead center
C	Celsius (centigrade)
cc	Cubic centimeters
cid	Cubic inch displacement
CDI	Capacitor discharge ignition
cu. in.	Cubic inches
ECT	Engine coolant temperature sensor
EVAP	Evaporative emission
F	Fahrenheit
ft.	Feet
ft.-lb.	Foot-pounds
gal.	Gallons
H/A	High altitude
Hp	Horsepower
ICM	Ignition control module
in.	Inches
in.-lb.	Inch-pounds
I.D.	Inside diameter
kg	Kilograms
kgm	Kilogram meters
km	kilometer
kPa	Kilopascals
L	Liter
m	Meter
MAG	Magneto
ml	Milliliter

(continued)

Table 4 TECHNICAL ABBREVIATIONS (continued)

mm	Millimeter
N•m	Newton-meters
O.D.	Outside diameter
oz.	Ounces
PAIR	Pulse secondary air injection system
psi	Pounds per square inch
pt.	Pint
qt.	Quart
RPM	Revolutions per minute
RTV	Room temperature vulcanization
TPS	Throttle position sensor

Table 5 METRIC TAP AND DRILL SIZES

Metric size	Drill equivalent	Decimal fraction	Nearest fraction
3 × 0.50	No. 39	0.0995	3/32
3 × 0.60	3/32	0.0937	3/32
4 × 0.70	No. 30	0.1285	1/8
4 × 0.75	1/8	0.125	1/8
5 × 0.80	No. 19	0.166	11/64
5 × 0.90	No. 20	0.161	5/32
6 × 1.00	No. 9	0.196	13/64
7 × 1.00	16/64	0.234	15/64
8 × 1.00	J	0.277	9/32
8 × 1.25	17/64	0.265	17/64
9 × 1.00	5/16	0.3125	5/16
9 × 1.25	5/16	0.3125	5/16
10 × 1.25	11/32	0.3437	11/32
10 × 1.50	R	0.339	11/32
11 × 1.50	3/8	0.375	3/8
12 × 1.50	13/32	0.406	13/32
12 × 1.75	13/32	0.406	13/32

Table 6 METRIC, INCH AND FRACTIONAL EQUIVALENTS

mm	in.	Nearest fraction	mm	in.	Nearest fraction
1	0.0394	1/32	26	1.0236	1 1/32
2	0.0787	3/32	27	1.0630	1 1/16
3	0.1181	1/8	28	1.1024	1 3/32
4	0.1575	5/32	29	1.1417	1 5/32
5	0.1969	3/16	30	1.1811	1 3/16
6	0.2362	1/4	31	1.2205	1 7/32
7	0.2756	9/32	32	1.2598	1 1/4
8	0.3150	5/16	33	1.2992	1 5/16
9	0.3543	11/32	34	1.3386	1 11/32
10	0.3937	13/32	35	1.3780	1 3/8
11	0.4331	7/16	36	1.4173	1 13/32
12	0.4724	15/32	37	1.4567	1 15/32
13	0.5118	1/2	38	1.4961	1 1/2
14	0.5512	9/16	39	1.5354	1 17/32
15	0.5906	19/32	40	1.5748	1 9/16
16	0.6299	5/8	41	1.6142	1 5/8
17	0.6693	21/32	42	1.6535	1 21/32
18	0.7087	23/32	43	1.6929	1 11/16
19	0.7480	3/4	44	1.7323	1 23/32
20	0.7874	25/32	45	1.7717	1 25/32
21	0.8268	13/16	46	1.8110	1 13/16
22	0.8661	7/8	47	1.8504	1 27/32
23	0.9055	29/32	48	1.8898	1 7/8
24	0.9449	15/16	49	1.9291	1 15/16
25	0.9843	31/32	50	1.9685	1 31/32

GENERAL INFORMATION

Table 7 GENERAL TORQUE RECOMMENDATIONS*

Fastener size or type	N•m	in.-lb.	ft.-lb.
5 mm screw	4	35	–
5 mm bolt and nut	5	44	–
6 mm screw	9	80	–
6 mm bolt and nut	10	89	–
6 mm flange bolt (8 mm head, small flange)	9	80	–
6 mm flange bolt (10 mm head) and nut	12	106	–
8 mm bolt and nut	22	–	16
8 mm flange bolt and nut	27	–	20
10 mm bolt and nut	35	–	26
10 mm flange bolt and nut	40	–	30
12 mm bolt and nut	55	–	40

*General torque recommendations are for fasteners without a specification. Refer to the torque specification table(s) at the end of respective chapter(s) for specific applications.

CHAPTER TWO

TROUBLESHOOTING

The troubleshooting procedures described in this chapter provide typical symptoms and logical methods for isolating the cause(s). There may be several ways to solve a problem, but only a systematic approach will be successful in avoiding wasted time and possibly unnecessary parts replacement. Gather as much information as possible to aid in diagnosis. Never assume anything and do not overlook the obvious. Make sure the engine stop switch is in the run position and there is fuel in the tank.

An engine needs the correct air/fuel mixture, compression and a spark at the correct time to run properly. If one of these basics is missing or not correct, the engine may not run or run poorly.

Learning to recognize symptoms makes troubleshooting easier. In most cases, expensive and complicated test equipment is not needed to determine whether repairs can be performed at home. On the other hand, be realistic and do not start procedures that are beyond your experience and equipment available. If the motorcycle requires the attention of a professional, describe symptoms and conditions accurately and fully. The more information a technician has available, the easier it is to diagnose the problem.

STARTING THE ENGINE

Starting System Operation

1. A sidestand ignition cut-off system is used on all models. The position of the sidestand can affect engine starting. Note the following:

   a. The engine cannot turn over when the sidestand is down and the transmission is in gear.
   b. The engine can turn over when the sidestand is down and the transmission is in neutral. The engine will stop when the transmission is shifted into gear with the sidestand down.
   c. The engine can turn over when the sidestand is up and the transmission is in neutral, or in gear with the clutch lever pulled in.

2. Before starting the engine, shift the transmission into neutral and confirm that the engine stop switch (A, **Figure 1**) is in the run position.

3. Turn the ignition switch on and confirm the following:

   a. The neutral indicator light is on (when transmission is in neutral).
   b. The low oil pressure warning light is on. The warning light should go off a few seconds after the engine starts. If the light stays on, turn the engine off and check the oil level (Chapter Three).

   NOTE
   *The low oil pressure indicator comes on when the ignition switch is turned on to show the indicator is working correctly. If the indicator did not come on after turning the ignition switch on, refer to **Oil Pressure Indicator and Oil Pressure Switch** in Chapter Nine.*

4. The engine is now ready to start. Refer to *Starting Procedure* in this section.

TROUBLESHOOTING

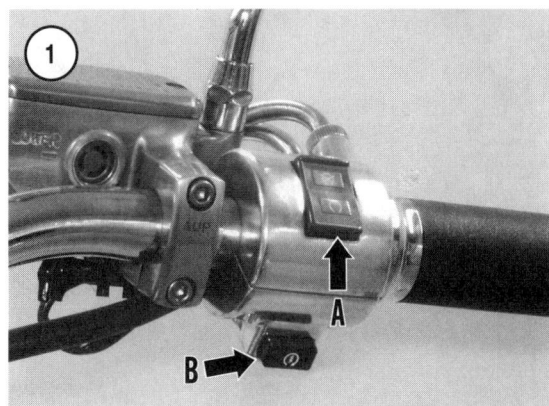

Starting Procedure

NOTE
Do not operate the starter for more than five seconds at a time. Wait approximately 10 seconds between starting attempts.

Cold engine with air temperature between 10-25° C (50-95° F)

1. Review *Starting System Operation* in this section.
2. Place the engine stop switch (A, **Figure 1**) in the run position.
3. Turn the fuel valve on (A, **Figure 2**, typical).
4. Turn the ignition switch on.
5. Pull the choke lever (B, **Figure 2**) to the fully on position.
6. Operate the starter button (B, **Figure 1**) and start the engine. Do not open the throttle when pressing the starting button.

NOTE
When the engine is started with the throttle open and the choke on, a lean mixture results and causes hard starting.

7. With the engine running, operate the choke lever as required to keep the engine idling.
8. After approximately 30 seconds, push the choke lever (B, **Figure 2**) to the fully off position. If the idle is rough, open the throttle lightly until the engine warms up.

Cold engine with air temperature of 10° C (50°F) or lower

1. Review *Starting System Operation* in this section.
2. Place the engine stop switch (A, **Figure 1**) in the run position.
3. Turn the fuel valve on (A, **Figure 2**).
4. Turn the ignition switch on.
5. Pull the choke lever (B, **Figure 2**) to the fully on position.
6. Operate the starter button (B, **Figure 1**) and start the engine. Do not open the throttle when pressing the starting button.

NOTE
When the engine is started with the throttle open and the choke on, a lean mixture results and causes hard starting.

7. Once the engine is running, open the throttle slightly to help warm the engine. Continue warming the engine until the choke can be turned off and the engine responds to the throttle cleanly.

Warm engine and/or high air temperature of 35°C (95° F) or higher

1. Review *Starting System Operation* in this section.
2. Place the engine stop switch (A, **Figure 1**) in the run position.
3. Turn the fuel valve on (A, **Figure 2**).
4. Turn the ignition switch on.
5. Open the throttle slightly (1/8-1/4 turn) and depress the starter button (B, **Figure 1**). Do not use the choke.

Engine flooded

If the engine does not start after a few attempts, it may be flooded. If a gasoline smell is present after attempting to start the engine, and the engine did not start, the engine is probably flooded. To start a flooded engine, perform the following:
1. Review *Starting System Operation* in this section.
2. Place the engine stop switch (A, **Figure 1**) in the run position.
3. Turn the fuel valve on (A, **Figure 2**).
4. Turn the ignition switch on.
5. Push the choke (B, **Figure 2**) off.

6. Open the throttle completely and depress the starter button (B, **Figure 1**) for five seconds. Note the following:
   a. If the engine starts but idles roughly, vary the throttle position as required until the engine idles and responds smoothly.
   b. If the engine does not start, turn the ignition switch off and wait approximately 10 seconds. Then repeat the steps under the warm engine starting procedure in this section. If the engine still does not start, refer to *Engine Will Not Start* in this chapter.

ENGINE WILL NOT START

Identifying the Problem

If the engine does not start, perform the following steps in order. Because there are so many things that can cause a starting problem, it is important to narrow the possibilities by following a specific troubleshooting procedure. If the engine fails to start after performing these checks, refer to the troubleshooting procedures indicated in the steps. If the engine starts, but idles or runs roughly, refer to *Poor Engine Performance* in this chapter.

NOTE
An accidentally triggered anti-theft device can cut-off power to the ignition system or starter, depending on how it is wired. If such a device is installed, check its operation for a short circuit.

1. Refer to *Starting the Engine* in this chapter to make sure the starting procedures are correct.
2A. If the starter does not turn over, perform these quick tests to isolate the starter problem:
   a. Check for a blown ignition/starter fuse as described in *Fuses* in Chapter Nine.
   b. Remove the seat (Chapter Fifteen) and check for loose or corroded battery terminals. Clean and/or tighten the cables as required.
   c. Perform the voltage test as described in *Battery* in Chapter Nine. Turn the ignition switch on and depress the starter button while reading the voltmeter. If the reading drops below 9.5 volts, the battery may have a weak or damaged cell. Recharge the battery (Chapter Nine) and repeat. If the reading is still below 9.5 volts, perform a battery load test as described in Chapter Nine.
   d. If the cables and connections are good, test the battery as described in Chapter Nine.
2B. If the starter is turning over correctly, continue with Step 3.

3. Check that there is a sufficient amount of fuel in the tank to start the engine and the fuel valve is in the on or reserve position.
4. If there is sufficient fuel in the fuel tank, remove one of the spark plugs immediately after attempting to start the engine. The plug's insulator should be wet, indicating that fuel is reaching the engine. Note the following:
   a. If the plug tip is dry, fuel is not reaching the engine. Confirm this condition by checking another spark plug from the other cylinder. A faulty fuel flow problem causes this condition. Refer to *Fuel System* in this chapter.
   b. If there is fuel on each spark plug and the engine will not start, the engine may not have adequate spark. Continue with Step 5.

NOTE
Remove the spark plug cap and examine it for the presence of water.

5. Make sure each spark plug cable is secure inside the cap. Push the cap back onto the plug and slightly rotate it to clean the electrical connection between the plug and the connector. Repeat for each cap. If the engine does not start, continue with Step 6.

NOTE
Cracked or damaged spark plug caps and cables can cause intermittent problems that are difficult to diagnose. If the engine occasionally misfires or cuts out, use a spray bottle to wet the spark plug cables and caps while the engine is running. Water that enters a damaged cap or cable causes an arc through the insulating material, resulting in an engine misfire.

6. Perform the *Spark Test* in this section. If there is a strong spark at each plug, perform Step 7. If there is no spark or if the spark is weak, refer to *Ignition System Testing* in Chapter Nine.

TROUBLESHOOTING

7. If the fuel and ignition systems are working correctly, perform a leakdown test as described in this chapter and cylinder compression test (Chapter Three). If the leakdown test indicates a problem with a cylinder(s) or the compression is low, refer to *Low Compression* in *Engine* in this chapter.

Spark Test

Perform a spark test to determine if the ignition system is producing adequate spark. This test can be performed by using a second set of spark plugs and grounding them against the engine. If available, a spark tester can also be used. Because the voltage required to jump the spark tester's gap is sufficiently larger than that of a normally gapped spark plug, the test results are more accurate than with a spark plug.

This test should be performed on a cold and hot engine. If the test results are positive for each test, the ignition system is working correctly.

WARNING
Do not perform this test if there are any fuel leaks on the motorcycle.

1. Support the motorcycle on its sidestand.
2. Remove the cylinder head shrouds (Chapter Fifteen).
3. Disconnect a spark plug cap from each cylinder. Leave the original spark plugs in the cylinder heads. Check for the presence of water in the plug caps.
4. Connect a separate spark plug to each of the spark plugs caps and ground them against the engine (**Figure 3**). If a spark tester is being used ([**Figure 4**] Motion Pro part No. 08-122), ground it the same way. Position the spark plugs and spark tester so the electrodes are visible.

WARNING
Do not hold the spark plug or spark tester; a serious electrical shock may result.

WARNING
If the original spark plugs were removed and are being used to perform the spark test, ground them away from the open spark plug holes. Otherwise, the spark firing across the spark plug could ignite the fuel.

5. Turn the ignition switch on and push the starter button to turn the engine over. A fat blue spark must be evident between the spark plug or spark tester terminals. Repeat the test at all four spark plug caps.
6. If there is a spark at each plug wire, the ignition system is functioning properly. Check for one or more of the following possible malfunctions:
   a. Faulty fuel system component.
   b. Flooded engine.
   c. Engine damage (low compression).
7. If the spark was weak or if there was no spark at one or more plugs, note the following:
   a. If there is no spark at all of the plugs, perform the peak voltage checks as described in *Ignition System Testing* in Chapter Nine.
   b. If there is no spark at one spark plug only, and the plug is in good condition, there is a problem with the spark plug wire or plug cap. Tighten the spark plug cap and repeat the test.
   c. If there is no spark with one ignition group (two spark plugs, same ignition coil), switch the ignition coils and retest. If there is now spark (both spark plugs), the ignition coil is faulty.
   d. If the problem cannot be found, refer to *Ignition System Testing* in Chapter Nine.

Starter Does Not Turn Over

If the engine will not turn over, the battery or starting system is usually at fault. Check the following steps in order:
1. Refer to *Starting the Engine* in this chapter for proper switch and sidestand operation.
2. Check the ignition/starter fuses as described in Chapter Nine.
3. Check the battery and battery cables as described in Chapter Nine.
4. Perform the tests in *Starter System Testing* in Chapter Nine.
5. Ignition system failure. Perform the peak voltage tests in *Ignition System Testing* in Chapter Nine.
6. Check for engine damage. Refer to Chapter Four and Chapter Five.

Starter Turns Over Slowly

For the starter to work correctly, the battery must be 75 percent charged and the battery cables clean and in good condition. Inspect and test the battery as described in Chapter Nine. If the battery and battery cables are in good condition, test the starter as described in Chapter Nine.

Starter Turns Over Correctly, but Engine Will Not Start

Perform the *Spark Test* in this section to isolate the problem to the fuel or ignition system. If the ignition and fuel systems are working correctly, the engine has low compression. Refer to *Low Compression* in *Engine* in this chapter.

Starter Turns over Correctly, but Engine Will Not Turn Over

Check for a damaged starter clutch as described in Chapter Nine.

Starter Relay Switch Clicks, But Engine Will Not Turn Over

1. Check for a damaged starter torque limiter or idle gear (Chapter Nine).
2. Check for engine damage. Refer to Chapter Four and Chapter Five.

POOR ENGINE PERFORMANCE

If the engine runs, but performance is unsatisfactory, refer to the following section(s) that best describes the symptom(s).

Engine Starts But Stalls and is Hard to Restart

Check for the following:
1. Check for proper fuel flow as described in *Fuel System* in this chapter. If the fuel flow is correct, continue with Step 2.

NOTE
*If a cold engine starts with the choke but cuts out when the choke is closed or if a warm engine will only start when the choke is on, check for a plugged pilot jet as described in **Carburetor** in Chapter Eight.*

2. Remove a spark plug from each cylinder and inspect them as described in *Spark Plugs* in Chapter Three. If the spark plugs are in good condition, continue with Step 3. If there is an excessive amount of fuel on the spark plugs, note the following:

a. Check for a dirty or contaminated air filter (Chapter Three).
b. Operate the choke knob to see if it is stuck in the on position.
c. Check the throttle cables to see if the carburetor throttle shaft is partially stuck open. Make sure there is some throttle cable free play as described in *Throttle Cable* in Chapter Three.
d. Remove the air filter housing and check for fuel leaks at the carburetor. If there is evidence of fuel overflowing from the carburetor or the carburetor was flooded, remove the carburetor and check the float and float valve as described in *Carburetor* in Chapter Eight.

3. If the spark plugs are in good condition, the fuel system could still be the problem. Refer to Chapter Eight and check the following:
   a. Incorrect carburetor adjustment.
   b. Leaking or damaged intake manifold.
   c. Leaking or damaged intake manifold base(s).
   d. Contaminated or stale fuel.
4. Check the ignition timing as described in Chapter Three and note the following:
   a. If the ignition timing is correct, continue with Step 5.
   b. If the ignition timing is incorrect, the ICM or ignition pulse generator may be faulty. Perform the *Ignition System Testing* in Chapter Nine.
5. Perform the *Engine Compression Test* in Chapter Three. If the compression reading for both cylinders is acceptable, repeat the checks in this section. If the compression reading is low for one or both cylinders, check for the following:
   a. Worn piston rings.
   b. Worn piston(s) and cylinder(s).
   c. Stuck or seized valve.
   d. Leaking cylinder head gasket.
   e. Incorrect valve timing.

Engine Backfires, Cuts Out or Misfires During Acceleration

A backfire occurs when fuel is burned or ignited in the exhaust system.
1. Lean air/fuel mixture.
2. Loose or damaged exhaust pipe-to-cylinder head connection.
3. Leaks in the intake system.
4. Incorrect ignition timing or a damaged ignition system can cause these conditions. Perform the *Ignition System Testing* in Chapter Nine to isolate the damaged ignition system component. Check the ignition timing as described in Chapter Three.
5. Check the following engine components:
   a. Broke valve springs.
   b. Stuck or leaking valves.

c. Worn or damaged camshaft lobes.
d. Incorrect valve timing due to incorrect camshaft installation or a mechanical failure.

Engine Backfires on Deceleration

If the engine backfires when the throttle is released, check the following:
1. Lean pilot circuit.
2. Damaged air cutoff valve.
3. Damaged pulse secondary air injection (PAIR) system:

NOTE
The PAIR system injects fresh air into the exhaust port.

   a. Clogged, damaged or disconnected PAIR system hoses.
   b. Damaged PAIR check valve.
   c. Damaged PAIR control solenoid valve.
4. Incorrect ignition timing or a damaged ignition system can cause these conditions. Perform the *Ignition System Testing* in Chapter Nine to isolate the damaged ignition system component. Check the ignition timing as described in Chapter Three.
5. Check the following engine components:
   a. Broke valve springs.
   b. Stuck or leaking valves.
   c. Worn or damaged camshaft lobes.
   d. Incorrect valve timing due to incorrect camshaft installation or a mechanical failure.

Poor Fuel Mileage

1. Dirty or clogged air filter.
2. Vacuum leak
3. Incorrect ignition timing.

Engine Will Not Idle or Idles Roughly

1. Clogged air filter element.
2. Partially blocked fuel tank breather hose.
3. Contaminated or stale fuel.
4. Clogged fuel feed hose.
5. Poor fuel flow.
6. Incorrect idle speed.
7. Incorrect pilot screw adjustment.
8. Incorrect float level.
9. Plugged carburetor pilot circuit.
10. Plugged carburetor choke circuit.
11. Damaged EVAP control system (California models only):
    a. Plugged EVAP hose.
    b. Damaged EVAP canister purge valve.
    c. Damaged EVAP CAV control valve.
12. Leaking head gasket(s) or vacuum leak.
13. Intake air leak.
14. Incorrect ignition timing due to an ignition component failure.
15. Low engine compression.

Low Engine Power

1. Turn the engine off.
2. Support the motorcycle on a workstand with the rear wheel off the ground, and then spin the rear wheel by hand. If the wheel spins freely, perform Step 2. If the wheel does not spin freely, check for the following conditions:
   a. Dragging brakes.

NOTE
After riding the motorcycle, come to a stop on a level surface (in a safe area away from all traffic). Turn the engine off and shift the transmission into neutral. Walk or push the motorcycle forward. If the motorcycle is harder to push than normal, check for dragging brakes.

   b. Damaged final gear bearings. Excessive noise from the final gear housing may indicate bearing or gear damage.
3. Test ride the motorcycle and accelerate quickly from first to second gear. If the engine speed increased according to throttle position, perform Step 4. If the engine speed did not increase, check for one or more of the following problems:
   a. Slipping clutch.
   b. Warped clutch plates/discs.
   c. Worn clutch plates/discs.
   d. Weak or damaged clutch springs.
4. Test ride the motorcycle and accelerate lightly. If the engine speed increased according to throttle position, perform Step 5. If the engine speed did not increase, check for one or more of the following problems:
   a. Clogged air filter.
   b. Restricted fuel flow.
   c. Pinched fuel tank breather hose.
   d. Clogged or damaged muffler. Tap the muffler with a rubber mallet and check for loose or broken baffles.

NOTE
A clogged muffler or exhaust system will prevent some of the burned exhaust gases from exiting the exhaust port at the end of the exhaust stroke. This condition effects the incoming air/fuel mixture on the intake stroke and reduces engine power.

5. Check for a retarded ignition timing as described in Chapter Three. A decrease in power results when the plugs fire later than normal.
6. Check for one or more of the following problems:
   a. Low engine compression.
   b. Worn spark plugs.
   c. Fouled spark plug(s).
   d. Incorrect spark plug heat range.
   e. Weak ignition coil(s).
   f. Incorrect ignition timing (defective ICM).
   g. Incorrect oil level (too high or too low).
   h. Contaminated oil.
   i. Worn or damaged valve train assembly.
   j. Engine overheating. Refer to *Overheating in Engine* in this chapter.
7. If the engine knocks when it is accelerated or when running at high speed, check for one or more of the following possible malfunctions:
   a. Incorrect fuel type.
   b. Lean fuel mixture.
   c. Advanced ignition timing (defective ICM).

NOTE
Other signs of advanced ignition timing are engine overheating and hard or uneven engine starting.

   d. Excessive carbon buildup in combustion chamber.
   e. Worn pistons and/or cylinder bores.

Poor Idle or Low Speed Performance

1. Check for leaking or damaged carburetor intake manifolds and loose or damaged air filter housing hose clamps. These conditions will cause an air leak.
2. Perform the spark test described in *Engine Will Not Start* in this chapter. Note the following:
   a. If the spark is good, go to Step 3.
   b. If the spark is weak, perform the *Ignition System Testing* described in Chapter Nine.
3. Check the ignition timing as described in Chapter Three. If ignition timing is correct, perform Step 4. If the timing is incorrect, perform the *Ignition System Testing* in Chapter Nine.
4. Check the fuel system as described in *Fuel System* in this chapter.

Poor High Speed Performance

1. Check ignition timing as described in Chapter Three. If ignition timing is correct, perform Step 2. If the timing is incorrect, perform the *Ignition System Testing* in Chapter Nine.

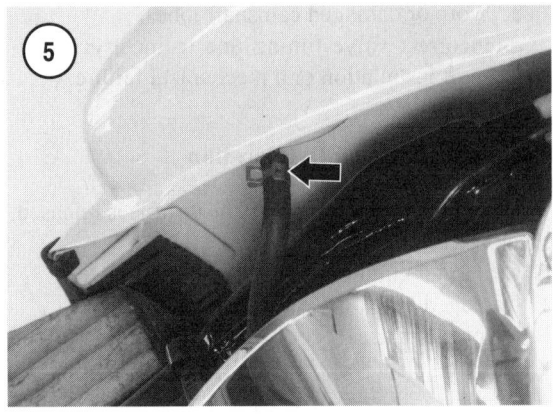

2. Check the fuel system as described in *Fuel System* in this chapter.
3. Check the valve clearance as described in Chapter Three. Note the following:
   a. If the valve clearance is correct, perform Step 4.
   b. If the clearance is incorrect, readjust the valves.
4. Incorrect valve timing and worn or damaged valve springs can cause poor high-speed performance. If the camshafts were timed just prior to the motorcycle experiencing this type of problem, the cam timing may be incorrect. If the cam timing was not set or changed, and all of the other inspection procedures in this section failed to locate the problem, inspect the camshafts and valve assembly.

FUEL SYSTEM

If the starter turns over and there is spark at each spark plug, poor fuel flow may be preventing the correct amount of fuel from being supplied to the carburetor. The following section determines if fuel is flowing from the fuel tank to the carburetor.

NOTE
On 2004-on models, a vacuum type fuel valve is used. Fuel is only supplied to the engine when the engine is being started or when running.

NOTE
*Refer to **Fuel Tank** in Chapter Eight to identify and service the hoses connected at the fuel tank and fuel valve described in this section.*

NOTE
All models covered in this manual were originally equipped with a filter screen mounted inside the carburetor and a filter screen mounted inside the fuel

TROUBLESHOOTING

tank. When working on an unfamiliar motorcycle, check for an external fuel filter installed by a previous owner.

1. Open the fuel fill cap and make sure there is an adequate amount of fuel in the tank. If a large amount of air is sucked into the tank, the fuel tank breather system is plugged. Note the following:
    a. On 49-state and Canada models, the fuel tank breather hose is connected onto the bottom of the fuel tank. On California models, the evaporative emission (EVAP) No. 1 hose is connected onto the bottom of the fuel tank. This hose is connected between the bottom of the fuel tank and the EVAP canister and serves the same function as a breather hose. Refer to **Figure 5** (all models). Check this hose for plugging or damage.
    b. On California models, if the hose connection at the fuel tank is correct, perform the tests in *Evaporative Emission Control System* in Chapter Eight.
2. After attempting to start the engine, remove one of the spark plugs (Chapter Three) and check for the presence of fuel on the plug tip. Note the following:
    a. If there is no fuel visible on the plug, or if you are unsure, check for fuel in the carburetor as described in Step 3.
    b. If fuel is present on the plug tip, and the engine has spark at all of the spark plugs, check for an excessive intake air leak or the possibility of contaminated or stale fuel.

NOTE
If the motorcycle was not used for some time, and was not properly stored, the fuel may have gone stale, where lighter parts of the fuel have evaporated. Depending on the condition of the fuel, a no-start condition can result.

   c. If there is an excessive amount of fuel on the plug, check for a clogged or plugged air filter.

Also check for a flooded carburetor, carburetor throttle valves partially stuck open and a stuck or inoperative choke mechanism.

3. To check for fuel in the carburetor float bowl, perform the following:
    a. Try to start the engine, and if it will not start, turn the ignition switch off.
    b. Remove the air filter housing (Chapter Eight).
    c. Connect a length of hose onto the float bowl fitting (A, **Figure 6**) adjacent to the drain screw and put the other end of the hose into a plastic container.
    d. Partially open the drain screw (B, **Figure 6**). Fuel should drain from the float bowl. Tighten the drain screw.
    e. If fuel drained from the float bowl, examine the fuel for water and other contaminants. If there is water in the fuel, drain and flush the fuel tank, then refill with fresh gasoline. If there are contaminants (rust and dirt) in the fuel, the fuel system including the fuel tank and carburetor should be removed and thoroughly cleaned.
    f. If no fuel drained from the carburetor, go to Step 4.
4A. On 2003 models, perform the following:
    a. Perform the *Fuel Pump Voltage Test* as described in *Fuel Pump and Fuel Filter* in Chapter Eight. If the fuel pump operation is correct, continue with substep b. If the fuel pump operation is faulty, replace the fuel pump (Chapter Eight) and retest the system.
    b. Perform the *Fuel Pump Flow Test* as described in *Fuel Pump and Fuel Filter* in Chapter Eight. If the fuel flow volume is less than specified, follow the inspection procedure in Chapter Eight. If the fuel volume is correct, continue with substep c.
    c. The carburetor may be contaminated and require cleaning.
4B. On 2004-on models, check fuel flow as follows:
    a. Turn the fuel valve (A, **Figure 2**) off and disconnect the fuel hose at the fuel tank. Connect a long clear hose to the fuel valve and place the open end into a plastic container.
    b. Turn the fuel valve on.
    c. Turn the ignition switch on and push the starter button. Fuel should flow through the hose once the starter button is pressed. Turn the ignition switch off.
    d. If fuel did not flow, test the diaphragm side of the fuel valve with a vacuum pump as described in *Fuel Valve* in Chapter Eight.
    e. If the diaphragm side of the fuel valve is working correctly but fuel is not flowing from the fuel valve, remove the fuel valve and check it and the fuel screen mounted inside the fuel

tank for plugging or damage. Refer to Chapter Eight.
f. If fuel flowed in substep c, check the fuel hose connected between the fuel tank and carburetor for clogging or other damage.
g. If there is fuel flow but the engine still will not start, the carburetor may be contaminated and require cleaning.

5. On California models, if the problem has not been located, perform the tests in *Evaporative Emission Control System* in Chapter Eight.

6. Reroute all hoses as required and check for fuel leaks.

ENGINE

Exhaust Smoke

The color of the exhaust can help diagnose engine problems or operating conditions.

Black

Black smoke is an indication of a rich air/fuel mixture where an excessive amount of fuel is being burned in the combustion chamber. Check for a partially or flooded carburetor.

Blue

Blue smoke indicates the engine is burning oil in the combustion chamber as it leaks past worn valve stem seals and piston rings. Excessive oil consumption is another indicator of an engine that is burning oil. Perform a compression test (Chapter Three) to isolate the problem.

White or steam

It is normal to see white smoke or steam from the exhaust after first starting the engine in cold weather. This is actually condensation formed by the engine during combustion. Once the engine heats up to normal operating temperature, the water evaporates and exits the engine through the crankcase vent system. However, if the motorcycle is ridden for short trips or repeatedly started and stopped without reaching operating temperature, water will start to collect in the crankcase. As this water mixes with the oil in the crankcase, sludge is produced. Sludge can eventually cause engine damage as it circulates through the lubrication system and blocks off oil passages.

Large amounts of steam that continue to exit the exhaust after the engine is running at operating temperature may indicate a cracked cylinder head or cylinder block surface. Perform the pressure test as described in *Cooling System* in Chapter Ten.

Low Compression

Problems with the engine top end will affect engine performance and drivability. When the engine is suspect, perform the cylinder leakdown test as described in this chapter and engine compression test as described in Chapter Three. Interpret the results as described in each procedure to troubleshoot the suspect area. A loss of engine compression can occur through the following areas:

1. Valves:
   a. Incorrect valve adjustment.
   b. Incorrect valve timing.
   c. Worn or damaged valve seats (valve and/or cylinder head).
   d. Bent valves.
   e. Weak or broken valve springs.
   f. Valve stuck open.
2. Cylinder head:
   a. Loose spark plug or damaged spark plug hole.
   b. Damaged cylinder head gasket.
   c. Warped or cracked cylinder head.

Overheating

Cooling system

A high coolant temperature indicator is located on the face of the speedometer. If the coolant temperature is above a preset level when the ignition switch is on, the indicator light on the speedometer face illuminates.

During normal operation the radiator fan does not operate constantly. It turns on when the temperature increases to a specified temperature. Problems in the cooling system can cause the engine to overheat. Because the system is not equipped with a temperature gauge, the actual engine temperature cannot be monitored. The coolant temperature indicator coming on may be the first indicator that the engine is overheating. If this happens, park in a safe spot and turn the engine off. Steam coming from the engine or a part in the cooling system indicates a leak. Do not touch the engine or parts of the cooling system until the engine cools down. Determine the cause of the overheating before operating the motorcycle.

> *WARNING*
> *Do not remove the radiator cap or disconnect any coolant hose immediately after or during engine operation. Scalding fluid and steam may be blown*

TROUBLESHOOTING

out under pressure and cause serious injury.

NOTE
To check the electrical part of the cooling system, perform the cooling system electrical tests in Chapter Nine.

1. Low coolant level.
2. Air in cooling system.
3. Clogged radiator, hose or engine coolant passages.
4. Thermostat stuck closed.
5. Worn or damaged radiator cap.
6. Open or short circuit in the cooling system wiring harness.
7. Damaged water pump.
8. Defective engine coolant temperature sensor.
9. Defective fan switch.
10. Damaged temperature indicator circuit.
11. Damaged fan.
12. Damaged radiator fan.

Engine

1. Improper spark plug heat range.
2. Low oil level.
3. Oil not circulating properly. Perform the *Engine Oil Pressure Check* in Chapter Three.
4. Valves leaking.
5. Heavy engine carbon deposits in the combustion chamber.
6. Dragging brake(s).
7. Clutch slipping.

Low Engine Temperature

1. Thermostat stuck open.
2. Defective engine coolant temperature (ECT) sensor.
3. Damaged temperature indicator circuit.
4. Defective fan switch.

NOTE
To check items in Steps 2-4, perform the cooling system electrical tests in Chapter Nine.

Preignition

Preignition is the premature burning of fuel and is caused by hot spots in the combustion chambers. Glowing deposits in the combustion chambers, inadequate cooling or an overheated spark plug(s) can all cause preignition. This is first noticed as a power loss but eventually causes damage to the internal parts of the engine because of higher combustion chamber temperatures.

Detonation

Commonly called spark knock or fuel knock, detonation is the violent explosion of fuel in the combustion chamber before the proper time of ignition. Engine damage can result. Use of low octane gasoline is a common cause of detonation.

Even when using a high octane gasoline, detonation can occur. Other causes are over-advanced ignition timing, lean air/fuel mixture at or near full throttle, inadequate engine cooling or the excessive accumulation of carbon deposits in the combustion chamber (cylinder head and piston crowns).

Power Loss

Refer to *Poor Engine Performance* in this chapter.

Noises

Unusual noises are often the first indication of a developing problem. Investigate any new noises as soon as possible. Something that may be a minor problem, if corrected, could prevent the possibility of more extensive damage.

Use a mechanic's stethoscope or a small section of hose held near your ear (not directly on your ear) with the other end close to the source of the noise to isolate the location. Determining the exact cause of a noise can be difficult. If this is the case, consult with a professional mechanic to determine the cause. Do not disassemble major components until all other possibilities have been eliminated.

Consider the following when troubleshooting engine noises:

1. Knocking or pinging during acceleration is caused by using a lower octane fuel than recommended. It may also be caused by poor fuel. Pinging can also be caused by an incorrect spark plug heat range or carbon buildup in the combustion chamber.
2. Slapping or rattling noises at low speed or during acceleration may be caused by excessive piston-to-cylinder wall clearance (piston slap). Piston slap is easier to detect when the engine is cold and before the pistons have expanded. Once the engine has warmed up, piston expansion reduces piston-to-cylinder clearance.
3. Knocking or rapping while decelerating is usually caused by excessive rod bearing clearance.

4. Persistent knocking and vibration occurring every crankshaft rotation is usually caused by worn rod or main bearing(s). It can also be caused by broken piston rings or damaged piston pins.

5. A rapid on-off squeal may be a compression leak around the cylinder head gasket or spark plug(s).

6. For a valve train noise, check the following:
   a. Excessive valve clearance.
   b. Worn or damaged camshaft.
   c. Damaged camshaft.
   d. Worn or damaged valve train components.
   e. Damaged valve lifter bore(s).
   f. Valve sticking in guide.
   g. Broken valve spring.
   h. Low oil pressure.
   i. Clogged cylinder oil hole or oil passage.

7. For rattles, start checking where the sound is coming from. If a rattle is coming from the lower, right side of the engine, check for a broken exhaust pipe flange assembly.

ENGINE LUBRICATION

An improperly operating engine lubrication system will quickly lead to engine seizure. Check the engine oil level and engine oil pressure as described in Chapter Three. Oil pump service is described in Chapter Five.

High Oil Consumption or Excessive Exhaust Smoke

1. Worn valve guides.
2. Worn or damaged piston rings.

Low Oil Pressure

1. Low oil level.
2. Worn or damaged oil pump.
3. Clogged oil filter.
4. Clogged oil-pump mounted oil strainer (Chapter Five).
5. Internal oil leak.
6. Broken oil pump drive chain (Chapter Six).
7. Damaged oil pump drive or driven sprockets (Chapter Six).

High Oil Pressure

1. Oil-pump mounted oil pressure relief valve stuck closed (Chapter Five).
2. Clogged oil filter.
3. Clogged oil gallery or oil jet(s).

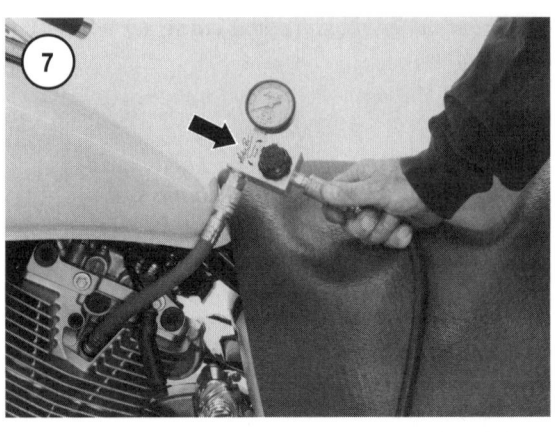

Engine Oil Pressure Warning Light Stays On

1. Low oil pressure.
2. No oil pressure.
3. Damaged oil pressure switch.
4. Short circuit in engine oil pressure switch circuit.

Oil Level Too Low

1. Oil level not maintained at the correct level.
2. Worn piston rings.
3. Worn cylinder.
4. Worn valve guides.
5. Worn valve stem seals.
6. Piston rings incorrectly installed during engine overhaul.
7. External oil leaks.

Oil Contamination

1. Work or damaged piston ring.
2. Oil and filter not changed at specified intervals or when operating conditions demand more frequent changes.

CYLINDER LEAKDOWN TEST

A cylinder leakdown test can locate engine problems from leaking valves, blown head gasket or broken, worn or stuck piston rings. This test is performed by applying compressed air to the cylinder and then measuring the leak percentage or pressure loss using a leakdown test tool (**Figure 7**).

Follow the manufacturer's directions along with the following information.

1. Start and run the engine until it is warm. Turn it off.
2. Remove a spark plug from the front cylinder as described in Chapter Three.

TROUBLESHOOTING

3. Set the No. 1 piston to top dead center (TDC) on its compression stroke as described in *Valve Clearance* in Chapter Three.

WARNING
The crankshaft may rotate when compressed air is applied to the cylinder. Remove any tools attached to the end of the crankshaft. To prevent the engine from turning over, shift the transmission into top gear and have an assistant apply the rear brake.

4. Thread the test adapter into the spark plug hole. Connect the air compressor hose to the tester.
5. Apply compressed air to the leakdown tester. Read the leak rate on the gauge. Note the following:

NOTE
If the engine is showing a 100 percent loss, the piston is probably not at TDC its compression stroke. If the timing marks are aligned, turn the crankshaft 360° and realign the timing marks.

   a. For a new or rebuilt engine, a pressure loss of 0 to 5 percent per cylinder is desired. A loss of 6 to 14 percent is acceptable.
   b. Note the difference between the cylinders. On a used engine, a pressure loss of 10 percent or less between cylinders is satisfactory. A pressure loss exceeding 10 percent between cylinders points to an engine in poor condition.

6. With air pressure still applied to the cylinder, listen for air escaping from the following areas. If necessary, use a mechanic's stethoscope to pinpoint the source.
   a. Air leaking through the exhaust pipe indicates a leaking exhaust valve.
   b. Air leaking through the throttle body indicates a leaking intake valve.
   c. Air leaking through the crankcase breather tube suggests worn piston rings or a worn cylinder bore.
   d. Air leaking into the cooling system causes the coolant to bubble in the radiator. Check by removing the radiator cap (when the engine is cool enough) and repeat the leakdown test. When this condition is indicated, check for a damaged cylinder head gasket, cylinder head or cylinder block surfaces.

7. Remove the leakdown tester and repeat these steps for the rear cylinder.

CLUTCH

Clutch service is covered in Chapter Six.

No Pressure at Clutch Lever

1. Incorrect clutch adjustment.
2. Broken clutch cable.
3. Damaged clutch release mechanism.

Clutch Lever Difficult to Pull In

1. Dry or damaged clutch cable.
2. Kinked or stuck clutch cable.
3. Incorrect clutch cable routing.
4. Damaged clutch release mechanism.
5. Damaged clutch release plate bearing

Rough Clutch Operation

Worn, grooved or damaged clutch hub and clutch housing slots.

Clutch Slip

If the engine speed increases without an increase in motorcycle speed, the clutch is probably slipping. The main causes of clutch slip are:
1. No clutch lever free play.
2. Worn clutch springs.
3. Worn clutch plates.
4. Sticking or damaged clutch release mechanism.
5. Clutch plates contaminated by engine oil additive.
6. Low engine oil level.

Clutch Drag

If the clutch will not disengage or if the motorcycle creeps with the transmission in gear and the clutch disengaged, the clutch is dragging. Some main causes of clutch drag are:
1. Excessive clutch lever free play.
2. Warped clutch plates.
3. Loose clutch housing locknut.
4. Damaged clutch pushrod.
5. Damaged clutch release mechanism.
6. Incorrect clutch release mechanism assembly after rebuild.
7. Clutch plates grabbing (not sliding) on clutch hub or clutch housing.
8. High oil level.
9. Incorrect oil viscosity.
10. Engine oil additive being used.

Difficult Shifting

Shifting problems caused by the clutch are:
1. Incorrect clutch adjustment.

2. Worn or damaged clutch components.
3. Incorrect clutch operation.

GEARSHIFT LINKAGE

The gearshift linkage assembly connects the shift pedal (external shift mechanism) to the shift drum (internal shift mechanism). Refer to Chapter Six and Chapter Seven to identify the components called out in this section.

Transmission Jumps Out of Gear

1. Damaged stopper arm.
2. Damaged stopper arm spring.
3. Damaged shift shaft, guide plate or spring assembly.
4. Worn or damaged shift drum cam or shift drum.
5. Bent shift fork shaft(s).
6. Bent or damaged shift fork(s).
7. Worn gear dogs or slots.

Difficult Shifting

1. Incorrect clutch operation.
2. Incorrect oil viscosity.
3. Loose or damaged stopper arm assembly.
4. Bent shift fork shaft(s).
5. Bent or damaged shift fork(s).
6. Worn gear dogs or slots.
7. Damaged shift drum grooves.
8. Damaged or incorrectly assembled shift shaft assembly.

Shift Pedal Does Not Return

Shift shaft return spring not centered on pin, due to broken spring or incorrect assembly.

TRANSMISSION

Transmission symptoms are sometimes difficult to distinguish from clutch symptoms. Before working on the transmission, make sure the clutch and gearshift linkage assembly are not causing the problem. Refer to Chapter Seven for transmission service procedures.

Difficult Shifting

1. Incorrect clutch operation.
2. Bent shift fork(s).
3. Damaged shift fork guide pin(s).
4. Bent shift fork shaft(s).
5. Bent shift shaft.
6. Damaged shift drum grooves.

Jumps Out of Gear

1. Loose or damaged shift shaft stopper arm.
2. Bent or damaged shift fork(s).
3. Bent shift fork shaft(s).
4. Damaged shift drum grooves.
5. Worn gear dogs or slots.
6. Weak or damaged shift shaft return spring.

Incorrect Shift Lever Operation

1. Bent shift pedal or linkage.
2. Stripped shift pedal splines.
3. Damaged shift shaft assembly.

Excessive Gear Noise

1. Worn or damaged transmission bearings.
2. Worn or damaged gears.
3. Excessive gear backlash.

Excessive Output Gear Noise

1. Worn or damaged bearings.
2. Worn or damaged gears.
3. Excessive output drive and driven gear backlash.
4. Incorrect shim adjustment.

ELECTRICAL TESTING

NOTE
Scan the QR code or search for "Clymer Manuals Youtube Tech Tips" to see an overview on electrical troubleshooting with a wiring diagram.

This section describes electrical troubleshooting and the use of test equipment.

Never assume anything and do not overlook the obvious, such as a blown fuse or an electrical connector that has separated. Test the simplest and most obvious items first and try to make tests at easily accessible points on the motorcycle. Make sure to troubleshoot systematically and never rule out the possibility of multiple problems.

Refer to the color wiring diagrams at the end of the manual for component and connector identification. Use the wiring diagrams to determine how the circuit should work by tracing the current paths from the power source through the circuit components to ground.

Preliminary Checks

Before starting any electrical troubleshooting, perform the following:
1. Inspect the fuse for the suspected circuit, and replace it if blown. Refer to *Fuses* in Chapter Nine.
2. Inspect the battery (Chapter Nine). Make sure it is fully charged and the battery leads are clean and securely attached to the battery terminals.
3. Electrical connectors are often the cause of electrical system problems. Never pull the wires when disconnecting a connector. Pull only on the connector housing. Inspect the connectors as follows:
   a. Make sure there are no bent terminals in the electrical connector. Make sure each terminal is clean and free of corrosion.
   b. Make sure the terminals are secure within the connector. If not, carefully push them in with a narrow blade screwdriver or a terminal tool.
   c. Check the wires where they attach to the terminals for damage.
   d. Push the connector halves together. Make sure the connectors are fully engaged and locked together.

Intermittent Problems

Problems that do not occur all the time can be difficult to isolate during testing. For example, when a problem only occurs when the motorcycle is ridden over rough roads (vibration) or in wet conditions (water penetration). Note the following:
1. Vibration. A loose or damaged electrical connector can fail to connect under a specific engine load (vibration).
   a. Perform a continuity test as described in the appropriate service procedure or in *Continuity Test* in this section.
   b. Lightly pull or wiggle the connectors while repeating the test. Do the same when checking the wiring harness and individual components, especially where the wires enter a housing or connector.
   c. A change in meter readings indicates a poor connection. Find and repair the problem or replace the part. Check for wires with cracked or broken insulation.

NOTE
An analog ohmmeter is useful when making this type of test. Slight needle movements are visibly apparent, which indicate a loose connection.

2. Heat. A loose or poor connection can heat up, and as the connection or joint expands, it separates and causes an open circuit. Components can also fail under specific heat ranges.
   a. Troubleshoot the problem to isolate the circuit.

CAUTION
A heat gun will quickly raise the temperature of the component being tested. Do not apply heat directly to the solid state devices or use heat in excess of 60° C (140° F) on any electrical component.

   b. To check a connector, perform a continuity test as described in the appropriate service procedure or in *Continuity Test* in this section. Then repeat the test while heating the connector with a heat gun. If the meter reading was normal (continuity) when the connector was cold, and then fluctuated or read infinity when heat was applied, the connection is bad.
   c. To check a component, allow the engine to cool, and then start and run the engine. Note operational differences when the engine is cold and hot.
   d. If the engine will not start, isolate and remove the suspect component. Test it at room temperature and again after heating it with a heat gun. A change in meter readings indicates a temperature problem.
3. Water. When the problem occurs when riding in wet conditions or in areas with high humidity, start and run the engine in a dry area. Then, with the engine running, spray water onto the suspected component/circuit. Water-related problems often stop after the component heats up and dries.

Test Light or Voltmeter

Use a test light to check for voltage in a circuit. Attach one lead to ground and the other lead to various points along the circuit. It does not make a difference which test lead is attached to ground. The bulb lights when voltage is present.

Use a voltmeter in the same manner as the test light to find out if voltage is present in any given circuit. The voltmeter, unlike the test light, also indicates how much voltage is present at each test point.

Voltage test

Unless otherwise specified, make all voltage tests with the electrical connectors still connected. Insert the test leads into the backside of the connector and make sure the test lead touches the electrical terminal within the connector housing. If the test lead only touches the wire insulation, it will cause a false reading.

Always check both sides of the connector because one side may be loose or corroded, thus preventing electrical flow through the connector. This type of test can be performed with a test light or a voltmeter.
1. Attach the voltmeter negative test lead to a confirmed ground location. If possible, use the battery ground connection. Make sure the ground is not insulated.
2. Attach the voltmeter positive test lead to the point to be tested (**Figure 8**).
3. Turn the ignition switch on. If using a test light, the test light will come on if voltage is present. If using a voltmeter, note the voltage reading. The reading should be within 1 volt of battery voltage. If the voltage is less there is a problem in the circuit.

Voltage drop test

The wires, cables, connectors and switches in the electrical circuit are designed to carry current with low resistance. This ensures current can flow through the circuit with a minimum loss of voltage. Voltage drop indicates where there is resistance in a circuit. A higher-than-normal amount of resistance in a circuit decreases the flow of current and causes the voltage to drop between the source and destination in the circuit.

Because resistance causes voltage to drop, a digital voltmeter is used to measure voltage drop when current is running through the circuit. If the circuit has no resistance, there is no voltage drop so the voltmeter indicates 0 volts. The greater the resistance in a circuit, the greater the voltage drop reading.

To perform a voltage drop:
1. Make sure the battery is fully charged (Chapter Nine).
2. Connect the positive meter test lead to the electrical source (where electricity is coming from). Connect the voltmeter negative test lead to the electrical load (where the electricity is going). Refer to **Figure 9**.
3. Turn the ignition switch on and activate the component(s) in the circuit. When the engine must be turned over (checking the starter circuit for ex-

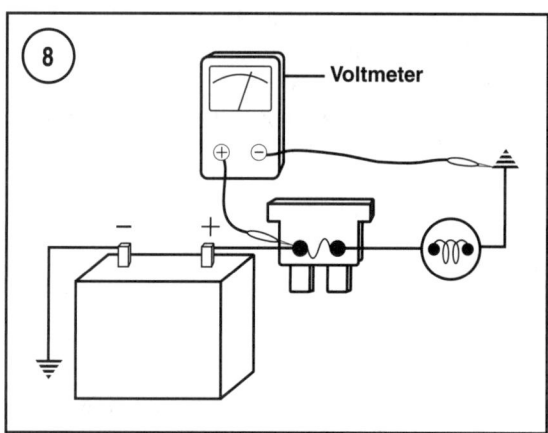

ample), disconnect all of the spark plugs caps and ground each one with a grounding tool as described in *Ignition Grounding Tool* in *Tools* in Chapter One. Then operate the starter button to turn the engine over without starting the engine. Limit cranking time to 5 seconds or less. Wait 10 seconds before cranking the starter again.
4. Read the voltage drop (difference in voltage between the source and destination) on the voltmeter. Note the following:
   a. The voltmeter should indicate a voltage drop of less than 0.4 volts. The actual number depends on the amount of current running through the system. If there is a drop of 1 volt or more, there is a problem within the circuit. A voltage drop reading of 12 volts indicates an open in the circuit.
   b. A voltage drop of 1 or more volts indicates that a circuit has excessive resistance.
   c. For example, consider a starting problem where the battery is fully charged but the starter turns over slowly. Voltage drop would be the difference in the voltage at the battery (source) and the voltage at the starter (destination) as the engine is being started (current is flowing through the battery cables). A corroded battery cable would cause a high voltage drop (high resistance) and slow engine cranking.
   d. Common sources of voltage drop are dirty or contaminated connectors, loose connectors and poor ground connections.

Peak voltage testing

Peak voltage tests check the voltage output of the ignition coil voltage pulse generator at normal cranking speed. These tests make it possible to identify ignition system problems quickly and accurately.

TROUBLESHOOTING

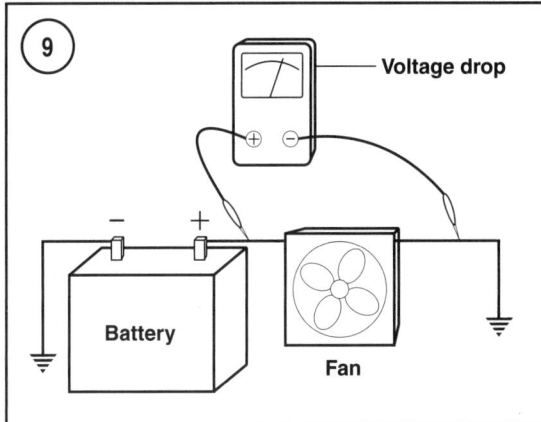

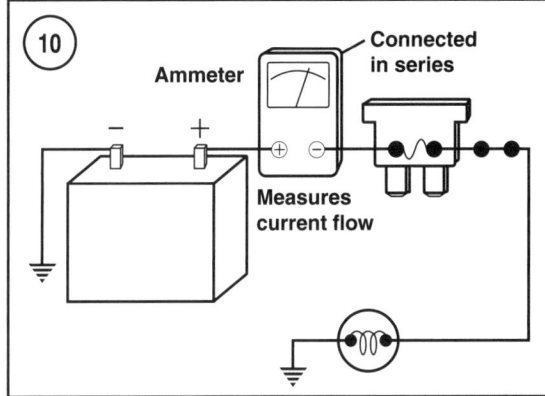

Peak voltage tests require a peak voltage adapter or tester. Refer to *Ignition System Testing* in Chapter Nine.

Testing For a Short with a Voltmeter

A test light may also be used.
1. Remove the blown fuse from the fuse panel.
2. Connect the voltmeter across the fuse terminals in the fuse panel. Turn the ignition switch on and check for battery voltage.
3. With the voltmeter attached to the fuse terminals, wiggle the wiring harness relating to the suspect circuit at approximately 15.2 cm (6 in.) intervals. Start next to the fuse panel and work systematically away from the panel. Note the voltmeter reading while progressing along the harness.
4. If the voltmeter reading changes (test light blinks), there is a short-to-ground at that point in the harness.

Ammeter

Use an ammeter to measure the flow of current (amps) in a circuit (**Figure 10**). When *connected in series* in a circuit, the ammeter determines if current is flowing through the circuit and if that current flow is excessive because of a short in the circuit. Current flow is often referred to as current draw. Comparing actual current draw in the circuit or component to current draw specification (if specified by the manufacturer) provides useful diagnostic information.

Self-powered Test Light

A self-powered test light can be constructed from a 12-volt light bulb, a pair of test leads and a 12-volt battery. When the test leads are touched together the light bulb should go on.

Never use a self-powered test light on circuits that contain solid-state devices. The solid-state devices may be damaged.

Use a self-powered test light as follows:
1. Touch the test leads together to make sure the light bulb goes on. If not, correct the problem.
2. Disconnect the motorcycle's battery or remove the fuse(s) that protects the circuit to be tested. Do not connect a self-powered test light to a circuit that has power applied to it.
3. Select two points within the circuit where there should be continuity.
4. Attach one lead of the test light to each point.
5. If there is continuity, the test light bulb will come on.
6. If there is no continuity, the test light bulb will not come on, indicating an open circuit.

Ohmmeter

CAUTION
To prevent damage to the ohmmeter, never connect it to a circuit that has power applied to it. Always disconnect the battery negative lead before using an ohmmeter.

Use an ohmmeter to measure the resistance (in ohms) to current flow in a circuit or component.

Ohmmeters may be analog type (needle scale) or digital type (LCD or LED readout). Both types of ohmmeters have a switch that allows the user to select different ranges of resistance for accurate readings. The analog ohmmeter also has a set-adjust control which is used to zero or calibrate the meter (digital ohmmeters do not require calibration). Refer to the ohmmeter's instructions to determine the correct scale setting.

Use an ohmmeter by connecting its test leads to the circuit or component to be tested. If an analog meter is used, it must be calibrated by touching the test leads together and turning the set-adjust knob until the meter needle reads zero. When the leads are uncrossed, the needle should move to the other end of the scale, indicating infinite resistance.

During a continuity test, a reading of infinite resistance indicates there is an open in the circuit or component. A reading of zero indicates continuity, that is, there is no measurable resistance in the circuit or component. A measured reading indicates the actual resistance to current flow that is present in that circuit. Even though resistance is present, the circuit has continuity.

Continuity test

Perform a continuity test to determine the integrity of a circuit, wire or component. A circuit has continuity if it forms a complete circuit; that is if there are no opens in either the electrical wires or components within the circuit. A circuit with an open, on the other hand, has no continuity.

This type of test can be performed with a self-powered test light or an ohmmeter. An ohmmeter gives the best results.

1. Disconnect the negative battery cable or disconnect the test circuit/component from its power source.
2. Attach one test lead (test light or ohmmeter) to one end of the part of the circuit to be tested.
3. Attach the other test lead to the other end of the part or the circuit to be tested.
4. The self-powered test light comes on if there is continuity. An ohmmeter reads 0 or low resistance if there is continuity. A reading of infinite resistance indicates no continuity; the circuit is open.
5. If testing a component, note the resistance and compare this to the specification if available.

Testing for short with an ohmmeter

An analog ohmmeter or one with an audible continuity indicator works best for short testing. A self-powered test light may also be used.

1. Disconnect the negative battery cable.
2. If necessary, remove the blown fuse from the fuse panel.
3. Connect one test lead of the ohmmeter to the load side (battery side) of the fuse terminal in the fuse panel.
4. Connect the other test lead to a confirmed ground location. Make sure the ground is not insulated. If possible, use the battery ground connection.
5. Wiggle the wiring harness relating to the suspect circuit at approximately 15.2 cm (6 in.) intervals. Watch the ohmmeter while progressing along the harness.
6. If the ohmmeter needle moves or the ohmmeter beeps, there is a short-to-ground at that point in the harness.

Jumper Wire

Use a jumper wire to bypass a potential problem and isolate it to a particular point in a circuit. If a faulty circuit works properly with a jumper wire installed, an open exists between the two jumped points in the circuit.

To troubleshoot with a jumper wire, first use the wire to determine if the problem is on the ground side or the load side of a device. Test the ground by connecting the wire between the lamp and a good ground. If the lamp comes on, the problem is the connection between the lamp and ground. If the lamp does not come on with the wire installed, the lamp's connection to ground is good, so the problem is between the lamp and the power source.

To isolate the problem, connect the wire between the battery and the lamp. If it comes on, the problem is between these two points. Next, connect the wire between the battery and the fuse side of the switch. If the lamp comes on, the switch is good. By successively moving the wire from one point to another, the problem can be isolated to a particular place in the circuit.

Note the following when using a jumper wire:

1. Make sure the wire gauge (thickness) is the same as that used in the circuit being tested. Smaller gauge wire rapidly overheats and could melt.
2. Make sure the jumper wire has insulated alligator clips. This prevents accidental grounding (sparks) or possible shock. Install an inline fuse/fuse holder in the jumper wire.
3. A jumper wire is a temporary test measure. Do not leave a jumper wire installed as a permanent solution. This creates a fire hazard.
4. Never use a jumper wire across any load (a component that is connected and turned on). This would cause a direct short and blow the fuse(s).

FINAL DRIVE

Oil Leaks

1. Clogged breather.
2. Oil level too high.
3. Loose or missing case cover mounting bolts.
4. Damaged oil seal(s).

Noise

1. Low oil level due to a leak.

TROUBLESHOOTING

2. Worn or damaged pinion and ring gears.
3. Worn or scored pinion and splines.
4. Excessive backlash between ring and pinion gears.

Rear Wheel Does Not Rotate Freely

1. Damaged drive shaft.
2. Damaged ring and pinion gears.
3. Worn or damaged universal joints.
4. Brake drag. Refer to *Brake System* in this chapter.

FRONT SUSPENSION AND STEERING

Steering is Sluggish

1. Low tire pressure.
2. Incorrect brake cable, cable or wiring harness routing.
3. Damaged steering bearings.
4. Incorrect steering adjustment (too tight).
5. Dragging brakes.
6. Weak fork springs.

Steers to One Side

1. Bent axle.
2. Bent frame.
3. Worn or damaged wheel bearings.
4. Loose or damaged front fork components.
5. Loose or damaged swing arm pivot bolts and/or bearings.
6. Bent swing arm.
7. Front and rear wheels are not aligned.
8. Front fork legs positioned unevenly in the steering stem.
9. Damaged tire.
10. Loose or damaged windshield mounts.
11. Unequal fork oil level.

Front Suspension Noise

1. Loose mounting fasteners.
2. Loose or damaged suspension components.
3. Damaged fork spring(s).
4. Worn or damaged fork tube and slider bushings.
5. Low fork oil capacity.
6. Loose or damaged front fender.
7. Loose or damaged windshield mounts.

Front Wheel Wobble/Vibration

1. Loose front wheel axle.
2. Loose or damaged wheel bearings.
3. Damaged wheel rim.
4. Damaged tire.
5. Flat spot on tire. A flat spot may develop during prolonged storage.
6. Unbalanced tire and wheel assembly.
7. Loose or damaged front windshield mounts.

Hard Suspension

Front fork

1. Excessive tire pressure.
2. Bent fork tube(s).
3. Fork oil level too high.
4. Incorrect fork oil weight.
5. Clogged front fork oil passages.

Rear shock absorber

1. Excessive rear tire pressure.
2. Bent damper rod.
3. Incorrect shock adjustment.
4. Damaged shock absorber bushing(s).
5. Damaged swing arm components.

Soft Suspension

Front fork

1. Low tire pressure.
2. Deteriorated fork oil.
3. Oil level too low.
4. Weak fork springs.
5. Incorrect fork oil weight.

Rear shock absorber

1. Low tire pressure.
2. Incorrect shock adjustment.
3. Weak or damaged shock spring.
4. Shock damper damaged (oil leak).

BRAKE SYSTEM

WARNING
The brake system is critical to riding performance and safety. Always check the brake operation before riding the motorcycle. Inspect the front and rear brakes frequently and repair any problem immediately. When replacing or refilling the brake fluid, use only DOT 4 brake fluid from a closed container. Refer to Chapter Three and Chapter Fourteen for brake inspection and service.

WARNING
If the brake level in the reservoir drops too low, air can enter the hydraulic system through the master cylinder. Air can also enter the system from loose or damaged hose fittings. Air in the hydraulic system causes a soft or spongy brake lever or pedal action. When it is suspected that air has entered the hydraulic system, flush the brake system and bleed the brakes as described in Chapter Fourteen.

Soft or Spongy Brake Lever or Pedal

Quickly operate the front brake lever or rear brake pedal and check to see if the lever/pedal travel distance increases. If the lever/pedal travel does increase while being operated, or feels soft or spongy, there may be air in the brake lines. In this condition, the brake system is not capable of producing sufficient brake force. When an increase in lever/pedal travel is noticed or when the brake feels soft or spongy, check the following possible causes:
1. Air in system.

NOTE
If different handlebars were installed, an extreme bar angle may affect the brake fluid level in the reservoir. Check the fluid level with the handlebar in both left and right lock positions.

2. Low brake fluid level.

NOTE
As the brake pads wear, the brake fluid level in the master cylinder reservoir drops. Whenever adding brake fluid to the reservoirs, visually check the brake pads for wear. If it does not appear that there is an increase in pad wear, check the brake hoses, lines and banjo bolts for leaks.

3. Leak in the brake system.
4. Contaminated brake fluid.
5. Plugged brake fluid passages.
6. Damaged brake lever or pedal assembly.
7. Worn or damaged brake pads.
8. Worn or damaged brake disc.
9. Warped brake disc.
10. Contaminated brake pads and disc.

NOTE
A leaking fork seal can allow oil to contaminate the brake pads and disc.

11. Worn or damaged master cylinder cups and/or cylinder bore.
12. Worn or damaged brake caliper piston seals.
13. Contaminated master cylinder assembly.
14. Contaminated brake caliper assembly.
15. Brake caliper not sliding correctly on fixed shafts.
16. Sticking master cylinder piston assembly.
17. Sticking brake caliper pistons.

Brake Drag

When the brakes drag, the brake pads are not capable of moving away from the brake disc when the brake lever or pedal is released. Any of the following causes, if they occur, would prevent correct brake pad movement and cause brake drag.
1. Warped or damaged brake disc.
2. Brake caliper not sliding correctly on fixed shafts.
3. Sticking or damaged brake caliper pistons.
4. Contaminated brake pads and disc.
5. Plugged master cylinder port.
6. Contaminated brake fluid and hydraulic passages.
7. Restricted brake hose joint.
8. Loose brake disc mounting bolts.
9. Damaged or misaligned wheel.
10. Incorrect wheel alignment.
11. Incorrectly installed brake caliper.
12. Damaged front wheel.

Hard Brake Lever or Pedal Operation

When the brakes are applied and there is sufficient brake performance but the brake lever or brake pedal operation feels excessively hard, check for the following possible causes:
1. Clogged brake hydraulic system.
2. Sticking caliper piston.
3. Sticking master cylinder piston.
4. Glazed or worn brake pads.
5. Mismatched brake pads.
6. Damaged front brake lever.
7. Damaged rear brake pedal.
8. Brake caliper not sliding correctly on fixed shafts.
9. Worn or damaged brake caliper seals.

Brakes Grab

1. Damaged brake pad pin bolt. Look for steps or cracks along the pad pin bolt surface.
2. Contaminated brake pads and disc.
3. Incorrect wheel alignment.
4. Warped brake disc.

TROUBLESHOOTING

5. Loose brake disc mounting bolts.
6. Brake caliper not sliding correctly on fixed shafts.
7. Mismatched brake pads.
8. Damaged wheel bearings.

Brake Squeal or Chatter

1. Contaminated brake pads and disc.
2. Incorrectly installed brake caliper.
3. Warped brake disc.
4. Incorrect wheel alignment.
5. Mismatched brake pads.
6. Incorrectly installed brake pads.

Leaking Brake Caliper

1. Damaged dust and piston seals.
2. Damaged cylinder bore.
3. Loose caliper body bolts.
4. Loose banjo bolt.
5. Damaged banjo bolt washers.
6. Damaged banjo bolt threads in caliper body.

Leaking Master Cylinder

1. Damaged piston secondary seal.
2. Damaged piston circlip/circlip groove.
3. Worn or damaged master cylinder bore.
4. Loose banjo bolt.
5. Damaged banjo bolt washers.
6. Damaged banjo bolt threads in master cylinder body.
7. Loose or damaged reservoir cap and/or diaphragm.

CHAPTER THREE

LUBRICATION, MAINTENANCE AND TUNE-UP

Tables 1-8 are at the end of this chapter. **Table 1** notes the maintenance and lubrication schedule.

TUNE-UP

An Emission Control Information Label is attached to the rear fender underneath the seat (2003-2007 models) or on the rear swing arm (2008-on models). Refer to **Table 2** for tune-up specifications. On 2003-2004 California models, a vacuum hose routing diagram is mounted on the rear fender. On 2005-on California models, this diagram is not used.

To perform a tune-up, service the following items as described in this chapter:
1. Air filter.
2. Spark plugs.
3. Engine compression.
4. Ignition timing.
5. Valve clearance.
6. Engine oil and filter.
7. Cooling system.
8. Wheels and tires.
9. Final drive oil.
10. Suspension components.
11. Brake system.
12. Fasteners.

ENGINE ROTATION

Normal engine rotation is clockwise when viewed from the right side (clutch side) of the engine. Use the primary drive gear mounting bolt to rotate the crankshaft, and always turn the crankshaft clockwise.

AIR FILTER

The air filter removes dust and abrasive particles from the air before the air enters the engine. A clogged air filter will decrease the efficiency and life of the engine. With a damaged air filter, very fine particles could enter the engine and cause rapid wear of the piston rings, cylinder and bearings. Never run the motorcycle without the air filter element installed.

Replace the air filter element at the service intervals specified in **Table 1** or when excessively contaminated or damaged. The service intervals in **Table 1** are for general use. However, replace the air filter more often if dusty areas are frequently encountered.

Removal/Inspection/Installation

1. Remove the screws, plastic washers and the air filter cover (**Figure 1**).
2. Remove the air filter (**Figure 2**).

LUBRICATION, MAINTENANCE AND TUNE-UP

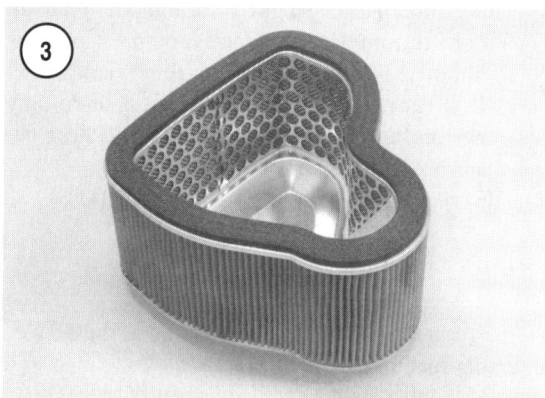

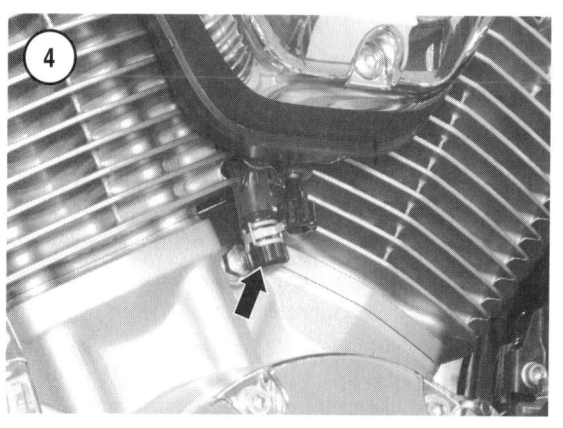

NOTE
*Do not clean the filter element (**Figure 3**) with air or any type of chemical cleaner or water.*

3. Inspect the air filter element (**Figure 3**) for excessive dirt buildup and/or damage. Check for holes or shredded filter seams. Check the foam seal for cuts, crushed or contaminated areas that would prevent the foam seal from sealing tightly. Do not run the motorcycle with a damaged air filter element or attempt to clean it as it may allow dirt to enter the engine. If the element is good, use it until the indicated time for replacement listed in **Table 1**.

4. Inspect the air filter housing for dirt and debris that may have passed through the element. Wipe the inside of the air filter housing and the air filter cover with a clean cloth.

5. Make sure the rubber seal seats fully in the air box cover groove. Replace the seal if deteriorated or damaged.

CAUTION
Overtightening the air filter cover bolts will crack the plastic cover.

6. Install the air filter element (**Figure 2**) and secure with the air filter cover (**Figure 1**), screws and plastic washers. Tighten the screws to 4 N•m (35 in.-lb.).

CRANKCASE BREATHER INSPECTION

The engine is equipped with a crankcase emission control system to prevent fumes and gases from being vented into the atmosphere. However, under various operating conditions, contaminants (water and blowby gas) that are not burned in the combustion chamber collect in the air filter housing. To remove these contaminants, a drain tube (**Figure 4**) is mounted on the bottom of the air filter housing. At the intervals in **Table 1**, inspect the drain tube for fluid. If necessary, remove the plug at the bottom of the drain tube and drain the contaminants into a container. Reinstall the plug securely onto the drain tube. Check the drain tube more frequently after riding the motorcycle in rain, after riding long distances under full-throttle, if the motorcycle is washed frequently, or after the motorcycle was dropped on its side.

ENGINE COMPRESSION TEST

A compression test can check the internal condition of the engine (piston rings, pistons, head gasket, valves and cylinders). By checking the compression at each tune-up, a running record may reveal developing problems.

Use the spark plug tool included in the motorcycle's tool kit and a screw-in type compression gauge with a flexible adapter; refer to *Compression Gauge* in *Measuring Tools* in Chapter One. Before using the gauge, check that the rubber gasket on the end of the adapter is not cracked or damaged; this gasket seals the cylinder to ensure accurate compression readings.

1. Make sure the battery is fully charged (Chapter Nine) to ensure proper engine cranking speed.
2. Run the engine until it reaches normal operating temperature, then turn it off.
3. Remove the cylinder head shroud from each cylinder head (Chapter Fifteen).
4. Grasp a spark plug cap (**Figure 5**) and twist it slightly to break it loose, then pull it from the spark plug. Disconnect all of the spark plug caps.
5. Remove one spark plug from one cylinder as described in this chapter.
6. Lubricate the threads of the compression gauge adapter with a small amount of antiseize compound and thread the gauge into one of the spark plug holes. Tighten the hose by hand to form a good seal.

CAUTION
*When the spark plug leads are disconnected, the electronic ignition will produce the highest voltage possible. This can damage the ICM or other ignition component. To protect the ignition system, install a grounding tool in each spark plug cap. Refer to **Ignition Grounding Tool** in **Tools** in Chapter One. Do not crank the engine more than necessary.*

7. Move the engine stop switch to its run position, then turn the ignition switch on. Open the throttle completely and using the starter, crank the engine while reading the compression gauge until there is no further rise in pressure. The compression reading should increase on each stroke. Maximum pressure is usually reached within 4-7 seconds of engine cranking. Record the reading.

NOTE
If a cylinder requires a longer cranking time to reach its maximum compression reading, there is a problem with that cylinder.

8. Install the spark plug.
9. Repeat for the other cylinder.
10. When interpreting the results, also note any difference between the readings. **Table 2** lists the standard compression pressure reading. Low compression indicates worn or broken rings, leaking or sticky valves, blown head gasket or a combination of all three. Readings that are lower than normal, but are relatively even among both cylinders indicates piston, ring and cylinder wear. Note the following:
   a. If the compression readings are within the specification and do not differ between cylinders by more than 10 percent, the rings and valves are in good condition.
   b. If a low reading (10 percent or more) is obtained on one of the cylinder, it indicates valve or ring trouble. To determine which, perform a wet compression test. Pour about a teaspoon of engine oil into the spark plug hole. Repeat the compression test and record the reading. If the compression increases significantly, the valves are good but the rings and/or cylinder wall are defective on that cylinder. If compression does not increase, the valves require servicing.
   c. If necessary, pinpoint the compression loss by performing the *Cylinder Leakdown Test* described in Chapter Two.
11. Reverse Steps 1-5 to complete installation.

SPARK PLUGS

Inspect and replace the spark plugs at the service intervals specified in **Table 1**.

Removal

Careful removal of a spark plug is important in preventing grit from entering the combustion chamber. It is also important to know how to remove a plug that is seized, or is resistant to removal. Forcing a seized plug can damage the threads in the cylinder head.

During removal, label each spark plug with its cylinder number and position in the cylinder head.

1. Remove the cylinder head shroud from each cylinder head (Chapter Fifteen).
2. Grasp a plug cap (**Figure 5**) and twist it slightly to break it loose, then pull it from the spark plug.

LUBRICATION, MAINTENANCE AND TUNE-UP

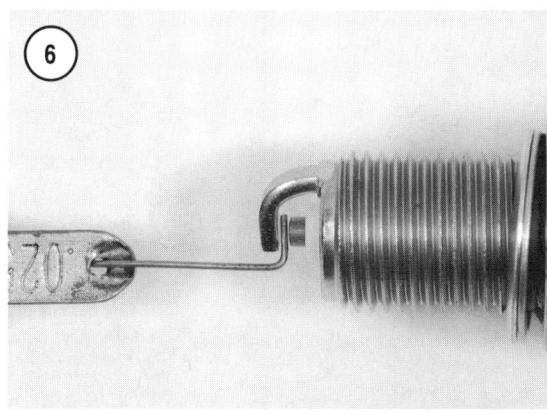

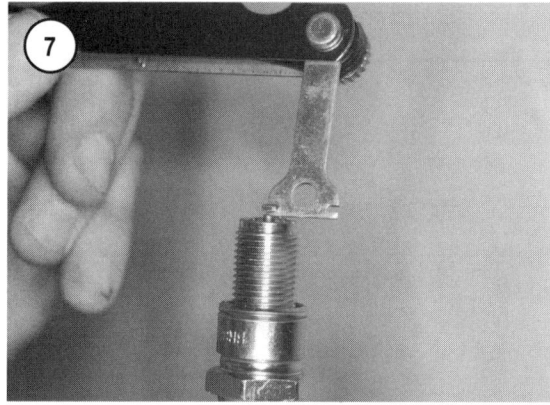

3. Blow any dirt that has accumulated around the spark plug.

> **CAUTION**
> *Dirt that falls through the spark plug hole causes rapid engine wear.*

4. Fit a spark plug wrench onto the spark plug, then remove it by turning the wrench counterclockwise. If the plug is seized or drags excessively during removal, stop and perform the following:
   a. Apply penetrating lubricant and allow it to stand for about 15 minutes.
   b. If the plug is completely seized, apply moderate pressure in both directions with the wrench. Only attempt to break the seal so lubricant can penetrate under the spark plug and into the threads. If this does not work, and the engine can still be started, install all of the spark plug caps and start the engine. Allow to completely warm up. The heat of the engine may be enough to expand the parts and allow the plug to be removed.
   c. When a spark plug is loose, but drags excessively during removal, apply penetrating lubricant around the spark plug threads. Turn the plug in (clockwise) to help distribute the lubricant onto the threads. Slowly remove the plug, working it in and out of the cylinder head while continuing to add lubricant. Do not reuse the spark plug.
   d. Inspect the threads in the cylinder head for damage. Clean and true the threads with a spark plug thread-chaser. Apply a thick grease onto the thread-chaser threads before using it. The grease will help trap some of the debris cut from the threads to prevent it from falling into the engine.

> **NOTE**
> *Damaged spark plug threads will require removal of the cylinder head (Chapter Four) and repair.*

5. Inspect the spark plug as described in this section.

> **NOTE**
> *The porcelain cover, found on the top of the spark plug, actually extends into the plug to prevent the spark from grounding through the plug metal body and threads. The porcelain cover can be easily damaged from mishandling. Make sure the spark plug socket fits the plug fully before turning the plug.*

Gap Measurement

Use *only* a wire feeler gauge when measuring spark plug gap.

1. If installing a new spark plug, remove it from the box and tighten the small terminal adapter installed on the end of the plug.
2. Refer to the spark plug gap listed in **Table 2**. Select the correct size wire feeler gauge and try to slide it past the gap between both electrodes (**Figure 6**). If there is a slight drag as the wire gauge passes through the gap, the setting is correct. If the gap is incorrect, adjust it with the spark plug gauge tool (**Figure 7**).

Installation

1. Wipe a small amount of antiseize compound to the plug threads before installing the spark plug. Do not allow the compound to get on the electrodes.

> **NOTE**
> *Do not overtighten the spark plug. This may crush the gasket and cause a compression leak or damage the cylinder head threads.*

2. Screw the spark plug in by hand until it seats. Very little effort should be required; if force is necessary, the plug may be cross-threaded. Unscrew it and try again. When the spark plug is properly seated, tighten it to 14 N•m (10 ft.-lb.).
3. Align and press the ignition plug cap (**Figure 5**) onto the spark plug.
4. Install the cylinder head cover shrouds (Chapter Fifteen).

Selection

The proper spark plug is very important in obtaining maximum performance and reliability. The condition of a used spark plug can tell a trained mechanic or experienced rider a lot about engine condition and carburetion.

If the engine is run in hot climates, at high speed or under heavy loads for prolonged periods, a spark plug with a colder heat range may be required. A colder plug quickly transfers heat away from its firing tip and to the cylinder head. This is accomplished by a short path up the ceramic insulator and into the body of the spark plug (**Figure 8**). By transferring heat quickly, the plug remains cool enough to avoid overheating and preignition problems. If the engine is run slowly for prolonged periods, this type of plug will foul and result in poor performance. A colder plug will not cool down a hot engine.

If the engine is run in cold climates or at a slow speed for prolonged periods, a spark plug with a hotter heat range may be required. A hotter plug slowly transfers heat away from its firing tip and to the cylinder head. This is accomplished by a long path up the ceramic insulator and into the body of the plug (**Figure 8**). By transferring heat slowly, the plug remains hot enough to avoid fouling and buildup. If the engine is run in hot climates for fast or prolonged periods, this type of plug will overheat, cause preignition problems and possible melt the electrode. Damage to the piston and cylinder assembly is possible.

When running a stock engine, changing to a different heat range plug is normally not required. Changing to a different heat range plug may be necessary when operating a motorcycle with a modified engine. This type of change is usually based on a recommendation made by the engine builder. Experience in reading spark plugs is also required when trying to determine if a different heat range plug is required. When installing a different heat range plug, go one step hotter or colder from the recommended plug. Do not try to correct fuel or ignition problems by using different spark plugs. This will only compound the existing problem(s) and possibly lead to severe engine damage.

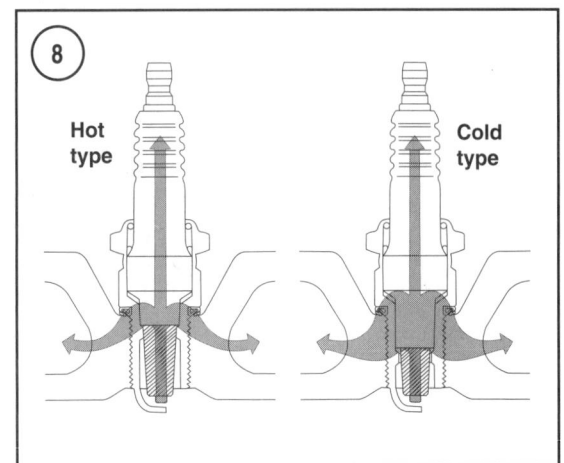

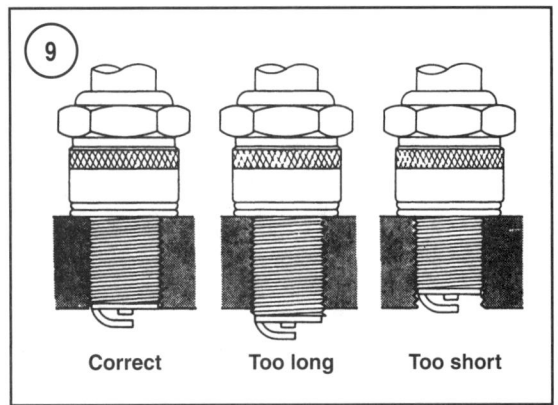

The reach (length) of a plug is also important (**Figure 9**). A shorter than normal plug causes hard starting, reduce engine performance and carbon buildup on the exposed cylinder head threads. These same conditions can occur if the correct length plug is used without a gasket. Trying to thread a spark plug into threads with carbon buildup may damage the threads in the cylinder head.

Reading/Inspection

The spark plug is an excellent indicator of how the engine is operating. By correctly evaluating the condition of the plug, engine problems can be diagnosed. To correctly read a spark plug, perform the following:
1. Refer to *Removal* and *Installation* in this section when removing and installing the spark plug during this procedure.
2. If a new plug was installed, ride the motorcycle for approximately 15 to 20 minutes so it will begin to color. Then continue with Step 3.
3. Accelerate on a straight road at full throttle. Then push the engine stop button, pull the clutch lever in

LUBRICATION, MAINTENANCE AND TUNE-UP

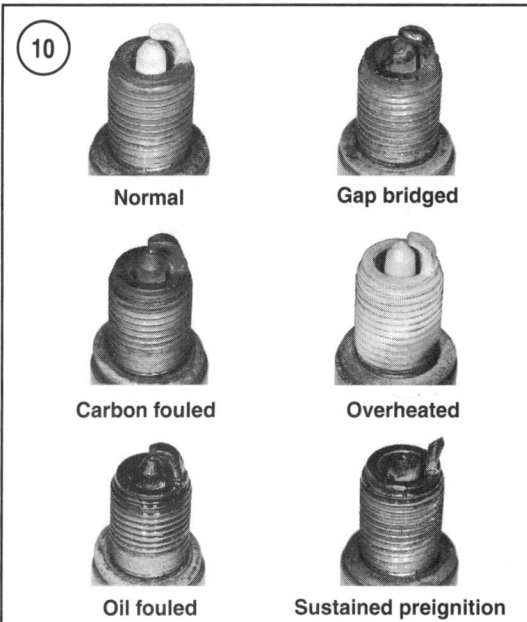

1. Clogged air filter.
2. Faulty fuel system.
3. Faulty ignition component.
4. Spark plug heat range too cold.
5. Low engine compression.
6. Engine not properly broken in.

Carbon fouled

The plug is black with a dry, sooty deposit on the entire plug surface. This dry sooty deposit is conductive and can create electrical paths that bypass the electrode gap. This often results in misfiring of the plug. Replace the spark plug. Possible causes:
1. Rich fuel mixture.
2. Faulty fuel system.
3. Spark plug heat range too cold.
4. Clogged air filter.
5. Faulty ignition component.
6. Low engine compression.

and coast to a stop. Do not stop by downshifting the transmission.
4. Remove the spark plug and examine its firing tip while noting the following:
   a. Inspect the spark plug with a magnifying glass or spark plug reader.
   b. Refer to **Figure 10** and the following paragraphs provide a description, as well as common causes for each of the conditions.

> **CAUTION**
> *In all cases, when a spark plug is abnormal, find the cause of the problem before continuing engine operation. Severe engine damage is possible when abnormal plug readings are ignored.*

Normal condition

The porcelain insulator around the center electrode is clean and colorless. There should be a gray ring around the center electrode where it separates from the porcelain. No erosion or rounding of the electrodes or abnormal gap is evident. This indicates an engine that has proper fuel mixture and ignition timing. This heat range of plug is appropriate for the conditions in which the engine has been operated. The plug can be reused.

Oil fouled

The plug is wet with black, oily deposits on the electrodes and insulator. The electrodes do not show wear. Replace the spark plug. Possible causes:

Overheating

The plug is dry and the insulator has a white or light gray cast. The insulator may also appear blistered. The electrodes may have a burnt appearance and there may be metallic specks on the center electrode and porcelain. This material is being removed from the piston crown. Replace the spark plug. Possible causes:
1. Lean fuel mixture.
2. Faulty fuel system.
3. Spark plug heat range too hot.
4. Faulty ignition component.
5. Air leak at the exhaust pipe or intake manifold.
6. Overtightened spark plug.
7. No crush washer on spark plug.
8. Spark plug heat range too hot.

Gap bridging

The plug is clogged with deposits between the electrodes. The engine may run with a bridged spark plug, but it will misfire. Replace the spark plug. Possible causes:
1. Incorrect oil type.
2. Incorrect fuel or fuel contamination.
3. Excessive carbon deposits in combustion chamber.

Preignition

The plug electrodes are severely eroded or melted. This condition can lead to severe engine damage. Replace the spark plug. Possible causes:

1. Faulty ignition system component.
2. Spark plug heat range too hot.
3. Air leak.
4. Excessive carbon deposits in combustion chamber.

Worn out

The center electrode is rounded from normal combustion. There is no indication of abnormal combustion or engine conditions.

IGNITION TIMING

The ignition control module (ICM) is not adjustable. However, checking the ignition timing can provide diagnostic information. If an ignition related problem is suspected, check the ignition timing to confirm proper ignition system operation. Also check the ignition timing after installing a new ignition system component to make sure it is working correctly.

1. Start the engine and warm to normal operating temperature, then turn the engine off.
2. Remove the Allen bolts and the timing hole cap cover (**Figure 11**).
3. Remove the timing hole cap (**Figure 12**) and its O-ring to access the timing marks.
4. Connect a timing light onto one of the front cylinder spark plug wires following the manufacturer's instructions.
5. Start the engine and check the idle speed (**Table 2**). If necessary, adjust the idle speed as described in this chapter.
6. Check the ignition timing as follows:
    a. Aim the timing light at the timing hole and pull the trigger. The ignition timing is correct if the F-F mark (A, **Figure 13**) on the primary drive gear aligns with the index mark (B) on the right crankcase cover while the engine is running at idle speed. Turn the engine off.
    b. Disconnect the timing light.
    c. Connect the timing light to one of the rear cylinder spark plug wires. Start the engine and recheck the ignition timing. The ignition timing is correct if the R-F mark (A, **Figure 14**) on the primary drive gear aligns with the index mark (B) on the right crankcase cover while the engine is running at idle speed.
7. Turn the engine off and disconnect the timing light.
8. If the ignition timing is correct for both cylinders, the ignition system is working correctly. If the ignition timing is incorrect, there is a problem with one or more ignition system components; refer to *Ignition System Testing* in Chapter Nine.

LUBRICATION, MAINTENANCE AND TUNE-UP

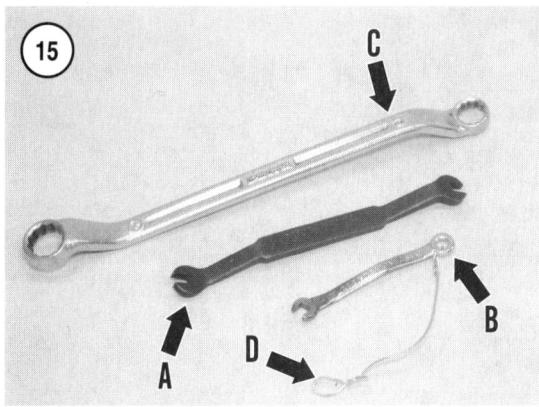

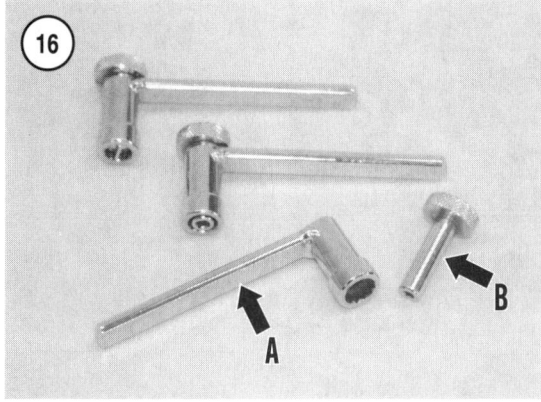

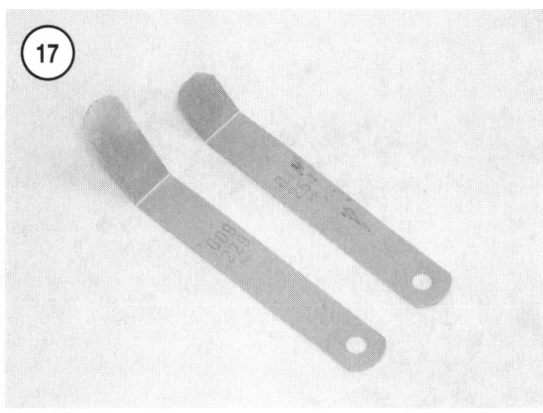

Tools

1. An offset 4-mm wrench is required to turn the valve adjusting screws. Use the Honda tappet wrench (part No. 07908-KE90100 [A, **Figure 15**]) or heat and bend a 4-mm wrench as shown in B, **Figure 15**. An offset 10-mm wrench (C, **Figure 15**) is required to turn the locknuts.
2. The Motion Pro Tappet Tool Set (part No. 08-0073) can also be used by combining the 10-mm wrench (A, **Figure 16**) with the 4-mm hex adjuster (B). These tools can also be used separately.
3. Bent or offset feeler gauges (**Figure 17**). If necessary, use aviation snips to trim the gauges so they can be operated without interference from the cylinder head cover opening, hoses and wiring harnesses. Take small bites with the snips to avoid twisting and damaging the gauge end. Remove burrs from the gauge ends with a file.

NOTE
Do not bend straight type feeler gauges as this may weaken the gauges and cause them to break off and fall inside the engine.

4. To retrieve the wrench or feeler gauges if they are dropped into the engine during the procedure, secure each with a piece of wire (D, **Figure 15**). Loop the end of the wire to prevent puncturing hands and fingers.

Inspection

Refer to **Table 2** for valve clearance specifications.

NOTE
Do not check or adjust the valve clearance when the air or engine temperature is above 35° C (95° F).

1. Support the motorcycle on a stand so the seat is level. This will make it easier to view the primary drive gear timing marks.
2. Remove the seat (Chapter Fifteen).
3. Remove the fuel tank (Chapter Eight).
4. Remove the cylinder head shrouds (Chapter Fifteen).
5. Remove the air filter housing (Chapter Eight).

NOTE
The hose routing shown in the following photographs are from a 2008 California model. Because the hose and wire harness routing is different for each model year, make sure to take notes while labeling and/or take digital photographs of the assembled parts before starting work.

9. Replace the O-ring on the timing hole cap if leaking or damaged.
10. Lubricate the timing hole cap (**Figure 12**) threads with grease and the O-ring with oil and tighten to 18 N•m (13 ft.-lb.).
11. Install the timing hole cap cover (**Figure 11**) and tighten the Allen bolts to 10 N•m (88 in.-lb.).

VALVE CLEARANCE

Check the valve clearance and adjust if necessary at the intervals specified in **Table 1**.

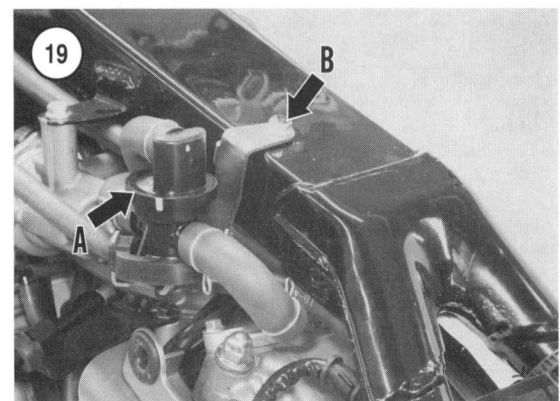

6. Disconnect the secondary air supply hose (**Figure 18**) from the rear cylinder head cover and at the pulse secondary air injection (PAIR) control valve (A, **Figure 19**) and remove the hose and its attached pipe from the right side of the frame.

7. Remove the bolt (B, **Figure 19**) securing the PAIR control valve mounting bracket to the frame. Then reposition the PAIR control valve assembly (**Figure 20**) or disconnect the hoses and remove the PAIR control valve assembly (**Figure 21**) from the motorcycle.

8. On 2008 California models, remove the sub-air cleaner and fuel cut-off solenoid valve as described in *Evaporative Emission Control System* in Chapter Eight.

9. Remove the right front and left rear air fin covers (Chapter Fifteen) to provide additional room for valve adjustment.

10. Block off the carburetor intake opening. Then clean the valve adjustment covers and the area around the covers with compressed air.

> *NOTE*
> *Make sure the hose clamps on the disconnected hoses are positioned or removed so they cannot fall into the engine.*

11. At the front cylinder head cover, remove the exhaust (A, **Figure 22**) and intake (B) valve adjustment covers and O-rings. Repeat at the rear cylinder head cover.

12. Remove the Allen bolts and the timing hole cap cover (**Figure 11**).

13. Remove the timing hole cap (**Figure 12**) and its O-ring to access the timing marks.

14. Remove one spark plug from each cylinder as described in this chapter. This makes it easier to turn the engine by hand. Cover the spark plug openings to prevent objects from falling into the engine.

15. Set the front cylinder piston at TDC on its compression stroke as follows:

LUBRICATION, MAINTENANCE AND TUNE-UP

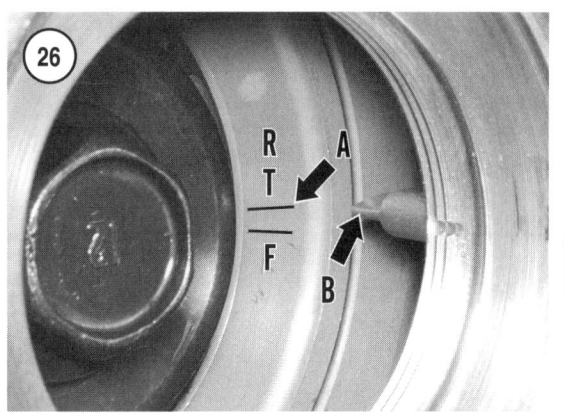

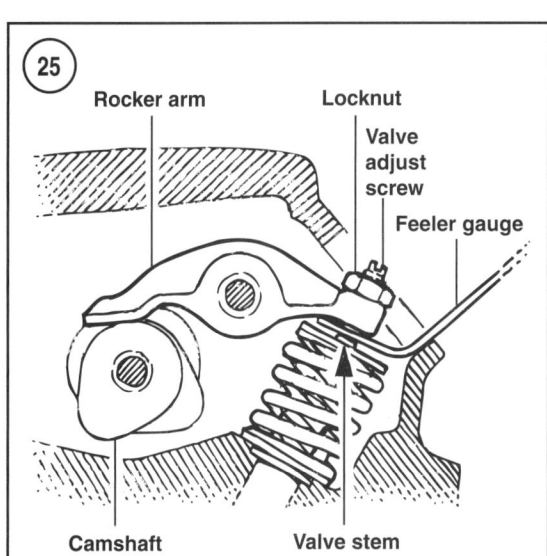

rotate the engine 360° (1 full turn) clockwise and realign the F-T mark.

16. Measure the clearance of the exhaust valve and both intake valves as follows:
   a. Refer to **Table 2** to select the correct feeler gauges for the valve to be checked.
   b. Insert the feeler gauge between the valve adjusting screw and the end of the valve stem (**Figure 25**). When the clearance is correct, there is a slight drag on the feeler gauge when it is inserted and withdrawn.
   c. If there is too much or too little drag, adjust the valve clearance as described in this section.
   d. When the front cylinder head valve clearances are correct, continue with Step 17 to check the rear cylinder head valve clearances.

17. Turn the crankshaft clockwise and align the R-T mark (A, **Figure 26**) on the primary drive gear with the index mark (B) on the right crankcase cover. Check that the rear cylinder head piston is at TDC on its compression stroke as described in Step 15. If all three rocker arms are tight (no free play), rotate the engine 360° (1 turn) clockwise and realign the R-T mark. Check the valve clearances as described in Step 16.

18. When the clearance of each valve is within specification, reverse Steps 1-14 while noting the following:
   a. Reinstall the spark plugs as described in this chapter.
   b. Replace the valve adjustment cover and timing hole cap O-rings if leaking or damaged. Lubricate the O-rings with oil.
   c. Lubricate the exhaust valve adjustment cover (A, **Figure 22**) threads with grease and tighten to 15 N•m (11 ft.-lb.). Install the intake valve adjustment covers (B, **Figure 22**) with the UP mark facing up and tighten the bolts securely.
   d. Replace the O-ring on the timing hole cap if leaking or damaged.

   a. Turn the crankshaft (**Figure 23**) clockwise and align the F-T mark (A, **Figure 24**) on the primary drive gear with the index mark (B) on the right crankcase cover.
   b. Try to move each front cylinder head rocker arm by hand. The exhaust rocker arm and both intake rocker arms should have some free play. If all three rocker arms are tight (no free play),

e. Lubricate the timing hole cap (**Figure 12**) threads with grease and the O-ring with oil and tighten to 18 N•m (13 ft.-lb.).

f. Install the timing hole cap cover (**Figure 11**) and tighten the Allen bolts to 10 N•m (88 in.-lb.).

Adjustment

Refer to **Figure 25**.

1. Set the cylinder to TDC on its compression stroke as described in this section.
2. Loosen the locknut on the valve adjust screw.
3. Turn the valve adjust screw until the valve clearance (slight drag on feeler gauge) is correct.
4. Hold the valve adjust screw to prevent it from turning and tighten the locknut to 22 N•m (16 ft.-lb.).
5. Recheck the valve clearance. If the clearance changed when the locknut was tightened, loosen the locknut and readjust the valve clearance. Repeat until the valve clearance is correct after the locknut is tightened.

IDLE SPEED ADJUSTMENT

Check idle speed at the intervals specified in **Table 1**.

> *WARNING*
> *With the engine idling, move the handlebar from side to side. If idle speed increases during this movement, the throttle cable needs adjusting or may be incorrectly routed through the frame. Correct this problem immediately. Do not ride the motorcycle in this unsafe condition.*

The engine idle speed is adjusted by turning the idle speed screw (**Figure 27**) on the right side of the engine.

1. Start the engine and let it warm up approximately 2-3 minutes.
2. Support the motorcycle on its sidestand. Turn the engine off.
3. Connect a portable tachometer following the manufacturer's instructions.
4. Restart the engine and set the idle speed by turning the idle speed screw (**Figure 27**). **Table 2** lists the correct idle speed.
5. Open and close the throttle a couple of times; check for variation in idle speed. Readjust if necessary.

> *NOTE*
> *If the engine runs roughly at idle, check for a dirty or contaminated air filter element.*

6. Turn the engine off and disconnect the portable tachometer.

FUEL SYSTEM HOSE INSPECTION

Inspect the fuel and vacuum (2004-on models) hoses at the intervals specified in **Table 1**.

> *WARNING*
> *Some fuel may spill from the hoses when disconnecting them for inspection or replacement. Because gasoline is extremely flammable and explosive, perform this procedure away from all open flames (including appliance pilot lights) and sparks. Do not smoke or allow smoking in the work area. Always work in a well-ventilated area. Wipe up any spills immediately.*

1. Refer to *Handling Gasoline Safely* in *Safety* in Chapter One.
2. Remove the fuel tank (Chapter Eight).

LUBRICATION, MAINTENANCE AND TUNE-UP

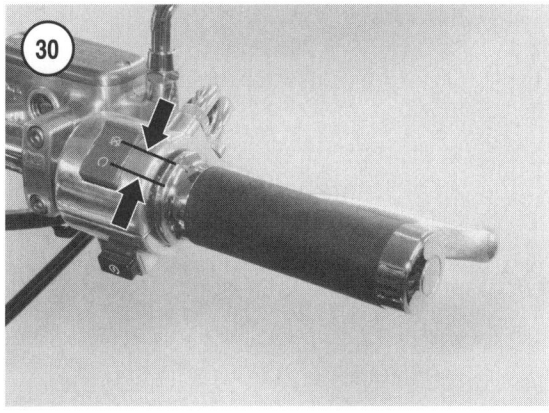

3. Remove the air filter housing (Chapter Eight).
4A. On 2003 models, inspect the hoses connected at the fuel valve, fuel pump and fuel filter for leaks, hardness, age deterioration or other damage. Follow the length of each hose to inspect it. Refer to *Fuel Pump and Fuel Filter* in Chapter Eight.
4B. On 2004-on models, perform the following:
   a. Inspect the fuel hose installed between the fuel valve and carburetor (A, **Figure 28**, typical) for leaks, hardness, age deterioration or other damage. Follow the length of the hose to inspect it.
   b. Make sure the wire guide (A, **Figure 29**) is positioned on the section of the fuel hose where it is connected at the carburetor. Also make sure the large rubber protector (B, **Figure 29**) is positioned between the rear cylinder head cover and fuel hose.
   c. Inspect the vacuum hose (B, **Figure 28**, typical) for leaks, hardness, age deterioration or other damage. Make sure the vacuum hose is connected to the T-connector, which is connected to a vacuum nozzle on the intake manifold.
5. Check the hose clamps for tightness, position and damage. Make sure the projections or handles on the hose clamps are positioned so they do not contact other hoses or wiring harnesses.

6. Replace damaged hoses and weak or damaged hose clamps as required.
7. Reverse Step 2 and Step 3.

FUEL FILTER

Removal/Installation
(2003 VTX1300S Models)

The manufacturer does not list a time or mileage interval for replacing the fuel filter. Refer to *Fuel Pump and Fuel Filter* in Chapter Eight.

THROTTLE CABLE

WARNING
An improperly adjusted, assembled or installed throttle grip assembly may cause the throttle to stick open and cause the rider to lose control of the motorcycle. Do not start or ride the motorcycle until the throttle grip is correctly installed, adjusted and snaps back when released.

Throttle Operation

Check the throttle operation at the intervals specified in **Table 1** or whenever the throttle operation feels too tight or loose.
Check for smooth throttle operation from the fully closed to fully open positions. Check at various steering positions. The throttle grip must return to the fully closed position without any hesitation.
Check the throttle cables for damage, wear or deterioration. Make sure the throttle cables are not kinked at any place.
If the throttle does not return to the fully closed position smoothly and the cables do not appear to be damaged, lubricate the throttle cables as described in this section. If the throttle still does not return properly, the cables are probably kinked or routed incorrectly. Replace damaged throttle cables.
Check free play at the throttle grip flange (**Figure 30**) and compare to the specifications in **Table 2**. If necessary, perform the adjustment procedure in this section.

Lubrication

Inspect the throttle operation at the intervals specified in **Table 1**. Lubricate the throttle cables whenever the throttle becomes stiff and sluggish and fails to snap back after releasing it.

The main cause of cable breaks or stiffness is improper lubrication. Periodic lubrication assures long service life. Inspect the cables for fraying, and check the sheath for chafing. Always replace both cables at the same time.

Because of their design, a cable lubricant tool cannot be mounted on the upper end of both throttle cables. To lubricate the cables at their upper ends, use a can of lubricant with a thin hollow tube. After disconnecting the cables at the carburetor, a cable lubricant tool can be mounted on the lower end of both throttle cables.

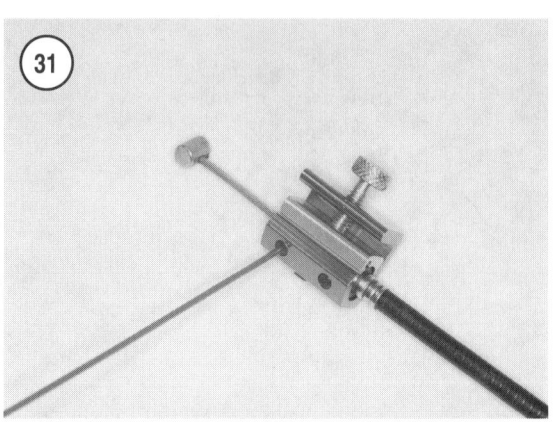

CAUTION
When servicing aftermarket cables, follow the manufacturer's cable lubrication requirements.

1. Disconnect the lower throttle cable ends as described in *Throttle Cable* in Chapter Eight.
2. Remove the throttle housing and disconnect the upper throttle cable ends as described in *Handlebar* in Chapter Twelve.
3. Lubricate the cables. **Figure 31** shows a cable lube tool and a cable lubricant. Lubricate each cable until fluid exits through the opposite end of the cable. Wipe up all excess lube from the end of the cable.

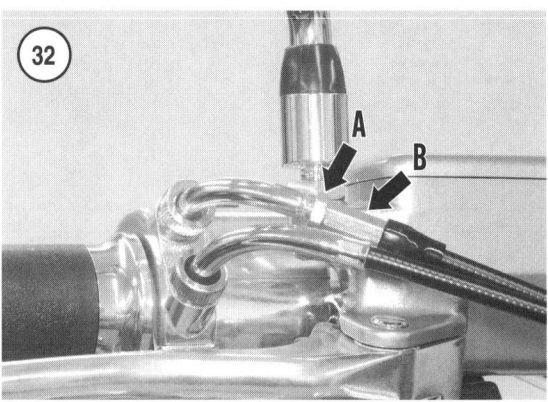

CAUTION
Do not use chain lube to lubricate control cables unless it is also advertised as a cable lubricant.

NOTE
When using an aerosol type lubricant, cover the area around the nozzle and tube with a plastic bag.

4. Lightly lubricate the upper cable ends with grease.
5. Installation is the reverse of removal. Adjust the throttle cables as described in this section.

Adjustment

Cable adjusters are provided at both ends of the pull cable. Minor cable adjustment is made at the upper adjuster at the handlebar. If this does not provide enough adjustment, continue by adjusting the lower adjuster at the carburetor.

WARNING
If the idle speed increases when the handlebar is turned, check the throttle cable routing. If the routing is correct, check for a damaged cable(s). Correct this problem immediately. Do not ride the motorcycle in this unsafe condition.

1. If minor adjustment is required, perform the following at the throttle grip:
   a. Loosen the locknut (A, **Figure 32**) and turn the upper adjuster (B) in or out to achieve the specified free play (**Table 2**).
   b. Tighten the locknut and recheck the adjustment. If there is not enough cable adjustment, continue with Step 2.
2. If major adjustment is necessary, perform the following:
   a. Remove the air filter housing (Chapter Eight).
   b. Loosen the upper cable locknut (A, **Figure 33**) and turn the adjuster (B) to achieve proper free play at the throttle grip (**Figure 30**). Tighten the locknut securely.

NOTE
*After tightening the cable locknut (A, **Figure 33**), make sure the lower locknut (C) is positioned against the bottom of the cable holder.*

   c. Recheck free play. If necessary, readjust the upper adjuster as described in Step 1.
3. Operate the throttle a few times. The throttle grip should now be adjusted correctly. If not, the throttle cables may be stretched. Replace cables if the specified free play cannot be obtained.

LUBRICATION, MAINTENANCE AND TUNE-UP

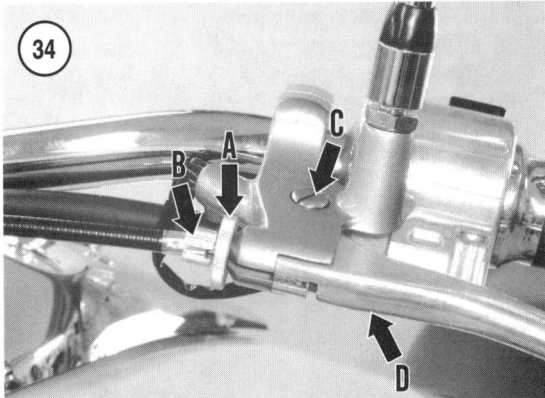

CAUTION
When servicing an aftermarket cable, follow the manufacturer's cable lubrication requirements.

1. Loosen the clutch cable locknut (A, **Figure 34**) and turn the adjuster (B) to provide as much cable slack as possible. Align the open slots in the cable locknut, adjuster and lever housing. Pull the clutch cable's outer sheath out of the adjuster, then slide the inner cable out through the open slots and disconnect it at the lever. If the cable is too tight to disconnect at the adjuster, loosen the cable at the lower adjuster.

CAUTION
Do not use chain lube to lubricate control cables unless it is also advertised as a cable lubricant.

NOTE
Cover the area around the nozzle and tube with a plastic bag.

2. Mount a cable lube tool onto the upper end of the cable (**Figure 31**) and lubricate the cable until fluid exits through the opposite end of the cable. Wipe up all excess lube from the end of the cable.
3. Lightly lubricate the upper cable end with grease.
4. Operate the clutch lever. If the clutch lever pivot bolt feels tight or dry, perform the following:
    a. Remove the locknut, pivot bolt (C, **Figure 34**) and clutch lever (D).
    b. Clean and dry all parts, including the threads in the clutch lever housing. Then lubricate the pivot bolt shoulder with grease. Do not lubricate the threads on the pivot bolt, locknut or inside the clutch lever housing.
    c. Install the clutch lever and pivot bolt and tighten securely. Operate the clutch lever to make sure it moves freely.
    d. Hold the pivot bolt and tighten the locknut securely. Recheck the clutch lever operation to make sure it moves freely.
5. Reconnect the clutch cable at the clutch lever.
6. Adjust the clutch cable by following the adjustment procedure in this section.

4. Reinstall all parts previously removed.
5. Open and release the throttle grip. Make sure it opens and closes (snaps back) without any binding or roughness. Then support the motorcycle and turn the handlebar from side to side, checking throttle operation at both steering lock positions.
6. Sit on the motorcycle and start the engine with the transmission in neutral. Turn the handlebars from lock-to-lock to check for idle speed variances due to improper cable adjustment, routing or damage.
7. Test ride the motorcycle, slowly at first, to make sure the throttle cables are operating correctly. Readjust if necessary.

CLUTCH CABLE AND CLUTCH LEVER

Lubrication

Lubricate the clutch cable whenever the clutch lever feels tight or the cable dry.

The main cause of cable breaks or stiffness is improper lubrication. Periodic lubrication assures long service life. Inspect the cable for fraying, and check the sheath for chafing.

A cable lubricant tool can be mounted on the upper end of the cable.

Adjustment

Check clutch lever free play at the intervals specified in **Table 1** and adjust when necessary to compensate for clutch cable stretching and drive plate wear. Excessive clutch lever free play prevents the clutch from disengaging and causes clutch drag. Too little or no clutch lever free play does not allow the clutch to

fully engage, resulting in clutch slippage. Both conditions cause clutch plate wear. Transmission wear can also result from incorrect clutch adjustment.
1. Operate the clutch lever a few times. If the cable feels tight or dry, lubricate it as described in this section. If clutch cable operation does not improve after lubricating it, replace the cable as described in Chapter Six.
2. With the engine turned off, pull the clutch lever until resistance is felt, then stop and measure the free play distance at the end of the clutch lever (**Figure 35**). Refer to **Table 2** for the specified free play.
3. Make minor adjustments at the clutch cable adjuster mounted at the clutch lever. Loosen the locknut (A, **Figure 34**) and turn the adjuster (B) as required to obtain the correct free play. Tighten the locknut and recheck the adjustment.

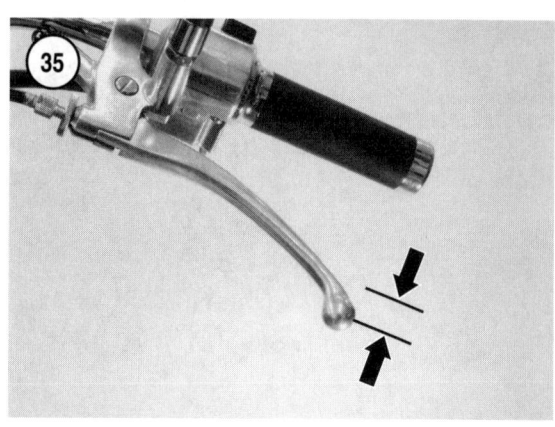

NOTE
If sufficient free play cannot be obtained at the hand lever, or there is too little thread engagement, use the adjuster at the bottom end of the clutch cable.

4. Loosen the lower clutch cable adjuster locknut (A, **Figure 36**).
5. At the hand lever, loosen the locknut (A, **Figure 34**) and turn the adjuster screw (B) in to loosen the clutch cable all the way, then turn it out one turn.
6. At the lower clutch cable adjuster, turn the adjust nut (B, **Figure 36**) until the adjustment is correct or almost correct. Tighten the locknut (A, **Figure 36**).
7. Turn the handlebar adjuster (B, **Figure 34**) as described in Step 3 and adjust the clutch cable. Tighten the locknut (A, **Figure 34**).
8. Check that all locknuts are tight and that both cable ends are properly seated.
9. Start the engine, then pull the clutch lever in and shift the transmission into first gear. Check that the clutch does not drag and that the motorcycle does not stall. Then slowly release the clutch lever while opening the throttle. The motorcycle should begin to move smoothly. If the clutch does not work correctly, turn the engine off and check the clutch adjustment. If the clutch does not work correctly, the clutch cable may be stretched or the drive plates are worn excessively. Service the clutch as described in Chapter Six.

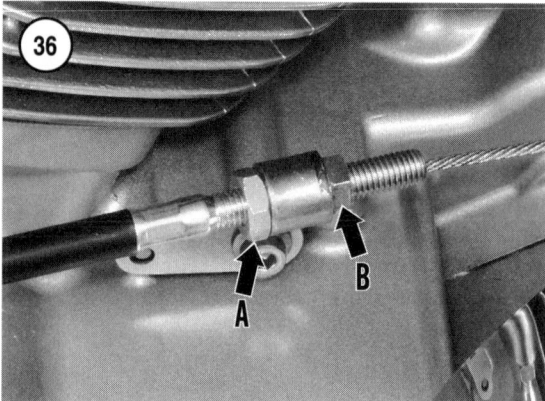

ENGINE OIL AND FILTER

Refer to **Table 1** for the recommended oil and filter check and change intervals. These intervals assume that the motorcycle is operated in moderate climates. If the motorcycle is operated infrequently, consider a time-based interval. If the motorcycle is operated under dusty conditions, the oil gets dirty quicker and should be changed more frequently than recommended.

Refer to *Lubricants and Fluids* in *Shop Supplies* in Chapter One for additional information on engine oil selection. Refer to **Table 3** for engine oil requirements and to **Table 4** for oil capacities.

WARNING
Prolonged contact with oil may cause skin cancer. Wear rubber gloves and wash hands thoroughly with soap and water after contacting engine oil.

Engine Oil Level Check

Check the engine oil level with the dipstick mounted on the right crankcase cover.
1. Support the motorcycle on its sidestand on a level surface.

CAUTION
To prevent an inaccurate oil level reading, do not snap the throttle when idling the engine in Step 2.

2. Start the engine and let idle for 3-5 minutes. Make sure the low oil pressure indicator turns off. If the indicator remains on, turn the engine off.

LUBRICATION, MAINTENANCE AND TUNE-UP

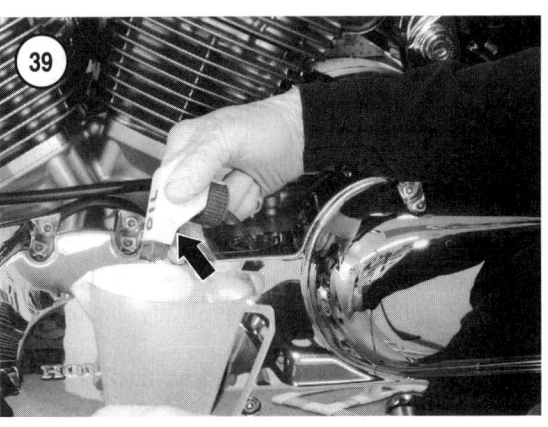

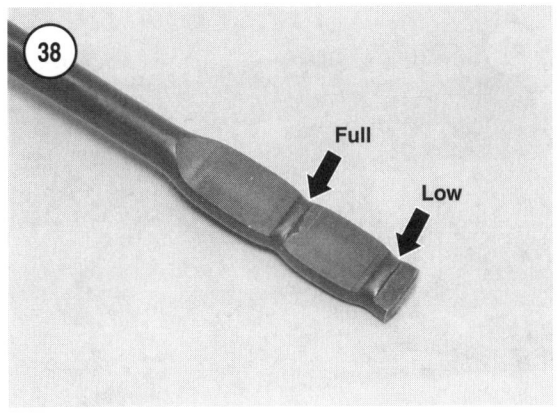

3. Shut off the engine and let the oil settle for 2-3 minutes.
4. Remove the oil filler cap/dipstick (**Figure 37**) and wipe it clean.

CAUTION
Do not check the oil level with the motorcycle on its sidestand; the oil will flow toward the dipstick, and result in a false reading.

5. Raise and position the motorcycle so the seat is level.
6. Reinsert the oil filler cap/dipstick until it seats against the cover opening. Do not screw it in.
7. Remove the oil filler cap/dipstick. The oil level should be between the full and low level marks (**Figure 38**).
8. If the oil level is near or below the low level mark (**Figure 38**), add the specified oil (**Table 3**) to correct the level. Add oil while checking the level to avoid overfilling.
9. Inspect the O-ring on the oil filler cap/dipstick. Replace it if it is starting to deteriorate or harden.
10. Install the oil filler cap/dipstick (**Figure 37**) and tighten securely.
11. If the oil level is too high, do the following:

NOTE
*A spray head attachment and its attached hose removed from a typical household cleaning container or spray bottle works well for removing excess oil from the crankcase (**Figure 39**). Flush the spray head attachment and its hose with clean engine oil before using it.*

a. Remove the oil filler cap/dipstick (**Figure 37**) and draw out the excess oil using a suitable pump.
b. Recheck the oil level and adjust if necessary.
c. Install the oil filler cap/dipstick and tighten securely.

Engine Oil and Filter Change

NOTE
Warming the engine heats the oil so it flows freely and carries out contamination and sludge.

1. Support the motorcycle on its sidestand when draining the engine oil. This ensures complete draining.

WARNING
The engine, exhaust pipes and oil are hot. Work carefully when removing the oil drain bolts and oil filter to avoid contacting the oil or hot engine parts.

2. Clean the area around the oil drain bolts and oil filter.
3. Place a clean drip pan under the crankcase and remove the front (A, **Figure 40**) and rear (B) oil drain bolts.
4. Remove the oil filler cap/dipstick (**Figure 37**) to help speed up the flow of oil. Allow the oil to drain completely.

5. To replace the oil filter, perform the following:
   a. Install a socket type oil filter wrench (A, **Figure 40**) squarely onto the oil filter (B) and turn the filter counterclockwise until oil begins to run out, then remove the oil filter.
   b. Hold the filter over the drain pan and pour out any remaining oil, then place the old filter in a plastic bag and dispose of it properly.
   c. Carefully clean the oil filter sealing surface on the crankcase. Do not allow any dirt or other debris to enter the engine.
   d. Lubricate the rubber seal and threads on the new oil filter with clean engine oil.
   e. Install the new oil filter onto the threaded fitting on the crankcase. Tighten the filter by hand until it contacts the crankcase. Then tighten an additional 3/4 turn. If using the oil filter socket, tighten the oil filter to 26 N•m (19 ft.-lb.).
6. Install the oil drain bolts (A and B, **Figure 40**) and new gaskets and tighten to 30 N•m (22 ft.-lb.).
7. Support the motorcycle on a stand with the seat in a level position.
8. Insert a funnel into the oil filler hole and fill the engine with the specified viscosity (**Table 3**) and quantity of oil (**Table 4**).
9. Remove the funnel and screw in the oil filler cap/dipstick and its O-ring (**Figure 37**).

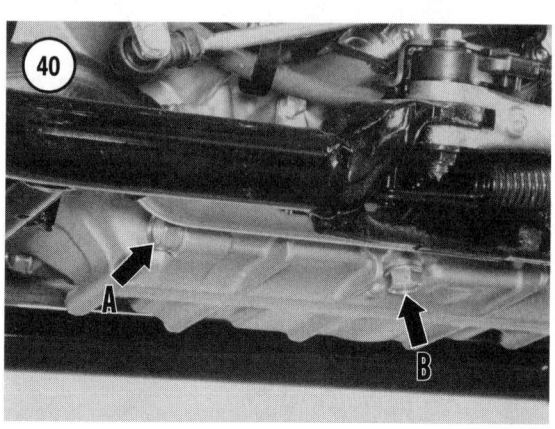

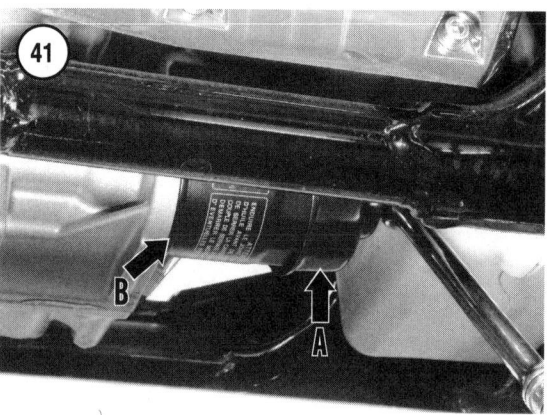

CAUTION
When starting a rebuilt engine for the first time, make sure the motorcycle is positioned with the seat in a level position to make sure oil is picked up by the oil pump and delivered under pressure to engine and transmission components.

10. Start the engine and let it idle.

NOTE
The oil pressure warning light should go out within 1-2 seconds. If it stays on, shut off the engine immediately and locate the problem. Do not run the engine with the oil pressure warning light on.

11. Check the oil filter and drain bolts for leaks.
12. Turn the engine off after 3-5 minutes and check the oil level as described in this section. Adjust the oil level if necessary.

ENGINE OIL PRESSURE CHECK

WARNING
The engine, exhaust pipes and oil are hot during this procedure. Work carefully to avoid contacting the oil or hot engine parts.

Check the engine oil pressure after reassembling the engine or when troubleshooting the lubrication system.

1. The following tools, or equivalent tools, are required to check the oil pressure:
   a. Oil pressure gauge: part No. 07506-3000001.
   b. Oil pressure adapter: part No. 07510-4220100.
2. Connect a tachometer to the engine following the manufacturer's instructions.
3. Start the engine and allow it to reach normal operating temperature. Turn the engine off.
4. Support the motorcycle on a stand so the seat is level.
5. Remove the oil pressure switch (Chapter Nine).

WARNING
Keep the gauge hose away from the exhaust pipe during this test. If the hose contacts the exhaust pipe, it may melt and spray hot oil.

6. Assemble the oil pressure adapter and gauge. Thread the oil pressure gauge adapter into the engine in place of the oil pressure switch. Make sure the fitting is tight and check for leaks.

LUBRICATION, MAINTENANCE AND TUNE-UP

CAUTION
The oil pressure indicator should go out within 1-2 seconds. If it stays on, shut off the engine immediately and locate the problem. Do not run the engine with the oil pressure indicator on.

7. Check the engine oil level as described in this chapter. Add oil if necessary.
8. Start the engine and let it idle until the operating temperature is 80° C (176° F). Check engine temperature with an infrared thermometer if available.
9. Increase engine speed to 5000 rpm and read the oil pressure on the gauge. Refer to the engine oil pressure specification in **Table 2**.
10. Allow the engine to return to idle, then shut it off and remove the test equipment.
11. If the oil pressure is lower or higher than specified, refer to *Engine Lubrication* in Chapter Two.
12. Install the oil pressure switch (Chapter Nine).
13. Check the engine oil level as described in this chapter. Add oil if necessary.
14. Disconnect and remove the tachometer.

COOLING SYSTEM

WARNING
When performing any service work on the engine or cooling system, never remove the radiator cap, coolant drain bolt or disconnect any coolant hose while the engine and radiator are hot. Scalding fluid and steam may be blown out under pressure and cause serious injury.

Check, inspect and service the cooling system at the intervals in **Table 1**. The specified coolant is listed in **Table 3**. Coolant capacities are listed in **Table 5**.

Coolant Selection

CAUTION
Many antifreeze solutions contain silicate inhibitors to protect aluminum parts from corrosion damage. However, these silicate inhibitors can cause premature wear to water pump seals. When selecting antifreeze, make sure it does not contain silicate inhibitors.

When adding coolant to the cooling system, use Pro Honda HP Coolant, a ready-to-use water/coolant blend pre-mixed 50:50 with silicate-free ethylene glycol antifreeze and purified, de-ionized water. If mixing antifreeze and water, use a 50:50 mixture of distilled water and antifreeze that does not contain silicate inhibitors. Use only soft or distilled water. Never use tap or saltwater, as these will damage engine parts.

Coolant Test

WARNING
Do not remove the radiator cap when the engine is hot.

1. Remove the fuel tank (Chapter Eight).
2. Remove the radiator cap (**Figure 42**).
3. Test the specific gravity of the coolant with an antifreeze tester to ensure adequate temperature and corrosion protection. A 50:50 mixture is recommended. Never allow the mixture become less than 40 percent antifreeze.
4. Reinstall the radiator cap (**Figure 42**).
5. Install the fuel tank (Chapter Eight).

Coolant Level

1. Start the engine and allow it to idle until it reaches normal operating temperature.
2. With the engine running at idle speed and the motorcycle positioned upright, the coolant level should be between the UPPER and LOWER level marks on the coolant reserve tank (**Figure 43**).
3. If necessary, add coolant as follows:
   a. Turn the engine off.
   b. Remove the left side cover (Chapter Fifteen).
   c. Position the motorcycle so that it is upright.
   d. Remove the coolant reserve tank cap (**Figure 44**) and add coolant into the reserve tank (not the radiator) to bring the level to the upper mark. Install the cap.
   e. Install the side cover.

f. Inspect the cooling system for leaks as described in Chapter Ten.

Coolant Change

WARNING
Antifreeze is toxic waste and should not be disposed of by flushing down a drain or poured onto the ground. Place old antifreeze into a suitable container and dispose of it properly. Do not store coolant where it is accessible to children or pets.

WARNING
Do not remove the radiator cap (Figure 42) if the engine is hot. The coolant is very hot and is under pressure. Severe scalding will result if hot coolant contacts skin.

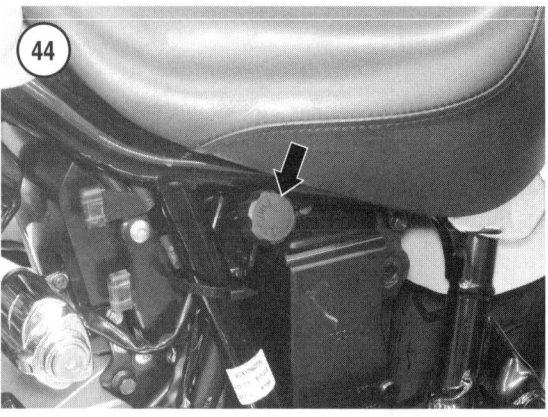

CAUTION
Be careful not to spill antifreeze on painted surfaces as it will damage some surfaces. Wash immediately with soapy water and rinse thoroughly.

Drain and refill the cooling system at the intervals listed in **Table 1**.

It is sometimes necessary to drain the cooling system when servicing the engine. If the coolant is still in good condition, the coolant can be reused if not contaminated. Drain the coolant into a clean pan and then pour into a container for storage.

Perform the following procedure when the engine is cold.
1. Place the motorcycle on a stand so the seat is level.
2. Remove the left side cover (Chapter Fifteen).
3. Remove the fuel tank (Chapter Eight).
4. Remove the left crankcase rear cover (Chapter Fifteen).

NOTE
If reusing the coolant, clean the lower frame rail to prevent debris from contaminating the coolant as it passes over it.

5. Place a drain pan under the coolant drain bolt (**Figure 45**). Remove the drain bolt and washer, then hold the drain pan at an angle in front of the drain bolt and remove the radiator cap (**Figure 42**). Allow the coolant to drain completely.
6. Install the drain bolt (**Figure 45**) with a new washer and tighten to 13 N•m (115 in.-lb.).
7. Disconnect the siphon hose (**Figure 46**) from the coolant reserve tank (**Figure 43**) and drain the coolant. Flush the tank with water. Check the end of the siphon hose for cracks, deterioration and other damage. Reinstall the siphon hose if in good condition and secure with its clamp.

CAUTION
*Do not use a higher percentage of antifreeze-to-water solution than is recommended in **Coolant Selection** in this section. A higher concentration of coolant will actually decrease the performance of the cooling system.*

8. Place a funnel in the radiator filler neck and refill the radiator and engine with a mixture of 50 percent antifreeze and 50 percent distilled water. Add the mixture slowly so it will expel as much air as possible from the cooling system. Refer to *Coolant Selection* in this section before purchasing and mixing coolant. **Table 5** lists engine coolant capacity.
9. Fill the coolant reserve tank to the upper level line (**Figure 43**).
10. After filling the radiator, bleed the cooling system as follows:
   a. Start the engine and allow it to idle for 2-3 minutes.
   b. Snap the throttle a few times to bleed air from the cooling system. When the coolant level

LUBRICATION, MAINTENANCE AND TUNE-UP

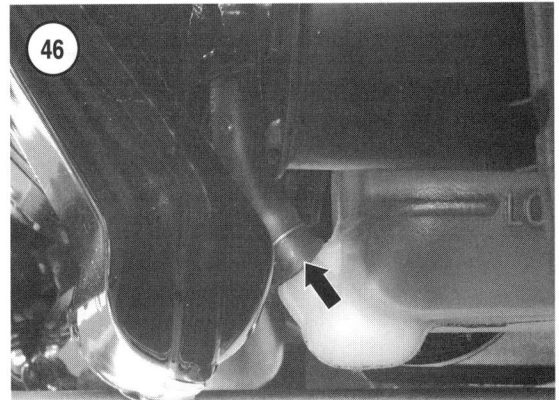

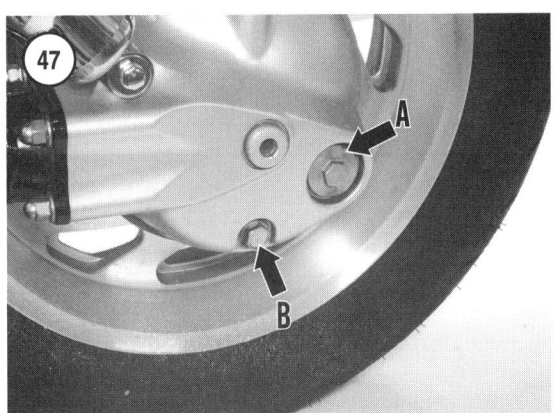

drops in the radiator, add coolant to bring the level to the bottom of the filler neck.

   c. When the radiator coolant level has stabilized, install the radiator cap (**Figure 42**).

11. Start the engine and let it run at idle speed until the engine reaches normal operating temperature. Make sure the coolant level in the coolant reserve tank stabilizes at the correct level. Add coolant to the coolant reserve tank as described in this section.

12. Test ride the motorcycle and readjust the coolant level in the reserve tank as required. Check the coolant drain bolt and coolant reserve tank for leaks.

PULSE SECONDARY AIR SUPPLY SYSTEM

All models are equipped with a pulse secondary air supply system. At the intervals specified in **Table 1**, inspect the system hoses and reed valves as described in Chapter Eight.

EVAPORATIVE EMISSION CONTROL SYSTEM

All California models are equipped with an evaporative emission control system. At the intervals specified in **Table 1**, check the system hoses and EVAP canister for damage. Refer to Chapter Eight.

BATTERY

The original equipment battery is a maintenance-free type. Maintenance-free batteries do not require periodic electrolyte inspection and water cannot be added. Refer to Chapter Nine for battery service, testing and replacement procedures.

FINAL DRIVE OIL

Oil Level Check

1. Support the motorcycle on its sidestand on level ground.
2. Clean the area around the final drive oil fill cap. Remove the cap (A, **Figure 47**).
3. The oil level must be even with the lower edge of the oil fill hole. If the oil level is low, add the recommended type gear oil (**Table 3**) to correct the level.
4. Inspect the oil fill cap O-ring and replace if leaking or damaged. Lubricate a new O-ring with grease.
5. Install and tighten the oil fill cap to 12 N•m (106 in.-lb.).

Final Drive Oil Change

The recommended oil change interval is listed in **Table 1**.

1. Ride the motorcycle to warm the oil in the final drive unit.
2. Place the motorcycle on its sidestand on level ground.
3. Place a drain pan under the final drive unit.
4. Remove the oil fill cap (A, **Figure 47**) and the drain bolt (B) to drain the oil.
5. Install a new washer on the drain bolt and tighten to 20 N•m (14 ft.-lb.).

6. Add the recommended type gear oil (**Table 3**) to bring the oil level even with the lower edge of the oil fill hole. **Table 6** lists final drive oil capacity.
7. Inspect the oil filler cap O-ring and replace if leaking or damaged. Lubricate a new O-ring with grease.
8. Install and tighten the oil fill cap to 12 N•m (106 in.-lb.).

TIRES AND WHEELS

Inspect the tires and wheels at the intervals specified in **Table 1**.

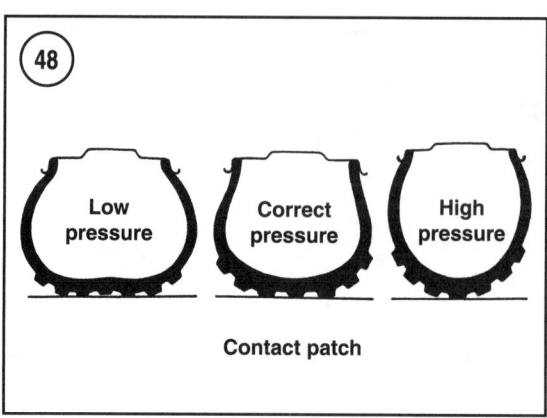

Tire Pressure

Check and adjust the tire pressure to maintain the tire profile, good traction and handling and to get the maximum life out of the tire. Check tire pressure when the tires are cold. When the motorcycle is ridden, the tire temperature rises. Never release air pressure from a warm or hot tire to match the recommended tire pressure listed in **Table 7**; doing so may cause the tire to be underinflated.

Tire Inspection

Inspect the tires periodically for excessive wear and damage. Inspect the tires for the following:
1. Deep cuts and imbedded objects, such as nails and stones. If a nail or other object is in a tire, mark its location with a light crayon prior to removing it. This helps to locate the hole for repair. Refer to Chapter Eleven for tire changing and repair information.
2. Flat spots. Storing the motorcycle with one or both wheels on the ground can cause flat spots.
3. Sidewall cracks and other damage.
4. Separating plies.
5. Bulges.
6. Improper tire centering on rim.
7. Damaged tire or tube stem.

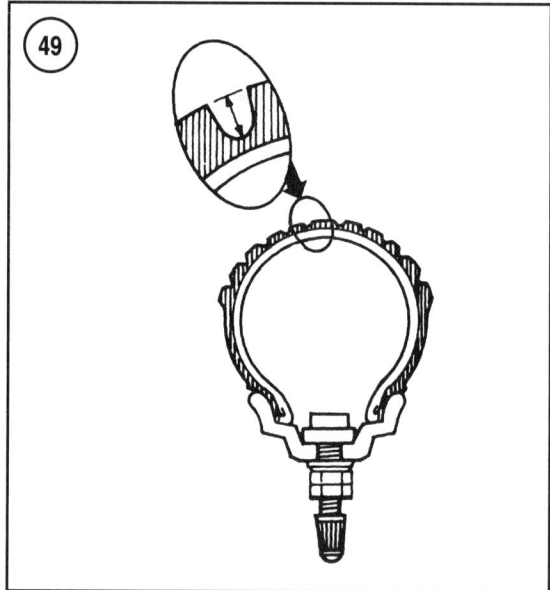

Tire Wear Inspection

Analyze abnormal tire wear to determine the cause. Common causes are:
1. Incorrect tire pressure. This is the biggest cause of abnormal tire wear. Compare the wear in the center of the contact patch with the wear at the edge of the contact patch (**Figure 48**). Check tire pressure and examine the tire tread. Note the following:
   a. If a tire shows excessive wear at the edge of the contact patch, but the wear at the center of the contact patch is normal, the tire has been underinflated. Underinflated tires will cause the sidewalls to flex excessively. This results in higher tire temperatures, hard or imprecise steering and abnormal tire wear on the tire edges.
   b. If a tire shows excessive wear in the center of the contact patch, but wear at the edge of the contact patch in normal, the tire has been overinflated. Overinflated tires will cause the tire to bulge in the center of the tread. This results in a hard ride and abnormal tire wear in the center of the tread. When a properly inflated tire hits a large bump in the road, it has a normal flex or give and is capable of absorbing much of the shock. However, an overinflated tire cannot flex or give and the tire casing (cord material) takes the shock. This weakens and breaks the tire cords and eventually causes tire failure.

NOTE
Large amounts of high-speed riding on straight roads will cause the tires to exhibit a similar wear pattern as described in substep b.

LUBRICATION, MAINTENANCE AND TUNE-UP

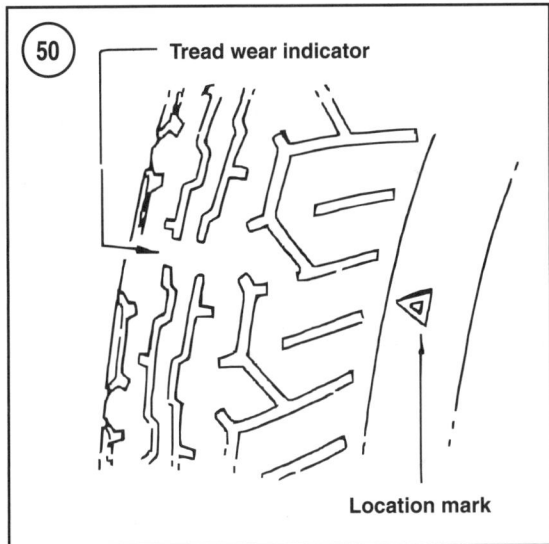

2. Overloading.
3. Incorrect wheel alignment.
4. Incorrect wheel balance: The tire and wheel assembly should be balanced when installing a new tire.
5. Worn or damaged wheel bearings.

Tread Depth

Measure the tread depth (**Figure 49**) in the center of the tire using a small ruler or a tread depth gauge. The manufacturer recommends replacing the original equipment tires before the center tread depth has worn to the minimum tread depth specified in **Table 7**.

Tires are also designed with tread wear indicators (**Figure 50**) that appear when a tire is worn out. When these are visible, the tire is no longer safe and must be replaced.

Wheel Bearing Inspection

Inspect the wheel bearings at the interval specified in **Table 1** and when the wheels are removed. Refer to *Front and Rear Hubs* in Chapter Eleven.

Spokes Tension

On models with laced wheels, check for loose or damaged spokes. Refer to *Wheel Service* Chapter Eleven for spoke service.

Wheel Inspection

Check the wheel rims for excessive runout, for cracks and other damage. Refer to Chapter Eleven for wheel service.

STEERING BEARINGS

Inspect the steering bearing adjustment at the intervals specified in **Table 1**.
1. Support the motorcycle on a stand with the front wheel off the ground.
2. Hold onto the handlebars and move them from side to side. Note any binding or roughness.
3. Support the motorcycle so both wheels are on the ground.
4. Sit on the motorcycle and hold onto the handlebars. Apply the front brake lever and try to push the front fork forward. Try to detect any movement in the steering head area. If so, the bearing adjustment is loose and requires adjustment.
5. If any roughness, binding or looseness was detected when performing Step 2 or Step 4, perform the *Steering Bearing Preload Check* in Chapter Twelve. Service the steering bearings if necessary.

FRONT SUSPENSION

> *CAUTION*
> *If any of the suspension fasteners are loose, refer to Chapter Twelve for procedures and torque specifications.*

Inspect the front suspension at the intervals specified in **Table 1**.
1. Use a soft wet cloth to wipe the front fork tubes to remove any dirt, road tar and debris. As this debris passes by the fork seals, it will eventually damage the seals and cause them to leak oil.
2. Check the front fork for any oil seal leaks or damage.
3. Apply the front brake and pump the fork up and down as vigorously as possible. Check for smooth operation.
4. Make sure the upper and lower fork tube pinch bolts are tightened to specification.
5. Check that the handlebar mounting bolts are tightened to specification.
6. Make sure the front axle is tightened to specification.

REAR SUSPENSION

> *CAUTION*
> *If any of the suspension fasteners are loose, refer to Chapter Thirteen for procedures and torque specifications.*

Inspect the rear suspension at the intervals specified in **Table 1**.

1. With both wheels on the ground, check the shock absorbers by bouncing on the seat several times.
2. Check the shock absorbers for oil leaks, loose mounting fasteners or other damage.
3. Check the swing arm bearings as described in Chapter Thirteen.
4. Check for loose or missing suspension fasteners.
5. Make sure the rear axle nut is tightened to specification.
6. To adjust the rear shock absorbers, refer to Chapter Thirteen.

BRAKES

All models are equipped with front and rear disc brakes. Check both brake assemblies at the intervals specified in **Table 1**. Immediately inspect the brake components when their operating condition has changed or when a scraping or grinding noise is detected.

Bleeding the brakes, replacing the brake pads and servicing the brake components are covered in Chapter Fourteen. Refer to Chapter Fourteen for brake system torque specifications.

Brake System Check

Check the front and rear brake operation as follows:
1. Support the motorcycle on its sidestand on level ground and shift the transmission into neutral.
2. Apply the front brake lever. Make sure it feels firm. If the lever feels soft or spongy, air has probably entered the system. Check the front brake hose and bleed the brake as described in Chapter Fourteen.
3. Apply the rear brake pedal. Make sure it feels firm. If the pedal feels soft or spongy, air has probably entered the system. Check the rear brake hose and bleed the brake as described in Chapter Fourteen.
4. With either brake applied, check the brake hose and brake line (rear brake) for leaks.
5. Check brake hose and brake line routing. Make sure there are no loose or missing fasteners and clamps.

Brake Hoses

Check the front and rear brake hoses between the master cylinders and brake calipers. If there are any leaks, tighten the banjo bolt(s) to specification and then bleed the brake system as described in Chapter Fourteen. If this does not stop the leak or if a brake line is obviously damaged, cracked or chafed, replace the brake hose(s) and bleed the system.

Brake Fluid Selection

Refer to *Brake Service* in Chapter Fourteen.

WARNING
Use DOT 4 brake fluid. Other fluid types may cause brake failure. Do not intermix different brands or types of brake fluid as they may not be compatible. Do not intermix silicone based (DOT 5) brake fluid as it can cause brake component damage leading to brake system failure.

CAUTION
Handle brake fluid carefully. Do not spill it on painted or plastic surfaces, as it will damage the surface. Wash the area immediately with soap and water and thoroughly rinse it off.

Front Brake Fluid Level Check

NOTE
A low brake fluid level usually indicates brake pad wear. As the pads wear (become thinner), the brake caliper pistons automatically extend farther out of their bores. As the caliper pistons move outward, the brake fluid level lowers in the reservoir to compensate for piston repositioning. However, if the brake fluid level is low and the brake pads are not worn excessively, check for a leak in the brake system.

1. Turn the handlebar so the brake master cylinder is level.
2. The brake fluid level must be above the lower level line (**Figure 51**) in the master cylinder window. If the brake fluid level is at or below the lower level line, continue with Step 3.

LUBRICATION, MAINTENANCE AND TUNE-UP

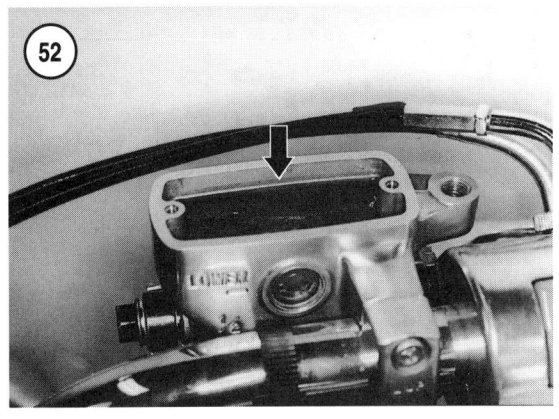

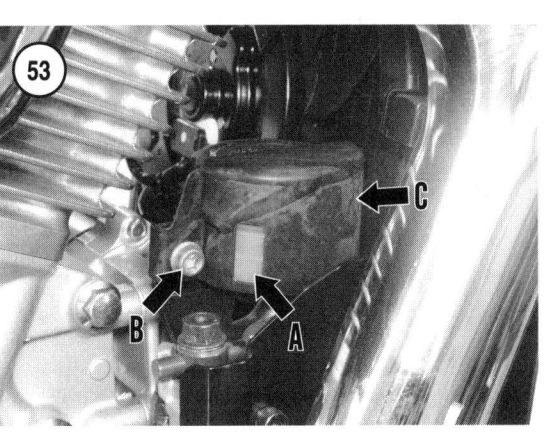

NOTE
If the reservoir is low, check for fluid leaks. If the reservoir is empty, air has probably entered the brake system. Bleed the brake as described in Chapter Fourteen.

3. Wipe off the master cylinder cover and remove the cover screws. Then remove the cover, diaphragm plate and diaphragm. The float can remain in the reservoir.
4. Add fresh DOT 4 brake fluid and fill the reservoir to the level mark inside the reservoir (**Figure 52**).
5. Install the diaphragm, diaphragm plate and cover. Install and tighten the cover screws to 1.5 N•m (13 in.-lb.).
6. If the brake fluid level was low, check the brake pads for excessive wear as described in this section.

Rear Brake Fluid Level Check

WARNING
Do not check the rear brake fluid level with the motorcycle resting on its sidestand. A false reading will result.

NOTE
A low brake fluid level usually indicates brake pad wear. As the pads wear (become thinner), the brake caliper piston automatically extends farther out of its bore. As the caliper piston moves outward, the brake fluid level lowers in the reservoir to compensate for piston repositioning. However, if the brake fluid level is low and the brake pads are not worn excessively, check for a leak in the brake system.

1. Support the motorcycle so the seat is level.
2. The brake fluid level must be between the upper and lower level marks on the reservoir housing (A,

Figure 53). If the brake fluid level is at or below the lower level line, continue with Step 3.

NOTE
If the reservoir is empty, air has probably entered the brake system. Bleed the brake as described in Chapter Fourteen.

3. Remove the bolt (B, **Figure 53**) and outer cover (C).
4. Wipe off the master cylinder cover and unscrew the cover. Then remove the cover, diaphragm plate and diaphragm. The float can remain in the reservoir. Place a paper towel underneath the reservoir.
5. Add fresh DOT 4 brake fluid to fill the reservoir to the upper level mark on the reservoir (A, **Figure 53**).
6. Install the diaphragm, diaphragm plate and cover and tighten securely. Remove the paper towel.
7. Install the outer cover (C, **Figure 53**) and tighten the mounting bolt (B) to 10 N•m (88 in.-lb.).
8. If the brake fluid level was low, check the brake pads for excessive wear as described in this section.

Disc Brake Fluid Change

Change the brake fluid at the intervals specified in **Table 1** or whenever the caliper or master cylinder is overhauled. To drain the fluid, refer to Chapter Fourteen.

Brake Pad Wear

Inspect the front and rear brake pads for wear at the intervals specified in **Table 1**.
1. Inspect the front and rear brake pads for uneven wear, oil contamination or other damage. Note the following:
   a. Binding or sticking caliper pistons or improper caliper bracket operation can cause uneven pad wear.

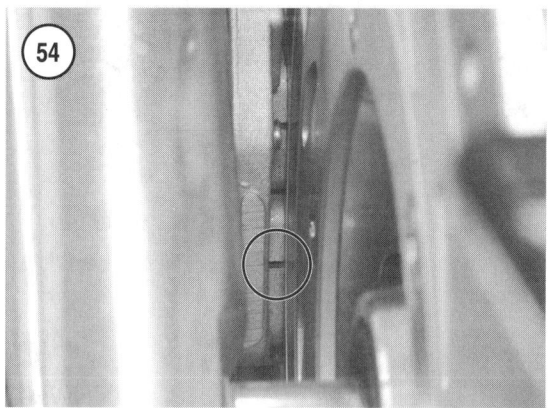

b. A damaged fork oil seal will allow oil to run down the fork tube and contaminate the front brake pads and caliper housing. Always check the pads for contamination when a leaking fork seal is detected and replace the seal immediately.

c. If there is no visible brake pad damage or contamination, perform Step 2.

NOTE
When checking the front brake pads, view the brake pads at the front and rear of the caliper.

2. Replace the front and rear brake pads in sets when a pad is worn to the bottom of the wear limit groove. Refer to **Figure 54** (front) and **Figure 55** (rear). Refer to Chapter Fourteen for removal/installation procedures.

Front Brake Lever Adjustment

There is no adjustment for the front brake lever.

Front Brake Light Switch Check

There is no adjustment for the front brake light switch. Check the front brake light switch operation at the intervals specified in **Table 1** or as part of a pre-ride safety check.
1. Turn the ignition switch on.
2. Operate the front brake lever. The brake light should come on just before the brake begins to work. If the brake light does not come on or stays on, test the front brake light switch as described in Chapter Nine. If the front brake light switch is okay, check for a blown bulb if the brake light did not come on.
3. Turn the ignition switch off.

Rear Brake Light Switch Adjustment

Check the rear brake light switch adjustment at the intervals specified in **Table 1**.
1. Turn the ignition switch on.
2. Depress the brake pedal. The brake light should come on just before the brake begins to work.
3. If the brake light stays on or comes on too late, continue with Step 4.

CAUTION
Do not turn the switch body when adjusting the rear brake light switch. This will damage the wires at the top of the switch. Hold the switch body and turn the adjusting nut.

4. Hold the brake light switch body and turn the adjusting nut (**Figure 56**) as required to make the brake light come at its proper time.
5. Recheck the rear brake light switch adjustment.
6. Turn the ignition switch off.

HEADLIGHT

Check the headlight adjustment at the intervals specified in **Table 1**. Refer to *Headlight Adjustment* in *Lighting System* in Chapter Nine.

LUBRICATION, MAINTENANCE AND TUNE-UP

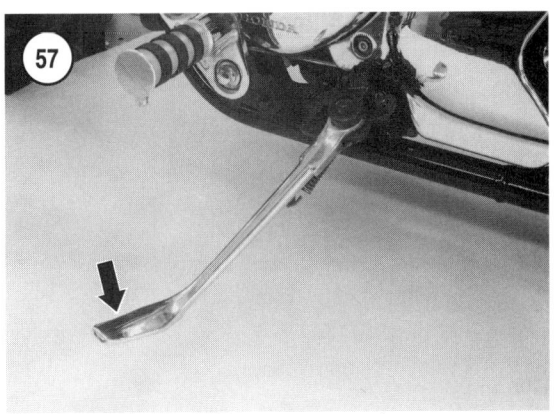

3. Check the sidestand ignition cut-off system as follows:
   a. Park the motorcycle so both wheels are on the ground.
   b. Sit on the motorcycle and raise the sidestand.
   c. Shift the transmission into neutral.
   d. Start the engine, then squeeze the clutch lever and shift the transmission into gear.
   e. Move the sidestand (**Figure 57**) down. When doing so, the engine should stop.
   f. If the engine did not stop as the sidestand was lowered, test the sidestand switch as described in Chapter Nine.

SIDESTAND AND IGNITION CUT-OFF SWITCH TEST

WARNING
Do not ride the motorcycle until the sidestand switch operates correctly. Riding the motorcycle with the sidestand down will cause the rider to lose control when the sidestand contacts the ground.

NOTE
*If the sidestand requires service as described in this section, refer to **Sidestand** in Chapter Fifteen.*

Check the sidestand and the ignition cut-off system operation at the intervals specified in **Table 1**.
1. Operate the sidestand to check its movement and spring tension. Replace the springs if weak or damaged.
2. Lubricate the sidestand pivot bolt if necessary.

FRONT FORK OIL

Oil Change

The manufacturer does not provide a service interval for changing the front fork oil. However, it is good practice to change the fork oil once a year. Because the forks are not equipped with drain screws, they must be removed and partially disassembled for fork oil replacement and oil level adjustment. Refer to Chapter Twelve.

FASTENER INSPECTION

Constant vibration can loosen many fasteners on a motorcycle.
1. Check the tightness of all exposed fasteners. Refer to the appropriate chapter for torque specifications.
2. Check that all hose clamps, cable stays and safety clips are properly installed. Replace missing or damaged items.

Table 1 MAINTENANCE AND LUBRICATION SCHEDULE[1]

Weekly/gas stop
- Check tire pressure cold; adjust to suit load and speed
- Check condition of tires
- Check brake fluid level; if low, check brakes for excessive wear
- Check brake operation
- Check throttle grip for smooth operation and return
- Check steering bearing play
- Check axle, suspension and control fasteners; tighten to specification if necessary
- Check engine oil level; add oil if necessary
- Check lights and horn operation
- Check brake light operation
- Check coolant level
- Check for any abnormal engine noises
- Check for coolant and oil leaks

(continued)

Table 1 MAINTENANCE AND LUBRICATION SCHEDULE[1] (continued)

First 600 miles (1000 km)
- Check valve clearance; adjust if necessary
- Replace engine oil and filter
- Check engine idle speed; adjust if necessary
- Check front and rear brake hoses and all connections for leaks
- Check brake fluid level
- Check brake pad wear
- Check clutch cable adjustment
- Check for loose or missing fasteners
- Check wheel runout and for damage
- Check tire wear and tread depth
- Check steering bearing adjustment; adjust if necessary

First 4000 miles (6400 km); thereafter every 4000 miles (6400 km)
- Check spark plug condition
- Drain crankcase breather hose[2]
- Check engine idle speed; adjust if necessary
- Check cooling system
- Check clutch cable adjustment
- Check brake pad wear
- Check brake fluid
- Check wheel runout and for damage
- Check tire wear and tread depth

At 8000 miles (12,800 km); thereafter every 8000 miles (12,800 km)
- Check fuel and vacuum (2004-on models) hoses
- Check throttle operation
- Check choke knob operation
- Replace spark plugs
- Check valve clearance; adjust if necessary
- Check coolant
- Check cooling system
- Check pulse secondary air supply system
- Check final drive oil level
- Check brake system
- Check brake light and brake switch operation
- Check headlight aim; adjust if necessary
- Check clutch system
- Check sidestand operation
- Check sidestand switch operation
- Check front and rear suspension
- Check for loose or missing fasteners
- Check steering bearing adjustment; adjust if necessary

Every 8000 miles (12,800 km) or 12 months
- Change engine oil and filter
- Inspect wheel bearing

At first 12,000 miles (19,200 km); thereafter every 12,000 miles (19,200 km)
- Replace air filter[3]
- Check evaporative emission control system (California models)
- Change brake fluid

Every 24,000 miles (38,400 km) or 2 years
- Change engine coolant
- Change final drive oil

1. Consider this schedule a guide to general maintenance and lubrication intervals. Harder than normal use and exposure to mud, water and high humidity will require more frequent attention to most maintenance items.
2. Increase service intervals when riding at full throttle or in rain.
3. Service more often when riding in wet or dusty conditions.

LUBRICATION, MAINTENANCE AND TUNE-UP

Table 2 TUNE-UP SPECIFICATIONS

Clutch lever free play	10-20 mm (3/8-3/4 in.)
Engine compression	1157 kPa (168 psi) @ 300 rpm
Engine idle speed	800-1000 rpm
Engine oil pressure	530 kPa (77 psi) @5000 rpm (80° C/176°F)
Spark plug gap	0.8-0.9 mm (0.031-0.035 in.)
Spark plug type	
Standard	NGK DCPR6E, Denso XU20EPR-U
Extended high speed riding	NGK DCPR7E, Denso XU22EPR-U
Throttle grip free play	2-6 mm (1/16-1/4 in.)
Valve clearance	
Intake	0.13-0.17 mm (0.005-0.007 in.)
Exhaust	0.28-0.32 mm (0.011-0.013 in.)

Table 3 RECOMMENDED LUBRICANTS AND FUEL

Brake fluid	DOT 4 brake fluid
Cooling system	
Type	Honda HP Coolant or equivalent[1]
Standard concentration	50:50 mixture coolant and purified water
Engine oil	
Classification	
JASCO T 903	MA
API	SG or higher[2]
Viscosity	SAE 10W-30
Final drive gear oil	Hypoid gear oil, SAE 80
Fork oil	Pro Honda Suspension Fluid SS-8 or equivalent 10 wt fork oil
Fuel	Unleaded gasoline with a pump octane number of 86 or higher

1. Coolant must not contain silicate inhibitors as they can cause premature wear to the water pump seals. Refer to text for further information.
2. API SG or higher classified oils not specified as ENERGY CONSERVING can be used. Refer to Chapter One for additional information.

Table 4 ENGINE OIL CAPACITY

	Liters	qt.
Engine oil change only	3.5	3.7
Engine oil and filter change	3.7	3.9
Engine disassembly	4.3	4.5

Table 5 COOLANT CAPACITY

	Liters	qt.
Radiator and engine	2.7	2.9
Reserve tank	0.95	1.0

Table 6 FINAL DRIVE OIL CAPACITY

	mL	oz.
After overhaul	150	5.1
Oil change	120	4.1

Table 7 TIRE INFLATION PRESSURE AND TREAD DEPTH*

	Front kPa (psi)	Rear kPa (psi)
Tire pressure		
Up to 90 kg (200 lb.) load	225 (33)	225 (33)
Maximum weight capacity	225 (33)	250 (36)
Tread depth (minimum)	1.5 mm (0.06 in.)	2.0 mm (0.08 in.)

*Specifications are for original equipment tires. Aftermarket tires may have different specifications.

Table 8 MAINTENANCE TORQUE SPECIFICATIONS

	N•m	in.-lb.	ft.-lb.
Air filter cover screw	4	35	–
Coolant drain bolt*	13	115	–
Engine oil drain bolts*	30	–	22
Engine oil filter	26	–	19
Exhaust valve adjustment cover*	15	–	11
Final drive oil drain bolt*	20	–	15
Final drive oil fill cap*	12	106	–
Front master cylinder reservoir cover screw	1.5	13	–
Rear brake reservoir cover mounting bolt	10	88	–
Spark plug	14	–	10
Spoke nipples	4.2	37	–
Timing hole cap*	18	–	13
Timing hole cap cover Allen bolt	10	88	–
Valve adjust screw locknut	22	–	16

*Refer to text for additional information.

CHAPTER FOUR

ENGINE TOP END

Tables 1-4 are at the end of the chapter.
Refer to Chapter Three for valve adjustment.

CYLINDER HEAD COVERS AND ROCKER ARMS

Each cylinder head cover is equipped with three rocker arms and two rocker arm shafts. A semi-drying sealer seals the cylinder head covers to the cylinder heads.

Removal

1. Remove the engine from the frame as described in *Engine* in Chapter Five.
2. Before removing the cylinder head covers, check for any oil leaks that may indicate a damaged gasket surface and mark the area if a leak is found. Check the water pipes for coolant leaks.

NOTE
The photographs in this procedure are for the front cylinder head cover. The procedure for the rear cylinder head cover is the same.

3. Remove the valve adjustment covers and O-rings.
4. Remove the bolts (A, **Figure 1**), cover (B, **Figure 1**) and the PAIR check valve (**Figure 2**).
5. Remove the Allen bolts and the timing hole cap cover.

NOTE
The primary drive gear and right crankcase cover must be installed on the engine to align the TDC timing marks.

6. Remove the timing hole cap (**Figure 3**) and its O-ring to access the timing marks.
7. Remove one spark plug from each cylinder as described in Chapter Three to make it easier to turn the engine by hand. Cover the spark plug openings to prevent objects from falling into the engine.
8. Set the piston for the cylinder head cover being serviced at TDC on its compression stroke as follows:
   a. Use a socket on the primary drive gear bolt and rotate the crankshaft clockwise.
   b. For the front cylinder head cover, align the F-T mark (A, **Figure 4**) on the primary drive gear with the index mark (B) on the right crankcase cover.
   c. For the rear cylinder head cover, align the R-T mark (A, **Figure 5**) on the primary drive gear with the index mark (B) on the right crankcase cover.
   d. Try to move the rocker arms for the cylinder head cover being removed. The exhaust rocker

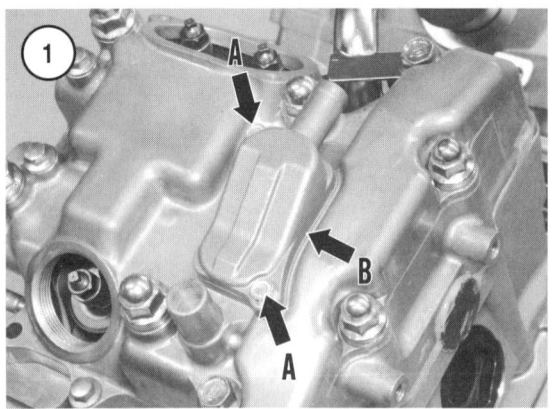

arm and both intake rocker arms should have some free play. If all three rocker arms are tight (no free play), rotate the engine 360° (1 full turn) clockwise and realign the F-T or R-T mark.

9. Loosen the following in order, then remove them:
   a. 6-mm bolt (A, **Figure 6**).
   b. Two 8-mm bolts (B, **Figure 6**) and water pipe (C). Discard the O-ring installed on the water pipe.
   c. Two 8-mm cap nuts and washers (D, **Figure 6**). Discard the washers.
   d. Four 10-mm cap nuts and washers (E, **Figure 6**). Discard the washers.

10. Remove the cylinder head cover (F, **Figure 6**). If the cover is stuck, tap around the edge with a soft-faced mallet. Do not pry it loose or the sealing surface may be damaged.
11. Remove the two rubber plugs (A, **Figure 7**).
12. Remove the oil passage dowel pin and O-ring (B, **Figure 7**). Discard the O-ring.
13. Remove the two dowel pins (C, **Figure 7**).
14. Inspect and service the cylinder head cover, rocker arms and shafts as described in this section.
15. If the cylinder studs are loose, service them as described in *Cylinder Stud* in this chapter.

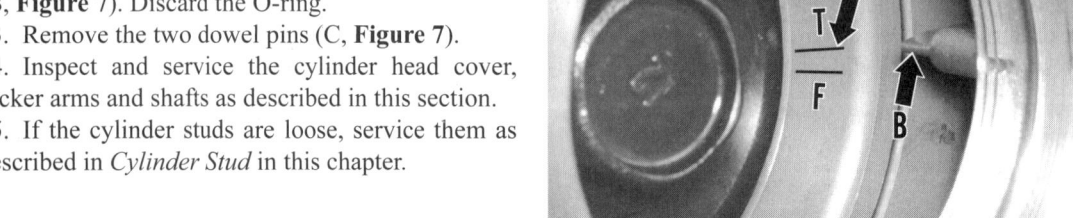

Installation

1. Remove sealer material from the cylinder head cover and cylinder head gasket surfaces.
2. Remove old sealer from the rubber plugs. Then check for damage and replace if necessary. Because of the work required to remove the engine from the frame, it is suggested to install new rubber plugs.
3. Clean and dry the cylinder head cover. Make sure the cylinder head cover oil passage is clean and dry.
4. If necessary, rotate the crankshaft clockwise until the camshaft lobes face down while aligning the F-T (**Figure 4**) or R-T (**Figure 5**) timing marks.
5. Reinstall the spark plugs (Chapter Three).
6. Install the two dowel pins (C, **Figure 7**).

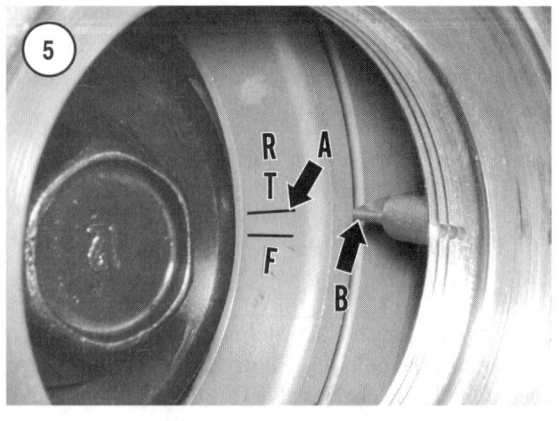

ENGINE TOP END

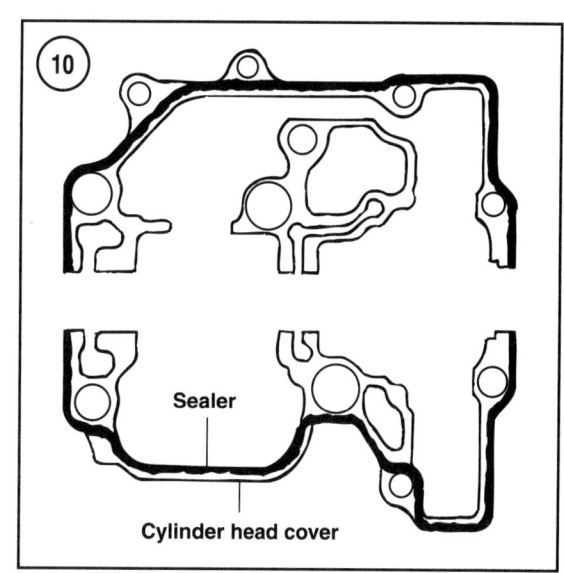

7. Lubricate a new oil passage O-ring with engine oil and install the dowel pin and O-ring (B, **Figure 7**).

8. Lubricate the following surfaces with molybdenum oil solution:
   a. Camshaft journals (D, **Figure 7**) and lobes (E).
   b. Rocker arm pads (**Figure 8**).

9. Clean oil from the cylinder head cover and cylinder head gasket surfaces with electrical contact cleaner and allow to dry.

NOTE
Oil remaining on the cylinder head cover and cylinder head gasket surface will prevent the sealer from curing properly, causing an oil leak.

NOTE
Use HondaBond 4, ThreeBond 1104 or Yamabond No. 4 gasket sealer when sealer is called for in the following steps.

10. Apply a thin coat of sealer to the cutouts (**Figure 9**) in the cylinder head.

11. Apply a thin coat of sealer to the sealing surface on each rubber plug and install them into the cylinder head cutouts with their closed side facing out (A, **Figure 7**).

NOTE
Make sure not to touch the cylinder head cover mating surface after applying sealer in Step 12.

12. Apply a thin coat of sealer to the cylinder head cover mating surface as shown in **Figure 10**.

13. Install the cylinder head cover over the studs while holding the rocker arms up with your fingers (**Figure 11**) to prevent them from pivoting down and

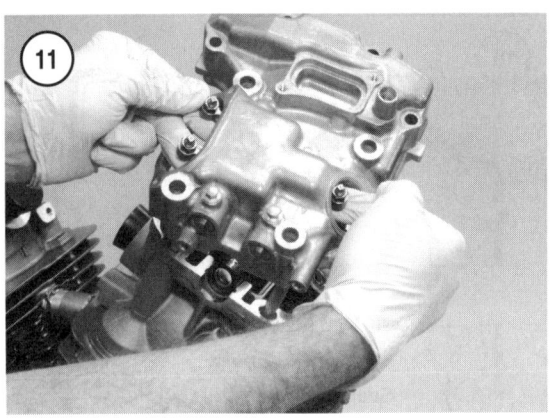

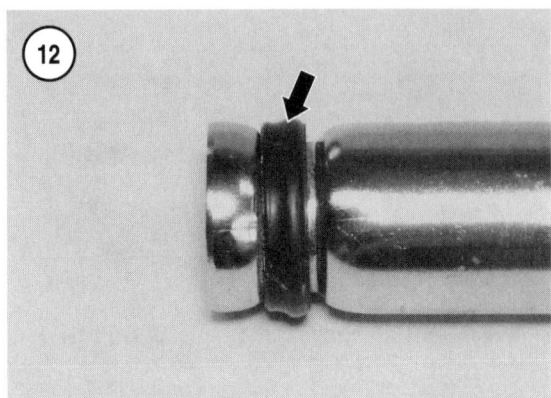

interfering with cover installation. Seat the cover fully, making sure it engages the rubber plugs and seats over the dowel pins. Check that the shoulder on each rubber plug seats squarely against the cylinder head cover and cylinder head surfaces.

14. Lubricate a new O-ring with engine oil and install it onto the water pipe in the direction shown in **Figure 12**.

15. Lubricate the seating surfaces and threads in each cap nut (**Figure 13**) with engine oil.

16. Install the cylinder head cover fasteners as follows:
    a. Install the four 10-mm cap nuts (E, **Figure 6**) with new washers and tighten hand-tight in a crossing pattern.
    b. Install the two 8-mm cap nuts (D, **Figure 6**) with new washers and tighten hand-tight.
    c. Install the water pipe (**Figure 14**) by pushing it into the cylinder head until the plate on the water pipe seats against the cylinder head cover.
    d. Install the two 8-mm bolts (B, **Figure 6**) and tighten hand-tight.
    e. Install the 6-mm bolt (A, **Figure 6**) and tighten hand-tight.

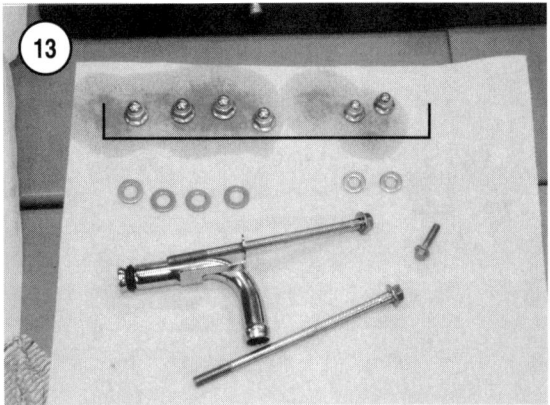

17. Tighten the cylinder head cover fasteners in a crossing pattern and in several steps in the following order:
    a. 10-mm cap nuts (E, **Figure 6**): 43 N•m (32 ft.-lb.).
    b. 8-mm bolts (B, **Figure 6**) and cap nuts (D): 26 N•m (19 ft.-lb.).
    c. Tighten the 6-mm bolt (A, **Figure 6**) securely.

18. Check and adjust the valves (Chapter Three).

19. Replace the valve adjustment cover and timing hole cap O-rings if leaking or damaged. Lubricate the O-rings with engine oil.

20. Lubricate the exhaust valve adjustment cover threads with grease and tighten to 15 N•m (11 ft.-lb.). Install the intake valve adjustment covers with their UP mark facing up and tighten the bolts securely.

21. Replace the O-ring on the timing hole cap if leaking or damaged.

22. Lubricate the timing hole cap (**Figure 3**) threads with grease and the O-ring with oil and tighten to 18 N•m (13 ft.-lb.).

23. Install the timing hole cap cover and tighten the Allen bolts to 10 N•m (88 in.-lb.).

24. Install the PAIR check valve as shown in **Figure 2** and its cover (B, **Figure 1**). Apply a medium strength threadlocking compound onto the cover mounting bolts (A, **Figure 1**) and tighten to 5.2 N•m (46 in.-lb.).

25. Install the engine into the frame as described in *Engine* in Chapter Five.

ENGINE TOP END

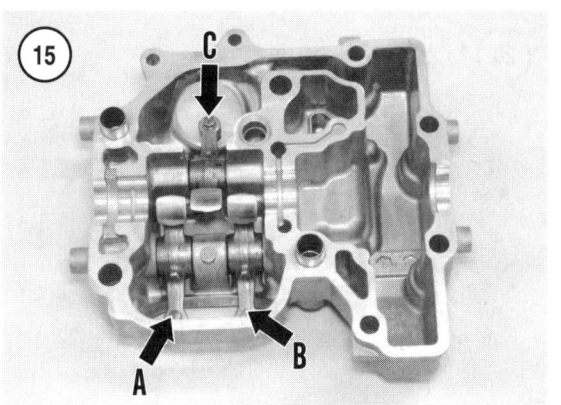

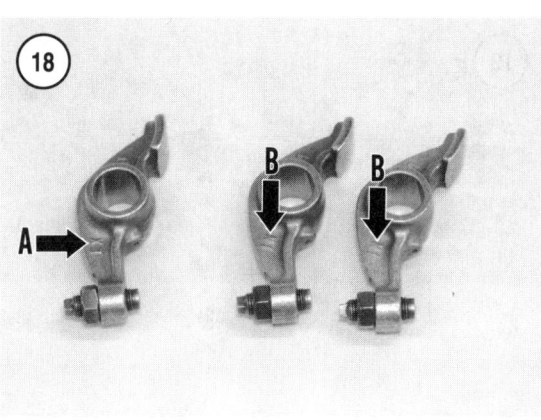

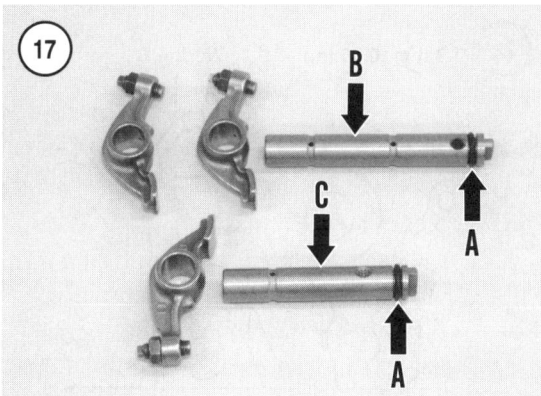

cover. Then remove the two intake rocker arms (A and B, **Figure 15**).
3. Repeat to remove the exhaust rocker arm shaft (C, **Figure 16**) and rocker arm (C, **Figure 15**).
4. Discard the O-ring used on each rocker arm shaft (A, **Figure 17**).
5. Inspect the rocker arms, shafts and cylinder head cover as described in this section.

Assembly

Lubricate components with molybdenum oil solution is this section.
1. Lubricate and install a new O-ring (A, **Figure 17**) on each rocker arm shaft.
2. Lubricate all rocker arm-to-rocker arm shaft sliding surfaces.
3. The rocker arms are identified as follows:
   a. Exhaust: EX (A, **Figure 18**).
   b. Intake: IN (B, **Figure 18**).

CAUTION
If reusing the intake rocker arms, install them in their original mounting positions by referring to the identification marks made during removal.

4. Install the intake rocker arms (A and B, **Figure 15**) with their pads facing toward the inside of the cover. Slide the intake rocker arm shaft (B, **Figure 17**) through the cover and rocker arms, making sure to turn the shaft as its O-ring enters the cover.
5. Repeat Step 4 for the exhaust rocker arm (C, **Figure 15**) and rocker arm shaft (C, **Figure 17**).
6. Align the holes in the shafts with the holes in the cover (**Figure 19**) and install the retaining bolts (A, **Figure 16**) with new washers. Tighten the retaining bolts securely.

Disassembly

Procedures for the front and rear cylinder head covers are identical.

NOTE
*Identify the two intake rocker arms (A and B, **Figure 15**) so they are installed in their original positions.*

1. Remove the retaining bolts and washers (A, **Figure 16**). Discard the washers.
2. With the rocker arms facing up, use pliers to pull the intake rocker arm shaft (B, **Figure 16**) out of the

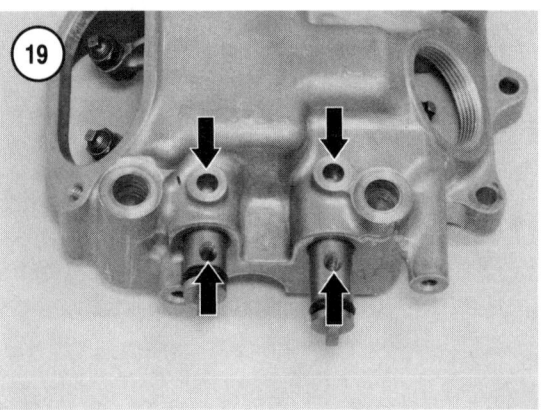

Inspection

Cylinder head cover

1. Remove sealer material from the cylinder head cover with a gasket scraper or razor blade and a chemical solvent. Take care to not damage the sealing surfaces or oil leaks will occur. Clean the oil passage (A, **Figure 20**) with compressed air. Recheck the passage carefully to make sure none of the sealer is trapped inside.
2. Inspect the camshaft bearing surfaces (B, **Figure 20**) in the cylinder head cover for scoring, cracks and other damage. If damage is noted, check the camshaft and cylinder head bearing surfaces for damage.
3. Check the rocker arm shaft bores for scoring, galling or other wear. If damage is noted, check the rocker arm shafts for damage.
4. Replace the cylinder head cover if damaged.

Rocker arms and shafts

Refer to the specifications in **Table 2**. Replace parts that are out of specification or show damage as described in this section.
1. Clean and dry the parts.
2. Inspect the rocker arm pad (A, **Figure 21**) where it contacts the cam lobe for flat spots, cracks, uneven wear and scoring.
3. Inspect the valve adjuster pads (B, **Figure 21**) for flat spots, cracks or other damage. Inspect the locknuts for damage.
4. Inspect the rocker arm shafts (C, **Figure 21**) for scoring, cracks or other damage.
5. Measure the rocker arm bore (D, **Figure 21**) inside diameter.
6. Measure the rocker arm shaft outside diameter at the rocker arm operating position(s).
7. Calculate the rocker arm-to-rocker arm shaft clearance as follows:
   a. Subtract the rocker arm shaft outside diameter from the rocker arm bore inside diameter.

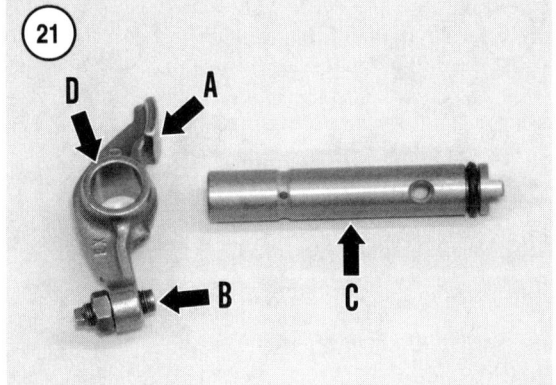
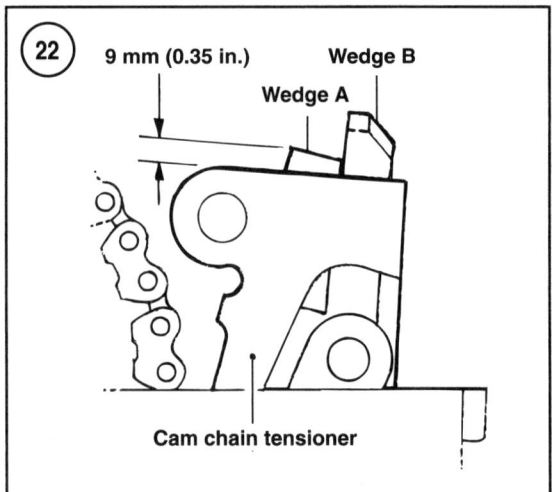

   b. Replace the rocker arm and/or the rocker arm shaft if the clearance is out of specification.
8. Repeat for each rocker arm and shaft.

CAMSHAFTS

Camshaft Removal

If removing both camshafts, remove the front camshaft first. If it is only necessary to remove one

ENGINE TOP END

camshaft, it is still necessary to remove both cylinder head covers to view the cam sprocket timing marks.
1. Remove the engine from the frame as described in *Engine* in Chapter Five.
2. Remove both cylinder head covers as described in this chapter.
3. Remove the crankshaft and timing hole cap from the right crankcase cover. The right crankcase cover must be installed on the engine when viewing the primary drive gear timing marks.
4. Remove one spark plug from each cylinder head (Chapter Three) to make it easier to turn the engine by hand. Cover the spark plug openings.

5. Inspect the cam chain for excessive wear as follows:
   a. Measure the exposed length of cam chain tensioner wedge A as shown in **Figure 22**.
   b. If the measurement exceeds 9 mm (0.35 in.), the cam chain is excessively worn and must be replaced as described in this chapter.
   c. Repeat for the opposite cam chain tensioner.

NOTE
*In the following steps, always turn the crankshaft clockwise, as viewed from the right side of the motorcycle. Turn the engine with a socket on the primary drive gear bolt. Refer to **Valve Clearance** in Chapter Three for additional information.*

NOTE
Rotate the engine and check the primary drive gear and cam sprocket timing marks a few times before actually removing the camshafts. Confirm that the timing marks and camshaft positions are correct while noting how the camshaft lobes are positioned when each cylinder is at TDC on its compression stroke.

6A. When removing the front camshaft, perform the following:
   a. Turn the crankshaft clockwise and align the primary drive gear F-T mark (A, **Figure 23**) with the right crankcase cover index mark (B).
   b. Check that the F mark on the front cam sprocket is aligned with the cylinder head surface (**Figure 24**). Then confirm that the front cylinder is at TDC on its compression stroke by viewing the camshaft flange mark. When the camshaft flange mark is facing up (A, **Figure 25**) the camshaft lobes (B) are facing down and the cylinder is on its compression stroke. If not, turn the crankshaft 360° (one turn) clockwise and realign the F-T mark. The front cylinder should now be at TDC on its compression stroke.

6B. When removing the rear camshaft, perform the following:
   a. Turn the crankshaft clockwise and align the primary drive gear R-T mark (A, **Figure 26**) with the right crankcase cover index mark (B).
   b. Check that the R mark on the rear cam sprocket is aligned with the cylinder head surface (**Figure 27**). Then confirm that the rear cylinder is at TDC on its compression stroke by viewing the position of the camshaft lobes. The cylinder is on its compression stroke when the

camshaft flange mark is facing up (A, **Figure 25**). If not, turn the crankshaft 360° (one turn) clockwise and realign the R-T mark. The rear cylinder should now be at TDC on its compression stroke.

7. Release the cam chain tensioner spring tension against the cam chain as follows:
   a. Refer to **Figure 28** to identify the A and B cam chain tensioner wedges.
   b. Cover the area around the cam chain tensioner to avoid dropping parts into the engine.
   c. Grab wedge B with a pair of pliers and pull it up, then push wedge A down with a screwdriver (**Figure 28**).
   d. Install a 2-mm pin through the hole in wedge B (**Figure 29**) to hold it in position and release spring tension against the cam chain.

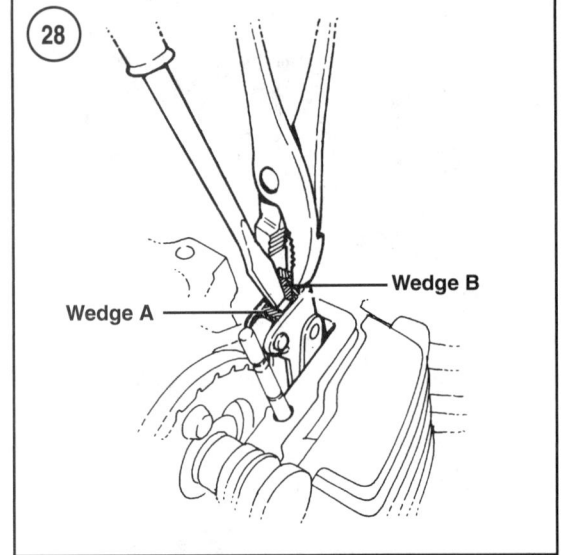

8. Loosen and remove the spark plug sleeve (A, **Figure 30**) with the fork tube holder attachment (Honda part No. 07930-KA50100 [A, **Figure 31**]), 27 mm holder (Yamaha part No. YM-1388 [B, **Figure 31**]) or a bolt that is 27 mm (1 1/16 in.) across the flats of the head. Discard the O-rings.

9. Turn the crankshaft clockwise until the camshaft lobes are facing up. Then hold the primary drive bolt to prevent the camshaft from turning and remove the exposed cam sprocket bolt (B, **Figure 30**, typical).

10. Turn the crankshaft clockwise 360° (one turn) until the camshaft flange mark is facing up (A, **Figure 25**). Then remove the other cam sprocket bolt (B, **Figure 30**).

11. Using a crossing pattern and several steps, loosen and remove the camshaft holder mounting bolts (A, **Figure 32**) and the camshaft holder (B). Note the dowel pins pressed into the holder.

12. Tie a piece of wire onto the cam chain.

13. Slide the cam sprocket off the camshaft and remove the camshaft.

14. Remove the cam sprocket from the cam chain.

NOTE
If both camshafts are to be removed, continue with Step 15 to remove the rear camshaft.

15. Hold the front cam chain up to prevent it from binding and turn the crankshaft clockwise to align the primary drive gear R-T mark (A, **Figure 26**) with

ENGINE TOP END

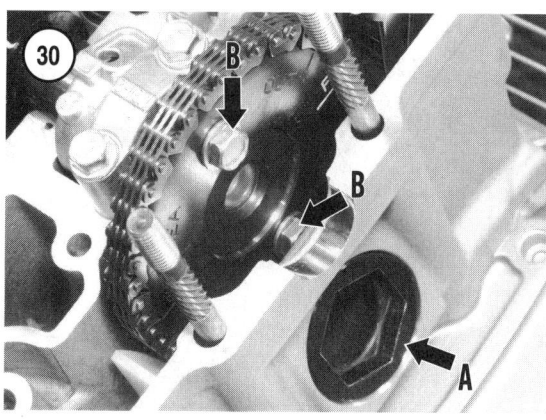

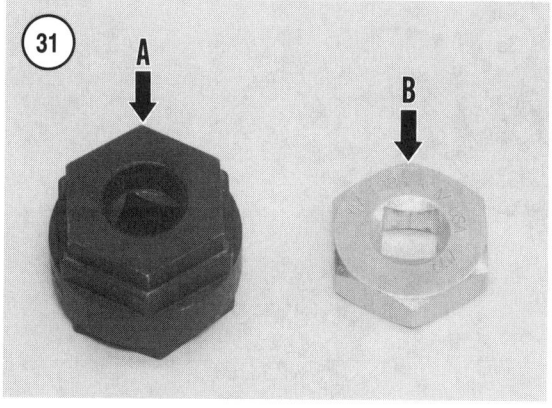

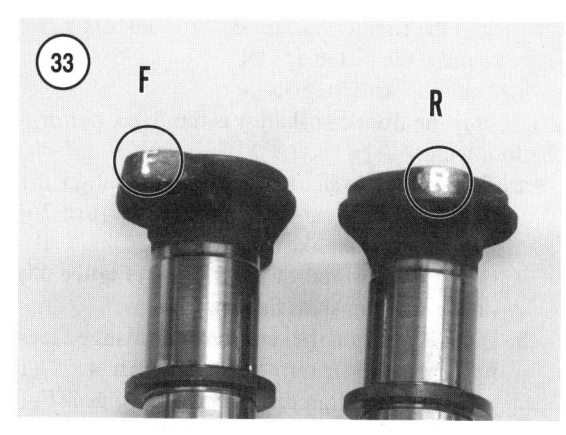

the right crankcase cover index mark (B). Check that the rear cylinder is at TDC on its compression stroke. Confirm by viewing the position of the camshaft lobes. The cylinder is on its compression stroke when all three cam lobes are facing down. If not, turn the crankshaft one full revolution (360°) clockwise and realign the RT mark. The cylinder should now be at TDC on its compression stroke.

16. Repeat Steps 7-14 to remove the rear camshaft.

CAUTION
If the crankshaft must be rotated while one or both camshafts are removed,
pull up on the cam chain(s) so it properly engages the crankshaft drive sprocket(s). Hold the chain taut on the drive sprocket while rotating the crankshaft. If this is not done, the cam chain could become kinked, which could damage the chain and drive sprocket.

17. Inspect the camshaft holders and camshafts as described in this section.

Camshaft Installation

1. Before installing the camshaft(s), note the following:
   a. Rotate the engine clockwise with a socket on the primary drive gear bolt.
   b. Rotating the crankshaft 360° (1 turn) rotates the camshafts 180° (1/2 turn).
   c. Identify the camshafts by the F (front) and R (rear) flange marks identified in **Figure 33**.
   d. When the camshaft flange marks (**Figure 33**) are facing up, the cam lobes are facing down.
   e. Both cam sprockets are identical; however, a different mark is used for each cylinder.
   f. If both camshafts were removed, install the front camshaft first, then the rear camshaft.
   g. If only one camshaft was removed, remove the opposite cylinder head cover so the timing mark on the installed cam sprocket can be viewed.

CAUTION
When rotating the crankshaft in the following steps, keep both cam chains taut to prevent them binding.

2A. If both camshafts were removed, perform the following:
   a. Turn the crankshaft clockwise and align the primary drive gear F- T mark (A, **Figure 23**)

with the right crankcase cover index mark (B) to place the piston at TDC.

b. Continue with Step 3.

2B. If only the front camshaft was removed, perform the following:

a. Turn the crankshaft clockwise and align the primary drive gear R-T mark (A, **Figure 26**) with the right crankcase cover index mark (B). Check the position of the R mark (**Figure 33**) on the rear camshaft flange.

b. If the R mark on the rear camshaft flange faces up (**Figure 34**), turn the crankshaft 412° (1 1/7 turn) and align the primary drive gear F-T mark (A, **Figure 23**) with the right crankcase cover index mark (B, **Figure 23**).

c. If the R mark on the rear camshaft flange faces down, turn the crankshaft clockwise 52° (1/7 turn) and align the primary drive gear F-T mark (A, **Figure 23**) with the right crankcase cover index mark (B).

d. Continue with Step 3 to install the front camshaft.

2C. If only the rear camshaft was removed, perform the following:

a. Turn the crankshaft clockwise and align the primary drive gear F-T mark (A, **Figure 23**) with the right crankcase cover index mark (B). Check the position of the F mark (**Figure 33**) on the front camshaft flange.

b. If the F mark faces up (**Figure 35**), turn the crankshaft 308° (6/7 turn) and align the primary drive gear R-T mark (A, **Figure 26**) with the right crankcase cover index mark (B, **Figure 26**). Continue with Step 3.

c. If the F mark faces down, turn the crankshaft 668° (360° + 308° [1 6/7 turn]) and align the primary drive gear R-T mark (A, **Figure 26**) with the right crankcase cover index mark (B). Continue with Step 3 to install the rear camshaft.

NOTE
After setting the engine position as described in Step 2, perform Steps 3-11 to either install the front or rear camshaft.

3. Apply molybdenum oil solution to the cylinder head camshaft journals, thrust surfaces and cam lobes.

4. Install the cam sprocket by meshing it with the cam chain so its timing mark faces outward and aligns with the cylinder head surface as shown in **Figure 36** (front) or **Figure 37** (rear).

5. Install the camshaft into the cylinder head with its F or R flange mark facing up and slide it through the cam sprocket. Refer to **Figure 38** (front) or **Figure 39** (rear).

6. Turn the camshaft to align its bolt holes with the cam sprocket.

7. Install the camshaft holder (B, **Figure 32**) with its two dowel pins and its two mounting bolts (A). Tighten the bolts in several crossing steps until securely tightened.

8. Apply a medium strength threadlocking compound onto both cam sprocket mounting bolt threads.

9. Install the first sprocket bolt finger-tight, then turn the crankshaft clockwise one turn and install the second bolt. Tighten the second bolt (B, **Figure 30**) to 23 N•m (17 ft.-lb.).

10. Turn the crankshaft clockwise one turn and tighten the first bolt (B, **Figure 30**) to 23 N•m (17 ft.-lb.).

ENGINE TOP END

NOTE
Perform Steps 14 and 15 to recheck the camshaft timing for both cylinders.

14. Turn the crankshaft clockwise and align the primary drive gear F-T mark (A, **Figure 23**) with the right crankcase cover index mark (B, **Figure 23**), then check the position of the front camshaft F flange mark (**Figure 24**) while noting the following:
   a. If the front camshaft F flange mark is facing up (**Figure 35**) and the front cam sprocket F mark is aligned with the cylinder head surface (**Figure 24**), continue with Step 15.
   b. If the front camshaft F flange mark is facing down, turn the crankshaft clockwise 360° (one turn) and realign the F-T mark (A, **Figure 23**) with the right crankcase cover index mark (B). If the camshaft flange and cam sprocket F marks are aligned as described in substep a, continue with Step 15.
15. Turn the crankshaft clockwise 308° (6/7 turn) and align the primary drive gear R-T mark (A, **Figure 26**) with the right crankcase cover index mark (B). The rear camshaft R flange mark (**Figure 34**) should be facing up and the rear cam sprocket R mark should align with the cylinder head surface (**Figure 27**).

CAUTION
The timing marks must align correctly at this time; otherwise, camshaft timing is incorrect. Do not proceed if the camshaft sprocket timing marks are positioned incorrectly.

16. Install the cylinder head covers as described in this chapter.
17. Adjust the valve clearance as described in Chapter Three.
18. Install the engine in the frame as described in *Engine* in Chapter Five.

Camshaft Inspection

Refer to the specifications in **Table 2**. Replace worn or damaged parts as described in this section.
1. Clean the camshafts in solvent and dry thoroughly. Flush the camshaft oil passages with solvent and compressed air.
2. Remove all threadlocking compound residue from the bolt and camshaft flange threads.
3. Check the cam lobes (A, **Figure 40**) for wear. Replace the camshaft if the lobes are pitted, scored, worn or damaged.
4. Measure each cam lobe height (**Figure 41**).
5. Check the camshaft bearing journals (B, **Figure 40**) for wear or scoring. Replace the camshaft if the journals are scored, worn or damaged.

11. Lubricate two new O-rings and install them into the grooves on the spark plug sleeve. Lubricate the threads on the spark plug sleeve (A, **Figure 30**) with engine oil and tighten to 18 N•m (13 ft.-lb.) with the same tool used during disassembly (**Figure 31**).
12. If both camshafts were removed and the front camshaft was just installed, perform Step 2C to position the engine for rear camshaft installation. Then perform Steps 3-11 to install the rear camshaft.
13. Remove the 2 mm pin from the cam chain tensioner (**Figure 29**, typical). Spring tension should pull wedge A into the tensioner. Repeat for the other cam chain tensioner, if necessary.

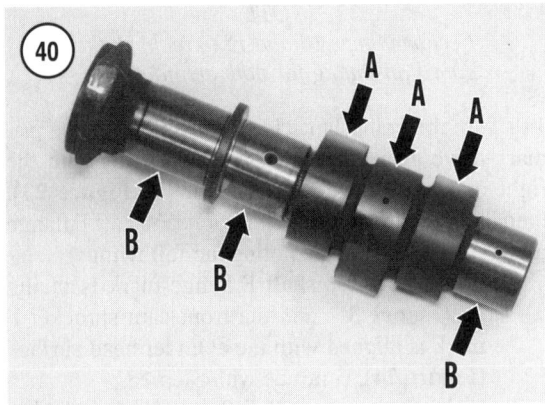

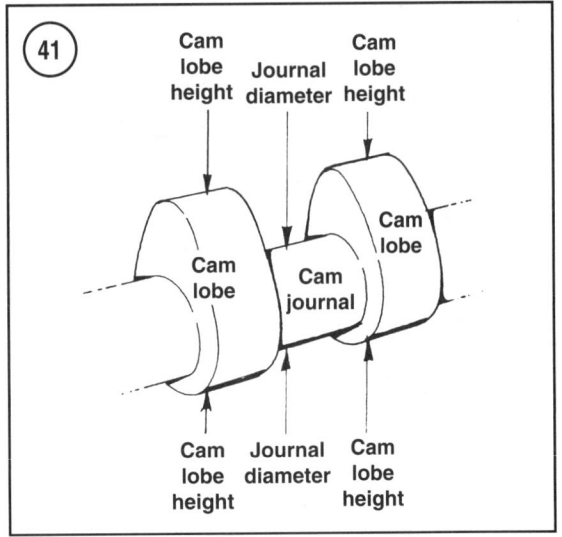

NOTE
Camshaft journal wear is determined in **Camshaft Oil Clearance Measurement** *as described in this section.*

6. If the camshaft lobes or journals are excessively worn or damaged, check the journal surfaces in the cylinder head cover, cylinder head and camshaft holder as described in this chapter.

7. Support the camshaft journals on a set of V-blocks or crankshaft truing stand and measure runout with a dial indicator. Note the following:
   a. If the runout is out of specification, replace the camshaft and measure the camshaft oil clearance as described in this section. If the clearance is out of specification, the camshaft holder and camshaft journals were damaged from the bent camshaft.
   b. If the camshaft was replaced, remeasure the camshaft oil clearance as described in this section with the new camshaft.

Cam Sprocket Inspection

1. Inspect the cam sprockets for broken or chipped teeth.
2. Inspect the cam chains and drive sprockets mounted on the crankshaft. Refer to *Cam Chain Tensioner and Cam Chain* in this chapter.

Camshaft Oil Clearance Measurement

Use Plastigage to measure the clearance between the journals on the cylinder head cover, camshaft, camshaft holder and cylinder head. The camshaft, camshaft holder and cylinder head cover must be installed on the cylinder head when performing this procedure.

1. Remove the rocker arms from the cylinder head cover as described in this chapter.
2. Clean the cylinder head cover, camshaft, camshaft holder and cylinder head journals. These surfaces must be clean and dry.

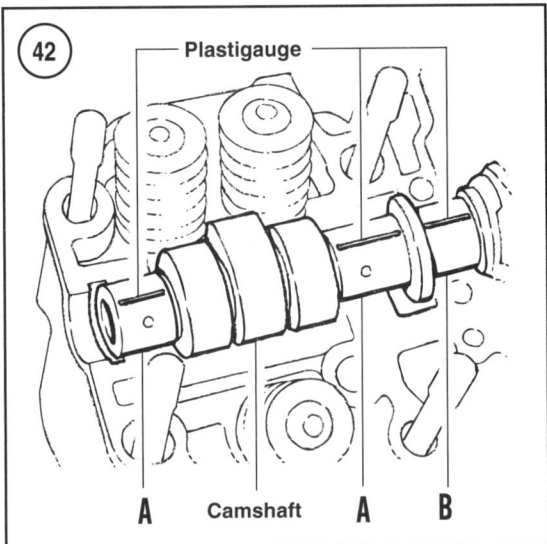

3. Identify the original equipment camshafts by the F (front) and R (rear) flange marks (**Figure 33**).
4. Install the camshaft into its cylinder head with its flange mark facing up as described in this section.
5. Cut a piece of Plastigage the width each camshaft bearing journal and place on the journals, parallel to the camshaft (**Figure 42**). Do not place the Plastigage across oil holes.
6. Install and tighten the camshaft holder (B, **Figure 32**) as described in this section.

CAUTION
Before installing the cylinder head cover, make sure the piece of wire connected to the cam chain is laying inside the engine so it cannot be pinched between the cover and cylinder head gasket surfaces.

ENGINE TOP END

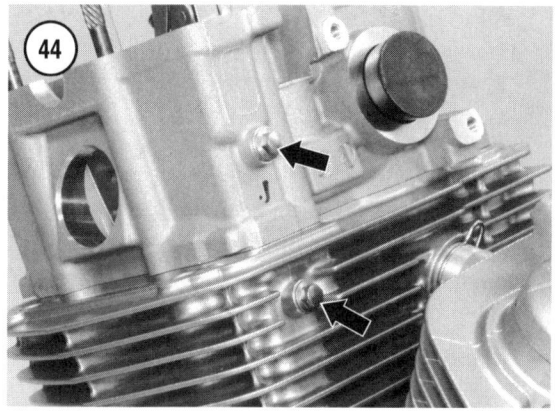

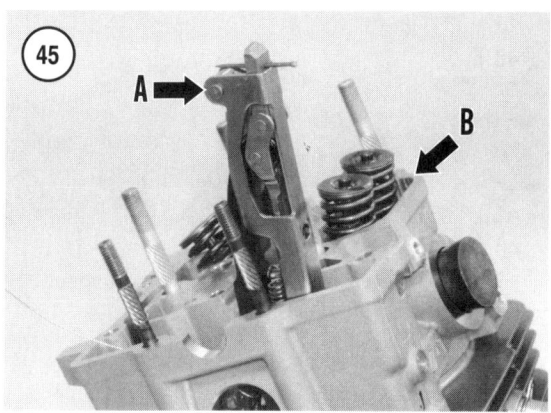

8. Remove the cylinder head cover as described in this chapter.
9. Remove the camshaft holder (B, **Figure 32**) as described in this section, making sure the camshaft does not rotate.
10. Measure the widest portion of the flattened Plastigage according to the manufacturer's instructions (**Figure 43**) and compare to the camshaft oil clearance A and B specification in **Table 2**. Note the following:
   a. Refer to **Figure 42** to identify the A and B measurement points specified in **Table 2**.
   b. If all the measurements are within specification, the cylinder head, camshaft and camshaft holder can be reused.
   c. If any measurement exceeds the service limit, replace the camshaft and recheck the oil clearance.
   d. If the new measurement exceeds the service limit with the new camshaft, replace the cylinder head cover, camshaft holder and cylinder head as a set.
11. Remove all Plastigage material from the cylinder head cover, camshaft, camshaft holder and cylinder head.
12. Install the rocker arms as described in this chapter.

CAM CHAIN TENSIONER AND CAM CHAIN

Each cylinder is equipped with a cam chain tensioner, chain guide and cam chain. Service procedures for the front and rear cylinders are the same.

Refer to *Cylinder Head* in this chapter to replace the chain guide.

Cam Chain Tensioner Removal/Inspection/Installation

1. Remove the engine as described in *Engine* in Chapter Five.
2. Remove the camshaft as described in this chapter.

7. Install and tighten the cylinder head cover as described in this chapter.

CAUTION
Do not rotate the camshafts with the Plastigage in place.

CAUTION
Loosen the camshaft holder bolts (A, Figure 32) as described in this section or the camshaft holder (B) may be damaged.

NOTE
Do not remove the pin and release the cam chain tension spring (installed during camshaft removal) when removing and inspecting the cam chain tensioner.

3. Remove the cam chain tensioner mounting bolts (**Figure 44**), washers and tensioner (A, **Figure 45**). Discard the washers.

4. Inspect the chain tensioner (**Figure 46**) for the following:
   a. Cracked or damaged tension spring.
   b. Worn or damaged tensioner arm.
5. Make sure the cam chain is properly meshed with the timing sprocket on the crankshaft. Refer to **Figure 47** (front) or **Figure 48** (rear).
6. Install the cam chain tensioner (A, **Figure 45**) by guiding the tensioner arm into the lower pocket in the crankcase. Refer to **Figure 47** (front) or **Figure 48** (rear).
7. Install a new sealing washer onto each cam chain tensioner mounting bolt (**Figure 44**) and tighten to 12 N•m (106 in.-lb.).
8. Install the camshaft as described in this chapter.

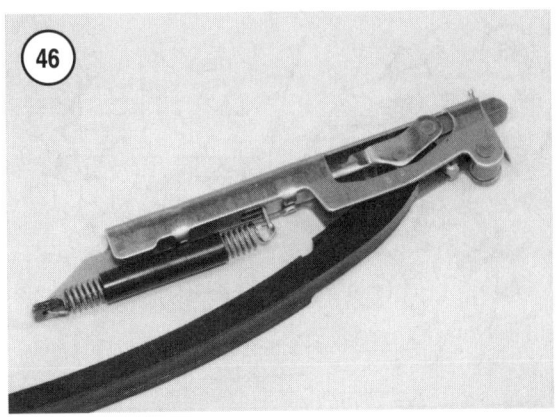

Cam Chain Removal/Installation

Do not cut the cam chains; replacement links are not available.

NOTE
*Before removing the camshaft in Step 1, make sure to measure the cam chain tensioner wedge as described in **Camshafts** in this chapter. Replace the cam chain if the measurement indicates a worn chain.*

1. Remove the engine as described in *Engine* in Chapter Five.
2. Remove the camshaft and spark plug sleeve as described in this chapter.
3. To replace the front cam chain, remove the flywheel (Chapter Nine).
4. To replace the rear cam chain, remove the primary drive gear (Chapter Six).
5. Remove the cam chain from the sprocket by squeezing the chain guide away from the cam chain. Refer to **Figure 47** (front) or **Figure 48** (rear). Pull the cam chain up through the chain tunnel and remove the chain.

NOTE
*If there is not enough clearance to remove the chain from the sprocket, remove the chain guide as described in **Cylinder Head** in this chapter.*

6. Install the cam chain by reversing these steps while making sure the cam chain is properly meshed with the timing sprocket on the crankshaft. Refer to **Figure 47** (front) or **Figure 48** (rear).

Component Inspection

If the cam chain or chain guides are excessively worn, the cam chain tensioner may not be working properly. Inspect the cam chain tensioner as described in this section.

1. Clean and dry the cam chain.
2. Inspect the cam chain for:
   a. Worn or damaged pins and rollers.
   b. Cracked or damaged side plates.
3. If the cam chain is excessively worn or damaged, inspect the drive (crankshaft) and driven (camshaft) sprockets for the same wear conditions. The driven sprocket can be replaced separately. Refer to *Primary Drive and Driven Gears and Oil Pump Chain and Sprockets* in Chapter Six An excessively worn or

ENGINE TOP END

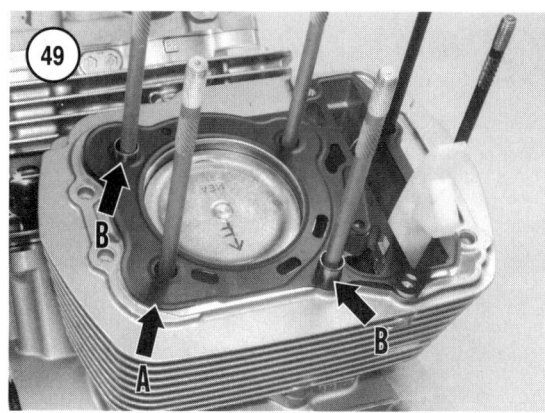

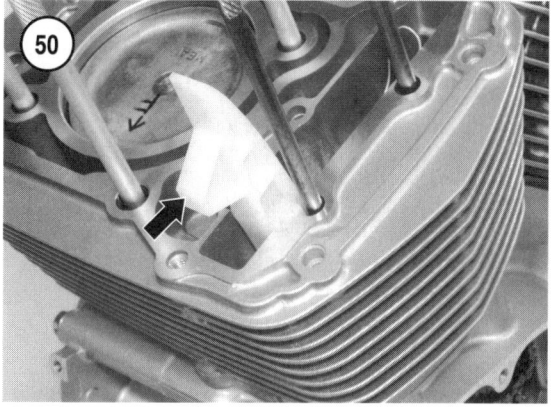

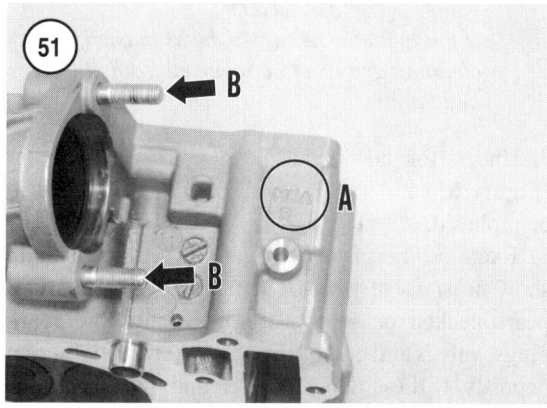

3. Place the cylinder head on wooden blocks to avoid damaging the gasket surfaces.
4. Remove the cylinder head gasket (A, **Figure 49**) and the two dowel pins (B).
5. Check the top and bottom gasket surfaces for any signs of leaks. Also, check the head and base gaskets. A blown gasket could indicate possible cylinder head or cylinder block warp or other damage.
6. Remove the chain guide (**Figure 50**).
7. Cover the cylinder block and chain tunnel with a clean shop cloth.
8. Inspect the cylinder head as described in this section.
9. Refer to *Valves and Valve Components* in this chapter to service the valve assembly.

Installation

1. Clean the cylinder head and cylinder block gasket surfaces.
2. Position the cam chain inside the chain tunnel so it does not interfere with the cylinder head.
3. Install the chain guide (**Figure 50**) by aligning its tabs with the slots in the cylinder. Make sure that the end of the chain guide seats into the pocket in the crankcase. Refer to **Figure 47** (front) or **Figure 48** (rear).
4. Install the two dowel pins (B, **Figure 49**).
5. Install a new cylinder head gasket (A, **Figure 49**).
6. Identify the cylinder heads by their F (front) or R (rear) cast mark (A, **Figure 51**).
7. Install the cylinder head over the dowel pins and against the head gasket. Check that the cylinder head is sitting flush against the head gasket.
8. Pull on the cam chain and make sure it is properly engaged with the drive sprocket on the crankshaft.
9. Install the chain tensioner, spark plug sleeve and camshaft as described in this chapter.

Inspection

1. Before removing the valves from the cylinder head, perform a solvent test to check the valve face-to-valve seat seal.
   a. Support the cylinder head with the exhaust port facing up (**Figure 52**). Pour solvent or kerosene into the port. Check the combustion chamber for fluid leaking past the exhaust valves. There should be no fluid entering the combustion chamber.
   b. Repeat Step 2 for the intake valves.
   c. If the combustion chamber is wet, the valve is not seating correctly.

damaged drive sprocket will require crankshaft replacement as described in Chapter Five.

CYLINDER HEAD

Removal

1. Remove the camshaft, spark plug sleeve and chain tensioner as described in this chapter.
2. Lift the cylinder head (B, **Figure 45**) off the engine. If the cylinder head is tight, tap it with a plastic hammer to break its seal. Do not use a metal hammer or pry the head off.

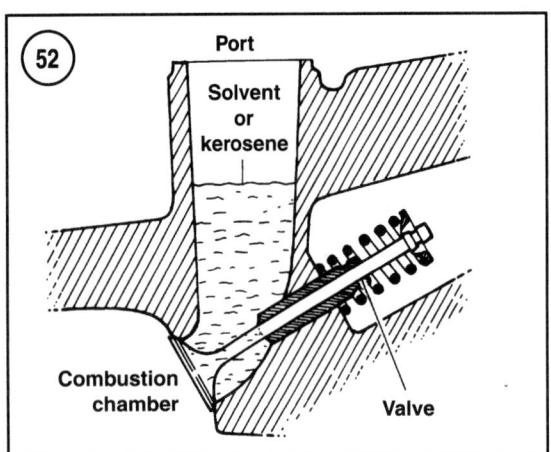

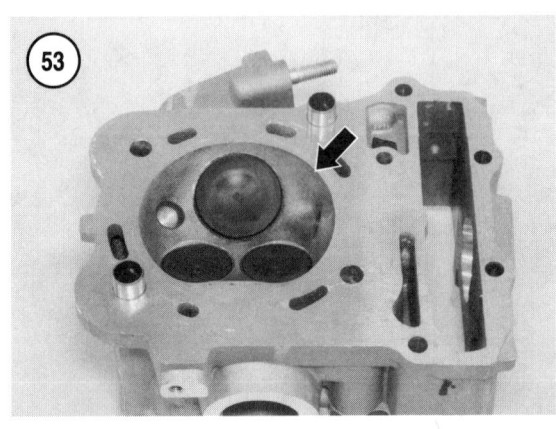

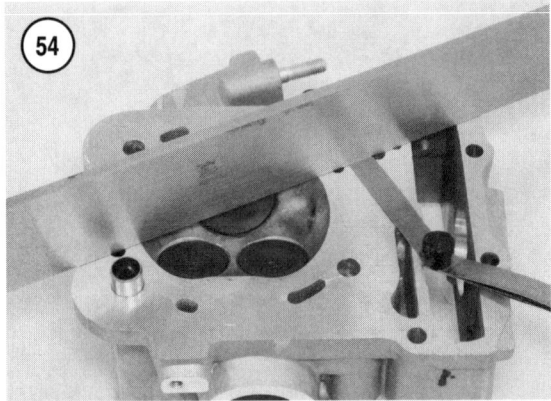

d. If there is a leak, check for a damaged valve stem, valve seat and/or face, or possibly a cracked combustion chamber.

2. Remove the spark plugs as described in Chapter Three.

3. Clean the cylinder head and cylinder block gasket surfaces. Do not scratch the gasket surface. If the gasket residue is hard to remove, place a solvent soaked rag across the cylinder head gasket surface to soften the deposits.

CAUTION
Cleaning the combustion chambers with the valves removed can damage the valve seat surfaces. A damaged or even slightly scratched valve seat causes poor valve seating.

4. Before removing the valves, remove all carbon deposits from the combustion chambers (**Figure 53**) with a wire brush. To protect the cylinder head surface, place the two dowel pins and the old head gasket onto the cylinder head and hold in place while cleaning the combustion chamber. Do not damage the head, valves or spark plug threads.

5. Examine the spark plug threads in the cylinder head for damage. If damage is minor or if the threads are contaminated with carbon, use a spark plug thread tap to clean the threads following the manufacturer's instructions. If thread damage is severe, repair the head by installing a steel thread insert.

CAUTION
When using a tap to clean spark plug threads, lubricate the tap with an aluminum tap cutting fluid or kerosene.

6. Clean the entire head in solvent. Make sure the coolant passageways are clear.

CAUTION
If the cylinder head was bead blasted, cleaning grit must be removed from all head areas.

7. Check for cracks in the combustion chamber (**Figure 53**) and exhaust port. A cracked head must be replaced.

8. Examine the piston crowns. The crowns should show no signs of wear or damage. If the crown appears pecked or spongy-looking, check the spark plugs, valves and combustion chamber for aluminum deposits. If these deposits are found, the cylinder is overheating.

CAUTION
Do not clean the piston crown while the piston is installed in the cylinder. Carbon scraped from the top of the piston may fall between the cylinder wall and piston and onto the piston rings. Because carbon grit is very abrasive, premature cylinder, piston and ring wear will occur. If the piston crowns have heavy deposits of carbon, remove the pistons as described in this chapter to clean them properly. Excessive carbon buildup on the piston crowns

ENGINE TOP END

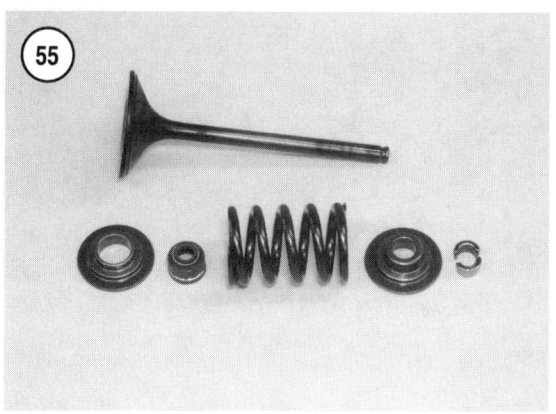

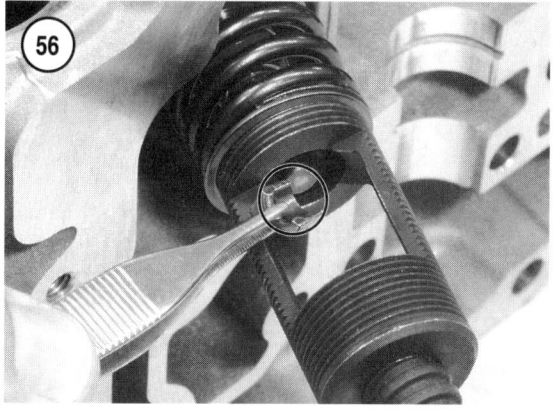

reduces piston cooling, raises engine compression and causes overheating.

9. Measure cylinder head warp with a feeler gauge and a straightedge (**Figure 54**). Check at several locations. Maximum allowable warp is listed in **Table 2**. If the warp exceeds this limit, the cylinder head must be resurfaced or replaced.
10. Check the exhaust pipe studs (B, **Figure 51**) for looseness or thread damage. Slight thread damage can be repaired with a thread file or die. If thread damage is severe, replace the damaged stud(s) as described in *Service Methods* in Chapter One. Install each stud so it extends 37.5-38.5 mm (1.48-1.52 in.) above the cylinder head surface.
11. Check the valves and valve guides as described in *Valves and Valve Components* in this chapter.

VALVES AND VALVE COMPONENTS

Due to the number of special tools and the skills required to use them, it is recommended that valve service be referred to a dealership.

All valve components should be identified and installed in their original position.

Valve Removal

1. Remove the cylinder head as described in this chapter.
2. Mark the parts (**Figure 55**) as they are removed so that they can be reinstalled in their original position.
3. Install a valve spring compressor squarely over the upper retainer with the other end of the tool placed against the valve head. Position the tool carefully to avoid damaging the cylinder head gasket surface.

NOTE
It is difficult to identify the tightly wound coils on the exhaust valve springs, which the manufacturer states should face down (toward the combustion chamber). The manufacturer does not specify any orientation for the intake valve springs. However, to ensure the valve springs are correctly installed, identify either the upper or lower end of each valve spring before removal.

4. Tighten the valve spring compressor until the valve keepers separate and remove them (**Figure 56**).
5. Remove the valve spring compressor from the head. Remove the upper retainer (A, **Figure 57**) and valve spring (B).

CAUTION
*Remove any burrs from the valve stem groove (A, **Figure 58**) before removing the valve; otherwise, the valve guide may be damaged as the valve stem passes through it.*

NOTE
If a valve is difficult to remove, it may be bent, causing it to stick in its valve guide. This condition will require valve and valve guide replacement as described in this section.

6. Remove the valve from the guide while rotating it slightly.

7. Use a pair of pliers to pull the oil seal (B, **Figure 58**) off the valve guide and discard it.
8. Remove the spring seat (C, **Figure 58**).
9. Repeat for the remaining intake and exhaust valves.

Valve Installation

Install the valves and their components in their original locations as recorded during removal.
1. Install the spring seat (C, **Figure 58**) with its shoulder facing up.
2. Lubricate the inside of a new oil seal with engine oil. Then push the seal (**Figure 59**) straight down the valve guide until it snaps into the groove in the top of the guide (B, **Figure 58**). Check that the oil seal is centered and seats squarely on top of the guide. If the seal is cocked to one side, oil will leak past the seal during engine operation. If it is necessary to remove a new seal, do not reuse it.
3. Install the valve as follows:
   a. Coat the valve stem with molybdenum oil solution.
   b. Install the valve partway into its guide and then slowly turn the valve as it enters the valve stem seal and continue turning it until the valve is installed all the way.
   c. Make sure the valve moves up and down smoothly.

NOTE
Refer to your orientation marks made on the valve springs. If installing new valve springs, use the orientation marks made on the original springs to help identify the tightly wound coils on the exhaust valve springs.

4. Install exhaust valve springs with their tightly wound coils facing down. Install the intake valve springs. Refer to B, **Figure 57**.
5. Install the retainer (A, **Figure 57**).

CAUTION
To avoid loss of spring tension, do not compress the spring any more than necessary when installing the valve keepers.

6. Compress the valve spring with a valve spring compressor tool and install the valve keepers (**Figure 56**) around the valve stem and into the hole in the top of the retainer. Then slowly release tension on the valve spring while watching the movement of the retainer and keepers. Make sure the keepers fit into the rounded groove in the valve stem. Gently tap the upper retainer with a plastic hammer to seat the keepers. Refer to **Figure 60**.

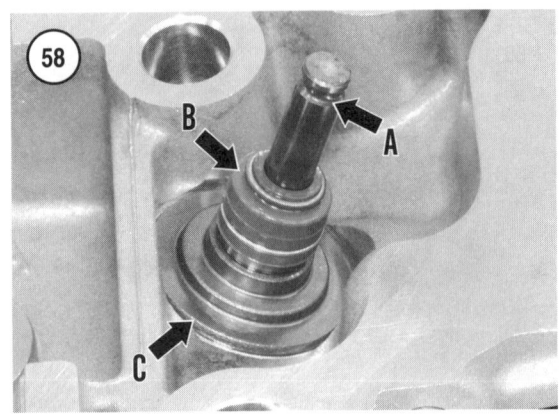

7. Repeat for the remaining valves.
8. Install the cylinder head, camshaft and camshaft holders as described in this chapter.
9. Check and adjust the valve clearance as described in Chapter Three.

Valve Inspection

Valve components

Refer to the specifications in **Table 2**. Replace parts that are damaged or out of specification as described in this section.

ENGINE TOP END

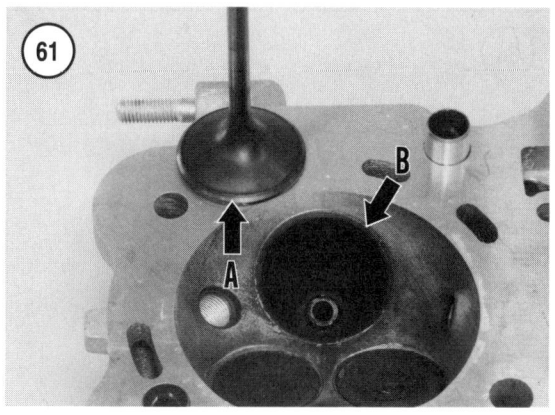

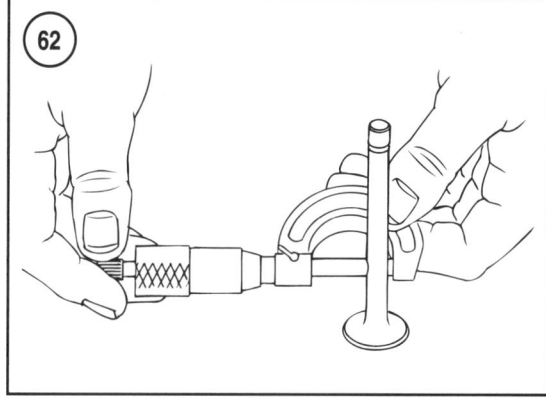

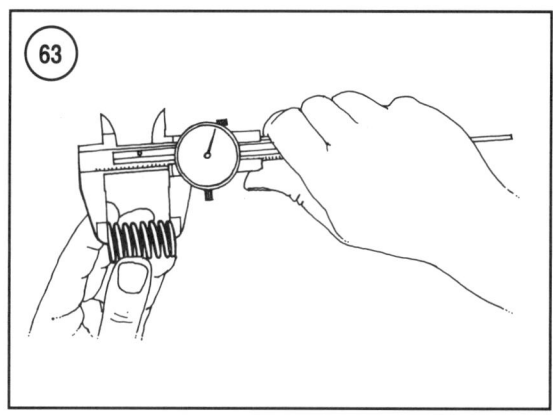

1. Clean the valve components in solvent. Do not damage the valve seating surface.
2. Inspect the valve face (A, **Figure 61**) for burning, pitting or other signs of wear. Unevenness of the valve face is an indication that the valve is not serviceable. If the wear on a valve is too extensive to be corrected by hand-lapping the valve into its seat, replace the valve. The face on the valve cannot be ground. Replace the valve if defective.
3. Inspect the valve stems for wear and roughness. Check the valve keeper grooves for damage.
4. Measure each valve stem outside diameter (**Figure 62**). Note the following:

   a. If a valve stem is out of specification, discard the valve.
   b. If a valve stem is within specification, record the measurement so it can be used to determine the valve stem-to-guide clearance in Step 7.

NOTE
The manufacturer recommends reaming the valve guides to remove any carbon buildup before checking and measuring the guides. For the home mechanic it is more practical to remove carbon and varnish from the valve guides with a stiff spiral wire brush. Then clean the valve guides with solvent to wash out all particles and dry with compressed air.

5. Insert each valve into its respective valve guide and move it up and down by hand. The valve should move smoothly.
6. Measure each valve guide inside diameter with a small hole gauge and record the measurements. Note the following:

NOTE
Because valve guides wear unevenly (oval shape), measure each guide at different positions. Use the largest inside diameter measurement when determining its size.

   a. If a valve guide is out of specification, replace it as described in this section.
   b. If a valve guide is within specification, record the measurement so it can be used to determine the valve stem-to-guide clearance in Step 7.

7. Subtract the valve stem outside diameter measurement from the valve guide inside diameter measurement to determine the valve stem-to-guide clearance. Note the following:

   a. If the clearance is out of specification, determine if a new guide would bring the clearance within specification.
   b. If the clearance would be out of specification with a new guide, replace the valve and guide as a set.

8. Inspect the valve springs as follows:

   a. Inspect each spring for any cracks or other visual damage.
   b. Measure the free length of each valve spring (**Figure 63**).
   c. Replace defective or worn springs.

9. Check the valve keepers for cracks and any surface spots. Replace both keepers.
10. Inspect the spring retainer and spring seat for damage.
11. Inspect the valve seats as described in this section.

Valve seat

The most accurate method for checking the valve seal is to use a marking compound (machinist's dye), available from auto parts and tool stores. Marking compound is used to locate high or irregular spots when checking or making close fits. Follow the manufacturer's directions.

NOTE
Because of the close operating tolerances within the valve assembly, the valve stem and guide must be within specification; otherwise the inspection results will be inaccurate.

1. Remove the valves as described in this section.
2. Clean the valve (A, **Figure 61**) and valve seat (B) mating areas with contact cleaner.
3. Clean all carbon deposits from the valve face with solvent and dry thoroughly.
4. Spread a thin layer of marking compound evenly on the valve face.
5. Slowly insert the valve into its guide and tap the valve against its seat several times (**Figure 64**) without spinning it.
6. Remove the valve and examine the impression left by the marking compound. If the impression (on the valve or in the cylinder head) is not even and continuous, and the valve seat width (**Figure 65**) is not within the specified tolerance listed in **Table 2**, the valve seat in the cylinder head must be reconditioned.
7. Examine the valve seat in the cylinder head (B, **Figure 61**). It should be smooth and even with a polished seating surface.
8. If the valve seat is not in good condition, recondition the valve seat as described in this chapter.

NOTE
The valve guides must be in good condition and serviced, if necessary, before regrinding the valve seats.

9. Repeat for the other valves.

Valve Guide Removal/Installation

Tools

The following tools (or equivalents) are required to remove and install the valve guides.
1. 6.6 mm valve guide driver (part No. 07942-6570100).
2. 6.6 mm valve guide reamer (part No. 07984-ZE2000D).

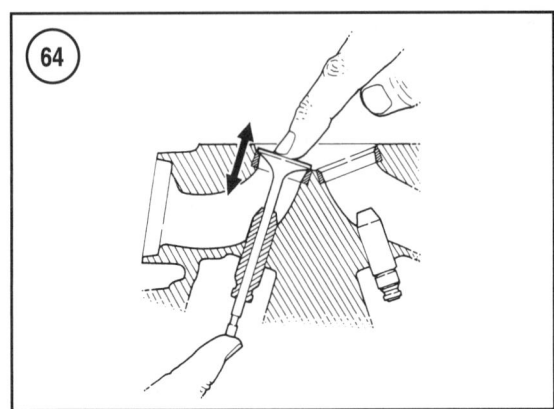

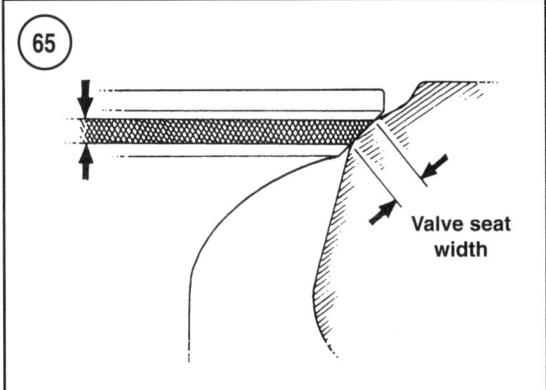

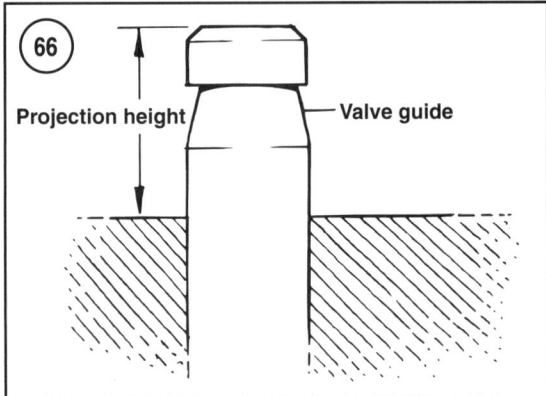

Procedure

1. Remove all of the valves and valve guide seals from the cylinder head as described in this section.
2. Place the new valve guides in the freezer for approximately one hour prior to heating the cylinder head. Chilling them will slightly reduce the outside diameter, while the cylinder is lightly larger due to heat expansion. This makes valve guide installation much easier. One at a time remove the guides as needed.
3. Measure the valve guide projection height above the cylinder head surface (**Figure 66**). Record the

ENGINE TOP END

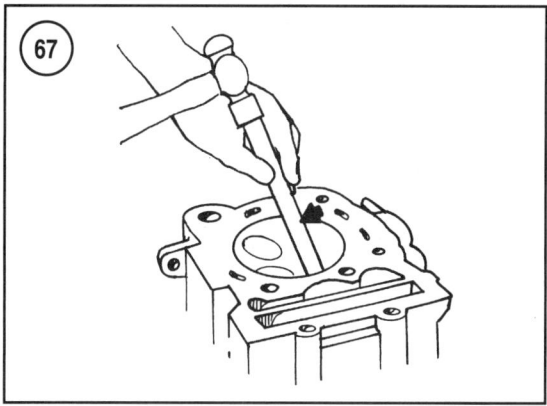

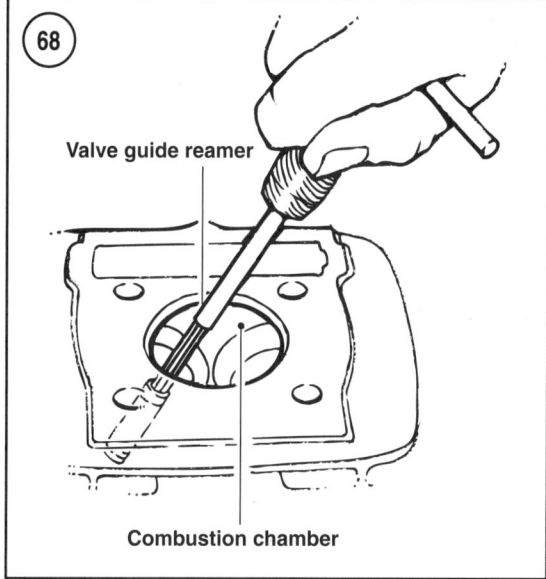

Valve guide reamer
Combustion chamber

projection height for each valve guide and compare to the valve projection height specification in **Table 2**.

WARNING
Wear protective gloves to prevent burns.

CAUTION
Do not heat the cylinder head with a torch. The direct heat can destroy the case hardening of the valve guide and may warp the cylinder head.

4. Place the cylinder head on a hot plate and heat to a temperature of 130-140° C (275-290° F). Do not exceed 150° C (300° F). Monitor the temperature with heat sticks, available at welding supply stores.
5. Remove the head from the hot plate. Place the head on wooden blocks with the combustion chamber facing *up*.
6. From the combustion chamber side of the head, drive out the valve guide with the valve guide remover (**Figure 67**). Quickly repeat this step for each guide to be replaced. Reheat the head as required. Discard the valve guides after removing them.

CAUTION
Do not attempt to remove the valve guides if the head is not hot enough. Doing so may damage the valve guide bore in the cylinder head and require replacement of the head.

7. Allow the head to cool.
8. Inspect and clean the valve guide bores. Check for cracks or any scoring along the bore wall.
9. Reheat the cylinder head as described in Step 4. Then remove it from the hot plate and place it on the wooden blocks with the valve spring side facing *up*. The valve guide is installed from this side.
10. Remove one new valve guide, either intake or exhaust, from the freezer.
11. Align the valve guide in the bore. Use the valve guide driver tool and a hammer to drive in the valve guide until the projection height (**Figure 66**) of the valve guide is within the specification in **Table 2**.
12. Repeat to install the remaining valve guides.
13. Allow the head to cool to room temperature.
14. Ream each valve guide as follows:
   a. Place the head on wooden blocks with the combustion chamber facing *up*. The guides are reamed from this side.
   b. Coat the valve guide and valve guide reamer with cutting oil.

CAUTION
*Always rotate the reamer **clockwise** through the entire length of the guide, both when reaming the guide and when removing the reamer. Rotating the reamer counterclockwise will reverse cut and damage (enlarge) the valve guide bore.*

CAUTION
Do not allow the reamer to tilt. Keep the tool square to the hole and apply even pressure and twisting motion during the entire operation.

   c. Rotate the reamer clockwise into the valve guide **Figure 68**.
   d. Slowly rotate the reamer through the guide, while periodically adding cutting oil.
   e. As the end of the reamer passes through the valve guide, maintain the clockwise motion and work the reamer back out of the guide while continuing to add cutting oil.
   f. Clean the reamer of all chips and relubricate with cutting oil before starting on the next guide. Repeat for each guide as required.

15. Thoroughly clean the cylinder head and all valve components in solvent, then with detergent and hot water to remove all cutting residue. Rinse in cold water. Dry with compressed air.
16. Measure the valve guide inside diameter. The measurement must be within the specification listed in **Table 2**.
17. Apply engine oil to the valve guides to prevent rust.
18. Lubricate a valve stem with engine oil and pass it through the valve guide, verifying that it moves without any roughness or binding.
19. Reface the valve seats as described in *Valve Seat Reconditioning* in this section.

Valve Seat Reconditioning

Tools

Before reconditioning the valve seats, inspect and measure them as described under *Valve Inspection* in this section.

The following tools are required:
1. Valve seat cutters (**Figure 69**). Follow the manufacturer's instructions.
2. Caliper.
3. Gear-marking compound.
4. Valve lapping tool.

Procedure

1. Rotate and insert the solid pilot into the valve guide. Be sure the pilot is correctly seated.
2. Install the 45° cutter and cutter holder onto the solid pilot.

> **CAUTION**
> Work slowly and make light cuts. Overcutting the valve seats will recede the valves into the cylinder head, reducing the valve adjustment range. If cutting is excessive, the ability to set the valve adjustment may be lost. This condition requires cylinder head replacement.

3. Using the 45° cutter, de-scale and clean the valve seat with one or two turns.
4. If the seat is still pitted or burned, turn the 45° cutter additional turns until the surface is clean.
5. Measure the valve seat width (**Figure 65**). Record the measurement to use as a reference point when performing the following.

> **CAUTION**
> The 32° cutter removes material quickly. Work carefully and check the progress often.

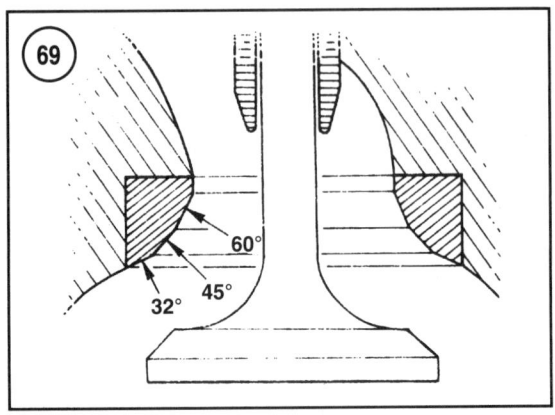

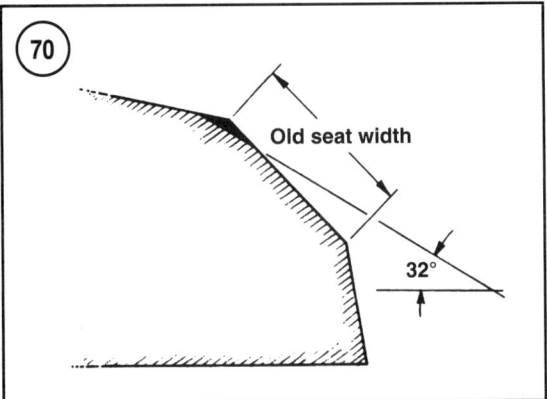

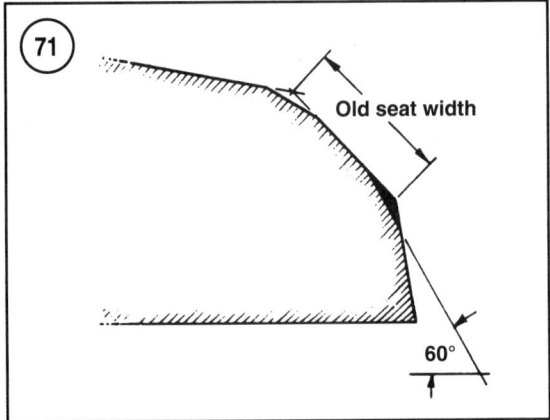

6. Install the 32° cutter onto the solid pilot and lightly cut the seat to remove 1/4 of the existing valve seat (**Figure 70**).
7. Install the 60° cutter onto the solid pilot and lightly cut the seat to remove 1/4 of the existing valve seat (**Figure 71**).
8. Measure the valve seat width (**Figure 65**). Then fit the 45° cutter onto the solid pilot and cut the valve seat to the specified width (**Figure 72**) listed in **Table 2**.
9. When the valve seat width is correct, check valve seating as follows:
   a. Clean the valve seat with contact cleaner.

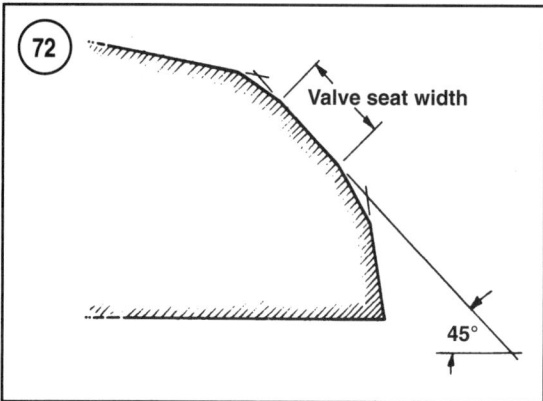

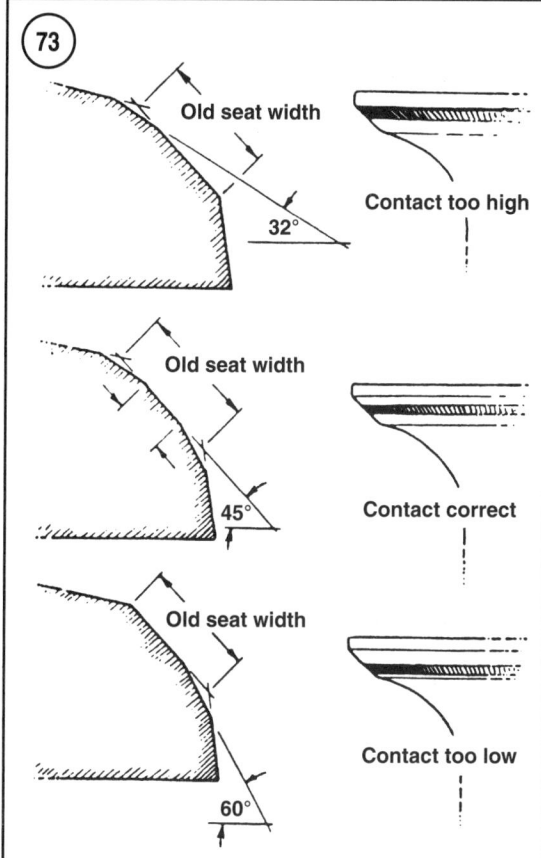

g. The valve contact should be approximately in the center of the valve seat area.

10. If the contact area is too high on the valve, or if it is too wide, use the 32° cutter and remove a portion of the top area of the valve seat material to lower and narrow the contact area on the valve (**Figure 73**).

11. If the contact area is too low on the valve, or too wide, use the 60° cutter and remove a portion of the lower area of the valve seat material to raise and narrow the contact area on the valve (**Figure 73**).

12. After the desired valve seat position and width is obtained, use the 45° cutter to lightly clean off any burrs that may have been caused by previous cuts.

13. When the contact area is correct, lap the valve as described in this section.

14. Repeat Steps 1-13 for all remaining valve seats.

15. Thoroughly clean the cylinder head and all valve components in solvent, then with detergent and hot water. Rinse in cold water and dry with compressed air. Lubricate the valve guides with engine oil to prevent rust.

Valve Lapping

Valve lapping can restore the valve seat without machining if the amount of wear or distortion is not too great.

Perform this procedure if the valve seat width and outside diameter are within specification. A valve lapping tool and compound are required.

1. Smear a light coating of fine grade valve lapping compound on the valve face seating surface.
2. Insert the valve into the head.
3. Wet the suction cup of the lapping stick and stick it onto the head of the valve. Spin the tool in both directions, while pressing it against the valve seat and lap the valve to the seat. Every 5 to 10 seconds, lift and rotate the valve 180° in the valve seat. Continue until the surfaces on the valve and seat are smooth and equal in size.
4. Examine the valve seat in the cylinder head (**Figure 65**). It should be smooth and even with a smooth, polished seating ring.
5. Repeat Steps 1-4 for the other valves.

CAUTION
Any compound left on the valves or in the cylinder head causes excessive wear to the engine components.

6. Thoroughly clean the cylinder head and all valve components in solvent, then with detergent and hot water. Rinse in cold water and dry with compressed air. Lubricate the valve guides with engine oil to prevent rust.

b. Spread a thin layer of marking compound evenly on the valve face.
c. Slowly insert the valve into its guide.
d. Support the valve with two fingers (**Figure 64**) and tap the valve up and down in the cylinder head several times. Do not rotate the valve or a false reading will result.
e. Remove the valve and examine the impression left by the marking compound.
f. Measure the valve seat width as shown in **Figure 65** and refer to **Table 2** for specified valve seat width.

7. Install the valve assemblies as described in this section.
8. Perform a solvent test as described in *Inspection* in *Cylinder Head* in this chapter. There should be no leaks past the seat. If fluid leaks past any of the seats, disassemble that valve assembly and repeat the lapping procedure.
9. After cleaning the cylinder head and valve components in detergent and hot water, apply a light coat of engine oil to all bare metal surfaces to prevent rust formation.

CYLINDER

Identify each set of parts so they installed in their original positions.

Removal

CAUTION
When rotating the crankshaft, pull up the cam chains so they do not bind.

1. Remove the cylinder head as described in this chapter.
2. Disconnect the water hose from the rear cylinder water pipe if it was not removed during engine removal. If necessary, remove the bolt (A, **Figure 74**) and the water pipe (B). Discard the O-ring installed on the end of the water pipe.

NOTE
If the water pipe is difficult to remove in Step 3, spray both ends with penetrating fluid (WD-40 or equivalent).

3. Remove the two clips (A, **Figure 75**) from the water pipe and slide the water pipe into one of the cylinders.
4. Slide the cylinder off the piston and cylinder studs. Hold the piston with one hand just before it clears the cylinder to prevent it from falling toward the cylinder studs and possibly damaging the piston rings.

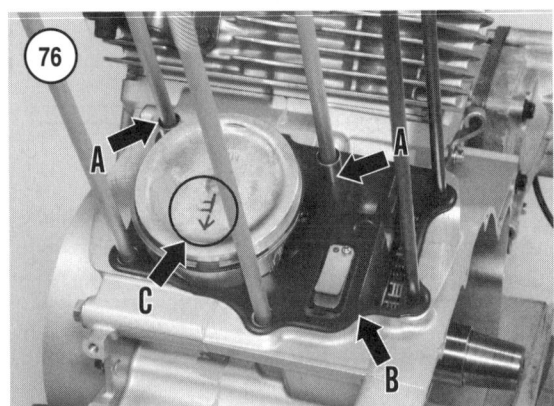

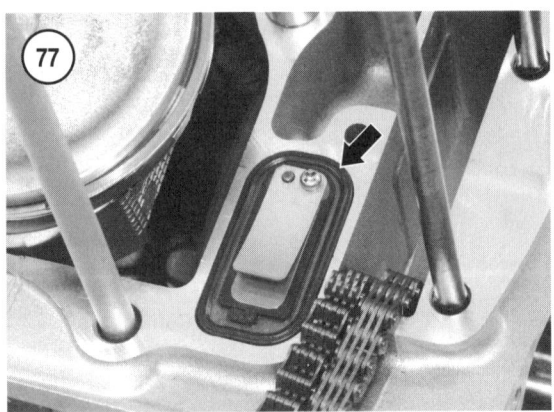

5. Remove the dowel pins (A, **Figure 76**).
6. Remove and discard the base gasket (B, **Figure 76**).
7. Slide a length of plastic hose down two of the cylinder studs and rest the piston and rings against them.
8. Remove the reed valve (**Figure 77**).
9. Cover the piston and crankcase opening.
10. Remove the water pipe (B, **Figure 75**) and discard both O-rings (**Figure 78**).

CAUTION
An oil jet is installed in the crankcase underneath the piston. When cleaning the

ENGINE TOP END

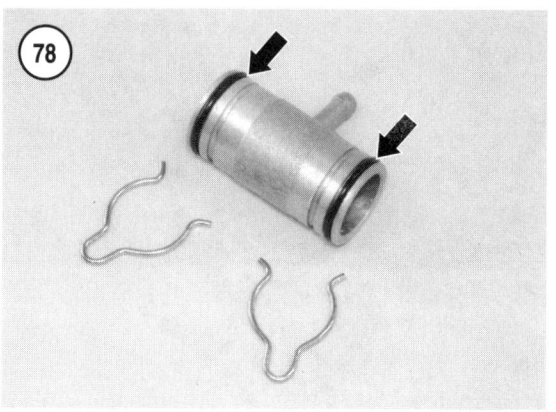

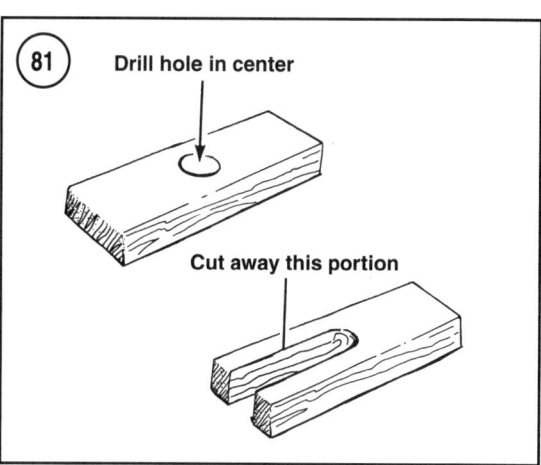

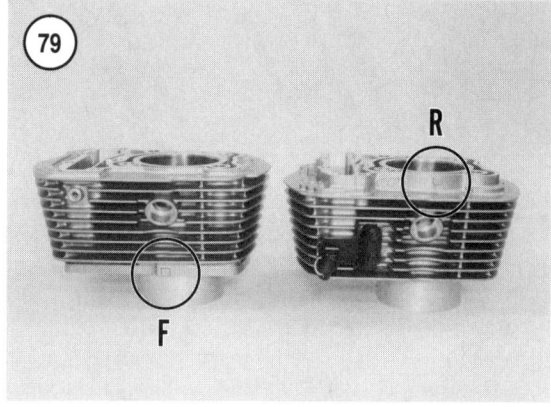

crankcase gasket surface, do not allow material to contaminate the oil jet opening. Refer to **Pistons and Piston Rings** in this chapter to service the oil jet.

11. Clean and inspect the cylinder as described in this section.

Installation

1. Measure the height of each cylinder stud to check for loose studs and reposition studs if necessary. Refer to *Cylinder Stud* in this chapter.

CAUTION
When rotating the crankshaft, pull up the cam chains so they do not bind.

2. Identify the cylinders by their F (front) and R (rear) marks (**Figure 79**).
3. If necessary, install the oil jet, piston and rings as described in this chapter.

CAUTION
Make sure the piston pin circlips are properly installed.

4. Install the reed valve (**Figure 77**).
5. Install the dowel pins (A, **Figure 76**) and a new base gasket (B).
6. Lubricate new O-rings with coolant and install them into the water pipe grooves (**Figure 78**).
7. Install a piston holding fixture (**Figure 80**) under the piston. If necessary, fabricate a wooden piston holding fixture from a piece of wood (**Figure 81**).
8. Lubricate the cylinder wall, piston and rings with engine oil. Liberally lubricate the oil control rings and spacer with oil.
9. Stagger the piston ring end gaps around the piston as shown in **Figure 82**.
10A. To install without a piston ring compressor, align the cylinder (A, **Figure 83**) with the cylinder studs and chain tunnel and lower it onto the piston. Compress each piston ring by hand as it enters the cylinder. Do not force the cylinder past the rings. Push the cylinder down until it bottoms on the piston holding fixture (B, **Figure 83**).
10B. If using a piston ring compressor, lubricate the part of the piston ring compressor that contacts the piston rings with engine oil. Install the compressor so it compresses all three rings (**Figure 84**), following the manufacturer's instructions. Tap the top of the cylinder evenly to push the cylinder over the rings and piston. Push the cylinder down until the

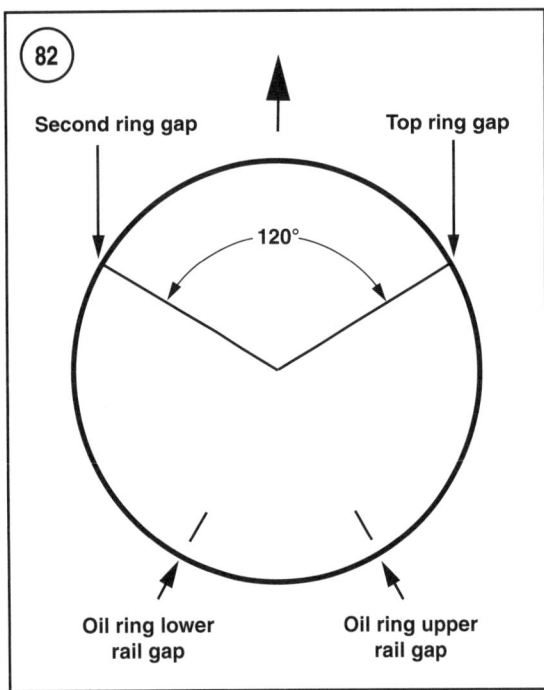

ring compressor bottoms on the piston holding fixture. Remove the ring compressor.

11. Remove the piston holding fixture and push the cylinder down into place over the dowel pins and against the base gasket.

12. Install a length of hose over one of the cylinder studs and secure it with a nut to hold the cylinder in place when the crankshaft is turned over in the following steps.

13. Pull up on both cam chains and rotate the crankshaft clockwise. The piston must move up and down in the bore with no binding or roughness. If there is any interference, a piston ring may have broken during cylinder installation.

14. Install the water pipe (A, **Figure 85**) fully into the cylinder just installed with its hose nozzle facing the left side (B).

NOTE
*The water pipe (A, **Figure 85**) cannot be installed when both cylinders are installed on the engine.*

15. Repeat these steps to install the other cylinder.

16. Lift one cylinder slightly and slide the water pipe (B, **Figure 75**) into the opposite cylinder and secure with the two clips (A). Make sure the clips seat in the grooves completely.

17. Install a new O-ring onto the water pipe and install it onto the rear cylinder. Tighten the bolt securely.

18. Install the cylinder heads as described in this chapter.

Inspection

Cylinder

Refer to the specifications in **Table 3**. Service the cylinder if it is out of specification or shows damage as described in this section.

1. Soak the cylinder block surfaces in solvent, then carefully remove gasket material from the top and bottom mating surfaces with a scraper. Do not nick or gouge the gasket surfaces or leaks may result.

2. Wash the cylinder block in solvent. Dry with compressed air.

3. Check the dowel pin holes for cracks or other damage.

4. Use a straight edge and feeler to check for upper cylinder block warp (**Figure 86**). Check at different locations. If the warp is excessive, check the cylinder head for the same conditions and refer service to a dealership.

5. Measure the cylinder bore inside diameter at the points shown in **Figure 87**. Measure in line with the piston pin and 90° to the pin. Use the largest measurement to determine cylinder bore. If the taper or out-of-round is greater than specifications, bore the cylinder oversize and install a new piston and rings.

ENGINE TOP END

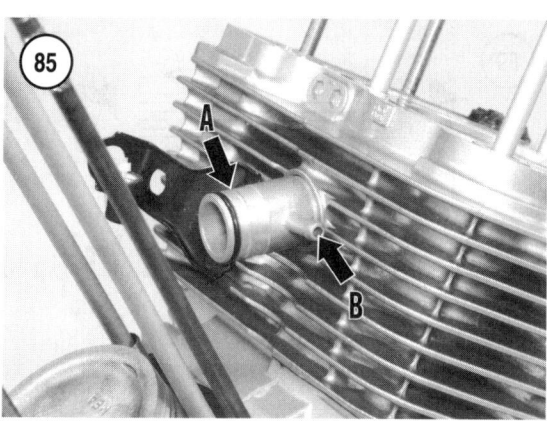

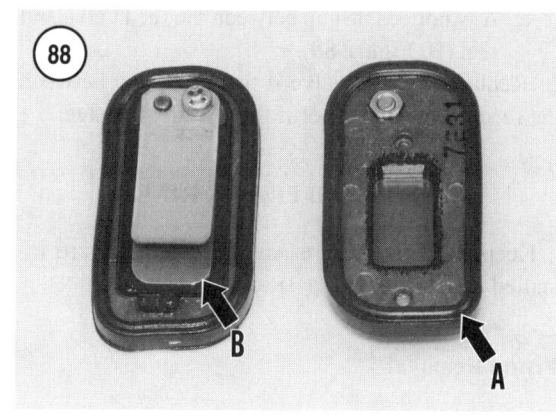

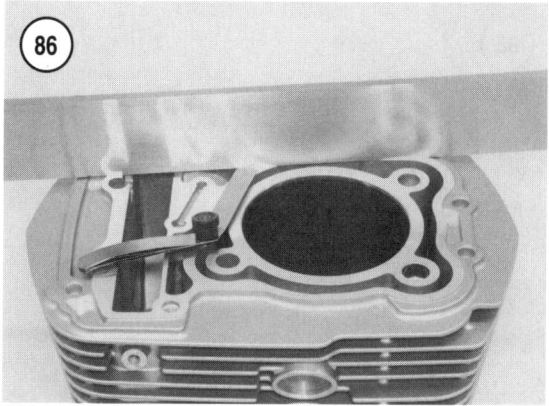

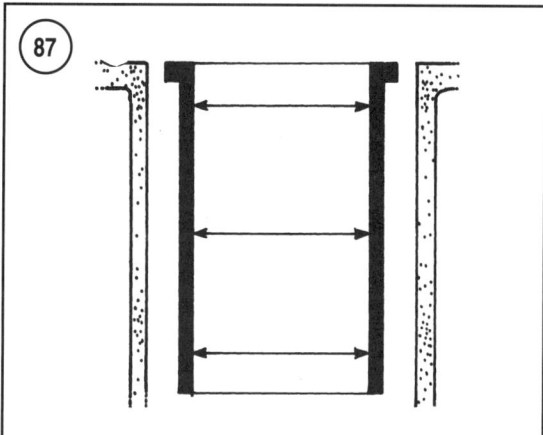

cylinder hone. As the hone deglazes the cylinder, a crosshatch pattern is left on the cylinder bore. The pattern provides a uniform surface, capable of spreading oil and allowing the rings to seat and seal against the cylinder. When deglazing the cylinder, apply plenty of honing lubricant to the hone and cylinder surface. Do not run the hone at high speed, or the crosshatch pattern will not develop. Move the hone at a moderate and consistent rate in an up and down motion for a time period specified by the manufacturer. Proper movement/speed of the hone is achieved when a 45° crosshatch pattern is visible on the cylinder wall.

CAUTION
Hot soapy water is required to completely clean the cylinder walls. Solvent and kerosene cannot wash fine grit out of cylinder crevices. Any grit left in the cylinder will cause the piston rings and other engine parts to wear unnecessarily.

9. After the cylinder has been serviced, clean the cylinder as follows:
   a. Wash the cylinder bore in hot soapy water.
   b. Also wash out any fine grit material from the cooling passages surrounding the cylinder.
   c. After washing the cylinder, wipe the cylinder wall with a clean white cloth. It should not show any traces of grit or debris. If the rag is the slightest bit dirty, the wall is not thoroughly cleaned and must be washed again.
   d. When the cylinder is clean, lubricate the liner with clean engine oil to prevent rust.
   e. Wrap the cylinder until engine reassembly.

6. Determine piston-to-cylinder clearance as described in *Piston Clearance* in *Piston and Piston Rings* this chapter.
7. If the cylinder is not worn past the service limit, check the bore for scratches or gouges. The bore still may require boring and reconditioning.
8. If the cylinder is within all service limits, and the current piston is reusable (refer to *Piston and Piston Rings* in this chapter), the cylinder must be deglazed to accommodate new piston rings. Cylinder glaze appears as a hard, shiny surface and is removed by a

Reed valve

1. Inspect the reed valve (**Figure 88**) for:
   a. Damaged rubber seat (A, **Figure 88**).
   b. Damaged reed valve.

c. Any noticeable gap between the reed valve and seat (B, **Figure 88**).

2. Replace the reed valve if there is a gap between the reed valve and seat or if there is any damage.

PISTON AND PISTON RINGS

Keep each set of parts identified so they are installed in their original positions.

Piston Removal

CAUTION
When rotating the crankshaft, pull up the cam chains so they do not bind.

CAUTION
Guide the pistons so they are not damaged while entering the crankcase.

1. Remove the cylinder as described in this chapter.
2. Clean the top of the piston and mark it with an identification letter (F or R) and a directional arrow pointing toward the front of the engine (C, **Figure 76**). If the carbon material on the top of the piston is too difficult to remove with the piston installed, lightly scratch the marks in the carbon with a scribe and then reapply marks after cleaning the piston. The original pistons do not have directional marks.
3. Block off the crankcase below the piston with a clean shop cloth to prevent the piston pin circlips from falling into the crankcase.
4. Before removing the piston, hold the rod and rock the piston (**Figure 89**). Any rocking motion (do not confuse with the normal sliding motion) indicates wear on the piston pin, rod bushing, pin bore, or a combination of all three.
5. Support the piston with a piston holder fixture (**Figure 80**), then install two plastic hoses over the cylinder studs to protect the piston rings when removing the circlips and piston pin.
6. Remove a circlip (**Figure 90**) from the side of the piston opposite the cam chain side.

CAUTION
The piston pin operates with a sliding fit and can be removed by hand. However, problems such as varnish on the piston pin, a burred pin bore or circlip groove, or a damaged piston can make it difficult to remove the piston pin. Do not drive the pin out as the piston and connecting rod assembly may be damaged.

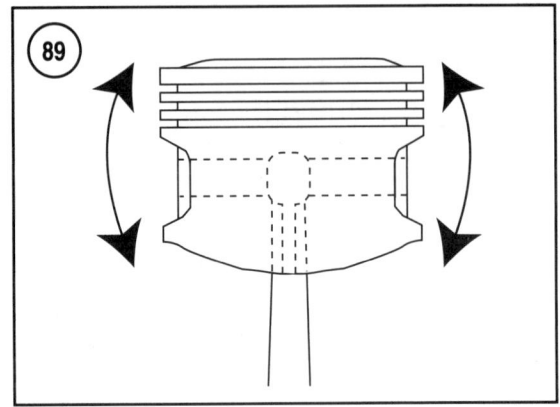

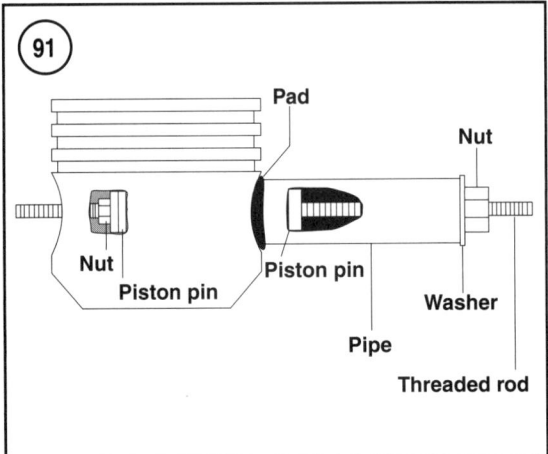

7. Push the piston pin out of the piston by hand. If the pin is tight, use a homemade tool (**Figure 91**) to remove it. Do not drive the piston pin out as this may damage the piston pin, connecting rod or piston. Heat can also be used to ease removal. Heat the piston crown (and not the side of the piston) with a heat gun.
8. Lift the piston off the connecting rod.
9. Remove the bolt (A, **Figure 92**) and oil jet (B) from the crankcase. Discard its O-ring. Store the oil jet in a plastic bag.

ENGINE TOP END

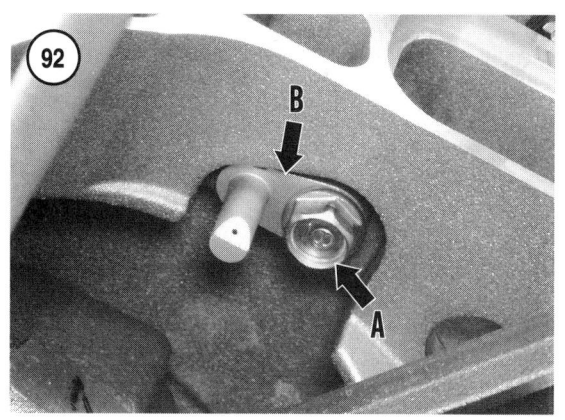

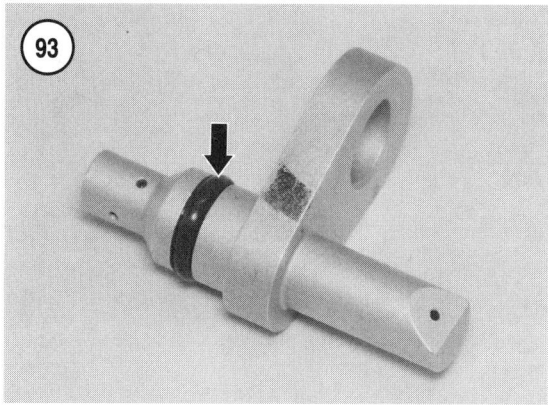

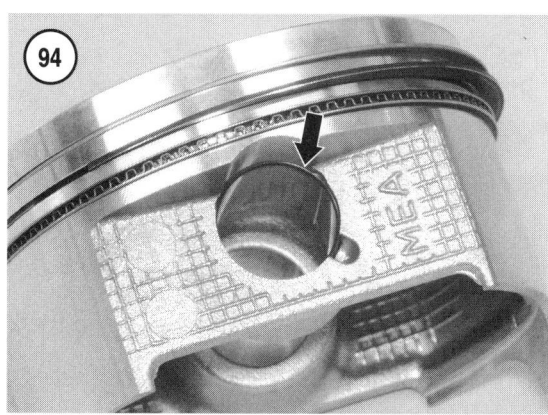

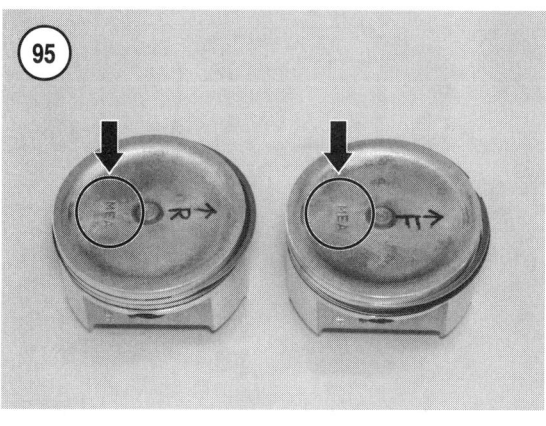

10. Inspect the pistons, piston pins, piston rings and oil jets as described in this section.

Piston Installation

CAUTION
When rotating the crankshaft, pull up the cam chains so they do not bind.

CAUTION
Guide the pistons so they are not damaged while entering the crankcase.

1. Make sure the crankcase gasket surface is clean.
2. Install the oil jet:
   a. Place a rag underneath the oil jet to avoid dropping its mounting bolt into the crankcase.
   b. Lubricate a new O-ring with engine oil and install it on the oil jet (**Figure 93**).
   c. Install the oil jet (B, **Figure 92**) into the crankcase and tighten its mounting bolt (A) securely.
   d. Remove the rag.
3. Install the piston rings onto the piston as described in this section.
4. Coat the connecting rod small end, piston pin and piston with engine oil.
5. Use the plastic hoses and piston fixture to support the piston and protect the piston rings as described under *Piston Removal* in this section.

CAUTION
Do not align the piston pin circlip end gap with the cut out in the piston.

6. Install a new piston circlip (**Figure 94**) into the piston on its cam chain side. Make sure the circlip seats in the groove completely.
7. Slide the piston pin into the piston until its end is flush with the piston pin boss.
8. Place the piston over the connecting rod:
   a. Install original pistons facing in their original positions. Refer to marks made during removal.
   b. Install new pistons with the MEA mark on the piston crown facing toward the rear of the engine. Refer to **Figure 95**.
9. Line up the piston pin with the hole in the connecting rod. Push the piston pin through the connecting rod and into the other side of the piston. Center the piston pin in the piston.
10. Block off the crankcase below the piston with a clean shop cloth to prevent the circlip from falling into the crankcase.

11. Install a new circlip (**Figure 90**) in the end of the piston pin boss. The first circlip was installed in Step 6. Make sure both circlips seat in the piston grooves completely.

Piston Inspection

1. Remove the piston rings as described in this section.
2. Soak the piston in solvent to soften the carbon deposits.

CAUTION
Do not wire brush the piston skirt.

3. Clean the carbon from the piston crown with a soft scraper or wire wheel mounted in a drill. A thick carbon buildup reduces piston cooling and results in detonation and piston damage. Relabel the piston as soon as it is cleaned.
4. After cleaning the piston, examine the crown. The crown must show no signs of wear or damage. If the crown appears pecked or spongy-looking, also check the spark plug, valves and combustion chamber for aluminum deposits. If these deposits are found, the engine is overheating.
5. Examine each ring groove (A, **Figure 96**) for burrs, dented edges or other damage. Pay particular attention to the top compression ring groove as it usually wears more than the others. Because the oil rings are bathed in oiled, these rings and grooves wear little compared to compression rings and their grooves. If there is evidence of oil ring groove wear or if the oil ring is tight and difficult to remove, the piston skirt may have collapsed due to excessive heat. Replace the piston.
6. Clean the oil control holes in the piston.
7. Check the piston skirt (**Figure 97**) for cracks or other damage. If the piston shows signs of partial seizure (bits of aluminum built up on the piston skirt), replace the piston.

NOTE
If the piston skirt is worn or scuffed unevenly from side-to-side, the connecting rod may be bent or twisted. Have it inspected by a machine shop or dealership.

8. Check the piston circlip grooves (B, **Figure 96**) for wear, cracks or other damage.
9. Measure piston-to-cylinder clearance as described in *Piston Clearance* in this section.

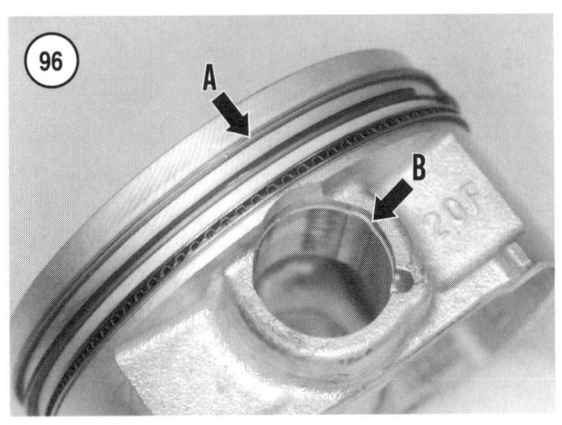

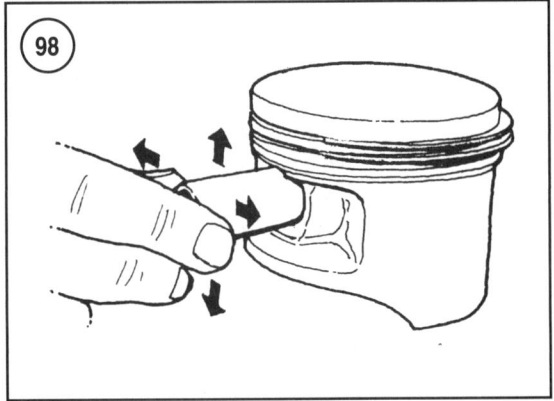

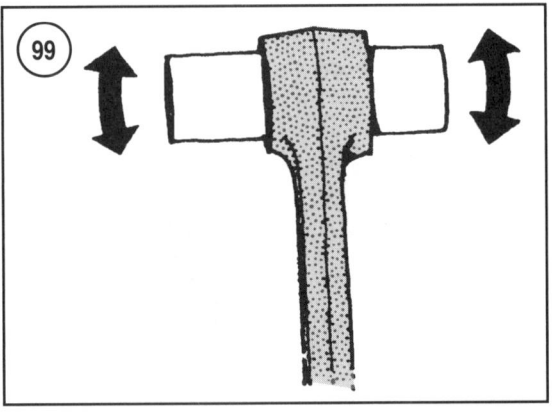

ENGINE TOP END

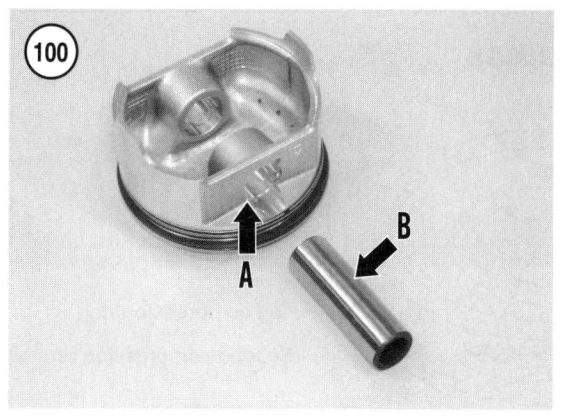

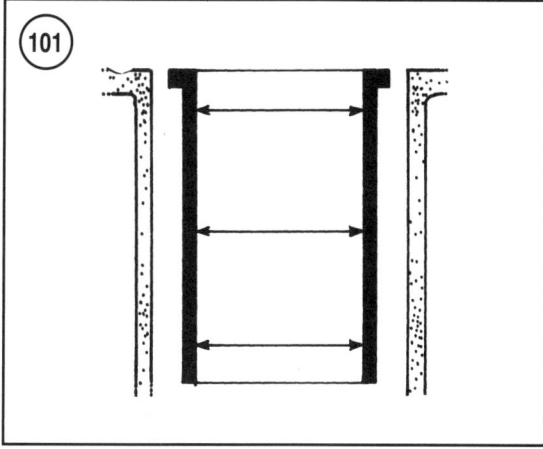

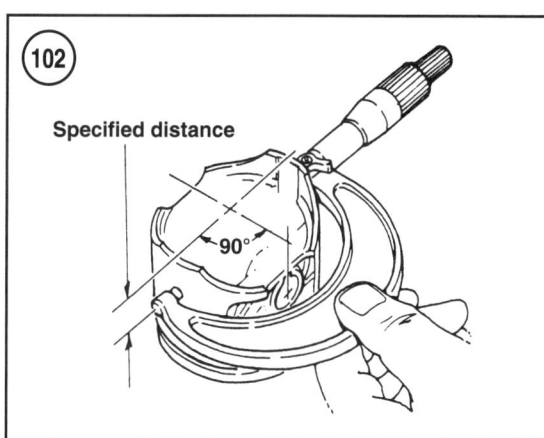

4. Lubricate the piston pin with engine oil and install it in the connecting rod. Slowly rotate the piston pin and check for radial play (**Figure 99**).
5. Measure the piston pin bore inside diameter (A, **Figure 100**).
6. Measure the piston pin (B, **Figure 100**) outside diameter.
7. Subtract the piston pin bore inside diameter from the piston pin outside diameter. The difference is the piston-to-piston pin clearance.

Connecting Rod Small End Inspection

1. Inspect the connecting rod small end for cracks or heat damage.
2. Measure the connecting rod small end inside diameter and compare to the dimension in **Table 3**. If out of specification, replace the connecting rod as described in Chapter Five.

Piston Clearance

1. Make sure the piston skirt and cylinder walls are clean and dry.
2. Measure the cylinder bore inside diameter at the points shown in **Figure 101**. Measure in line with the piston pin and 90° to the pin. Use the largest measurement to determine cylinder bore diameter. If the cylinder bore is out of specification, replace the piston and bore the cylinder oversize. If the cylinder bore is within specification, continue with Step 3.
3. Measure the piston outside diameter at a right angle to the piston pin bore. Measure up 15 mm (0.6 in.) from the bottom edge of the piston skirt (**Figure 102**).
4. Subtract the piston diameter from the largest bore diameter. The difference is piston-to-cylinder clearance. If clearance exceeds the service limit in **Table 3**, determine if the piston, cylinder or both are worn. If necessary, take the cylinder to a dealership that can rebore the cylinder to accept an oversize piston.

Piston Ring Inspection and Removal

A 3-ring type piston and ring assembly is used (**Figure 103**). The top and second rings are compression rings. The lower ring is an oil control ring assembly consisting of two ring rails and a spacer.

Refer to the specifications in **Table 3**. Replace the piston rings as a set if out of specification or if they show damage as described in this section.
1. Measure the side clearance of each ring in its groove with a flat feeler gauge (**Figure 104**):
   a. If the clearance is greater than specified, replace the rings. If the clearance is still excessive with new rings, replace the piston.

Piston Pin Inspection

Refer to the specifications in **Table 3**. Replace the piston pin if out of specification or if it shows damage as described in this section.
1. Clean and dry the piston pin.
2. Inspect the piston pin for chrome flaking or cracks.
3. Lubricate the piston pin with engine oil and install it in the piston. Slowly rotate the piston pin and check for tightness or excessive play (**Figure 98**).

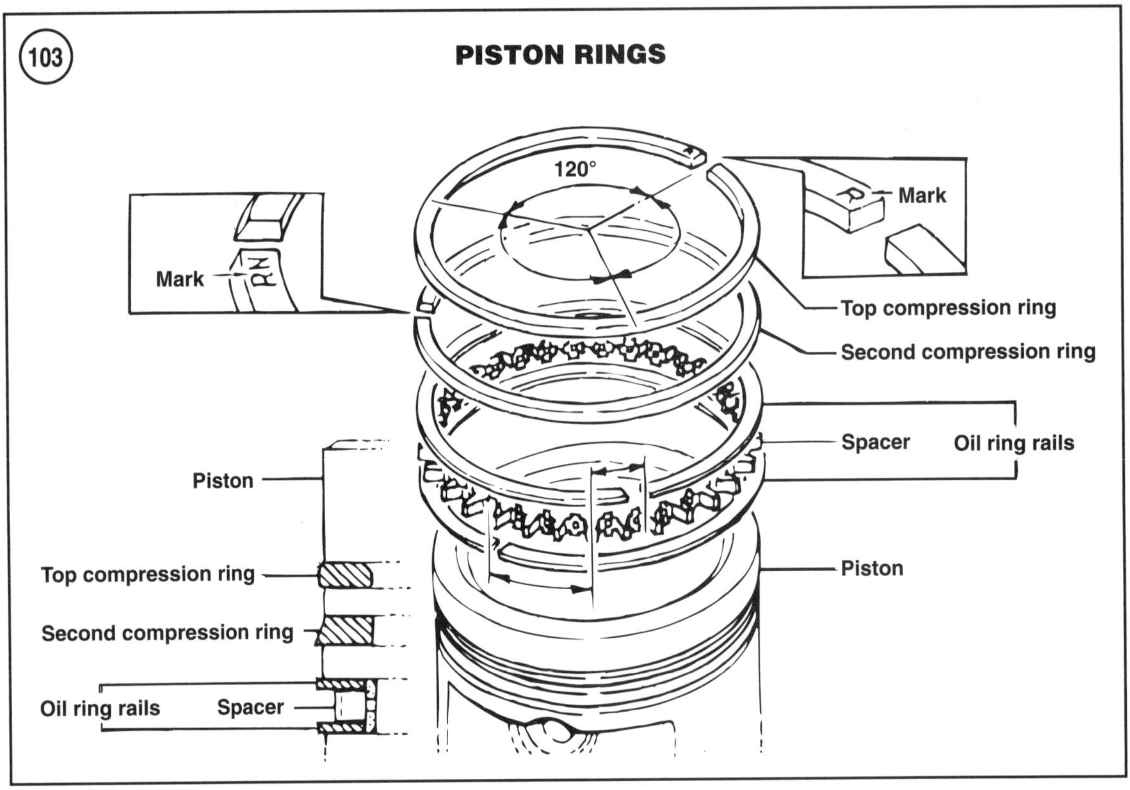

CHAPTER FOUR

PISTON RINGS

b. If the clearance is too small, check the ring and ring groove for carbon and oil residue. Clean the ring without removing any metal from its surface. Clean the piston ring groove as described in Step 4.

2. Remove the compression rings with a ring expander tool (**Figure 105**) or spread the ring ends by hand (**Figure 106**). Store the rings in order of removal.

3. Remove the oil ring assembly by first removing the upper (**Figure 103**) and then the lower ring rails. Remove the spacer.

4. Remove carbon and oil residues from the piston ring grooves (**Figure 107**) with a broken piston ring. Do not remove aluminum material from the ring grooves as this will increase the side clearance.

5. Inspect the ring grooves for burrs, nicks or broken or cracked lands. Replace the piston if necessary.

6. Check the end gap of each ring. Insert the ring into the bottom of the cylinder bore and square it with the cylinder wall by tapping it with the piston (**Figure 108**). Measure the end gap with a feeler gauge (**Figure 108**). Replace the rings if the gap is too large. If the gap on the new ring is smaller than specified, hold a small file in a vise. Then grip the ends of the ring with your fingers and slowly enlarge the gap.

NOTE
When measuring the oil control ring end gap, measure the upper and lower

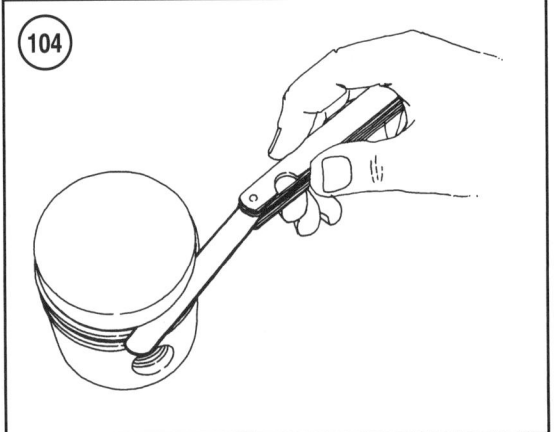

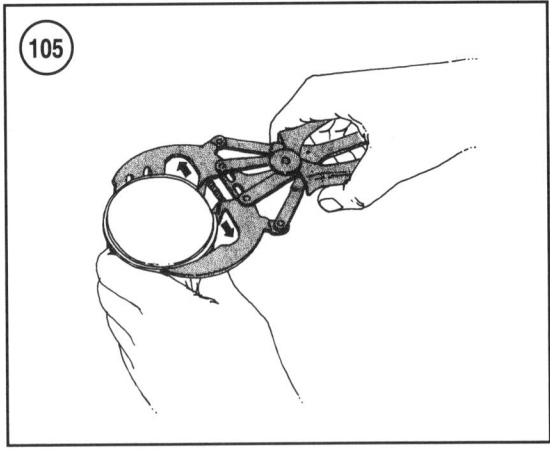

ENGINE TOP END

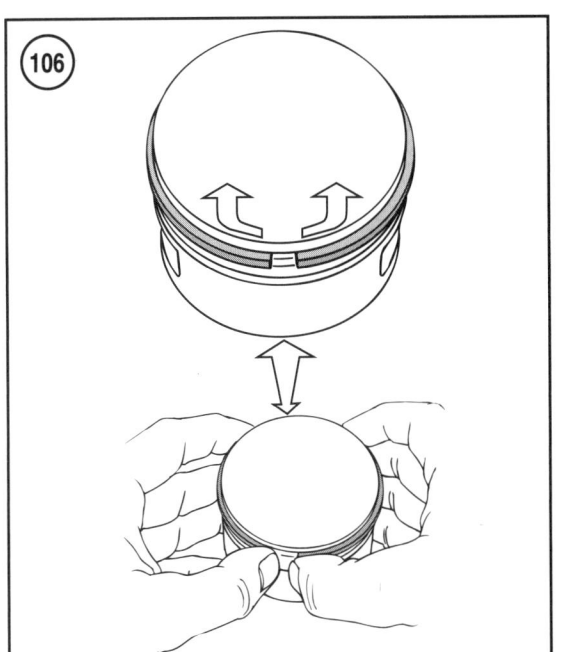

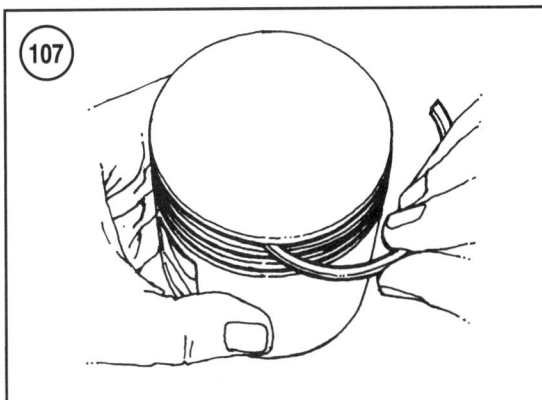

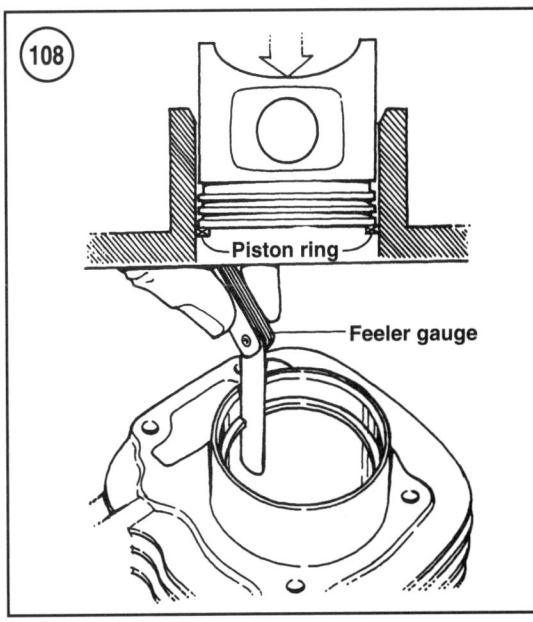

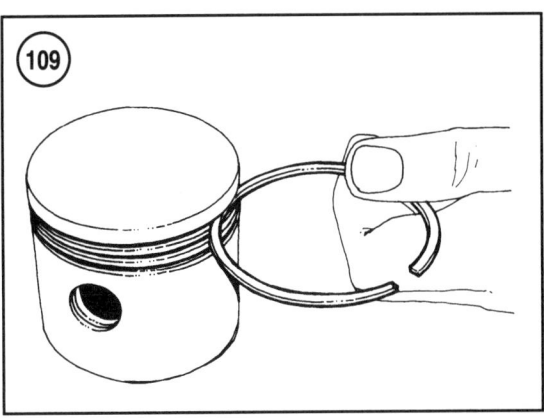

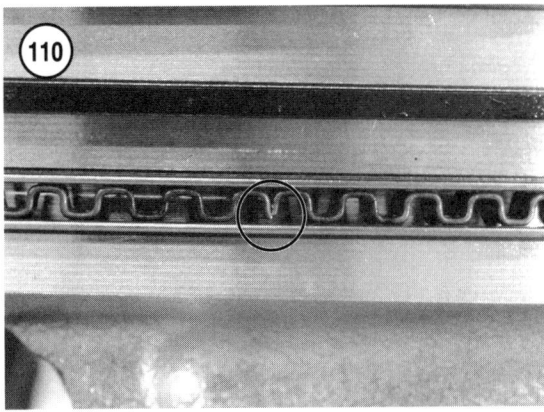

ring rail end gaps only. Do not measure the spacer (**Figure 103**).

7. Roll each compression ring around its piston groove (**Figure 109**) to check for binding. Repair minor binding with a fine-cut file.

Piston Ring Installation

1. When installing new piston rings, hone or deglaze the cylinder wall. This will help the new rings to seat in the cylinder. Refer to *Cylinder* in this chapter or refer this service to a dealership. After honing, measure the end gap of each ring and compare to the dimensions in **Table 3**.
2. Clean the cylinder as described in *Inspection* in *Cylinder* in this chapter.
3. Clean and dry the piston and rings.
4. Install the piston rings as follows:
   a. Install the oil ring assembly into the bottom ring groove. Install the spacer first, and then the bottom and top ring rails (**Figure 103**). Make sure the ends of the spacer butt together (**Figure 110**). They should not overlap. If reassembling used parts, install the ring rails in their original positions.

b. Install the compression rings with a ring expander tool (**Figure 105**) or by spreading the ring ends by hand (**Figure 106**).
c. Install the compression rings with their marks (**Figure 103**) facing up.
d. Install the second compression ring. This ring has a slight taper (**Figure 103**) and is marked with the letters RN.
e. The top compression ring is marked with the letter R.

5. Make sure the rings are seated completely in their grooves all the way around the piston and that the end gaps are distributed around the piston as shown in **Figure 103**. To prevent combustion from escaping past them, the ring gaps must not align.
6. If new parts were installed, follow the *Engine Break-In* procedure in Chapter Five.

Oil Jet Inspection

Inspect the oil jet (**Figure 93**) for any debris that may be clogging the oil holes. If the engine suffered any type of lubrication failure, replace the oil jets. Store the oil jet in a plastic bag until reassembly.

CYLINDER STUD

Removal/Installation

Stud height is critical to ensure the mounting nuts do not bottom out when tightened. This could damage the top of the nut (Acorn nut design) and cause an oil leak through the top of the nut.

1. Remove the cylinders as described in this chapter.
2. Measure each stud height (**Figure 111**) and compare to the specifications in **Figure 112**. Note the following:
   a. If the cylinder stud height is correct, continue with Step 3 to inspect them.
   b. If the cylinder stud height is incorrect, inspect and service the studs as described in this section.
3. Check for loose, bent or damaged studs. Retighten or replace damaged studs as described in the following steps.
4. Remove the stud as described in *Service Methods* in Chapter One.
5. Roll the stud on a flat surface to check for bending.
6. Clean the threaded hole in the crankcase. Check for any debris or damaged threads.
7. Lubricate the stud's lower end threads with engine oil and install to the dimensions in **Figure 112** using a stud installation tool (**Figure 113** [Motion Pro part No. 08-0152]) or reverse the tool setup used in Step 4.
8. Recheck the height of each stud.

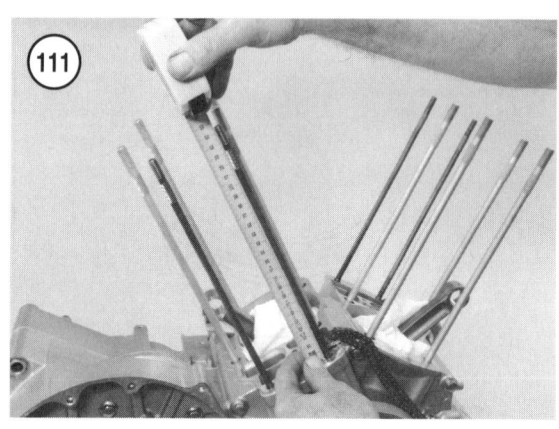

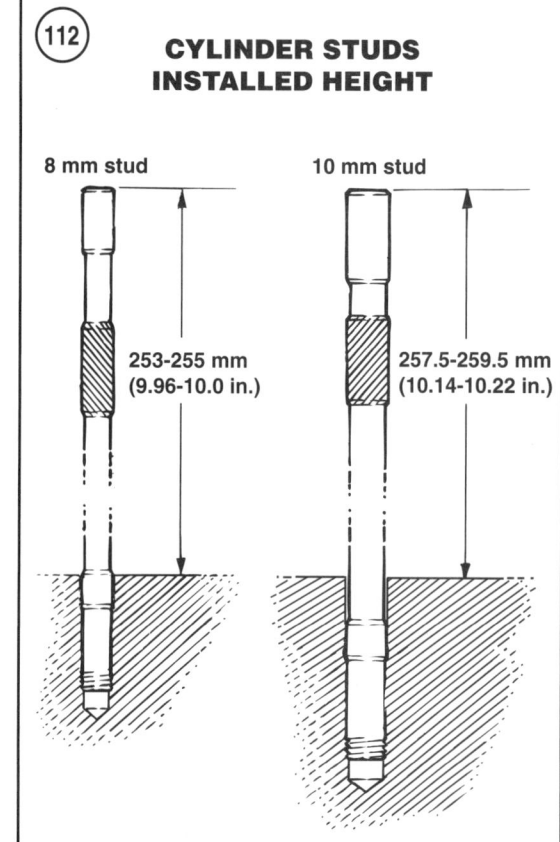

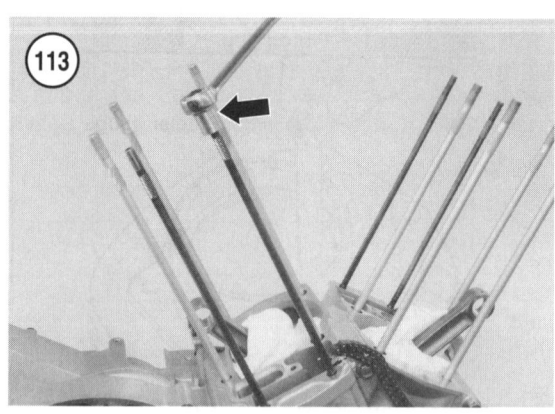

ENGINE TOP END

Table 1 GENERAL ENGINE SPECIFICATIONS

Bore and stroke	89.5 × 104.3 mm (3.52 × 4.11 in.)
Compression ratio	9.2:1
Cylinder alignment	52° V-Twin
Displacement	1312 cc (80.0 cu.-in.)
Engine firing order	Front (308°), rear (412°)
Valve timing	
Intake valve	
Opens	0° BTDC @ 1 mm (0.04 in.) lift
Closes	50° ABDC @ 1 mm (0.04 in.) lift
Exhaust valve	
Opens	
Front	46° BBDC @ 1 mm (0.04 in.) lift
Rear	54° BBDC @ 1 mm (0.04 in.) lift
Closes	
Front	4° ATDC @ 1 mm (0.004 in.) lift
Rear	-4° ATDC @ 1 mm (0.004 in.) lift

Table 2 CYLINDER HEAD AND VALVE SERVICE SPECIFICATIONS

	New mm (in.)	Service limit mm (in.)
Camshaft		
Lobe height		
Intake	38.886-39.080 (1.5309-1.5386)	38.86 (1.530)
Exhaust	39.050-39.250 (1.5374-1.5453)	39.03 (1.537)
Oil clearance		
A measurement points	0.040-0.101 (0.0016-0.0040)	0.120 (0.0047)
B measurement point*	0.055-0.121 (0.0022-0.0048)	0.140 (0.0055)
Runout	–	0.04 (0.002)
Cylinder head warp	–	0.10 (0.004)
Cylinder stud installed height		
8 mm	–	253-255 (9.96-10.0)
10 mm	–	257.5-259.5 (10.14-10.22)
Rocker arm and shaft		
Rocker arm bore inside diameter	14.000-14.018 (0.5512-0.5519)	13.95 (0.549)
Rocker arm shaft outside diameter	13.966-13.984 (0.5498-0.5506)	13.91 (0.548)
Rocker arm-to-rocker arm shaft clearance	0.016-0.052 (0.0006-0.0020)	0.15 (0.006)
Valve		
Valve stem outside diameter		
Intake	6.575-6.590 (0.2589-0.2594)	6.57 (0.259)
Exhaust	6.560-6.575 (0.2583-0.2589)	6.545 (0.258)
Valve guide inside diameter	6.600-6.615 (0.2598-0.2604)	6.635 (0.2612)
Valve stem-to-guide clearance		
Intake	0.010-0.040 (0.0004-0.0016)	0.08 (0.003)
Exhaust	0.025-0.055 (0.0010-0.0022)	0.115 (0.0045)
(continued)		

Table 2 CYLINDER HEAD AND VALVE SERVICE SPECIFICATIONS (continued)

	New mm (in.)	Service limit mm (in.)
Valve (continued)		
Valve guide projection above cylinder head		
Intake	14.5 (0.57)	–
Exhaust	15.5 (0.61)	–
Valve seat width	0.9-1.1 (0.035-0.043)	1.5 (0.06)
Valve spring free length		
Intake	45.70 (1.799)	43.90 (1.728)
Exhaust	43.50 (1.713)	41.80 (1.646)

*Refer to text to identify measurement points.

Table 3 PISTON, RINGS AND BORE SPECIFICATIONS

	New mm (in.)	Service limit mm (in.)
Connecting rod small end inside diameter	20.016-20.034 (0.7880-0.7887)	20.044 (0.7891)
Connecting rod-to-piston pin clearance	0.016-0.040 (0.0006-0.0016)	0.063 (0.0025)
Cylinder		
Block warp	–	0.10 (0.004)
Bore inside diameter	89.500-89.515 (3.4236-3.5242)	89.55 (3.526)
Out-of-round	–	0.10 (0.004)
Taper	–	0.10 (0.004)
Piston-to-cylinder clearance	0.010-0.045 (0.0004-0.0018)	0.32 (0.013)
Piston		
Outside diameter*	89.470-89.490 (3.5224-3.5232)	89.41 (3.520)
Piston pin bore inside diameter	20.002-20.008 (0.7875-0.7877)	20.018 (0.7881)
Piston pin		
Outside diameter	19.994-20.000 (0.7872-0.7874)	19.984 (0.7868)
Piston-to-piston pin clearance	0.002-0.014 (0.0001-0.0006)	0.034 (0.0013)
Piston rings		
Piston ring-to-ring groove side clearance		
Top ring	0.015-0.050 (0.0006-0.0020)	0.070 (0.0028)
Second ring	0.015-0.045 (0.0006-0.0018)	0.065 (0.0026)
Piston ring end gap		
Top ring	0.200-0.300 (0.0079-0.0118)	0.315 (0.0124)
Second ring	0.300-0.400 (0.0118-0.0157)	0.415 (0.0163)
Oil side rail	0.425-0.475 (0.0167-0.0187)	0.495 (0.0195)

*Refer to text for piston measuring point.

Table 4 ENGINE TOP END TORQUE SPECIFICATIONS

	N•m	in.-lb.	ft.-lb.
Cam chain tensioner bolt*	12	106	–
Cam sprocket bolt*	23	–	17
Cylinder head cover			
8 mm cap nut*	26	–	19
8 mm bolt	26	–	19
10 mm cap nut*	43	–	32
Exhaust valve adjustment cover*	15	–	11
PAIR check valve cover bolt*	5.2	46	–
Spark plug sleeve*	18	–	13
Spark plug	14	–	10
Timing hole cap*	18	–	13
Timing hole cap cover Allen bolt	10	88	–

*Refer to text for additional information.

CHAPTER FIVE

ENGINE LOWER END

This chapter provides service procedures for lower end components. These include the crankcase, crankshaft, connecting rods, oil pump and output gear. This chapter also includes removal and installation procedures for the transmission and internal shift mechanism assemblies. However, service procedures for these components are described in Chapter Seven.

Tables 1-6 are at the end of this chapter.

SERVICING ENGINE IN FRAME

1. The following components can be serviced with the engine mounted in the frame:
   a. Carburetor.
   b. Alternator and starter clutch.
   c. Clutch, primary drive and external shift linkage.
   d. Starter.
   e. Clutch release housing.
   f. Water pump.
2. The following components require engine removal for service:
   a. Cylinder head covers.
   b. Camshafts and cylinder heads.
   c. Cylinders and pistons.
   d. Crankshaft.
   e. Transmission and internal shift mechanism.
   f. Oil pump.
   g. Output gear.

ENGINE

Preliminary Information

Before servicing the engine, note the following:
1. Review *Service Methods* and *Measuring Tools* in Chapter One.
2. Prior to removing and disassembling the engine, clean the engine and frame with a degreaser. Keep the work environment as clean as possible.
3. Viewed from the engine's right side, crankshaft rotation is clockwise (**Figure 1**).
4. Throughout the text there are references to the left and right side of the engine. This refers to the engine as it is mounted in the frame, not how it may sit on the workbench.
5. Always replace worn or damaged fasteners with those of the same size, type and torque requirements. If a specific torque value is not in **Table 6**, refer to the general torque recommendation table at the end of Chapter One.
6. Use special tools where noted.
7. Store parts and assemblies in well-marked plastic bags and containers. Use masking tape and a permanent, waterproof marking pen to label parts.
8. Use a box of assorted size and color vacuum hose identifiers, such as those shown in **Figure 2** (Lisle part No. 74600), to identify hoses and fittings during

ENGINE LOWER END

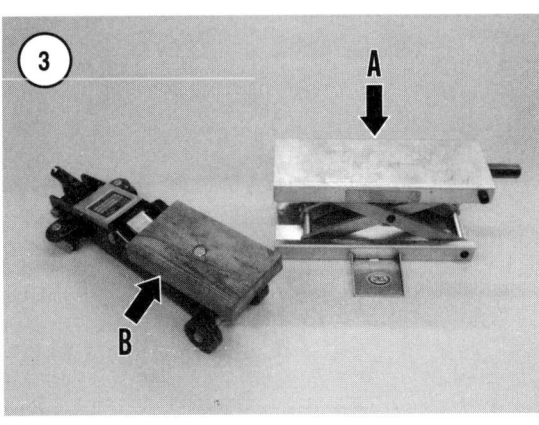

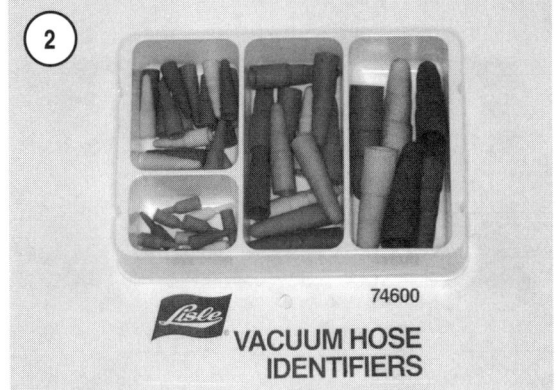

engine removal and disassembly. Automotive and parts suppliers carry this kit, or similar equivalents.
9. Use a vise with protective jaws to hold parts.
10. Use a press or special tools when force is required to remove and install parts. Do not try to pry, hammer or otherwise force them on or off.
11. Replace all O-rings and seals during reassembly. Apply a small amount of grease to the inner lips of each new seal to prevent damage when the engine is first started.
12. Complete engine top and lower end gasket kits can be purchased from the manufacturer. However, the gaskets, washers and O-rings in these kits are not identified. During disassembly, do not discard washers and O-rings after removing them. Label these parts so they can be used to identify the replacement parts.
13. If possible, take photographs of the hose and wire routing before engine removal.
14. When removing the thermostat and the emission control assemblies, disconnect the hoses as close to the engine assembly as possible. This will allow most of the hoses to remain attached to the assembly being removed and help with routing and reassembly.
15. The dry weight for an assembled VT1300 engine is approximately 109 kg (240 lbs). At least three people will be required to remove and install the engine.

16. Two jacks will be required during engine removal. Use a scissor jack, such as the K&L MC450 Center Jack (part No. 37-9841) shown in A, **Figure 3**, to level and support the motorcycle. Use a floor jack (B, **Figure 3**, typical) to secure and position the engine in and out of the frame.

Removal

The VT1300 engine is difficult to remove and install as a complete assembly. If possible, lighten the engine by removing its subassemblies while it is mounted in the frame.
1. Support the motorcycle securely on a scissor jack.
2. Remove the seat and both side covers (Chapter Fifteen).
3. Remove the fuel tank (Chapter Eight).
4. Remove the cylinder head shrouds (Chapter Fifteen).
5. If possible, perform a compression test (Chapter Three) and cylinder leakdown test (Chapter Two) before dismantling the engine.
6. Disconnect the negative battery cable from the battery (Chapter Nine). Place an insulator over the cable end so it cannot fall back across the battery, causing a short.
7. Drain the engine oil (Chapter Three).
8. Drain the engine coolant (Chapter Three).
9. Remove the front ignition coils (Chapter Nine).
10. Remove the exhaust system (Chapter Fifteen).
11. Remove the left case half rear cover and its two mounting brackets (Chapter Fifteen).
12. Remove both footrest or footpeg assemblies (Chapter Fifteen).
13. Remove the air filter housing (Chapter Eight).
14. On 2008-on California models, remove the fuel cutoff solenoid valve as described in *Evaporative Emission Control System* in Chapter Eight.
15. Remove the carburetor (Chapter Eight).
16. Remove the radiator (Chapter Ten).

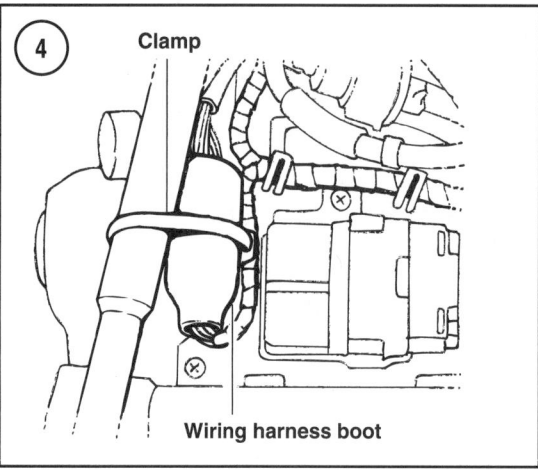

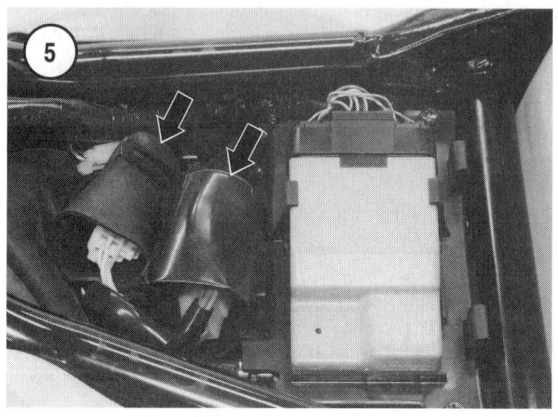

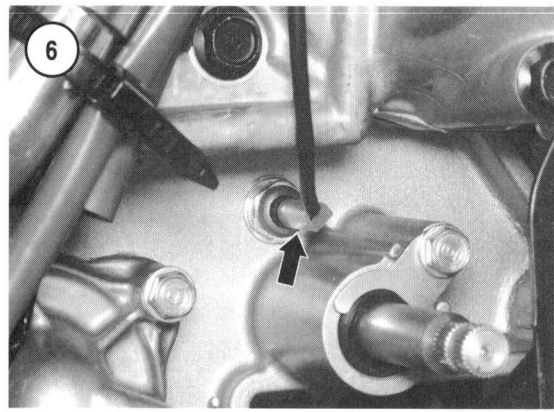

NOTE
Note the routing and alignment of all switch connector wiring harnesses before disconnecting them.

17A. On 2003-2004 models, release the clamp from the wiring harness boot (**Figure 4**).

17B. On 2005-on models, release the clamp securing the wiring harness boots (**Figure 5**).

18. Disconnect the following electrical connectors located in the wiring harness boot(s) described in Step 17:
    a. Ignition switch 3-pin connector.
    b. Ignition pulse generator 2-pin connector.
    c. Neutral switch light green wire connector.
    d. Alternator 3-pin connector (2005-on models).

19. Disconnect the neutral switch connector (**Figure 6**).

20. Disconnect the two clamps (A, **Figure 7**) and disconnect the following electrical connectors (B):
    a. Alternator 3-pin connectors (2003-2004 models).
    b. Speed sensor 3-pin connector.
    c. Sidestand switch 2-pin connector. Then release the sidestand switch wiring harness (C, **Figure 7**) from the cover clamp.

21. Disconnect the water hose (D, **Figure 7**) at the water pump.

22. Remove the clutch cable holder bolt (A, **Figure 8**) and holder, then disconnect the clutch cable (B) from its release lever.

23. Remove the bolt and the battery ground wire (C, **Figure 8**).

24. Remove the ignition switch (Chapter Nine). It is unnecessary to disconnect the ignition switch electrical connector from the main wiring harness; wrap the switch housing with a thick rag and rubber band and set it aside on the frame.

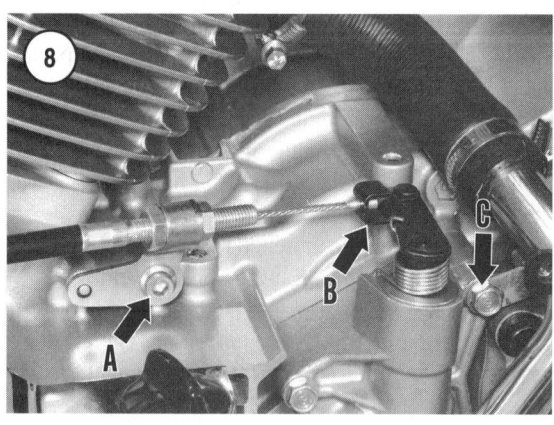

ENGINE LOWER END

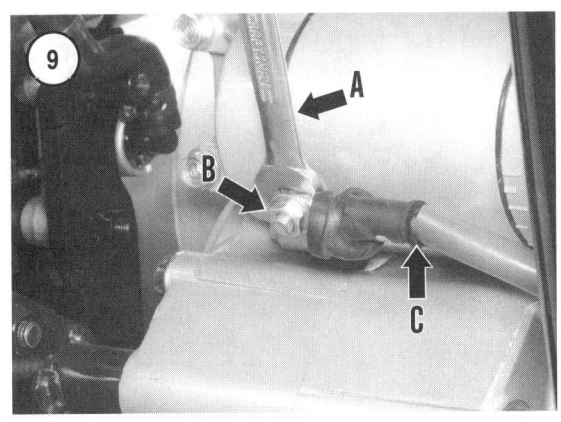

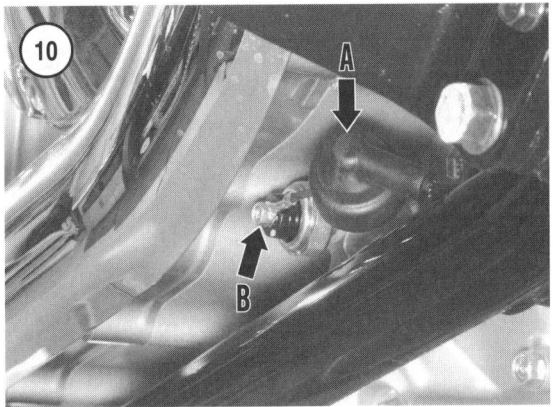

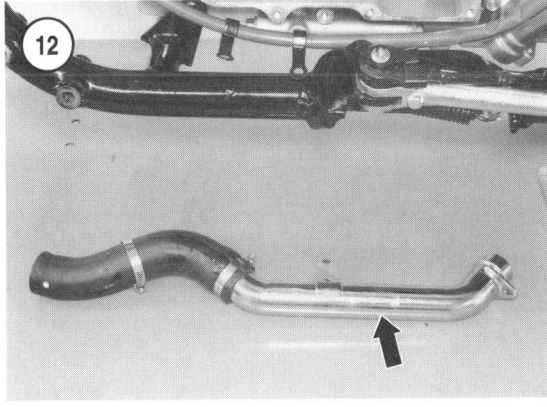

CAUTION
Failure to hold the inner cable nut may allow the terminal bolt to turn and damage its insulator inside the starter. The insulator is not available separately.

25. Hold the inner nut on the starter terminal with a wrench (A, **Figure 9**) to prevent it from turning, then remove the outer nut (B) and disconnect the starter cable (C). Trace the cable toward the engine and disconnect it from the clamps on the alternator cover.

26. Slide the rubber boot (A, **Figure 10**) off of the oil pressure switch. Remove the bolt and disconnect the wire (B, **Figure 10**) from the switch. Trace the wire forward and disconnect it from the clamp on the frame.

27. Disconnect the rear spark plug caps (A, **Figure 11**) at the spark plugs. Then disconnect the rear spark plug cables from the clamp (B, **Figure 11**).

28. If the engine will be disassembled or to lighten the engine for removal, remove the following subassemblies:
    a. Starter (Chapter Nine).
    b. Alternator cover, flywheel and starter clutch (Chapter Nine).
    c. Water pump (Chapter Ten).
    d. Clutch release assembly (Chapter Six).
    e. Right crankcase half cover and clutch (Chapter Six).
    f. Primary drive and driven gears (Chapter Six).
    g. External shift mechanism (Chapter Six).

29. Remove the bolt and the water pipe (**Figure 12**) connected between the radiator and water pump.

30. Remove the pulse secondary air injection (PAIR) control valve assembly (Chapter Eight). Make sure to remove the hose (C, **Figure 11**) routed between the cylinder head cover and frame.

31. Disconnect the water hose from each cylinder head water pipe; refer to A, **Figure 13** (front) and D, **Figure 11** (rear). Then remove the thermostat housing assembly (B, **Figure 13**) as described in Chapter Ten with these two water hoses attached at the thermostat.

32. Disconnect the crankcase breather hose (C, **Figure 13**) at the front cylinder head cover.

33. Check the engine for any remaining hoses or electrical connectors that were not disconnected and disconnect them now. If desired, remove any additional components that will make engine removal and handling easier.

34. Secure a thick wooden block onto a floor jack to protect the engine and position the jack (A, **Figure 14**) underneath the engine. Adjust this jack as required to relieve pressure on the engine when removing the engine mounting bolts in the following steps. The engine must remain balanced on the jack when all mounting hardware is removed.

35. To protect the frame, wrap the right side of the frame with pieces of rubber cut from old inner tubes (B, **Figure 14**) and secure them in place with plastic tie wraps. For areas difficult to cover with rubber inner tubes, use Scotch Blue Tape (part No. 2080) and overlap areas as required to provide adequate protection.

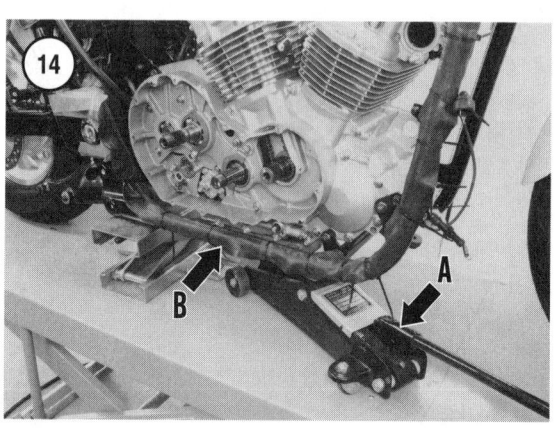

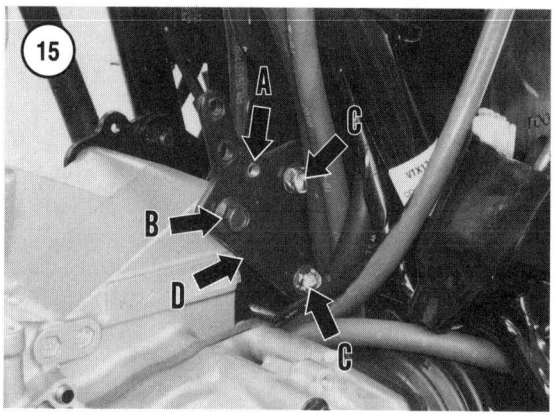

NOTE
While the engine can be made narrower by removing subassemblies from each side, the engine's height cannot be changed. Thus it is difficult to maneuver the engine out of the frame without the rear cylinder head cover contacting the portion of the wiring harness routed underneath the upper frame tube. To provide additional room for engine removal and installation, it is suggested to remove the swing arm and disconnect the drive shaft and universal joint from the output gear shaft. The engine, however, can be removed without removing these parts.

36. Remove the swing arm, drive shaft and universal joint (Chapter Thirteen).

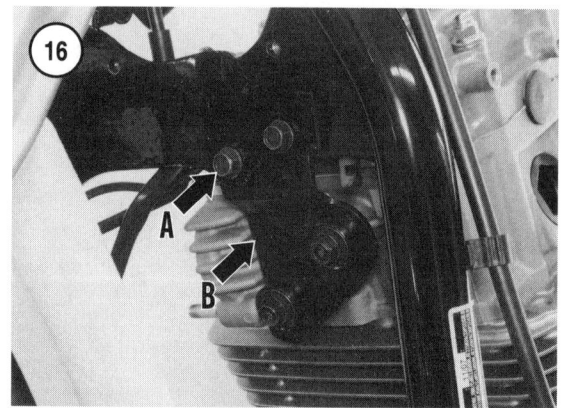

NOTE
Identify the engine hanger plates and fasteners when removing them in the following steps.

37. Remove the engine mounting nuts, bolts and brackets as follows:

WARNING
When removing the bolts, be aware that the engine may shift in the frame. Keep hands protected and check the stability of the motorcycle and engine after removing each set of bolts.

a. Note and photograph the position of all remaining cables and hoses on how they are routed around the frame, engine and engine mounts

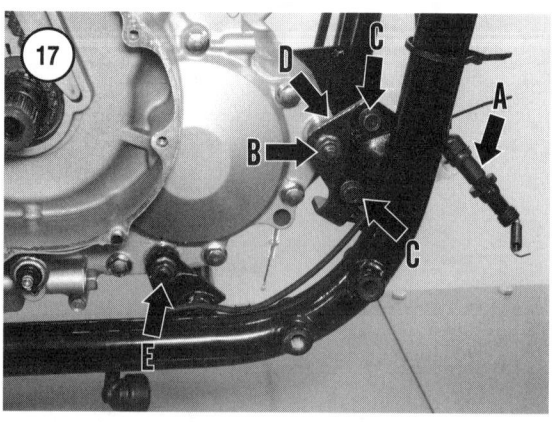

ENGINE LOWER END

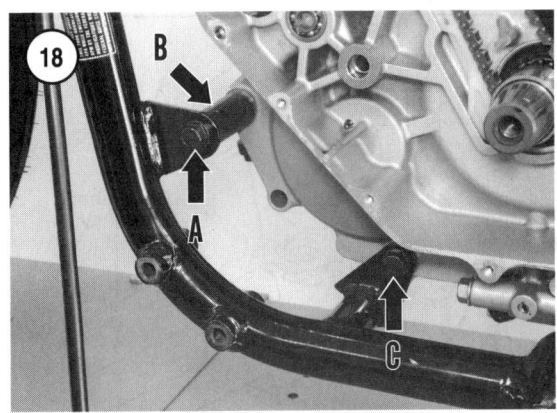

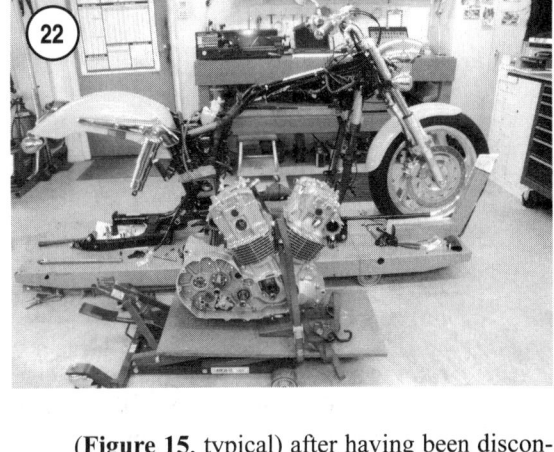

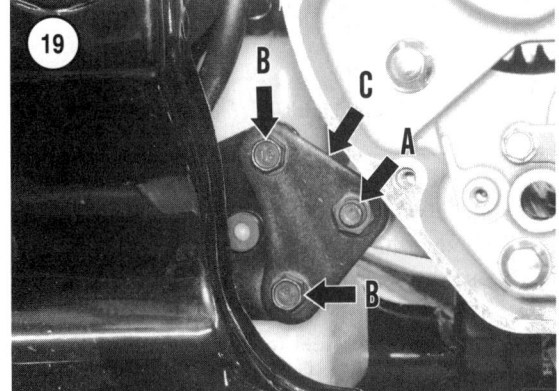

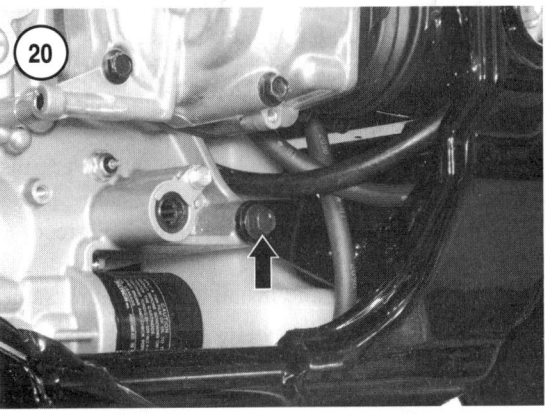

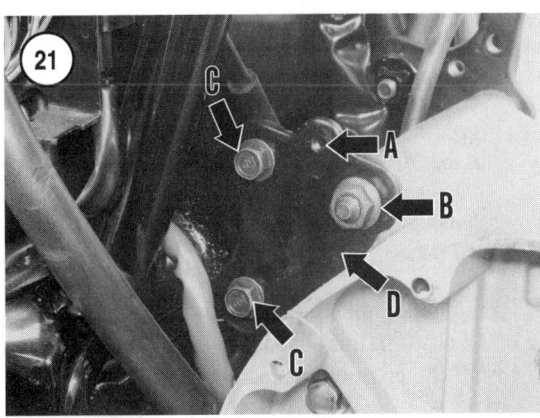

(**Figure 15**, typical) after having been disconnected and/or rerouted during the previous steps. While some of the routing positions may differ from original mounting positions, this is how they must be positioned when reinstalling the engine. In some cases, it may be impossible to reroute some of the cables and hoses once the engine is reinstalled in the frame.

b. Note the position and orientation of all brackets, bolts, nuts and washers.

NOTE
Loosen all of the following fasteners in order, then remove them.

c. Front center hanger plate bolts (A, **Figure 16**) and hanger plate (B).
d. Front brake light switch (A, **Figure 17**).
e. Front upper mounting nut (B, **Figure 17**), bolt (A, **Figure 18**) and spacer (B, **Figure 18**).
f. Front hanger plate bolts (C, **Figure 17**) and hanger plate (D).
g. Front bottom mounting nut (E, **Figure 17**) and bolt (C, **Figure 18**).
h. Rear lower mounting nut (A, **Figure 19**) and bolt (**Figure 20**).
i. Rear lower hanger plate bolts (B, **Figure 19**) and hanger plate (C).
j. Lower ignition coil cover Allen bolts if the cover was not previously removed. A, **Figure 21** and A, **Figure 15** show the bolts mounting position.
k. Rear upper mounting nut (B, **Figure 21**) and bolt (B, **Figure 15**).
l. Rear right upper hanger plate bolts (C, **Figure 21**) and hanger plate (D).
m. Rear left upper hanger plate bolts (C, **Figure 15**) and hanger plate (D).

38. Remove the engine from the frame as follows (**Figure 22**):

WARNING
The following steps require the aid of helpers to safely remove the engine assembly from the frame.

CAUTION
There is little clearance between the engine and top of the frame. Take your time and be careful not to damage the wiring harness or drop the engine against the frame.

a. If the swing arm was not removed, release the boot from the output gear case on the engine. Then slowly move the jack and engine forward to release the output shaft from the universal joint in the swing arm (**Figure 23**). Have an assistant hold the cylinders to keep the engine centered.
b. Lift the engine and remove it from the right side of the frame.
c. Take the engine to a workbench and support it with wooden blocks to prevent it from falling over.

39. Before removing the jack used to support the engine, measure the pad's raised height position so it can be set to the same approximate position when installing the engine in the frame.

Inspection

After engine removal, perform the following:
1. Inspect the frame for cracks or other damage. If found, have the frame inspected by a dealership or frame alignment specialist.
2. Touch up the frame with paint as required.
3. Inspect and replace any worn or damaged coolant hoses and clamps.
4. Inspect and replace any damaged vacuum hoses.
5. Check all engine mounting fasteners for corrosion and thread damage. Clean each fastener in solvent. Replace worn or damaged fasteners before reassembly.
6. Inspect the wiring harness for signs of damage that may have occurred when removing the engine. Repair damaged wires as required.

Installation

1. If the swing arm is mounted in the frame, perform the following:
    a. Make sure the universal joint (**Figure 23**) is mounted on the drive shaft.
    b. Lubricate the output shaft splines (**Figure 23**) with Honda Moly 60 paste.

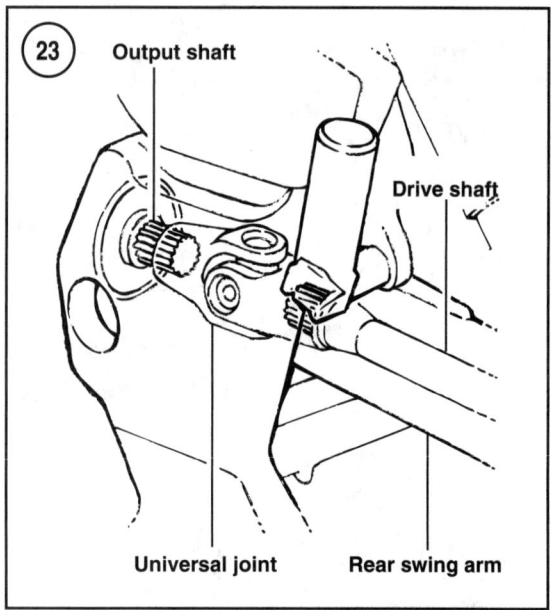

c. Make sure the rubber boot is mounted on the swing arm.
d. Use the scissor jack to raise the frame so the rear wheel just clears the ground. This will allow the rear wheel to turn when aligning the output shaft and the universal joint splines.
e. Shift the transmission into gear so the output shaft will not turn when meshing it with the universal joint later in this procedure.

2. Install the engine in the frame as follows:
    a. Position the engine on the right side of the frame (**Figure 22**).
    b. Position the floor jack between the lower rails to support the engine when it is installed in the frame. Raise the jack pad to the height recorded during removal.
    c. Lift the engine and install it through the frame from the right side and place it on the jack pad. If the swing arm is mounted on the motorcycle, mesh the output shaft with the universal joint (**Figure 23**). If necessary, turn the rear wheel to mesh the shaft and universal joint splines.

CAUTION
Do not tighten the hanger plate and engine mount fasteners (nuts and bolts) until all of the hanger plates and fasteners are installed. Make sure the fastener threads are clean and dry. Do not oil them.

3. Position the cables and hoses as noted during Step 37 of *Removal* in this section.
4. Install the engine brackets, bolts and nuts as follows:

ENGINE LOWER END

  a. Front bottom mounting bolt (C, **Figure 18**) and nut (E, **Figure 17**).
  b. Front hanger plate (D, **Figure 17**) and bolts (C).
  c. Front upper mounting bolt spacer (B, **Figure 18**), bolt (A, **Figure 18**) and nut (B, **Figure 17**).
  d. Rear left upper hanger plate (D, **Figure 15**) and bolts (C).
  e. Rear right upper hanger plate (D, **Figure 21**) and bolts (C).
  f. Rear upper mounting bolt (B, **Figure 15**) and mounting nut (B, **Figure 21**).
  g. Lower ignition coil cover Allen bolts if the cover was not previously removed. A, **Figure 21** and A, **Figure 15** show the bolt mounting positions.
  h. Rear lower hanger plate (C, **Figure 19**) and bolts (B).
  i. Rear lower mounting bolt (**Figure 20**) and mounting nut (A, **Figure 19**).
  j. Front center hanger plate (B, **Figure 16**) and bolts (A).
5. Tighten the fasteners in the following order:
  a. 8-mm hanger plate mounting bolts to 27 N•m (20 ft.-lb.).
  b. 10-mm mounting nuts to 39 N•m (29 ft.-lb.).
6. Reposition the rear brake light switch (A, **Figure 17**) into the front hanger plate's light switch bracket.
7. If the swing arm is installed on the motorcycle, install the boot over the output gear case. Make sure there are no gaps between the boot and output gearcase.
8. Clean electrical connections and apply dielectric grease before reconnecting.
9. Reverse Steps 1-32 in *Removal* in this section to complete engine installation, plus the following steps.
10. Reconnect the clutch cable (B, **Figure 8**) at the release lever. Then tighten the clutch cable holder bolt (A, **Figure 8**) to 12 N•m (106 in.-lb.).
11. Clean the starter cable end and install it onto the starter terminal. Hold the inner nut on the starter terminal with a wrench (A, **Figure 9**) and tighten the outer nut (B) to 7 N•m (62 in.-lb.).
12. Refill the engine with coolant as described in Chapter Three. Check all of the coolant hoses for leaks.
13. If the oil filter was removed, install a new oil filter (Chapter Three).
14. Fill the engine with oil as described in Chapter Three.
15. Reconnect the negative battery cable at the battery as described in Chapter Nine.
16. Remove the jack from underneath the frame.
17. Start the engine and check for oil leaks.
18. Operate all controls and adjust as needed.
19. Shift the transmission into gear and check clutch and transmission operation.
20. Slowly test ride the motorcycle to ensure all systems are operating correctly.
21. If the engine top-end was rebuilt, perform a compression test as described in Chapter Three. Record the results for future reference.
22. Refer to *Engine Break-In* in this chapter.

CRANKCASE

The crankcase must be disassembled to service the crankshaft, balancer shaft, oil pump, transmission and output gear housing.

Disassembly

As components are removed, keep each part/assembly separated from the other components. Keep seals and O-rings oriented with their respective parts to help with inspection, identification of new parts and reassembly.

Remember that the right and left side of the engine relates to the engine as it sits in the frame, not as it may sit on the workbench.

1. Remove the engine from the frame as described in this chapter.
2. Remove all engine assemblies as described in this chapter and other related chapters.

WARNING
Even with all of the engine assemblies removed from the engine, the crankcase is still heavy and awkward to handle.

CAUTION
Do not move or lift the crankcase assembly by grabbing the cylinder studs. Bent or damaged cylinder studs may cause oil leaks.

NOTE
*To ensure that the crankcase bolts are correctly located during assembly, make an outline of the right case half on a piece of cardboard (A, **Figure 24**). Punch holes in the cardboard at the same locations as the bolts. Place the bolts in their respective holes.*

3. Place the engine on wooden blocks with the right case half (B, **Figure 24**) facing up and perform the following:
  a. Loosen and remove the 6-mm bolts identified by the arrows in **Figure 25**.

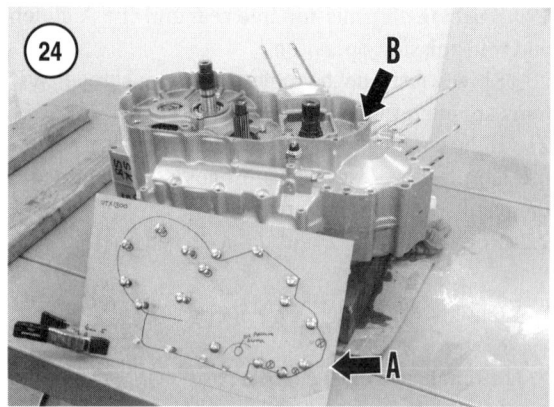

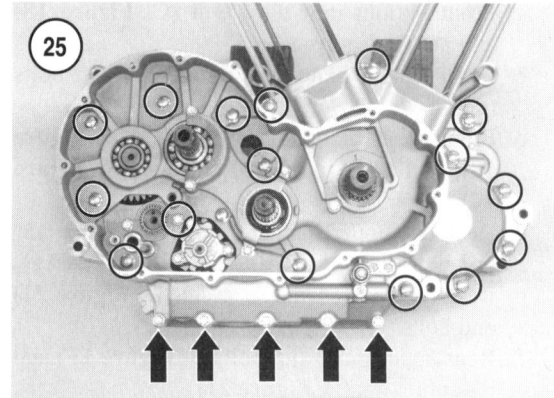

b. Working in a crossing pattern and in several steps, loosen and remove the 8-mm bolts identified by the circles in **Figure 25**. Remove the washer used on the 8-mm bolt identified in **Figure 26**. Make sure all bolts are removed.

4. Remove the right case half as follows:

CAUTION
Sealer is used to seal the case halves and there are no press fits between the shafts and the right case half bearings. If the right case half is tight and will not separate, check for a missed mounting bolt. A rusted dowel pin can also bind the cases and make separation difficult.

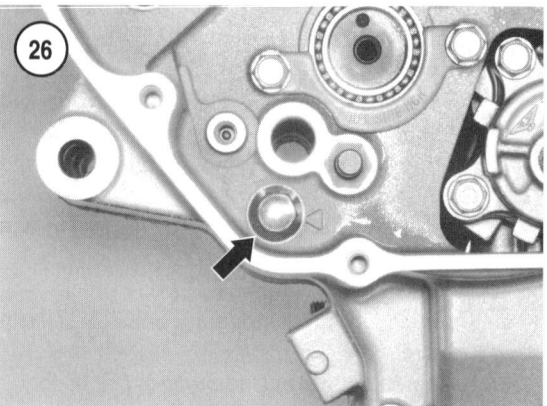

CAUTION
Do not hammer or pry on areas of the engine cases that are not reinforced. Never pry between the case halves. Doing so may result in oil leaks, requiring replacement of the case halves.

a. Locate the pry points around the mating surfaces of the engine cases and carefully pry the right case half upward with a screwdriver (**Figure 27**) to break the case seal and separate the case halves. Do *not* pry between the gasket surfaces.

b. When the right case half is free of the dowel pins and the gap around the case halves is even (**Figure 28**), carefully lift and remove it from the left case half. If necessary, wiggle or walk the right case half up and off the shafts. If the mainshaft moved and is binding against its right case half bearing, have an assistant tap on the end of the mainshaft while removing the right case half. Do not allow the right case half or mainshaft to bind. If necessary, reseat the right crankcase half and start again.

c. Remove the right case half.

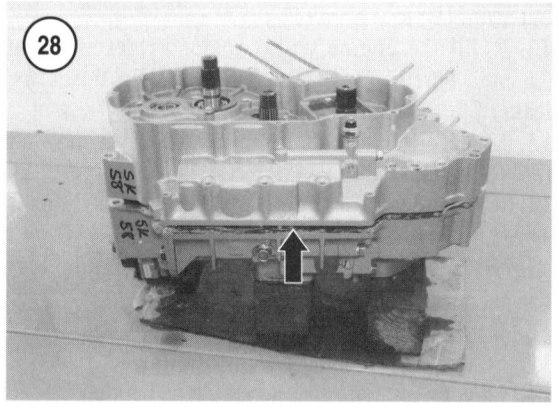

ENGINE LOWER END

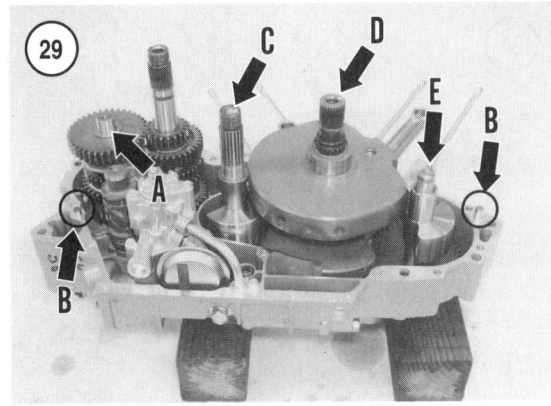

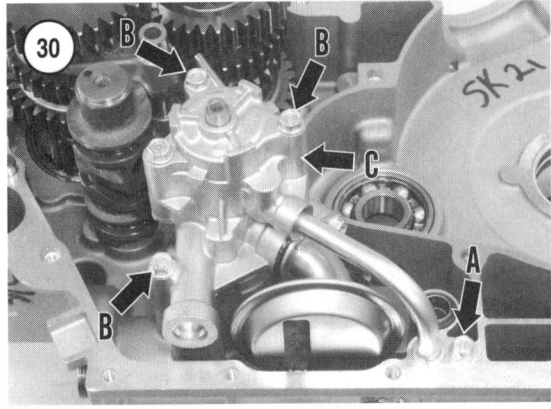

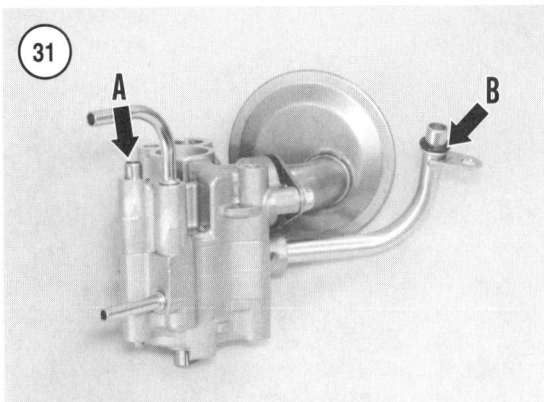

    d. Locate the thrust washer (A, **Figure 29**) installed on the end of the countershaft. Reinstall if necessary.

    e. Remove the two solid dowel pins (B, **Figure 29**) if they are not stuck.

5. Turn the rear balancer shaft (C, **Figure 29**) to position its counterweight away from the crankshaft and remove it. If necessary, turn the crankshaft to provide additional room for balancer shaft removal.

6. Lift out the crankshaft (D, **Figure 29**) and place in a plastic bag to prevent contamination.

7. Remove the front balancer shaft (E, **Figure 29**).

8. Remove the oil pump and oil pressure relief valve as follows:

    a. The oil pipe mounting bolt (A, **Figure 30**) is secured with threadlocking compound. Loosen and remove the bolt. If the bolt still turns under considerable resistance after loosening it, work the bolt back and forth several times to weaken the threadlocking compound.

    b. Remove the three oil pump mounting bolts (B, **Figure 30**) and the oil pump (C) with the oil pipe attached.

    c. Remove the dowel pin (A, **Figure 31**) and O-ring (B) from the oil pump and oil pipe.

    d. Remove the two dowel pins and O-rings (A, **Figure 32**) from the left case half.

    e. Remove the oil pressure relief valve (B, **Figure 32**) and its O-ring.

    f. Store the oil pump and pressure relief valve in plastic bags to prevent contamination.

NOTE
If shifting problems were occurring, inspect the transmission assembly before removing it. Look for severe wear or damaged parts. Spin the mainshaft and turn the shift drum by hand to shift the transmission. Check the movement and operation of each shift fork and sliding gear. Look for hard shifting and incomplete gear dog engagement. Check also for seized gears and bushings.

9. Remove the transmission assembly from the left case half as follows:

NOTE
Gears on the left side of both shafts are not secured with snap rings and can slide off when the shafts are removed.

    a. Remove the shift fork shaft (A, **Figure 33**).

    b. Pivot the shift forks away from the shift drum and remove the shift drum (B, **Figure 33**).

    c. Remove the shift forks (C, **Figure 33**).

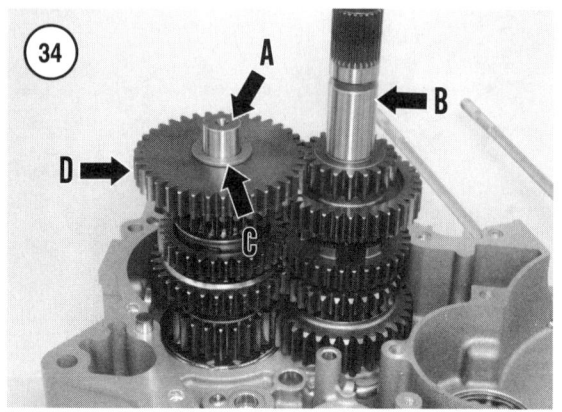

NOTE
The countershaft (A, Figure 34) is part of the output gear assembly. Some of the gears are removed from the countershaft while the output gear assembly is mounted on the engine. The remaining countershaft gears are removed with the mainshaft (B, Figure 34) assembly.

d. Remove the thrust washer (C, **Figure 34**) and the countershaft first gear (D).
e. Remove the needle bearing (A, **Figure 35**).
f. Remove the bushing (B, **Figure 35**).
g. Remove the thrust washer (C, **Figure 35**).
h. Remove the countershaft fourth gear (D, **Figure 35**).
i. Remove the spline collar (**Figure 36**).
j. Slide the remaining countershaft gears off the countershaft while removing the mainshaft at the same time (**Figure 37**).

10. Remove the oil orifice bolt and washer (C, **Figure 32**). Discard the washer.
11. Remove the oil pipe (A, **Figure 38**) as follows:
    a. The oil pipe mounting bolts (B, **Figure 38**) are secured with a threadlocking compound. Loosen and remove the bolts. If the bolts still turn under considerable resistance after loosening them, work the bolts back and forth several times to weaken the threadlocking compound.
    b. Remove the oil pipe and discard the two O-rings.
12. Remove the four output gear mounting bolts (A, **Figure 39**) and the output gear assembly (B). Account for the dowel pin.

NOTE
The oil jet removed in Step 13 is directional. The side with the chamfered hole faces toward the left case half.

13. Remove the oil jet and both O-rings (**Figure 40**). Discard the O-rings.

ENGINE LOWER END

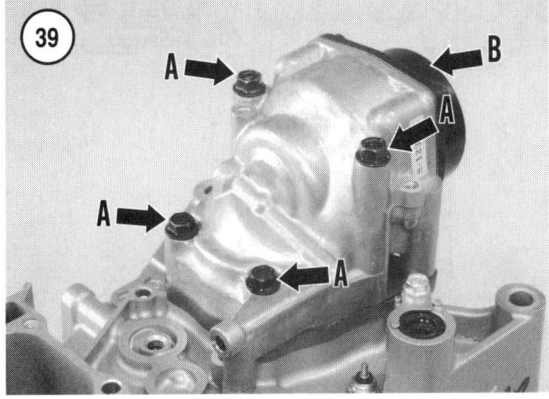

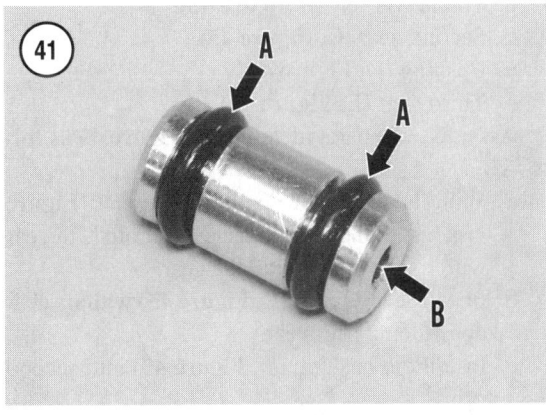

14. Inspect the case halves, crankshaft, connecting rods, balancer shafts, oil pump and output gear assemblies as described in this chapter.
15. Service and inspect the transmission assembly as described in Chapter Seven.
16. Clean and inspect the case halves as described in *Inspection* in this section.

Assembly

1. Lubricate two new O-rings with engine oil and install onto the oil pipe (A, **Figure 38**). Install the oil pipe, making sure both ends bottom against the crankcase. Apply a medium strength threadlocking compound onto the bolt threads and tighten securely (B, **Figure 38**).
2. Install the output gear housing as follows:
   a. Clean the oil jet (**Figure 41**) with compressed air, then inspect its passage for debris.
   b. Lubricate two new O-rings with engine oil and install them into the oil jet grooves (A, **Figure 41**).
   c. Install the oil jet with its chamfered hole end (B, **Figure 41**) facing *toward* the left case half. Refer to **Figure 40**.
   d. Lubricate a new O-ring with engine oil and install it into the output gear housing groove (A, **Figure 42**).
   e. Make sure the dowel pin is installed in the output gear housing (B, **Figure 42**).
   f. Install the output gear housing (B, **Figure 39**) onto the left case half.
   g. Clean the bolt surfaces on the output gear housing of all engine oil. The threads must be dry to achieve the specified torque. Then install the output gear housing mounting bolts (A, **Figure 39**) and tighten in a crossing pattern and in two steps to 31 N•m (23 ft.-lb.).

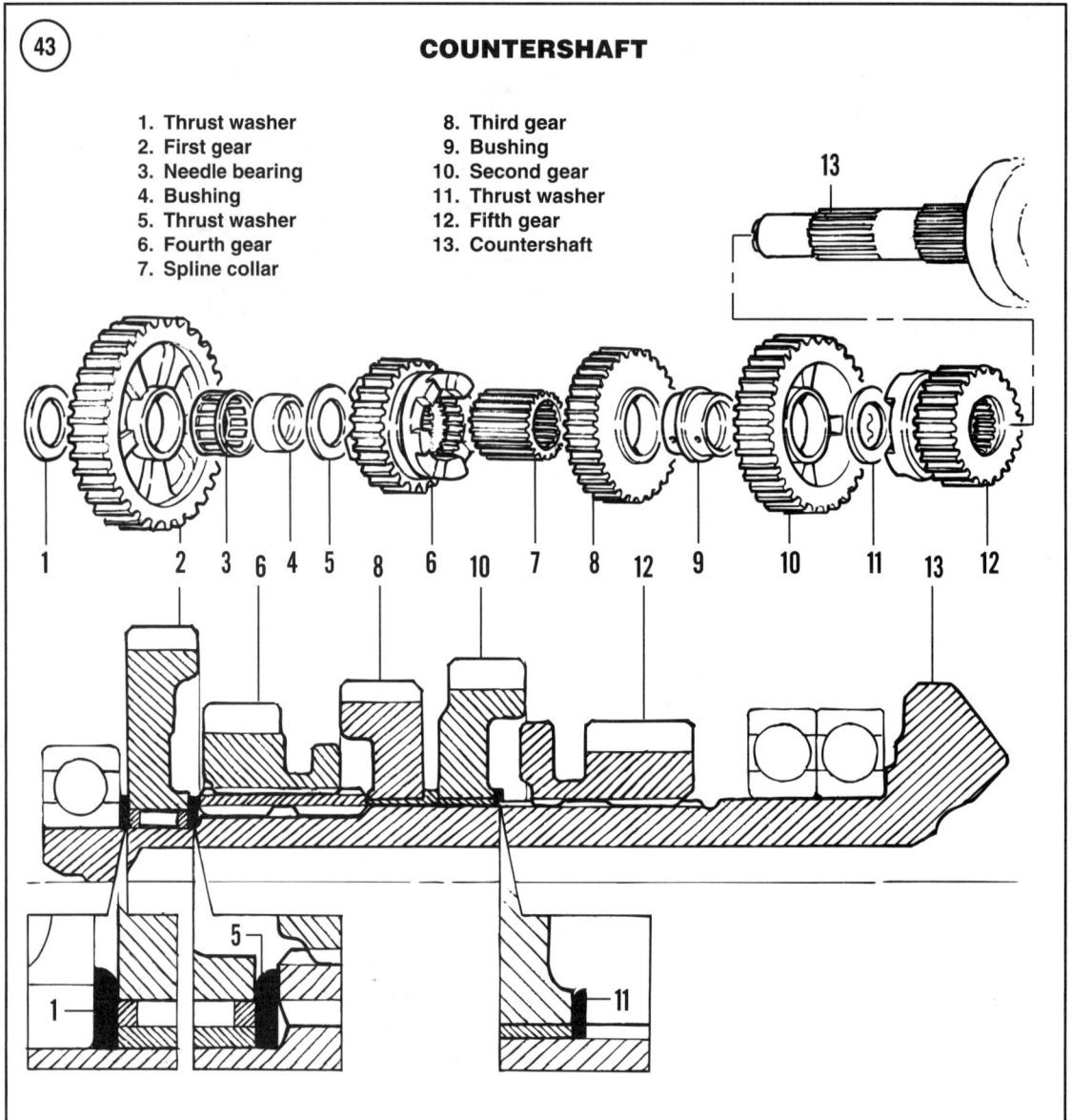

43 COUNTERSHAFT

1. Thrust washer
2. First gear
3. Needle bearing
4. Bushing
5. Thrust washer
6. Fourth gear
7. Spline collar
8. Third gear
9. Bushing
10. Second gear
11. Thrust washer
12. Fifth gear
13. Countershaft

NOTE
*Refer to **Transmission** in Chapter Seven to make sure the mainshaft is properly assembled.*

3. Support the left case half on wooden blocks with the countershaft facing up.

4. Lubricate the countershaft, thrust washers, bushing and gear bores with engine oil.

5. Identify the countershaft assembly (**Figure 43**) as follows:

   a. The A components in **Figure 44** will be assembled on the bench and then meshed with the mainshaft before they are installed over the countershaft.

   b. The B components in **Figure 44** will be installed separately over the countershaft.

6. Lay out the countershaft parts in the following order:

   a. Fifth gear (A, **Figure 45**).
   b. Thrust washer (B, **Figure 45**).
   c. Second gear (C, **Figure 45**).
   d. Bushing (D, **Figure 45**).
   e. Third gear (E, **Figure 45**).

7. Assemble the parts identified in **Figure 45** as follows:

   a. With the fifth gear dogs facing up (A, **Figure 45**), install the thrust washer (B) onto fifth gear with its flat side facing the gear.

   b. Install second gear (C, **Figure 45**) with its gear dogs facing fifth gear.

   c. Install the bushing (D, **Figure 45**) into second gear.

ENGINE LOWER END

d. Install third gear (E, **Figure 45**) over the bushing with its gear dogs facing away from the bushing.

e. The countershaft gear cluster should now appear as shown in **Figure 46**.

8. Mesh the countershaft gear cluster with the mainshaft (**Figure 47**).

NOTE
*Do not allow the washer (**Figure 47**) to fall off the mainshaft in Step 9.*

9. Install the countershaft gear cluster over the countershaft while installing the mainshaft into its crankcase bearing (**Figure 48**).

10. The transmission assembly should appear as shown in **Figure 49**.

11. Align the oil holes (A, **Figure 50**) and install the spline collar (B) over the countershaft.

12. Install countershaft fourth gear with its shift fork groove (A, **Figure 51**) facing down and with the gear and spline collar oil holes aligned (B). Refer to A, **Figure 52**.

13. Install the thrust washer (B, **Figure 52**) with its flat side facing down.

14. Install the bushing (C, **Figure 52**) and needle bearing (D).

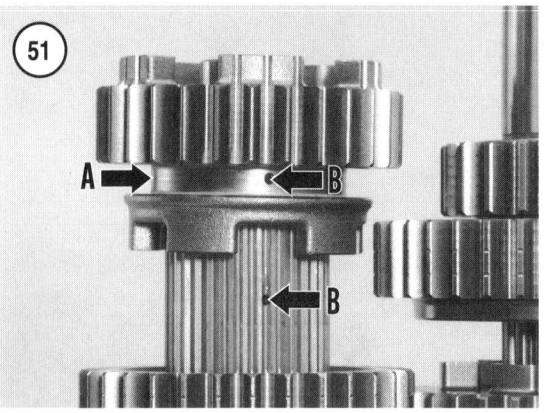

15. Install first gear with its flat side (A, **Figure 53**) facing up.
16. Install the thrust washer (B, **Figure 53**) with its flat side facing up.
17. Identify the shift forks by their letter mark (**Figure 54**):
    a. L (left shift fork).
    b. C (center shift fork).
    c. R (right shift fork).

NOTE
Install each shift fork with its letter mark (L, C or R) facing up.

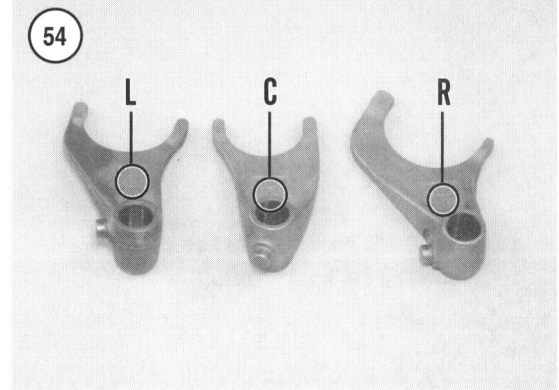

18. Install the L shift fork into the countershaft fifth gear groove (A, **Figure 55**).
19. Install the C shift fork into the mainshaft second/third gear groove (B, **Figure 55**).
20. Install the R shift fork into the countershaft fourth gear groove (C, **Figure 55**).
21. Install the shift drum and mesh each shift fork pin with its mating shift drum groove (**Figure 56**).
22. Lubricate the shift fork shaft (**Figure 57**) with engine oil and slide it through each shift fork and bottom it in its bore.
23. Spin the mainshaft and turn the shift drum by hand to check transmission operation. Check that each shift fork travels through its operating groove in

ENGINE LOWER END

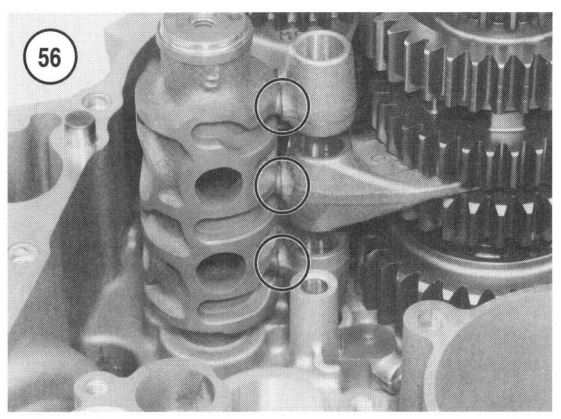

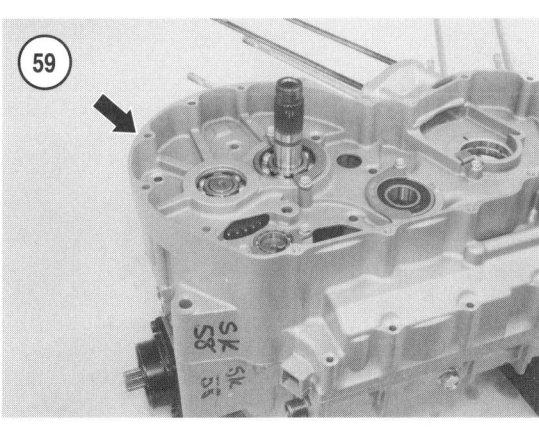

the shift drum and bottoms against both groove ends (**Figure 58**).

24. Check shifting as follows:
    a. Temporarily install the right case half (**Figure 59**) with the two solid dowel pins.
    b. Install the stopper lever without its spring (A, **Figure 60**) and shift drum cam assembly (B) as described in *External Shift Mechanism* in Chapter Six.
    c. Spin the mainshaft and turn the shift drum so that the stopper lever aligns with the drum's raised detent position (C, **Figure 60**). This is the neutral position and both shafts should turn separately of each other.
    d. Turn the mainshaft and shift drum to check shifting into each gear. The transmission shifts into a different gear each time the stopper lever moves into a different shift drum cam groove.
    e. Reverse substep a and b to remove the parts. Make sure the thrust washer is installed on the countershaft (B, **Figure 53**).

25. Install the oil orifice bolt (A, **Figure 61**) with a new washer and tighten to 14 N•m (10 ft.-lb.).

26. Lubricate a new O-ring with engine oil and install it onto the oil pressure relief valve. Install the oil pressure relief valve with its O-ring side (**Figure 62**) facing down. Push the valve down into its bore until it bottoms (B, **Figure 61**).

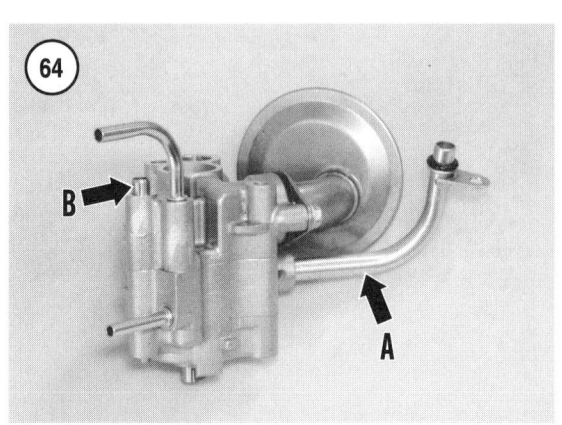

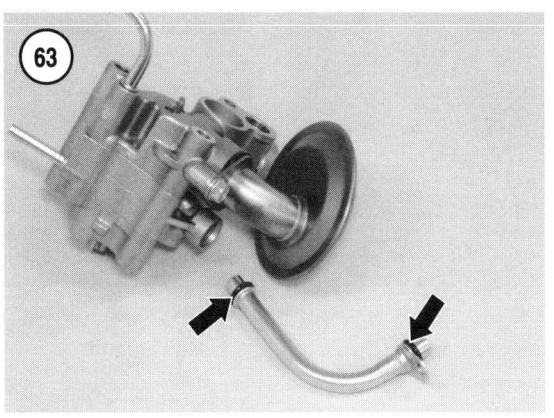

27. Lubricate two new O-rings with oil and install with the dowel pins (C, **Figure 61**) into the left case half bores.
28. Install the oil pump as follows:
    a. Lubricate two new O-rings (**Figure 63**) with engine oil and install them onto the oil pipe.
    b. Install the oil pipe (A, **Figure 64**) into the oil pump.
    c. Install the dowel pin (B, **Figure 64**) into the oil pump.
    d. Install the oil pump/oil pipe assembly (A, **Figure 65**) by inserting the dowel pin and oil pipe into the crankcase. Install and tighten the mounting bolts (B, **Figure 65**) securely.
    e. Apply a medium strength threadlocking compound onto the oil pipe mounting bolt (C, **Figure 65**).
29. Install the front balancer shaft as follows:
    a. Lubricate the balancer shaft's left journal with engine oil.
    b. Align the balancer shaft driven gears by inserting a screwdriver through the gear holes as shown in **Figure 66**. Only a small portion of the screwdriver should extend through the bottom side of the hole.
    c. Install the front balancer shaft with the screwdriver into its left case half bearing (A, **Figure 67**).

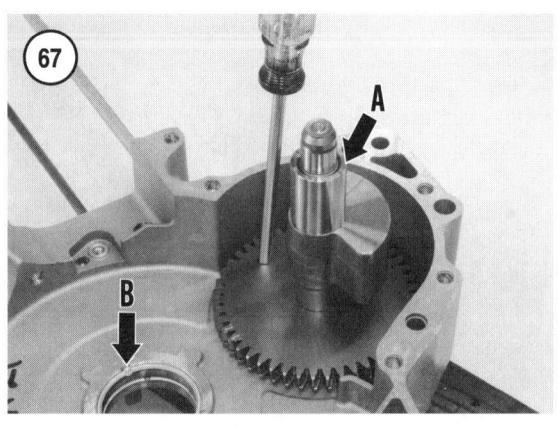

ENGINE LOWER END

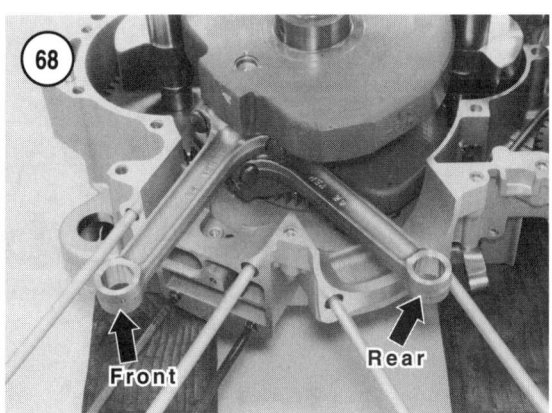

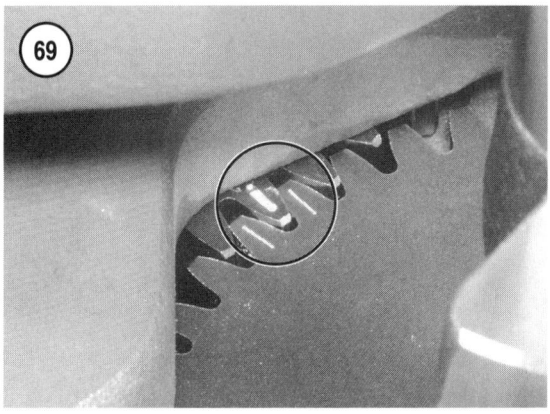

30. Lubricate the left case half main bearing journal (B, **Figure 67**) with molybdenum oil solution.
31. Install the crankshaft in two steps as follows:
    a. With the crankshaft's tapered shaft end facing toward the left case half, position the front and rear connecting rods with the front and rear cylinder openings as shown in **Figure 68**.
    b. Align the timing mark on the crankshaft drive gear with the two timing marks on the front balancer shaft driven gear (**Figure 69**).
    c. When the crankshaft (A, **Figure 70**) is properly installed, remove the screwdriver (B). Turn the crankshaft and recheck the timing marks.
32. Lubricate the rear balancer shaft's left journal with engine oil and install in the left case half (**Figure 71**) with its counterweight facing away from the crankshaft. If necessary, turn the crankshaft so that the narrow part of its counterweight is facing toward the balancer shaft to provide room for installation.
33. Lubricate all of the exposed shaft journals (A, **Figure 72**) with engine oil.
34. Thoroughly clean the mating surfaces on both case halves with contact cleaner and a clean lint-free cloth. Check the mating surfaces to make sure they are clean and dry.
35. Make sure the O-ring and dowel pin (B, **Figure 72**) are installed in the left case half.
36. Use one of the following semi-drying liquid gasket sealers: HondaBond 4, ThreeBond 1104 or YamaBond No. 4.
37. Apply a light coat of gasket sealer to the left case half sealing surface as shown in **Figure 73**.
38. Install the two solid dowel pins into the left case half (C, **Figure 72**).
39. Align and install the right case half over the shafts and seat it against the left case half. Make sure there are no gaps between the case halves.
40. Install and tighten the crankcase bolts and washer as follows:

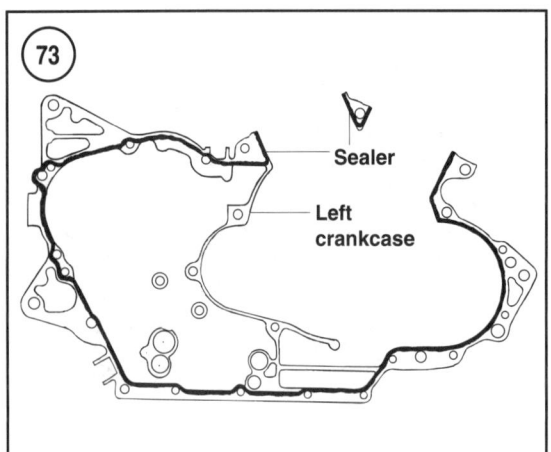

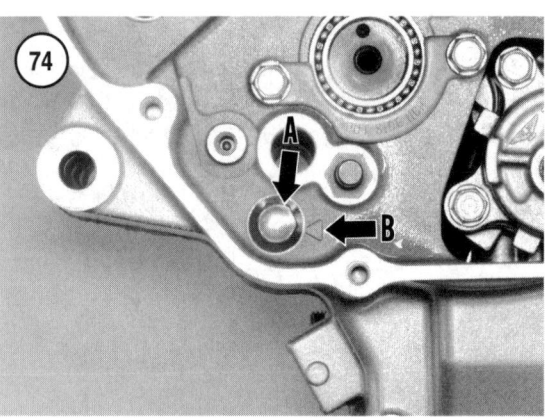

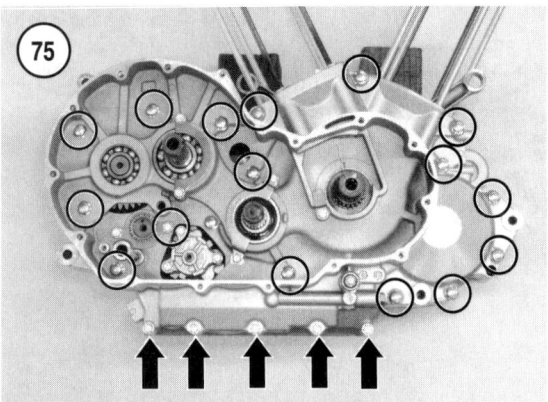

a. Use the cardboard template made during disassembly to identify the right case half bolts and washer.
b. Install a new washer on the 8-mm bolt identified in A, **Figure 74**. The bolt hole in the right case half is identified with an arrow mark (B, **Figure 74**).
c. Install the bolts with dry threads.
d. Tighten the 8-mm bolts (circles, **Figure 75**) in a crossing pattern and in two steps to 26 N•m (19 ft.-lb.).
e. Tighten the 6-mm bolts (arrows, **Figure 75**) to 12 N•m (106 in.-lb.).
f. Allow the engine to remain in this position to allow the sealer to set and dry.

41. Turn the crankshaft and both transmission shafts. All shafts must turn freely.
42. Repeat Step 24 to check shifting.
43. Reverse Steps 1 and 2 in *Disassembly* in this section to complete installation.

Inspection

1. Remove all sealer residue from the gasket surfaces with solvent and a scraper. If a silicone based sealer was used, use Permatex Silicone Stripper Gel Gasket Remover (part No. 80647) to remove the silicone residue with minimal scraping. Remove sealer residue from the threaded holes in both case halves with a small brush.
2. Remove the oil pressure switch (A, **Figure 76**) and the oil passage bolt (B) from the right case half to allow the oil passages to be cleaned and flushed with solvent and compressed air.

NOTE
*Make sure to remove the oil jet installed underneath each cylinder before cleaning the crankcase halves. Refer to **Piston and Piston Rings** in Chapter Four.*

3. Remove and discard the shift shaft oil seal as described in *Crankcase Seal and Bearing* in this chapter. The needle bearing is a slip fit and can be removed for cleaning and inspection.

CAUTION
*Do not damage the crankshaft main bearings (**Figure 77**) when cleaning and servicing the case halves. These bearings cannot be replaced separately. If damaged, the case half must be replaced.*

4. Clean the crankcase halves with solvent.

ENGINE LOWER END

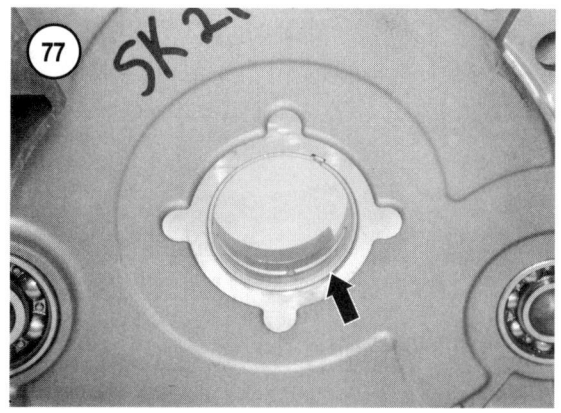

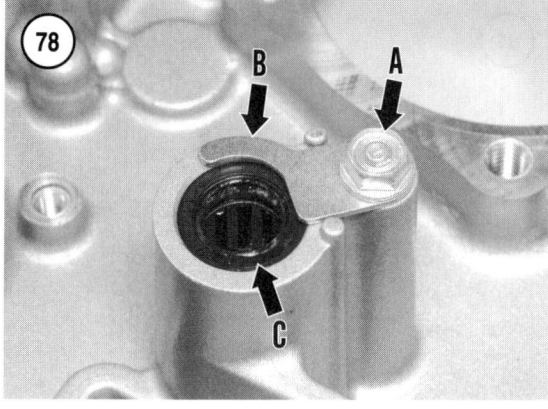

8. Dry the crankcase halves with compressed air. Blow through the oil holes to clean the passages leading through the crankshaft main bearings.

WARNING
When drying a bearing with compressed air, do not allow the inner bearing race to spin. The air can spin the bearing at excessive speed, possibly damaging the bearing.

9. Blow through each oil passage with compressed air. Then inspect the passages with a flashlight. When the passages are clean and dry, install the following parts:
   a. Install the oil pressure switch as described in *Piston and Piston Rings* in Chapter Nine.
   b. Install a new washer on the right case half oil passage bolt (B, **Figure 76**) and tighten securely.
   c. Install a new washer on both engine oil drain bolts and tighten to 30 N•m (22 ft.-lb.).
   d. Refer to Chapter Nine and reinstall the oil pressure switch.

10. Lightly oil the engine bearings with new engine oil before inspecting their condition. A dry bearing will exhibit more sound and looseness than a properly lubricated bearing.

11. Inspect the bearings for roughness, pitting, galling and play. Replace any bearing that is not in good condition. Always replace the opposite bearing at the same time. Refer to *Crankcase Seal and Bearing* in this chapter.

12. Retighten or replace damaged cylinder studs. Refer to *Cylinder Stud* in Chapter Four.

CRANKCASE SEAL AND BEARING

Refer to *Service Methods* in Chapter One for general bearing removal and installation techniques.
Refer to this section to identify the shift shaft seal and crankcase bearings.

Shift Seal and Bearing Removal/Installation

This seal and bearing can be replaced with the engine mounted in the frame and the shift shaft removed. Refer to *External Shift Mechanism* in Chapter Six for shift shaft removal procedures.

1. Remove the bolt (A, **Figure 78**), plate (B) and seal (C). Discard the seal.
2. Slide the needle bearing out of its bore (**Figure 79**).
3. Inspect the needle bearing. The rollers should be smooth and polished with no flat spots, burrs or other

5. Inspect the crankcases for fractures around all mounting and bearing bosses, stiffening ribs and threaded holes. If repair is required, have a dealership inspect the case halves.

NOTE
The left and right case halves can be replaced separately.

6. Using clean solvent, flush each bearing.
7. Check all threaded holes for damage or debris buildup. Clean threads with the correct size metric tap. Lubricate the tap with kerosene or aluminum tap fluid.

damage. Inspect the bearing cage for cracks or other damage. Replace the bearing if necessary.

4. Lubricate the bearing needles with engine oil and install it into its bore.

5. Lubricate the new seal lip with grease and install the seal with its closed side facing out (C, **Figure 78**).

6. Installation is the reverse of removal. Apply a medium strength threadlocking compound to the bolt threads and tighten securely.

Bearing Removal/Installation

1. When replacing crankcase bearings, note the following:
   a. Identify and record the size code of each bearing before it is removed from the crankcase. This will eliminate confusion when installing the bearings.
   b. Record the orientation of each bearing in its bore. Note if the size code faces toward the inside or outside of the crankcase.
   c. Heat the crankcase area around the bearing or bearing bore to approximately 80° C (176° F) before removing and installing the bearing.
   d. Remove bearings that are only accessible from one side with a blind bearing puller (**Figure 80**). The puller is fitted through the bearing, then expanded to grip the back-side of the bearing.
   e. Refer to *Crankshaft* in this chapter to inspect the crankshaft main bearings.
2. Identify the *left* case half bearings as follows:
   a. Shift shaft bearing (**Figure 79**).
   b. Mainshaft bearing (A, **Figure 81**).
   c. Rear balancer shaft bearing (B, **Figure 81**).
   d. Crankshaft main bearing (C, **Figure 81**).
   e. Front balancer shaft bearing (D, **Figure 81**).
   f. Starter drive bearing (**Figure 82**).
3. Identify the *right* case half bearings as follows:
   a. Front balancer shaft bearing (A, **Figure 83**).
   b. Mainshaft bearing (B, **Figure 83**).
   c. Rear balancer shaft bearing (C, **Figure 83**).
   d. Mainshaft bearing (D, **Figure 83**).
   e. Countershaft bearing (E, **Figure 83**).
   f. Shift drum bearing (F, **Figure 83**).
4. When reinstalling the right case half bearing plates (**Figure 84**), note the following:
   a. Install bearing plates with their identification marks facing out.
   b. Remove all threadlock residue from bolt and case half threads.
   c. Apply a medium strength threadlocking compound to the bolt threads and tighten to 12 N•m (106 in.-lb.).

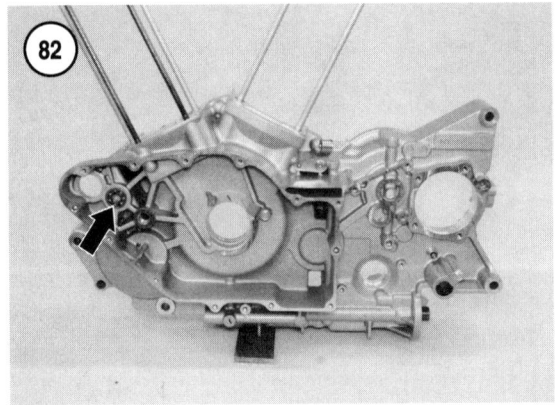

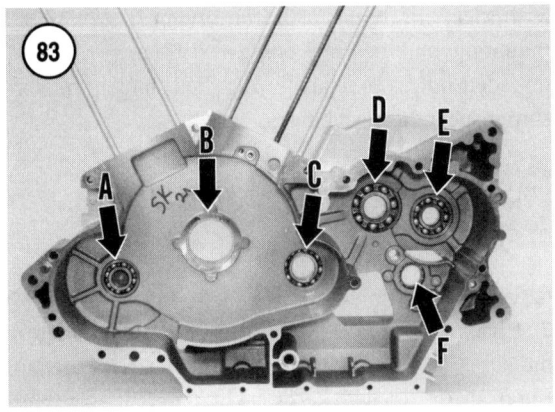

ENGINE LOWER END

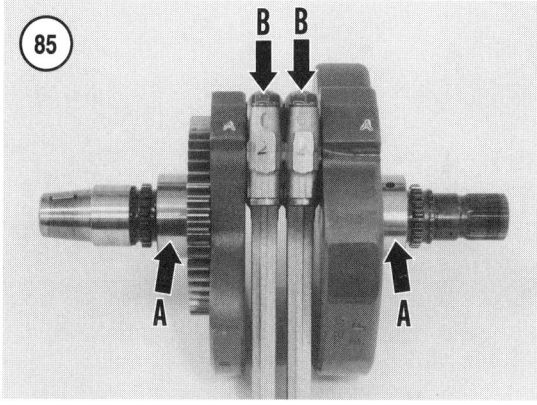

CRANKSHAFT

Removal/Installation

Remove and install the crankshaft as described in *Crankcase* in this chapter.

Crankshaft Inspection

1. Clean the crankshaft and connecting rods thoroughly with clean solvent. Clean the crankshaft oil passageways with compressed air. Dry the crankshaft with compressed air and lubricate all bearing surfaces with a light coat of engine oil.

2. Inspect each crankshaft main journal (A, **Figure 85**) for scratches, ridges, scoring, nicks or heat discoloration. Very small nicks and scratches may be removed with crocus cloth. Anything more serious must be referred to a dealership.

3. To determine main journal wear, perform the *Main Bearing Inspection and Clearance Check* in this section.

4. Inspect the crankshaft splines, flywheel taper and drive gears for damage.

5. Measure crankshaft runout with the crankshaft mounted between centers on a crankshaft truing stand or in a lathe and check the amount of runout at each crankshaft journal. If the runout exceeds the service limit in **Table 1** after rotating the crankshaft two full turns, replace the crankshaft.

Main Bearing Inspection and Clearance Check

Each case half is equipped with an insert-type main bearing (**Figure 77**). The main bearing inserts cannot be replaced. If severely worn or damaged, the case half must be replaced. Do not remove the inserts when inspecting them in the following steps.

1. Inspect the inside surface of each bearing insert (**Figure 77**) for severe wear, bluish or burned appearance, flaking and scoring. If the insert is questionable, replace the case half.

2. Clean the crankshaft main bearing journal (A, **Figure 85**) and case half bearing insert (**Figure 77**) surfaces.

3. Measure the main bearing clearance by performing the following steps:

   a. Measure the bearing insert inside diameter (**Figure 77**) with a bore gauge or inside micrometer.
   b. Measure the crankshaft main bearing journal outside diameter with a micrometer (**Figure 86**).
   c. Subtract the main bearing journal outside diameter from the main bearing insert inside diameter to determine the main bearing journal oil clearance. If the main bearing journal oil clearance exceeds the service limit in **Table 1**, replace the case half. Recheck the clearance with the new case half. If the clearance is still excessive, replace the crankshaft.

CONNECTING RODS

Removal/Installation

Identify the connecting rods, bearings and caps so they can be reinstalled in their original mounting positions.

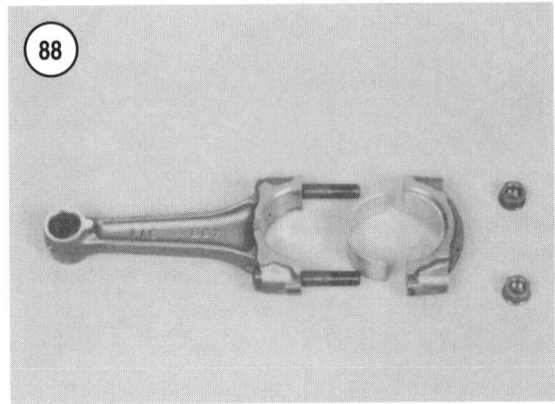

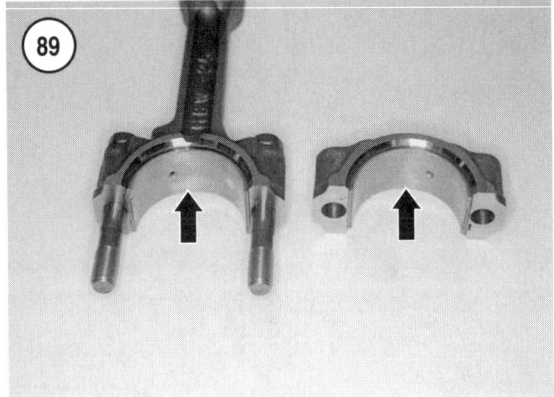

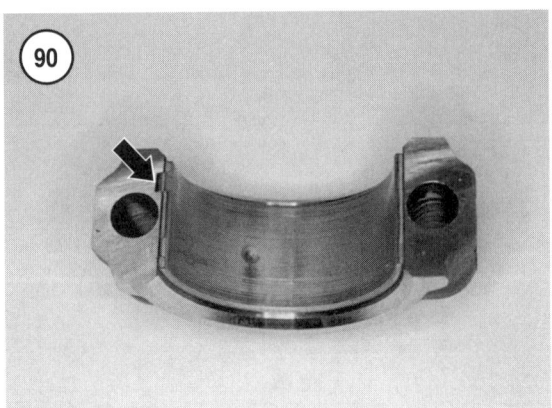

1. Remove the crankshaft as described in *Crankcase* in this chapter.
2. Measure the connecting rod side clearance by inserting a feeler gauge between the connecting rod and crankshaft machined surfaces (**Figure 87**). Compare to the connecting rod side clearance limit in **Table 1**. Measure each connecting rod. If the measurement is out of specification, replace the connecting rod as described in this chapter. Recheck the clearance with the new rod.
3. Remove the nuts (B, **Figure 85**) securing the connecting rod caps and remove the caps.
4. Carefully remove the connecting rod from the crankshaft so the studs on the rod do not contact the crankshaft rod journal surface. Mark the rod, bearing and cap to show its correct cylinder and rod journal position for reassembly (**Figure 88**).
5. Remove and identify each bearing insert (**Figure 89**) as to its upper or lower position.
6. Clean these parts and the crankshaft in solvent and dry with compressed air.
7. Inspect the connecting rods and bearings as described in this section.
8. If new bearing inserts are being installed, check the connecting rod bearing oil clearance as described in this chapter.
9. Clean the bearing inserts, connecting rod and cap contact surfaces with isopropyl alcohol. There must be no oil, lint or debris on the contact surfaces when installing the inserts.
10. Install the bearing inserts into each connecting rod and cap (**Figure 89**). Make sure they are locked in place (**Figure 90**).

CAUTION
If the old bearing inserts are reused, they must be installed in their original positions; otherwise, engine damage may occur.

11. Apply molybdenum oil solution to the bearing inserts and rod journal bearing thrust surfaces.
12. Install the connecting rod onto the crankshaft so it is facing in its original position, as noted during removal.
13. Match the code number on the end of the cap with the mark on the rod (A, **Figure 91**) and install the cap.

NOTE
The fine threads used on the connecting rod studs and cap nuts are easily damaged. Carefully start the nuts by hand.

14. Lubricate the bearing cap nut threads and seating surfaces with engine oil and install the cap nuts

ENGINE LOWER END

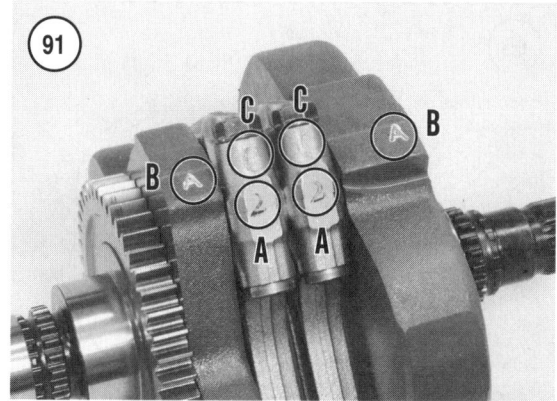

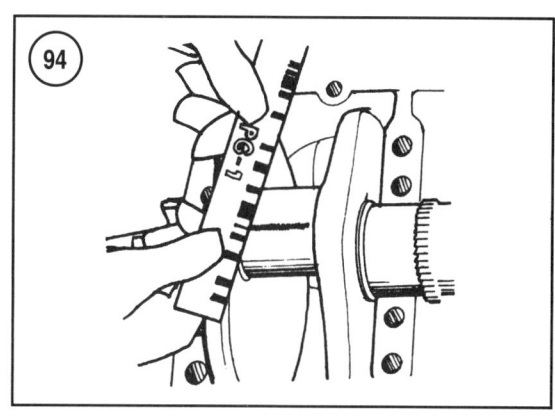

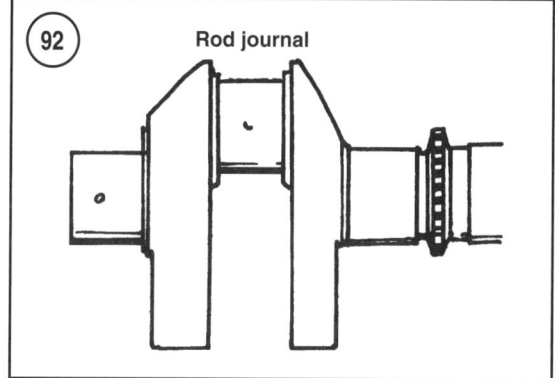

Rod journal

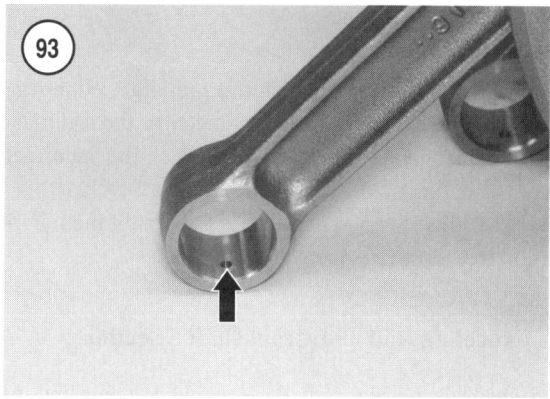

(B, **Figure 85**). Tighten the cap nuts in several steps to 59 N•m (44 ft.-lb.).
15. Rotate the connecting rod several times to check there is no binding or roughness.
16. Repeat for the other connecting rod.

Inspection

1. Remove and identify the connecting rods from the crankshaft as described in this section.
2. Clean the connecting rods and inserts in solvent and dry with compressed air.
3. Inspect the crankshaft rod journal for scratches, ridges, scoring and other damage.

4. Inspect each bearing insert (**Figure 89**) for evidence of wear, abrasion and scoring. They are reusable if in good condition.
5. Measure the rod journal (**Figure 92**) and check for out-of-roundness and taper. If the rod journal is not straight, refer further inspection to a dealership.
6. Check each connecting rod big end for signs of seizure, bearing or connecting rod damage.
7. Check each connecting rod small end (**Figure 93**) for signs of excessive heat (blue coloration), cracks and other damage.
8. Measure the connecting rod small end inside diameter (**Figure 93**) with an inside micrometer or small hole gauge. Replace the connecting rod if the small end inside diameter exceeds the service limit specified in **Table 1**.
9. If all of the parts are within specification, check the connecting rod bearing oil clearance as described in this section.

Connecting Rod Bearing Oil Clearance

Measurement

1. Clean any oil from the bearing insert and rod journal surfaces.
2. Place a strip of Plastigage over the rod bearing journal parallel to the crankshaft as shown in **Figure 94**. Do not place the Plastigage material over the oil hole.

NOTE
Do not rotate the connecting rod while the Plastigage strip is in place.

3. Install the bearing inserts into each connecting rod and cap. Make sure they are locked in place correctly (**Figure 90**).

NOTE
The bearing inserts must be installed in their original mounting position.

4. Install the connecting rod onto the crankshaft so that it is facing in its original position.

5. Match the code number on the end of the cap with the mark on the rod (A, **Figure 91**) and install the cap.
6. Lubricate the bearing cap nut threads and seating surfaces with engine oil and install the cap nuts (B, **Figure 85**). Tighten the cap nuts in several steps to 59 N•m (44 ft.-lb.).
7. Repeat to install the other connecting rod and cap.
8. Remove the rod cap nuts and rod cap for both connecting rods.
9. Measure the width of the flattened Plastigage (**Figure 94**) at its widest point following the manufacturer's instructions. If the connecting rod bearing oil clearance exceeds the wear limit in **Table 1**, select new bearings as described in this section.
10. Remove all of the Plastigage material from the crankshaft journal and connecting rod bearing inserts.
11. If the bearing oil clearance is greater than specified, new inserts must be installed. Select new inserts as described in this section.

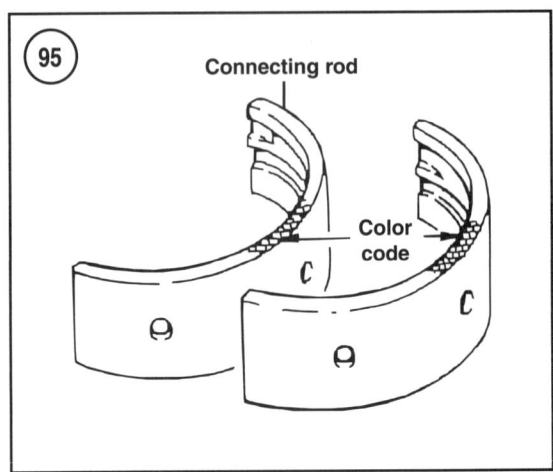

Selection

A code number stamped on the side of each connecting rod and cap (A, **Figure 91**) identifies the connecting rod inside diameter. Half the number is stamped on the rod and the other half is stamped on the cap. A code letter stamped on each crankshaft web (B, **Figure 91**) identifies the rod journal outside diameter.

NOTE
If a code on either part is undecipherable, refer selection to a dealership.

1. Record the connecting rod inside diameter code number (1 or 2) on the rod and cap (A, **Figure 91**).
2. Record the rod journal outside diameter code letter (A or B) on the crankshaft web (B, **Figure 91**).
3. Select new bearings by cross-referencing the rod journal outside diameter code letter (B, **Figure 91**) in the vertical column of **Table 2** to the connecting rod inside diameter code number (A) in the horizontal column. Where the two columns intersect, the new bearing insert color is indicated. **Table 3** identifies the different bearing colors and thicknesses. The bearing identification colors are painted on the side of the bearings (**Figure 95**). For example, if the rod journal outside diameter code letter is A and the connecting rod inside diameter code number is 2, the new bearing insert color is yellow.

CAUTION
Installing the wrong bearing insert can cause severe engine damage.

4. After installing the new bearing inserts, recheck the connecting rod bearing oil clearance as described in this section and note the following:

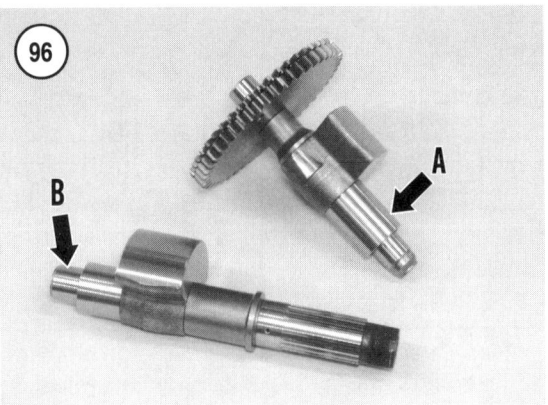

a. If the bearing clearance is too large, either the connecting rod inside diameter or the rod journal outside diameter is worn or the incorrect bearing size was installed.
b. If the bearing clearance is too small, the incorrect bearing size was installed.

Connecting Rod and Crankshaft Selection

The connecting rods are matched according to weight. A code letter stamped on the side of each connecting rod cap (C, **Figure 91**) identifies the connecting rod weight.

When replacing a connecting rod, replace it with the same weight code found on the original rod (C, **Figure 91**). If the same weight code is unavailable, select one from **Table 4** that is a match.

BALANCER SHAFTS

Removal/Installation

Remove and install the balancer shafts as described under *Crankcase* in this chapter.

ENGINE LOWER END

Inspection

1. Clean and dry the front (A, **Figure 96**) and rear (B) balancer shaft assemblies.
2. Inspect the balancer shaft bearing journals and splines for damage.
3. Service the front balancer shaft as follows:
   a. The front balancer shaft can be partially disassembled to inspect the springs and gears. However, replacement parts are not available. If damage is noted, replace the front balancer shaft as an assembly.
   b. Remove the snap ring (A, **Figure 97**), washer (B), outer gear (C) and springs.
   c. Inspect the springs for cracks and other damage. Compare the length of the three springs. If there is an appreciable difference in spring height, replace the balancer shaft assembly.
   d. Inspect the gears for tooth damage.
   e. Install the outer gear with its OUT (D, **Figure 97**) mark facing out. Install a spring into each gear slot.
   f. Install the washer (B, **Figure 97**) and secure the assembly with the snap ring (A). Make sure the snap ring seats in the groove completely.

OIL PUMP

The oil pump can be disassembled to measure and inspect its internal components. However, because individual parts are not available, the oil pump can only be replaced as a complete unit.

Removal/Installation

Remove and install the oil pump as described in *Crankcase* in this chapter.

Disassembly

Refer to **Figure 98**.

1. Remove the oil pipe (A, **Figure 99**) and O-rings.
2. Remove the bolt (B, **Figure 99**), oil strainer (C, **Figure 99**) and seal (**Figure 100**).

NOTE
Identify the rotors so they can be reinstalled facing in the same direction and in their original locations.

3. Remove the bolt (A, **Figure 101**) and front cover (B).
4. Remove the scavenge rotor assembly (A, **Figure 102**).
5. Remove the drive pin (B, **Figure 102**) and dowel pins (C).
6. Remove the pump body (A, **Figure 103**) and dowel pins (B).
7. Remove the washer (C, **Figure 103**), drive pin (D) and shaft (E).
8. Remove the feed rotor assembly (**Figure 104**).

NOTE
*Do not remove the seal (**Figure 105**) from the pump body or damage it when cleaning the oil pump. A replacement seal is not available.*

Inspection

Refer to **Table 5** for oil pump specifications. If any measurement is out of specification, or if any component shows visual damage, replace the oil pump assembly. Internal parts are not available.

1. Clean and dry all parts.
2. Inspect the covers and housing for cracks.
3. Check both rotor sets and bores (A and B, **Figure 106**) for scoring and other damage.
4. Inspect the oil strainer screen (A, **Figure 107**) and seal (B) for damage.
5. Inspect the shaft, drive pins and washer for cracks or other damage.
6. Inspect the seal (**Figure 105**) in the pump body for tearing and other visible damage.
7. Install the scavenge rotors into the front cover (A, **Figure 106**) with the groove on the inner rotor facing up.
8. Measure the axial clearance between the rotors and pump housing with a straightedge and flat feeler gauge (**Figure 108**).
9. Install the drive pin into the shaft and install the shaft and pin into the inner rotor.
10. Measure the tip clearance between the inner and outer rotors with a flat feeler gauge (**Figure 109**).
11. Measure the side clearance between the outer rotor and housing bore with a flat feeler gauge (**Figure 110**).

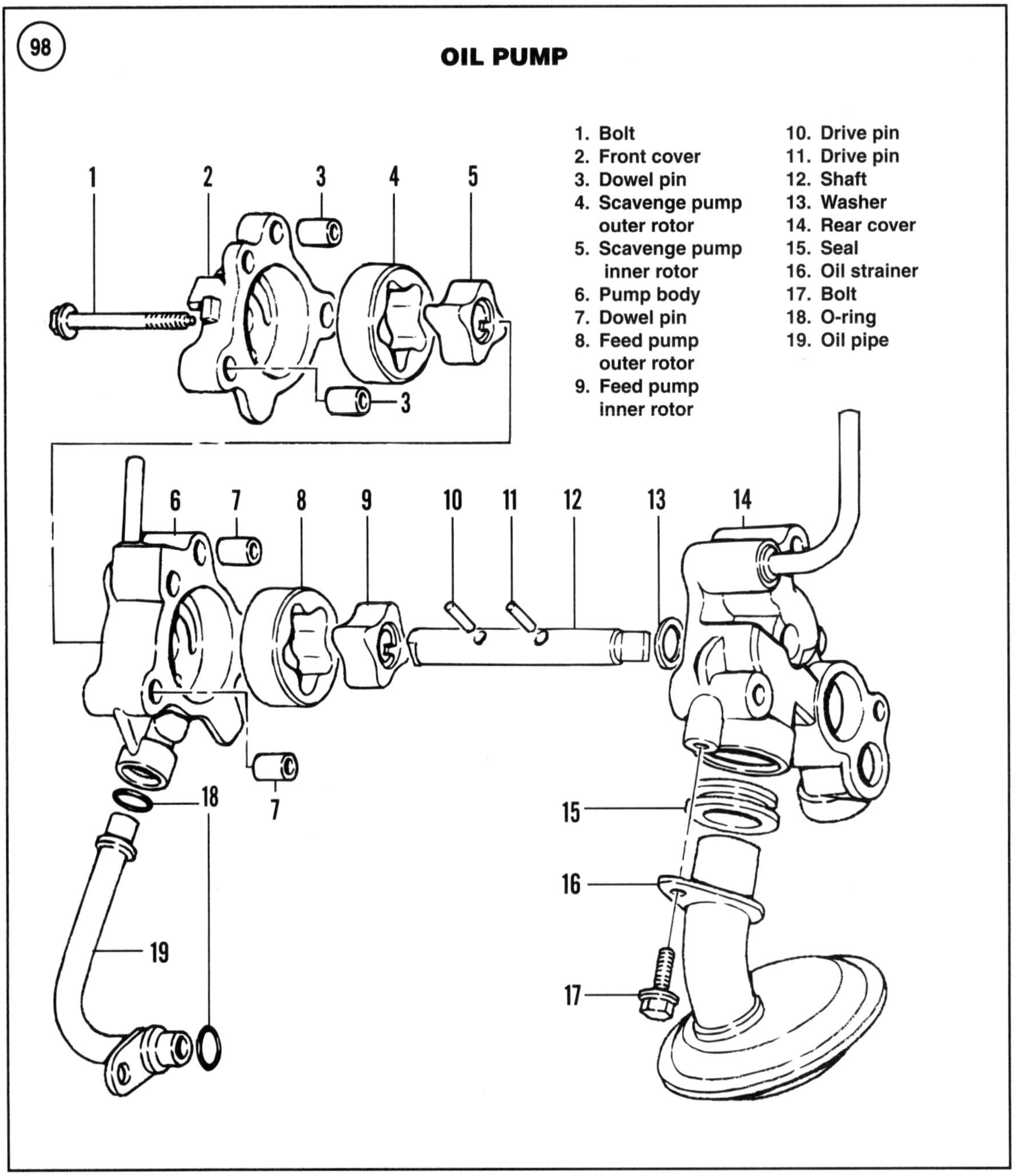

CHAPTER FIVE

OIL PUMP

1. Bolt
2. Front cover
3. Dowel pin
4. Scavenge pump outer rotor
5. Scavenge pump inner rotor
6. Pump body
7. Dowel pin
8. Feed pump outer rotor
9. Feed pump inner rotor
10. Drive pin
11. Drive pin
12. Shaft
13. Washer
14. Rear cover
15. Seal
16. Oil strainer
17. Bolt
18. O-ring
19. Oil pipe

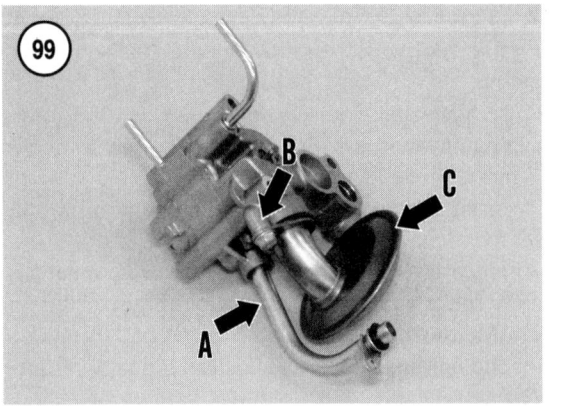

ENGINE LOWER END

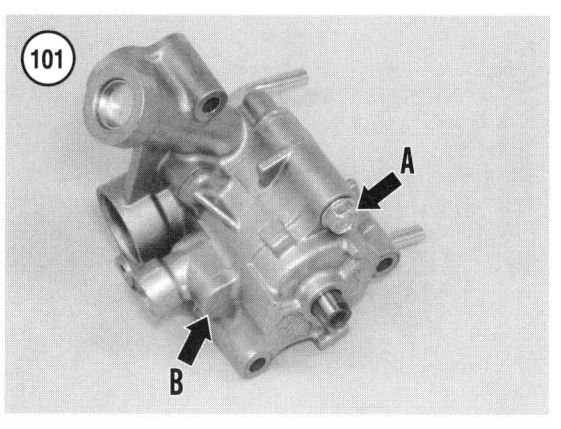
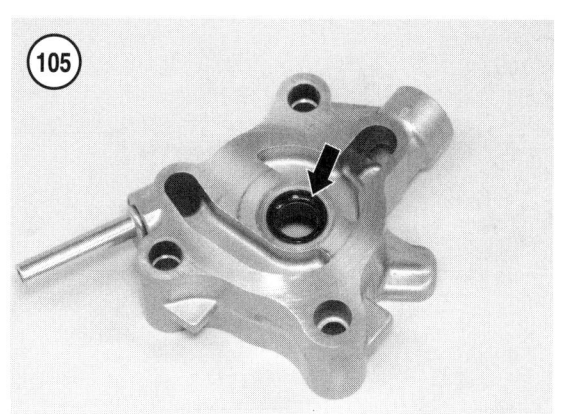
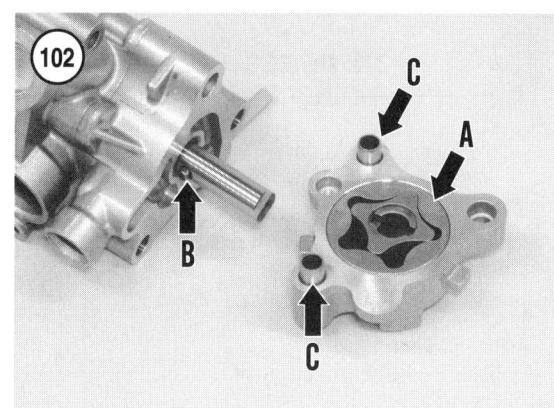
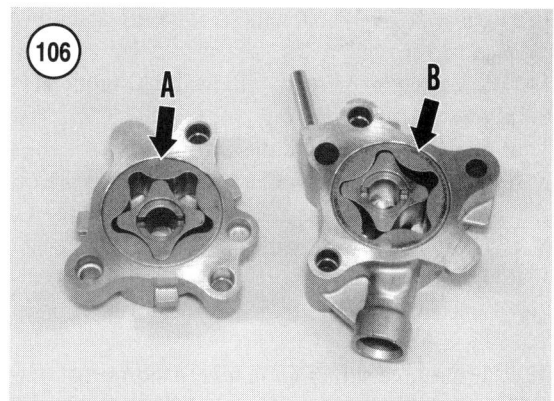
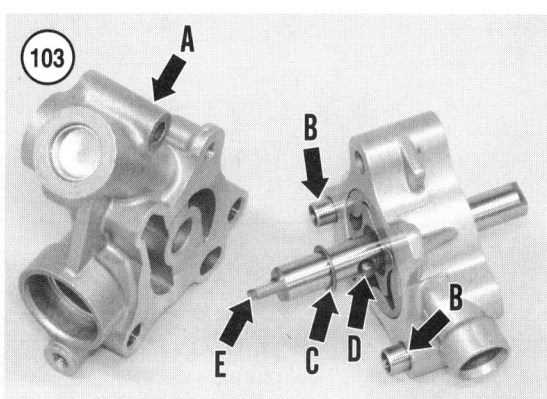
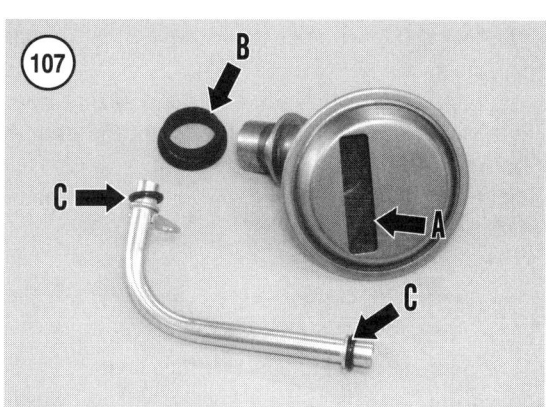
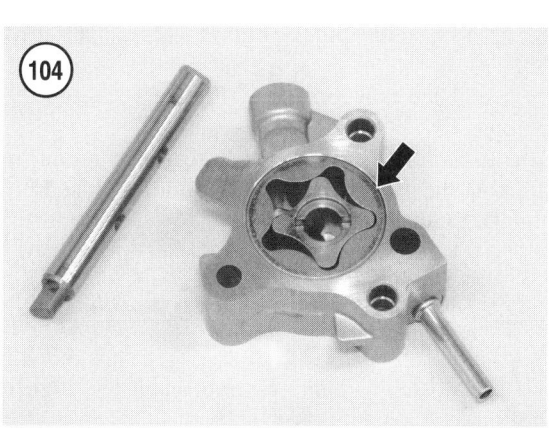
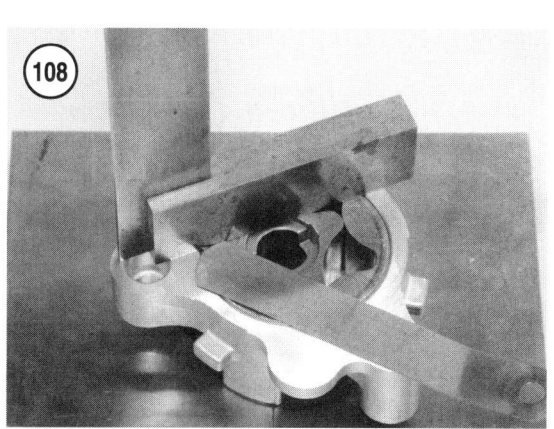

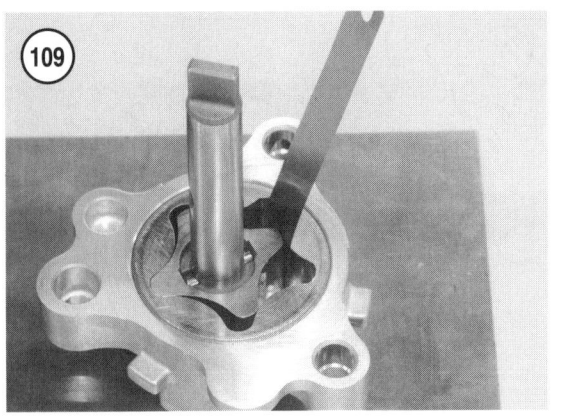

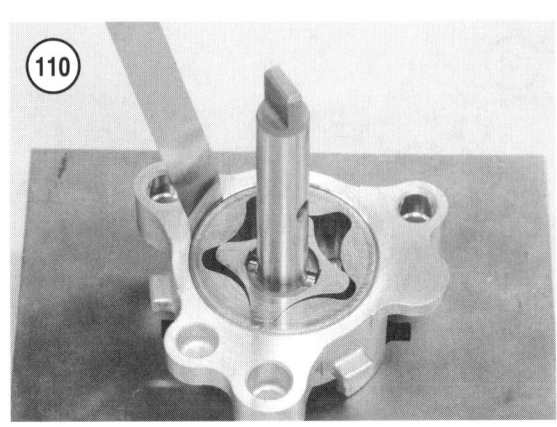

12. Repeat Steps 7-11 for the feed pump assembly (B, **Figure 106**).
13. Inspect the oil pressure relief valve (**Figure 111**) as follows:
    a. Remove and discard the O-ring.
    b. Remove the snap ring and disassemble the oil pressure relief valve assembly.
    c. Clean and dry all parts.
    d. Inspect the valve bore and piston outside diameter for scratches or wear. Replace if damaged.
    e. Inspect the spring for cracks, distortion or other damage. Replace the spring if any damage is noted.
    f. Make sure the holes in the valve body are not clogged.
    g. Install the piston, spring, washer and snap ring. Make sure the snap ring seats in the groove completely.
    h. Install a new O-ring into the valve body groove.

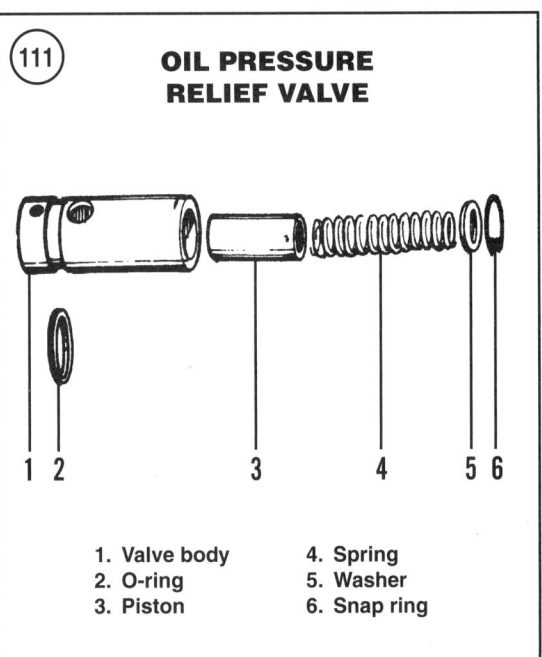

OIL PRESSURE RELIEF VALVE

1. Valve body
2. O-ring
3. Piston
4. Spring
5. Washer
6. Snap ring

Assembly

Use new engine oil to lubricate the parts.

1. Lubricate the rotors, rotor bores, shaft and washer.
2. Lubricate the seal (**Figure 105**) in the pump body.

NOTE
Refer to your disassembly marks and install both rotor sets facing in their original direction. The grooves in the inner rotors must face out.

3. Install the feed rotors (B, **Figure 106**) into the pump body.
4. Install the shaft with its water pump drive end facing as shown in E, **Figure 103**. Install the drive pin (D, **Figure 103**) and washer (C).
5. Push the shaft through the rotors until the drive pin engages the groove in the inner rotor.
6. Install the dowel pins (B, **Figure 103**) and install the rear cover against the pump body.
7. Install the scavenge rotors (A, **Figure 102**) into the front cover.
8. Install the drive pin (B, **Figure 102**) into the shaft hole.
9. Install the dowel pins (C, **Figure 102**) into the pump body.
10. Install the front cover and scavenge rotors by aligning the groove in the inner rotor with the drive pin (B, **Figure 102**).

NOTE
The threads on the oil pump assembly bolt must be clean and dry.

11. Install the oil pump assembly bolt (A, **Figure 101**) and tighten to 13 N•m (115 in.-lb.).

ENGINE LOWER END

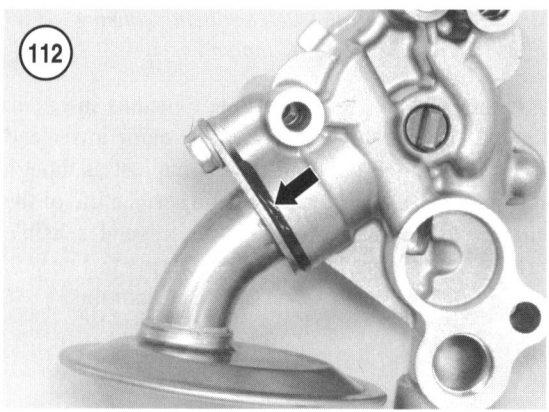

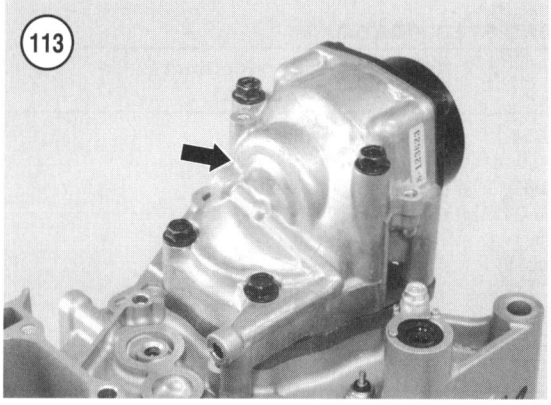

12. Turn the oil pump shaft to make sure the rotors turn freely.
13. Lubricate a new seal and install onto the oil strainer in the direction shown in **Figure 100**.
14. Install the oil strainer (C, **Figure 99**) and tighten its mounting bolt (B) to 13 N•m (115 in.-lb.). The seal must seat flush between the two parts as shown in **Figure 112**.
15. Lubricate two new O-rings and install on the oil pipe (C, **Figure 107**).
16. Install the oil pipe as shown in A, **Figure 99**.

OUTPUT GEAR

Inspection

Replacement gears, adjustment shims and internal O-rings are not available to reshim or rebuild the output gear assembly (**Figure 113**). If the output gear assembly is suspected of damage or wear, refer inspection to a dealership.

Seal Removal/Installation

If the output gearcase seal is leaking oil, replace it as follows:

1. Remove the rear swing arm (Chapter Thirteen). Thoroughly clean the swing arm boot of oil that leaked through the output gearcase seal.
2. Place a drain pan underneath the output gearcase.
3. Clean the seal and the area around the seal to prevent dirt from entering the output gearcase.
4. Remove the snap ring (A, **Figure 114**). Replace the snap ring if weak or damaged.
5. Remove the oil seal (B, **Figure 114**) from the output gearcase.

NOTE
If it is difficult to remove the seal, remove the engine as described in this chapter.

6. Clean the seal bore and check it for any damage that may have occurred when removing the seal.
7. Clean the output shaft and splines. Check the shaft for any visible wear or damage where it operates against the seal.
8. Lubricate the lip on the new seal with grease.

NOTE
Before installing the new seal, check the splines on the end of the output gear shaft for burrs and other conditions that could damage the new seal.

9. Lightly lubricate the shaft splines with the same grease used on the seal lip.
10. Carefully install the new seal over the shaft with its closed side facing out while turning it slightly to prevent the splines from tearing the seal lip. When the seal is positioned squarely against the housing, drive it into its bore until it bottoms and the snap ring groove is visible.
11. Install the snap ring, making sure it seats completely in the housing groove.
12. Clean the shaft splines of all grease applied in Step 9.
13. Install the swing arm (Chapter Thirteen).

14. Check the engine oil level (Chapter Three).
15. After riding the motorcycle, look inside the swing arm boot to check the new seal for leaks.

ENGINE BREAK-IN

CAUTION
Because oil consumption during break-in may be higher than normal, check the engine oil level frequently during beak-in. Refer to Chapter Three.

If the rings were replaced, new pistons installed, the cylinders rebored or honed or major lower end work performed, break in the engine just as though it were new. The performance and service life of the engine depends greatly on a careful and sensible break-in for the initial 300 miles. During this period, avoid full-throttle starts and hard acceleration.

Table 1 ENGINE LOWER END SPECIFICATIONS

	New mm (in.)	Service limit mm (in.)
Main bearing journal oil clearance	0.030-0.054 (0.0012-0.0021)	0.068 (0.0027)
Connecting rod bearing oil clearance	0.038-0.062 (0.0015-0.0024)	0.070 (0.0028)
Connecting rod side clearance	0.10-0.25 (0.004-0.010)	0.28 (0.011)
Connecting rod small end inside diameter	20.016-20.034 (0.7880-0.7887)	20.044 (0.7891)
Crankshaft runout	–	0.05 (0.002)

Table 2 CONNECTING ROD BEARING SELECTION

Rod journal outside diameter code letter	Connecting rod inside diameter code number	
	Number 1	Number 2
Letter A	Pink	Yellow
Letter B	Yellow	Green

Table 3 CONNECTING ROD BEARING THICKNESS

Bearing color	Thickness
Green	1.495-1.499 mm (0.0589-0.0590 in.)
Yellow	1.491-1.495 mm (0.0587-0.0589 in.)
Pink	1.487-1.491 mm (0.0585-0.0587 in.)

Table 4 CONNECTING ROD WEIGHT SELECTION

Replacement rod weight code	Original rod weight code						
	A	B	C	D	E	F	G
C	–	–	0	0	0	0	0
D	–	0	0	0	0	0	–
E	0	0	0	0	0	–	–
Cross mating OK: 0							
Cross mating unacceptable: –							

ENGINE LOWER END

Table 5 OIL PUMP SPECIFICATIONS

Feed and scavenge pump	New mm (in.)	Service limit mm (in.)
Axial clearance	0.15-0.21 (0.006-0.008)	0.35 (0.014)
Side clearance	0.02-0.07 (0.001-0.003)	0.10 (0.004)
Tip clearance	0.15 (0.006)	0.20 (0.008)

Table 6 ENGINE LOWER END TORQUE SPECIFICATIONS

	N•m	in.-lb.	ft.-lb.
Clutch cable holder bolt	12	106	–
Connecting rod bearing cap nut*	59	–	44
Engine 8-mm hanger plate bolts	27	–	20
Engine 10-mm mounting nuts	39	–	29
Engine oil drain bolts*	30	–	22
Oil passage bolt*	14	–	10
Oil pressure switch*	12	106	–
Oil pump assembly bolt	13	115	–
Oil strainer bolt	13	115	–
Output gear housing mounting bolt*	31	–	23
Rear balancer shaft bearing setting plate bolt*	12	106	–
Right case half bearing plate bolts*	12	106	–
Right crankcase assembly bolts			
6-mm	12	106	–
8-mm*	26	–	19
Starter cable outer nut	7	62	–

*Refer to text for additional information.

CHAPTER SIX

CLUTCH AND EXTERNAL SHIFT MECHANISM

This chapter covers procedures for the right crankcase cover, clutch, clutch release assembly, primary drive and driven gears, external shift mechanism and clutch cable.

Table 1 and **Table 2** are at the end of this chapter.

RIGHT CRANKCASE COVER

Removal/Installation

1. Drain the engine oil (Chapter Three).
2. Remove the exhaust system (Chapter Fifteen).
3. Remove the timing hole cover mounting bolts and cover (A, **Figure 1**).
4. Remove the clutch cover mounting bolts and cover (B, **Figure 1**). The bolt identified in C, **Figure 1** is a position bolt and does not require removal.

NOTE
Different length bolts are used to retain the right crankcase cover. Sketch the right crankcase cover and each mounting bolt position on a piece of cardboard. Punch holes in the cardboard and place each bolt in its correct position for reassembly (Figure 2).

CAUTION
Because the right crankcase cover is sealed with a gasket sealer, it can be difficult to break loose. If necessary, use a small knock puller (Figure 3) threaded into one of the cover threaded holes to break the cover loose. Do not pry behind the cover.

5. Remove the right crankcase cover mounting bolts and cover (**Figure 4**).
6. Remove the dowel pins (**Figure 5**), if necessary.
7. Remove sealer residue from the crankcase and cover gasket surfaces. Do not damage the sealing surface or leaks will occur.
8. Installation is the reverse of removal. Note the following:
   a. Clean and dry the cover and crankcase mating surfaces. Clean the crankcase bolt holes of all oil and sealer debris.
   b. Clean and dry the cover mounting bolts.
   c. Apply HondaBond 4, ThreeBond 1104 or Yamabond No. 4 gasket sealer to the crankcase cover gasket surface (**Figure 6**).
   d. Tighten the right crankcase cover mounting bolts in a crossing pattern and in several steps.

NOTE
Allow the gasket sealer to set per the manufacturer's instructions before filling the engine with oil.

CLUTCH AND EXTERNAL SHIFT MECHANISM

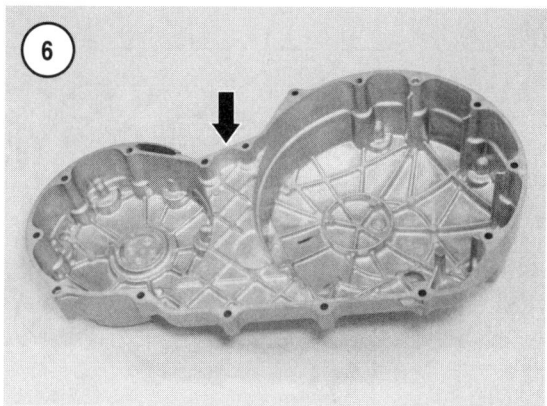

e. Refill the engine with the recommended type and quantity of oil as described in Chapter Three. Check for oil leaks.

f. Tighten the timing hole cap cover Allen bolts (A, **Figure 1**) to 10 N•m (88 in.-lb.).

g. Tighten the clutch cover mounting bolts (B, **Figure 1**) to 10 N•m (88 in.-lb.).

CLUTCH

The clutch (**Figure 7**) is a multi-plate type that operates immersed in the engine oil supply. The clutch assembly consists of a clutch hub (13, **Figure 7**) and clutch housing (16). The gear-driven clutch housing is mounted on the transmission mainshaft. The housing receives power from the primary drive gear mounted on the crankshaft. The tabs on the drive plate (6, **Figure 7**) engage with slots in the clutch housing (16). If the clutch is engaged, the plates are locked together. This transfers power via the drive plates which are always spinning, to the driven plates (7, **Figure 7**) splined to the clutch hub (13). The clutch hub is splined to the mainshaft and drives the transmission mainshaft. The clutch plates are engaged by springs and disengaged by a cable operated clutch release system.

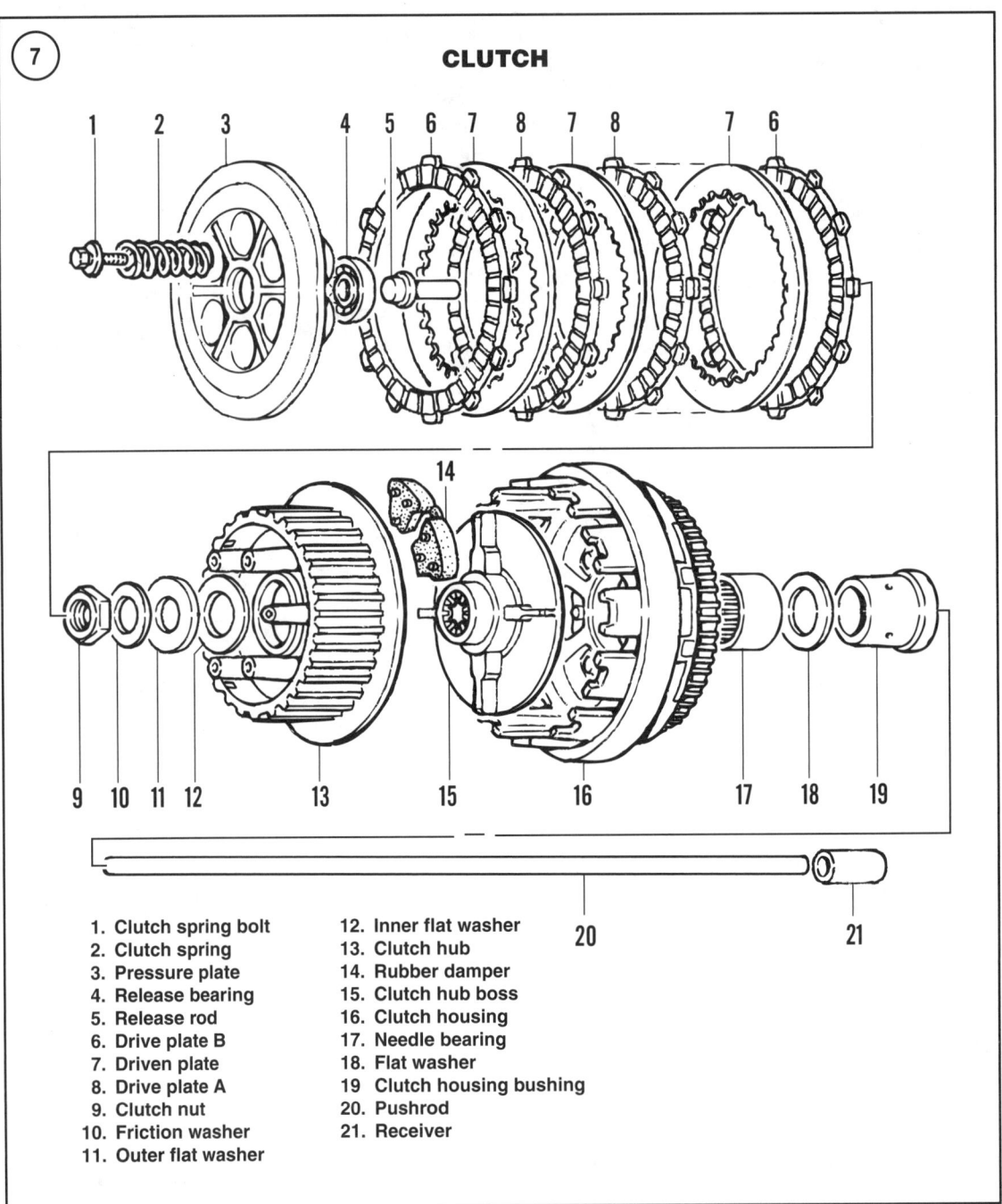

⑦ CLUTCH

1. Clutch spring bolt
2. Clutch spring
3. Pressure plate
4. Release bearing
5. Release rod
6. Drive plate B
7. Driven plate
8. Drive plate A
9. Clutch nut
10. Friction washer
11. Outer flat washer
12. Inner flat washer
13. Clutch hub
14. Rubber damper
15. Clutch hub boss
16. Clutch housing
17. Needle bearing
18. Flat washer
19. Clutch housing bushing
20. Pushrod
21. Receiver

Component Identification

Some clutch parts have two or more names, which can cause confusion. The following lists the terms used in the manual and often used alternatives:

1. Drive plate (6, **Figure 7**)–Clutch disc, clutch plate, friction disc, friction plate and outer plate.
2. Driven plate (7, **Figure 7**)–Aluminum plate, clutch disc, clutch plate, inner plate and steel plate.
3. Clutch plates–When clutch plates are used in the text, it refers to both the drive and driven plates as an assembly.
4. Clutch hub (13, **Figure 7**)–Clutch boss, clutch center and inner hub.
5. Clutch housing (16, **Figure 7**)–Clutch basket, clutch outer, outer clutch hub and primary driven gear basket.

Tools

The clutch holder (part No. 07JMB-MN50301 or 07HGB-001010B [**Figure 8**]) and collar set A (part No. 07HGB-001020B [**Figure 8**]) is required to hold

CLUTCH AND EXTERNAL SHIFT MECHANISM

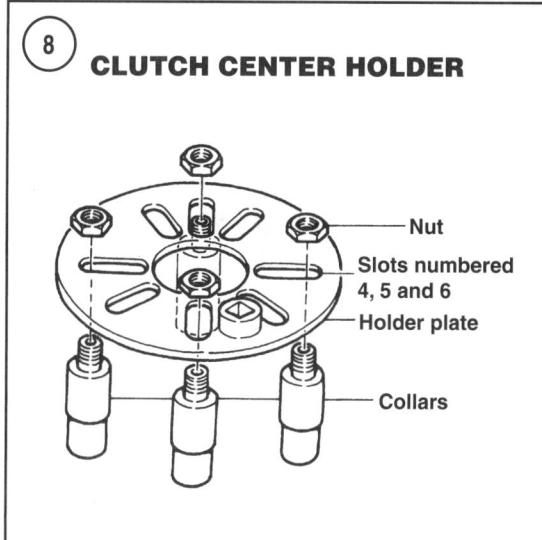

Removal/Disassembly

1. Remove the right crankcase cover as described in this chapter.
2. Loosen the clutch bolts (A, **Figure 9**) in a crossing pattern and in several steps. Remove the bolts and springs.
3. Remove the pressure plate (B, **Figure 9**).
4. Remove the release rod (A, **Figure 10**) and pushrod (B).

NOTE
*The first and last drive plates (6, **Figure 7**) are different from the drive plates (8) installed between them. During removal, place a zip-tie on these two drive plates to help identify them.*

5. Remove the clutch plates from the clutch assembly in the order shown in **Figure 7**.
6. Carefully grind the staked portion of the clutch nut (**Figure 11**) with a small grinding stone to weaken it. Do not grind through the nut or the mainshaft will be damaged.
7. Hold the clutch hub with the holder plate (A, **Figure 12**). Then hold the holder plate (B, **Figure 12**) and loosen the clutch nut (C). Remove the tool.
8. Remove the clutch nut and discard it.
9. Remove the friction washer (A, **Figure 13**).

the clutch hub when removing and tightening the clutch nut. The tool consists of a holder plate with eight slots and a set of holder collars and nuts. The slots in the holder plate are marked with the numbers 4, 5 or 6. These numbers correspond to the number of springs used in the clutch assembly. Before using the tool, set the holder collars to the No. 6 holder slot position.

10. Remove the outer (B, **Figure 13**) and inner (**Figure 14**) flat washers.
11. Remove the clutch hub (A, **Figure 15**).
12. Remove the clutch hub boss (**Figure 16**) and the four rubber dampers (**Figure 17**) installed in the back of the clutch hub.
13. Remove the clutch housing (B, **Figure 15**) and needle bearing (**Figure 18**).
14. Remove the flat washer (A, **Figure 19**) and the clutch housing bushing (B).
15. Inspect all parts as described in this section.

Assembly/Installation

Refer to **Figure 7**.

> *NOTE*
> *If removed, install the external shift mechanism, oil chain and sprockets and the primary driven gear as described in this chapter before installing the clutch.*

> *NOTE*
> *Molybdenum oil solution is a 1:1 mixture of engine oil and molybdenum disulfide grease.*

1. Lubricate the clutch housing bushing with molybdenum oil solution. Lubricate all other parts with engine oil before reassembly.
2. Install the clutch housing bushing with its shoulder facing in (B, **Figure 19**).
3. Install the flat washer (A, **Figure 19**) and seat it against the bushing shoulder.
4. Install the needle bearing (**Figure 18**) and seat it against the washer.
5. Install the clutch housing (B, **Figure 15**).
6. Install the four rubber dampers (**Figure 17**) so the connecting band on each set of dampers fits over the arms on the clutch hub. Lubricate the shoulder on the clutch hub boss with engine oil and install the hub with its arms positioned between the gaps in the rubber dampers. Refer to **Figure 16**.
7. Install the clutch hub (A, **Figure 15**).
8. Install the inner flat washer (A, **Figure 20**) and seat it against the shoulder on the clutch hub (**Figure 14**).
9. Install the outer flat washer (B, **Figure 20**). Refer to B, **Figure 13**.
10. Install the friction washer (C, **Figure 20**) with its OUT mark facing out. Refer to A, **Figure 13**.
11. Lubricate the mainshaft threads with engine oil.
12. Lubricate the threads on a new clutch nut (**Figure 11**) and its seating surface with engine oil, and then

CLUTCH AND EXTERNAL SHIFT MECHANISM

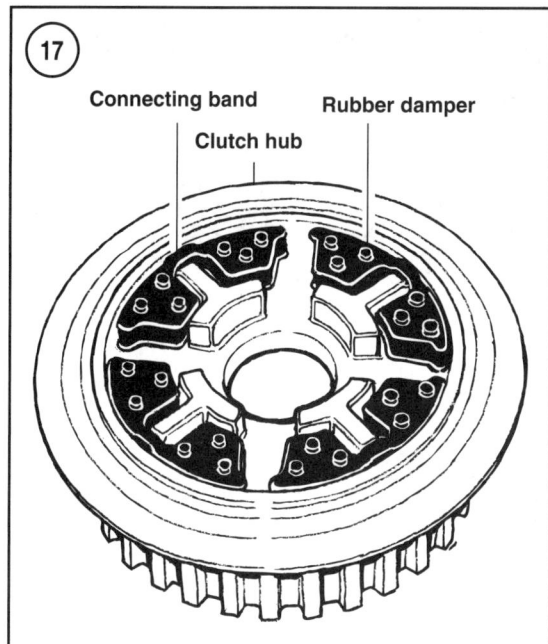

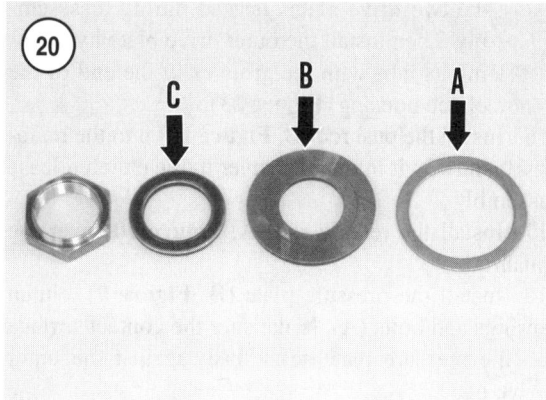

install it with its shoulder side facing out. Tighten the nut finger-tight.

13. Hold the clutch hub with the holder plate tool (**Figure 21**) and tighten the clutch nut to 186 N•m (137 ft.-lb.).

CAUTION
*In Step 14, stake the clutch nut into the groove in the mainshaft. Do **not** stake the nut against any other part of the mainshaft.*

14. Use a punch and stake a portion of the clutch nut shoulder into the groove in the mainshaft (**Figure 11**).
15. Install the clutch plate assembly as follows:
    a. Refer to **Figure 7** to identify the clutch plates.
    b. The driven plates (7, **Figure 7**) are stamped during manufacturing and have one flat side and one chamfered side. Install all of the driven plates with their flat side facing in the same direction (either in or out).
    c. The two outer drive plates (6, **Figure 7**) are different from the other six drive plates (8) installed between them. The two outer drive plates have green paint (A, **Figure 22**) on the edge of one tab. The inner drive plates have black paint on the edge of one tab (B, **Figure 22**).
    d. Lubricate all of the drive and driven plates with engine oil. Before installing new drive plates, soak them in clean engine oil for a few minutes before installation.
    e. Install the clutch plate assembly in the order shown in **Figure 7**. Remove the zip-tie from

the two drive plates if used during disassembly. Then install the outer drive plate by aligning its tabs with the grooves in the end of the clutch housing (**Figure 23**).

16. Install the pushrod (B, **Figure 10**) into the mainshaft and seat it into the receiver in the clutch release assembly.

17. Install the release rod (A, **Figure 10**) over the pushrod.

18. Install the pressure plate (B, **Figure 9**), clutch springs and bolts (A). Make sure the contact surface on the pressure plate seats flush against the outer drive plate.

19. Tighten the clutch spring bolts (A, **Figure 9**) securely in several steps and in a crossing pattern until tight. Then tighten to 12 N•m (106 in.-lb.).

20. Adjust the clutch cable as described in Chapter Three.

21. Pull the clutch lever and hold in position while watching the clutch assembly. The pressure plate should move outward, thus removing pressure from the plates where they can be moved by hand. Release the clutch lever so pressure is applied against the clutch plates and they cannot be moved by hand.

22. Install the right crankcase cover as described in this chapter.

23. Shift the transmission into neutral and start the engine. After the engine warms up, pull the clutch in and shift the transmission into first gear. Note the following:
   a. If the clutch makes a loud grinding and spinning noise immediately after the engine is started and then stops, either the engine oil level is low or the new drive plates were not lubricated with oil.
   b. If the motorcycle jumps forwards and stalls, or creeps with the transmission in gear and the clutch pulled in, the clutch adjustment is incorrect or the drive plates are excessively worn.
   c. If the clutch adjustment is correct but the clutch is not working correctly, the clutch may have been assembled incorrectly or there is a broken part in the clutch. Disassemble the clutch and inspect the parts as described in this section.

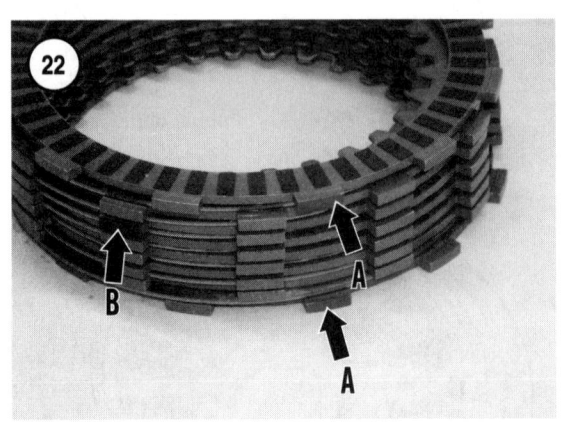

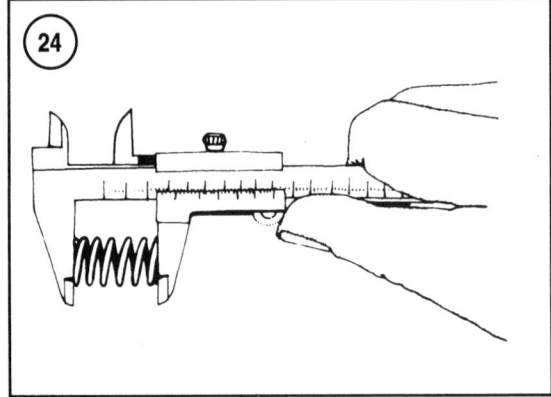

Inspection

Always replace drive plates, driven plates or clutch springs as a set if individual components do not meet specifications (**Table 1**). If parts show other signs of wear or damage, replace them regardless of their specifications.

1. Clean and dry all parts.
2. Inspect the clutch springs for cracks and blue discoloration (heat damage).

CLUTCH AND EXTERNAL SHIFT MECHANISM

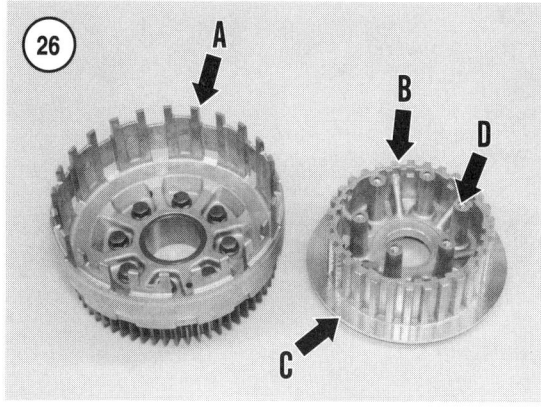

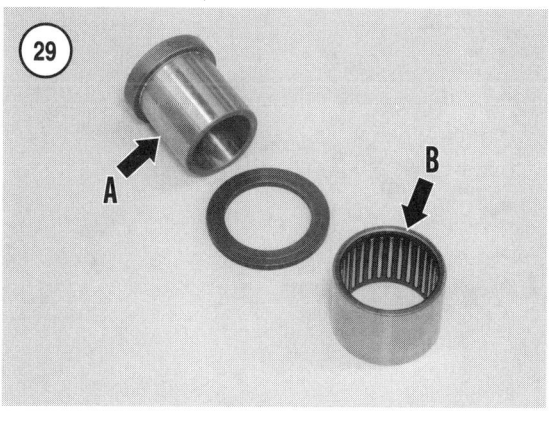

3. Measure the free length of each clutch spring (**Figure 24**). Replace the springs as a set if any one spring is out of specification.
4. Inspect each drive plate (6 and 8, **Figure 7**) as follows:
   a. Inspect the friction material for excessive or uneven wear, cracks and other damage.
   b. Inspect the tabs for cracks, grooves and noticeable wear. The tabs must be smooth so the drive plates can slide in the clutch housing grooves when the clutch is released.

NOTE
If the drive plate tabs are damaged, inspect the clutch housing grooves for damage as described in this section.

   c. Measure the thickness of each drive plate (**Figure 25**) at different locations around the plate.
5. Inspect each driven plate (7, **Figure 7**) as follows:
   a. Inspect the driven plates for cracks, damage or color change. Overheated driven plates will have a blue discoloration.
   b. After washing the driven plates in solvent, check them for an oil glaze buildup. Remove by lightly sanding both sides of each plate with 400-grit sandpaper placed on a surface plate or piece of glass.
   c. Inspect the inner teeth for wear, grooves and other damage. The teeth must be able to slide smoothly on the clutch hub when the clutch is released.
   d. Check each driven plate for warp by placing it on a flat surface and measuring any gap around its perimeter with a feeler gauge.
6. Check the clutch housing (A, **Figure 26**) as follows:
   a. Inspect the clutch housing slots (**Figure 27**) for notches, grooves or other damage. Repair minor damage with a fine-cut file. If damage is excessive, replace the clutch housing. The slots must be smooth so the drive plates can move when the clutch is released.

NOTE
Filing the clutch housing slots is only a temporary fix as removing metal from the sides of the slots provides more room for the plates to move around and start wearing new grooves.

   b. Check the clutch housing bore (A, **Figure 28**) for scoring, cracks, pitting or other damage. If damage is noted, inspect the bushing (A, **Figure 29**) and needle bearing (B) for similar damage.

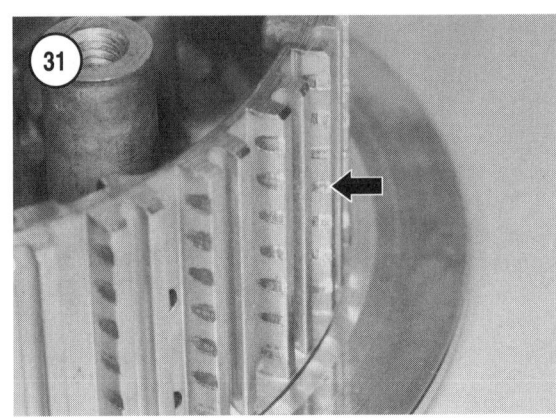

c. Check the primary driven gear (B, **Figure 28**) for excessive wear, pitting chipped gear teeth or other damage.

7. Inspect the clutch housing bushing (A, **Figure 29**) and needle bearing (B) as follows:
   a. Check the bushing for grooves, cracks and other damage. The inner and outer diameters must be smooth. Then measure the bushing's inside diameter. Replace the bushing if its inside diameter is not to specification.
   b. Inspect the needle bearing. The rollers should be smooth and polished with no flat spots, burrs or other damage. Inspect the bearing cage for cracks or other damage. Replace the bearing if necessary.

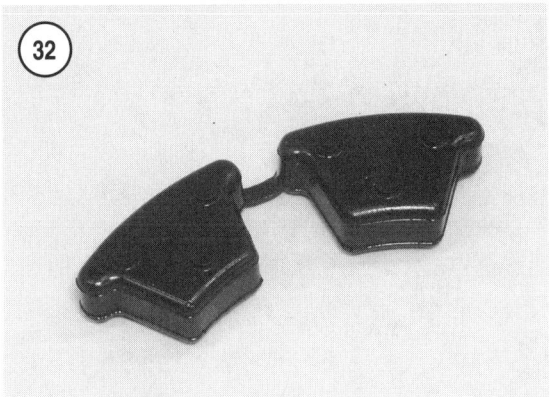

8. Measure the mainshaft outside diameter at the clutch housing bushing operating area (**Figure 30**). If out of specification, disassemble the crankcase (Chapter Five) and replace the mainshaft as described in *Transmission* in Chapter Seven.

9. Inspect the clutch hub (B, **Figure 26**) as follows:
   a. Inspect the outer splines (**Figure 31**) for rough spots, grooves or other damage. Repair minor damage with a file or oil stone. If the damage is excessive, replace the clutch hub. The splines must smooth so the driven plates can move when the clutch is released.

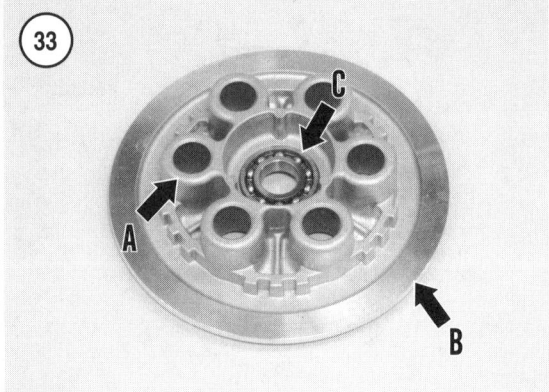

   b. Check the drive plate surface (C, **Figure 26**) for cracks and other damage. This surface must be smooth.
   c. Check for damaged spring towers and threads (D, **Figure 26**).
   d. Check the rubber dampers (**Figure 32**) for deterioration and other damage.
   e. Check the rubber damper grooves in the clutch hub and clutch hub boss (15, **Figure 7**) for damage.

10. Check the pressure plate as follows:
    a. Inspect for damaged spring towers (A, **Figure 33**).

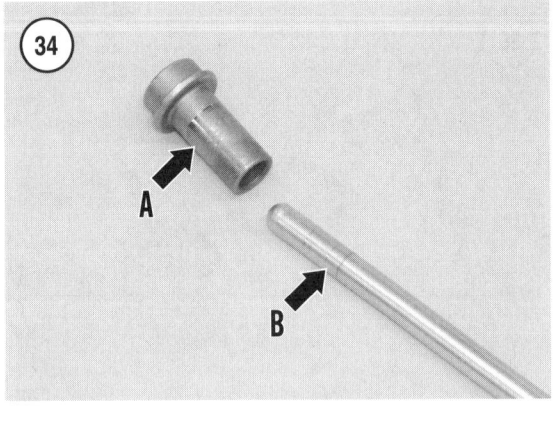

CLUTCH AND EXTERNAL SHIFT MECHANISM

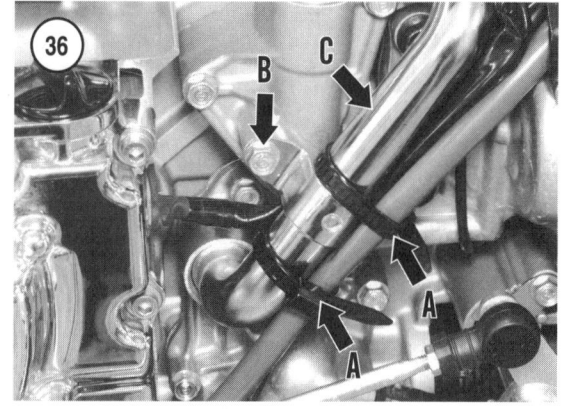

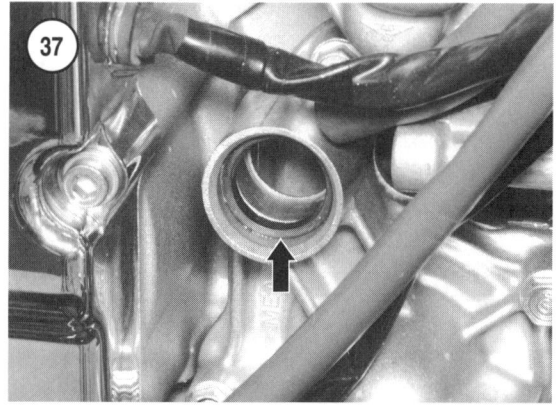

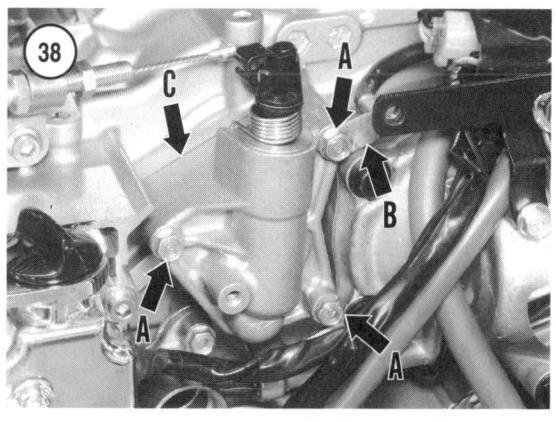

b. Check the drive plate surface (B, **Figure 33**) for cracks and other damage. This surface must be smooth.

c. Inspect the release bearing (C, **Figure 33**). Turn the bearing inner race and check for any roughness, catching or binding. The outer bearing race should fit in the plate bore without any play. If damaged, replace the bearing as described in *Bearings* in *Service Methods* in Chapter One. At the same time, check the bearing bore for cracks or damage.

11. Inspect the release rod (A, **Figure 34**) and the pushrod ends (B) for damage. Check the pushrod for straightness by rolling it on a flat surface. Replace if not straight.

12. Check all of the washers for cracks, scoring and other damage.

CLUTCH RELEASE ASSEMBLY

The clutch release assembly is mounted on the left side of the engine and can be serviced without removing the clutch.

Removal/Disassembly

1. Support the motorcycle on a stand so the seat is level.
2. Remove the left crankcase rear cover (Chapter Fifteen).
3. Drain the coolant (Chapter Three).
4. At the handlebar, loosen the clutch cable adjuster locknut.
5. At the engine, loosen the clutch cable locknut (A, **Figure 35**) and adjust nut (B) and disconnect the clutch cable from the clutch release arm.
6. Remove the two clamps (A, **Figure 36**) securing the starter cable to the water pipe.
7. Loosen the hose clamp (C, **Figure 35**) securing the water pipe to the rear cylinder coolant hose.
8. Remove the water pipe mounting bolt (B, **Figure 36**) and pull the water pipe (C) out of the water pump while disconnecting it from the rear cylinder coolant hose. Locate the O-ring installed on the lower end of the water pipe as it may instead remain in the water pump (**Figure 37**).
9. Remove the bolts (A, **Figure 38**) and ground cable (B) and the clutch release housing (C).
10. Remove the two dowel pins (A, **Figure 39**), if necessary.
11. Remove the O-ring (**Figure 40**) from the clutch release housing.
12. Turn the release arm (A, **Figure 41**) and remove the receiver (B) from the housing.

13. Pull and remove the release arm (A, **Figure 42**), tension spring (B) and washer (C) from the housing.
14. Check the seal (A, **Figure 43**) for leaks, tearing and other damage. If necessary, pry the seal out of the housing with a small screwdriver, making sure not to damage the needle bearing underneath it.
15. Inspect the needle bearings (B, **Figure 43**). The rollers should be smooth and polished with no flat spots, burrs or other damage. Insert the release arm into the bearings and turn it by hand to check the bearings. If the release arm was difficult to remove or install or turns roughly, the bearings/and or release arm are damaged. If the bearings are damaged, replace the release arm housing. The bearings are not available separately.
16. Check the release arm (A, **Figure 42**) for wear and damage. Check for wear grooves where the seal operates against the release arm. This surface should be smooth and uniform in size. Check the rivet securing the cable end for looseness or damage. The cable end should pivot smoothly with no binding, roughness or excessive play. Check the receiver shoulder in the bottom of the release arm for cracks and other damage. The surface edges on the shoulder should be sharp.
17. Check the tension spring (B, **Figure 42**) for cracked coils and damaged ends. Check the washer (C, **Figure 42**) for warp, cracks and other damage.
18. Check the receiver (B, **Figure 41**) for wear and damage.
19. Clean and dry the release arm housing assembly.

Assembly/Installation

1. Lubricate the needle bearings (B, **Figure 43**) with engine oil.
2. If removed, lubricate the lip of a new seal with grease. Then use fingers or a small socket and install the seal with its flat side facing up (A, **Figure 43**).
3. Install the tension spring and washer onto the clutch release arm. Hook the spring's curved end against the release arm as shown in **Figure 44**.

NOTE
Install the clutch release arm carefully to prevent the arm from tearing the seal.

4. Lubricate the clutch release arm with oil and insert into the seal and bearing while positioning the spring's free end against the housing shoulder as shown in **Figure 45**.
5. Lubricate the receiver (B, **Figure 41**) with oil and insert it into the housing with its open side facing out. Turn the clutch release arm (A, **Figure 41**) counterclockwise (against spring tension) until the lifter piece falls and seats into the shoulder on the clutch

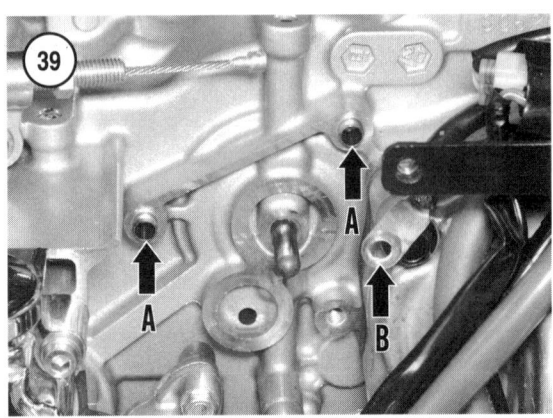

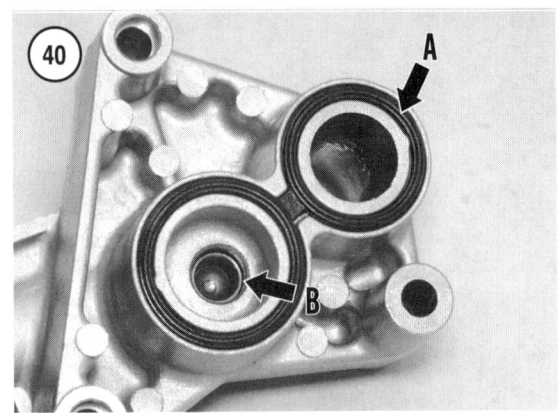

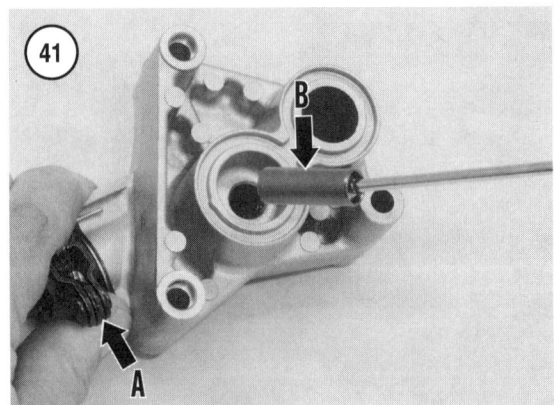

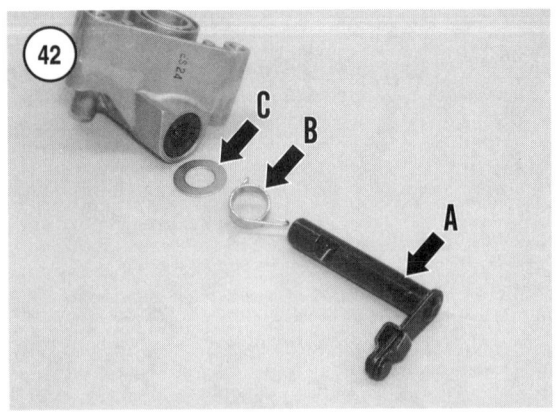

CLUTCH AND EXTERNAL SHIFT MECHANISM

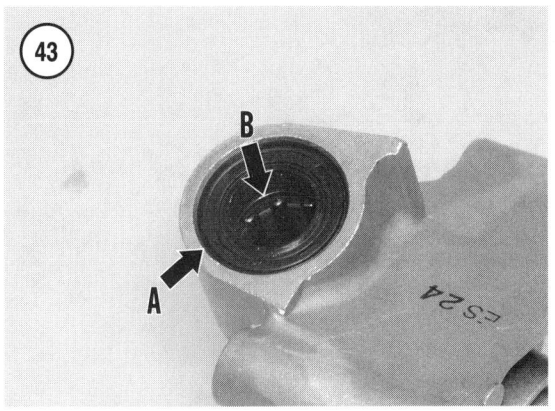

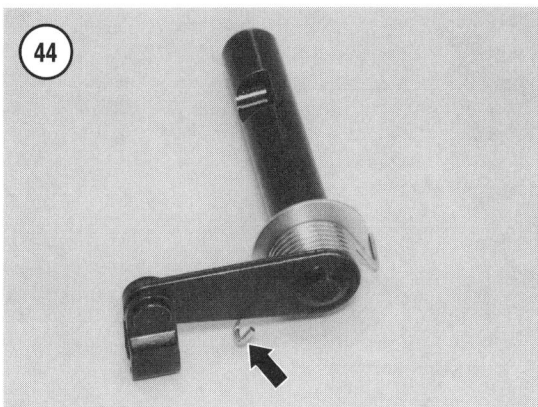

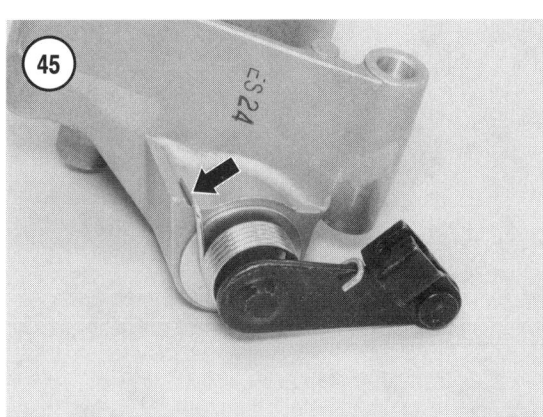

release arm, and then release the arm. When properly installed, the receiver's upper edge will be slightly below the top of the housing bore (B, **Figure 40**).

6. Lubricate a new O-ring with oil and install it into the housing groove (A, **Figure 40**).
7. Clean the ground cable end (B. **Figure 39**) with sandpaper.
8. Install the two dowel pins (A, **Figure 39**), if removed.
9. Install the clutch release arm housing (C, **Figure 38**) over the dowel pins, while making sure the pushrod enters the receiver and the O-ring stays in the housing groove.
10. Install the ground cable (B, **Figure 38**) and the mounting bolts (A). Tighten the mounting bolts securely.
11. Lubricate a new O-ring with oil and install it onto the lower end of the water pipe.
12. Install the water pipe (C, **Figure 36**) into the water pump, making sure the O-ring enters the water pump squarely. Install the water pipe's upper end into the rear cylinder coolant hose and tighten the hose clamp (C, **Figure 35**) securely.
13. Install the water pipe mounting bolt (B, **Figure 36**) and tighten securely.
14. Install the two clamps (A, **Figure 36**) around the water pipe and starter cable.
15. Reconnect the clutch cable at the clutch release arm and adjust the clutch as described in Chapter Three.
16. Fill the engine with coolant and bleed the cooling system (Chapter Three). Check the water hose for leaks.
17. Shift the transmission into neutral and start the engine. Pull the clutch in and shift the transmission into first gear, then slowly release the clutch lever to make sure the clutch releases and engages properly.
18. Install the left crankcase rear cover (Chapter Fifteen).

PRIMARY DRIVE AND DRIVEN GEARS AND OIL PUMP CHAIN AND SPROCKETS

The primary drive (A, **Figure 46**) and driven (B) gears and the oil pump chain and sprockets (C) are mounted behind the right crankcase cover. If both gear sets and the oil pump driven sprocket will be removed at the same time, loosen their fasteners first (D, E and F, **Figure 46**), and then remove the gears.

Tools

A small gear tooth holding tool is required to hold the primary gears when loosening and tightening their fasteners:

1. Gear holder, 2.5 (part No. 07724-0010100 or 07724-001A100 [A, **Figure 47**]).
2. Make a tool by cutting a section of gear teeth (B, **Figure 47**) from a discarded gear.

Primary Drive and Driven Gears
Removal/Inspection/Installation

1. Remove the right crankcase cover as described in this chapter.
2. If the primary driven gear (B, **Figure 46**) will be removed, perform the following:
   a. Remove the clutch as described in this chapter.
   b. Carefully grind the staked portion of the primary driven gear nut (**Figure 48**) with a small grinding stone to weaken it. Do not grind through the nut or the balancer shaft will be damaged.

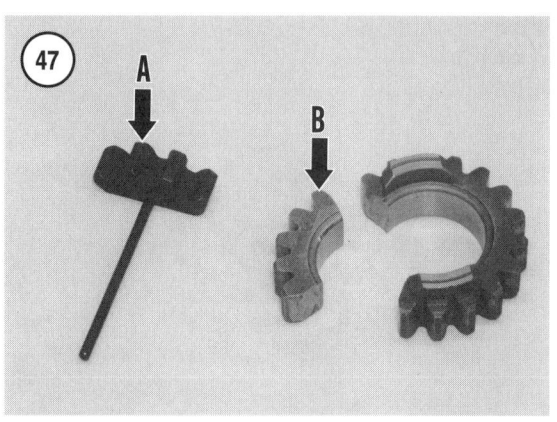

NOTE
Step 3 instructs to align the primary drive and driven gear timing marks before removing the gears. Do this if the engine will not be disassembled (crankshaft will not be turned) as it will ease installation and timing of the gears. If the engine will be disassembled (or the crankshaft turned), it is unnecessary to align the timing marks.

NOTE
If the crankshaft is difficult to turn to align the timing marks, remove one spark plug from each cylinder as described in Chapter Three.

3. Using a socket on the primary drive gear bolt, turn the crankshaft clockwise and align the timing mark on the primary drive gear with the timing mark on the primary driven gear (**Figure 49**).
4. Place the holding tool in mesh with the primary drive and driven gears as shown in **Figure 50**.
5. Loosen the primary drive gear bolt (D, **Figure 46**).
6. Remove the holding tool and place in mesh with the primary drive and driven gears as shown in **Figure 51**.
7. Loosen the primary driven gear nut (E, **Figure 46**).
8. Remove the holding tool.
9. Remove the bolt (D, **Figure 46**), washer and primary drive gear (A).
10. Remove the nut (E, **Figure 46**), washer and primary driven gear (B). Discard the nut.

11. If necessary, remove the oil pump chain and sprockets (C, **Figure 46**) as described in this section.
12. Check the primary gears for:
   a. Broken or chipped teeth.
   b. Worn or damaged internal splines.

NOTE
Do not attempt to disassemble the primary drive gear assembly. If a part on the gear is damaged, replace the primary drive gear assembly.

13. Check the primary drive gear bolt (D, **Figure 46**) and the washers for damage and replace if necessary.

CLUTCH AND EXTERNAL SHIFT MECHANISM

16. Install the primary drive gear (A, **Figure 46**) as follows:
    a. Align the gear's wide spline groove with the crankshaft's wide spline tooth (B, **Figure 52**). At the same time, align the timing marks on the primary drive and driven gears as shown in **Figure 49**. If necessary, turn the crankshaft and balancer shaft to align the timing marks.

    NOTE
    If the engine lock ups when turning the crankshaft, turn the primary driven gear to reposition the weight on the balancer shaft so the crankshaft can be turned to align the timing marks.

    b. Lubricate the primary drive gear bolt threads, washer and seating surfaces with engine oil.
    c. Install the washer and primary drive gear bolt. Tighten the bolt finger-tight.

17. Place the holding tool in mesh with the primary drive and driven gears as shown in **Figure 51** and tighten the primary drive gear bolt (D, **Figure 46**) to 138 N•m (102 ft.-lb.).

18. Remove the holding tool and place it in mesh with the primary drive and driven gears as shown in **Figure 50** and tighten the primary driven gear nut (E, **Figure 46**) to 186 N•m (137 ft.-lb.).

19. Remove the holding tool.

    CAUTION
    *Stake the nut into the groove in the balancer shaft. Do **not** stake the nut against any other part of the balancer shaft.*

20. Use a punch and stake a portion of the balancer shaft nut shoulder (**Figure 48**) into the groove in the balancer shaft.

21. If removed, install the clutch as described in this chapter.

22. Install the right crankcase cover as described in this chapter.

14. If removed, install the oil pump chain and sprockets (C, **Figure 46**) as described in this section.

15. Install the primary driven gear (B, **Figure 46**) as follows:
    a. Install the primary driven gear assembly with its smaller gear facing out and by aligning its wide spline groove with the balancer shaft's wide spline tooth (A, **Figure 52**).
    b. Install the washer with its OUT mark facing out.
    c. Lubricate the balancer shaft threads and the threads and seating surface on a new nut with engine oil and install the nut finger-tight.

Oil Pump Chain and Sprockets
Removal/Inspection/Installation

1. Remove the right crankcase cover as described in this chapter.
2. Remove the clutch as described in this chapter.
3. Loosen the oil pump driven sprocket bolt (F, **Figure 46**).
4. Remove the primary drive and driven gears as described in this section.
5. Remove the oil pump driven sprocket bolt and washer (F, **Figure 46**). The washer is permanently fixed onto the bolt. Do not attempt to remove it.

6. Remove the oil pump driven sprocket (A, **Figure 53**), drive chain (B) and oil pump drive sprocket (C) as a set.
7. Clean and dry all parts. Remove threadlocking compound residue from the oil pump driven sprocket bolt.
8. Perform the following:
   a. Check both sprockets for broken or chipped teeth.
   b. Check the drive sprocket for worn or damaged internal splines.
   c. Check the driven sprocket for a worn or damaged engagement hole.
   d. Check the drive chain for damage.
   e. If damage is noted on the drive chain or sprockets, replace all three components as a set.

9. Assemble the drive chain over the sprockets with the OUT mark on the driven sprocket (A, **Figure 54**) facing out, and the wide flat surface on the drive sprocket (B) facing out.
10. Install the sprockets and drive chain as an assembly. Align the flats on the driven sprocket and oil pump shaft, and the drive sprocket's wide spline groove (C, **Figure 54**) with the balancer shaft's wide spline tooth (A, **Figure 52**). The OUT mark on the oil pump driven sprocket must face out (D, **Figure 53**). Make sure the drive chain is running true on both sprockets.

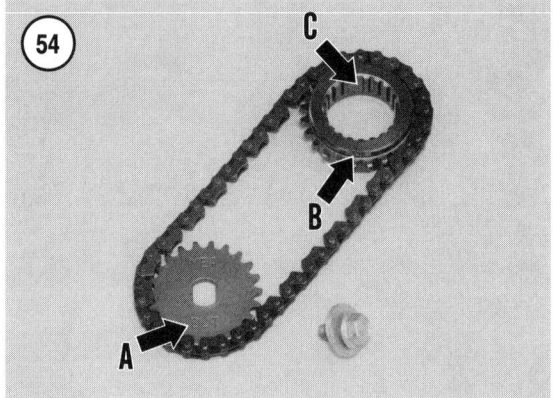

11. Apply a medium strength threadlocking compound onto the oil pump driven sprocket bolt threads and install the bolt finger-tight.
12. Install the primary driven gear as described in this section.
13. Tighten the oil pump driven sprocket bolt (F, **Figure 46**) to 18 N•m (13 ft.-lb.).
14. Install the primary drive gear as described in this section.
15. Install the clutch as described in this chapter.
16. Install the right crankcase cover as described in this chapter.

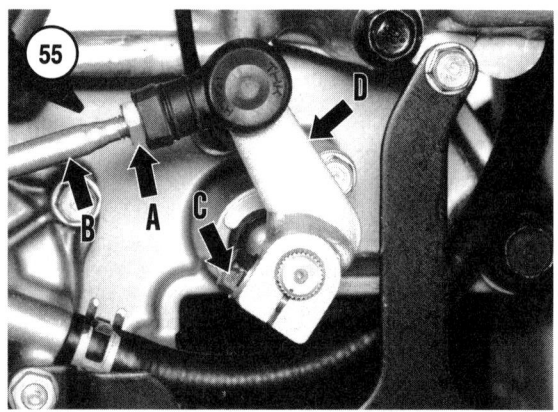

EXTERNAL SHIFT MECHANISM

The external shift mechanism consists of the shift pedal and linkage, shift shaft, stopper arm assembly and shift cam assembly. The parts serviced in this section can be removed with the engine mounted in the frame. Access to the shift drum and shift forks requires removing the engine and splitting the crankcase (Chapter Five).

Shift Linkage Adjustment

The shift pedal is connected to the shift arm with an adjustable linkage rod. Turning the linkage rod

CLUTCH AND EXTERNAL SHIFT MECHANISM

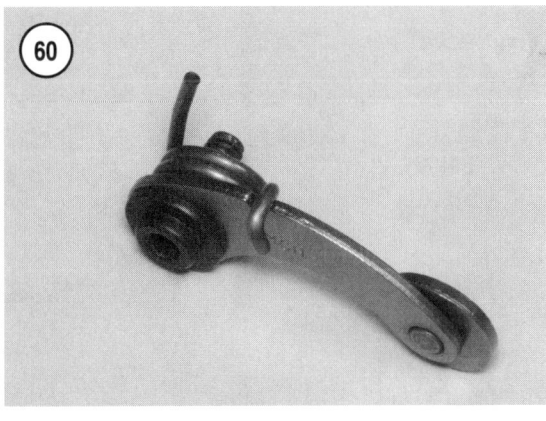

changes the shift pedal's height position, moving it closer to or farther away from your foot.

1. Remove the left crankcase rear cover (Chapter Fifteen).
2. Loosen the locknut (A, **Figure 55**) at each end of the shift linkage rod.
3. Turn the linkage rod (B, **Figure 55**) to raise or lower the shift pedal. Then hold the linkage rod with a pair of locking pliers and tighten both locknuts. Pad the locking plier jaws so the rod is not damaged.
4. Recheck the pedal position.
5. Install the left crankcase rear cover (Chapter Fifteen).

Shift Mechanism

Removal

1. Shift the transmission into neutral.
2. Remove the right crankcase cover and clutch as described in this chapter.
3. Remove the left crankcase rear cover (Chapter Fifteen).

> **NOTE**
> *If troubleshooting a shifting problem, inspect the external shift mechanism before removing it. Refer to **Gearshift Linkage** in Chapter Two.*

4. Remove the pinch bolt (C, **Figure 55**) and slide the shift arm (D) off the shift shaft.
5. Remove the shift shaft (A, **Figure 56**) and thrust washer (B) from the engine.

> **NOTE**
> *Cover the area underneath the shift cam to prevent the dowel pin located behind the shift cam from falling into the engine.*

6. Turn the shift cam Allen bolt (A, **Figure 57**) counterclockwise until the shift cam stops, then loosen and remove the Allen bolt.
7. Remove the shift cam (B, **Figure 57**) and dowel pin (A, **Figure 58**).
8. Remove the bolt (B, **Figure 58**), stopper arm (C), washer and return spring.
9. Inspect the components as described in this section.

Installation

1. Install the stopper arm assembly (**Figure 59**) as follows:
   a. Assemble the stopper arm as shown in **Figure 60**. Install the washer between the stopper arm and spring.

b. Install the stopper arm as shown in C, **Figure 58**. Finger-tighten the stopper arm pivot bolt while making sure the spring is aligned around the bolt's shoulder and against the crankcase.

c. Pry the stopper arm with a screwdriver, and then release it. When properly installed, the stopper arm will move and return under spring tension. If the stopper arm will not move, the spring is pinched against the shoulder on the pivot bolt. Loosen the bolt to center the stopper arm on the bolt's shoulder. Tighten the stopper arm pivot bolt (B, **Figure 58**) to 12 N•m (106 in.-lb.).

2. Install the shift cam as follows:
   a. Apply a medium strength threadlocking compound onto the shift cam Allen bolt threads. Set the bolt nearby for installation later.
   b. Insert the dowel pin (A, **Figure 58**) into the shift drum hole.
   c. Raise the stopper arm with a screwdriver, and then install the shift cam by aligning the cam's notch identified in **Figure 61** with the dowel pin. Install the shift cam and hold in position, then release the stopper arm. Do not release the shift cam.
   d. Install and tighten the shift cam Allen bolt (A, **Figure 57**) to 23 N•m (17 ft.-lb.).

3. Install the shift shaft as follows:
   a. On the left side of the engine, clean the shift shaft oil seal and lubricate the seal lips with grease.
   b. Install the thrust washer (B, **Figure 56**) onto the shift shaft (A).
   c. Slowly install the shift shaft through the engine and seal while centering the return spring (C, **Figure 56**) around the spring pin (D), then push the shaft until it bottoms against and engages with the shift cam. Refer to **Figure 62**.

4. Install the shift arm by aligning its groove with the punch mark on the end of the shift shaft (**Figure 63**). Install the pinch bolt (C, **Figure 55**) and tighten to 12 N•m (106 in.-lb.).

5. Support the motorcycle with the rear wheel off the ground and check the shifting as follows:
   a. Mount a plate across the crankcase to hold the shift shaft in position (**Figure 64**).
   b. Slowly turn the rear wheel and shift the transmission into first gear, then shift to neutral and the remaining forward gears.

NOTE
Figure 65 shows the shift cam in neutral.

c. If the shift shaft moves and then locks in place, the return spring may not be centered on the spring pin.

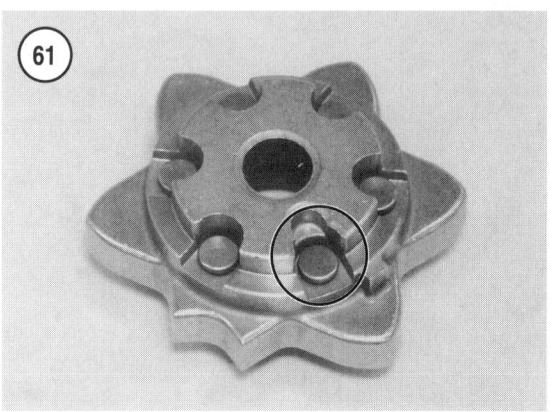

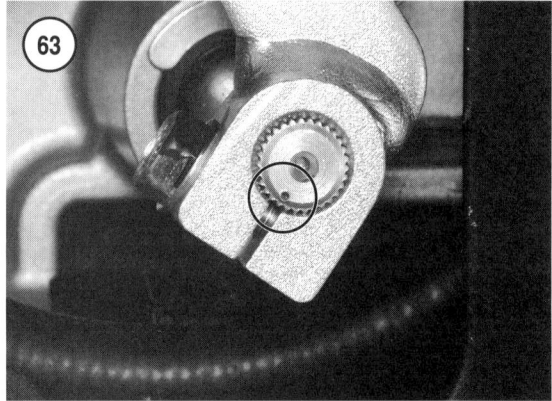

CLUTCH AND EXTERNAL SHIFT MECHANISM

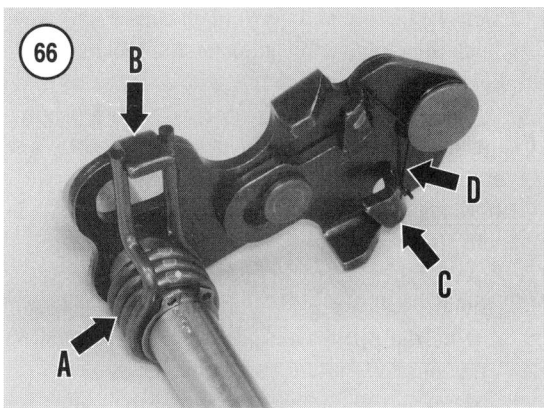

d. If the transmission over-shifts, check for an incorrectly assembled stopper arm assembly.
e. If the transmission does not shift properly, check for an incorrectly installed shift shaft return spring. Then check the shift lever assembly.
f. Remove the plate (**Figure 64**).

6. Install the clutch and right crankcase cover as described in this chapter.
7. Install the left crankcase rear cover as described in Chapter Fifteen.

Inspection

Worn or damaged shift linkage components will cause missed shifts and wear to the transmission gears, shift forks and shift drum. Replace parts that show excessive wear or damage.

1. Clean and dry the parts. Remove all threadlocking compound residue from the shift cam Allen bolt threads.
2. Inspect the shift shaft assembly (**Figure 66**) as follows:
   a. Inspect the splines for damage.
   b. Inspect the shaft for straightness.
   c. Inspect the return spring (A, **Figure 66**) for damage.
   d. Make sure the return spring is positioned correctly (B, **Figure 66**).
   e. Inspect the shift pawl (C, **Figure 66**) for excessive wear or damage.
   f. Inspect the tension spring (D, **Figure 66**) for damage.
3. Check the stopper arm (**Figure 59**) assembly for:
   a. Weak or damaged return spring.
   b. Bent, cracked or damaged stopper arm. Check roller for flat spots.
   c. Pivot bolt and washer damage.
4. Check the shift cam (**Figure 67**) as follows:
   a. Inspect the ramps in the front side of the cam for wear and damage. If the sides of the ramps are rounded or damaged, the stopper arm roller can slip and the transmission will jump out of gear.
   b. Inspect the pins in the front side of the shift cam. The pins must not be worn or shifting will be incorrect.
   c. Inspect the dowel pin for damage.
   d. Inspect the Allen bolt for damage.

CLUTCH CABLE

Removal/Installation

1. Note the original clutch cable routing (**Figure 68**, typical) from the handlebar cable adjuster to the

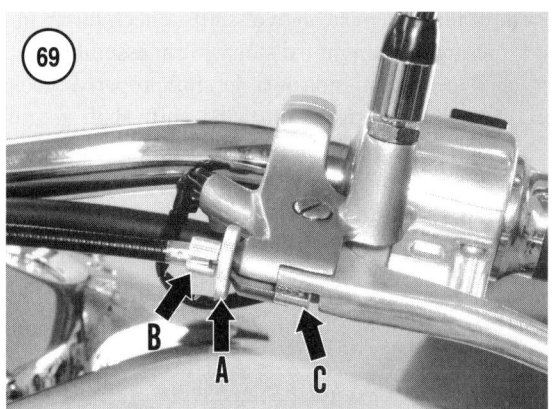
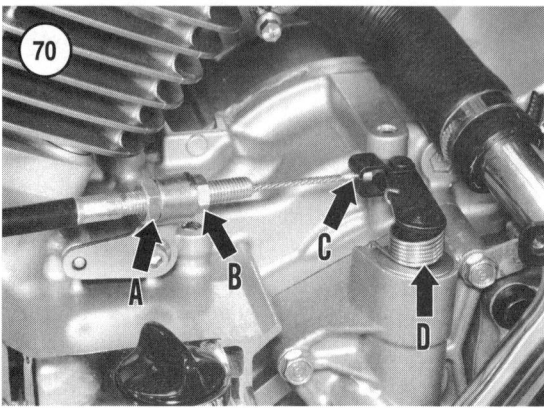

clutch release lever so the new cable can be routed correctly.

NOTE
If it seems the clutch cable routing is incorrect, ask a dealership service department about the correct routing.

2. At the handlebar, loosen the clutch cable adjuster locknut (A, **Figure 69**) and turn the adjuster (B) to loosen the cable. Align the locknut and adjuster slots with the clutch lever bracket and clutch lever slots (C, **Figure 69**).
3. At the clutch release housing, loosen the locknut (A, **Figure 70**) and the adjust nut (B). Then remove the cable from the adjust bracket and disconnect the cable from the clutch release lever (C, **Figure 70**).
4. Disconnect the clutch cable at the upper adjuster.
5. Open the two cable guides on the frame's left down tube and remove the clutch cable.
6. Compare the old and new clutch cables.
7. Check the clutch cable adjuster and locknut at the handlebar and replace if damaged.
8. Install the original clutch cable locknut (A, **Figure 70**) and adjust nut (B) onto the new clutch cable. The locknut is larger and should be installed first.
9. Lubricate the new clutch cable as described in Chapter Three.
10. Reverse these steps to install the new clutch cable. Note the following:
   a. Wipe the upper cable end with grease before reconnecting it at the clutch lever.
   b. Make sure the tension spring at the clutch release lever is attached between the housing shoulder and clutch release lever as shown in D, **Figure 70**.
   c. Make sure each cable end is properly seated.
   d. Adjust the clutch cable and check the clutch operation as described in Chapter Three.

Table 1 CLUTCH SPECIFICATIONS

	New mm (in.)	Service limit mm (in.)
Clutch housing bushing inside diameter	27.995-28.012 (1.1022-1.1028)	28.80 (1.134)
Drive plate thickness	3.72-3.88 (0.146-0.153)	3.10 (0.122)
Driven plate warp	—	0.30 (0.012)
Mainshaft outside diameter at clutch housing bushing	27.980-27.993 (1.1016-1.1021)	27.97 (1.101)
Spring free length	58.2 (2.29)	56.7 (2.23)

CLUTCH AND EXTERNAL SHIFT MECHANISM

Table 2 CLUTCH TORQUE SPECIFICATIONS

	N•m	in.-lb.	ft.-lb.
Clutch cover bolt	10	88	–
Clutch nut*	186	–	137
Clutch spring bolt	12	106	–
Oil pump driven sprocket bolt*	18	–	13
Primary drive gear bolt*	138	–	102
Primary driven gear nut*	186	–	137
Shift arm pinch bolt	12	106	–
Shift cam Allen bolt*	23	–	17
Stopper arm pivot bolt	12	106	–
Timing hole cap cover Allen bolt	10	88	–

*Refer to text for additional information.

CHAPTER SEVEN

TRANSMISSION AND INTERNAL SHIFT MECHANISM

This chapter describes disassembly and reassembly of the mainshaft and internal shift mechanism. The countershaft is part of the output gear assembly and is removed during engine disassembly and reassembly as described in *Crankcase* in Chapter Five. Countershaft inspection is covered in this chapter.

Refer to Chapter Two for transmission troubleshooting.

Tables 1-4 are at the end of the chapter.

TRANSMISSION

Operation

The engine is equipped with a 5-speed constant-mesh transmission. The gears on the mainshaft (A, **Figure 1**) are meshed with the gears on the countershaft (B). Each pair of meshed gears represents one gear ratio. For each pair of gears, one of the gears freewheels on its shaft. Next to each freewheeling gear is a gear that is splined to the shaft. Each splined gear can slide on the shaft and lock onto the freewheeling gear, making that gear ratio active. Any time the transmission is in gear, one pair of meshed gears are locked to their shafts, and that gear ratio is selected. All other meshed gears are freewheeling, making those ratios inoperative.

To engage and disengage the various gear ratios, the splined gears are moved by shift forks. The shift forks are guided by grooves in the shift drum, which is operated by a shift pedal and linkage assembly. As the transmission is upshifted and downshifted, the shift drum rotates and guides the forks to engage and disengage pairs of gears on the transmission shafts.

Removal/Installation

The engine crankcase must be split to remove the transmission and shift assemblies (**Figure 1**). The mainshaft (A, **Figure 1**) is removed as a complete assembly. The countershaft gears (B, **Figure 1**) are removed from the countershaft, which is part of the output gear assembly, before the output gear assembly is removed from the engine. Refer to *Crankcase* in Chapter Five.

Service

1. Clean and dry the mainshaft assembly before disassembly. The countershaft gears were removed from the countershaft during engine disassembly (Chapter Five) and should be cleaned separately.

TRANSMISSION AND INTERNAL SHIFT MECHANISM

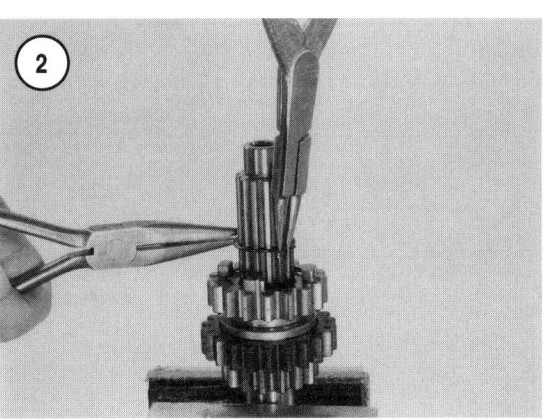

2. As the mainshaft is disassembled, store the individual parts in a divided container, or make an identification mark on each part to indicate orientation. Use marking pens, such as those made by Speedry, to identify gears and other metal parts. These pens can be purchased in different colors at tool and bearing supply stores.

3. Install new mainshaft snap rings during reassembly. The snap rings will fatigue and distort when they are removed. Do not reuse them, although they may appear to be in good condition.

4. To install new snap rings without distorting them, use the following installation technique:
   a. Open the new snap ring with a pair of snap ring pliers while holding the back of the snap ring with a pair of pliers (**Figure 2**).
   b. Slide the snap ring down the shaft and seat it into its correct groove.
   c. This technique can also be used to remove the snap rings from a shaft once they are free from their grooves.

Mainshaft

Refer to **Figure 3**.

Disassembly

1. Remove the thrust washer.
2. Remove fifth gear and its bushing.
3. Remove the spline washer and snap ring.
4. Remove second/third gear.
5. Remove the snap ring and spline washer.
6. Remove fourth gear and its bushing.

> *NOTE*
> *First gear is an integral part of the mainshaft.*

7. Inspect the mainshaft assembly as described in *Inspection* in this section.

Assembly

Before beginning assembly, have two new snap rings on hand. Throughout the procedure, the orientation of parts is made in relationship to first gear (A, **Figure 4**), which is part of the mainshaft.

> *CAUTION*
> *The snap rings and washers used on the mainshaft are stamped types. One edge is rounded, while the other is sharp. The side with the sharp edge, referred to as the flat side, must be installed so the flat side always faces away from the part producing the thrust. The sharp edge prevents the snap ring from rolling out of its groove when thrust is applied. Refer to **Figure 3** and **Figure 5**.*

1. Clean and dry all parts before assembly. Lubricate the bushing surfaces with a 1:1 solution of molybdenum oil and engine oil. Lubricate all other parts with engine oil.

2. Install fourth gear (B, **Figure 4**) and its bushing (C) on the mainshaft. The gear dogs (**Figure 6**) on fourth gear must face away from first gear.

> *CAUTION*
> *Install the snap ring so its ends align with a groove in the splines (**Figure 7** and **Figure 8**).*

3. Install the spline washer (D, **Figure 4**) and a new snap ring (E) onto the shaft. The flat side of both parts must face away from first gear. The snap ring must seat fully in the groove in the shaft.

4. Install second/third gear so the larger gear (A, **Figure 9**) faces toward first gear. Align the oil hole in the gear's shift fork groove (B, **Figure 9**) with the oil hole in the shaft (C).

5. Install a new snap ring into the shaft groove (**Figure 10**) so that its flat side faces toward first gear.

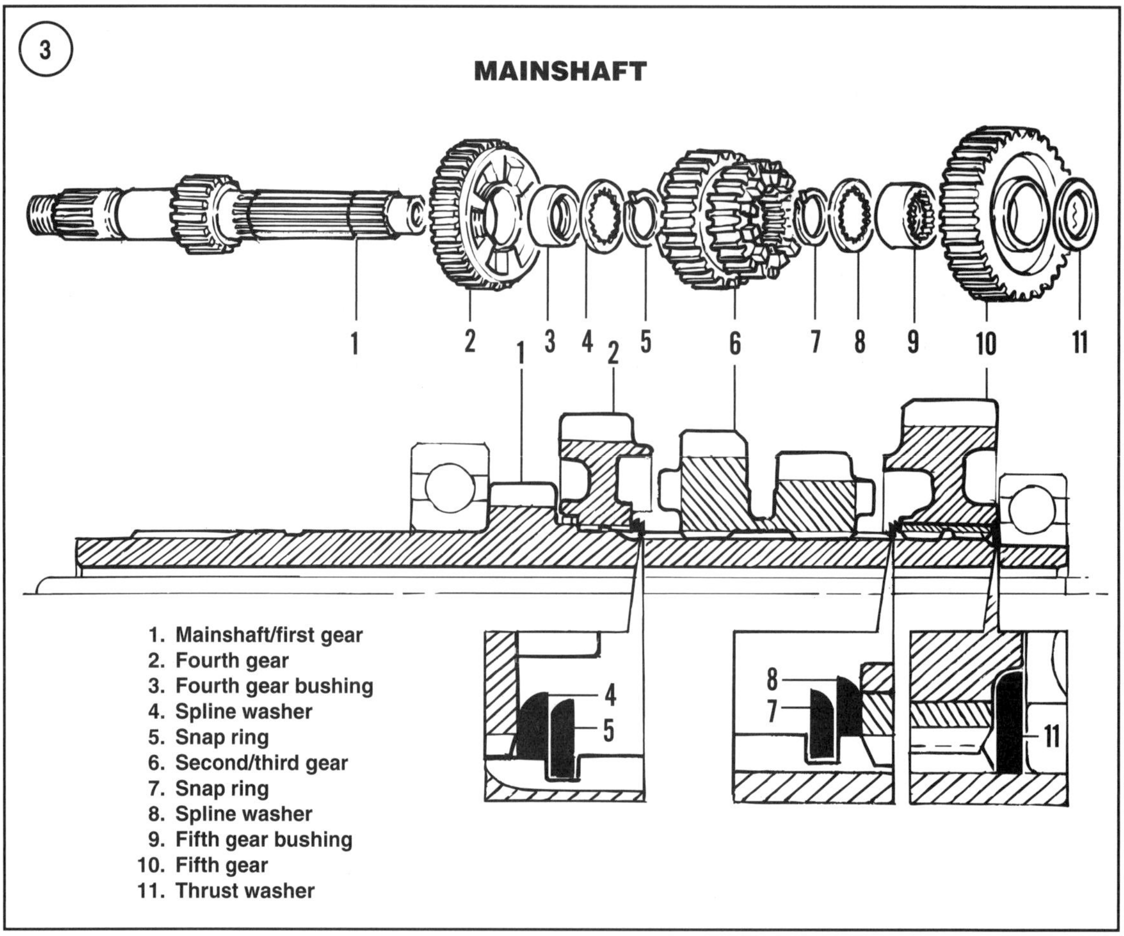

MAINSHAFT

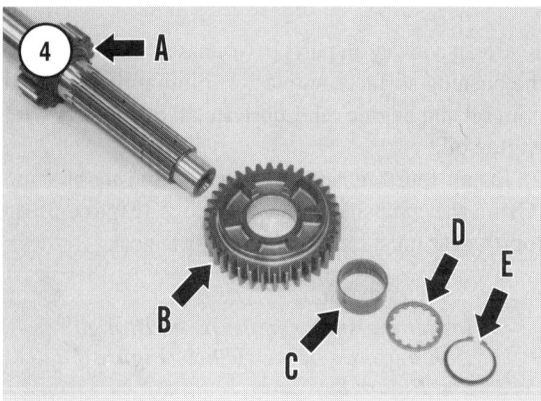

1. Mainshaft/first gear
2. Fourth gear
3. Fourth gear bushing
4. Spline washer
5. Snap ring
6. Second/third gear
7. Snap ring
8. Spline washer
9. Fifth gear bushing
10. Fifth gear
11. Thrust washer

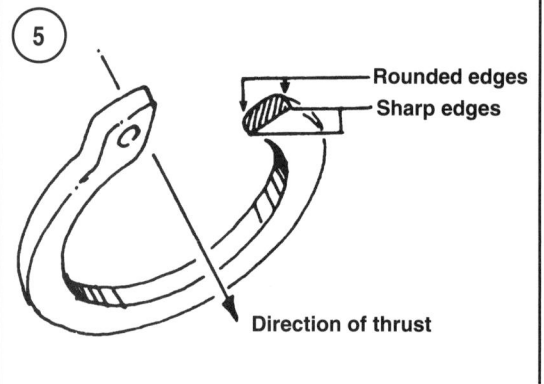

CAUTION
*Install the snap ring so its ends align with a groove in the splines (**Figure 8**).*

6. Install the spline washer (A, **Figure 11**) and seat it against the snap ring so its flat side faces toward first gear.

7. Install the fifth gear bushing (B, **Figure 11**) and seat it against the snap ring. Align the oil hole in the bushing (A, **Figure 12**) with the oil hole in the shaft (B).

8. Install fifth gear (C, **Figure 11**) so that its closed side faces away from first gear. Refer to A, **Figure 13**.

9. Install the thrust washer (D, **Figure 11**) and seat it against fifth gear so that its round side faces toward first gear. Refer to B, **Figure 13**.

10. Refer to **Figure 3** and **Figure 14** for the correct placement of the mainshaft gears, snap rings and washers.

11. Wrap a heavy rubber band around the end of the shaft to prevent parts from sliding off the shaft.

TRANSMISSION AND INTERNAL SHIFT MECHANISM

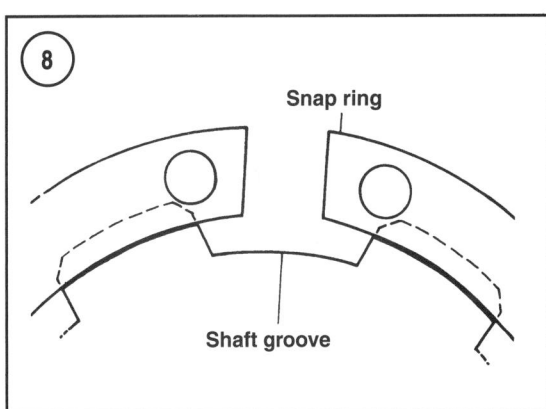

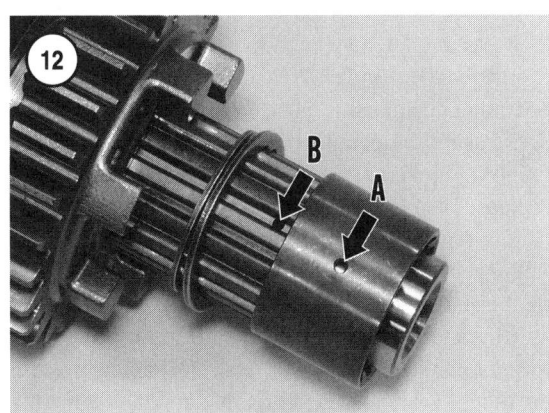

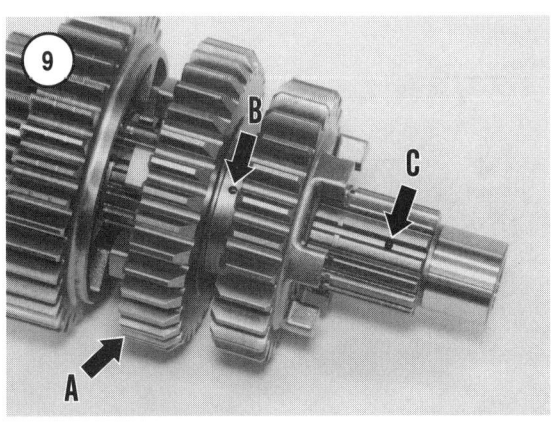

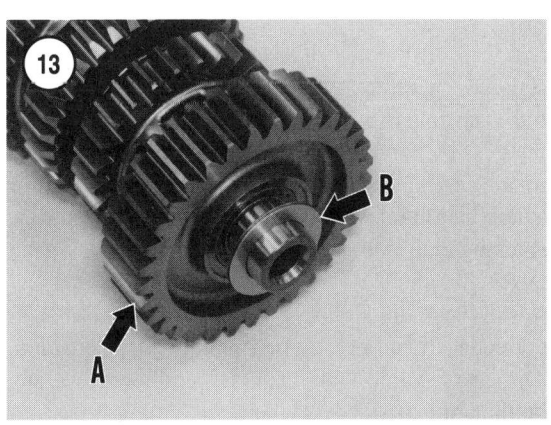

Countershaft

The countershaft (**Figure 15**) is mounted on the output gear assembly. The countershaft assembly (B, **Figure 1**) is disassembled and assembled onto the countershaft while the output gear assembly is mounted on the engine. Refer to *Crankcase* in Chapter Five. Inspect the countershaft and gears as described in this section.

Inspection

When measuring the transmission components in this section, compare the actual measurements to the specifications in **Table 2** and **Table 3**. Replace parts that are worn or damaged.

> *NOTE*
> *Maintain the alignment of the transmission components when cleaning and inspecting the parts in this section.*

1. Inspect the mainshaft (**Figure 16**) and countershaft (**Figure 15**) for:
   a. Worn or damaged splines.
   b. Missing, broken or chipped first gear teeth (A, **Figure 16**) on the mainshaft.
   c. Worn or damaged bearing surfaces.
   d. Cracked or rounded-off snap ring grooves.
2. Measure the mainshaft outside diameter at its fourth gear (B, **Figure 16**) and clutch outer guide (C) operating positions.
3. Measure the countershaft outside diameter at its first (A, **Figure 17**) and second/third (B) gear operating positions. If either measurement is out of specification, replace the output gear assembly (C, **Figure 17**). Replacement parts are not available to overhaul the assembly.
4. Check each gear for excessive wear, burrs, pitting, or chipped or missing teeth. Check the splines on sliding gears and the bore on stationary gears for excessive wear or damage.
5. To check stationary gears for wear, install them and their bushing on their correct shaft and in their original operating position. If necessary, use the old snap rings to secure them in place. Then spin the gear by hand. The gear should turn smoothly. A rough turning gear indicates heat damage. Check for a dark blue color or galling on the operating surfaces. Rocking indicates excessive wear, either to the gear, bushing or shaft.
6. To check the sliding gears, install them on their correct shaft and in their original operating position. The gears should slide back and forth without any binding or excessive play.

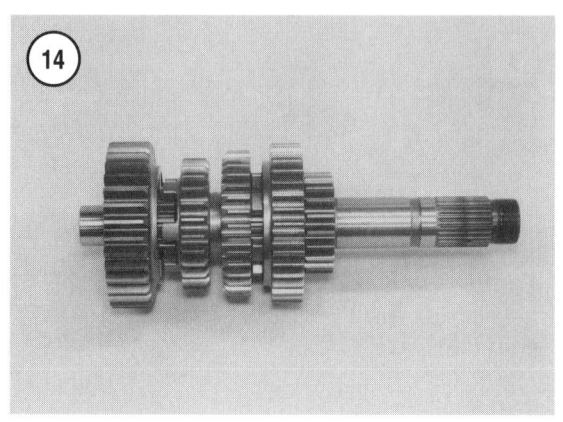

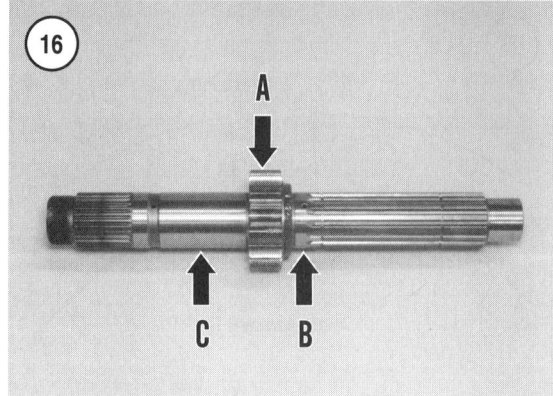

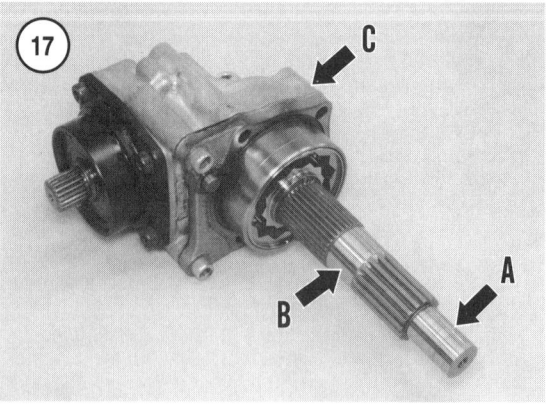

TRANSMISSION AND INTERNAL SHIFT MECHANISM

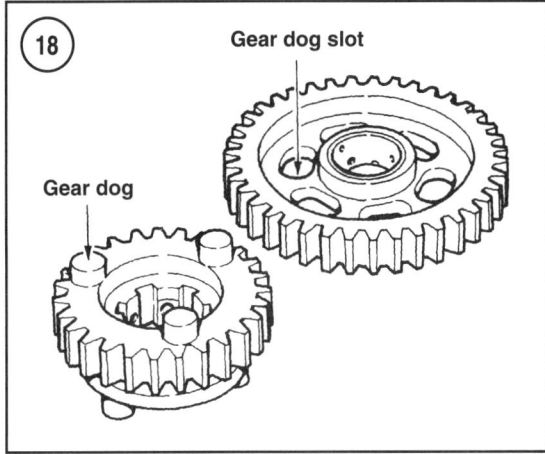

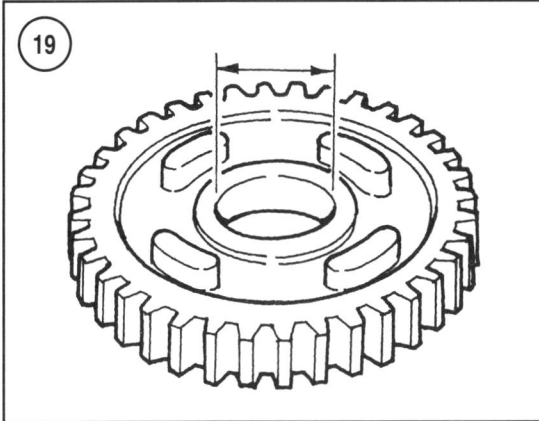

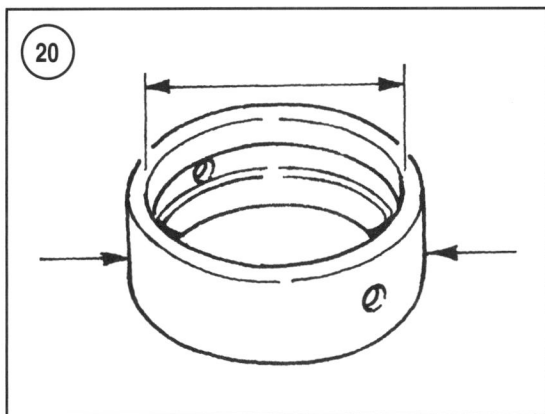

NOTE
The side of the gear dogs that carries the engine load will wear and eventually become rounded. The unloaded side of the dogs remains unworn. Rounded dogs cause the transmission to jump out of gear.

7. Check the dogs and dog slots (**Figure 18**) on the gears for excessive wear, rounding, cracks or other damage. Any wear on the dogs and mating recesses should be uniform. If the dogs are not worn evenly, the remaining dogs will be overstressed and possibly fail.

8. Check engaging gears by installing both gears on their respective shafts and in their original operating position, and then twist the gears together to engage the dogs. Check for positive engagement in both directions. If damage is evident, also inspect the condition of the shift forks, as described in this chapter.

9. Check for worn or damaged shift fork grooves. Check the gear groove and its mating shift fork.

10. Measure the mainshaft fourth and fifth gear inside diameters (**Figure 19**).

11. Measure the countershaft first and second/third gear inside diameters (**Figure 19**).

12. Check the bushings for:
   a. Severely worn or damaged bearing surface.
   b. Worn or damaged splines or bore.
   c. Cracked or scored gear bore (on the mating gear).

13. Measure the mainshaft fourth and fifth gear bushing outside diameters. Also measure the fourth gear bushing inside diameter (**Figure 20**).

14. Measure the countershaft first and second/third gear bushing inside and outside diameters (**Figure 20**).

15. Using the measurements recorded in the previous steps, determine the bushing-to-shaft and gear-to-bushing clearances specified in **Table 2** (mainshaft) and **Table 3** (countershaft). Replace worn parts to correct any clearance not within specification. Though they may not show equal wear or damaged, always replace defective gears and their mating gear at the same time.

16. Inspect the spline washers. The teeth in the washer should be uniform.

17. Inspect the thrust washers. The washers should be smooth and not worn or heat damaged (bluing).

INTERNAL SHIFT MECHANISM

As the transmission is upshifted and downshifted, the shift drum and fork assembly engages and disengages pairs of gears on the transmission shafts. Gear shifting is controlled by the shift forks, which are guided by cam grooves in the shift drum.

The shift drum grooves, shift forks and mating gear grooves must be in good condition. Too much wear between the parts will cause poor engagement of the gears. This can lead to premature wear of the gear dogs and other parts.

Shift Drum Inspection

1. Clean and dry the shift drum.

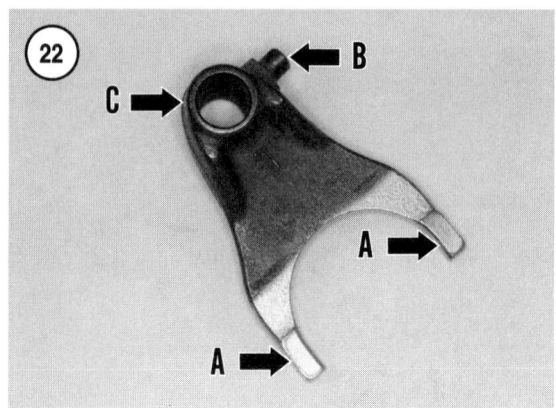

2. Check the shift drum (**Figure 21**) for wear and damage as follows:
   a. The shift drum grooves should be a uniform width. Worn grooves can prevent complete gear engagement, which can cause rough shifting and allow the transmission to disengage.
   b. Check the journal. The journal surface must not be worn or show overheating discoloration due to lack of lubrication.

Shift Fork and Shaft Inspection

Refer to **Table 4**. Replace the shift forks and shaft if out of specification or if they show damage as described in this section.

1. Inspect each shift fork (**Figure 22**) for wear or damage. Examine the shift fork claw where it contacts the slider gear (A, **Figure 22**). These surfaces must be smooth without excessive wear, bending, cracks, heat discoloration or other damage.
2. Check each shift fork for arc-shaped wear or burn marks. These marks indicate a bent shift fork.
3. The guide pin (B, **Figure 22**) should be symmetrical and not flat on the sides.

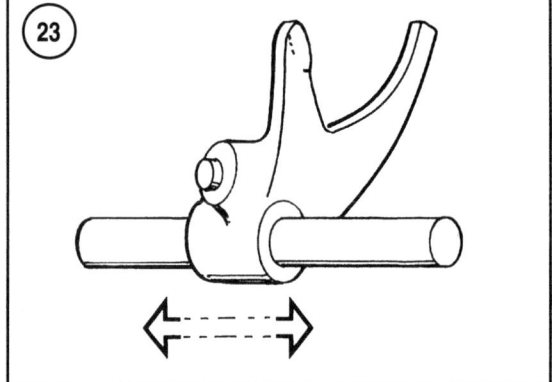

4. Check the shift fork shafts for bending or other damage. Install each shift fork on the shaft and slide it back and forth (**Figure 23**). Each shift fork must slide smoothly with no binding or tight spots. If any fork binds, check the shaft for bending.
5. Measure the thickness of each shift fork claw (A, **Figure 22**).
6. Measure the inside diameter (C, **Figure 22**) of each shift fork.
7. Inspect the shift fork shaft for wear and damage. Measure the shift fork shaft outside diameter.

Table 1 TRANSMISSION SPECIFICATIONS

Transmission type	5-speed, constant mesh
Shift pattern	1-N-2-3-4-5
Primary reduction	1.935 (60/31)
Secondary reduction (output drive)	0.944 (17/18)
Final reduction ratio	2.818 (31/11)
Gear ratios	
First gear	1.900 (38/20)
Second gear	
2003-2007 models	1.148 (31/27)
2008-on models	1.231 (32/26)
Third gear	0.912 (31/34)
Fourth gear	0.778 (28/36)
Fifth gear	0.697 (23/33)

TRANSMISSION AND INTERNAL SHIFT MECHANISM

Table 2 MAINSHAFT SERVICE SPECIFICATIONS

	New mm (in.)	Service limit mm (in.)
Bushing inside diameter		
Fourth gear	27.985-28.006 (1.1018-1.1025)	28.03 (1.104)
Bushing outside diameter		
Fourth and fifth gear	30.950-30.975 (1.2185-1.2195)	30.94 (1.218)
Bushing-to-shaft clearance		
Fourth gear	0.005-0.047 (0.0002-0.0019)	0.067 (0.0026)
Gear inside diameter		
Fourth and fifth gear	31.000-31.025 (1.2205-1.2215)	31.035 (1.2218)
Gear-to-bushing clearance		
Fourth and fifth gear	0.025-0.075 (0.0010-0.0030)	0.095 (0.0037)
Mainshaft outside diameter		
Clutch outer guide position	27.980-27.993 (1.1016-1.1021)	27.970 (1.1012)
Fourth gear position	27.959-27.980 (1.1007-1.1016)	27.940 (1.1000)

Table 3 COUNTERSHAFT SERVICE SPECIFICATIONS

	New mm (in.)	Service limit mm (in.)
Bushing inside diameter		
First gear	22.050-22.150 (0.8681-0.8720)	22.170 (0.8728)
Second/third gear	30.000-30.030 (1.1811-1.1823)	30.050 (1.1831)
Bushing outside diameter		
First gear	25.987-26.000 (1.0231-1.0236)	25.977 (1.0227)
Second/third gear	32.950-32.965 (1.2972-1.2978)	32.94 (1.297)
Bushing-to-shaft clearance		
First gear	0.057-0.170 (0.0022-0.0067)	0.190 (0.0075)
Second/third gear	0.020-0.071 (0.0008-0.0028)	0.091 (0.0036)
Gear inside diameter		
First gear	30.000-30.025 (1.1811-1.1821)	30.035 (1.1825)
Second/third gear	33.000-33.025 (1.2992-1.3002)	33.035 (1.3006)
Gear-to-bushing clearance		
Second and third gear	0.035-0.075 (0.0014-0.0030)	0.095 (0.0037)
Countershaft outside diameter		
First gear position	21.980-21.993 (0.8654-0.8659)	21.97 (0.865)
Second/third gear position	29.959-29.980 (1.1795-1.1803)	29.94 (1.179)

Table 4 SHIFT FORK AND SHIFT SHAFT SERVICE SPECIFICATIONS

	New mm (in.)	Service limit mm (in.)
Shift fork claw thickness	5.93-6.00 (0.233-0.236)	5.83 (0.230)
	(continued)	

Table 4 SHIFT FORK AND SHIFT SHAFT SERVICE SPECIFICATIONS (continued)

	New mm (in.)	Service limit mm (in.)
Shift fork inside diameter	14.000-14.018 (0.5512-0.5519)	14.04 (0.553)
Shift fork shaft outside diameter	13.966-13.984 (0.5498-0.5506)	13.956 (0.5494)

CHAPTER EIGHT

FUEL AND EMISSION CONTROL SYSTEMS

This chapter services the fuel tank, air filter housing, fuel tank, carburetor, fuel pump and fuel filter (2003 VTX1300S models) and emission control system.

Refer to Chapter Three for air filter service, throttle cable adjustment and lubrication.

Before working on the fuel system, refer to *Safety* in Chapter One.

Tables 1-3 are at the end of the chapter.

FUEL SYSTEM DIFFERENCES

On 2003 VTX1300S models, a fuel pump assembly was used to supply fuel to the carburetor. 2004-on models use a vacuum operated fuel valve assembly.

Major differences are noted in the procedures. Minor differences not shown in all of the photographs include the type and number of hoses used and their routing, which can affect service procedures. Before and during the procedure, take notes and photographs to identify hoses before disconnecting them. Also, use a vacuum hose identifier kit to identify hoses and connection points before disconnecting them. A typical kit is described in *Preliminary Information* in *Engine* Chapter Five.

FUEL TANK

Draining Fuel Tank

The fuel tank can be drained while installed on the motorcycle. A vacuum pump is required on 2004-on models.

1. Disconnect the negative battery cable (Chapter Nine).
2. Turn off the fuel valve (A, **Figure 1**).
3. Disconnect the fuel hose (B, **Figure 1**) at the fuel valve. Then connect a length of hose onto the fuel valve (A, **Figure 2**) and insert the other end into a fuel storage can.
4. On 2004-on models, disconnect the vacuum hose (C, **Figure 1**) at the fuel valve and connect a vacuum pump onto the fuel valve vacuum hose fitting (B, **Figure 2**). Operate the vacuum pump to apply a vacuum at the fuel valve.
5. Turn the fuel valve to its reserve position to drain the fuel tank.
6. Turn off the fuel valve and disconnect the vacuum pump, if used.
7. Reconnect the hose(s).
8. Reconnect the negative battery cable (Chapter Nine).

Removal/Installation

1. Remove the seat (Chapter Fifteen).
2. Disconnect the negative battery cable (Chapter Nine).
3. Turn off the fuel valve (A, **Figure 1**).
4. If necessary, drain the fuel tank as described in this section. Handling the fuel tank will be easier during removal and installation.
5. Remove the right front cylinder head shroud (Chapter Fifteen).
6. Remove the fuel tank mounting bolt (**Figure 3**), washer and collar.
7. Disconnect the fuel hose (B, **Figure 1**) at the fuel valve.
8. On 2004-on models, disconnect the vacuum hose (C, **Figure 1**) at the fuel valve.
9. Lift the rear of the fuel tank and disconnect the breather (49-state models) or No. 1 (California models) hose (**Figure 4**).
10. Disconnect the two speedometer 7-pin connectors (**Figure 5**) underneath the right front side of the fuel tank.
11. Lift the rear of the fuel tank slightly and slide it back and off the frame.
12. Installation is the reverse of these steps, plus the following:
    a. Make sure a rubber damper is installed on each side of the frame and at the rear of the fuel tank. Replace any rubber damper that is deteriorated or damaged.
    b. Make sure the instrument panel wiring harness is routed through the guide on the fuel tank (**Figure 6**).
    c. Tighten the fuel tank mounting bolt (**Figure 3**) to 19 N•m (14 ft.-lb.).
    d. Refill the fuel tank if previously drained.
    e. On 2003 models, turn on the ignition switch. Then turn on the fuel valve and check for fuel leaks.
    f. On 2004-on models, check for fuel leaks.
    g. Turn on the ignition switch (if off) and make sure the fuel gauge is registering the amount of fuel in the tank.
    h. Turn off the ignition switch.

FUEL VALVE

Troubleshooting (2004-On Models)

Fuel valve operation is controlled by vacuum, which is relayed by a hose connected between the intake manifold and fuel valve. Vacuum is present when the engine is being started and when the engine is running. If there is a fuel supply problem, test the fuel valve as follows:

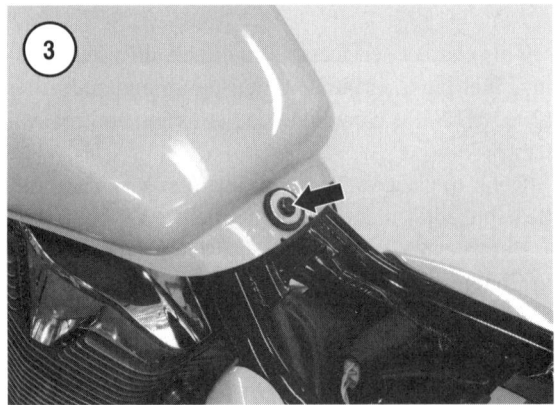

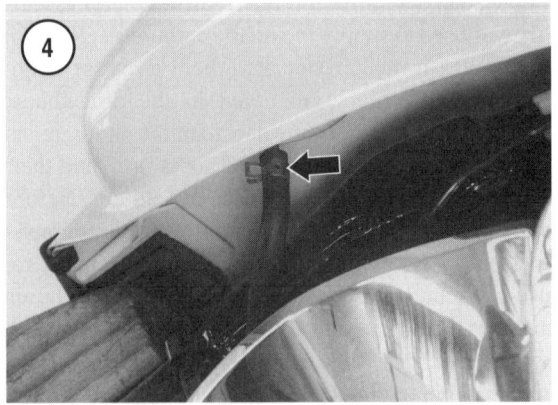

FUEL AND EMISSION CONTROL SYSTEMS

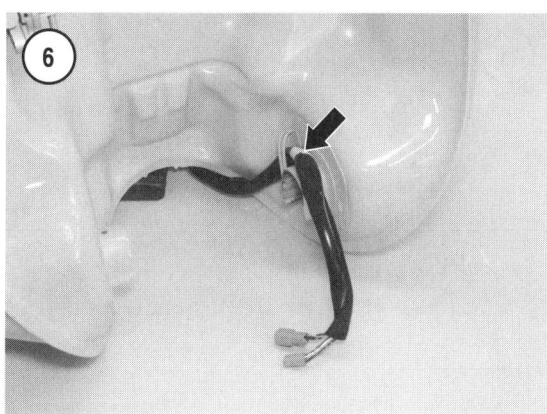

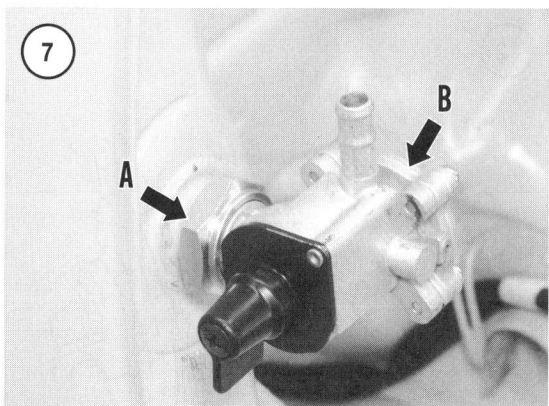

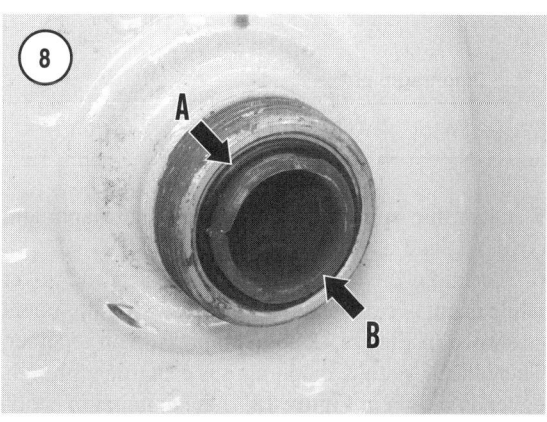

1. Remove the left front shroud (Chapter Fifteen).
2. Make sure the vacuum hose (C, **Figure 1**) is connected to the fuel valve. If not, reconnect the hose and attempt to start the engine. If the vacuum hose is connected, disconnect it at the fuel valve and check it and all connections leading toward the intake manifold for cracks and other damage. If the vacuum hose is okay, do not reconnect it and continue with Step 3.
3. Disconnect the fuel hose (B, **Figure 1**) at the fuel valve.
4. Connect a length of hose to the fuel hose fitting on the fuel valve (A, **Figure 2**). Insert the open end into a fuel storage can.
5. Connect a vacuum pump onto the vacuum hose fitting on the fuel valve (B, **Figure 2**).
6. Turn the fuel valve (A, **Figure 1**) to its reserve position.
7. Operate the vacuum pump to apply a vacuum to the fuel valve. Fuel should begin to flow out of the fuel hose and continue as long as a vacuum is applied and until the tank runs dry. If fuel flows in the reserve position, repeat the test with the fuel valve in the on position. Note the following:
   a. If fuel flows when the vacuum pump is applying vacuum, but does not flow when the vacuum hose is connected to the fuel valve, check for a plugged or damaged vacuum hose.
   b. If fuel does not flow with either vacuum source, remove the fuel valve vacuum diaphragm as described in this section. Inspect the diaphragm for damage and the internal fuel valve port for clogging.

NOTE
There is also a fuel strainer screen inside the carburetor fuel hose fitting.

   c. If the vacuum diaphragm appears in good condition, the fuel strainer screen attached to the fuel valve may be clogged. Remove and inspect the fuel strainer screen as described in this section.
8. Reverse the steps required to disconnect the vacuum pump and reconnect the hoses.

Removal/Installation

1. Drain and remove the fuel tank as described in this chapter.
2. Place the fuel tank on a padded surface to prevent scratches.
3. Loosen the nut (A, **Figure 7**) and remove the fuel valve assembly (B).
4. Remove the O-ring (A, **Figure 8**) and fuel strainer (B) from the fuel tank if they did not come off with the fuel valve.

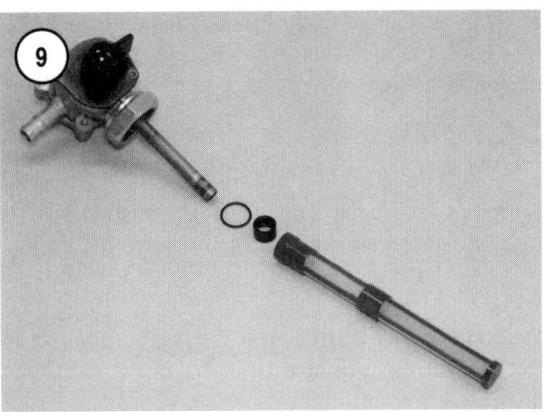

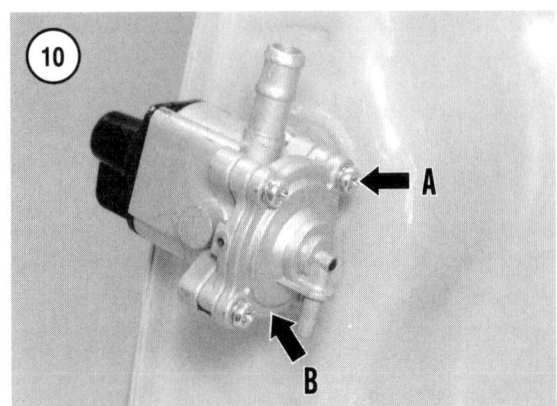

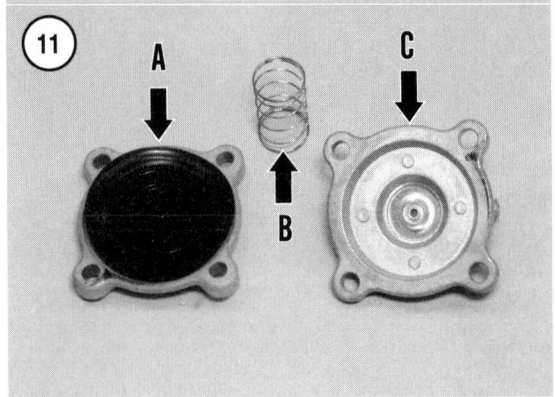

5. If the fuel strainer remains attached onto the fuel valve, remove the strainer, guide and O-ring (**Figure 9**).
6. Replace the O-ring if cracked or if the fuel valve previously leaked at its mounting nut.
7. Clean the fuel strainer and then check the screen for damage. Replace the fuel strainer if the screen cannot be cleaned or is torn.
8. Installation is the reverse of these steps. Note the following:
    a. Install the O-ring over the fuel valve pickup tube and seat against the fuel valve. Then install the guide over the tube and the fuel strainer.
    b. Align the fuel valve so its on/off knob faces out and tighten the nut (A, **Figure 7**) to 34 N•m (25 ft.-lb.).
    c. Partially fill the tank with fuel and check for fuel leaks.
    d. If the fuel valve does not leak, install the fuel tank as described in this chapter.

Diaphragm Removal/Installation
(2004-On Models)

The diaphragm assembly can be replaced with the fuel valve mounted on the fuel tank. However, the fuel tank must be removed to ensure the diaphragm plate and cover are properly centered on the fuel valve.
1. Drain and remove the fuel tank as described in this chapter.
2. Scribe an alignment mark across the fuel valve, diaphragm plate and diaphragm cover so the parts can be reinstalled facing in their original direction or used as reference to align the new parts.
3. Remove the screws (A, **Figure 10**), diaphragm cover (B), spring and diaphragm plate.
4. Inspect the diaphragm (A, **Figure 11**) for tearing, deterioration and other damage. Replace the diaphragm assembly if necessary.

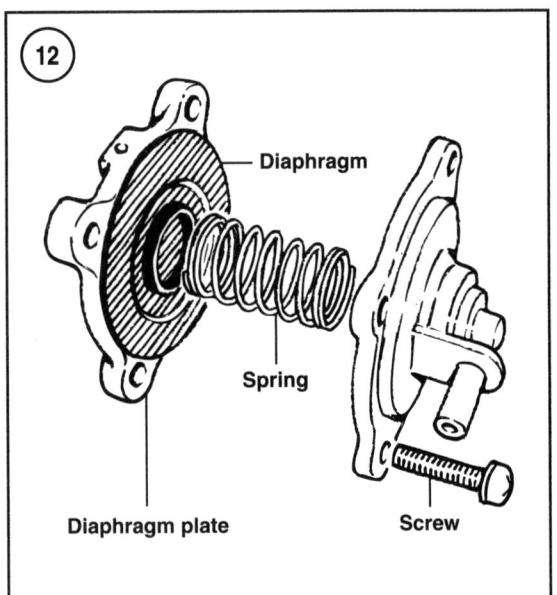

5. Clean the spring (B, **Figure 11**) and diaphragm cover (C) and check for damage.
6. Assemble the diaphragm plate, spring and cover while using two of the mounting screws for alignment as shown in **Figure 12** and compress them together. Then check that the diaphragm is centered within its cover as shown in **Figure 13**. If the diaphragm is off-

FUEL AND EMISSION CONTROL SYSTEMS

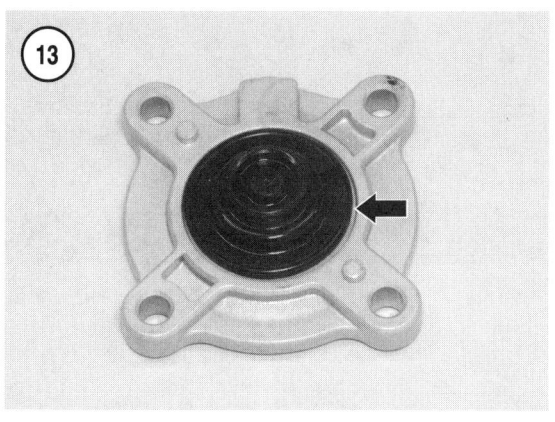

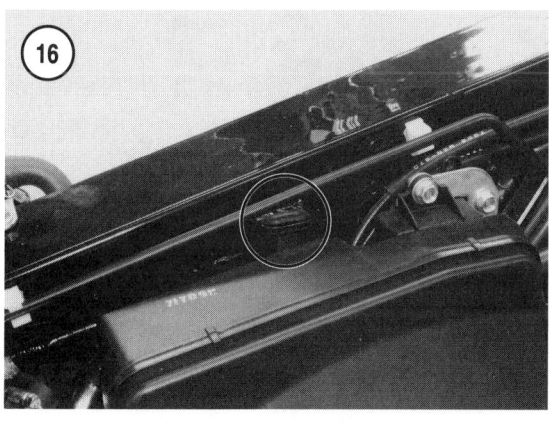

center, reassemble the parts. An off-center diaphragm can cause a fuel leak or fuel starvation.

7. Install the diaphragm assembly onto the fuel valve by aligning the pins on the diaphragm plate with the holes in the fuel valve while also aligning the marks made during Step 2. Install the screws (A, **Figure 10**) and tighten securely in a crossing pattern.

8. Install the fuel tank as described in this section and check for fuel leaks. Before riding the motorcycle, verify that the fuel valve is operational by checking fuel flow as described in *Fuel Tank* in this chapter.

AIR FILTER HOUSING

Removal/Installation

1. Remove the fuel tank as described in this chapter.
2. Remove the air filter as described in Chapter Three.
3. Remove the bolt (A, **Figure 14**) and the three screws (B) from inside the air filter housing.
4. Push the idle speed screw knob out of the grommet (**Figure 15**) at the bottom of the air filter housing.
5. Pull the air filter housing down to release its metal tab from the frame grommet (**Figure 16**).
6. Disconnect the crankcase breather hose (A, **Figure 17**) and the air supply hose (B) from the backside of the air filter housing, then remove the housing.
7. Check the O-ring in the carburetor groove (**Figure 18**) for flat spots, cracks and other damage. Replace if necessary.
8. Reverse this procedure to install the air filter housing. Note the following:
   a. Make sure the O-ring (**Figure 18**) is installed in the carburetor groove.
   b. Tighten the mounting bolt (A, **Figure 14**) to 10 N•m (88 in.-lb.).
   c. Tighten the three air filter mounting screws (B, **Figure 14**) to 3.7 N•m (32.7 in.-lb.).

CARBURETOR

Removal

1. Disconnect the battery negative cable (Chapter Nine).
2. Remove the fuel tank as described in this chapter.
3. Drain the engine coolant as described in Chapter Three.
4. Remove the air filter housing as described in this chapter.
5. Install a length of hose onto the float bowl drain nozzle (A, **Figure 19**) and put the other end of the hose into a clean plastic container. Open the drain screw (B, **Figure 19**) and drain the float bowl. Tighten the drain screw and pour the fuel back into the fuel tank or into a fuel storage can.
6. Open the clamp and disconnect the fuel hose (A, **Figure 20**) from the carburetor. Note the fuel filter installed inside the top of the carburetor hose fitting.

NOTE
On California models, the original equipment emission hoses are labeled with the same numbers called out in the text.

7. On California models, disconnect the No. 6 hose (B, **Figure 20**) from the carburetor.
8. Loosen the starting enrichment (SE) valve nut (**Figure 21**) and remove the SE valve (**Figure 22**) from the carburetor. Pull the spring up, then disconnect and remove the SE valve and spring from the cable.
9. Pull the wiring harness down and away from the frame at the point shown in **Figure 23**. Then disconnect the throttle position sensor (TPS) electrical connector (**Figure 24**). Lift the female connector's center tab to unlock/disconnect the connector.
10. Disconnect the throttle cables as follows:
    a. Disconnect the right front spark plug cap (A, **Figure 25**).
    b. Remove the two bolts and the air fin cover (B, **Figure 25**) as described in Chapter Fifteen. Do

FUEL AND EMISSION CONTROL SYSTEMS

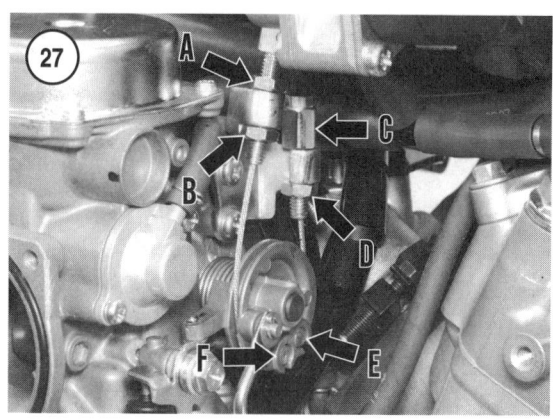

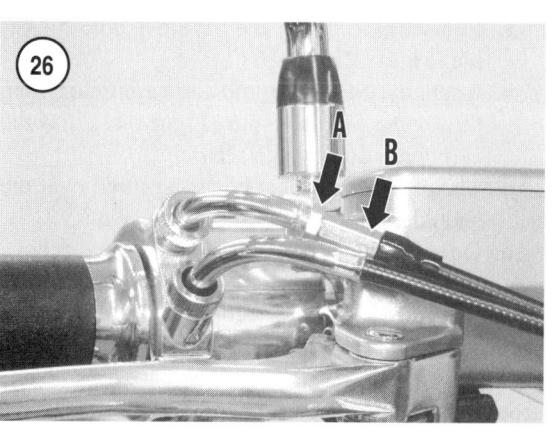

not lose the two grommets installed at the bottom of the air fin cover.

c. At the handlebar, loosen the pull cable adjuster locknut (A, **Figure 26**) and turn the adjuster (B) until it contacts the cable housing.

d. At the carburetor, loosen and turn the pull cable upper locknut (A, **Figure 27**) counterclockwise until it contacts the cable housing. Then push the cable down and turn the lower locknut (B, **Figure 27**) clockwise until the cable can be released from the cable holder. At this point, do not attempt to disconnect the pull cable from the throttle drum.

e. Hold the return cable (C, **Figure 27**) and loosen its locknut (D) until the cable can be released from the cable holder. Then disconnect the return cable (E, **Figure 27**) from the throttle drum.

f. Disconnect the pull cable (F, **Figure 27**) from the throttle drum.

11. Disconnect the vacuum hose (**Figure 28**) from the carburetor air cutoff valve cover.

12. On California models, disconnect the No.5 (**Figure 29**) and No. 11 (**Figure 30**) hoses from the carburetor.

13. Loosen the carburetor hose clamp (**Figure 31**) and remove the carburetor from the insulator.

14. Disconnect the two water hoses (**Figure 32**) from the carburetor heater and remove the carburetor.
15. Plug the insulator opening to prevent dirt and other debris from entering the engine.
16. Note the routing of all cables and hoses disconnected from the carburetor so they can be correctly positioned when installing the carburetor.

Installation

1. Position the hose clamp onto the insulator so its hole fits over the round shoulder on the insulator and with the screw is facing as shown in **Figure 33**.
2. Remove the plug from the insulator opening.
3. Connect the two water hoses onto the carburetor heater (**Figure 32**) and secure with the clamps.

CAUTION
*Make sure to position the hose clamps (**Figure 32**) with their tabs facing away from the opposite water hose; otherwise, the tabs could contact a hose and cause a coolant leak.*

NOTE
If the rear water hose is difficult to reconnect at the carburetor heater, trace the hose to its T-connection on the left side of the engine and disconnect the hose there. Connect the hose at the carburetor heater first, then at the T-connection. After reconnecting the hose, make sure it is properly routed.

4. Reconnect the throttle position sensor (TPS) electrical connector (**Figure 24**) and position the wiring harness in its original position.
5. On California models, reconnect the No. 5 hose (**Figure 29**) and the No. 11 hose (**Figure 30**) at the carburetor.
6. Reconnect the choke cable as follows:

a. Reinstall the spring and SE valve onto the cable (**Figure 22**).
b. Insert the SE valve into the carburetor, then thread the SE valve nut (**Figure 21**) into the carburetor and tighten securely.
c. Make sure the rubber boot is secured over the shoulder on the top of the SE valve nut.
d. Open and close the choke knob to check choke operation.

7. On California models, reconnect the No. 6 hose (B, **Figure 20**) at the carburetor.
8. Align the raised tab on the carburetor with the groove in the insulator (**Figure 34**) and install the

FUEL AND EMISSION CONTROL SYSTEMS

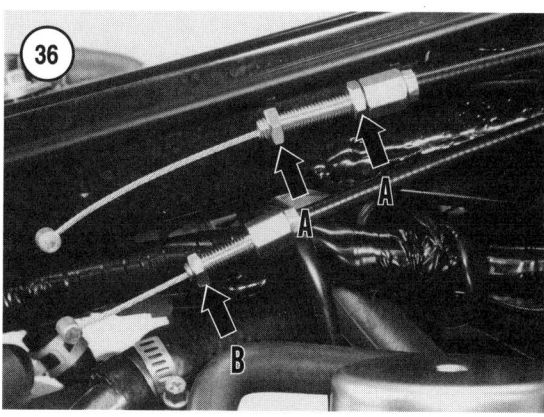

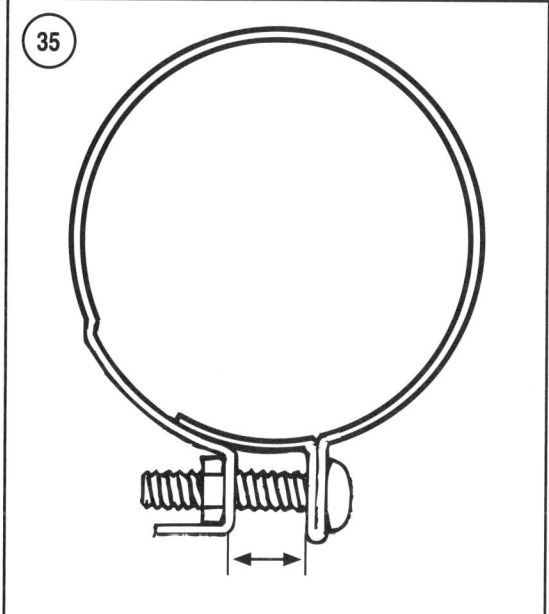

carburetor fully into the insulator. Tighten the hose clamp so the distance between the clamp ends (**Figure 35**) is 3-5 mm (0.12-0.20 in.).

9. Reconnect the vacuum hose (**Figure 28**) at the carburetor air cutoff valve cover. Route this hose between the carburetor and throttle cable bracket to make sure it does not interfere with throttle cable operation. This hose does not have an identification number.

10. Reconnect the throttle cables as follows:
 a. Position the two pull cable locknuts as shown in A, **Figure 36**.
 b. Position the return cable locknut as shown in B, **Figure 36**.
 c. Reconnect the pull cable (F, **Figure 27**) onto the throttle drum.
 d. Reconnect the return cable (E, **Figure 27**) onto the throttle drum.
 e. Lift the return cable and install it in the cable guide. Hold the cable (C, **Figure 27**) and tighten its locknut (D) securely.
 f. Install the pull cable (B, **Figure 27**) in the cable guide. Note that both locknuts are still loose.
 g. Adjust the throttle cables as described in Chapter Three, making sure the pull cable locknuts are tightened.
 h. Make sure the two collars and grommets are installed on the bottom of the air fin cover (B, **Figure 25**). Install the air fin cover so the two grommets fit into the cylinder head holes and tighten the air fin bolts securely. Refer to Chapter Fifteen.
 i. Reconnect the spark plug cap (A, **Figure 25**).

11. Install the fuel filter into the carburetor hose fitting (if removed). Then reconnect the fuel hose (A, **Figure 20**) and secure with the clamp.

12. Install the air filter housing as described in this chapter.

13. Reconnect the battery negative lead (Chapter Nine).

14. Fill and bleed the cooling system as described in Chapter Three. Use an accessory fuel tank to supply fuel to the engine when bleeding the cooling system.

15. Install the fuel tank as described in this chapter.

16. Turn the fuel valve on and start the engine to check for fuel leaks.

186 CHAPTER EIGHT

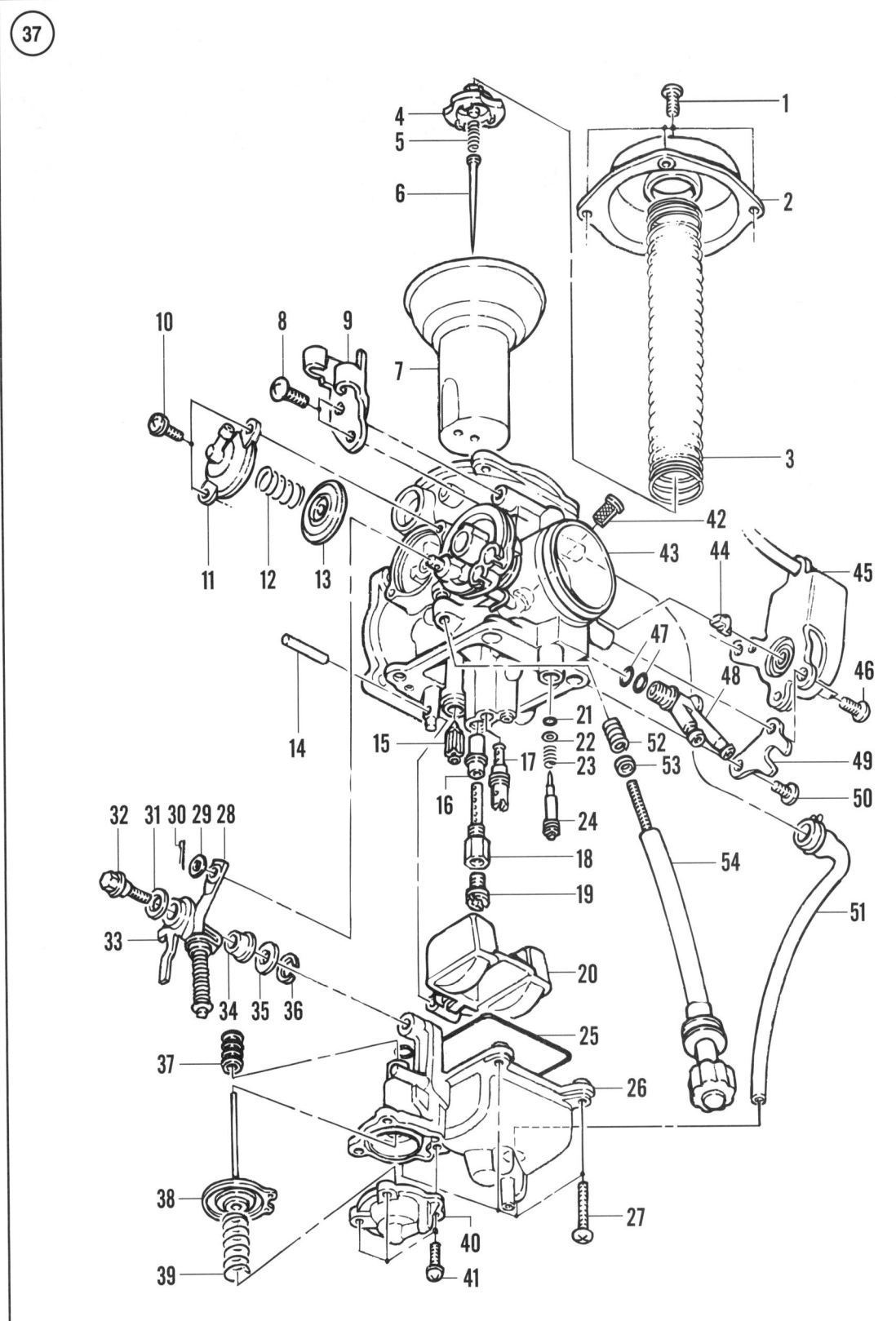

FUEL AND EMISSION CONTROL SYSTEMS

CARBURETOR

1. Screw
2. Diaphragm cover
3. Spring
4. Jet needle holder
5. Spring
6. Jet needle
7. Vacuum piston assembly
8. Screw
9. Throttle cable holder
10. Screw
11. Air cutoff valve cover
12. Spring
13. Diaphragm
14. Float pin
15. Float valve
16. Needle jet
17. Pilot jet
18. Needle jet holder
19. Main jet
20. Float
21. O-ring
22. Washer
23. Spring
24. Pilot screw
25. O-ring
26. Float bowl
27. Screw
28. Accelerator pump rod
29. Washer
30. Cotter pin
31. Plastic washer
32. Bolt
33. Accelerator pump arm
34. Collar
35. Washer
36. Washer
37. Boot
38. Diaphragm
39. Spring
40. Accelerator pump cover
41. Screw
42. Fuel filter
43. Body
44. Connector joint
45. Throttle position sensor (TPS)
46. Screw
47. O-ring
48. Carburetor heater
49. Alignment bracket
50. Screw
51. Air vent hose
52. Spring
53. Washer
54. Idle speed screw

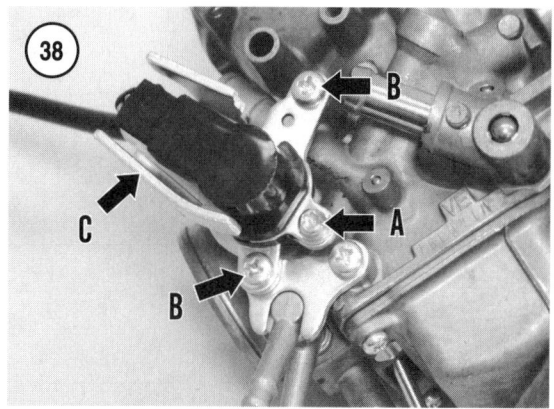

17. Confirm the throttle cable operation is correct with the fuel tank mounted. Refer to *Throttle Cable* in Chapter Three.

Disassembly

The carburetor does not have to be completely disassembled so service some of the components. Disassemble the carburetor only as far as necessary to inspect/clean/replace the damaged part. During disassembly, keep all parts identified and organized. Refer to **Figure 37**.

NOTE
*Do not loosen the Torx screw (A, **Figure 38**) securing the throttle position sensor to its mounting bracket. The sensor is preset on its mounting bracket and secured with the Torx screw. The sensor is removed with its mounting bracket.*

1. Remove the two Phillips screws (B, **Figure 38**) and the throttle position sensor (TPS) and its mounting bracket (C).
2. Remove the connector joint (**Figure 39**) from the end of the throttle shaft.

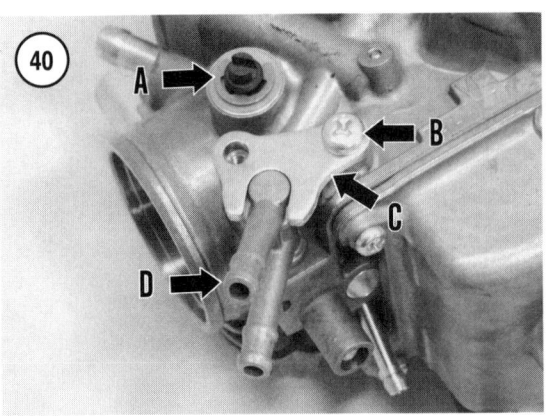

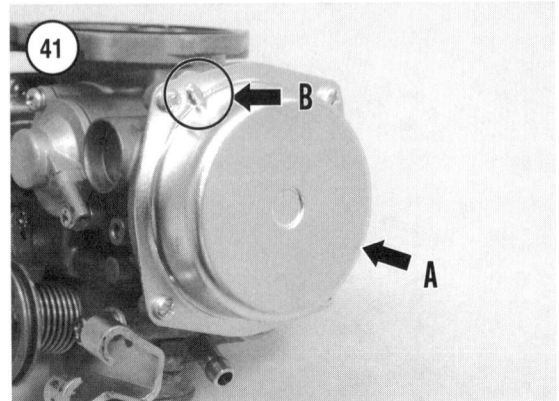

CAUTION
Do not remove the E-clip or the connector joint socket (A, Figure 40) from the end of the throttle shaft. The connector joint socket is not a replaceable part.

3. Remove the screw (B, **Figure 40**), bracket (C) and carburetor heater (D). Discard the O-rings.
4. Remove the diaphragm cover, vacuum piston and jet needle as follows:
    a. Remove the diaphragm cover (A, **Figure 41**). The cover is under slight pressure. Hold the cover in place as the screws are removed, then lift off the cover.
    b. Remove the spring (A, **Figure 42**).

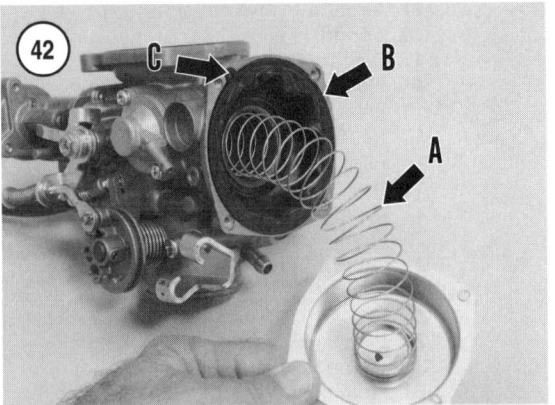

CAUTION
Do not lift or hold the vacuum piston by the diaphragm. Do not damage the jet needle.

    c. From the intake side, push up on the vacuum piston and lift it from the carburetor (B, **Figure 42**).
    d. Push the jet needle holder (**Figure 43**) in with a Phillips screwdriver or socket and turn it counterclockwise to release it.
    e. Remove the jet needle holder, spring and jet needle (**Figure 44**).
5. Remove the air cutoff valve assembly as follows:
    a. Remove the screws from the cover (**Figure 45**). The cover is under strong spring pressure. Keep pressure on the cover as the screws are removed.
    b. Remove the spring (A, **Figure 46**) and diaphragm (B).
6. Remove the accelerator pump assembly as follows:
    a. Remove the screws from the cover (**Figure 47**). The cover is under spring pressure. Keep pressure on the cover as the screws are removed.
    b. Remove the spring (A, **Figure 48**).

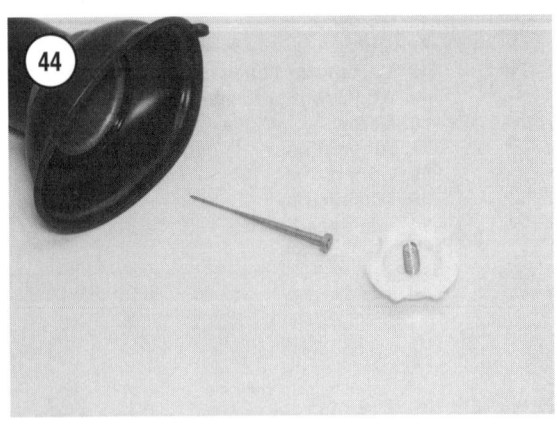

FUEL AND EMISSION CONTROL SYSTEMS

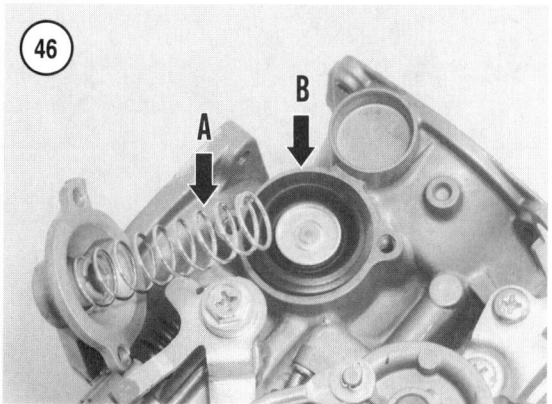

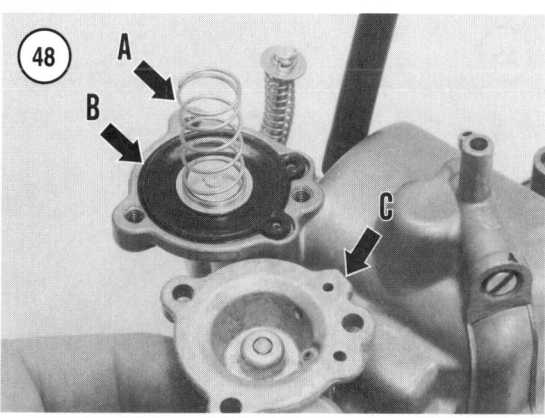

c. Carefully remove the diaphragm (B, **Figure 48**) with its attached rod.
d. Remove the boot (**Figure 49**).
7. Remove the float bowl as follows:

NOTE
*The accelerator pump rod (A, **Figure 50**) is attached to the throttle drum with a cotter pin and washer. Do not disconnect the accelerator pump rod unless necessary.*

a. Remove the bolt (B, **Figure 50**) securing the accelerator pump arm to the float bolt. Then remove the plastic washer, accelerator pump arm and the two steel washers.
b. Remove the collar (A, **Figure 51**) from the accelerator pump arm (B).
c. Unless damaged, leave the accelerator pump arm (B, **Figure 51**) attached to the accelerator pump rod (C) and the rod attached to the throttle drum.
d. Remove the screws (A, **Figure 52**) and the float bowl (B).
e. Remove the O-ring from the float bowl.
f. Remove the drain screw and its O-ring from the float bowl.
8. Remove the float assembly as follows:

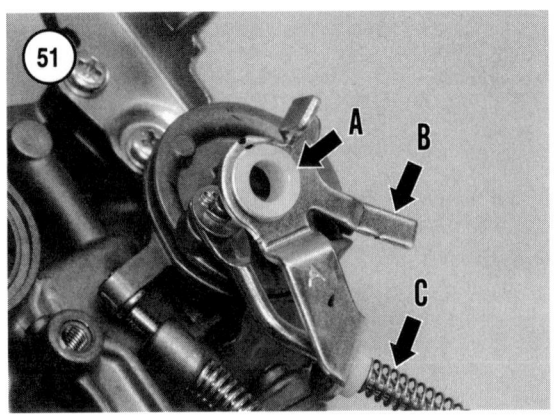

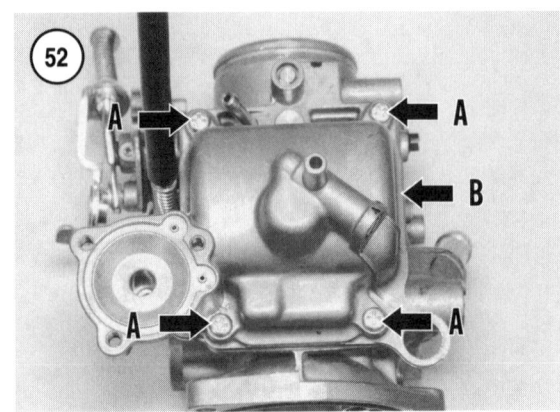

a. Remove the float pin (A, **Figure 53**) and float (B).
b. Slide the float valve (**Figure 54**) off the float arm.
9. Remove the pilot jet (A, **Figure 55**).
10. Hold the needle jet holder (B, **Figure 55**) and remove the main jet (C) or remove the needle jet holder with the main jet attached.
11. Working from the top side of the carburetor, carefully push the needle jet (**Figure 56**) out through the bottom side.

CAUTION
The pilot screw tip is easily damaged. Do not overtighten the pilot screw when setting it in Step 12. If the pilot screw tip breaks off, its removal from the pilot screw bore may be impossible.

NOTE
*The pilot screw requires a D-shaped tool to turn and remove it. Suitable tools are described in **Pilot Screw Adjustment (Idle Drop Procedure)** in this chapter.*

12. Lightly seat the pilot screw, recording the number of turns for reassembly reference, then remove the screw (**Figure 57**), spring, washer and O-ring.

CAUTION
Do not remove the throttle valve or throttle shaft assembly from the carburetor. Replacement parts are not available.

13. Clean and inspect all parts as described in this section.

Assembly

1. Install the spring, washer and O-ring onto the pilot screw (24, **Figure 37**).

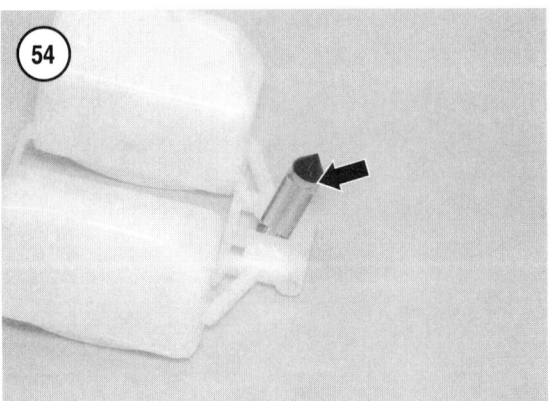

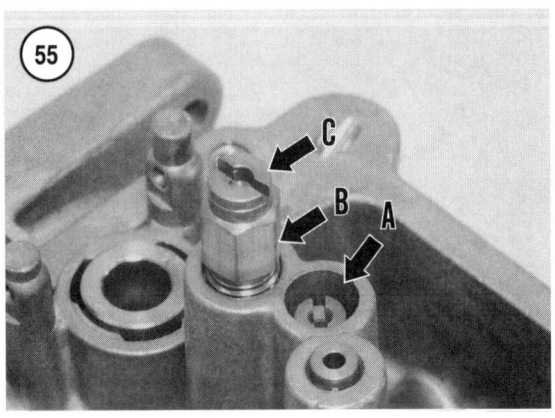

FUEL AND EMISSION CONTROL SYSTEMS

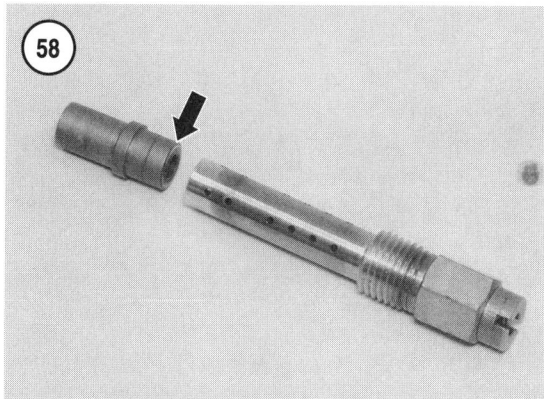

2. Install the pilot screw (**Figure 57**) and lightly seat it, then back it out the number of turns recorded during removal. If the number of turns is not known, or if installing a new pilot screw, set it to the initial setting listed in **Table 1**. Then perform the *Pilot Screw Adjustment (Idle Drop Procedure)* in this chapter after reassembling and installing the carburetor onto the motorcycle.
3. Install the needle jet (**Figure 56**) through the bottom side of the carburetor so its curved end will seat against the needle jet holder. Refer to **Figure 58**.
4. Install the needle jet holder (B, **Figure 55**) and tighten securely.
5. If removed, hold the needle jet holder and install and tighten the main jet (C, **Figure 55**).
6. Install and tighten the pilot jet (A, **Figure 55**).
7. Install the float assembly as follows:
    a. Hook the float valve onto the float as shown in **Figure 54**.
    b. Install the float valve into its seat, then install the float pin (A, **Figure 53**) through pedestals and float (B).
    c. Measure the float level as described in this section.
8. Install the float bowl as follows:
    a. Install the drain screw and a new O-ring and tighten securely.
    b. Install a new O-ring into the float bowl groove.
    c. Install the float bowl (B, **Figure 52**) and tighten the screws (A) securely.
    d. Install the collar into the accelerator pump arm as shown in A, **Figure 51**.
    e. Install the accelerator pump arm onto the float bowl by installing the following as shown in **Figure 37**: washer (36), washer (35), plastic washer (31) and bolt (32). With the accelerator pump arm positioned as shown in C, **Figure 50**, tighten the bolt (B) securely.
9. Install the accelerator pump assembly as follows:
    a. Position the boot underneath the accelerator pump arm and into the bore funnel as shown in **Figure 49**.
    b. Slide the accelerator pump shaft through its bore and the boot until the end of the shaft contacts the accelerator pump arm (A, **Figure 59**). Make sure the bottom end of the boot remains seated into the bore funnel (B, **Figure 59**).
    c. Seat the diaphragm into the bowl groove as shown in B, **Figure 48**.
    d. Install the spring (A, **Figure 48**) onto the center of the diaphragm.
    e. Align the two passage holes in the cover (C, **Figure 48**) with the two holes in the bowl and install the cover, making sure the diaphragm remains seated at its edge.

f. Compress the cover (**Figure 47**), then install and tighten the screws securely.
10. Install the air cutoff valve as follows:
    a. Seat the diaphragm (B, **Figure 46**) into its groove with its shaft seating into the hole in the carburetor.
    b. Install the spring (A, **Figure 46**) over the cover shoulder, then center the spring onto the diaphragm and compress the cover (**Figure 45**), making sure the diaphragm remains seated at its edge.
    c. Install the screws and washers and tighten securely.
11. Install the jet needle, vacuum piston and diaphragm cover as follows:
    a. Install the jet needle (**Figure 44**) into the vacuum piston.
    b. Install the jet needle holder and spring (**Figure 44**) into the vacuum piston, then compress and turn the holder 90° clockwise with a screwdriver until it clicks and locks in place (**Figure 43**).
    c. Hold the carburetor upright and install the vacuum piston by inserting the jet needle into the needle jet and while aligning the tab on the diaphragm with the air hole on the carburetor (C, **Figure 42**).
    d. Lift the bottom of the vacuum piston slightly to help seat the edge of diaphragm (B, **Figure 42**) into the groove in the carburetor.
    e. Install the spring (A, **Figure 42**) and cover, making sure the diaphragm remains seated at its edge. The raised section on the cover (B, **Figure 41**) must align with the tab on the diaphragm (C, **Figure 42**). Hold the cover in place and install and tighten the screws securely.
    f. Lift the bottom of the vacuum piston and release it. The vacuum piston should move and return under slight resistance. If there is any binding or roughness, remove the cover and check the spring and diaphragm.
12. Lightly coat two new O-rings with engine oil and install them into the carburetor heater grooves (**Figure 60**). Then install the carburetor heater (D, **Figure 40**) and secure with the bracket (C) and screw (B).
13. Install the throttle position sensor (TPS) as follows:
    a. Install the connector joint (**Figure 39**) into the end of the throttle shaft.
    b. Align the slot in the throttle position sensor (A, **Figure 61**) with the connector joint (B) and install the sensor.
    c. Install the two screws (B, **Figure 38**) and tighten securely.
14. Store the carburetor in a plastic bag until installation.

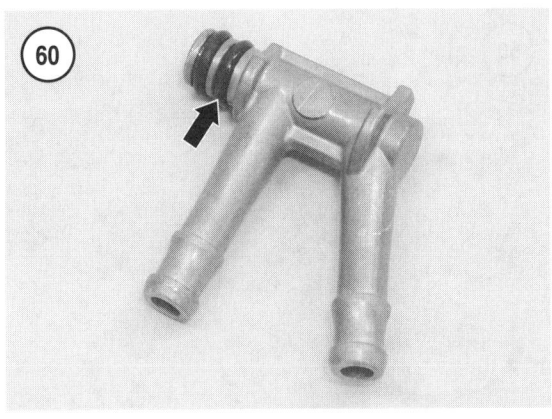

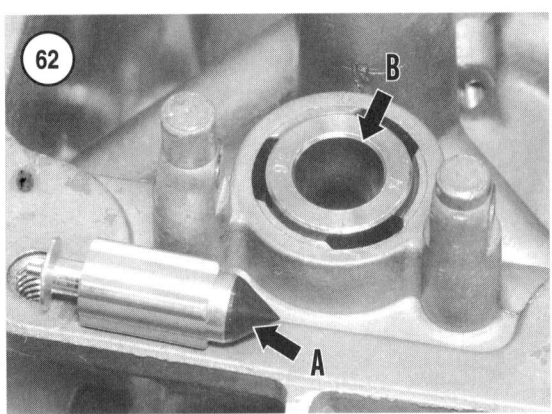

Cleaning/Inspection

CAUTION
Because the carburetor body cannot be completely disassembled, it is not recommended to soak the carburetor in a carburetor cleaner unless the cleaner will not damage plastic or rubber parts that may be installed on the throttle shaft. Follow the manufacturer's instructions when using a cleaner.

1. Clean the carburetor:

FUEL AND EMISSION CONTROL SYSTEMS

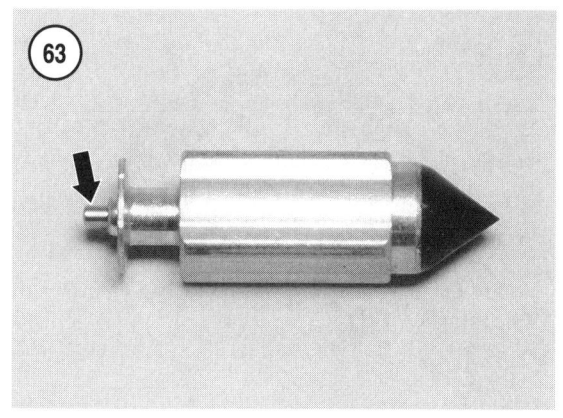

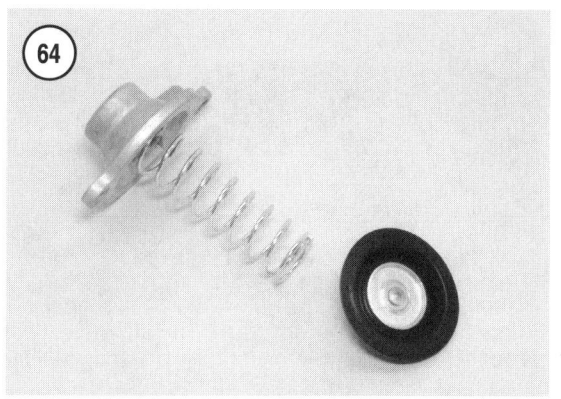

a. Use an aerosol carburetor cleaner with a plastic tube to clean fuel and air passages.
b. Used compressed air to clean all passages, orifices and vents in the carburetor body.
c. Do not clean the jets or seats with wire or drill bits. These items can scratch the surfaces and alter flow rates, or cause leaks.
d. Clean rubber and plastic parts with a clean towel. If passages in the carburetor or carburetor jets are plugged and cannot be opened, have the parts cleaned by a dealership with an ultrasonic cleaner.
e. After cleaning the carburetor, clean it again with soapy water and then rinse with clear water and dry thoroughly with compressed air. Make sure all passages are clean and dry.

2. Inspect the main jet assembly and pilot jet. Check that all holes are clean and undamaged.
3. Inspect the pilot screw and choke plunger:
   a. Inspect the screw and plunger tips for dents and wear.
   b. The spring coils should be evenly spaced and not crushed or spread apart.
4. Inspect the diaphragm and vacuum piston assembly (7, **Figure 37**). If either part is damaged, replace the assembly.
   a. Inspect the vacuum piston for wear and scratches. Install the vacuum piston into the carburetor and check for smooth operation. The vacuum piston should move up and down freely.
   b. Inspect the diaphragm for cracks, tears and holes. The diaphragm must be undamaged in order to isolate the pressure differences that are above and below the diaphragm. A leaking diaphragm will prevent the vacuum piston from reaching/maintaining its normal level, for any off idle throttle position. Engine performance will be noticeably diminished.
5. Inspect the diaphragm cover (2, **Figure 37**) and the jet needle assembly (6).
   a. The diaphragm cover must be undamaged in order to maintain low pressure in the upper chamber of the carburetor. A cracked or loose cover will affect engine performance similarly to a damaged diaphragm.
   b. The jet needle must be smooth and evenly tapered. If it is stepped, dented, worn or bent, replace the needle.
   c. The spring coils (3, **Figure 37**) must be uniform and not damaged.
6. Inspect the float and float valve assembly.
   a. Inspect the tip of the float valve (A, **Figure 62**) and replace if the rubber part is not smooth.
   b. Lightly press on the spring-loaded pin (**Figure 63**) in the float valve. The pin should easily move in and out of the valve. If there is any roughness or binding, replace the float valve.
   c. Inspect the float valve seat (B, **Figure 62**) for steps and other damage. If the tapered seat is not smooth and it is determined that fuel is leaking past the seat (even with a new float valve), replace the carburetor assembly. The float valve seat is not replaceable.
   d. Submerge the float in water and check for leaks. Replace the float if there is fuel or water in the float.
   e. Check that the float pin is smooth and straight.
7. Inspect the float bowl:
   a. Removal all residue from the interior of the float bowl.
   b. Make sure all fuel and air passages are clear.
   c. Replace the float bowl and drain screw O-rings.
8. Inspect the air cutoff valve assembly (**Figure 64**):
   a. Check the diaphragm (A, **Figure 65**) for cuts, tears and age deterioration. Hold the diaphragm up to a light to check for pin holes.
   b. Check the diaphragm shaft (B, **Figure 65**) for burrs and other damage. Check the shaft operating hole in the carburetor (A, **Figure 66**) for debris and damage. These surfaces must be smooth.

c. The small air hole (B, **Figure 66**) and passage in the diaphragm chamber must be clear.
d. The spring must be in good condition to apply pressure against the diaphragm.

9. Inspect the accelerator pump assembly (**Figure 67**):
   a. Check the diaphragm for cuts, tears and age deterioration. Hold the diaphragm up to a light to check for pin holes.
   b. Check the diaphragm shaft for burrs and other damage. Check the shaft operating hole in the float bowl for debris and damage.
   c. The small air holes and passages in the cover and diaphragm chamber must be clear.
   d. The spring must be in good condition to apply pressure against the diaphragm.
   e. Replace the boot (37, **Figure 37**) if damaged.

10. Inspect the throttle valve assembly:
    a. The spring must be clean and in good condition.
    b. The throttle valve plate must fully open and close, and be tightly secured to the shaft.
    c. The shaft must not be loose or bind.

11. Clean the fuel filter (42, **Figure 37**) and inspect for damage. Replace if the screen is plugged or damaged.

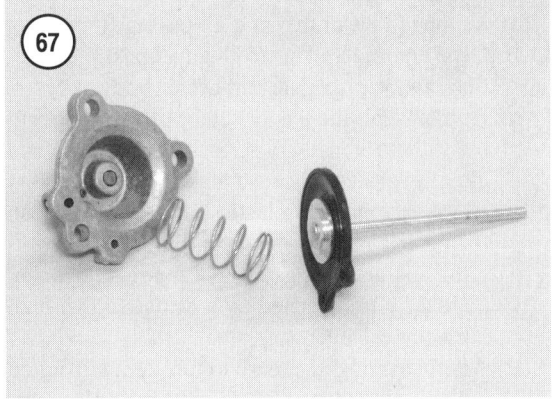

Float Level Measurement

Check the float level whenever the carburetor has been disassembled, when the carburetor is overflowing or when troubleshooting a rich air/fuel mixture.

1. Remove the carburetor as described in this section.
2. Remove the float bowl as described in *Disassembly* in this section.
3. Position the carburetor so the float and hangs freely and the float valve is open. Tilt the carburetor until the float valve closes and the tab on the float lightly touches the spring-loaded pin in the valve. The float tab must not compress the pin.
4. Measure the distance from the carburetor gasket surface to the highest point on the float (**Figure 68**). Refer to **Table 1** for the required float level.
5. If the float level is incorrect, replace the float as described in this section. The float is not adjustable. Remeasure the float level with the new float.
6. Install the float bowl and carburetor as described in this section.

INTAKE MANIFOLD

Removal

1. Remove the carburetor as described in this chapter.

2. With the insulator opening covered, clean the area around the intake manifold with compressed air.

NOTE
Compare the vacuum and water hose routing on and around the intake manifold shown in the procedure with the manifold being worked on and note any differences so the parts can be assembled correctly. Make diagrams and take picture to aid in assembly. The intake manifold shown in this procedure is used on a 2008 California model.

FUEL AND EMISSION CONTROL SYSTEMS

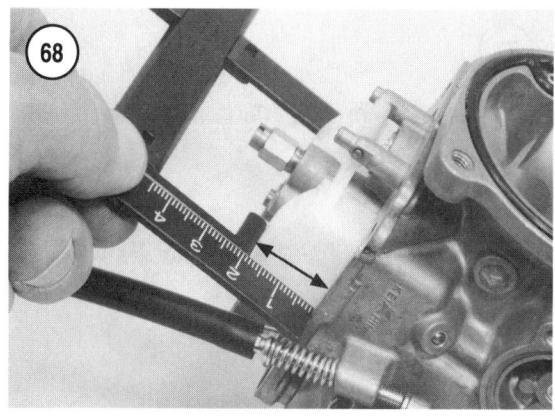

3. Disconnect the water hose at the cylinder water pipe (A, **Figure 69**). It is easier to remove the intake manifold with the water hose attached to the manifold.

4. Disconnect the vacuum hose from the intake manifold. B, **Figure 69** shows the vacuum hose position used on 2004-on models. On 2003 models, the vacuum hose connects into the top of the intake manifold and can be reached from the right side.

NOTE
If necessary, remove the choke cable mounting bracket (C, Figure 69) from the intake manifold and the front and rear cylinder head air fins (Chapter Fifteen) to provide additional room when loosening the Allen bolts. Otherwise, the intake manifold can be removed with the choke cable mounting bracket attached.

NOTE
The Allen wrench must fit the Allen bolts fully. Otherwise, the wrench could strip the Allen bolt recesses and damage the bolts so they are difficult to remove. Make sure the Allen bolt recesses are clean and the Allen wrench flats are straight and not rounded. Grind the end of the Allen wrench or use a new Allen wrench if necessary.

5. Remove the four Allen bolts (A and B, **Figure 70**) securing the front and rear intake manifold bases to the cylinder heads.

6. Slide the intake manifold (C, **Figure 70**) outward with both manifold bases attached to the manifold. Refer to **Figure 71**.

7. Plug or tape over both cylinder head openings to prevent dirt from entering the engine.

8. Remove the bolts and the choke cable bracket (A, **Figure 71**) from the top of the intake manifold.

9. Loosen the hose clamps and remove the carburetor insulator (B, **Figure 71**) and the front (C) and rear (D) intake manifold bases from the intake manifold. Remove and discard the O-ring (**Figure 72**) installed inside each manifold base.

10. Clean and dry all parts.

11. While accessible, inspect the vacuum and water hoses for cracks or damage and replace if necessary. Inspect and replace weak or damaged hose clamps.

Installation

Remove all tape or plugs from the cylinder head intake ports when assembling and installing the parts as described in this section.

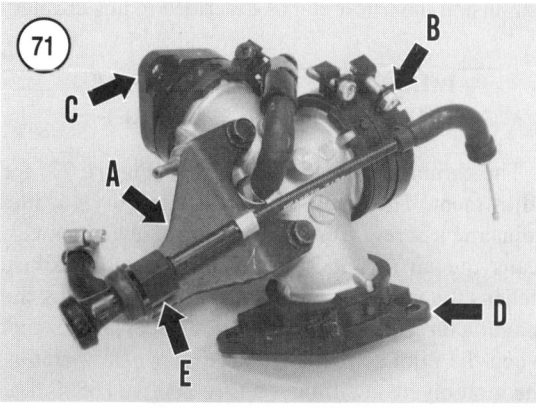

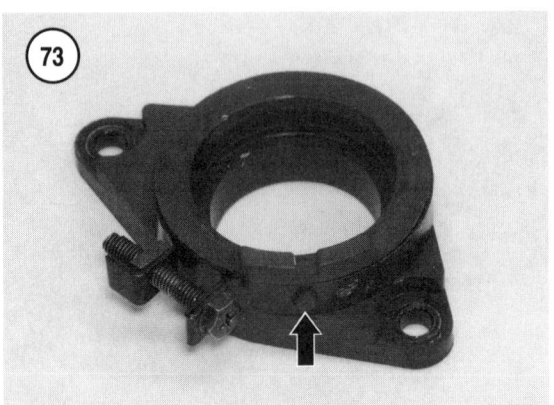

1. Install a new O-ring (**Figure 72**) into the groove in each intake manifold base groove.

NOTE
*During installation, align the hose clamps by inserting the hole in each hose clamp over the round shoulder on the manifold base or carburetor insulator (**Figure 73**, typical).*

2. Install the front intake manifold base (A, **Figure 74**) onto the cylinder head and tighten the two Allen bolts (B) to 10 N•m (88 in.-lb.).
3. Install the rear intake manifold base by aligning the slot in the base with the raised tab (A, **Figure 75**) on the intake manifold. Tighten the hose clamp so the distance between the clamp ends (**Figure 76**) is 2-4 mm (0.08-0.12 in.).
4. Install the carburetor insulator with its CARB UP mark (B, **Figure 75**) facing out while aligning the slot in the insulator with the raised tab (C) on the intake manifold.
5. Install the choke cable bracket (A, **Figure 71**) and tighten the two bolts securely.
6. Install the intake manifold into the front cylinder intake manifold base while positioning the rear cylinder intake manifold base against the cylinder head. Make sure the O-ring in the rear intake manifold base is not pinched between the manifold base and cylinder head.
7. Install the two rear intake manifold base Allen bolts and tighten to 10 N•m (88 in.-lb.).
8. Tighten the front intake manifold base hose clamp so the distance between the clamp ends (**Figure 76**) is 2-4 mm (0.08-0.12 in.).
9. Tighten the carburetor insulator hose clamp so the distance between the clamp ends (**Figure 76**) is 3-5 mm (0.12-0.20 in.).
10. Reconnect the intake manifold's left water hose at the cylinder hose nozzle (A, **Figure 69**).
11. Reconnect the vacuum hose (B, **Figure 69**, typical) at the intake manifold.

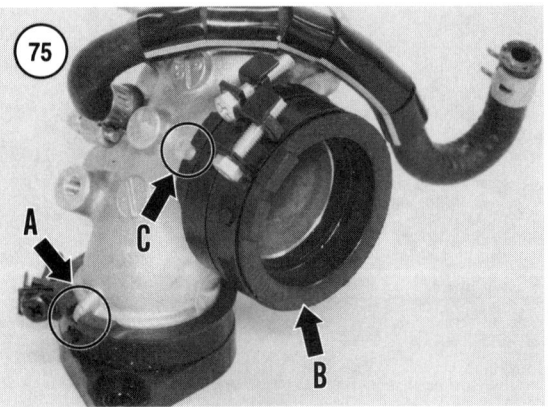

12. Install the carburetor as described in this chapter.

PILOT SCREW ADJUSTMENT (IDLE DROP PROCEDURE)

The carburetor uses a pilot screw (**Figure 77**) for adjustment. The screw is also referred to as a fuel adjustment screw. Turning the pilot screw clockwise leans the air/fuel mixture while counterclockwise richens the mixture. The pilot screw is preset by the manufacturer. Adjustment is not necessary except when the pilot screw is replaced or when operating the motorcycle at altitudes above 2000 m (6500 ft.).

FUEL AND EMISSION CONTROL SYSTEMS

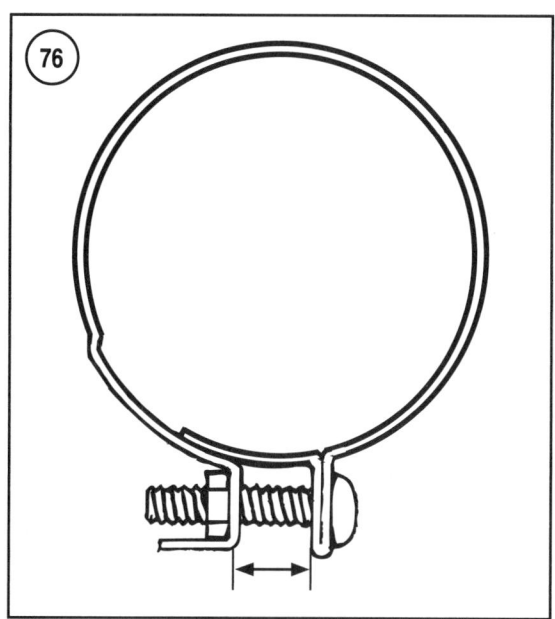

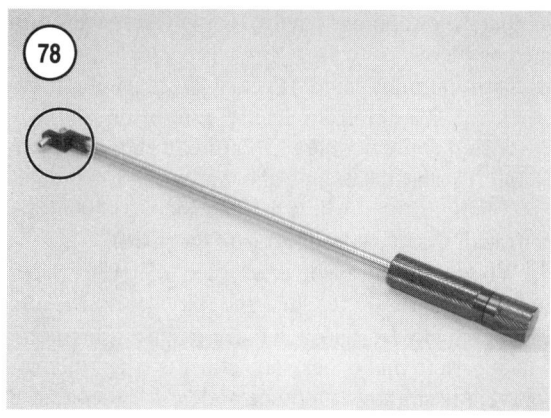

b. Pilot screw wrench, D type (part No. 07KMA-MN9A100).

2. Shop tachometer that can read rpm changes of 50 rpm or less.

Procedure

Before adjusting the carburetor, read the procedure through to understand the tools and steps required.

1. If necessary, replace the air filter (Chapter Three).

CAUTION
The pilot screw tip is small and easily damaged. Do not overtighten the pilot screw when seating it in Step 2. If the pilot screw tip breaks off, its removal from the pilot screw bore may be impossible.

NOTE
***Figure 77** shows the pilot screw position with the carburetor removed for clarity.*

2. Working from the left side, insert the tool between the cylinders and mount it onto the pilot screw (**Figure 79**). Turn the pilot screw clockwise until it lightly seats, then back out the number of turns listed in **Table 1**. This is the initial setting.

3. Start the engine and warm to normal operating temperature (approximately 10 minutes), then turn the engine off.

4. Connect a shop tachometer to the engine following the manufacturer's instructions.

5. Start the engine and turn the idle speed screw (**Figure 80**) to set the engine idle speed to 1300-1500 rpm.

6. Turn the pilot screw in or out to obtain the highest engine idle speed.

7. Turn the idle speed screw to reset the engine idle speed to 800-1000 rpm.

Tools

1. The pilot screw uses a D-shaped head and requires a D-shaped driver head tool mounted on a 90° holder for adjustment. Note the following options:
   a. 90° 1/4 in. Hex Driver (Motion Pro part No. 08-0229 [**Figure 78**]).

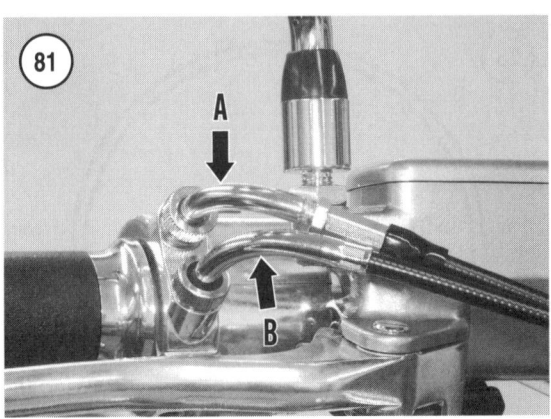

8. Slowly open the throttle two or three times (less than 1/4 throttle) and release it, then turn the idle speed screw to reset the engine idle speed to 800-1000 rpm.
9. While reading the tachometer, turn the pilot screw in until the engine speed drops 50 rpm.
10. Turn the pilot screw counterclockwise 3/4 of a turn. This is the final pilot screw adjustment.
11. Turn the idle speed screw to reset the engine idle speed to 800-1000 rpm.
12. Open the throttle and check throttle response. If the engine rpm does not increase smoothly, repeat these steps.
13. Turn the engine off and remove the tachometer.

HIGH ALTITUDE ADJUSTMENT

CAUTION
Operating the motorcycle at altitudes lower than 1500 m (5000 ft.) with the carburetor adjusted for high altitude may cause the engine to idle roughly and stall. Overheating may also cause engine damage.

If the motorcycle is ridden for a sustained period at an elevation above 2000 m (6500 ft.), readjust the carburetor to improve engine performance and decrease emissions. Otherwise, the standard jetting will be too rich. This will cause hard starting and spark plug fouling, reduce engine performance and increase fuel consumption.

NOTE
If a dealership performs this adjustment they place a Vehicle Emission Control Information Update label on the rear fender (2003-2007 models) or on the fuel tank (2008-on models). When working on an unfamiliar motorcycle, check for this label before making the adjustment.

NOTE
*Refer to **Pilot Screw Adjustment (Idle Drop Procedure)** in this chapter for tools required to turn the D-shaped pilot screw.*

1. Start the engine and warm to normal operating temperature (approximately 10 minutes), then turn the engine off.
2. Turn the pilot screw (**Figure 77** and **Figure 79**) clockwise 1/2 turn from the preset position.
3. With the motorcycle at an altitude above 2000 m (6500 ft), start the engine and warm to normal operating temperature. Adjust the idle speed to 800-1000 rpm with the idle speed screw (**Figure 80**).
4. When the motorcycle is returned to elevations below 2000 m (6500 ft.), turn the pilot screw 1/2 turn counterclockwise and reset the engine idle speed. Make sure to make these adjustments when the motorcycle is at a lower altitude and with the engine at operating temperature.

THROTTLE CABLE

WARNING
Do not ride the motorcycle with an improperly routed and/or adjusted throttle cable.

FUEL AND EMISSION CONTROL SYSTEMS

Removal/Installation

The throttle uses two cables. Always replace both cables at the same time.
1. Remove the fuel tank as described in this chapter.
2. Remove the air filter housing as described in this chapter.
3. Note how the cables are routed.
4. At the carburetor, disconnect the cables as described in *Removal* in *Carburetor* in this chapter.
5. At the handlebar, disconnect the cables as described in *Removal* in *Handlebar* in Chapter Twelve.
6. Note the throttle cable routing from the throttle drum to the carburetor and remove the throttle cables.
7. Lubricate the new throttle cables as described in Chapter Three.
8. Clean the throttle assembly and handlebar.
9. Install the new throttle cables by routing them along their original path.
10. Identify the throttle cables as follows:
    a. Pull cable: A, **Figure 81** and A, **Figure 82**.
    b. Return cable: B, **Figure 81** and B, **Figure 82**.
11. At the handlebar, reconnect the cables (**Figure 81**) as described in *Installation* in *Handlebar* in Chapter Twelve.
12. At the carburetor, reconnect the cables (**Figure 82**) as described in *Installation* in *Carburetor* in this chapter.
13. Adjust the throttle cables as described in Chapter Three.
14. Install the air filter housing and fuel tank as described in this chapter.
15. Start the engine and run at idle speed with the transmission in neutral. Turn the handlebar from side to side without operating the throttle. The idle speed must remain constant with no increase in idle speed. If the idle speed increases when turning the handlebar, the throttle cable routing and/or adjustment is incorrect. Reroute and/or readjust the throttle cables as required.

CHOKE CABLE

Removal/Installation

NOTE
***Figure 71** shows the intake manifold removed for clarity.*

The choke cable is mounted on a bracket (A, **Figure 71**) that is bolted on the intake manifold. The choke cable can be replaced with the intake manifold and carburetor mounted on the engine.
1. Remove the fuel tank as described in this chapter.
2. On California models, disconnect the No. 6 hose (A, **Figure 83**) from the carburetor.
3. Note the choke cable routing from its mounting bracket to the carburetor.
4. Loosen the starting enrichment (SE) valve nut (**Figure 84**) and remove the SE valve (**Figure 85**) from the carburetor. Pull the spring up, then disconnect and remove the SE valve and spring from the cable.
5. Note the end of the choke cable and how it is angled toward the carburetor.

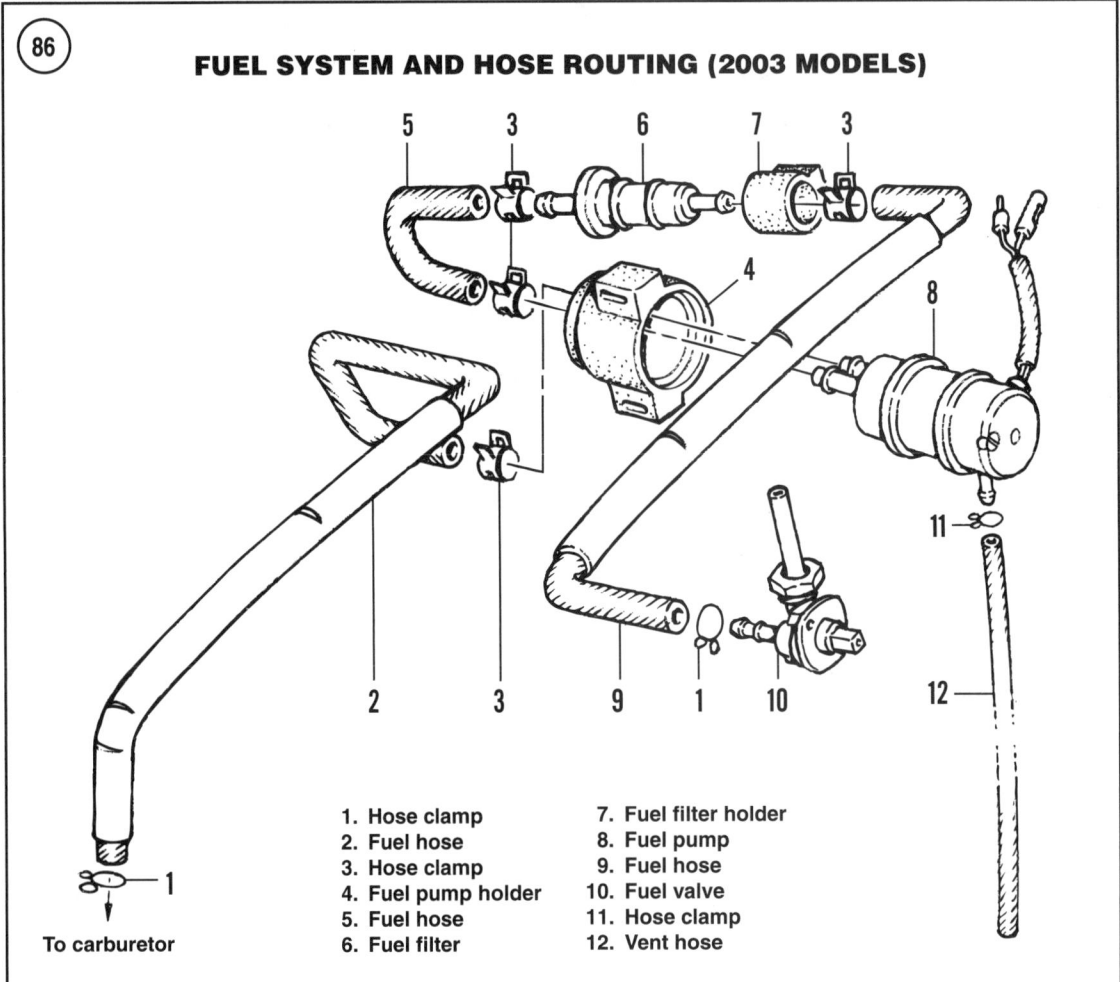

86 FUEL SYSTEM AND HOSE ROUTING (2003 MODELS)

1. Hose clamp
2. Fuel hose
3. Hose clamp
4. Fuel pump holder
5. Fuel hose
6. Fuel filter
7. Fuel filter holder
8. Fuel pump
9. Fuel hose
10. Fuel valve
11. Hose clamp
12. Vent hose

6. Remove the two bolts securing the choke cable mounting bracket to the intake manifold and remove the mounting bracket and choke cable assembly.
7. Loosen the locknut (E, **Figure 71**) and remove the choke cable from the mounting bracket.
8. Route the new choke cable across the mounting bracket and secure it with the locknut (E, **Figure 71**).
9. Install the choke cable mounting bracket while routing the cable toward the carburetor and following its original path. Tighten the bolts securely.
10. The end of the choke cable should fall in the same approximate position as noted before removal. If necessary, loosen the locknut (E, **Figure 71**) and readjust the cable's position, then tighten the locknut.
11. Clean the SE valve and spring.
12. Reconnect the choke cable as follows:
    a. Reinstall the spring and SE valve onto the choke cable (**Figure 85**).
    b. Insert the SE valve into the carburetor, then thread the SE valve nut (**Figure 84**) into the carburetor and tighten securely.
    c. Make sure the rubber boot is secured over the shoulder on the top of the SE valve nut.
    d. Open and close the choke knob to check choke operation.
13. On California models, reconnect the No. 6 hose (A, **Figure 83**) at the carburetor.
14. Reinstall the fuel tank as described in this chapter.

FUEL PUMP AND FUEL FILTER (2003 MODELS)

An electrical fuel pump mounted below the battery delivers fuel from the fuel tank to the carburetor. Fuel is pumped through an inline fuel filter before it enters the fuel pump to prevent dirt from entering the fuel pump and carburetor. Refer **Figure 86**.

Fuel Pump Voltage Check

1. Remove the right side cover (Chapter Fifteen).

FUEL AND EMISSION CONTROL SYSTEMS

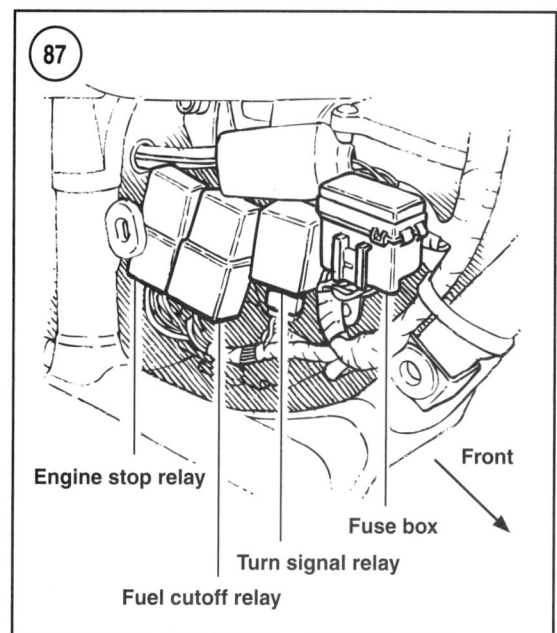

87
- Engine stop relay
- Fuse box
- Turn signal relay
- Fuel cutoff relay
- Front

2. Disconnect the connector at the fuel cutoff relay (**Figure 87**).
3. Connect a voltmeter between the wire harness connector black (+) terminal and a good engine ground (−). Turn the ignition switch on. The voltmeter should read battery voltage. Turn the ignition switch off and note the following:
   a. If there is battery voltage, continue with Step 4.
   b. If there is no battery voltage, check for an open circuit in the black wire.
4. Connect a voltmeter between the wire harness connector blue/yellow (+) terminal and a good engine ground (−). Turn the ignition switch on and the engine stop switch to its run position. The voltmeter should read battery voltage. Turn the ignition switch off and note the following:
   a. If there is battery voltage, continue with Step 5.
   b. If there is no battery voltage, check for an open circuit in the blue/yellow wire.
5. Remove the seats (Chapter Fifteen).
6. Connect a jumper wire between the fuel cutoff relay black/blue and black connector terminals. Disconnect the two fuel pump single pin connectors (black/blue and green wires). Turn the ignition switch on and measure voltage between the black/blue (+) and green (−) wire harness side connectors. The voltmeter should read battery voltage. Turn the ignition switch off and note the following:
   a. If there is no battery voltage, check for an open circuit in the black/blue and green wires.

   b. If there is battery voltage, but there is still a problem with the fuel pump, perform the *Fuel Pump Flow Test* described in this section.
7. Reconnect all connectors and reinstall all parts previously removed.

Fuel Pump Flow Test

1. Remove the air filter housing as described in this chapter.
2. Remove the right side cover (Chapter Fifteen).
3. Turn the fuel valve to its on position, then turn the ignition switch on for a few seconds to fill the fuel lines. Turn the fuel valve to its off position and remove the fuel tank as described in this chapter.
4. Disconnect the connector at the fuel cutoff relay (**Figure 87**).
5. Connect a jumper wire between the fuel cutoff relay black/blue and black connector terminals.
6. Disconnect the fuel hose (B, **Figure 83**) at the carburetor and place it in a plastic graduated beaker.

WARNING
Wear safety glasses when performing Step 7.

7. Turn the ignition switch on for 5 seconds, then turn it off.
8. Measure the amount of fuel in the beaker and multiply it by 12 to determine the fuel pump flow rate for one minute. Compare the actual fuel pump fuel flow rate to the specification in **Table 2** and note the following:
   a. If there was no fuel flow, check for a plugged fuel filter (**Figure 86**). If the fuel filter is okay, replace the fuel pump as described in this section.
   b. If the fuel flow rate is correct, but the fuel pump does not operate when the engine is running, replace the fuel cutoff relay.
   c. If the fuel flow rate is correct, the fuel pump and fuel cutoff relay are operating correctly.
   d. Pour the fuel back into the fuel tank.
9. Reconnect the fuel hose (B, **Figure 83**) at the carburetor.
10. Remove the jumper wire and reconnect the fuel cutoff relay.
11. Reinstall the right side cover (Chapter Fifteen).
12. Reinstall the fuel tank (this chapter).

Fuel Filter Removal/Installation

The manufacturer does not list an interval for replacing the fuel filter. To prevent a plugged fuel filter from causing a starting or drivability problem,

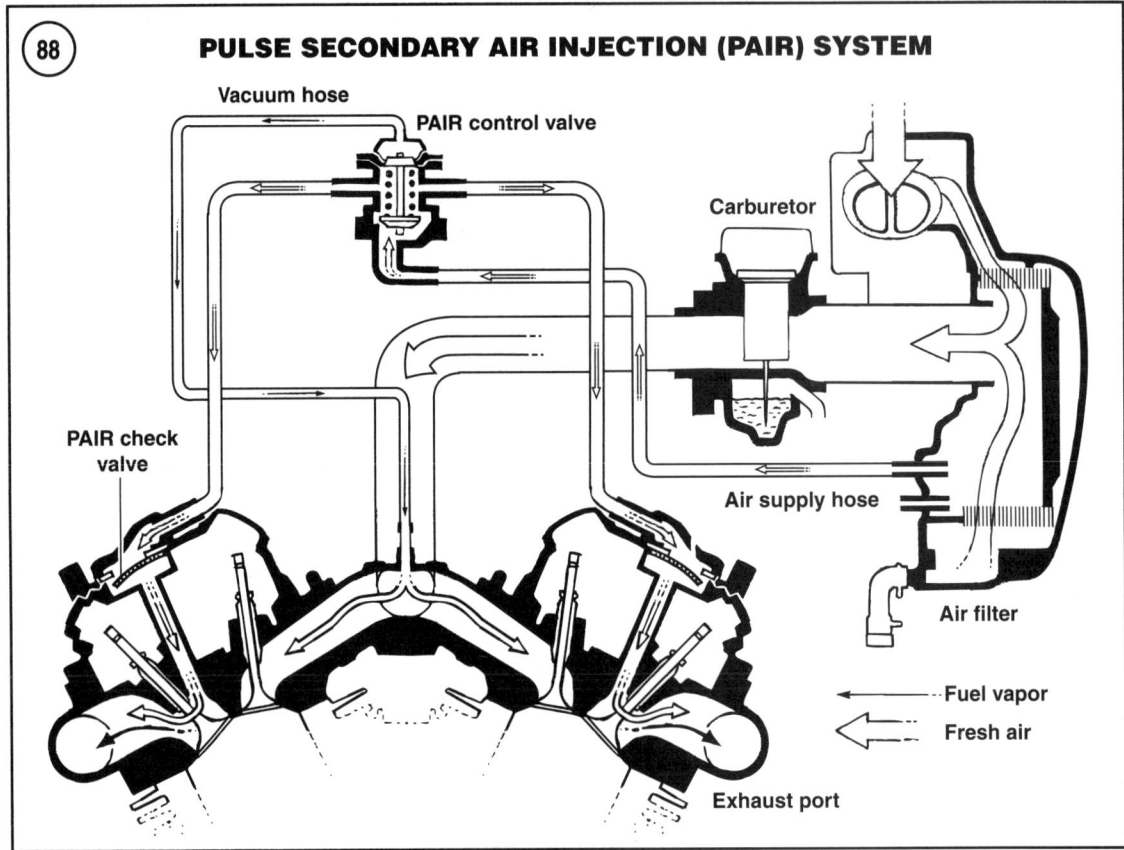

88 PULSE SECONDARY AIR INJECTION (PAIR) SYSTEM

replace the fuel filter every couple of years when the motorcycle is frequently operated.

Refer to **Figure 86**.

1. Turn the ignition switch off.
2. Turn the fuel valve off.
3. Remove the seats (Chapter Fifteen).
4. Compare the fuel filter and fuel hose alignment with **Figure 86**.
5. Pinch the arms on the clamps and slide them up the hoses and away from the fuel filter. Then disconnect the hoses at the fuel filter. Slide the filter holder off its mounting bracket. Turn the fuel filter over and drain as much fuel as possible into a fuel storage can.
6. Remove the fuel filter (6, **Figure 86**) from its holder.
7. Inspect the fuel hoses for cracks, age deterioration and other damage and replace if necessary.
8. Replace weak or damaged hose clamps.
9. Install the new fuel filter into its holder in the direction shown in **Figure 86**.
10. Reconnect the fuel hoses at the fuel filter and secure each hose end with a clamp as shown in **Figure 86**. Position the clamps (3, **Figure 86**) with their arms facing up.
11. Install the filter holder onto its mounting bracket.
12. Turn the ignition switch on to allow the fuel system to pressurize and check for fuel leaks. Repeat two or three times. If there are no fuel leaks, start the engine and check for leaks.

Fuel Pump Removal/Installation

Refer to **Figure 86**.

1. Remove the battery box (Chapter Nine).
2. Before removing the fuel pump, note the following:
   a. Note the fuel hose and wiring harness routing.
   b. Note the hose clamps installed position so they can be installed facing in their original directions to prevent their tabs from contacting the fuel hoses.
3. Disconnect the fuel pump electrical connectors.
4. Pull the fuel pump and the fuel filter holders from the center cover. Disconnect the vent hose from the fuel pump.

WARNING
There will be a significant amount of fuel remaining in the fuel pump. Handle the fuel pump carefully during removal.

5. Disconnect the fuel hoses from the fuel pump and remove the pump.

FUEL AND EMISSION CONTROL SYSTEMS

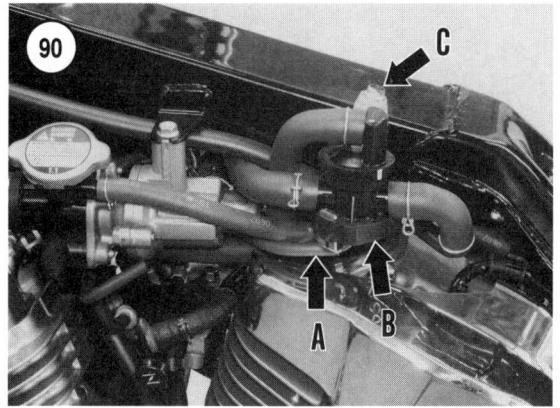

6. Remove the fuel pump (8, **Figure 86**) from its holder. Hold the fuel pump over a plastic container to drain fuel trapped inside.
7. Remove the holder (4, **Figure 86**) and install onto the new pump. Replace the holder if damaged.
8. Inspect the fuel hoses for cracks, age deterioration and other damage and replace if necessary.
9. Replace weak or damaged hose clamps.
10. Install the fuel pump by reversing these steps. Note the following:
    a. Install a new fuel filter as described in this section if installing a new fuel pump.
    b. Install the fuel pump with its holder as shown **Figure 86**. Secure the end of each hose with a clamp and with the clamp arms facing in their original directions.
    c. Make sure the hoses are correctly routed.
    d. After installing the battery box (Chapter Nine), turn the ignition switch on to allow the fuel system to pressurize and check for fuel leaks. Repeat two or three times. If there are no fuel leaks, start the engine and check for leaks.

CRANKCASE BREATHER SYSTEM

The engine is equipped with a closed crankcase breather system. The system draws blow-by gasses from the crankcase and recirculates them into the combustion chamber to be burned.

Liquid residues collect in the air box breather drain tube. These must be emptied at periodic intervals. Refer to *Crankcase Breather Inspection* in Chapter Three for service intervals and procedures.

PULSE SECONDARY AIR SUPPLY SYSTEM

All models are equipped with a pulse secondary air supply system that lowers emissions output by introducing filtered secondary air into the exhaust ports. The introduction of air raises the exhaust temperature, which consumes some of the unburned fuel in the exhaust.

The system uses the momentary pressure variance created by the exhaust gas pulses to introduce air into the exhaust ports. During deceleration the PAIR control valve shuts off the air flow to the exhaust. This prevents exhaust backfire due to the rich mixture conditions on deceleration. The PAIR check valves prevents the reverse flow of air back through the PAIR control valve.

The system consists of a PAIR control valve, PAIR check valves and the vacuum and outlet hoses (**Figure 88**).

Inspection

1. Start and warm the engine up to normal operating temperature, then turn it off.
2. Remove the air filter element (Chapter Three).
3. Check the secondary air intake port (**Figure 89**) in the air filter housing for carbon deposits. If carbon deposits are found, remove and inspect the PAIR check valves for damage as described in this section.
4. Remove the fuel tank as described in this chapter.
5. Remove the air filter housing as described in this chapter.
6. Disconnect the vacuum hose at the PAIR control valve. Refer to **Figure 88** (2003-2007 models) and A, **Figure 90** (2008-on models). Plug the end of the hose to prevent a vacuum leak and connect a vacuum pump to the vacuum hose nozzle on the PAIR control valve.
7. Start the engine and slightly open the throttle. Check that air is being drawn into the air supply hose (**Figure 91**). If not, check for a clogged or damaged air supply hose.
8. With the engine running, apply 470 mm (18.5 in.) HG of vacuum to the PAIR control valve with the vacuum pump. With vacuum applied, check that the air supply hose (**Figure 91**) stops drawing air. Then check that the vacuum does not bleed off.

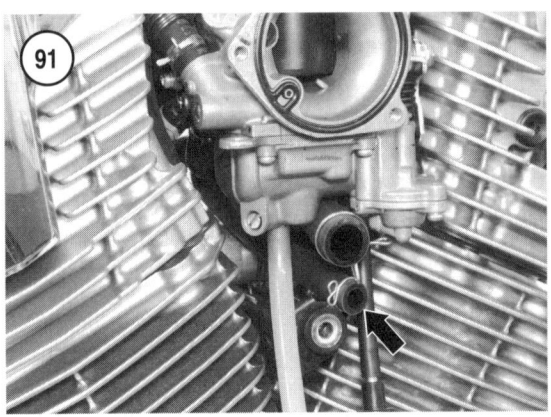

9. If air is drawn in or if the specified vacuum is not maintained, the PAIR control valve is defective and must be replaced.

10. If backfiring occurs on deceleration and the tests just performed were all correct, the air cutoff valve installed on the carburetor may be defective. Refer to *Disassembly* in *Carburetor* in this chapter.

11. Disconnect the vacuum pump and reconnect the vacuum hose at the PAIR control valve.

12. Install the air filter housing, air filter and fuel tank.

PAIR Control Valve Removal/Installation

1. Remove the fuel tank as described in this chapter.
2. Label and then disconnect the hoses at the PAIR control valve (B, **Figure 90**, typical).
3. Remove the bolt (C, **Figure 90**) and the PAIR control valve.
4. Installation is the reverse of removal.

PAIR Check Valves Removal/Inspection/Installation

1. Remove the fuel tank as described in this chapter.
2. To remove the front check valve, remove the left front cylinder head shroud (Chapter Fifteen).
3. To remove the rear check valve, remove the right rear cylinder head shroud (Chapter Fifteen). Then disconnect the right rear spark plug cap.
4. Disconnect the hose from the check valve cover. Then remove the bolts and cover. Refer to **Figure 92** (front) and **Figure 93** (rear).
5. Remove the check valve (**Figure 94**) from the cylinder head cover.

NOTE
Do not disassemble the check valves. Do not bend the stopper or remove the screws to remove and turn the reed plate over.

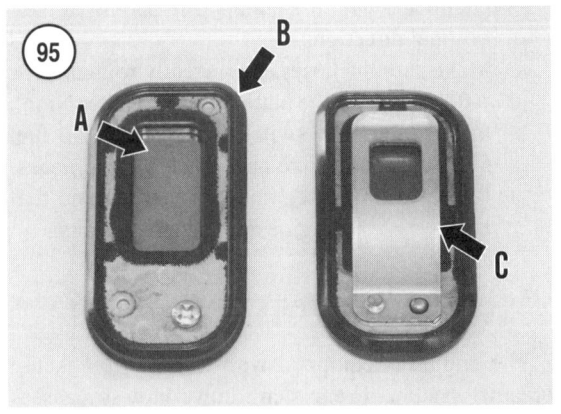

FUEL AND EMISSION CONTROL SYSTEMS

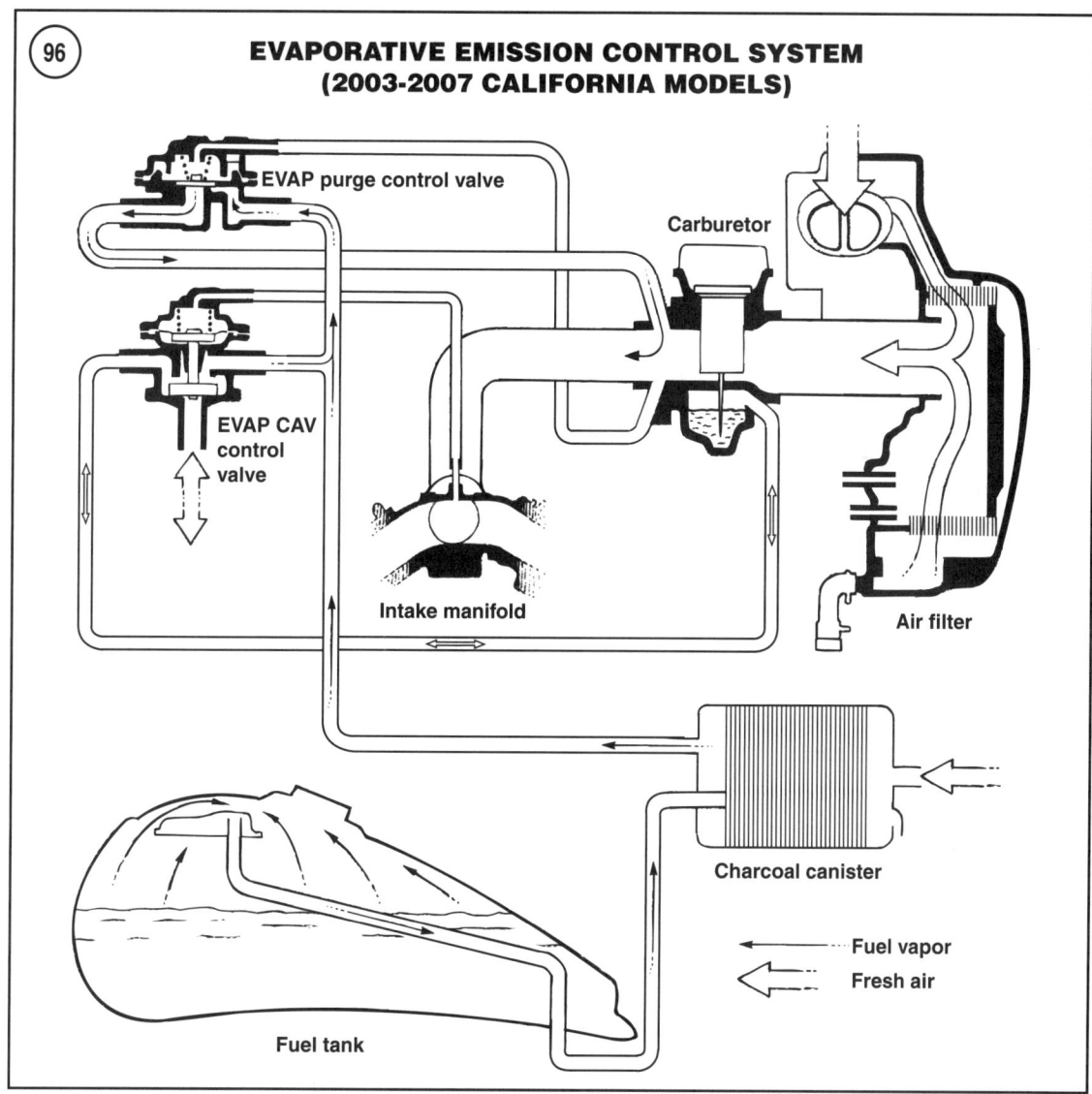

96. EVAPORATIVE EMISSION CONTROL SYSTEM (2003-2007 CALIFORNIA MODELS)

6. Inspect each check valve assembly (**Figure 95**) for fatigue, damage and carbon deposits. The reed plate (A, **Figure 95**) must set flush against its seat. Inspect the rubber seat (B, **Figure 95**) on the check valve body for cracks, flat spots, deterioration and other damage. Make sure the reed plate (C, **Figure 95**) is secured tightly and not damaged. If damaged or wear is noted, or if the mounting screw is loose, replace the check valve assembly.
7. Clean the check valve mounting area in the cylinder head cover with a rag.
8. Install the check valve into the cylinder head cover as shown in **Figure 94**.
9. Install the PAIR check valve cover with the hose fitting facing as shown in **Figure 92** (front) or **Figure 93** (rear). Apply a medium strength threadlocking compound onto the screw threads and tighten to 5.2 N•m (46 in.-lb.).
10. Reverse Steps 1-3.

EVAPORATIVE EMISSION CONTROL SYSTEM (CALIFORNIA MODELS)

The evaporative emission control (EVAP) system captures fuel system vapors and stores them in a charcoal canister so they cannot be released into the atmosphere. When the engine is started, the stored vapors are drawn from the charcoal canister. They pass through the EVAP purge control valve, flow into the carburetor and then into the engine where they are burned. At the same time, the EVAP CAV control valve opens so air is drawn into the carburetor. On 2008-on models, a fuel cutoff solenoid valve, which is controlled by the ICM, was added to stop fuel flow to the carburetor when the rev limiter is operated or when the engine stop switch is turned off when the engine is running. Refer to **Figure 96** (2003-2007 models) or **Figure 97** (2008-on models).

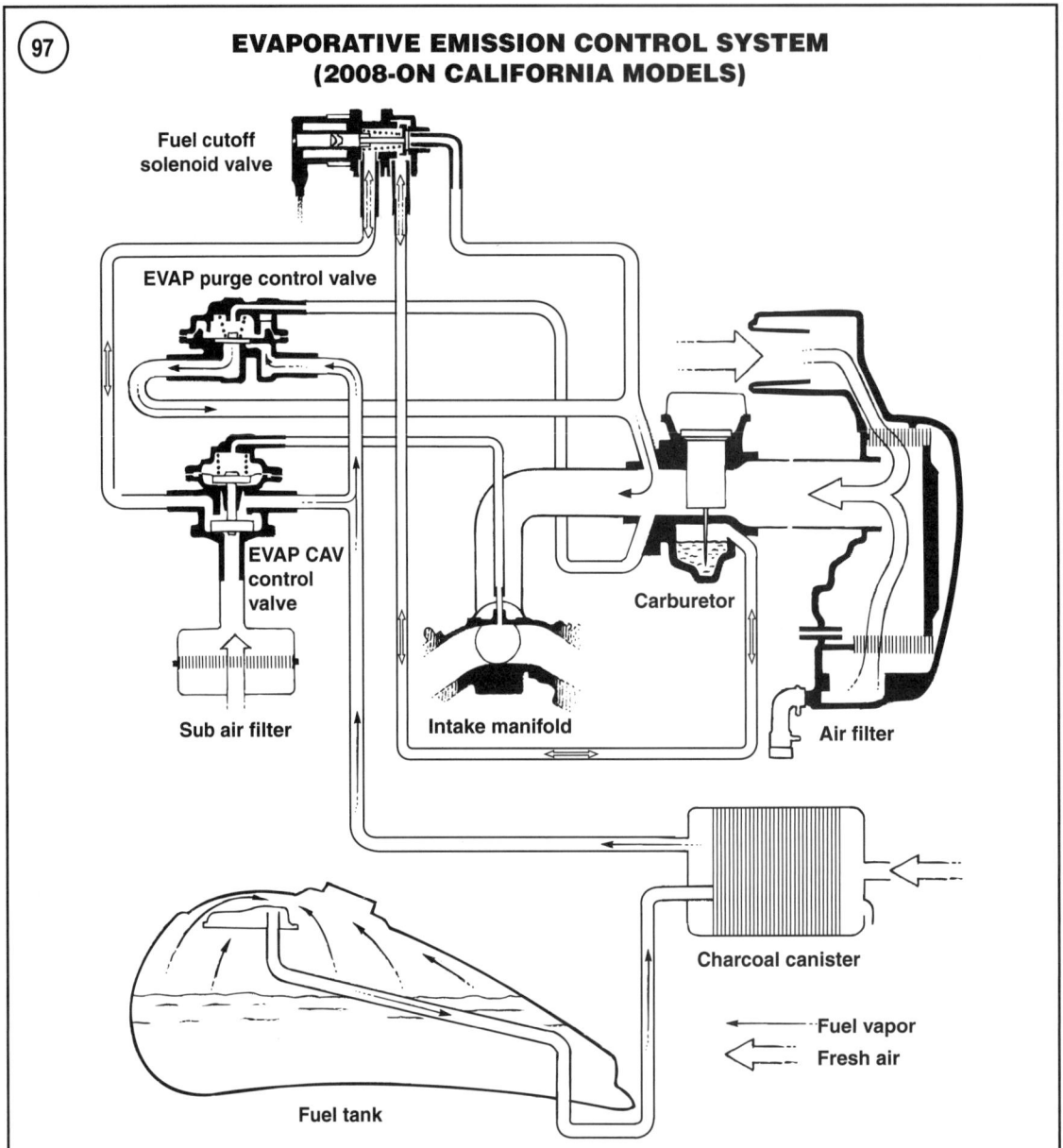

97 EVAPORATIVE EMISSION CONTROL SYSTEM (2008-ON CALIFORNIA MODELS)

Make sure all hoses are correctly routed, properly attached to the different components and all hose clamps are tight. Check all hoses for deterioration, and replace them as necessary.

There are many vacuum hoses used on this system. Without clear identifying marks, reconnecting the hoses can be difficult.

Charcoal (EVAP) Canister Removal/Installation

1. Support motorcycle on workstand.
2. Disconnect the No. 2 hose (A, **Figure 98**) from left side of canister.
3. Remove the two bolts (B, **Figure 98**) and lower the canister (C).
4. Disconnect the No. 1 hose (A, **Figure 99**) and No. 4 hose (B) from the right side of the canister and remove the canister.
5. Installation is the reverse of these steps. Tighten the bolts (B, **Figure 98**) securely.

Evaporative Emission Carburetor Air Vent (EVAP CAV) Control Valve

If the engine is difficult to restart when hot, test the EVAP CAV control valve as described in this section.

Removal/installation

1. Remove the fuel tank as described in this chapter.

FUEL AND EMISSION CONTROL SYSTEMS

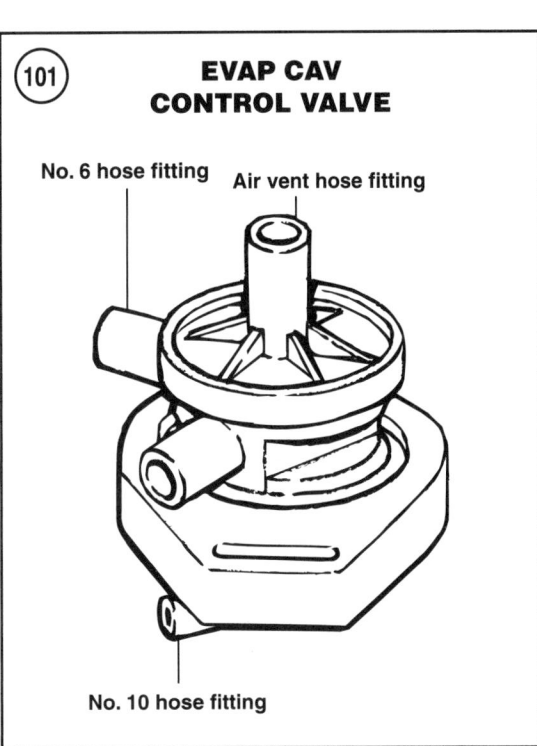

2. Label and disconnect the hoses from the EVAP CAV control valve (A, **Figure 100**).
3. Remove the EVAP CAV control valve off its mounting bracket.
4. Reverse these steps to install the EVAP CAV control valve.

Testing

Refer to **Figure 101**.

A hand-operated vacuum pump with gauge and pressure pump are required.

1. Remove the EVAP CAV control valve as described in this section.

2. Connect a vacuum pump to the No. 10 hose fitting and apply 500 mm (19.7 in.) HG of vacuum. The vacuum should hold. If the vacuum does not hold, replace the EVAP CAV control valve.
3. Disconnect the vacuum pump.
4. Connect the vacuum pump to the air vent hose fitting and apply vacuum to the EVAP CAV control valve. The vacuum should hold. If the vacuum does not hold, replace the EVAP CAV control valve.
5. Disconnect the vacuum pump.
6. Connect the vacuum pump to the No.10 hose fitting and a pressure pump to the air vent hose fitting.

CAUTION
Use only a hand-operated pressure pump. Using air from a high-pressure source in Step 7 and Step 9 may damage the EVAP CAV control valve.

7. Apply vacuum to the No. 10 hose fitting, then pump air through the air vent tube fitting. Air must flow through the valve and exit through the No. 6 hose fitting. Release the vacuum from the valve.
8. Plug the No. 6 hose fitting.
9. Apply vacuum to the No. 10 hose fitting, then pump air through the air vent tube fitting. The air pressure pumped through the air vent tube fitting should hold steady. If the air pressure does not hold, replace the EVAP CAV control valve.
10. Disconnect the vacuum and pressure pumps.
11. Install the EVAP CAV control valve as described in this section.

EVAP CAV Control Valve Sub-Air Filter (2008-On Models) Removal/Cleaning/Installation

The sub-air filter (A, **Figure 102**) for the EVAP CAV control valve is mounted on the fuel cutoff solenoid valve mounting bracket.
1. Remove the fuel tank as described in this chapter.
2. Disconnect the hose (B, **Figure 102**) from the filter housing.
3. Remove the bolt (C, **Figure 102**) and filter housing.
4. Remove the bottom cover and filter.
5. If dirty, remove and clean the sub-air filter with soapy water and rinse with clear water. Replace the filter if deteriorated or damaged.
6. Installation is the reverse of these steps.

Evaporative Emission (EVAP) Purge Control Valve

If the engine is difficult to restart when hot, test the EVAP purge control valve as described in this section.

Removal/installation

1. Remove the fuel tank as described in this chapter.
2. Remove the EVAP CAV control valve as described in this section.
3. Label and disconnect the hoses from the EVAP purge control valve (B, **Figure 100**).
4. Remove the EVAP purge control valve off its mounting bracket.
5. Reverse these steps to install the EVAP purge control valve.

Testing

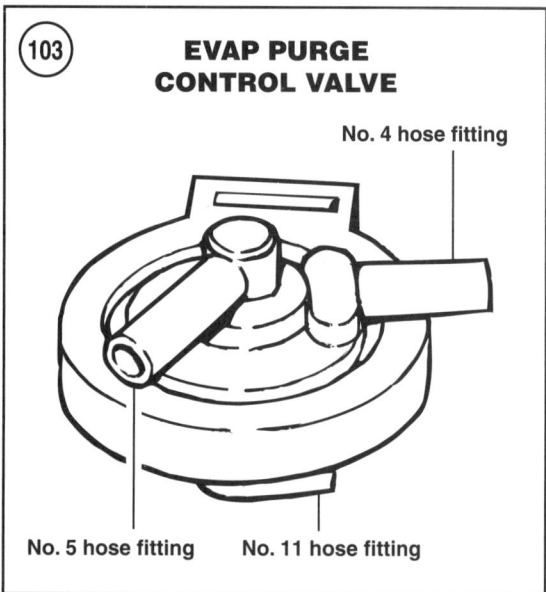

Refer to **Figure 103**.
A hand-operated vacuum pump with gauge and pressure pump are required.
1. Remove the EVAP purge control valve as described in this section.
2. Connect a vacuum pump to the No. 5 hose fitting and apply 40 mm (1.6 in.) HG of vacuum. The vacuum should hold. If the vacuum does not hold, replace the EVAP purge control valve.
3. Disconnect the vacuum pump.
4. Connect the vacuum pump to the No. 11 hose fitting and apply 250 mm (9.8 in.) HG of vacuum. The vacuum should hold. If the vacuum does not hold, replace the EVAP purge control valve. If continuing, leave the vacuum pump connected to the No. 11 hose fitting and perform Step 5.

CAUTION
Use only a hand-operated pressure pump. Using air from a high-pressure source in Step 5 may damage the EVAP purge control valve.

5. Connect a pressure pump to the No.4 hose fitting and apply 25 mm (1.0 in.) HG of vacuum, then pump air through the No. 11 hose fitting. Air should flow through the No. 5 hose fitting. If air did not flow through the No. 5 hose fitting, replace the EVAP purge control valve.
6. Disconnect the vacuum and pressure pumps.
7. Install the EVAP purge control valve as described in this section.

Evaporative Emission (EVAP) Fuel Cutoff Solenoid Valve (2008-On Models)

Removal/installation

1. Remove the fuel tank as described in this chapter.

FUEL AND EMISSION CONTROL SYSTEMS

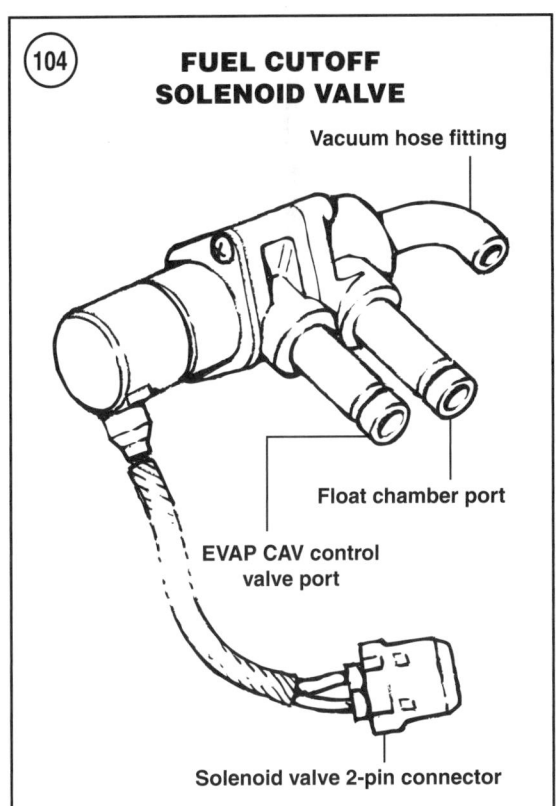

104 FUEL CUTOFF SOLENOID VALVE
- Vacuum hose fitting
- Float chamber port
- EVAP CAV control valve port
- Solenoid valve 2-pin connector

2. Label and disconnect the hoses from the fuel cutoff solenoid valve (D, **Figure 102**) and the sub-air filter housing (B).
3. Remove the bolt (E, **Figure 102**) and the fuel cutoff solenoid valve assembly.
4. Reverse these steps to install the fuel cutoff solenoid valve.

Testing

Refer to **Figure 104**.

A hand-operated vacuum pump with gauge and pressure pump are required.

1. Remove the fuel cutoff solenoid valve as described in this section.
2. Connect a vacuum pump to the vacuum hose fitting and apply 250 mm (9.8 in.) HG of vacuum. The vacuum should hold. If the vacuum does not hold, replace the fuel cutoff solenoid valve.
3. Disconnect the vacuum pump.

CAUTION
Use only a hand-operated pressure pump. Using air from a high-pressure source in Step 4 and Step 7 may damage the fuel cutoff solenoid valve.

4. Connect a pressure pump to the EVAP CAV control valve fitting and pump air into the valve. Air must flow through the valve and exit through the float chamber port. If air did not exit through the float chamber port, replace the fuel cutoff solenoid valve.
5. Remove the pressure pump.
6. Perform the following test:
   a. Connect the vacuum pump to the EVAP CAV control valve fitting.
   b. Connect a 12-volt battery to the fuel cutoff solenoid valve 2-pin electrical connector. Connect the positive battery lead to the black terminal and the negative battery lead to the green terminal.
   c. Apply 250 mm (9.8 in.) HG of vacuum. The vacuum should hold. If the vacuum does not hold, replace the fuel cutoff solenoid valve.
   d. Disconnect the battery test leads and the vacuum pump.
7. Perform the following test:
   a. Connect the pressure pump to the vacuum hose fitting.
   b. Connect a 12-volt battery to the fuel cutoff solenoid valve 2-pin electrical connector. Connect the positive battery lead to the black terminal and the negative battery lead to the green terminal.
   c. Pump air through the vacuum port. Air should flow through the valve and exit through the float chamber port. If air did not exit through the float chamber port, replace the fuel cutoff solenoid valve.
   d. Disconnect the battery test leads and the pressure pump.
8. Install the fuel cutoff solenoid valve as described in this section.

Table 1 CARBURETOR SPECIFICATIONS

Carburetor identification number	
2003 models	
49-state and Canada	VE7BA
California	VE7BB
	(continued)

Table 1 CARBURETOR SPECIFICATIONS (continued)

Carburetor identification number (continued)	
2004 models	
VT1300C models	
49-state and Canada	VE7CA
California	VE7CB
VT1300S models	
49-state and Canada	VE7BE
California	VE7BF
2005 models	
49-state and Canada	VE7BE
California	VE7BF
2006-2007 models	
49-state and Canada	VE7BG
California	VE7BH
2008-on models	
49-state and Canada	VE7BK
California	VE7BL
Float level	18.5 mm (0.73 in.)
Idle speed	800-1000 rpm
Main jet	
2003-2007 models	195
2008-on models	190
Pilot jet	55
Pilot screw	
Initial setting	
2003 models	1 5/8 turns out
2004-2007 models	1 3/4 turns out
2008-on models	1.0 turn out
Pilot screw high altitude adjustment	Refer to text

Table 2 FUEL PUMP SPECIFICATIONS (2003 VTX1300S MODELS)

Fuel pump flow capacity per minute (minimum)	700 ml (23.7 oz.)

Table 3 FUEL SYSTEM TORQUE SPECIFICATIONS

	N•m	in.-lb.	ft.-lb.
Air filter cover screw	4	35	–
Air filter mounting bolt	10	88	–
Air filter mounting screw	3.7	32.7	–
Fuel tank mounting bolt	19	–	14
Fuel valve nut	34	–	25
Intake manifold base Allen bolt	10	88	–
Intake manifold vacuum joint	2.5	22.1	–
PAIR check valve cover screw*	5.2	46.0	–

*Refer to text for additional information.

CHAPTER NINE

ELECTRICAL SYSTEM

Tables 1-10 are at the end of this chapter.

ELECTRICAL COMPONENT REPLACEMENT

Most motorcycle dealerships and parts suppliers will not accept the return of any electrical part. If you cannot determine the exact cause of any electrical system malfunction, have a dealership retest that specific system to verify your test results. If you purchase a new electrical component(s), install it, and then find that the system still does not work properly, you will probably not be able to return the unit for a refund.

Consider any test result carefully before replacing a component that tests only *slightly* out of specification, especially resistance. A number of variables can affect test results dramatically. These include the testing meter's internal circuitry, ambient temperatures and conditions under which the motorcycle has been operated. All instructions and specifications have been checked for accuracy; however, successful test results depend largely upon individual accuracy.

ELECTRICAL CONNECTORS

Corrosion-causing moisture can enter electrical connectors and cause poor electrical connections leading to component failure. Before reconnecting electrical connectors, pack them with a dielectric grease compound. Do not use a substitute that may interfere with the current flow within the electrical connector. Do not use silicone sealant.

BATTERY

A sealed, maintenance-free battery is installed on all models. The battery electrolyte level cannot be serviced. When replacing the battery, use a sealed type; do not install a non-sealed battery. Never attempt to remove the sealing cap from the top of the battery. The battery does not require periodic electrolyte inspection or refilling. Refer to **Table 1** for battery specifications.

To prevent accidental shorts that could blow a fuse when working on the electrical system, always disconnect the negative battery cable from the battery.

Safety Precautions

WARNING
Although the battery is a sealed type, protect your eyes, skin and clothing; electrolyte is corrosive and can cause severe burns and permanent injury. The battery case may be cracked and leaking electrolyte. If electrolyte gets into your eyes, flush your eyes thoroughly with clean, running water and get immediate medical attention. Always wear safety goggles when servicing the battery.

WARNING
While batteries are being charged, highly explosive hydrogen gas forms in each cell. Some of this gas escapes through a vent opening and may form an explosive atmosphere in and around the battery. This condition can persist for several hours. Sparks, an open flame or a lighted cigarette can ignite the gas, causing an internal battery explosion and possible serious personal injury.

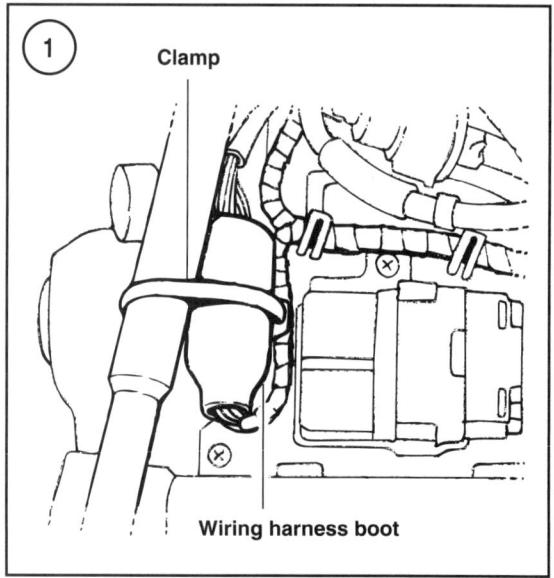

Take the following precautions:
1. Do not disconnect live circuits at the battery. A spark usually occurs when a live circuit is broken.
2. Do not smoke or permit any open flame near any battery being charged or which has been recently charged.
3. Take care when connecting or disconnecting a battery charger. Be sure the power switch is off before making or breaking connections. Poor connections are a common cause of electrical arcs, which cause explosions.
4. Keep children and pets away from the charging equipment and battery.

Removal/Installation

NOTE
Recycle the old battery. Most motorcycle dealerships accept old batteries in trade when purchasing a new one. Never place an old battery in the trash.

1. Read *Safety Precautions* in this section.
2. Turn the ignition switch off.
3. Remove the seats (Chapter Fifteen).
4. On 2003-2004 models, remove the clamp securing the wiring harness to the left side frame tube (**Figure 1**) and move the wiring harness away from the cover.

5. Remove the screws and the battery box cover (A, **Figure 2**) with the ignition control module (ICM [B]) attached, or the ICM can be removed first, and then the cover.
6. Disconnect the negative battery lead (A, **Figure 3**) first. Then remove the positive lead (B, **Figure 3**).

NOTE
If only the negative battery terminal is being disconnected, insulate the cable or battery terminal so it cannot accidentally reconnect the battery circuit.

7. Thread a long 6-mm bolt into each battery terminal (A, **Figure 4**) and use them to lift the battery (B) out of the battery box. Remove the bolts from the battery terminals.
8. After servicing the battery, install it by reversing these removal steps while noting the following:

CAUTION
Be sure the battery cables are connected to their proper terminals. Connecting

ELECTRICAL SYSTEM

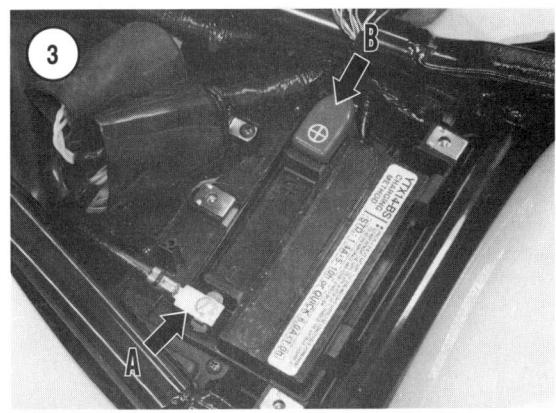

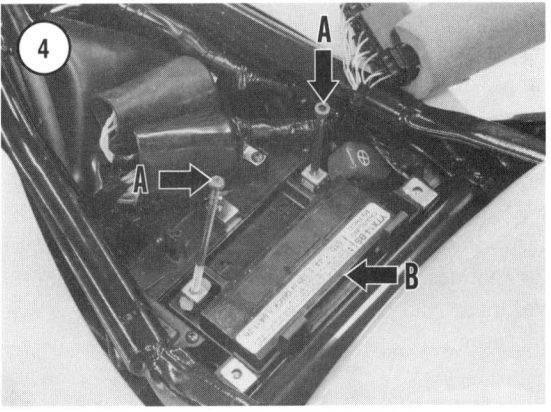

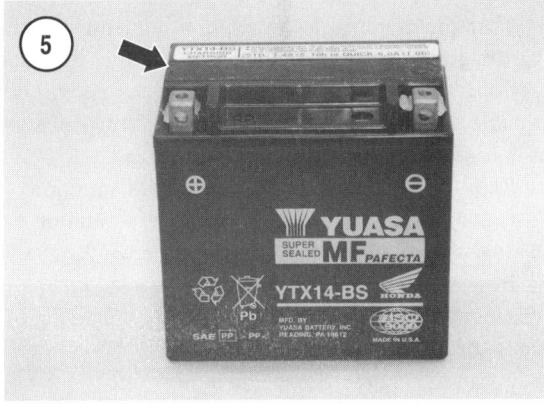

the battery backward reverses the polarity and damages components in the electrical system. When installing a replacement battery, make sure the negative and positive battery cables are in the same positions.

a. Always connect the positive cable (B, **Figure 3**) first, and then the negative cable (A).
b. Coat the battery leads with dielectric grease or petroleum jelly.
c. Make sure the clamp is secured around the wiring harness.

Cleaning/Inspection

The battery electrolyte level cannot be serviced. *Never* attempt to remove the sealing bar cap from the top of the battery (**Figure 5**). The battery does not require periodic electrolyte inspection or refilling.

1. Read *Safety Precautions* in this section.
2. Remove the battery from the motorcycle as described in this section. Do not clean the battery while it is mounted in the motorcycle.
3. Clean the battery case with a solution of warm water and baking soda. Rinse thoroughly with clean water.
4. Inspect the physical condition of the battery. Look for bulges or cracks in the case, leaking electrolyte or corrosion buildup.
5. Check the battery terminal bolts, spacers and nuts for corrosion and damage. Clean parts with a solution of baking soda and water and rinse thoroughly. Replace if damaged.
6. Check the battery cable clamps for corrosion and damage. If corrosion is minor, clean the battery cable clamps with a stiff brush. Replace excessively worn or damaged cables.

Voltage Test

Use a digital voltmeter to test the battery while it is mounted on the motorcycle. Refer to **Table 1** for battery voltage readings.

1. Remove the battery cover as described in this section.

NOTE
To prevent false test readings, do not test the battery if the battery terminals are corroded. Remove and clean the battery and terminals as described in this section, then install and test the battery.

2. Connect a digital voltmeter between the battery positive (+) and negative (−) terminals.
   a. If the battery voltage is 13.0-13.2, the battery is fully charged.
   b. If the battery voltage is below 12.3 volts, the battery is undercharged and requires charging.
3. If the battery is undercharged, recharge it as described in this section. Then test the charging system as described in *Charging System* in this chapter.

Load Test

A load test checks the battery's performance with a current draw or load applied and is the best indication of battery condition.

A battery load tester is required for this procedure. When using a load tester, follow the manufacturer's instructions for the procedure.

Charging

> **WARNING**
> *During the charging process, highly explosive hydrogen gas is released from the battery. Charge the battery only in a well-ventilated area away from any open flames (including pilot lights on home gas appliances). Do not allow any smoking in the area. Never check the charge of the battery by connecting screwdriver blades or other metal objects between the terminals; the resulting spark can ignite the hydrogen gas.*

Refer to *Safety Precautions* in this section. Refer to *New Battery Setup* in this section if the battery is new.

To recharge a maintenance-free battery, use an automatic battery charger with variable voltage and amperage outputs. Excessive voltage and amperage from an unregulated charger can damage the battery and shorten service life.

The battery should only self-discharge approximately one percent of its given capacity each day. If a battery not in use, without any loads connected, loses its charge within one week after charging, the battery is defective.

1. Remove the battery as described in this section.
2. Measure the battery voltage as described in *Voltage Test* in this section. Voltage specifications are in **Table 2**.
3. Clean the battery terminals and case as described in this section.
4. Connect the positive (+) charger lead to the positive battery terminal and the negative (−) charger lead to the negative battery terminal.

> **CAUTION**
> *When using an adjustable battery charger, follow the manufacturer's instructions. Do not use a larger output battery charger or increase the charge rate on an adjustable battery charger to reduce charging time. Doing so can cause permanent battery damage.*

> **NOTE**
> *If the voltage reading is low, internal resistance in the battery may prevent it from recovering when following normal charging attempts. When a battery's state of charge is 25 percent or less, it is necessary to increase the charging voltage of the battery by applying a low current rate to allow the battery to recover. This will require an adjustable battery charger with a separate amp and volt meter or a battery charger that can do this automatically. Automatic battery chargers that can diagnose and recover deep-discharged batteries can also be used without overcharging or overheating the battery.*

5. Charge the battery following the manufacturer's instructions. Set the charger at 12 volts and switch it on. Charge the battery at a slow charge rate of 1/10 its given capacity. To determine the current output in amps, divide the battery amp hour capacity by 10. Refer to Charging Current in **Table 1**.
6. After the battery has been charged for 4-5 hours or within the time determined by the automatic battery charger, turn the charger off, disconnect the leads and allow the battery to set for a minimum of 30 minutes. Then check the battery with a digital voltmeter and compare to the voltage specifications in **Table 2**.

Battery Storage

When the motorcycle is ridden infrequently or put in storage for an extended amount of time, the battery must be periodically charged to ensure it will be capable of working correctly when returned to service. Use an automatic battery charger.

1. Remove the battery as described in this section.
2. Clean the battery and terminals with a solution of baking soda and water.
3. Inspect the battery case for any cracks, leaks or bulging. Replace the battery if the case is leaking or damaged.
4. Clean the battery box in the motorcycle.
5. Charge the battery to 100 percent. Store the battery in a cool dry place. Continue to charge the battery once a month when stored in temperatures below 16° C (61° F) and every two weeks when stored in temperatures above 16° C (61° F).

New Battery Setup

Read *Safety Precautions* in this section.

When ordering a new battery from a mail order company, it will be necessary to fill and charge the battery. Follow the battery manufacturer's instructions while observing the following guidelines when activating a new battery:

ELECTRICAL SYSTEM

CAUTION
A new battery must be fully charged before installation. Failure to do so reduces the life of the battery. Using a new battery without an initial charge causes permanent battery damage. That is, the battery will never be able to hold more than an 80 percent charge. Charging a new battery after it has been used will not bring its charge to 100 percent. When purchasing a new battery, verify its charge status. If necessary, have the initial or booster charge performed before accepting the battery.

1. Use the electrolyte that comes with the battery. Do not use electrolyte from a common container.
2. Fill the battery with all of the electrolyte included with the battery kit.
3. Allow the battery to sit for one hour. This allows the plates to absorb the electrolyte for optimum performance.
4. Loosely install the sealing cap over the battery filling holes.
5. Charge the battery following the manufacturer's instructions.
6. When the battery is fully charged, press the sealing cap (**Figure 5**) firmly to seal each of the battery fill holes. Make sure the cap seats flush into the battery.

CAUTION
Never remove the sealing cap or add additional electrolyte to the battery.

BATTERY BOX

Removal/Installation

Refer to **Figure 6**.
1. Remove the battery as described in this chapter.
2. On 2003 models, perform the following:
   a. Remove the fuel filter (Chapter Eight).
   b. Remove the screws and the fuel filter mounting bracket.
3. Remove the screws and the tool box cover.
4. Remove the two bolts from inside the box.
5. Remove the two bolts securing the battery box to the frame and remove the battery box.
6. Installation is the reverse of these steps, plus the following:
   a. Bosses on the bottom of the battery box fit into grommets mounted in the frame. Make sure the grommets are in place before installing the battery box.
   b. Fit the bosses on the battery box into the grommets, then install and tighten the mounting bolts.
   c. On 2003 models, check the fuel filter for leaks.

CHARGING SYSTEM

The charging system supplies power to operate the engine and electrical system components and keeps the battery charged. The charging system consists of the battery, alternator and a voltage regulator/rectifier. A 30-amp fuse protects the circuit. Refer to the appropriate wiring diagram at the end of this manual.

Alternating current generated by the alternator is rectified to direct current. The voltage regulator maintains constant voltage to the battery and electrical loads despite variations in engine speed and load.

Troubleshooting

Because the charging system is not equipped with an indicator system (light or gauge), slow cranking may be the first indication of a charging system problem.
1. A fully charged battery is required to accurately test the charging system. If the battery is damaged or worn out, the charging system may not be at fault.
2. Check all of the connections to make sure they are tight and free of corrosion. Use the correct wiring diagram at the end of this manual to identify and locate the appropriate connectors.
3. Perform the *Current Draw Test* as described in this section. If the current draw is incorrect, continue with Step 4. If the current draw is correct, go to Step 5.
4. Disconnect the regulator/rectifier connector as described in this section. Repeat the *Current Draw Test*. If the current draw is acceptable, the regulator/rectifier is faulty. Replace the regulator/rectifier as described in this section and retest. If the current draw is high, the problem is probably caused by a short in the wiring or the ignition switch is faulty. Check for a short circuit in the charging system by disconnecting the connectors one at a time while repeating the current draw test performed in Step 3. Reconnect the connector before disconnecting another connector. If the current draw returns to normal when a connector is disconnected, the circuit is shorting to ground. If a short circuit cannot be located, test the ignition switch as described in this chapter.
5. Check the stator coil resistance as described in *Stator Coil, Ignition Pulse Generator and Left Crankcase Cover* in this chapter. If the stator coil re-

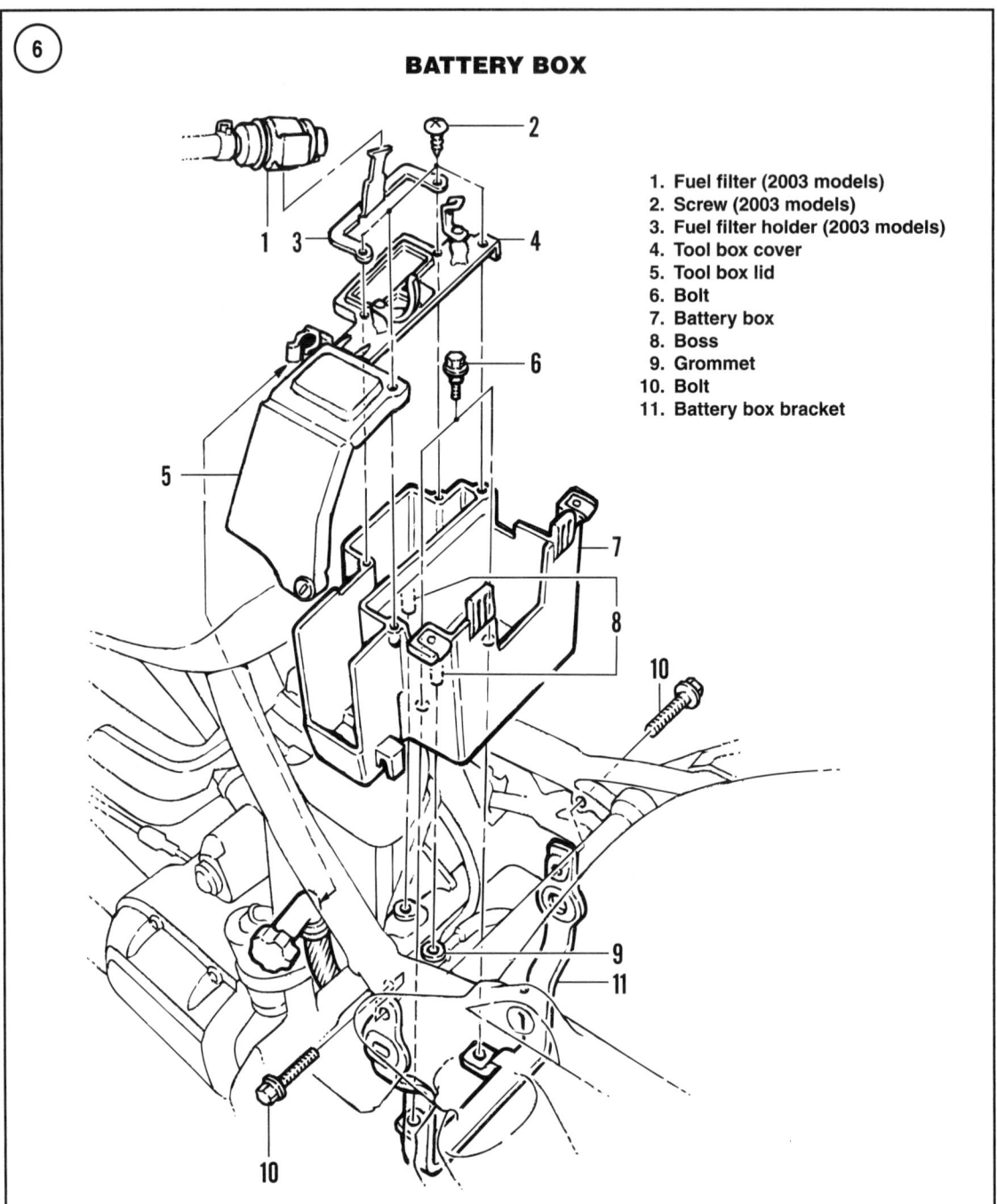

BATTERY BOX

1. Fuel filter (2003 models)
2. Screw (2003 models)
3. Fuel filter holder (2003 models)
4. Tool box cover
5. Tool box lid
6. Bolt
7. Battery box
8. Boss
9. Grommet
10. Bolt
11. Battery box bracket

sistance is incorrect, the charge coil is damaged and should be replaced. If the resistance is correct, continue with Step 6.

6. Perform the *Charging Voltage Test* in this section. If the voltage reading is incorrect, continue with Step 7. If the voltage reading is correct, the battery is damaged. Replace the battery and retest.

7. Perform the *Wiring Harness Test* in this section. If all of the tests are correct, the regulator/rectifier is damaged and must be replaced. If one or all of the tests are incorrect, check for an open circuit in the related circuit wire. Then check for loose or contaminated connector terminals and for a short circuit in the wiring harness.

8. Once a repair has been made, repeat the *Charging Voltage Test* in this section to confirm the charging system is working correctly.

Current Draw Test

A short circuit will increase current draw and drain the battery. Perform this test before troubleshooting

ELECTRICAL SYSTEM

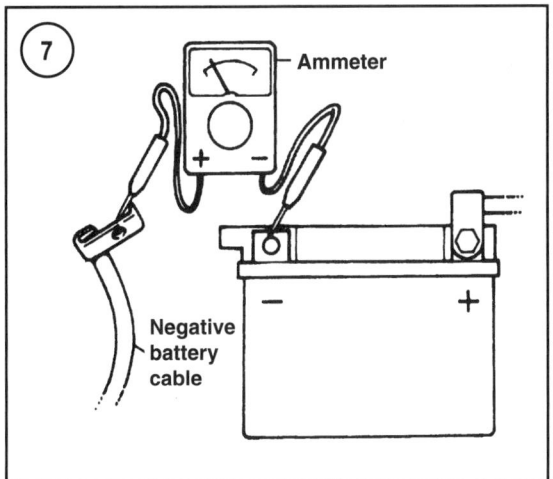

the charging system or performing the charging voltage test to determine if the current draw is normal or excessive. If the battery discharges because of a short, the charging system may not be at fault.

NOTE
When installing electrical accessories, do not wire them into a live circuit where they stay on all the time. Refer to the manufacturer's instructions.

1. Turn the ignition switch off.
2. Disconnect the negative battery cable as described in *Battery* in this chapter.

CAUTION
Before connecting the ammeter into the circuit, set the meter to its highest amperage scale. This prevents a large current flow from damaging the meter or blowing the meter's fuse.

3. Connect an ammeter between the negative battery cable and the negative battery terminal as shown in **Figure 7**. Do *not* turn the ignition switch on once this connection is made.
4. Switch the ammeter to its lowest scale and note the reading. The maximum current draw is 2.0 mA or less. A current draw that exceeds 2.0 mA will discharge the battery.
5. If the current draw is excessive, consider the following probable causes:
   a. Damaged battery.
   b. Faulty voltage regulator/rectifier.
   c. Short circuit in the system.
   d. Loose, dirty or faulty electrical connectors.
   e. Aftermarket electrical accessories incorrectly added to the electrical system.
6. To find the short circuit that is causing the excessive current draw, refer to the wiring diagram at the end of this book. Then disconnect different electrical connectors one by one while monitoring the ammeter. When the current draw returns to an acceptable level, the faulty circuit is indicated. Test the circuit further to find the problem.
7. Disconnect the ammeter.
8. Reconnect the negative battery cable.

Charging Voltage Test

This procedure tests charging system operation. It does not measure maximum charging system output.

To obtain accurate test results, the battery must be fully charged (13.0-13.2 volts).
1. Start and run the engine until it reaches normal operating temperature, then turn the engine off.
2. Remove the battery box cover as described in *Battery* in this chapter.
3. Connect a digital voltmeter to the battery terminals (positive-to-positive and negative-to-negative). To prevent a short, make sure the voltmeter leads attach firmly to the battery terminals. Record the voltage reading.

CAUTION
Do not disconnect either battery cable when making this test. Doing so may damage the voltmeter or electrical accessories.

4. Start the engine and allow it to idle. Turn the headlight to HI beam. Gradually increase engine speed to 5000 rpm and read the voltage indicated on the voltmeter. The voltmeter should show a reading greater than the measured battery voltage recorded in Step 3 and less than 15.5 volts.

NOTE
*If the battery is often discharged, but the charging voltage tested normal during Step 4, the battery may be damaged. Perform a battery load-test as described in **Battery** in this section to accurately test the battery.*

5. If the voltage reading is incorrect, perform the *Wiring Harness Test* in this section, while noting the following:
   a. If the charging voltage is too low, check for an open or short circuit in the charging system wiring harness, an open or short in the alternator, high resistance in the alternator-to-battery cable or a damaged regulator/rectifier.
   b. If the charging voltage is too high, check for a poor regulator/rectifier ground, damaged regulator/rectifier or a damaged battery.

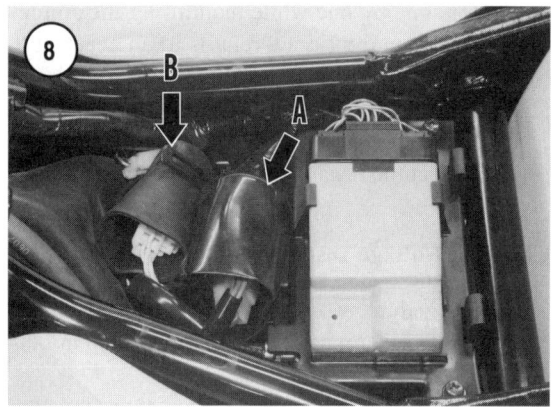

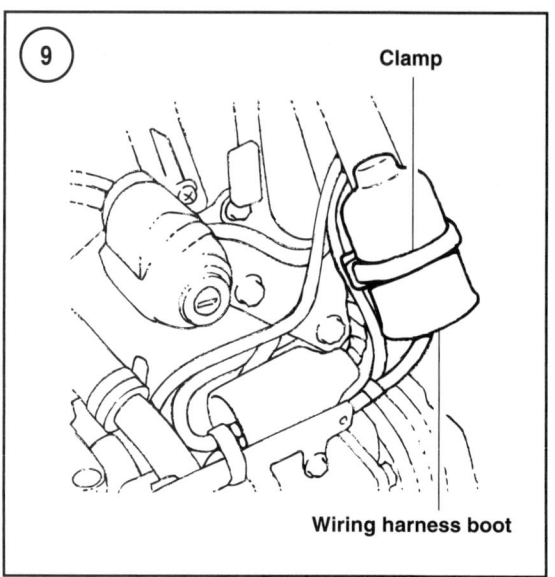

Wiring Harness Test

This procedure tests the integrity of the wires and connectors attached to the regulator/rectifier.

Use the appropriate wiring diagram at the end of this manual to identify the connectors and wire colors called out in this test.

1. Remove the seats (Chapter Fifteen).
2A. On 2003-2004 models, remove the clamp securing the wiring harness boot (**Figure 1**) to the frame. Disconnect the regulator/rectifier 4-pin connector located inside the wiring harness boot.
2B. On 2005-on models, open the clamp and disconnect the regulator/rectifier 4-pin connector located inside the wiring harness boot (A, **Figure 8**).
3. Check for loose or corroded terminals in the alternator, regulator/rectifier and wiring harness connectors.

NOTE
Perform all of the tests on the wiring harness connector side, not on the regulator/rectifier connector side.

4. Check the battery charge line as follows:
   a. Connect a voltmeter between the red/white wire (+) and a good engine ground (–).
   b. The voltmeter should read battery voltage at all times (ignition switch on or off).
   c. If there is no voltage, check both of the red/white wires for an open circuit.
   d. Disconnect the voltmeter leads.
5. Check the ground circuit as follows:
   a. Connect the ohmmeter between the green wire and a good engine ground.
   b. The ohmmeter should read continuity.
   c. If there is no continuity, check both of the green wires for an open circuit.
6. Check the charge coil circuit as described in *Stator Coil, Ignition Pulse Generator and Left Crankcase Cover* in this chapter.
7. Reverse Step 1 and Step 2 to complete the procedure.

Regulator/Rectifier Removal/Installation

1. Remove both seats (Chapter Fifteen).
2A. On 2003-2004 models, perform the following:
   a. Remove the clamp securing the wiring harness boot (**Figure 1**) to the frame. Disconnect the regulator/rectifier 4-pin connector located inside the wiring harness boot.
   b. Remove the left side cover (Chapter Fifteen).
   c. Remove the clamp securing the wiring harness boot (**Figure 9**) to the frame. Disconnect the alternator 3-pin connector located inside the wiring harness boot.
2B. On 2005-on models, perform the following:
   a. Open the clamp and disconnect the regulator/rectifier 4-pin connector located inside the wiring harness boot (A, **Figure 8**).
   b. Disconnect the alternator 3-pin connector located inside the wiring harness boot (B, **Figure 8**).
3. If used, remove the charcoal canister as described in *Evaporative Emission Control System* in Chapter Eight.
4. Note the regulator/rectifier wiring harness routing.
5. Remove the bolts (A, **Figure 10**) and the regulator/rectifier (B).
6. Installation is the reverse of removal. Tighten the bolts securely.

STATOR COIL, IGNITION PULSE GENERATOR AND LEFT CRANKCASE COVER

The stator coil and ignition pulse generator are mounted inside the left crankcase cover.

ELECTRICAL SYSTEM

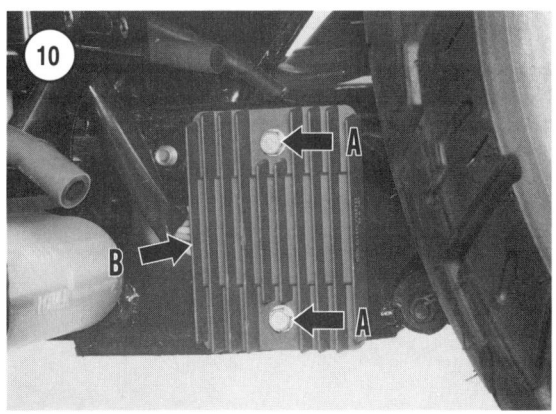

Left Crankcase Cover Removal/Installation

1. Drain the engine oil (Chapter Three).
2. Remove the following as described in Chapter Fifteen:
   a. Both seats.
   b. Left side cover.
   c. Left footrest or footpeg assembly.
   d. Left crankcase rear cover.

NOTE
Note the wiring harness routing before removing the left crankcase cover.

3A. On 2003-2004 models, perform the following:
   a. Remove the clamp securing the wiring harness boot (**Figure 1**) to the frame. Disconnect the ignition pulse generator 2-pin connector and the neutral switch connector located inside the wiring harness boot.
   b. Remove the clamp securing the wiring harness boot (**Figure 9**) to the frame. Disconnect the alternator 3-pin connector located inside the wiring harness boot.
3B. On 2005-on models, perform the following:
   a. Open the clamp and disconnect the ignition pulse generator 2-pin connector and the neutral switch connector located inside the wiring harness boot (A, **Figure 8**).
   b. Disconnect the alternator 3-pin connector located inside the wiring harness boot (B, **Figure 8**).

NOTE
If the alternator wiring harness connector (A, Figure 11) is difficult to remove between the water hose and case half, remove the water hose mounting bolt (B).

4. Disconnect the neutral switch electrical connector (**Figure 12**).
5. Place a clean drain pan underneath the left crankcase cover.

NOTE
Some engine oil will drain out when the left crankcase cover is removed.

NOTE
To ensure that the left crankcase cover bolts are installed correctly during assembly, make an outline of the left crankcase cover on a piece of cardboard. Punch holes in the cardboard at the same locations as the bolts. Place the bolts in their respective holes.

6. Remove the bolts securing the left crankcase cover (**Figure 13**) to the engine, noting the position of the wiring harness clamps and remove the cover. If necessary, lightly tap the cover to loosen it from the engine. If the cover is tight, mount a small knock puller (**Figure 14**) into the cover's threaded hole and operate the puller to loosen the cover from the engine. Do not pry the cover off.
7. Remove the dowel pins (A, **Figure 15**).
8. If necessary, service the stator coil and ignition pulse generator as described in this section.
9. Do not clean the cover or stator coils in solvent. Wipe the coils and cover with a clean rag.

10. Installation is the reverse of removal. Note the following:

NOTE
Because a liquid sealer is used on the left crankcase cover, clean the parts and mating surfaces as described in the following steps to prevent an oil leak.

a. Carefully remove all sealer from the cover and crankcase mating surfaces. Block off the crankcase opening to prevent the sealer from entering the engine lower end.
b. Spray the crankcase bolt holes with an aerosol cleaner to remove all oil and sealer residue. If necessary, use a brush to loosen the sealer from the threads.
c. Clean the cover mounting bolts to remove all oil and sealer residue.
d. Make sure the starter drive gears (B, **Figure 15**) are properly installed. Refer to *Flywheel, Starter Clutch and Starter Drive Gears* in this chapter.
e. Make sure the grommet (A, **Figure 16**) on the stator coil wiring harness is positioned firmly into the cover notch.
f. Apply a light coat of gasket sealer onto the left crankcase cover gasket surface (B, **Figure 16**). Use HondaBond 4, ThreeBond 1104 or Yamabond 4.
g. Install the two dowel pins (A, **Figure 15**) and the left crankcase cover (**Figure 13**). Make sure there are no gaps between the cover and engine.
h. Use the cardboard template made during disassembly to identify the cover bolts and clamps and install them. Tighten the bolts in a crossing pattern and two steps to 12 N•m (106 in.-lb.).

NOTE
Allow the gasket sealer to set according to the manufacturer's instructions before adding engine oil to the crankcase.

i. Make sure the electrical connectors are free of corrosion. Check the wiring harness routing.
j. Refill the engine with oil (Chapter Three).
k. Check the cover for oil leaks.

Stator Coil Resistance Test

The stator coil (C, **Figure 16**) is mounted inside the left crankcase cover. The stator coil can be tested while the left crankcase cover is mounted on the engine.
1A. On 2003-2004 models, perform the following:
  a. Remove the left side cover (Chapter Fifteen).
  b. Remove the clamp securing the wiring harness boot (**Figure 9**) to the frame. Disconnect the alternator 3-pin connector located inside the wiring harness boot.
1B. On 2005-on models, perform the following:
  a. Remove the seats (Chapter Fifteen).
  b. Disconnect the alternator 3-pin connector located inside the wiring harness boot (B, **Figure 8**).
2. Measure the resistance between each yellow wire on the alternator side of the connector. Refer to **Table 3** for the specified stator coil resistance. The test must be made at an ambient temperature of 20°C (68°F). Do not test when the engine or component is hot.
3. Replace the stator coil assembly if any resistance reading is incorrect.

ELECTRICAL SYSTEM

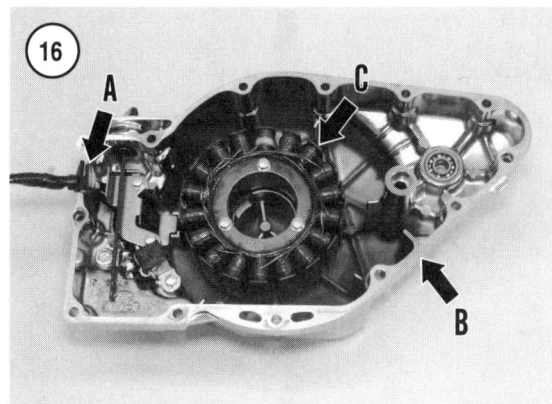

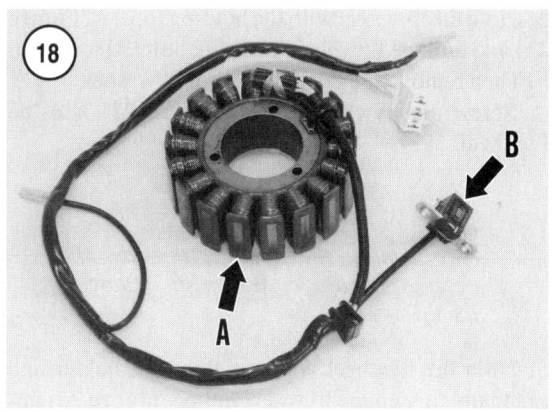

4. Check continuity from each yellow stator wire to ground. Replace the stator coil if any yellow terminal has continuity to ground, indicating a short within the stator coil winding.
5. If the stator coil (C, **Figure 16**) fails either of these tests, replace it as described in this section.
6. Make sure the electrical connector is secure and corrosion free.

Stator Coil and Ignition Pulse Generator Removal/Installation

1. Remove the left crankcase cover as described in this section.
2. Remove the bolts and the wire harness guide plate (A, **Figure 17**). Note the stator coil and ignition pulse generator wire harness routing before removing them.
3. Remove the stator coil (B, **Figure 17**) and ignition pulse generator (C) mounting bolts.
4. Pull the grommet out of the cover and remove the stator coil and ignition pulse generator.

NOTE
Do not separate the stator coil (A, Figure 18) and ignition pulse generator (B) wiring harnesses. Both com-

ponents are assembled and sold as a complete assembly.

5. Clean and dry the left crankcase cover. Clean the mounting bolt holes of all threadlock residue.
6. Installation is the revere of removal. Apply a medium strength threadlocking compound onto all the stator coil, ignition pulse generator and wire harness guide plate mounting bolts and tighten them to 10 N•m (88 in.-lb.).

FLYWHEEL, STARTER CLUTCH AND STARTER DRIVE GEARS

The flywheel (alternator rotor) is mounted on the left end of the crankshaft. The starter clutch is mounted on the back of the flywheel. The starter drive gears can be removed without removing the flywheel.

Tools

CAUTION
Do not try to remove the flywheel without the correct puller. Doing so may damage the flywheel and crankshaft.

The following tools, or their equivalents, are required to remove the flywheel (alternator rotor):
1. Flywheel puller (M22 × 1.5 right-hand threads): Motion Pro part No. 08-0074 (A, **Figure 19**) or Honda part No. 07733-002001 or 07933-3290001 (U.S. only).
2. Flywheel holder: part No. 07725-0040000 or STVS17 (U.S. only) (B, **Figure 19**).

Removal

1. Remove the left crankcase cover as described in this chapter.
2. Remove the torque limiter (A, **Figure 20**), shaft (B) and the starter idle gear (C).

3. Hold the flywheel with the holding tool (A, **Figure 21**) and turn the flywheel mounting bolt (B) to loosen it. Then remove the flywheel bolt and washer.
4. Screw the flywheel puller (**Figure 22**) into the flywheel.

CAUTION
Do not force the puller. Excessive force may damage the flywheel threads. If necessary, have a dealership remove the flywheel.

5. Hold the flywheel with the flywheel holder and gradually tighten the flywheel puller (**Figure 22**) until the flywheel pops off the crankshaft taper. Remove the flywheel while also holding onto the starter driven gear installed on the back of the flywheel.
6. Do not remove the Woodruff key (A, **Figure 23**) from the crankshaft unless it is loose. If it is loose, check both the crankshaft keyway and Woodruff key for damage.
7. Remove the holder and puller from the flywheel.
8. Remove the starter driven gear (A, **Figure 24**), needle bearing (B, **Figure 24**) and washer (**Figure 25**) from the flywheel.
9. Inspect the components as described in this section.

Installation

1. If removed, install the Woodruff key (A, **Figure 23**) into the crankshaft keyway.
2. Install the washer (**Figure 25**) into the flywheel.
3. Lubricate the needle bearing and the starter reduction gear shoulder with engine oil.
4. Install the needle bearing (B, **Figure 24**) into the starter driven gear (A) and install the gear into the starter clutch.
5. Degrease the crankshaft outer taper (B, **Figure 23**) and the flywheel inner taper with an aerosol parts cleaner. Allow both tapers to dry before installing the flywheel.
6. Align the flywheel keyway with the Woodruff key and install the flywheel.
7. Lubricate the flywheel bolt threads and washer with engine oil and install the bolt finger-tight.
8. Hold the flywheel with the flywheel holder (A, **Figure 21**) and tighten the flywheel mounting bolt (B) to 138 N•m (102 ft.-lb.). Remove the flywheel holder.
9. Lubricate the torque limiter (A, **Figure 20**), shaft (B) and starter idler gear (C) operating surfaces with engine oil.
10. Install the starter idler gear (C, **Figure 20**), shaft (B) and torque limiter (A).
11. Install the left crankcase cover as described in this chapter.

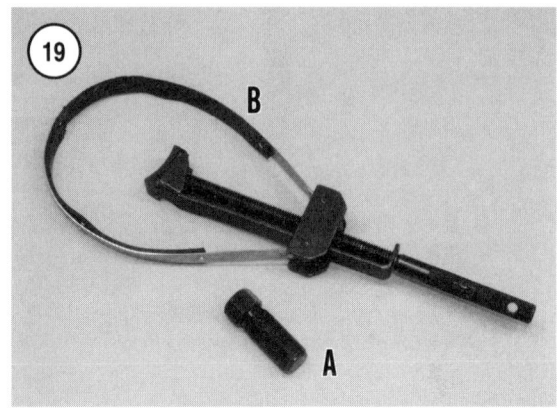

ELECTRICAL SYSTEM

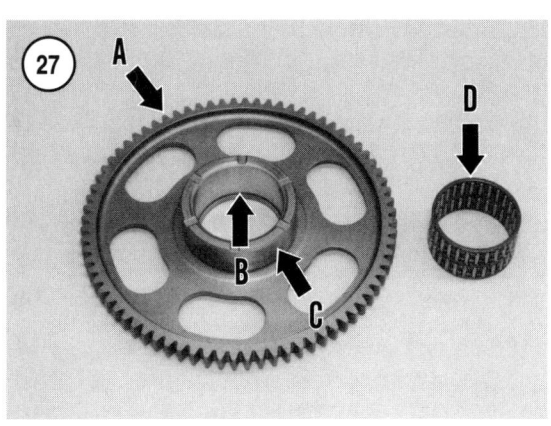

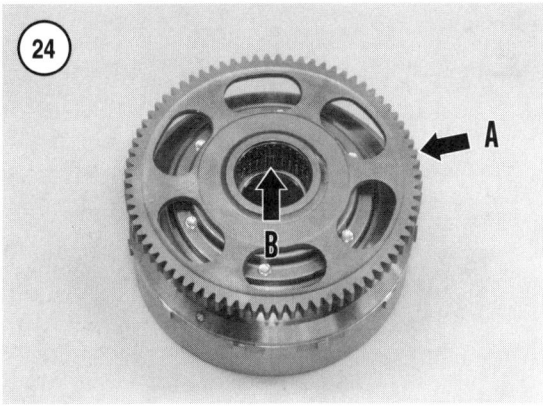

Inspection

> *WARNING*
> *Replace a cracked or chipped flywheel. A damaged flywheel can fly apart at high engine speeds.*

1. Clean the flywheel/starter clutch assembly and the starter gears in solvent and dry with compressed air.
2. Check the flywheel for cracks or breaks.
3. Check the flywheel tapered bore and the crankshaft taper for pitting and other damage.
4. Inspect the flywheel keyway for damage.
5. Inspect the starter clutch assembly as follows:
    a. Inspect the one-way clutch roller cage (**Figure 26**) for overheating, pitting or flaking. If damaged, replace the starter clutch as described in this section.
    b. Inspect the starter driven gear for damaged gear teeth (A, **Figure 27**). Then inspect the needle bearing (B, **Figure 27**) and starter clutch (C) operating surfaces for pitting, cracks and other damage.
    c. Measure the starter driven gear inside (B, **Figure 27**) and outside (C) diameters and compare to the specifications in **Table 4**. Replace the gear if any measurement is out of specification.
    d. Inspect the needle bearing (D, **Figure 27**) for damage. Check the cage for cracks or areas where the needles can fall out. Check the needles for flat spots, pitting and other damage.
    e. If there is no visible damage, perform Step 6 to check the starter clutch operation.
6. Insert the starter driven gear (A, **Figure 24**) into the starter clutch. Hold the flywheel and try to turn the gear clockwise and then counterclockwise. The gear should only turn *counterclockwise* (**Figure 28**). If the gear turns clockwise, replace the starter clutch as described in this section.
7. Inspect the torque limiter (**Figure 29**), idle gear (A, **Figure 30**) and shaft (B) for:

a. Broken or chipped gear teeth.
b. Worn or scored gear bores.
c. Pitted or damaged shaft surfaces.

8. Inspect the flywheel mounting bolt and washer for damage. Replace only with original equipment parts.

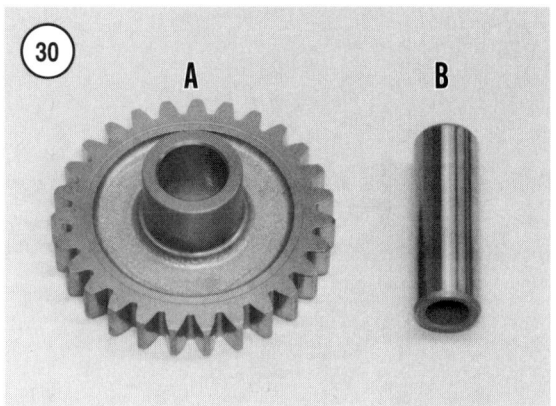

Starter Clutch Disassembly/Assembly

The starter clutch (**Figure 31**) can be inspected while assembled and installed on the flywheel. Do not remove the starter clutch unless replacement is necessary.

1. Inspect the starter clutch as described in this section.
2. Secure the flywheel with the flywheel holder (A, **Figure 32**) used to remove the flywheel. Then remove the Torx bolts (B, **Figure 32**) securing the starter clutch assembly to the flywheel. Remove the starter clutch housing (2, **Figure 31**) from the flywheel.
3. Remove the one-way clutch (3, **Figure 31**) from the starter clutch housing. Discard the one-way clutch.

NOTE
If the one-way clutch was going to be reused but the center spring band slipped off the one-way clutch, most of the small parts that make up this assembly will probably fall off. This will require replacement of the one-way clutch.

4. Clean and dry all parts. Remove all threadlocking compound residue from the Torx bolts and starter clutch housing threads.
5. Install the new one-way clutch (3, **Figure 31**) into the starter clutch housing in the direction shown in **Figure 31**.
6. Install the starter clutch housing onto the flywheel.
7. Apply a medium strength threadlocking compound onto the threads of each starter clutch Torx bolt (B, **Figure 32**) and tighten to 29 N•m (21 ft.-lb.).
8. Insert the starter driven gear (A, **Figure 24**) into the starter clutch. Hold the flywheel and try to turn

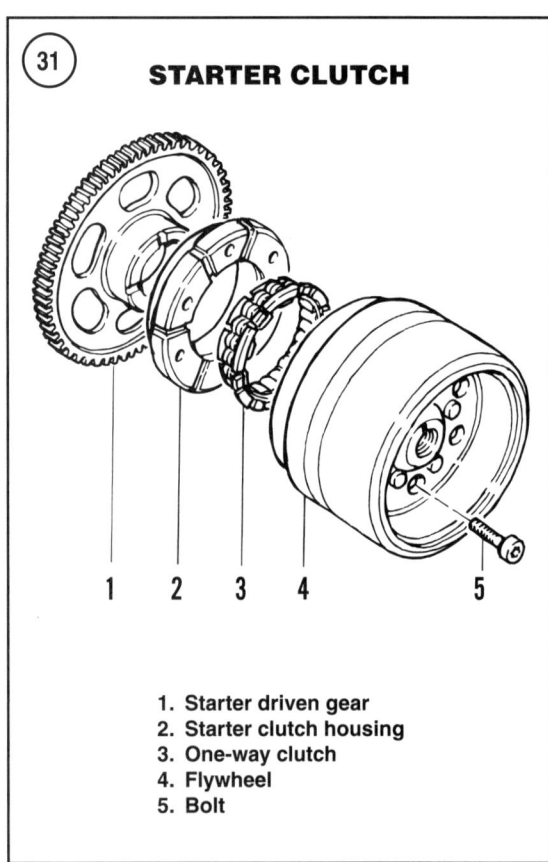

1. Starter driven gear
2. Starter clutch housing
3. One-way clutch
4. Flywheel
5. Bolt

ELECTRICAL SYSTEM

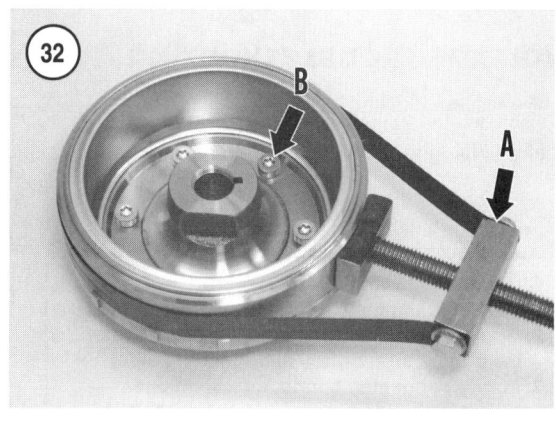

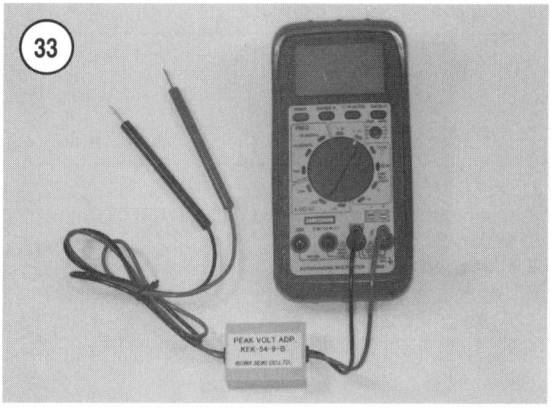

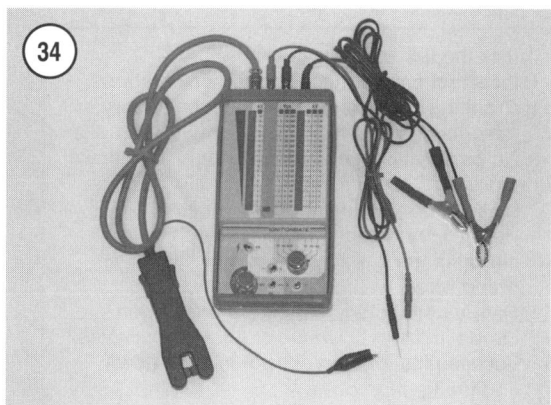

the gear clockwise and then counterclockwise. The gear should only turn *counterclockwise* (**Figure 28**). If the gear turns clockwise, the one-way clutch was installed incorrectly or is damaged.

IGNITION SYSTEM TESTING

WARNING
High voltage is present during ignition system operation. Do not touch ignition components, wires or test leads while cranking or running the engine.

Peak voltage tests check the voltage output of the ignition coils and pulse generator at normal cranking speed. These tests make it possible to accurately test the voltage output under operating conditions.

The peak voltage specifications listed in **Table 5** are minimum values. If the measured voltage meets or exceeds the specification, the test results are satisfactory. In some cases, the voltage may greatly exceed the minimum specification.

Tools

A peak voltage tester is required to measure peak voltage. Use one of the following testers or an equivalent. Refer to the manufacturer's instructions when using these tools.

1. Peak voltage adapter (Kowa Seiki part No. KEK-54-9B). This tool must be used in combination with a digital multimeter with a minimum impedance of 10M ohms/DCV (**Figure 33**). A meter with a lower impedance will not display accurate measurements. The peak voltage adapter plugs directly into the multimeter and the peak voltage readings are read directly off the meter. This tool is shown in the following procedures.
2. Ignition Mate (part No. MTP07-0286 [**Figure 34**]).

Preliminary Checks

Before testing the ignition system, make the following checks:
1. Make sure the battery is fully charged and in good condition. A weak battery will result in a slow engine cranking speed and incorrect peak voltage readings.
2. Perform the *Spark Test* as described in *Engine Will Not Start* in Chapter Two. If a crisp, blue spark is noted, the ignition system is working correctly. Test each spark plug and note the following:
   a. If there is no spark at all spark plugs, check for a disconnected or contaminated connector or a damaged ignition switch or engine stop switch. Test each switch as described in this chapter.
   b. If the spark test shows there is no spark at one coil group (front or rear cylinder), switch the ignition coils and repeat the spark test. If the inoperative cylinder now has spark, the original ignition coil is defective. Replace it and retest. However, if the inoperative cylinder still does not have spark, check the ignition coil wires for an open circuit.
   c. Check for a fouled or damaged spark plug, loose spark plugs caps or water in the spark plugs caps.

IGNITION COIL PRIMARY PEAK VOLTAGE TROUBLESHOOTING

NOTE: Initial voltage is the recorded battery voltage before cranking the engine with the starter.

No peak voltage.

Check the following in order:
1. Damaged engine stop switch.
2. Open circuit in the black/white wire between the engine stop switch and ignition coil(s).
3. Poorly connected connectors or an open circuit in the ignition coil primary circuit.
4. Damaged ignition control module (ICM) when all of the above are normal.

Peak voltage reading is normal, but there is no spark.

Check the following in order:
1. Open circuit in the ignition coil ground or secondary circuits.
2. Damaged ignition coil.
3. Loose spark plug cap.
4. Damaged spark plug wire.

Initial voltage is normal, but drops to 2-4 volts when engine is cranked.

Check the following in order:
1. Incorrect peak voltage adapter connections.
2. Cranking speed is too low. Test the battery as described in this chapter.
3. No battery voltage at the black ignition control module (ICM) connector. Check also for a loose or contaminated ICM connector.
4. Poorly connected connectors or an open circuit in the ignition control module (ICM) green wire.
5. Poorly connected connectors or an open circuit in the yellow/blue or blue/yellow wires between the ignition control module (ICM) and the ignition coils.
6. Short circuit in ignition coil primary circuit.
7. Damaged neutral switch.
8. Damaged sidestand switch.
9. Poorly connected connectors or an open circuit in the following:
    a. Neutral switch circuit light green wire.
    b. Sidestand switch green/white wire.
10. Damaged ignition pulse generator. Check peak voltage at ignition pulse generator as described in this chapter.
11. Damaged ignition control module (ICM) when all of the above are normal.

(continued)

ELECTRICAL SYSTEM

35 (continued)

| Initial battery voltage is normal, but there is no peak voltage reading when engine is cranked. | → | Check the following in order:
1. Incorrect peak voltage adapter connections.
2. Damaged peak voltage adapter or test unit.
3. Damaged ignition control module (ICM) when all of the above are normal. |

| Initial battery voltage is normal, but peak voltage reading is lower than the minimum. | → | Check the following in order:
1. Meter impedance is too low.
2. Cranking speed is too low. Test battery as described in this chapter
3. The test sampling and measured pulse were not synchronizing. If measured voltage is over the minimum voltage at least once, the system is normal.
4. Damaged ignition control module (ICM) when all of the above are normal. |

3. If the problem has not been found and the spark plugs, plug caps and all electrical system connectors are in good working order, the problem is probably due to a defective switch or ignition system component. Perform the peak voltage tests in this section to locate the damaged component.

Ignition Coil Peak Voltage Test

Refer to **Figure 35**.
1. Remove the seats (Chapter Fifteen).
2. Remove the cylinder head shrouds (Chapter Eight).

3. Check engine compression as described in Chapter Three. If the compression is low in one or both cylinders, the following test results will be inaccurate.
4. Check all of the ignition component electrical connectors and wiring harnesses. Make sure the connectors are clean and properly connected.
5. Disconnect each spark plug cap. Then connect a new spark plug to each plug cap and ground the plug against the cylinder head (**Figure 36**). Do not remove the spark plugs installed in the cylinder heads. These must remain in the cylinder heads.
6. Assemble the peak voltage adapter and multimeter as shown in **Figure 33**.

NOTE
*Refer to **Ignition Coils** in this chapter to identify the ignition coils.*

NOTE
Do not disconnect the ignition coil primary connectors when performing Step 7.

7. Locate the ignition coil to be checked and connect the peak voltage test leads as follows:
   a. At the front cylinder ignition coil, connect the positive test lead to the blue/yellow termi-

nal (**Figure 37**) and the negative test lead to ground.

    b. At the rear cylinder ignition coil, connect the positive test lead to the yellow/blue ignition coil terminal at its 2-pin connector (A, **Figure 38**) and the negative test lead to ground.

8. Shift the transmission into neutral.
9. Turn the ignition switch on and the engine stop switch to run.
10. The meter should read battery voltage. Note the following:

    a. If there is no battery voltage or the voltage reading is low, refer to the test results in **Figure 35**. Perform the steps in order to find the problem.

    b. If the battery voltage reading is correct, continue with Step 11.

> *WARNING*
> *High voltage is present during ignition system operation. Do not touch spark plugs, ignition components, connectors or test leads while cranking the engine.*

11. Press the starter button while reading the meter.
12. Release the starter button, then connect the test lead to the other ignition coil primary as described in Step 7 and repeat.
13. Turn the ignition switch off and interpret the test results as follows:

> *NOTE*
> *All peak voltage specifications in the text and **Table 5** are **minimum** voltages. As long as the measured voltage meets or exceeds the specification, consider the test results satisfactory. On some components, the voltage may greatly exceed the minimum specification.*

    a. The minimum ignition coil peak voltage reading is 100 volts minimum.

    b. The individual peak voltage reading recorded for each ignition coil can vary as long as the voltage readings are higher than the specified minimum value.

    c. If the peak voltage reading for one or both ignition coils is less than 100 volts, refer to the test results in **Figure 35** and perform the steps in order to find the problem.

14. Disconnect the test leads.
15. Remove the spark plugs from the plug caps, then reconnect the plug caps onto the spark plugs installed in the cylinder head.
16. Reverse Step 1 and Step 2 to complete installation.

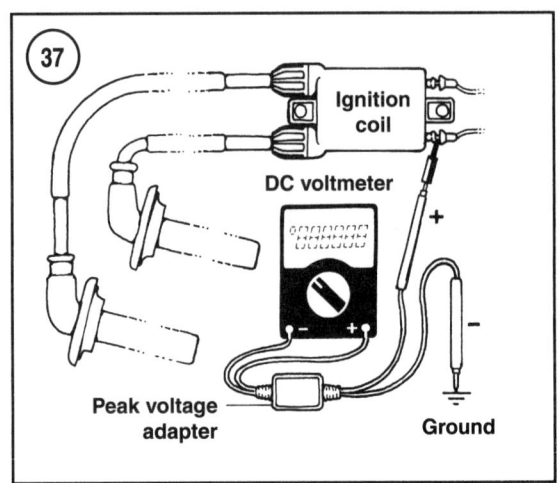

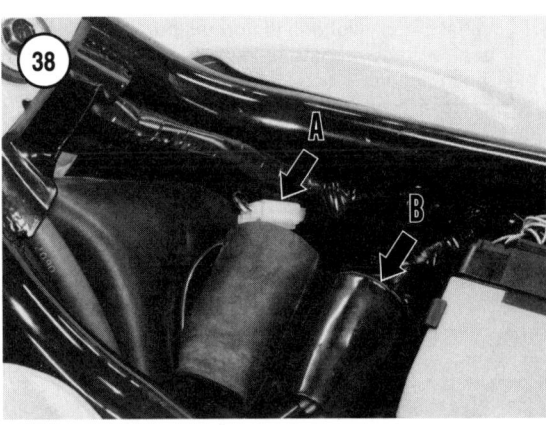

Ignition Pulse Generator Peak Voltage Test

Refer to **Figure 39**.

1. Support the motorcycle on a workstand so the sidestand can be raised during this test.
2. Remove the seats (Chapter Fifteen).
3. Check engine compression as described in Chapter Three. If the compression is low in one or both cylinders, the following test results will be inaccurate.
4. Check all of the ignition component electrical connectors and wiring harnesses. Make sure the connectors are clean and properly connected.
5. Remove the ignition control module (ICM) from the battery box cover as described in *Battery* in this chapter. Disconnect the 22-pin connector (**Figure 40**).
6. Assemble the peak voltage adapter and multimeter as shown in **Figure 33**.
7. Connect the peak voltage positive test lead to the white/blue connector terminal and the negative test lead to the green connector terminal in the 22-pin connector (**Figure 41**).
8. Shift the transmission into neutral.
9. Raise the sidestand.
10. Turn the ignition switch on and the engine stop switch to run.

ELECTRICAL SYSTEM

(39)

IGNITION PULSE GENERATOR PEAK VOLTAGE TROUBLESHOOTING

No peak voltage. → Check:
1. Incorrect peak voltage adapter connections.
2. Damaged ignition pulse generator.

Low peak voltage. → Check the following in order:
1. Meter impedance is too low.
2. Cranking speed is too low. Test the battery as described in this chapter.
3. The test sampling and measured pulse were not synchronizing. If measured voltage is over the minimum voltage at least once, the system is normal.
4. Damaged ignition pulse generator when all of the above are normal.

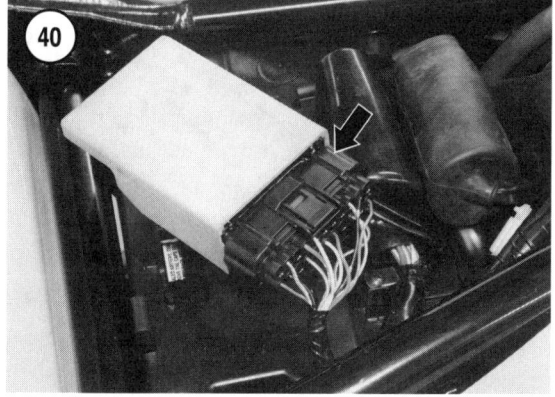

WARNING
High voltage is present during ignition system operation. Do not touch spark plugs, ignition components, connectors or test leads while cranking the engine.

NOTE
All peak voltage specifications in the text and **Table 5** *are* **minimum** *voltages. If the measured voltage meets or exceeds the specification, consider the test results satisfactory. On some components, the voltage may greatly exceed the minimum specification.*

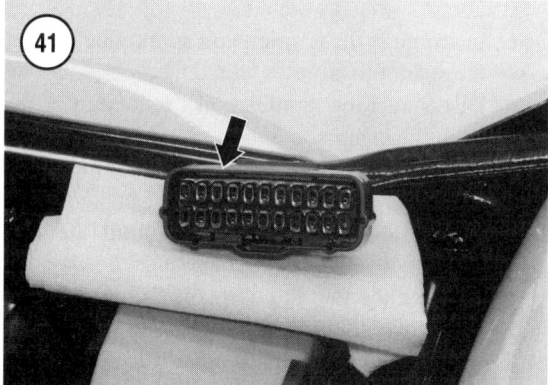

11. Press the starter button while reading the meter. The meter should indicate a minimum peak voltage reading of 0.7 volts DC. If the reading is less than this, continue with Step 12.

12. Measure the peak voltage at the ignition pulse generator connector:
   a. Turn the ignition switch off.

NOTE
Refer to the appropriate wiring diagram at the end of this manual to identify the ignition pulse generator 2-pin connector and its wire colors.

b. On 2003-2004 models, remove the band securing the wiring harness boot (**Figure 42**) to the frame. Disconnect the ignition pulse generator 2-pin connector located inside the wiring harness boot next to the ICM.

c. On 2005-on models, open the clamp and disconnect the ignition pulse generator 2-pin connector located inside the wiring harness boot (B, **Figure 38**) next to the ICM.

d. Connect the peak voltage positive test lead to the white/blue connector terminal and the negative test lead to the green connector terminal in the 2-pin connector. Connect the test leads to the ignition pulse generator side of the connector, not to the wire harness side.

e. Turn the ignition switch on and the engine stop switch to run.

f. Press the starter button while reading the meter. The meter should indicate a minimum peak voltage reading of 0.7 volts DC. If the reading is now correct, check the white/blue and green wires between the ignition pulse generator and the ICM connector for an open or short circuit. At the same time, check the connectors for loose terminals or contamination. If the reading is still incorrect, refer to the test results in **Figure 39**.

13. Install the previously removed parts to complete assembly.

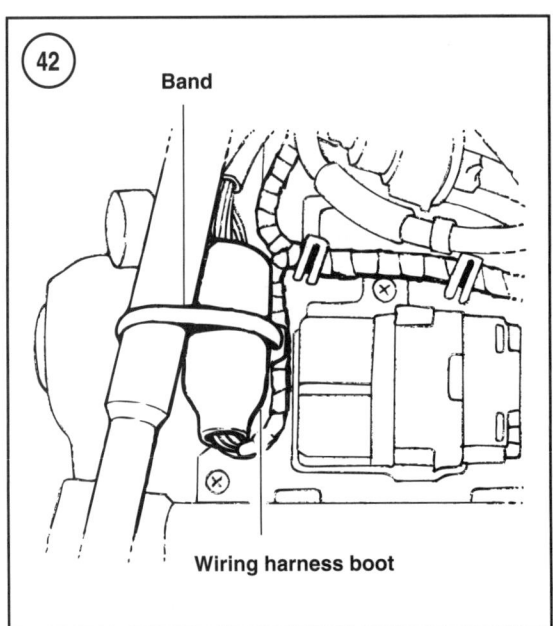

IGNITION COILS

Removal/Installation

1. Turn the ignition switch off.
2. Remove the fuel tank (Chapter Eight).

NOTE
Note the wiring harness routing for both ignition coils before removing them.

3A. Remove the front ignition coil as follows:
   a. Remove the cylinder head shrouds (Chapter Fifteen).
   b. Remove the right side steering side cover (Chapter Fifteen).
   c. Disconnect the ignition coil spark plug caps at the spark plugs.
   d. Remove the bolts (A, **Figure 43**), ground wire terminal (B) and spacers. The spacers are U-shaped and fit around the ignition coil mounting hole bosses.
   e. Label and disconnect the two primary wires (C, **Figure 43**) from the coil and remove the coil.

3B. Remove the rear ignition coil as follows:

NOTE
*The rear ignition coil (**Figure 44**) is mounted on the center cover, which is installed behind the rear cylinder.*

   a. Remove the battery box as described in this chapter.
   b. Disconnect the ignition coil spark plug caps at the spark plugs.
   c. Disconnect the ignition coil's secondary wires from the clamps.
   d. On 2003 models, remove the fuel pump from the center cover as described in Chapter Eight. Do not disconnect the hoses from the fuel pump. Move the fuel pump out of the way.
   e. Remove the two ignition coil mounting bolts, disconnect the primary wires, and remove the ignition coil from the center cover.

4. Installation is the reverse of removal.

ELECTRICAL SYSTEM

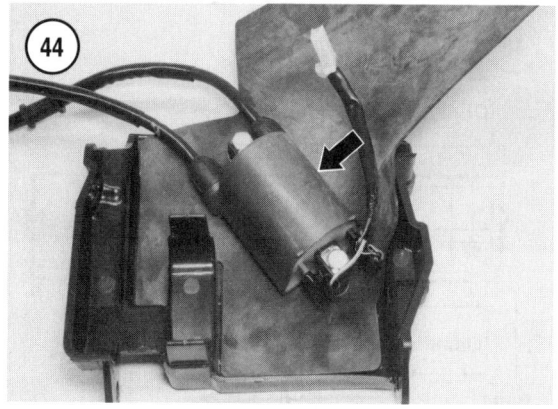

tion coil. Check the ignition coil terminal for any rust or corrosion and clean with a small file or sandpaper. Insert the secondary wire into the ignition coil, then install and tighten the cap.

IGNITION PULSE GENERATOR

The ignition pulse generator is permanently assembled with the stator coil assembly. Do not separate the stator coil (A, **Figure 18**) and ignition pulse generator (B) wiring harnesses. Refer to *Stator Coil, Ignition Pulse Generator and Left Crankcase Cover* in this chapter.

IGNITION CONTROL MODULE (ICM)

The ignition control module (ICM) controls the ignition system and the fuel cutoff solenoid valve (2008-on California models).

Testing

No testing procedure is available. If all other ignition components and systems have been tested, replace the ICM and recheck the ignition system operation. Faulty wiring and connections cause many electrical problems. Make sure to check all wires and connections before presuming the ICM is faulty. Because electrical components are not returnable, if possible, have a dealership install a known good ICM for testing and check operation before purchasing a new unit. Refer to *Electrical Component Replacement* in this chapter.

Removal/Installation

1. Remove the seats (Chapter Fifteen).
2. Remove the ICM (**Figure 45**) from the battery box cover.
3. Disconnect the 22-pin connector (**Figure 40**) and remove the ICM.
4. Installation is the reverse of these steps.

IGNITION TIMING

Refer to Chapter Three.

THROTTLE POSITION SENSOR (TPS)

The throttle position sensor (TPS) is mounted on the carburetor.

Testing

1. Remove the seats (Chapter Fifteen).

Spark Plug Cap and Secondary Wire Removal/Installation

The spark plug caps and secondary wires can be replaced separately.

1. To replace the spark plug cap, perform the following:
    a. Before removing the spark plug cap, note the angled position of the cap on the secondary wire so the new cap can be reinstalled correctly.
    b. Hold the secondary wire and twist the spark plug cap to break its seal and loosen it. Do not pull the cap as this may damage the secondary wire. Continue to unscrew the cap until it is free. Check the end of the secondary wire for any rust or corrosion and clean with a small file or sandpaper. Hold the secondary wire and turn the spark plug cap until its screw threads into the end of the wire and the cap bottoms.

NOTE
All four secondary wires have different part numbers. Match and replace one secondary wire at a time until they are all replaced.

2. To replace the secondary wire, unscrew the cap and pull the secondary wire out of the end of the igni-

2. Remove the ICM (**Figure 45**) from the battery box cover and disconnect the 22-pin connector (**Figure 40**).

3. Measure resistance between the yellow/red and blue/green connector wiring harness side terminals (**Figure 46**). The correct reading is 4-6 K ohms.

4. Connect the ohmmeter between the red/yellow and blue/green connector wiring harness side terminals and note the following while operating the throttle grip:
   a. When opening the throttle grip from its fully closed to full open position, the resistance should increase.
   b. When closing the throttle grip from its fully open to fully closed position, the resistance should decrease.

5. If either test result in Step 3 or Step 4 was incorrect, continue with Step 6. If the test results in Step 3 and Step 4 were correct, continue with Step 9.

6. Remove the air filter housing (Chapter Eight).

7. Disconnect the TPS 3-pin connector (**Figure 47**).

8. Repeat the resistance tests in Step 3 and Step 4 at the TPS 3-pin connector sensor side terminals. Note the following:
   a. If both test results are incorrect, remove the carburetor and replace the TPS as described in Chapter Eight.
   b. If one or both test results are correct, check the wiring harness between the TPS 3-pin connector and the ICM 22-pin connector for an open or short circuit. Then check for loose, corroded or damaged terminals in both connectors. After making these checks, repeat the tests.

9. Reconnect the ICM 22-pin connector (**Figure 40**).

10. Turn the ignition switch on and the engine stop switch to run.

11. Measure input voltage between the yellow/red (+) and blue/green (+) TPS 3-pin connector wiring harness side terminals. The voltmeter should read 4.7-5.3 volts. Note the following:
   a. If the reading is correct, continue with Step 12.
   b. If the reading is incorrect or there was no reading, check the wiring harness between the TPS 3-pin connector and the ICM 22-pin connector for an open or short circuit. Then check for loose, corroded or damaged terminals in both connectors.

12. Installation is the reverse of removal.

STARTER SYSTEM TROUBLESHOOTING

The starting system consists of the battery, starter, starter relay switch, start button, starter mechanism and related wiring.

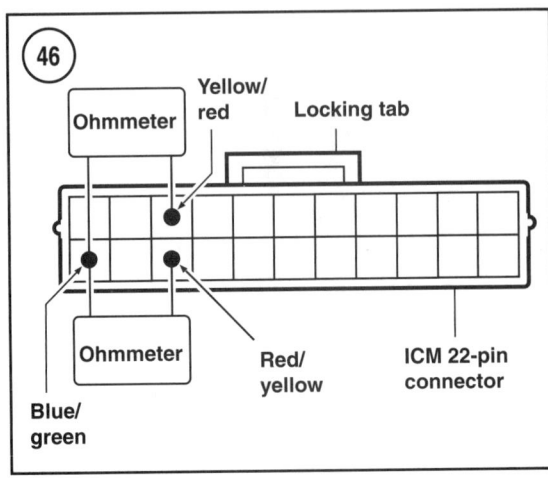

When the ignition is turned on and the start button is pushed, current is transmitted from the battery to the starter relay switch. When the relay is activated, it activates the starter solenoid that mechanically engages the starter with the engine.

A starting system problem may be an electrical or mechanical problem. Refer to *Engine Will Not Start* in Chapter Two for general troubleshooting procedures to help isolate the starting problems.

1. If troubleshooting a starting system problem, check the following before proceeding with more in-depth testing:
   a. Make sure the battery is fully charged and has passed a battery load test as described in this chapter.
   b. Make sure the battery cables are the proper size and length. Replace damaged or undersized cables.
   c. Make sure all electrical connections are clean and tight. High resistance caused from dirty or loose connections can affect voltage and current levels.
   d. Make sure the wiring harness is in good condition, with no worn or frayed insulation or lose harness sockets.
   e. Make sure the fuel tank is filled with an adequate supply of fresh gasoline.
   f. Make sure the spark plugs are in good condition and properly gapped (Chapter Three).
   g. Perform a *Spark Test* as described in *Engine Will Not Start* in Chapter Two to make sure the ignition system is working correctly.

2. If the starter does not turn over, perform these tests to isolate the problem:
   a. Turn the ignition switch on and shift the transmission into neutral. The headlight should come on. If not, check the main fuse and appropriate subfuse. Refer to *Fuses* in this chapter. If the fuses are good, test the battery as described in this chapter.

ELECTRICAL SYSTEM

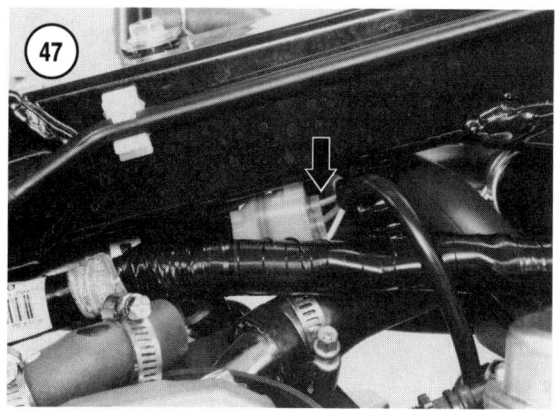

47

b. If the headlight came on, push the starter button to start the engine. The solenoid should click. If not, the problem is in the wiring to the solenoid, ignition switch or the solenoid is faulty.

c. If the solenoid did click but the starter did not turn the engine over, the problem may be due to excessive voltage drop in the starter circuit or the starter is damaged. This could be due to worn brushes or a shorted commutator. The problem can also be in the starter drive system or engine.

3. If the problem is traced to the starter circuit, refer to *Symptom-Based Tests* in this section and find the procedure that matches the starting problem.

Symptom-Based Tests

The following symptom related sections are:
1. Starter spins slowly.
2. Starter relay switch clicks but engine does not turn over.
3. Starter operates but engine does not turn over.
4. Starter does not spin.
5. Starter spins with the transmission in neutral but does not turn with the transmission in gear with the clutch lever pulled in and the sidestand up.

CAUTION
Never operate the starter for more than 5 seconds at a time. Allow the starter to cool 10 seconds before reusing it. Failing to allow the starter to cool after continuous starting attempts can damage the starter.

Starter spins slowly

If the starter operates but does not turn the engine over at normal speed, check the following:
1. Test the battery as described in this chapter.
2. Check for the following:
   a. Loose or corroded battery terminals.
   b. Loose or corroded battery ground cable.
   c. Loose starter cable.
3. If the battery is fully charged and passes a load test, and the cables are in good condition, the starter may be faulty. Remove, disassemble and bench test the starter as described in this chapter.

Starter relay switch clicks but engine does not turn over

Check the following:
1. Test the battery as described in this chapter.
2. Make sure all connections are clean and tight.
3. Damaged starter idle gear.
4. Damaged starter reduction gear.
5. Crankshaft cannot turn over because of mechanical failure.

Starter operates but engine does not turn over

Check the following:
1. If the starter was just overhauled, it may have been assembled incorrectly.
2. Damaged starter clutch.
3. Damaged starter gears.

Starter does not spin

Perform the following:
1. Check for a blown main or subfuse as described in this chapter. If the fuses are good, continue with Step 2.
2. Check the starter cable for an open circuit or dirty or loose-fitting terminals. Repair any dirty, loose fitting or damaged connectors or wiring.
3. Check the starter relay connectors for dirty or loose-fitting terminals. Clean and repair as required. Reconnect the connectors and continue with Step 4.
4. Check the starter relay switch as follows. Turn the ignition switch on and push the starter button while listening for a click at the starter relay. Turn the ignition switch off and note the following:
   a. If the starter relay clicks, continue with Step 5.
   b. If there was no click, go to Step 6.

CAUTION
Because of the large amount of current that will flow from the battery to the starter in Step 5, use a large diameter cable when making the connection. To avoid damaging the starter, do not leave the battery connected for more than 5 seconds.

5. Remove the starter from the motorcycle as described this chapter. Using an auxiliary battery, ap-

ply battery voltage directly to the starter (**Figure 48**). The starter should turn when battery voltage is applied directly to the starter.

   a. If the starter did not turn, remove, disassemble and inspect the starter as described in this chapter. Test the starter components and replace worn or damaged parts as required.

   b. If the starter turned, check for loose or damaged starter cables. If the cables are good, remove and test the starter relay switch as described in this chapter. Replace the starter relay switch if necessary.

   c. Reinstall the starter (this chapter).

6. Check the starter relay switch ground line for continuity as described in *Starter Relay Switch* in this chapter. There should be continuity.

   a. If there is continuity, continue with Step 7.

   b. If there is no continuity, check for a loose or damaged connector or an open circuit in the wiring harness. If these items are good, test the following items as described in this chapter: sidestand switch, neutral switch, clutch switch diode.

   c. Reconnect the starter relay switch electrical connector.

7. Check the starter relay for voltage as described in *Starter Relay Switch* in this chapter. There should be voltage when the ignition switch is on and the starter button is pushed.

   a. If there is battery voltage, continue with Step 8.

   b. If there is no battery voltage, check for a blown main or subfuse in this chapter. If the fuses are good, check for an open circuit in the wiring harness or for dirty or loose-fitting terminals. If the wiring and connectors are in good condition, check for a faulty ignition and/or starter switch as described in this chapter.

8. Perform the starter relay switch operational check as described under *Starter Relay Switch* in this chapter.

   a. If the starter relay switch is normal, check for dirty or loose-fitting connector terminals.

   b. If the starter relay switch is faulty, replace it and retest.

Starter works with the transmission in neutral but does not turn with the transmission in gear with the clutch lever pulled in and the sidestand up

1. Test the clutch switch as described in this chapter.

   a. If the clutch switch is good, perform Step 2.

   b. If the clutch switch is defective, replace the switch and retest.

2. Test the sidestand switch as described in this chapter.

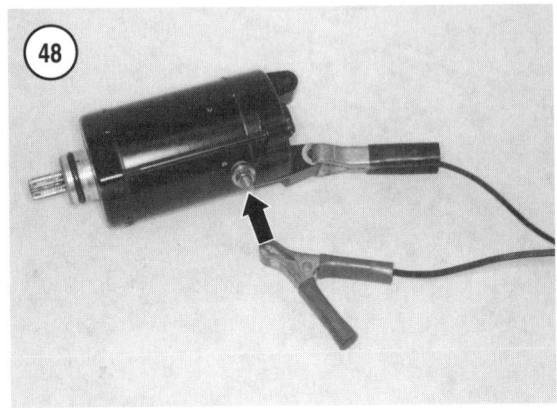

   a. If the sidestand switch is good, perform Step 3.

   b. If the sidestand switch is defective, replace switch and retest.

3. Check for an open circuit in the wiring harness. Check for loose or damaged electrical connector.

WARNING
Before riding the motorcycle, make sure the sidestand switch is working properly. Riding the motorcycle with the sidestand down can cause loss of control.

STARTER

CAUTION
Do not operate the starter for more than 5 seconds at a time. Wait approximately 10 seconds between starting attempts.

Removal/Installation

1. Disconnect the negative battery cable at the battery as described in this chapter.
2. Remove the radiator (Chapter Ten).

ELECTRICAL SYSTEM

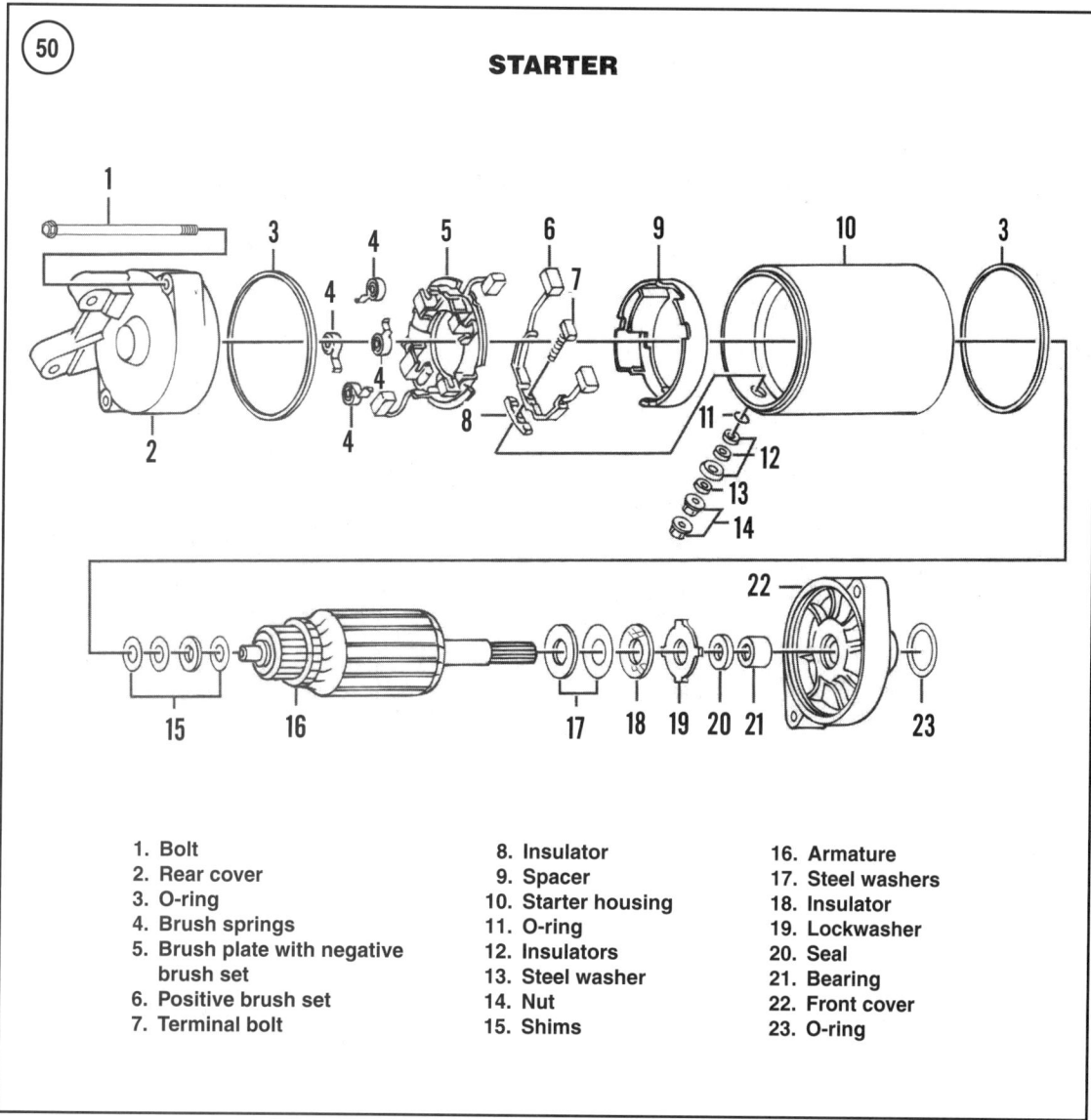

50 STARTER

1. Bolt
2. Rear cover
3. O-ring
4. Brush springs
5. Brush plate with negative brush set
6. Positive brush set
7. Terminal bolt
8. Insulator
9. Spacer
10. Starter housing
11. O-ring
12. Insulators
13. Steel washer
14. Nut
15. Shims
16. Armature
17. Steel washers
18. Insulator
19. Lockwasher
20. Seal
21. Bearing
22. Front cover
23. O-ring

3. Pull the rubber cap (A, **Figure 49**) off the starter terminal.

NOTE
The insulator described in Step 4 cannot be purchased separately. If this part is damaged, the starter must be replaced, or a salvage starter located.

4. Disconnect the starter cable by holding the inner nut with a wrench (B, **Figure 49**) and removing the outer nut (C). Holding the inner nut prevents the terminal bolt from turning and damaging the insulator installed inside the starter.

5. Remove the mounting bolts (D, **Figure 49**) and ground cable (E).

6. Pull the starter toward the right side to disconnect it from the starter drive mechanism and remove it.

7. Install by reversing these removal steps, plus the following:
   a. Lubricate the starter O-ring with engine oil.
   b. Remove all corrosion from the starter cables.
   c. Tighten the starter mounting bolts securely.
   d. Hold the inner nut (B, **Figure 49**) and tighten the outer starter cable nut (C) to 7 N•m (62 in.-lb.).
   e. Fit the rubber cover (A, **Figure 49**) securely over the starter cable. Replace the cover if damaged.
   f. Operate the starter to make sure it works correctly.

Disassembly

Refer to **Figure 50**.

1. Find the alignment marks across the armature housing and both end covers. If necessary, scribe or paint the marks to identify them.

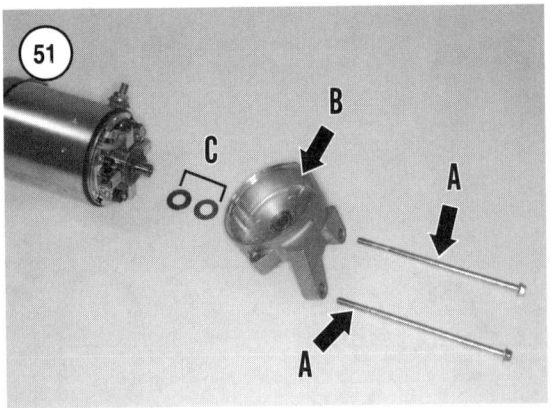

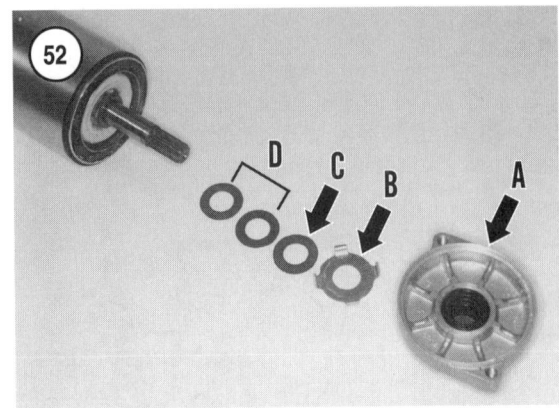

2. Remove the bolts (A, **Figure 51**).

NOTE
The number of shims used in each starter varies. The shims and washers must be reinstalled in their correct order and number. Failing to install the correct number of shims and washers may increase armature end play and cause the starter to draw excessive current. Record the thickness and alignment of each shim and washer removed during disassembly.

NOTE
If disassembling the starter to only check brush condition, remove only the rear cover. The brushes can be inspected and the cover installed if further disassembly is not required. When doing so, locate and reinstall the shims onto the armature shaft.

3. Remove the rear cover (B, **Figure 51**) and shims (C).
4. Remove the front cover (A, **Figure 52**) and the lockwasher (B).

NOTE
Do not remove the seal from the front cover. It is not available as a replacement part.

5. Remove the insulated washer (C, **Figure 52**) and shim(s) (D).
6. Remove the armature (16, **Figure 50**) from the housing.
7. Before removing the brush holder, test the brushes and terminal bolt as follows:

NOTE
The positive brushes have insulated sleeves installed over the wire leads.

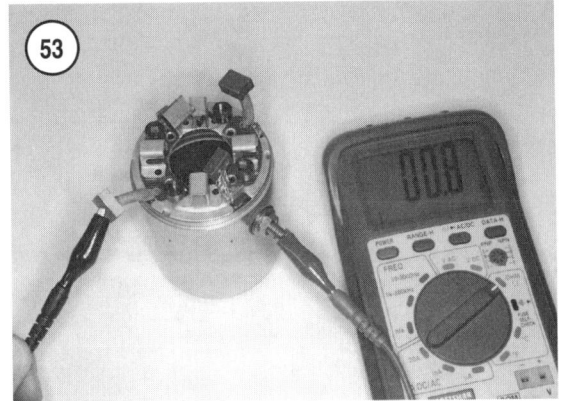

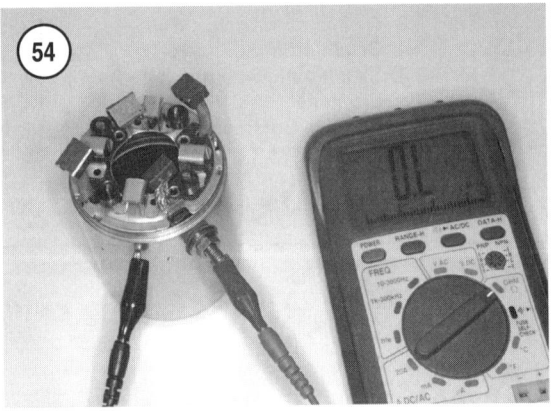

a. Check for continuity between the terminal bolt and each positive brush (**Figure 53**). There should be continuity. If there is no continuity, replace the positive brush holder during reassembly.
b. Check for continuity between the terminal bolt and starter housing (**Figure 54**). There should be no continuity. If there is continuity, check for damaged, missing or improperly installed insulators. Compare the alignment of the installed insulators before removing them.
c. Check for continuity between the positive and negative brushes (**Figure 55**). There should

ELECTRICAL SYSTEM

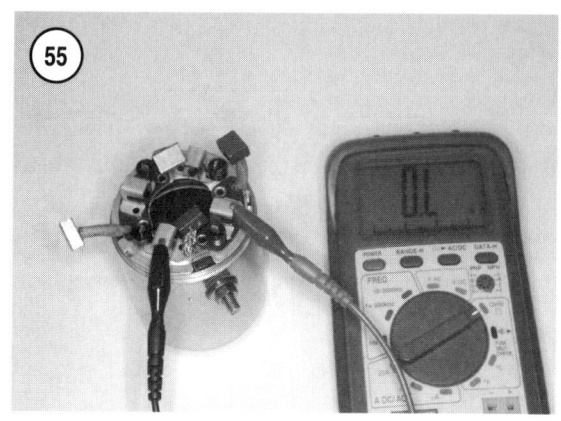

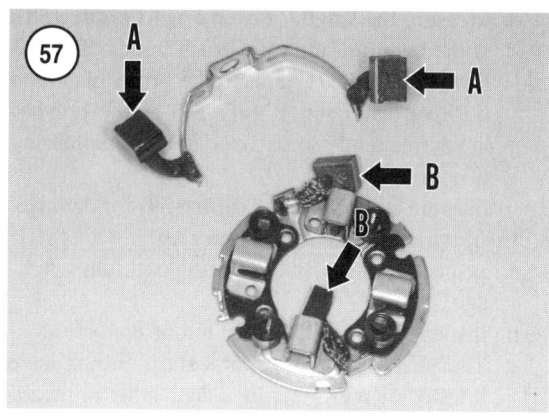

be no continuity. If there is continuity, check the positive brush wires for damaged insulation sleeves. The insulation sleeves must be installed through the brush holder plate so the positive brush wires cannot short out.

8. Remove the terminal nut (14, **Figure 50**) and remove the steel washer, insulators and O-ring.
9. Remove the brush plate, terminal bolt and positive brush set (**Figure 56**).
10. Remove the insulator (8, **Figure 50**) and terminal bolt (7) and separate the positive brush set from the brush plate. Refer to **Figure 57**.
11. Clean all grease, dirt and carbon from the armature, starter housing and end covers as described in *Inspection* in this section.

Inspection

If any starter component (other than O-rings and brush sets) are severely worn or damaged, the starter must be replaced as an assembly. Individual replacement parts are not available.

A salvage starter may provide a source for individual parts. It may also be possible to source parts from another model of starter that uses the same internal parts.

1. The internal parts in a used starter are often contaminated with carbon and copper dust released from the brushes and commutator. Because a starter can be damaged from improper cleaning, note the following:
   a. Clean all parts (except the armature, insulated washers and starter housing) in solvent. Use a rag lightly damped with solvent to wipe off the armature, insulated washers and the starter housing (inside and outside).
   b. Use a fine grade sandpaper to clean the brushes. Do not use emery cloth as its fibers may insulate the brushes.
   c. Use only crocus cloth to clean the commutator. Do not use emery cloth or sandpaper. Any abrasive material left on or embedded in the commutator may cause excessive brush wear. Do not leave any debris on or between the commutator bars.
2. Replace the starter housing O-rings (3, **Figure 50**) if damaged.

NOTE
The bushing, seal and bearing used in the end covers are not available separately.

3. Inspect the bushing in the front cover for wear or damage.
4. Inspect the seal and needle bearing in the rear cover for damage. Do not remove the seal to check the bearing.
5. Check the lockwasher, shims and insulated washers for damage.
6. Inspect the brushes (A and B, **Figure 57**) as follows:
   a. Inspect each brush for cracks and other damage.
   b. Inspect the insulation on the positive brushes (A, **Figure 57**) for tearing and other damage.
   c. Check each brush where it is fixed to its holder (A or B, **Figure 57**) for looseness or damage.

d. Measure the length of each brush (**Figure 58**). If the length of any one brush is out of specification (**Table 7**), replace the brush plate and positive brush set (**Figure 57**) as the brushes are permanently fixed to the holders. Soldering is not required.
7. Inspect the brush springs (**Figure 59**) for damage.
8. Inspect the armature (A, **Figure 60**):
   a. Inspect both shafts for scoring and other damage.
   b. Inspect the windings for obvious damage.
   c. To check the armature for a short circuit, have it tested on a growler by a dealership or an automotive electrical repair shop.
9. Inspect the commutator (B, **Figure 60**):
   a. Inspect the commutator bars for visual damage.
   b. Clean the commutator surface as described in Step 1.
   c. The mica must be below the surface of the copper bars. On a worn commutator the mica and copper bars may be worn to the same level (**Figure 61**).
   d. If the mica level is too high or if its shape is too narrow or V-shaped, undercut the mica with a hacksaw blade.
   e. Inspect the commutator copper bars for discoloration. If a pair of bars are discolored, grounded armature coils are indicated.
   f. Check for continuity across all adjacent pairs of commutator bars (**Figure 62**). There should be continuity across all pairs of bars. If an open circuit exists between a pair of bars, replace the starter.
   g. Check for continuity between the armature shaft and each commutator bar (**Figure 63**). There should be no continuity. If there is continuity, replace the starter.
   h. Check for continuity between the armature coil core and each commutator bar. There should be no continuity. If there is continuity, replace the starter.
10. Inspect the starter housing for cracks or other damage. Then inspect for loose, chipped or damaged magnets.

Assembly

1. Assemble the positive brush set (A, **Figure 57**) and brush plate (B) as follows:
   a. Install the positive brush wires through the two notches in the brush plate as shown in A, **Figure 64**.
   b. Install the terminal bolt through the positive brush holder, then install the insulator (B, **Figure 64**) and O-ring (C).

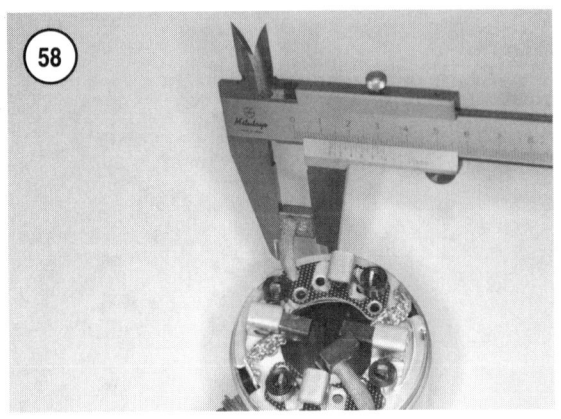

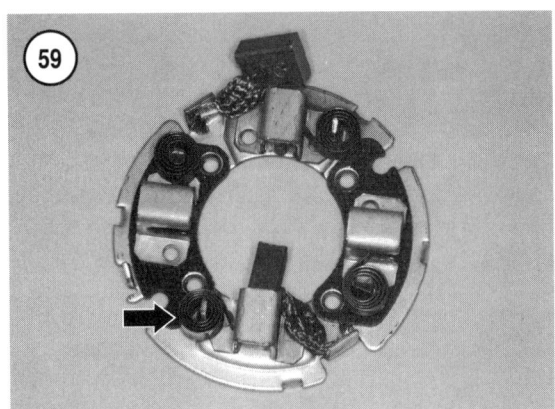

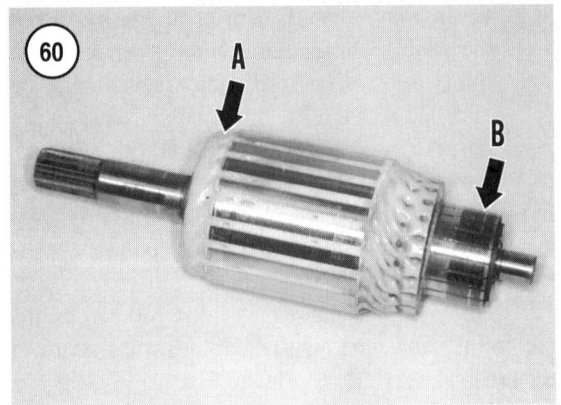

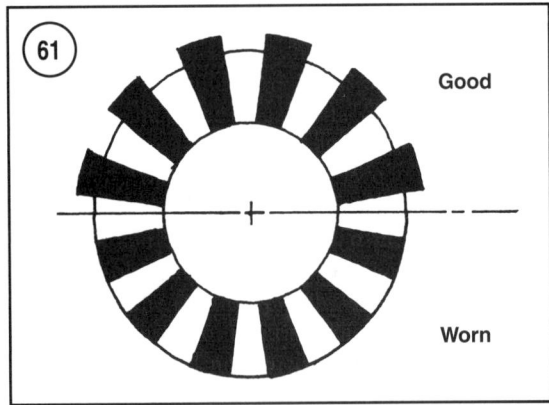

ELECTRICAL SYSTEM

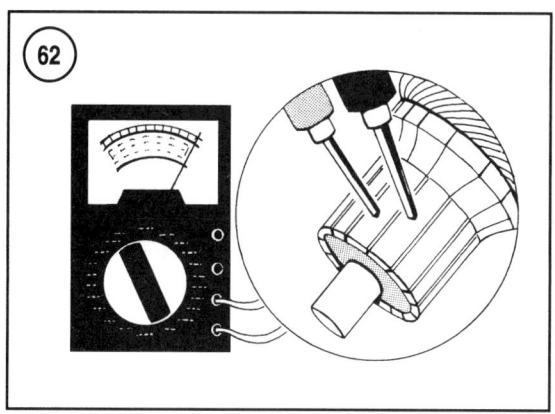

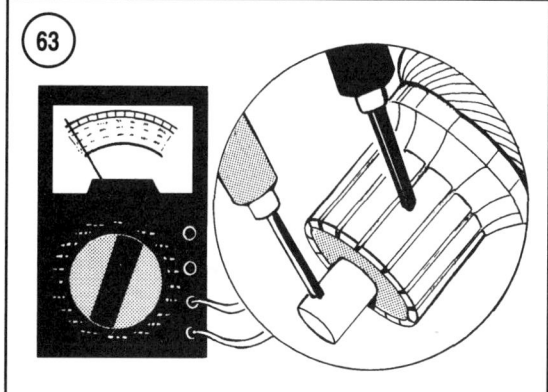

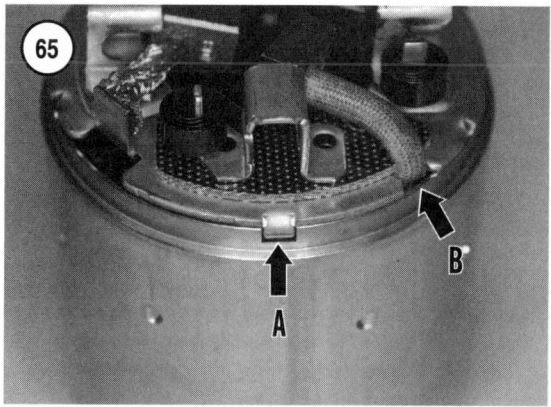

2. Install the terminal bolt through the hole in the starter housing while aligning the tab on the brush plate with the notch in the starter housing (A, **Figure 65**). Make sure the positive brush wires remain in their notches in the brush plate so they are not pinched between the plate and housing. Refer to B, **Figure 65**.

NOTE
In the next step, reinstall all parts in the order described to insulate the positive brushes from the case.

3. Install the two small insulators, large insulator, steel washer and nut to secure the terminal bolt to the starter housing. Refer to **Figure 50**. Tighten the nut securely.
4. Perform the two continuity checks described under *Disassembly*, Step 7 to check the positive brushes and terminal bolt for proper installation.
5. Install the brushes into their holders as follows:
   a. To keep spring pressure off the four brushes when installing the armature, insert strips of stiff plastic between each spring and brush holder (**Figure 66**).
   b. Install the brushes into their holders (**Figure 66**).

NOTE
In Step 6, magnetic force will pull the armature against the coils inside the starter housing. Hold the armature tightly when installing it to avoid damaging the coils or brushes.

6. Install the armature into the starter housing until the commutator is aligned with the brush holders. Then remove the plastic strips to release the brush springs and allow them to push the brushes against the commutator. Check that each brush seats squarely against the commutator (**Figure 67**).
7. Install the shims (C, **Figure 51**) onto the armature shaft.
8. Install the O-ring onto the commutator side of the starter housing.

9. Apply a thin coat of grease onto the armature shaft.
10. Install the rear cover over the armature shaft and seat it against the O-ring/housing. Align the index mark on the rear cover with the mark on the housing.
11. Install the O-ring onto the front side of the starter housing.
12. Lubricate the front cover oil seal lips and bearing with grease.
13. Refer to **Figure 52** and install the front cover as follows:
    a. Install the steel shims (D, **Figure 52**) onto the armature shaft. The number of shims on the starter may differ from the shims shown in **Figure 52**.
    b. Install the insulator (C, **Figure 52**) and seat it against the shims.
    c. Install the lockwasher (B, **Figure 52**) onto the front cover.
    d. Install the front cover by aligning the index mark on the cover with the mark on the housing. Set the cover against the O-ring/housing.
14. Install the starter assembly bolts and tighten to 6.4 N•m (56.6 in.-lb.).

NOTE
If one or both bolts will not pass through the starter, the end covers and/or the brush plate are installed incorrectly.

15. Lubricate the O-ring with grease and install it into the front cover groove.
16. Hold the starter and turn the armature shaft by hand. The armature should turn with some resistance, but should not bind or lockup. If the armature does not turn properly, disassemble the starter and check the shim, insulated washer and lockwasher alignment.

CAUTION
Because of the large amount of current that will flow from the battery to the starter, use a large diameter cable when making the connection. To avoid damaging the starter, do not leave the battery connected for more than 5 seconds.

17. Use an auxiliary battery and apply battery voltage directly to the starter (**Figure 68**). The starter should turn when battery voltage is applied directly to the terminal bolt. If the starter did not turn, disassemble and inspect the starter as described in this section.

STARTER RELAY SWITCH

The starter relay switch (**Figure 69**) is mounted behind the right side cover.

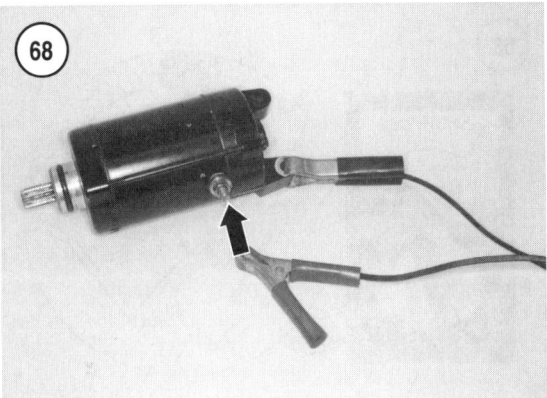

Starter Relay Switch Testing

1. Refer to *Starter System Troubleshooting* in this chapter to test the starting circuit. If the problem has been isolated to the starter relay switch, perform the following test.
2. Remove the left side cover (Chapter Fifteen).
3. Shift the transmission into neutral.
4. Turn the ignition switch on and press the starter button. The starter relay should click.
    a. Yes. The starter relay switch is working correctly.
    b. No. Continue with Step 5.
5. Disconnect the 4-pin connector (A, **Figure 69**) at the starter relay switch. Clean or repair any dirty, loose fitting or damaged terminals in the connector or at the starter relay switch. If the terminals are in good condition, leave the connector disconnected and continue with Step 6.
6. Ground line connection test: Shift the transmission into neutral. Check for continuity between the green/red wire terminal in the starter relay switch connector and ground. There should be continuity or a slight resistance reading.

NOTE
There should also be continuity when the clutch is released (clutch lever

ELECTRICAL SYSTEM

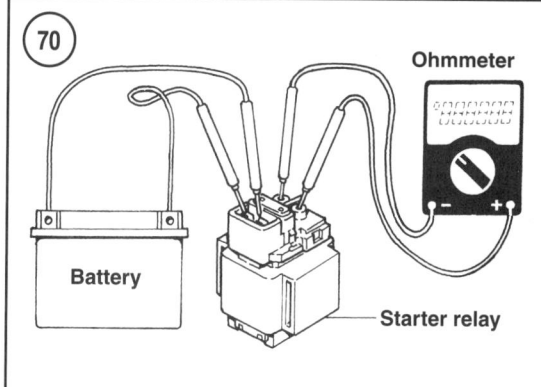

pulled in) and the sidestand is locked in its up position.

NOTE
Normally the ohmmeter will read 0 ohms when making a ground test. However, because of the diode in the circuit, it is normal for the ohmmeter to show a slight resistance reading.

   a. Continuity: Go to Step 7.
   b. No continuity: Repair the open circuit in the green/red wire between the starter relay switch connector and the left handlebar switch connector.

7. Starter relay switch voltage check: Reconnect the starter relay 4-pin connector (A, **Figure 69**). Turn the ignition switch on and measure voltage between the starter relay switch yellow/red wire at the 4-pin connector and ground when pressing the starter button. There should be battery voltage.
   a. Battery voltage: Go to Step 8.
   b. No battery voltage: Repair the open in the yellow/red wire between the starter/relay switch connector and the starter in the right-handlebar switch connector.
8. Bench test the starter relay switch as follows:

   a. Remove the starter relay switch as described in this section. Clean the switch electrical contacts.
   b. Connect ohmmeter test leads across the two large leads on the starter relay switch (**Figure 70**). There should be no continuity.
   c. If there is continuity, replace the starter relay switch.
   d. If there is no continuity, leave the ohmmeter connected to the switch and continue with sub-step e.
   e. Connect the positive lead from a fully charged 12 volt battery to the starter relay switch yellow/red wire terminal and the negative battery lead to the green/red wire terminal (**Figure 70**). There should be continuity.
   f. If there is no continuity, replace the starter relay switch.
   g. If there is continuity, the starter relay switch is operational. Reinstall the starter relay switch and check the wires and cables in the starting circuit.
9. Install all parts previously removed.

Removal/Installation

1. Remove the right side cover (Chapter Fifteen).
2. Disconnect the negative battery lead as described in this chapter.
3. Label the connectors and cables before disconnecting them from the starter relay switch.
4. Disconnect the starter relay switch electrical connector (A, **Figure 69**) at the switch.
5. Disconnect the battery (B, **Figure 69**) and starter (C) cables at the starter relay switch.
6. Remove the starter relay switch from the frame.
7. Installation is the reverse of removal. Clean the battery and starter cable leads before connecting them to the relay.

CLUTCH DIODE

The clutch diode is part of the starter circuit and is wired between the clutch switch and neutral switch. The diode prevents the flow of current from the neutral switch back through the clutch switch.

Suspect a faulty clutch diode if the neutral light comes on when the transmission is in gear and the clutch is disengaged. Also, look for a dirty or loose clutch diode connection if the starter does not operate when the transmission is in neutral.

Testing/Removal/Installation

1. Remove the right side cover (Chapter Fifteen).

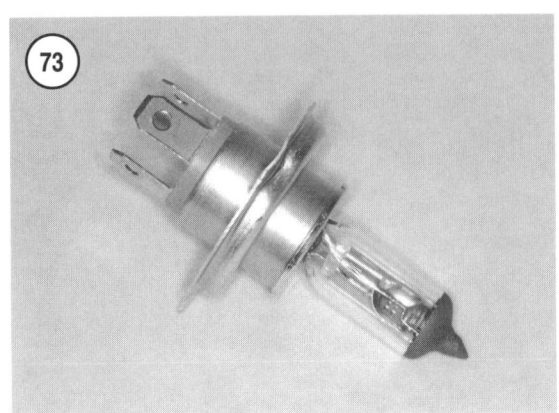

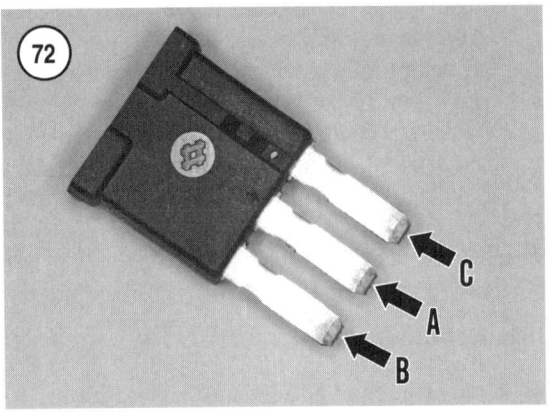

2. Open the fuse box cover and remove the diode (**Figure 71**) from the fuse box.

3. Connect an ohmmeter test lead to the A terminal (**Figure 72**). Then touch the opposite ohmmeter test lead to the B and then the C terminals. Reverse the first test lead attached to the A terminal and check continuity in the opposite direction at the B, then the C terminals. Each pair should have continuity in one direction and no continuity when the test leads are reversed.

4. Replace the diode if it fails any part of this test.

5. Install the diode by aligning the raised tab on the diode with the slot in the fuse box.

LIGHTING SYSTEM

Refer to **Table 8** for bulb specifications. Always use the correct wattage bulb. Using the wrong size bulb gives a dim light or causes the bulb to burn out prematurely.

Headlight Lens Removal/Installation (Bulb Removal/Installation)

WARNING
If the headlight just burned out or it was just turned off it will be hot. Do not touch the bulb until it cools off.

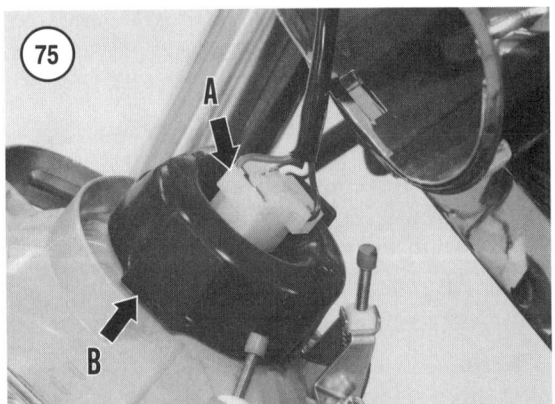

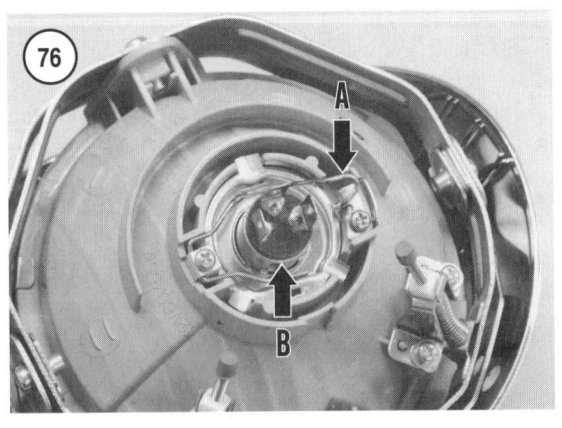

ELECTRICAL SYSTEM

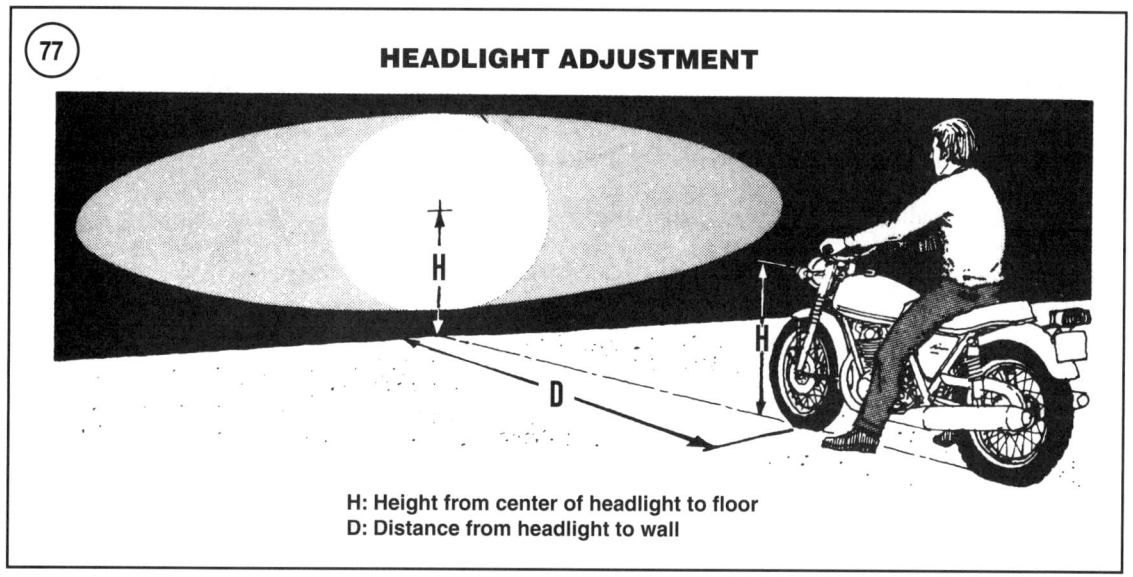

HEADLIGHT ADJUSTMENT

H: Height from center of headlight to floor
D: Distance from headlight to wall

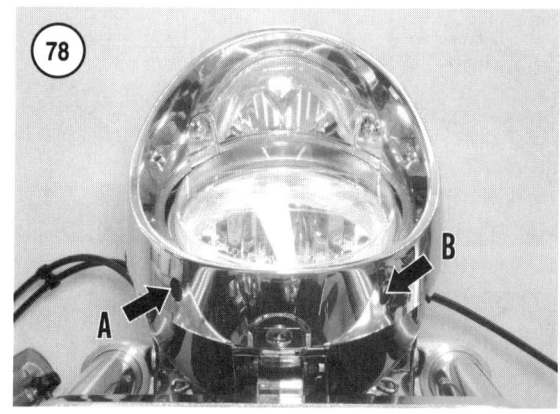

CAUTION
*All models use a quartz-halogen bulb (**Figure 73**). Because traces of oil on the glass will reduce the life of the bulb, do not touch the bulb glass. Clean any oil or other chemicals from the bulb glass with an alcohol-moistened cloth.*

1. Place a towel on the front fender.
2. Remove the two screws (**Figure 74**) and the headlight from the housing.
3. Disconnect the electrical connector (A, **Figure 75**) at the bulb and remove the headlight assembly.
4. Remove the dust cover (B, **Figure 75**) from around the bulb.
5. Unhook the bulb retainer (A, **Figure 76**) and remove the bulb (B).
6. Install the bulb and headlight lens by reversing these removal steps. Note the following:
   a. Align the tabs on the bulb with the notches in the bulb holder and install the bulb.
   b. Install the dust cover (B, **Figure 75**) with its TOP mark at the top of the housing.
   c. Hook the tab at the bottom of the lens into the retainer at the bottom of the headlight housing, then pivot the lens into the housing and install the two screws (**Figure 74**) and tighten securely.
   d. Turn the ignition switch on and check the headlight operation. If necessary, perform the *Headlight Adjustment* in this section.

Headlight Adjustment

Adjust the headlight as follows or according to local regulations if they differ from the following:
Refer to **Figure 77**.
1. Check tire inflation pressure (Chapter Three).
2. Park the motorcycle on a level surface 7.6 m (25 ft.) from a wall.
3. Draw a horizontal line on the wall the same height as the center of the headlight.
4. Have an assistant with the same approximate weight as the primary rider sit on the seat.
5. Turn the ignition switch on and the light switch to HIGH beam. Turn the handlebars so they point straight ahead and the beam is centered with the horizontal mark on the wall.
6. Check the headlight beam alignment. The broad, flat pattern of light (main beam of light) must be centered on the horizontal light with an equal area of light above and below the line.
7. Check the headlight beam lateral alignment. With the front wheel pointed straight ahead, there should be an equal area of light to the left and right of center.
8. If the beam is incorrect, adjust it as follows:
   a. To adjust the headlight vertically, turn the screw on the right side of the headlight (A, **Figure 78**).

b. To adjust the headlight horizontally, turn the screw on the left side of the headlight (B, **Figure 78**).

Headlight Housing Removal/Installation

1. Remove the headlight lens as described in this section.
2. Disconnect the connectors mounted inside the headlight housing.
3. Note how the wire harness clamps are installed and routed inside the headlight housing.
4. Remove the cap nuts and bolts (**Figure 79**, typical) securing the headlight housing to the lower steering bracket and remove the headlight housing.
5. Installation is the reverse of removal. Note the following:
    a. Turn the ignition switch on and check the operation of all switches and indicators.
    b. Check the headlight adjustment as described in this section.

Turn Signal Bulb Removal/Installation

1. Remove the screws, lens and gasket.
2. Replace the gasket if damaged.
3. Push the bulb (**Figure 80**, typical) in and turn it counterclockwise to remove it.
4. Install the new bulb and lens by reversing these steps. Do not overtighten the screws or the lens may crack.

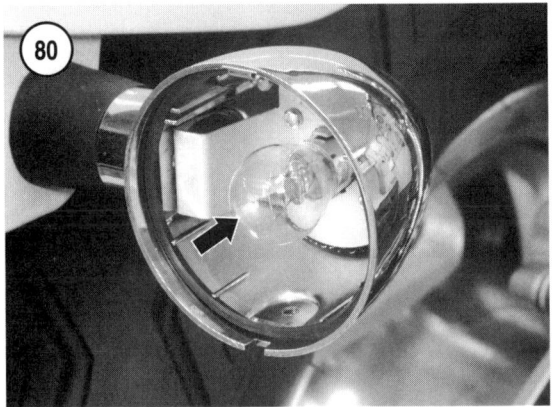

Front Turn Signal Assembly Removal/Installation

VTX1300C

1. Note the wiring harness routing from the turn signal to the headlight housing.
2. Remove the headlight lens as described in this chapter and disconnect the turn signal connectors located inside the headlight housing.
3. Release the wiring harness from the clamp and pull the harness out of the headlight housing.
4. Remove the bolt (A, **Figure 81**), clamp, collar, index nut and turn signal assembly.
5. Installation is the reverse of these steps, plus the following:
    a. Lower the front turn signal and insert the arm on the end of the index nut (B, **Figure 81**) into the slot in the fork bridge. Tighten the pinch bolt to secure the turn signal assembly to the fork tube.
    b. Route the wiring harness correctly and secure it with the clamp.

c. Turn the ignition switch on and check the operation of both front turn signals and the headlight.

VTX1300R/S/T

1. Note the wiring harness routing from the turn signal to the headlight housing.
2. Remove the headlight lens as described in this chapter and disconnect the turn signal connectors located inside the headlight housing.
3. Release the wiring harness from the clamp and pull the harness out of the headlight housing.

ELECTRICAL SYSTEM

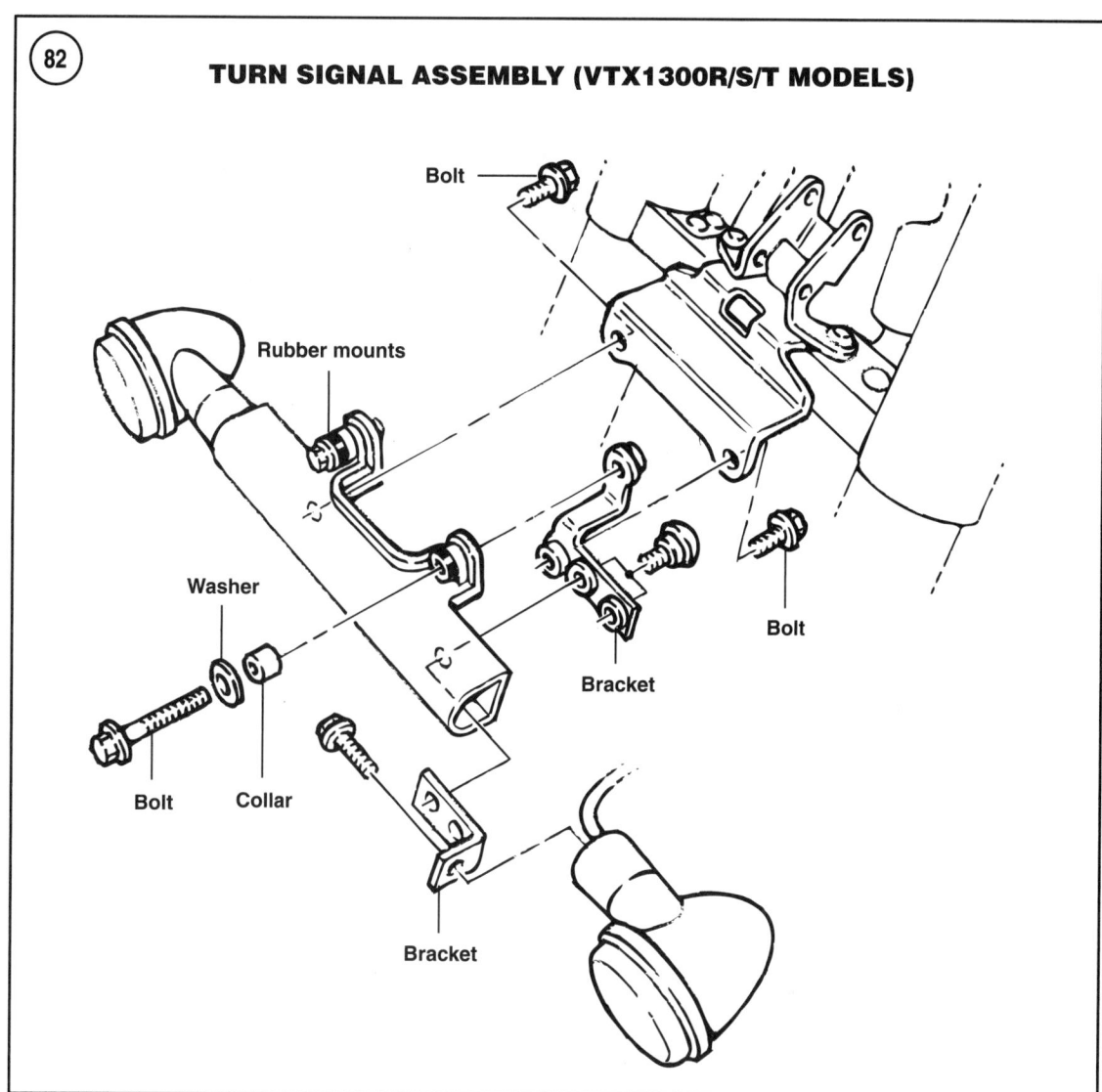

82. TURN SIGNAL ASSEMBLY (VTX1300R/S/T MODELS)

4. Remove the bolts, washers and collars securing the turn signal assembly to the mounting bracket and remove the turn signal assembly (**Figure 82**).
5. To remove the turn signal assemblies from the cover assembly, refer to **Figure 82**.
6. Installation is the reverse of these steps. Note the following:
   a. Route the wiring harness correctly and secure it with the clamp.
   b. Turn the ignition switch on and check the operation of both front turn signals and the headlight.

Rear Turn Signal Assembly Removal/Installation

1. Remove the rear fender (Chapter Fifteen).
2. Remove the turn signal wiring harness from the clamps on the rear fender.
3. Remove the bolt and the rear turn signal assembly.
4. Installation is the reverse of removal. Turn the ignition switch on and check the operation of both rear turn signals.

Tail/Brake Light Bulb Removal/Installation

WARNING
Do not ride the motorcycle without a properly operating taillight and brake light.

1. Remove the screws, lens and gasket.
2. Replace the gasket if damaged.
3. Push the bulb (**Figure 83**) in and turn it counterclockwise to remove it.
4. Install the new bulb and lens by reversing these steps. Note the following:

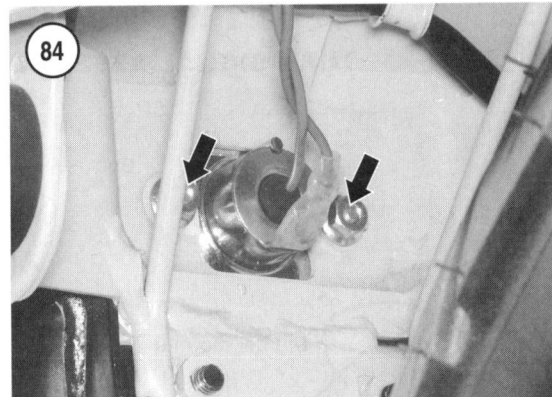

a. Do not overtighten the screws or the lens may crack.
b. Turn the ignition switch on and check the taillight and brake light operation.

Tail/Brake Light Housing Removal/Installation

1. Remove the rear fender (Chapter Fifteen).
2. Release the wiring harness from the clamps on the inside of the rear fender.
3. From inside the rear fender, remove the bolts and collars securing the tail/brake light housing and its rubber mount to the rear fender.
4. Installation is the reverse of these steps.

License Plate Light Bulb/Housing Removal/Installation (VTX1300C Models)

1. Remove the nuts (**Figure 84**) and washers located on the inside of the rear fender, then remove the cover and lens (**Figure 85**). Push the bulb in and turn counterclockwise to remove.
2. Installation is the reverse of removal. Turn the ignition switch on and check the license plate operation.

License Plate Light (VTX1300R/S/T Models)

Bulb removal/installation

Refer to **Figure 86**.
1. From inside the rear fender, remove the bolt and bulb cover.
2. Turn the bulb socket counterclockwise and remove it.
3. Pull the blown bulb out of the socket and replace it.
4. Installation is the reverse of removal, plus the following:
   a. Align the tab on the bulb cover with the notch in the rear fender.

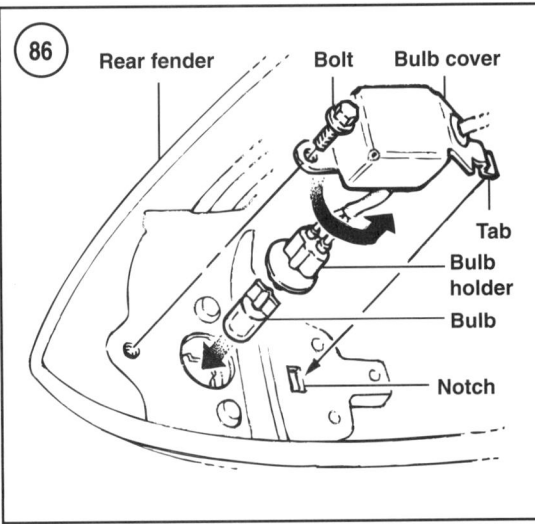

b. Turn the ignition switch on and check the license plate operation.

Housing removal/installation

Refer to **Figure 87**.
1. Remove the license plate bulb as described in this section.
2. Remove the bolts and the license plate bracket.

ELECTRICAL SYSTEM

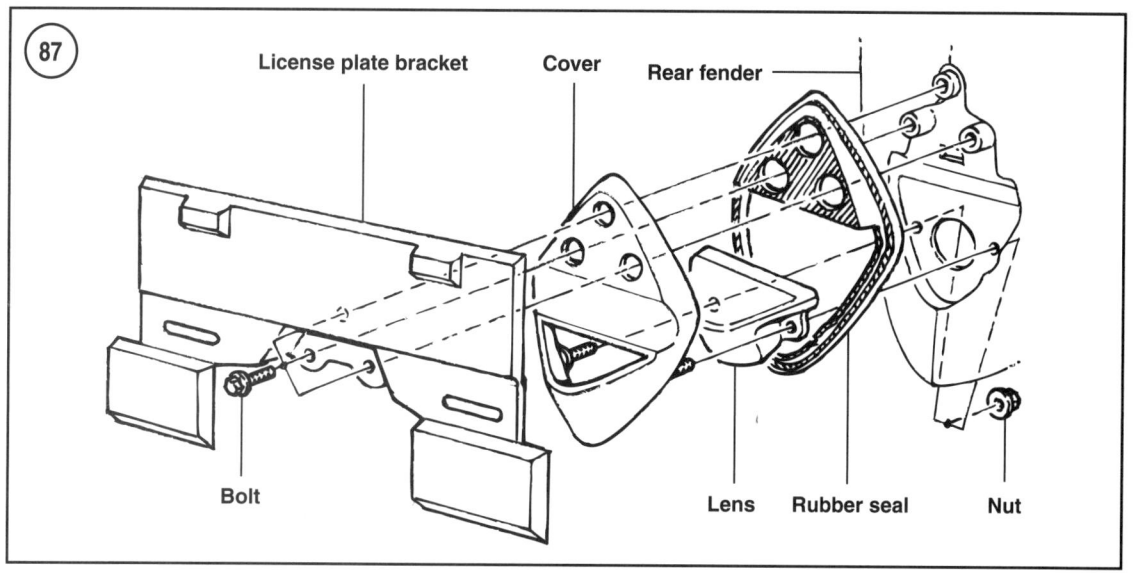

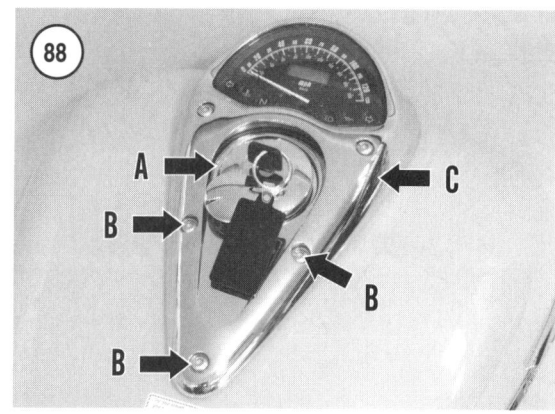

3. Remove nuts and bolts and the license plate light cover, lens and rubber seal.
4. Installation is the reverse of these steps.

METER ASSEMBLY

The meter box is mounted on the fuel tank cover and consists of the speedometer, reset switch and indicator display. LEDs provide illumination for the meter assembly. If the speedometer function fails or an LED does not come on, replace the meter assembly. The reset switch can be replaced separately.

Meter Box Illumination

An LED is used to illuminate the meter box (speedometer and all indicators). The LED should come on when the ignition switch is turned on. If the LED does not come on, perform the tests in this section. If damage is noted, and individual LED cannot be replaced separately; replace the meter box assembly.

Fuel Tank Cover/Meter Assembly Removal/Installation

1. Remove the fuel tank (Chapter Eight).
2. Remove the wiring harness from the clamp on the fuel tank.
3. Open the fuel tank cap (A, **Figure 88**) with the ignition key and remove it.
4. Remove the screws and washers (B, **Figure 88**) securing the fuel tank cover/meter assembly (C) to the fuel tank.
5. Reinstall the fuel tank cap.
6. Installation is the reverse of these steps. Tighten the fuel tank cover/meter assembly screws (B, **Figure 88**) to 3.5 N•m (31 in.-lb.).

Meter Assembly and Reset Switch Removal/Installation

The reset switch can be replaced separately.
1. Remove the fuel tank cover/meter box assembly as described in this section.
2. Note the wiring harness routing before removing the reset switch or meter box.
3. Remove the reset switch button (7, **Figure 89**) from the cover.
4. Remove the screws and washers securing the mounting bracket (4, **Figure 89**) to the cover and remove the cover with the meter assembly. Then remove the reset switch (5, **Figure 89**) from the cover.
5. Remove the screws (1, **Figure 89**) securing the meter assembly to the mounting bracket and remove the meter assembly and reset switch.
6. Refer to **Figure 90** to replace the reset switch or remove the lens and visor from the meter assembly.
7. Installation is the reverse of these steps.

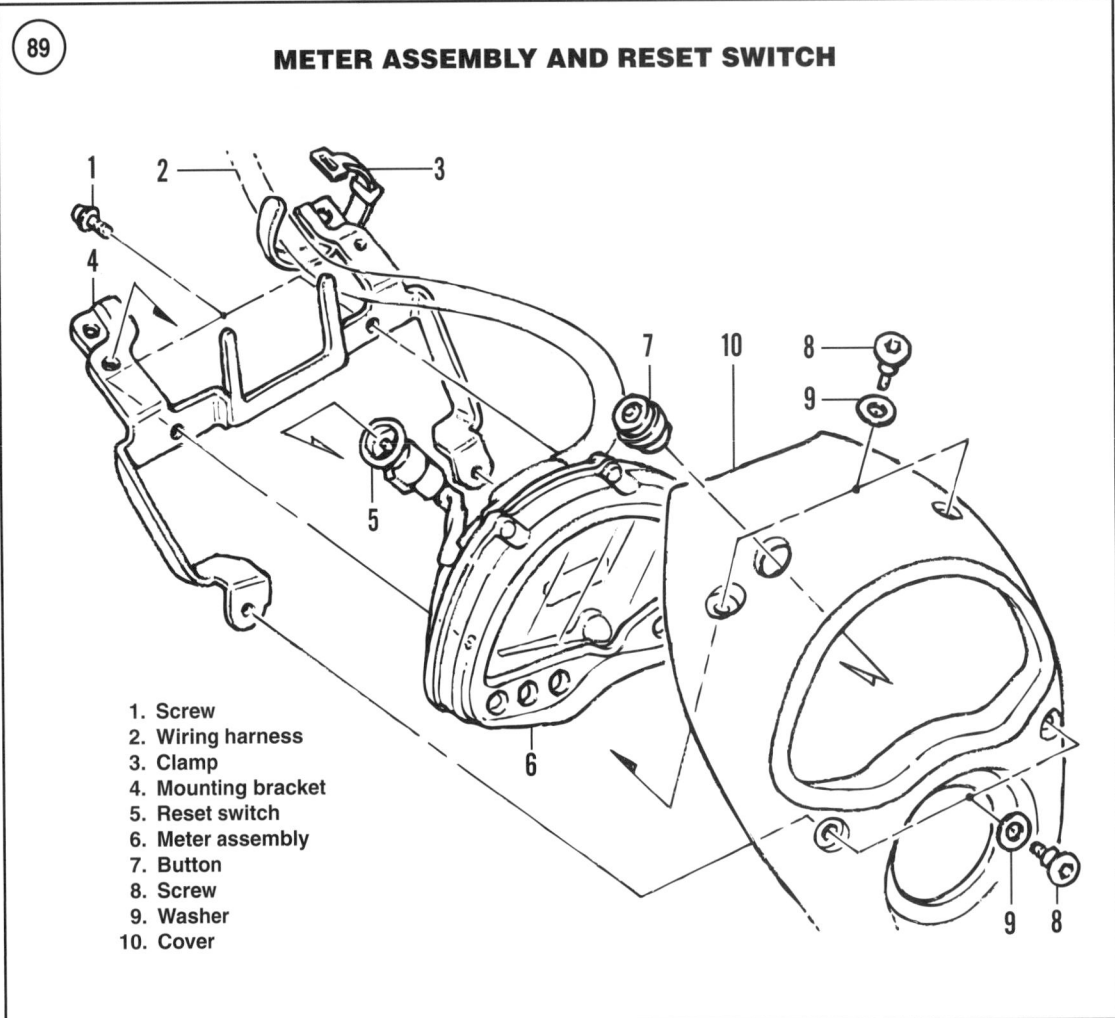

(89) METER ASSEMBLY AND RESET SWITCH

1. Screw
2. Wiring harness
3. Clamp
4. Mounting bracket
5. Reset switch
6. Meter assembly
7. Button
8. Screw
9. Washer
10. Cover

Power/Ground Line Test

NOTE
Refer to the appropriate wiring diagram at the end of the manual to identify the electrical connectors referred to in this procedure.

If none of the indicators on the meter assembly work correctly, perform the following:

1. Check for a blown taillight/meter fuse as described in this chapter. If the fuse is good, continue with Step 2.
2. Remove the right cylinder head shroud (Chapter Fifteen).
3. Disconnect the two speedometer 7-pin connectors (**Figure 91**) underneath the right front side of the fuel tank.
4. To test the power line circuit, turn the ignition switch on and measure voltage between the black/brown (+) terminal in the speedometer 7-pin connector and ground (−). There should be battery voltage.
   a. If there is battery voltage, go to Step 5.
   b. If there is no battery voltage, and the fuse is good (Step 1), check the black/brown wire between the speedometer 7-pin connector and fuse box for an open circuit.
5. To test the ground line circuit, check for resistance between the green connector terminal in the speedometer 7-pin wiring harness connector and ground. If there is no continuity, check the green wire for an open circuit.

NOTE
Perform Step 6 if the odometer/trip meter does not work.

6. Measure voltage between the red/green (+) terminal in the speedometer 7-pin connector and ground (−). There should be battery voltage at all times (ignition switch on and off). If there is no battery voltage, perform the following:

ELECTRICAL SYSTEM

METER ASSEMBLY

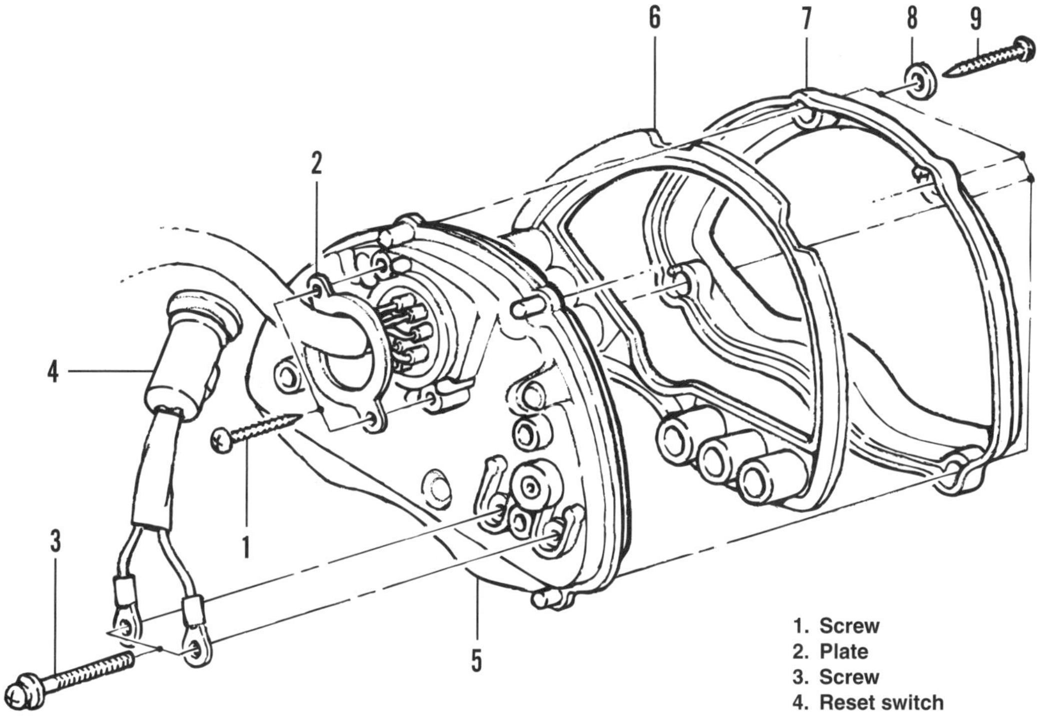

1. Screw
2. Plate
3. Screw
4. Reset switch
5. Meter assembly
6. Visor
7. Lens
8. Washer
9. Screw

a. Check for a blown odometer fuse as described in this chapter.
b. Check for an open circuit in the red/green wire between the speedometer 7-pin connector and the fuse box.
c. Check for an open circuit in the red wire between the fuse box and ignition switch.
7. Reverse Steps 1-3.

Speedometer Test

If the speedometer does not operate, perform the following:

NOTE
Refer to the appropriate wiring diagram at the end of the manual to identify the electrical connectors referred to in this procedure.

1. If none of the indicators on the meter assembly work correctly, perform the *Power/Ground Line Test* in this section. If the indicators work correctly, go to Step 2.
2. Reconnect the two speedometer 7-pin connectors (**Figure 91**) underneath the right front side of the fuel tank if they were previously disconnected.
3. Support the motorcycle with the rear wheel off the ground.
4. Shift the transmission into neutral.
5. Turn the ignition switch on and slowly turn the rear wheel while measuring voltage between white (+) and

green/black (–) terminals in the speedometer 7-pin connector. The voltmeter should read 0-5 volts (intermittently). Interpret the results in Step 6A or 6B.

6A. If the voltage reading is correct, replace the meter assembly as described in this section.

6B. If the voltage reading is incorrect, perform the following:
   a. Check the green/black wire for an open circuit.
   b. Check the white wire for an open or short circuit.
   c. If the green/black and white wires are in good condition, test the vehicle speed sensor as described in this chapter.

7. Lower the motorcycle so both wheels are on the ground and the motorcycle is supported by the sidestand.

8. Make sure all connectors are properly fastened. Install any removed body work.

VEHICLE SPEED SENSOR (VSS)

Removal/Installation

1. Remove the left crankcase rear cover (Chapter Fifteen).
2. Remove the coolant reserve tank (Chapter Ten).
3. Trace the vehicle speed sensor wiring harness from the sensor (**Figure 92**) to its 3-pin connector. Disconnect the connector (**Figure 93**).
4. Clean the area around the vehicle speed sensor to prevent dirt from entering the engine.
5. Unbolt and remove the vehicle speed sensor (**Figure 92**) and its O-ring from the crankcase. Discard the O-ring.
6. Installation is the reverse of removal. Lubricate a new O-ring with engine oil and install it onto the sensor. Tighten the sensor bolts securely.

Testing

The inspection adapter (part No. 07GMJ-ML80100 [**Figure 94**]) is required for this test.

1. Disconnect the vehicle speed sensor 3-pin connector as described in this section. Check both connector halves for dirty, loose or damaged terminals.
2. Connect the inspection adapter (**Figure 94**) between the vehicle speed sensor and wiring harness connectors.

NOTE
The clip colors called out in the following steps corresponds to the clip colors on the Honda inspection adapter.

3. Turn the ignition switch on and measure voltage between the white clip (+) and red clip (–). There should be battery voltage.
   a. If there is battery voltage, go to Step 4.
   b. If there is no battery voltage, check the black/brown and green/black wires for an open circuit.
4. Support the motorcycle with its rear wheel off the ground and shift the transmission into neutral. Then turn the ignition switch on and slowly turn the rear wheel while measuring voltage between green clip (+) and red clip (–). The voltmeter should read 0-5 volts (intermittently). If the voltage reading is incorrect, replace the vehicle speed sensor.
5. Remove the inspection adapter and reconnect the vehicle speed sensor and wiring harness connectors.
6. Reverse the removal steps.

COOLANT TEMPERATURE INDICATOR AND ENGINE COOLANT TEMPERATURE (ECT) SENSOR

CAUTION
The engine coolant temperature sensor can be damaged if dropped. Handle the sensor carefully during service and testing.

ELECTRICAL SYSTEM

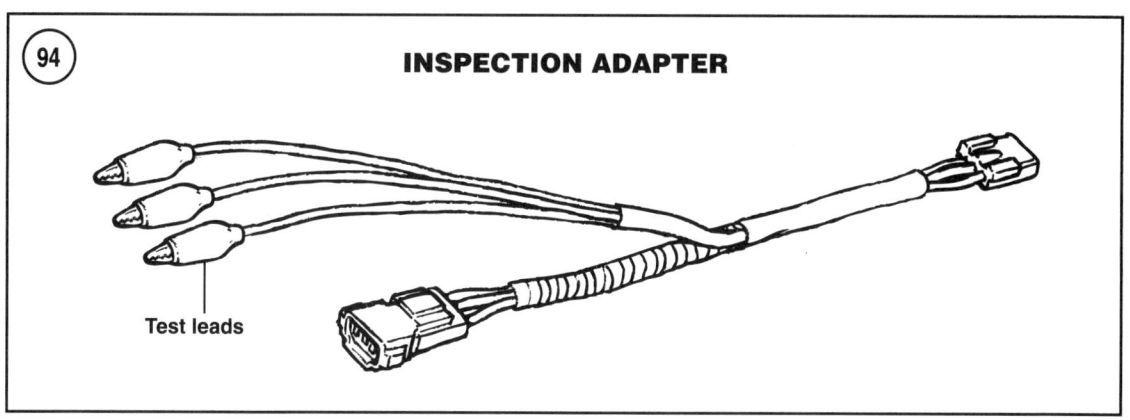

94 INSPECTION ADAPTER — Test leads

95

The engine coolant temperature sensor threads into the thermostat housing (**Figure 95**) and controls current flow to the coolant temperature indicator according to coolant temperature. When the coolant temperature is below 108° C (226° F), the sensor is open and no current can flow to the indicator and the indicator is off. When the coolant temperature increases to 112-118° C (234-244° F), the sensor closes and current flows to the indicator and turns it on, indicating an overheating condition.

Removal/Installation

1. Remove the fuel tank (Chapter Eight).
2. Remove the air filter housing (Chapter Eight).
3. Drain the engine coolant (Chapter Three).
4. Disconnect the engine coolant temperature sensor connector at the sensor (**Figure 95**) and remove the sensor.
5. Installation is the reverse of removal. Note the following:
   a. Clean the engine coolant temperature sensor and thermostat housing threads of all sealant residue.
   b. Apply sealant onto the engine coolant temperature sensor threads and tighten to 8 N•m (71 in.-lb.).
   c. Fill and bleed the cooling system (Chapter Three).

Testing

The coolant indicator lights, but the engine coolant temperature is low

1. Disconnect the engine coolant temperature sensor connector at the sensor (**Figure 95**) as described in *Removal/Installation* in this section.
2. Turn the ignition switch on and check the coolant temperature indicator on the meter assembly:
   a. If the indicator came on, check the grey wire between the engine coolant temperature sensor and the meter assembly for a short circuit. If the grey wire is in good condition, replace the meter assembly as described in this chapter.
   b. If the indicator did not come on, replace the engine coolant temperature sensor as described in this section.

The coolant indicator does not light when the engine temperature is too high

1. Shift the transmission into neutral and turn the ignition switch on. The neutral and oil pressure indicators should come on. Note the following:
   a. If both indicators did not come on, perform the *Power/Ground Line Test* in *Meter Assembly* in this chapter.
   b. If both indicators came on, go to Step 2.
2. Disconnect the engine coolant temperature sensor connector at the sensor (**Figure 95**) as described in *Removal/Installation* in this section.
3. Connect a jumper wire between the engine coolant temperature sensor wiring harness connector and a good engine ground. Turn the ignition switch on and note the following:

a. If the indicator came on, replace the engine coolant temperature sensor as described in this section.
b. If the indicator did not come on, check the grey wire between the engine coolant temperature sensor and the meter assembly for a short circuit. If the grey wire is in good condition, replace the meter assembly as described in this chapter.

4. Remove the jumper wire and reconnect the engine coolant temperature sensor.

FAN SWITCH

The fan switch is mounted on the bottom of the radiator and controls the radiator fan according to engine coolant temperature.

Removal/Installation

1. Disconnect the connectors at the horn, then remove the bolt (A, **Figure 96**) and horn (B).
2. Remove the two radiator mounting bolts (C, **Figure 96**), plate (D) and the radiator grill (E). Note the collars installed in the grommets in the top of the radiator grill.
3. Drain the cooling system (Chapter Three).
4. Disconnect the electrical connector (A, **Figure 97**) at the fan switch.
5. Remove the fan switch (B, **Figure 97**) and O-ring.
6. Installation is the reverse of these steps, plus the following:
   a. Tighten the radiator mounting bolts securely.
   b. Install a new O-ring onto the fan switch.
   c. Tighten the fan switch to 17 N•m (13 ft.-lb.).
   d. Align the horn bracket with the shoulder on the frame bracket. Then tighten the horn mounting bolt to 21 N•m (15 ft.-lb.).
   e. Fill and bleed the cooling system (Chapter Three). Check for leaks.
   f. Turn the ignition switch on and verify the horn works correctly.

Testing

Fan does not stop

1. Turn the ignition switch off.
2. Remove the radiator grill as described in *Removal/Installation* in this section.
3. Disconnect the fan switch connector (A, **Figure 97**), then turn the ignition switch on and note the operation of the fan.
4. If the fan stops, replace the fan switch as described in this section.

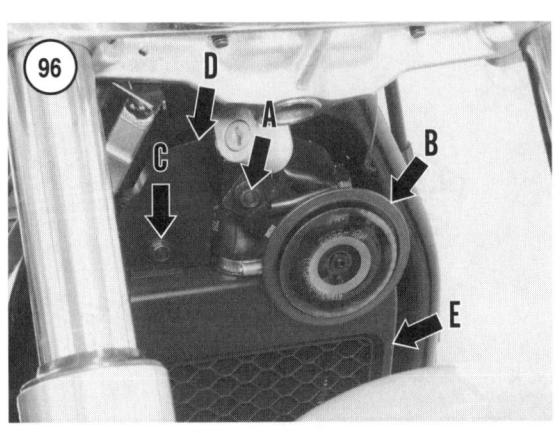

5. If the fan did not stop, check for a short circuit in the black wire between the fan switch and fan.
6. Reconnect the fan switch connector (A, **Figure 97**).
7. Reverse Step 2.

Fan does not start

1. Check for a blown fan fuse as described in this chapter. If the fuse is good, continue with Step 2.
2. Check that the ground terminal mounted on the fan (**Figure 98**) is clean. Check the bolt for tightness. If necessary, remove the bolt and remove any paint or corrosion from the attachment area, then reinstall.
3. Remove the radiator grill as described in *Removal/Installation* in this section.
4. Disconnect the connector at the fan switch (A, **Figure 97**).
5. Connect a jumper wire between the fan switch connector and ground. Then turn the ignition switch on. The fan should run.
   a. If the fan runs, continue with Step 6.
   b. If the fan did not run, go to Step 7.
6. Check the connector at the fan switch for a dirty or loose fitting terminal. If the connector is good, replace the fan switch and retest.

ELECTRICAL SYSTEM

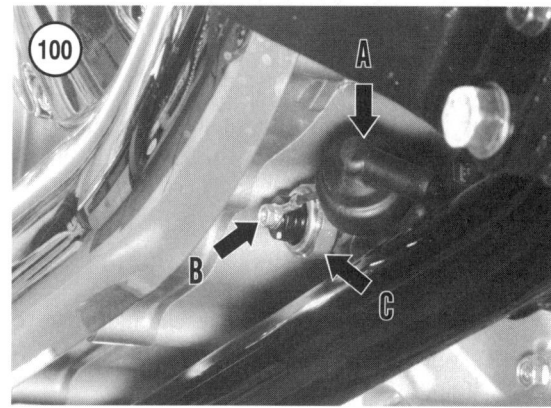

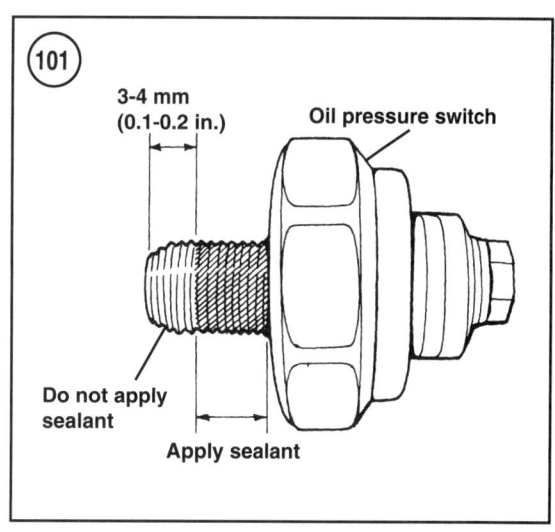

connector and the fuse box. If the wire is in good condition, continue with Step 10.

10. Check for the following conditions:
    a. Dirty or damaged wiring between the ignition switch and fuse box.
    b. Damaged ignition switch. Test the ignition switch as described in this chapter.
11. Reconnect the fan switch connector (A, **Figure 97**).
12. Reverse Step 3 and Step 7.

OIL PRESSURE SWITCH AND OIL PRESSURE INDICATOR

Oil Pressure Switch Removal/Installation

1. Support the motorcycle on its sidestand.
2. Slide the rubber cover (A, **Figure 100**) off the oil pressure switch.
3. Clean the switch and the area around the switch of all debris.
4. Remove the screw (B, **Figure 100**) and disconnect the wire at the oil pressure switch.
5. Loosen and remove the oil pressure switch (C, **Figure 100**).
6. Clean the oil pressure switch and crankcase threads of all sealant and oil residue.
7. Apply an RTV sealant to the oil pressure switch threads as shown in **Figure 101**. Do not apply sealant within 3-4 mm (0.1-0.2 in.) from the end of the switch threads.

NOTE
Allow the RTV sealant to set for 10-15 minutes before installing the oil pressure switch.

8. Install the oil pressure switch and tighten to 12 N•m (106 in.-lb.).

7. Remove the left cylinder head shroud (Chapter Fifteen).
8. Disconnect the 2-pin fan switch connector located in the wiring harness behind the radiator (**Figure 99**).
9. Turn the ignition switch on and measure voltage between black/blue (+) and green (−) wires in the wire harness side of the 2-pin connector. There should be battery voltage.
    a. If there is battery voltage, the fan is damaged. Replace the fan (Chapter Ten).
    b. If there is no battery voltage, check for an open circuit in the black/blue wire between the 2-pin

9. Reconnect the wire onto the switch and tighten the screw. Then slide the rubber cover over the switch.

NOTE
The oil pressure indicator should go out within 1-2 seconds after starting the engine. If it stays on, shut off the engine immediately and locate the problem. Do not run the engine with the oil pressure indicator on.

10. Follow the sealer manufacturer's recommendations for drying time, then start the engine and check for leaks.

CAUTION
Do not exceed the torque specification of the switch to correct an oil leak as this may strip the crankcase threads. If oil leaks from the switch after installing it, remove the switch and reclean the threads. Reseal and reinstall the switch.

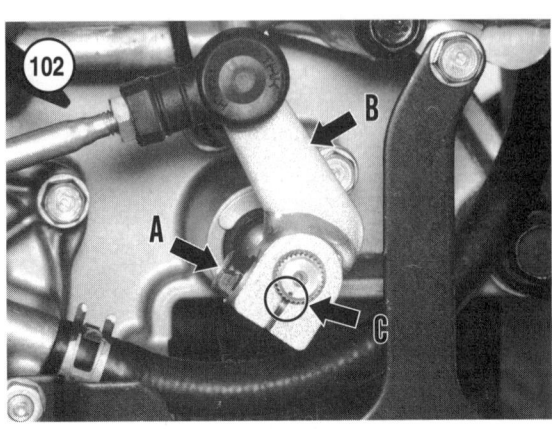

Troubleshooting

When the ignition switch is turned on, the oil pressure indicator comes on and will remain on until the engine is started. When the engine is started, the oil pressure rises and the oil pressure indicator turns off (usually within 1-2 seconds). If the indicator fails to operate as specified, perform the test that matches the indicator's operating condition.

NOTE
Make sure the engine oil level (Chapter Three) is correct before making the following tests.

Oil pressure indicator does not come on when ignition switch is turned on

1. Shift the transmission into neutral and turn the ignition switch on. The neutral and coolant temperature indicators should come on. Note the following:
   a. If both indicators did not come on, perform the *Power/Ground Line Test* in *Meter Assembly* in this chapter.
   b. If both indicators came on, go to Step 2.
2. Slide the rubber cover (A, **Figure 100**) off the oil pressure switch. Then remove the screw (B, **Figure 100**) and disconnect the wire at the oil pressure switch.
3. Ground the oil pressure switch wire with a jumper wire.
4. Turn the ignition switch on. The oil pressure indicator should come on.
   a. If the indicator came on, replace the oil pressure switch and retest.
   b. If the indicator did not come on, check the blue/red wire between the oil pressure switch and meter assembly for an open circuit or dirty or damaged connector terminals.
5. Remove the ground wire and reverse Step 2 to complete installation.

Oil pressure indicator stays on when engine is running

1. Turn the engine off and check the engine oil level (Chapter Three).
2. Support the motorcycle on its sidestand.
3. Slide the rubber cover (A, **Figure 100**) off the oil pressure switch. Then remove the screw (B, **Figure 100**) and disconnect the wire at the oil pressure switch.
4. Check for continuity between the oil pressure switch wire and ground. There should be no continuity.
   a. If there is no continuity, check the oil pressure as described in Chapter Three. If the oil pressure is normal, replace the oil pressure switch.
   b. If there is continuity, check the blue/red wire between the oil pressure switch and meter assembly for a short circuit.

CAUTION
Do not ride the motorcycle until the problem is corrected. Low oil pressure will damage the engine.

5. Reverse Steps 3 to complete installation.

NEUTRAL SWITCH

Removal/Installation

1. Support the motorcycle so it is upright.
2. Remove the left crankcase rear cover (Chapter Fifteen).

ELECTRICAL SYSTEM

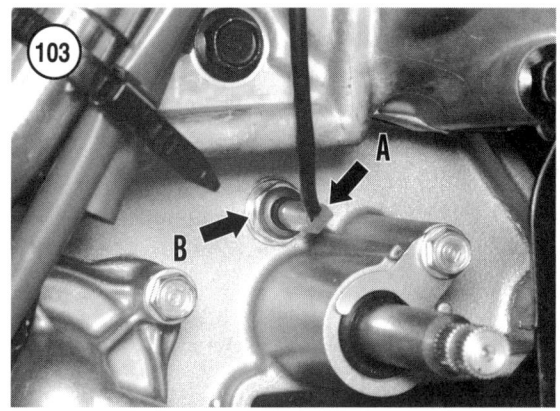

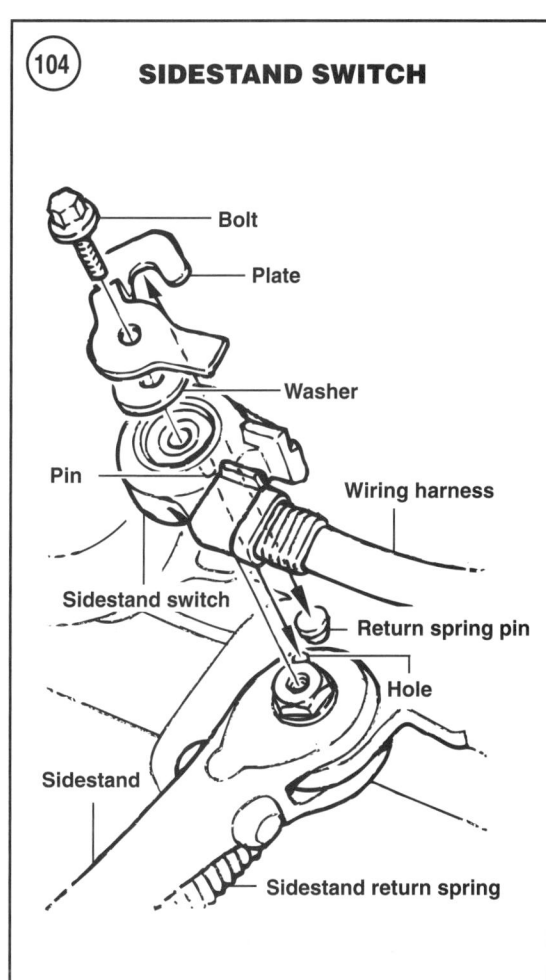

3. Remove the pinch bolt (A, **Figure 102**) and slide the shift boss (B) off the shift shaft.
4. Disconnect the wire (A, **Figure 103**) at the neutral switch.
5. Remove the neutral switch (B, **Figure 103**) and sealing washer.
6. Install the neutral switch with a new sealing washer and tighten to 12 N•m (106 in.-lb.). Reconnect the wire at the neutral switch.

7. Reverse Step 2 and Step 3 to complete installation. Align the slot in the shift boss with the punch mark (C, **Figure 102**) on the end of the shift shaft. Tighten the pinch bolt to 12 N•m (106 in.-lb.).
8. Turn the ignition switch on and shift the transmission into neutral. The neutral indicator light should come on.

Testing

1. Shift the transmission into neutral and turn the ignition switch on. The neutral indicator should come on.
   a. If the neutral indicator came on, the system is normal.
   b. If the neutral indicator did not come on, continue with Step 2.
2. Disconnect the wire (A, **Figure 103**) at the neutral switch as described in *Removal/Installation* in this section.
3. Check for continuity between the terminal on the neutral switch and ground. There should be continuity with the transmission in neutral and no continuity with the transmission in any gear (except neutral).
   a. Replace the neutral switch if it failed either test.
   b. If the switch is good, check for an open circuit in the light green/red wire.
4. Reverse Step 2 to complete installation.

SIDESTAND SWITCH

WARNING
Do not ride the motorcycle until the sidestand switch operates correctly. Riding the motorcycle with the sidestand down will cause the rider to lose control when the sidestand contacts the ground.

The sidestand switch is part of the ignition cutoff system. This system is designed to prevent the motorcycle from being ridden when the sidestand is down. When the sidestand is down, the engine will only start when the transmission is in neutral. When the sidestand is up, the engine can be started in neutral, or in gear when the clutch lever is pulled in. If the engine is started with the transmission in neutral and the sidestand down, the engine cuts off if the transmission is shifted into gear before the sidestand is raised.

Removal/Installation

Refer to **Figure 104**.

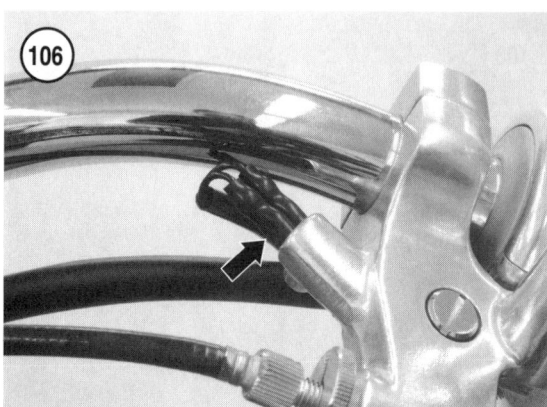

1. Support the motorcycle on a workstand so the sidestand can be serviced.
2. Remove left crankcase rear cover (Chapter Fifteen).

NOTE
Note the sidestand switch wiring harness routing before disconnecting and removing the switch.

3. Trace the wiring harness from the sidestand switch (**Figure 105**) to the main wiring harness and disconnect the sidestand switch 2-pin connector.
4. Remove the bolt, plate, washer and sidestand switch. Discard the bolt.
5. Install the sidestand switch by inserting the pin on the switch into the hole in the sidestand.
6. Install the washer and plate. Align the tab on the plate with the groove in the switch and the groove on the plate with the return spring pin.
7. Install a new sidestand switch mounting bolt and tighten to 10 N•m (88 in.-lb.).
8. Route the sidestand switch wiring harness along its original path and reconnect its connector.
9. Test the sidestand switch as described in this section.
10. Install the left crankcase rear cover (Chapter Fifteen).
11. Perform the *Sidestand and Ignition Cut-off Switch Test* in Chapter Three.

Testing

A problem in the sidestand switch circuit can prevent the engine from starting or can cause the engine to cut-out.
1. Support the motorcycle on a workstand so the sidestand can be operated by hand.
2. Remove left crankcase rear cover (Chapter Fifteen).

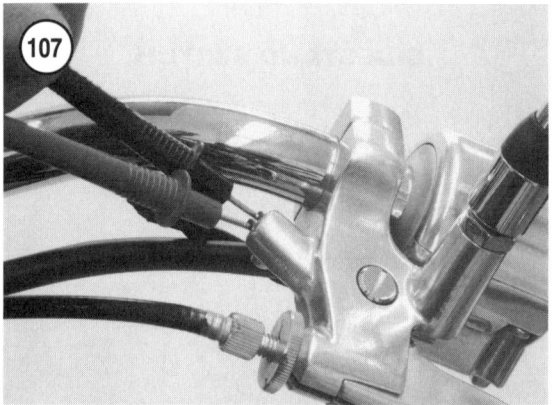

NOTE
Note the sidestand switch wiring harness routing before disconnecting the switch in this section.

3. Trace the wiring harness from the sidestand switch (**Figure 105**) to the main wiring harness and disconnect the 2-pin sidestand switch connector.

NOTE
Make the test on the switch side of the connector, not on the wire harness side.

4. Test the sidestand switch as follows:
   a. Check for continuity between the 2-pin connector green/white and green terminals.
   b. There should be continuity with the sidestand up.
   c. There should be no continuity with the sidestand down.
5. Replace the sidestand switch if it failed any part of this test.
6. Reverse Steps 1-3 to complete installation.

CLUTCH SWITCH

The clutch switch is mounted inside the clutch lever housing.

ELECTRICAL SYSTEM

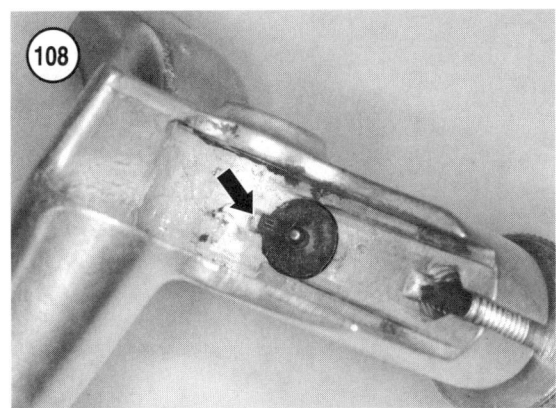

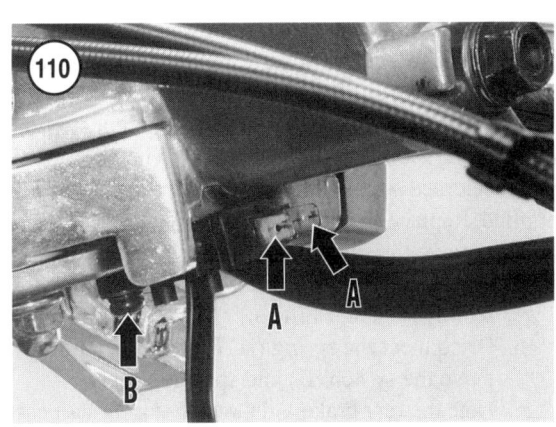

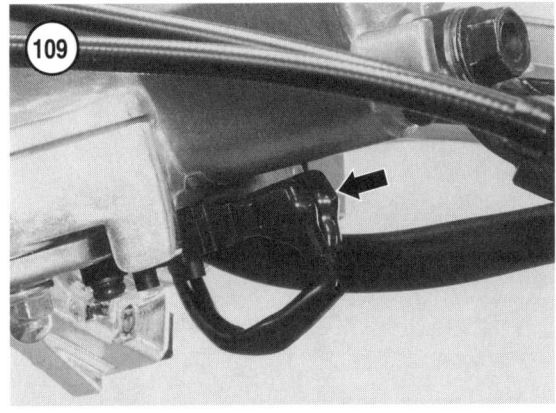

Testing/Removal/Installation

1. Disconnect the two electrical connectors at the clutch switch (**Figure 106**).
2. Connect ohmmeter leads across the two clutch switch terminals (**Figure 107**). There should be continuity with the clutch lever applied and no continuity with the clutch lever released. Replace the switch if faulty.
3. Replace the clutch switch as follows:
   a. Disconnect the clutch cable from the clutch lever at the handlebar.
   b. Remove the nut, pivot bolt and clutch lever.
   c. Gently push the clutch switch out of the housing.
   d. Install the clutch switch by aligning the tab on the switch with the notch in the housing (**Figure 108**). Push the switch into the housing until it bottoms.
4. Clean the clutch lever and pivot bolt. Tighten the pivot bolt securely. Then hold the pivot bolt and tighten the nut. Check that the clutch lever pivots smoothly.
5. Reconnect the clutch cable and adjust the clutch (Chapter Three).
6. Reconnect the electrical connectors at the clutch switch.

FRONT BRAKE LIGHT SWITCH

The front brake light switch is mounted on the bottom of the front master cylinder.

Testing/Removal/Installation

WARNING
Do not ride the motorcycle without a correctly operating brake light.

1. Disconnect the two electrical connectors (**Figure 109**) from the switch terminals.
2. Check for continuity between the switch terminals (A, **Figure 110**). There should be continuity with the brake lever applied and no continuity with the brake lever released. Replace the switch if faulty.
3. Replace the switch by removing the screw (B, **Figure 110**) and switch.
4. Installation is the reverse of removal. Note the following:
   a. Make sure all connectors are plugged tightly into the switch.
   b. Turn the ignition switch on and operate the front brake lever to check the brake light operation.

REAR BRAKE LIGHT SWITCH

The rear brake light switch is mounted on the rear brake pedal assembly.

Testing/Removal/Installation

WARNING
Do not ride the motorcycle without a correctly operating brake light.

1. Remove the left steering side cover (Chapter Fifteen).

2. Disconnect the rear brake light switch 2-pin connector (**Figure 111**) from the wiring harness connector located in front of the ignition coil.
3. Check for continuity between the switch terminals. There should be no continuity with the brake pedal released and continuity with the brake pedal applied. Replace the switch if faulty.
4. To remove the switch:
   a. Remove the right footpeg or right footrest assembly (Chapter Fifteen).
   b. Disconnect the spring (A, **Figure 112**) and remove the switch (B) and spring.
   c. Note the rear brake light switch wiring harness routing and remove it.
5. Installation is the reverse of removal.
6. Adjust the rear brake light switch (Chapter Three).

IGNITION SWITCH

The ignition switch is mounted on the left side of the motorcycle.

Testing/Removal/Installation

1. Remove the seats and the left side cover (Chapter Fifteen).
2. Disconnect the ignition switch 4-pin connector located in the connector pouch underneath the seat.
3. Test the ignition switch as described in *Switch Continuity Test* in this chapter. Refer to the wiring diagram at the end of this manual for the ignition switch continuity diagram. Replace the switch if faulty.
4. Replace the ignition switch as follows:
   a. Note the ignition switch wiring harness routing. Remove any clamps securing the wiring harness in place.
   b. Remove the screw (A, **Figure 113**) and the chrome cover (B).
   c. Remove the bolts (A, **Figure 114**) and the ignition switch (B).
5. Installation is the reverse of removal. Note the following:
   a. Tighten the ignition switch mounting bolts to 10 N•m (88 in.-lb.).
   b. If installing a new ignition switch, record the new key number in the *Quick Reference Data* section at the front of this manual.
   c. Check the switch operation.

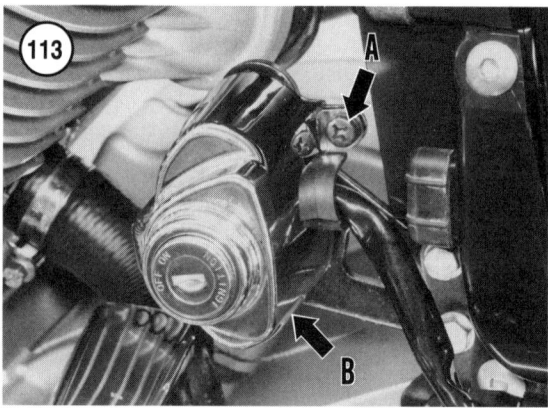

HANDLEBAR SWITCH

The left handlebar switch housing (**Figure 115**) includes the headlight dimmer switch, turn signal switch and horn button.

The right handlebar switch housing (**Figure 116**) includes the engine stop switch and the starter switch.

Testing/Removal/Installation

WARNING
Do not ride the motorcycle unless each switch works properly.

1. Remove the headlight lens as described in this chapter.
2. Trace the switch wiring harness from the switch assembly to the connectors in the headlight housing

ELECTRICAL SYSTEM

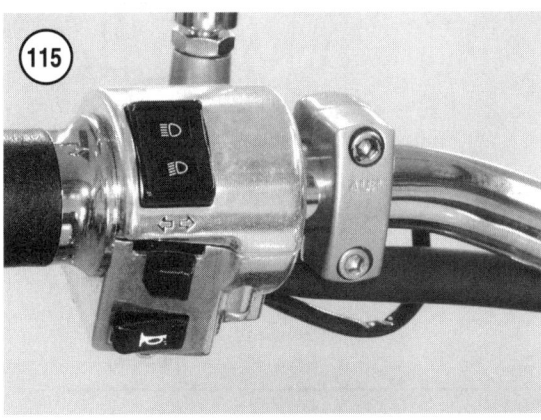

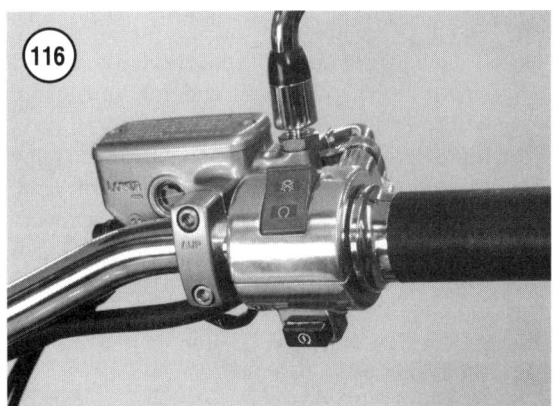

IGNITION SWITCH

	FAN	IG	BAT 1
ON	●———————————	●——————————	———●
OFF			
LOCK			
Color	Blue/orange	Red/black	Red

and disconnect them. Refer to the appropriate wiring diagram at the end of this manual to identify the connectors and wire colors for each switch.

3. Test the switch as described in *Switch Continuity Test* in this chapter. Note the following:
   a. If the continuity test indicates a faulty switch, continue with Step 4 to replace the switch assembly.
   b. If the switch is good, reconnect the connectors and install the headlight lens.

4. Note how the switch wiring harness is routed from the switch to the headlight housing. Then carefully pull the wiring harness and connectors from the headlight housing.

5. Remove the left (**Figure 115**) and right (**Figure 116**) side handlebar switches from the handlebar as described in *Handlebar* in Chapter Twelve.

6. Installation is the reverse of removal. Check each switch function for proper operation.

SWITCH CONTINUITY TEST

Test the switches for continuity using an ohmmeter or a self-powered test light (refer to *Electrical System Fundamentals* in Chapter One) at the switch connector by operating the switch in each of its operating positions. Compare the results with its switch operation diagram. For example, **Figure 117** shows a typical continuity diagram for the ignition switch. The horizontal line indicates which terminals should show continuity when the switch is in that position. Continuing with the example, in the ON position there should be continuity between all three terminals. When the switch is in the OFF position, there should be no continuity between any of the terminals.

1. Refer to the appropriate switch procedure in this chapter to access the switch connectors. Some switches do not use a continuity diagram for testing. Instead, follow the procedure in its appropriate section.

2. Check the subfuse as described in *Fuses* in this chapter.

3. Check the battery as described in *Battery* in this chapter. Charge the battery to the correct state of charge, if required.

4. Disconnect the negative battery cable at the battery if the switch connectors are not disconnected from the circuit.

CAUTION
Do not attempt to start the engine with the battery disconnected.

5. When separating two connectors, unlock and pull on the connector housings and not the wires.
6. After locating a defective circuit, check the connectors to make sure they are clean and properly connected. Check all wires going into a connector to make sure each wire is properly positioned and the wire ends are not loose.
7. Before disconnecting two connectors, check them for any locking tabs or arms that must be pushed or opened. If connectors are difficult to separate, do not force them as damage may occur.
8. When reconnecting electrical connector halves, push them together until they click or snap into place.
9. If the switch is operating erratically, the contacts may be oily, dirty or corroded. Disassemble the switch housing to access the switch contacts. Clean the contacts as required.
10. If a switch or button does not perform properly, replace the switch assembly as described in its appropriate section in this chapter. The individual switches cannot be replaced separately.

TURN SIGNAL RELAY

Testing/Removal/Installation

1. If only one bulb or individual side does not work, check for a blown bulb or a disconnected turn signal connector. If the turn signals do not work, test the turn signal relay as described in this procedure.
2. Remove the right side cover (Chapter Fifteen).
3. Remove the turn signal relay (**Figure 118**) from its mounting position and disconnect its connector.
4. Check for loose, bent or corroded turn signal relay terminals. Then check the socket terminals in the connector for corrosion or damage.
5. Connect a jumper wire between the white/green and gray terminals in the wiring harness side connector. Turn the ignition switch on and operate the turn signal switch. The turn signals should light and stay

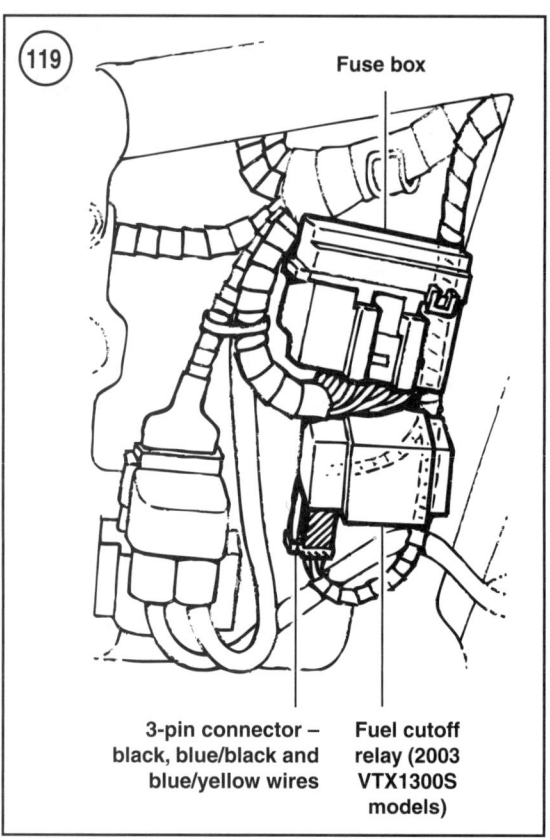

3-pin connector – black, blue/black and blue/yellow wires

Fuel cutoff relay (2003 VTX1300S models)

on. Turn the turn signal off and the ignition switch off. Disconnect the jumper wire.
 a. If the light did not come on, check for an open circuit in the white/green and gray turn signal wires.
 b. If the light came on, either the turn signal relay connector is dirty or damaged or the turn signal relay is damaged. Check and clean the connector first and retest. If the turn signals still do not work, replace the turn signal relay.
6. Installation is the reverse of removal. Install the turn signal relay, turn the ignition switch on and check the turn signal operation.

FUEL CUTOFF RELAY (2003 MODELS)

Removal/Installation

1. Remove the right side cover (Chapter Fifteen).
2. Remove the fuel cutoff relay (**Figure 119**) from its mounting position and disconnect its connector.
3. Reverse to install the new relay.

NOTE
For information on when to replace the fuel cutoff relay when troubleshooting a fuel flow problem, refer to **Fuel Pump Flow Test** *in Fuel Pump and Fuel Filter in Chapter Eight.*

ELECTRICAL SYSTEM

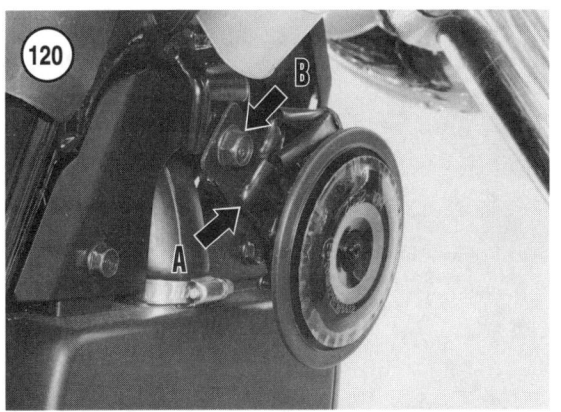

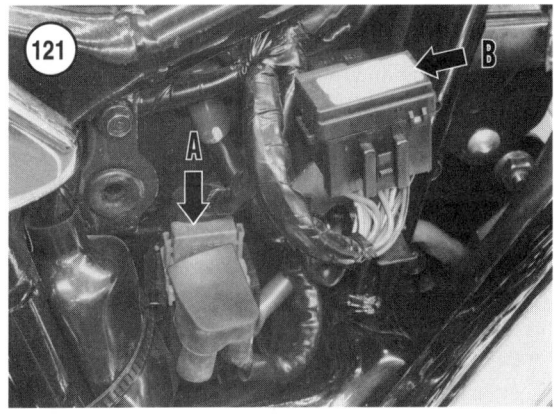

HORN

The horn is an important safety device and must be kept in good working order.

Testing

1. Disconnect the electrical connectors (A, **Figure 120**) from the horn.
2. Connect a 12-volt battery across the horn terminals. The horn must sound loudly. If not, replace the horn.

Removal/Installation

WARNING
Do not operate the motorcycle without a correctly operating horn.

1. Disconnect the electrical connectors from the horn (A, **Figure 120**).
2. Remove the bolt (B, **Figure 120**) and the horn assembly.
3. Install by reversing these removal steps. Note the following:
   a. Align the horn bracket with the shoulder on the frame bracket.
   b. Tighten the horn mounting bolt to 21 N•m (15 ft.-lb.).
   c. Make sure the electrical connections are secure and corrosion-free.
   d. Check the horn operation. If the horn does not work properly, test the horn as described in this section.

FUSES

WARNING
Never substitute any metal object for a fuse. Never use a higher amperage fuse than specified. An overload could cause a fire.

CAUTION
If replacing a fuse, make sure the ignition switch is turned off. This lessens the chance of a short circuit.

Whenever a fuse blows, determine the cause before replacing the fuse. Usually, the trouble is a short circuit in the wiring caused by worn-through insulation or a short to ground from a disconnected or damaged wire.

Main Fuse

The 30 amp main fuse is mounted in a fuse holder located on the starter relay switch.
1. Turn the ignition switch off.
2. Remove the right side cover (Chapter Fifteen).
3. Disconnect the electrical connector (A, **Figure 121**) from the starter relay switch.
4. Remove the main fuse (**Figure 122**) and inspect it. Replace the fuse if blown (**Figure 123**).

NOTE
A spare 30-amp fuse is stored in the bottom of the starter relay switch rubber holder.

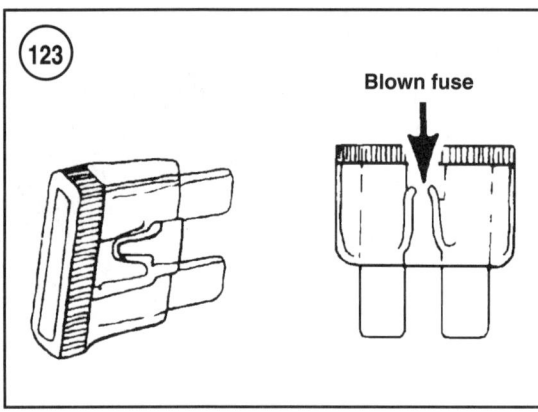

Blown fuse

5. Reconnect the starter relay switch connector.
6. Reinstall the right side cover (Chapter Fifteen).

Fuse Box (Subfuses)

All of the subfuses are mounted inside the fuse box located behind the right side cover. To identify an individual fuse and its amperage, refer to the printed information on the fuse box cover (B, **Figure 121**) and **Table 9**.
1. Turn the ignition switch off.
2. Remove the right side cover (Chapter Fifteen).
3. Open the fuse box cover (B, **Figure 121**).
4. Remove and inspect the fuse (**Figure 124**). Replace the fuse if blown (**Figure 123**).
5. Close and secure the fuse box cover.
6. Install the right side cover (Chapter Fifteen).

WIRING DIAGRAMS

Color wiring diagrams for all models are located at the end of this manual.

NOTE
Scan the QR code or search for "Clymer Manuals Youtube Tech Tips" to see an overview on electrical troubleshooting with a wiring diagram.

Table 1 BATTERY SPECIFICATIONS

Type	Maintenance-free (sealed)*
Capacity	12 volts, 12 amp hour
Charging current	
Normal	1.4 amps × 5-10 hours
Quick	6.0 amps × 1 hour
Voltage (at 20° C [68° F])	
Fully charged	13.0-13.2 volts
Needs charging	Below 12.3 volts

*See text

Table 2 MAINTENANCE-FREE BATTERY VOLTAGE READINGS

State of charge	Voltage reading
100%	13.0-13.2
75%	12.8
50%	12.5
25%	12.2
0%	12.0 volts or less

ELECTRICAL SYSTEM

Table 3 ALTERNATOR AND CHARGING SYSTEM SPECIFICATIONS

Alternator	
Type	Triple phase
Charging system output	364 watts @5000 rpm
Charging voltage test (regulated voltage)	Refer to text
Current draw	2.0 mA maximum
Stator coil resistance*	0.22-0.34 ohms

*Test must be made at an ambient temperature of 20° C (68° F). Do not test when the engine or component is hot.

Table 4 STARTER CLUTCH SPECIFICATIONS

	New mm (in.)	Service limit mm (in.)
Starter driven gear		
Inside diameter	44.000-44.016 (1.7323-1.7329)	44.10 (1.736)
Outside diameter	57.759-57.768 (2.2740-2.2743)	57.639 (2.2692)

Table 5 IGNITION SYSTEM SPECIFICATIONS

Ignition coil primary peak voltage	100 volts minimum
Ignition pulse generator peak voltage	0.7 volts minimum
Ignition timing	4.1° BTDC at idle

Table 6 SENSOR TEST SPECIFICATIONS

Fan switch	
Start to close (ON)	98-102° C (208-216° F)
Start to open (OFF)	93-97° C (199-207° F)
Instrumentation ECT switch	
Start to close (ON)	112-118° C (234-244° F)
Stop to open (OFF)	108° C (226° F) minimum
Throttle position sensor (TPS)	
Input voltage	4.7-5.3 volts
Resistance	
Red/yellow and blue/green terminals	4-6 K ohms

Table 7 STARTING SYSTEM SPECIFICATIONS

Starter brush length	
New	12.0-13.0mm (0.47-0.51 in.)
Service limit	4.5 mm (0.18 in.)

Table 8 BULB SPECIFICATIONS

Item	Specification
Headlight (Hi/Low beam)	60/55W
Brake/taillight	21/5W
License light	5W
Front turn signal/position light	21/5W
Rear turn signal light	21W

Table 9 FUSE SPECIFICATIONS

	Rating
Fan	
2003-2005 models	10 amp
2006-on models	20 amp
Headlight	10 amp
Horn/brake light/turn signal	10 amp
Ignition/starter	10 amp
Main fuse	30 amp
Meter/taillight	10 amp
Odometer	
2003-2005 models	5 amp
2006-on models	10 amp

Table 10 ELECTRICAL SYSTEM TORQUE SPECIFICATIONS

	N•m	in.-lb.	ft.-lb.
Engine coolant temperature sensor*	8	71	–
Fan switch	17	–	13
Flywheel mounting bolt*	138	–	102
Fuel tank cover/meter assembly screw	3.5	31	–
Horn mounting bolt	21	–	15
Ignition pulse generator mounting bolt*	10	88	–
Ignition switch mounting bolt	10	88	–
Left crankcase cover mounting bolt	12	106	–
Neutral switch	12	106	–
Oil pressure switch*	12	106	–
Shift boss pinch bolt	12	106	–
Sidestand switch mounting bolt*	10	88	–
Starter cable outer nut	7	62	–
Starter clutch Torx mounting bolt*	29	–	21
Starter housing assembly bolt	6.4	56.6	–
Stator coil mounting bolt*	10	88	–
Timing hole cap*	18	–	13
Timing hole cap cover Allen bolt	10	88	–
Wire harness guide plate	10	88	–

*Refer to text for additional information.

CHAPTER TEN

COOLING SYSTEM

Table 1 and **Table 2** are at the end of this chapter. For routine maintenance, refer to Chapter Three.

WARNING
*Do not remove the radiator cap (A, **Figure 1**) or any cooling system component that is under pressure when the engine is hot. The coolant is very hot and under pressure. Severe scalding could result if the coolant touches skin. The cooling system must be cool before removing or disconnecting any system component.*

CAUTION
Do not reuse the old coolant as it deteriorates with use. Do not operate the cooling system with only distilled water (even if freezing temperatures are not expected). The antifreeze inhibits internal engine corrosion and provides lubrication of moving parts in the water pump.

COOLING SYSTEM

Inspection

1. If steam is observed at the muffler after the engine has sufficiently warmed up, a head gasket might be damaged. If enough coolant leaks into a cylinder(s), the cylinders could hydrolock. This would prevent the engine from being turned over. Coolant may also be present in the engine oil. If the oil visible in the oil level inspection window is foamy or milky-looking, there is coolant in the oil. If so, correct the problem before returning the motorcycle to service.
2. Refer *Cooling System* in Chapter Three to check the coolant level.
3. Check the radiator for clogged or damaged fins.
4. Check the radiator for loose or missing mounting bolts.
5. Check all coolant hoses for cracks or damage. With the engine cold, squeeze the hoses by hand. If a hose collapses easily, it is damaged and must be replaced. Make sure the hose clamps are tight, but not so tight that they cut the hoses. Refer to *Hoses* in this section.
6. Make sure the siphon tube (B, **Figure 1**) is connected to the radiator and is not clogged or damaged.
7. To check the cooling system for leaks, pressure test it as described in this section.
8. If coolant is leaking from underneath the water pump, refer to *Water Pump* in this chapter to check for a damaged seal.

Hoses

After removing any cooling system component, inspect the adjoining hose(s) to determine if replacement is necessary. Hoses deteriorate with age and should be inspected for conditions that may cause them to fail. Loss of coolant will cause the engine to overheat, and spray from a leaking hose can injure the rider. A collapsed hose prevents coolant circulation and will cause overheating. Observe the following when servicing hoses:

1. Make sure the cooling system is cool before removing any coolant hose or component.
2. Use original equipment replacement hoses; they are formed to a specific shape and dimension for correct fit.
3. Loosen the hose clamps on the hose that is to be replaced. Slide the clamps back off the component fittings.
4. Before disconnecting a formed hose, look for a paint mark on the end of the hose. This mark usually aligns with a raised boss on the connecting part to ensure the hose is properly aligned.

CAUTION
Do not use excessive force when attempting to remove a stubborn hose. Also, use caution when attempting to loosen hoses with hose pliers. The aluminum radiator and water pump hose joints are easily damaged.

5. Twist the hose to release it from the joint. If the hose is difficult to break loose, insert a small screwdriver between the hose and joint and spray WD-40 or a similar lubricant into the opening and carefully twist the hose to break it loose.

NOTE
Remove all lubricant residue from the hose and hose fitting before reinstalling the hose.

6. Examine the fittings for cracks or other damage. Repair or replace as necessary. If the fitting is good, use a wire brush and clean off any hose residue that may have transferred to the fitting. Wipe clean with a cloth.
7. Inspect the hose clamps for rust and corrosion. Replace if necessary.
8. If a hose is difficult to install on the joint, soak the end in hot water to make it more pliable. Do not use any lubricant when installing hoses.
9. Formed hoses must be properly installed. Refer to Step 4.
10. With the hose correctly installed, position and tighten the clamp securely. Position the clamp head so it is accessible for future removal and does not contact other parts.

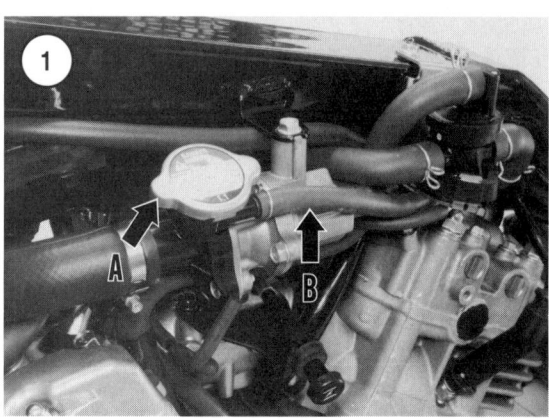

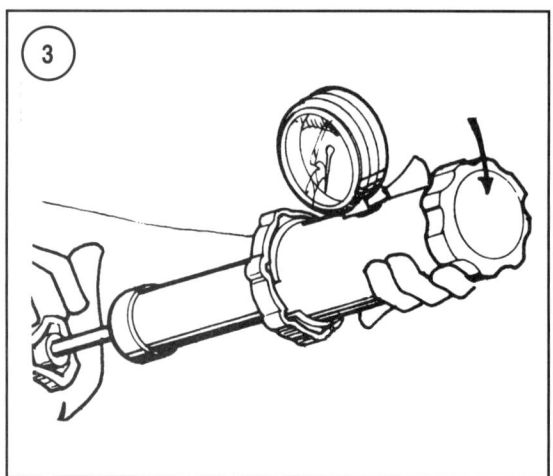

Pressure Test

1. Remove the fuel tank (Chapter Eight).
2. With the engine cold, remove the radiator cap (A, **Figure 1**).
3. Add coolant to the radiator to bring the level up to the filler neck.
4. Check the rubber seals on the radiator cap (**Figure 2**). Replace the cap if the seals show signs of deterioration, cracking or other damage. If the radiator cap is good, perform Step 5.

COOLING SYSTEM

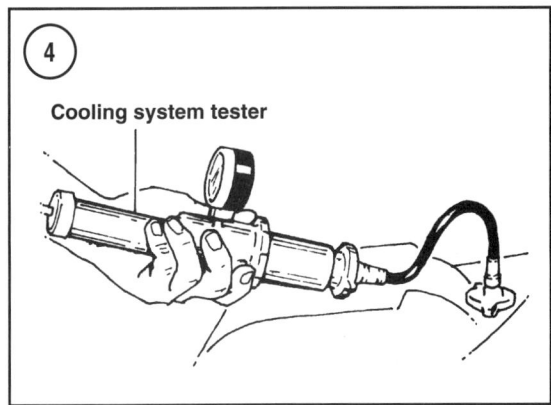

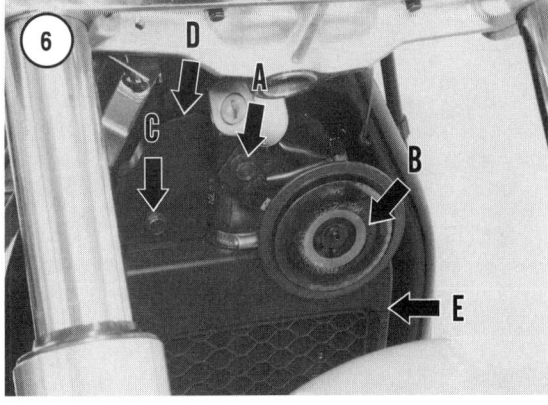

CAUTION
Do not exceed 137 kPa (20 psi) or the cooling system components may be damaged.

5. Lubricate the rubber washer on the bottom of the radiator cap with coolant and install it on a cooling system pressure tester (**Figure 3**). Apply 108-137 kPa (16-20 psi) and check for a pressure drop. Replace the cap if it cannot hold this pressure for six seconds.
6. Mount the pressure tester onto the thermostat housing filler neck (**Figure 4**) and pressure test the cooling system to 108-137 kPa (16-20 psi). If the system cannot hold this pressure for six seconds, check for a coolant leak at the following points:
  a. Radiator cap. If the radiator cap passed the pressure test in Step 5, but is now leaking, inspect the thermostat filler neck and cap mounting flange for damage.
  b. Leaking or damaged coolant hoses.
  c. Damaged or deteriorated O-rings installed in coolant hose connectors.
  d. Damaged water pump mechanical seal.
  e. Water pump.
  f. Loose coolant drain bolt.
  g. Warped cylinder head or cylinder mating surfaces.

NOTE
*If the test pressure drops rapidly, but there are no visible coolant leaks, coolant may be leaking into one of the cylinder heads. To check, perform a **Cylinder Leakdown Test** as described in Chapter Two.*

7. Check all cooling system hoses for damage or deterioration. Replace any questionable hose. Make sure all hose clamps are tight.
8. Remove the tester and install the radiator cap (A, **Figure 1**).
9. Install the fuel tank (Chapter Eight).

RADIATOR

Removal/Installation

1. Drain the cooling system (Chapter Three).
2. Remove the front left cylinder head shroud (Chapter Fifteen).
3. Disconnect the fan switch connector (**Figure 5**). Then remove the connector half leading from the fan from the frame mount.
4. Place a towel on the front fender to protect the fender when removing the radiator.
5. Disconnect the connectors at the horn, then remove the bolt (A, **Figure 6**) and horn (B).
6. Remove the two radiator mounting bolts (C, **Figure 6**), plate (D) and grill (E). Note the collars installed in the grommets in the top of the radiator grill.
7. Disconnect the lower hose at the radiator.
8. Lift the radiator and disconnect its locating pin (A, **Figure 7**) from the grommet (B).
9. Disconnect the upper hose at the radiator (**Figure 8**) and remove the radiator with the fan.
10. Installation is the reverse of removal. Note the following:

a. Replace hoses that are hard, cracked or show signs of deterioration. Hold each hose and flex it in several directions to check for damage.
b. Replace missing or damaged rubber dampers.
c. Install clamps in their original positions.
d. Tighten the radiator mounting bolts securely.
e. Align the horn bracket with the shoulder on the frame bracket. Then tighten the horn mounting bolt to 21 N•m (15 ft.-lb.).
f. Fill and bleed the cooling system (Chapter Three). Check for leaks.
g. Turn the ignition switch on and verify the horn works correctly.

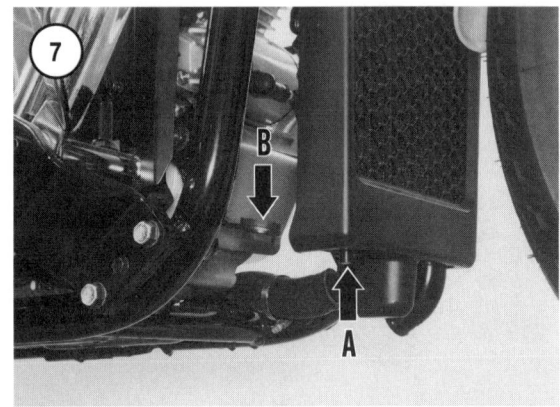

Inspection

CAUTION
Do not press too hard or the cooling fins and tubes may be damaged.

1. Clean the exterior of the radiator with a garden hose on low pressure. Spray the front and back sides to remove all debris. Carefully use a whisk broom or stiff paint brush to remove any stubborn dirt.
2. Check for bent cooling fins. Straighten bent cooling fins with a screwdriver. If a large area of the cooling surface is damaged, replace the radiator.
3. Check the seams and other soldered connections for corrosion (green residue). If corrosion is evident, there could be a leak in that spot. Perform a cooling system pressure check as described in this chapter.
4. Fill the radiator with water and check the flow rate out of the radiator. If the flow rate is slow, or if corrosion or other buildup is seen, take the radiator to a radiator repair shop to have it flushed and pressure checked.
5. If paint has been worn off in any area of the radiator, repaint with a quality black spray paint. This will help to prolong the radiator life by cutting down on oxidation from the outside. Do not apply too much paint to the cooling fin area as this will cut down on the cooling capabilities of the radiator.
6. Replace the upper (A, **Figure 9**) and lower (B, **Figure 7**) rubber dampers if damaged.
7. Inspect the rubber seals (**Figure 2**) on the radiator cap. Replace the cap if they are hardened or starting to deteriorate.

COOLING FAN

Removal/Installation

1. Remove the radiator as described in this chapter.
2. Disconnect the fan switch connector (B, **Figure 9**) at the bottom of the radiator.

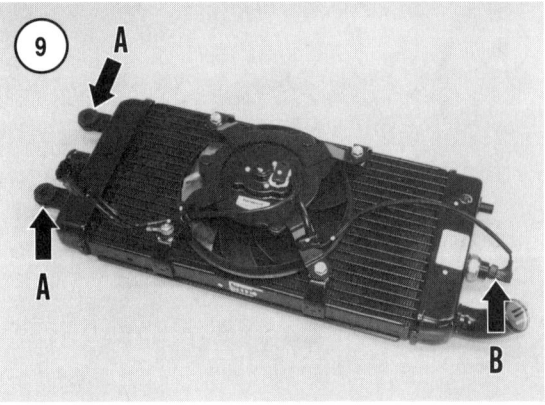

3. Remove the wiring harnesses from the clamps on the fan.
4. Remove the fan mounting bolts (A, **Figure 10**) and ground wire (B), then remove the fan (C) and its mounting bracket from the radiator.
5. To separate the fan blade from the fan, remove the nut and the fan blade.
6. Remove the nuts and the fan from the mounting bracket.
7. Installation is the reverse of removal. Note the following:
   a. Tighten the nuts securing the fan to the mounting bracket to 5.1 N•m (45 in.-lb.).

COOLING SYSTEM

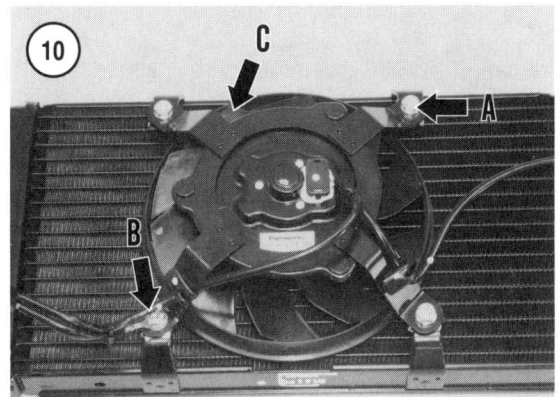

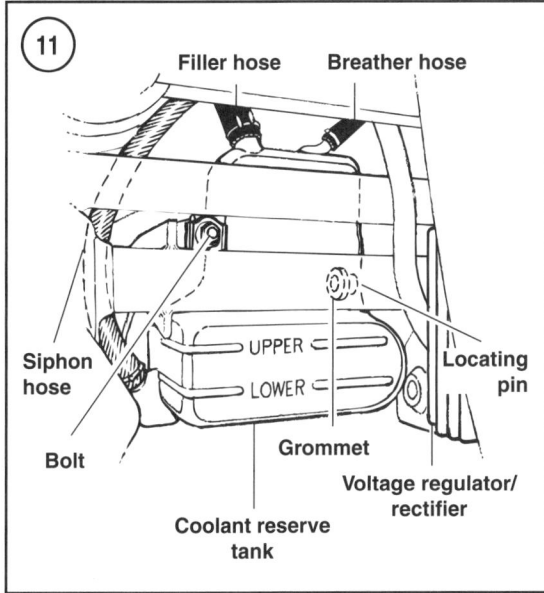

b. Install the fan blade onto the fan shaft by aligning the flat surfaces. Apply a medium strength threadlocking compound onto the cooling fan blade nut threads and tighten to 2.7 N•m (24 in.-lb.).

c. Tighten the fan assembly mounting bolts to 8.3 N•m (7.3 in.-lb. [2003-2006 models]) or to 8.4 N•m (74.3 in.-lb. [2007-on models]).

d. Check the wire harness routing before installing the radiator.

Testing

Refer to *Fan Switch* in Chapter Nine to test he fan switch and its related circuit.

COOLANT RESERVE TANK

Removal/Installation

Refer to **Figure 11**.

1. Support the motorcycle securely on a workstand.
2. Remove the left crankcase rear cover (Chapter Fifteen).
3. On California models, remove the charcoal canister as described in *Evaporative Emission Control System* in Chapter Eight.
4. Disconnect the coolant siphon hose from the bottom of the coolant reserve tank and drain the tank.
5. Disconnect the filler and breather hoses from the top of the tank.
6. Remove the mounting bolt and slide the tank toward the left side to release its locating pin from the mounting grommet, then remove the tank.
7. Flush the tank with clean water. Check the tank for cracks or other damage.
8. Inspect and replace damaged hoses. Replace weak or damaged hose clamps.
9. Install the coolant reserve tank by reversing these steps.
10. Fill the reserve tank as described in *Cooling System* in Chapter Three. Check the tank for leaks.

THERMOSTAT

The thermostat is a temperature sensitive valve used to control the flow of coolant into the radiator. When the engine is cold, the thermostat is closed and coolant bypasses the radiator. This helps the engine warm up quickly. When the engine reaches operating temperature, the thermostat opens and coolant flows between the engine and radiator.

Removal/Installation

1. Remove the fuel tank (Chapter Eight).
2. Drain the cooling system until the coolant level is below the thermostat housing or drain all the coolant as described in Chapter Three.
3. Place a rag underneath the thermostat to catch any residue coolant spilled from the thermostat housing.
4. Disconnect the siphon hose (A, **Figure 12**).

5. Remove mounting bolt (B, **Figure 12**).
6. Remove the two cover bolts (C, **Figure 12**) and separate the housing cover from the housing.
7. Remove the thermostat (A, **Figure 13**).
8. Remove the O-ring (**Figure 14**) from the housing cover.
9. Rinse the thermostat with clean water.
10. Inspect the thermostat for damage. Make sure the spring (**Figure 15**) has not sagged or broken.
11. Inspect the thermostat valve and valve seat for any gaps, indicating a stuck thermostat.
12. If necessary, test the thermostat as described in this section.
13. Clean the thermostat housing, filler neck and all mating surfaces.
14. Installation is the reverse of removal. Note the following:
   a. Install a new O-ring (**Figure 14**) in the housing cover groove.
   b. Install the thermostat with its vent hole (B, **Figure 13**) facing up.
   c. Tighten the thermostat cover bolts (C, **Figure 12**) securely.
   d. Align the tab on the thermostat housing with the mounting bracket groove (D, **Figure 12**) and install the thermostat housing mounting bolt (B). Tighten the bolt securely.
   e. Fill and bleed the cooling system (Chapter Three). Check for coolant leaks.

Testing

A stuck thermostat causes the engine to warm up slowly (when stuck open) or causes overheating (when stuck partially or fully closed). Check by starting the engine (when cold) and allow it to warm to normal operating temperature. During this time, carefully touch the top radiator hose. If the hose becomes hot quickly, the thermostat is probably stuck open. This condition causes the engine to run colder for a longer period. If the hose gradually warms and

then becomes hot, the thermostat is probably operating correctly. However, if the upper hose and radiator do not feel hot after the engine has run long enough to warm to normal operating temperature, the thermostat is probably stuck closed and is blocking coolant flow through the radiator. This condition causes the engine to overheat.

1. Support the thermostat and a thermometer (rated higher than the test temperature) in a pan of water (**Figure 16**). The thermostat and thermometer must not touch the sides or bottom of the pan or a false reading will result.
2. Gradually heat the water and continue to gently stir the water until it reaches 80-84° C (176-183° F). At this temperature, the thermostat valve should start to open.
3. At 95° C (203° F), the minimum valve lift should be 8 mm (0.31 in.).

NOTE
Valve operation can be slow. It may take 3-5 minutes for the valve to operate properly.

4. If the valve fails to operate at the listed temperatures, or if the valve lift is below minimum at the specified temperature, replace the thermostat.

COOLING SYSTEM

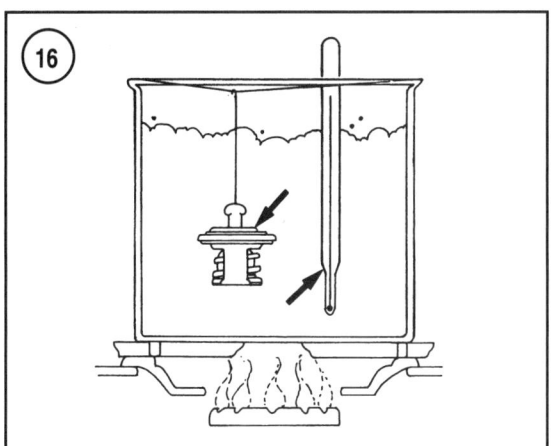

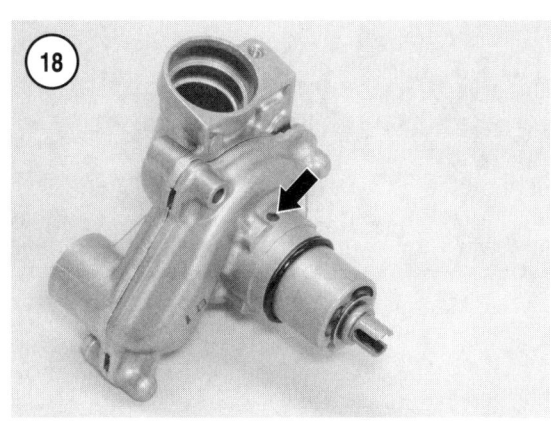

4. Disconnect the hoses at the thermostat housing and filler neck (A, **Figure 12**).
5. Disconnect the engine coolant temperature sensor electrical connector (**Figure 17**).
6. Remove the thermostat housing.
7. Installation is the reverse of removal. Refill the cooling system as described in Chapter Three.

Engine Coolant Temperature (ECT) Sensor

Refer to Chapter Nine to test and service the engine coolant temperature sensor.

WATER PUMP

The water pump is mounted on the bottom, left side of the engine. The water pump can be removed with the engine in the frame. The water pump is not rebuildable.

Mechanical Seal Check

An inspection or weep hole is built into the bottom of the water pump (**Figure 18**). When coolant leaks from the hole, the mechanical seal in the water pump is damaged and the water pump must be replaced.

1. Check for signs of coolant or coolant stains on the bottom of the water pump or on the ground underneath the motorcycle where it is parked. If there is coolant in this area, first check the condition of the two hoses and hose clamps mounted on the water pump. Check the hose clamps for tightness.
2. Clean up any spilled coolant so it does not contact the rear tire.

Removal/Installation

1. Remove the left crankcase rear cover (Chapter Fifteen).

Always replace the thermostat with one of the same temperature rating.

THERMOSTAT HOUSING

The thermostat housing contains the thermostat, filler neck and serves as a hose manifold. Hoses route the coolant from the cylinders to the manifold, while a bypass hose directs coolant to the water pump when the thermostat is closed. The engine coolant temperature sensor is mounted in the thermostat housing.

The thermostat housing can be removed as an assembly without removing the thermostat. To remove the thermostat only, refer to *Thermostat* in this chapter.

Removal/Installation

1. Remove the fuel tank (Chapter Eight).
2. Drain the cooling system until the coolant level is below the thermostat housing or drain all the coolant as described in Chapter Three.
3. Remove the thermostat housing mounting bolt (B, **Figure 12**).

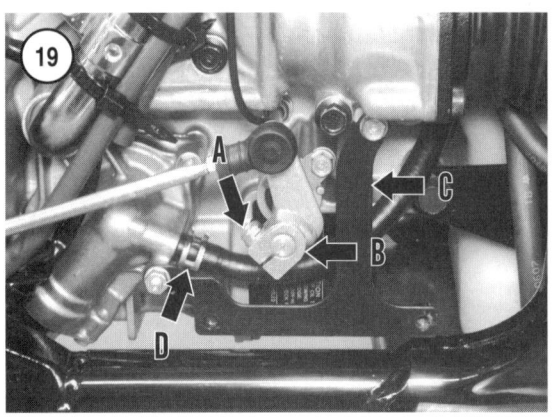
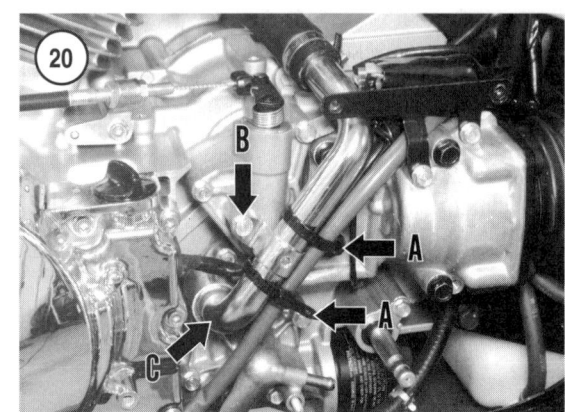

2. Drain the engine oil (Chapter Three).
3. Drain the cooling system (Chapter Three).
4. Support the motorcycle on a workstand. Position the workstand so it is not directly underneath the water pump as the water pump is removed in this area.
5. Note the wiring harness and cable routing around the water pump/water pipe assembly so the parts can be installed and routed correctly.
6. Remove the pinch bolt (A, **Figure 19**) and the shift arm (B) and set aside.
7. Remove the nut, bolt and plate (C, **Figure 19**).
8. Disconnect the coolant hose (D, **Figure 19**) at the water pump.
9. Disconnect the two plastic ties (A, **Figure 20**) securing the cable to the water pipe.
10. Remove the bolt (B, **Figure 20**) and disconnect the rear cylinder water pipe (C) at the water pump. Remove the O-ring installed on the end of the water pipe or from inside the water pump.
11. Remove the bolt (**Figure 21**) and disconnect the front coolant pipe on the bottom of the water pump. Remove the O-ring (**Figure 22**) installed on the end of the water pipe or from inside the water pump.

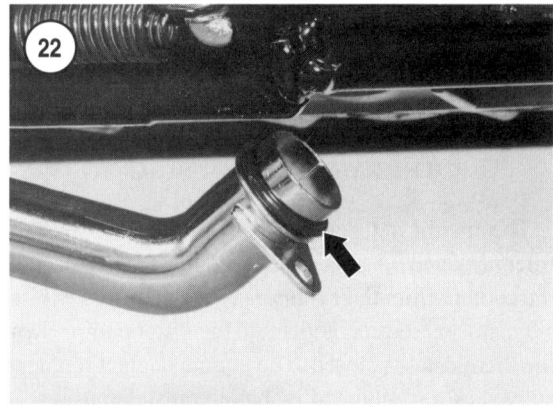

NOTE
The water pump can be removed as an assembly or the front cover can be removed separately and the pump removed in two parts.

12A. To remove the assembled water pump, remove bolts A and B in **Figure 23**. A sealing washer is installed on bolt A, **Figure 23**.
12B. To remove the water pump in two parts, remove the four bolts (A, B and C, **Figure 23**). Remove the cover (D, **Figure 23**) and then the housing (A, **Figure 24**) and O-ring (B, **Figure 24**). A sealing washer is installed on bolt A, **Figure 23**.
13. Inspect the water pump as described in this section.

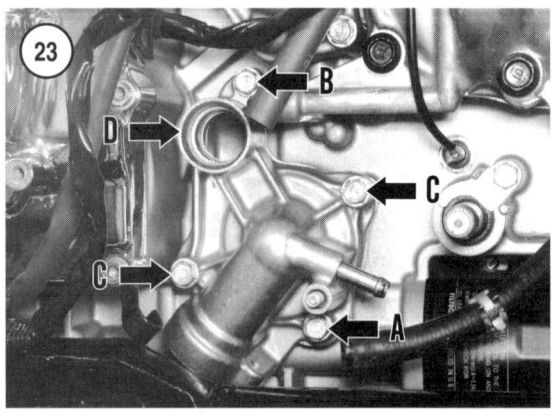

COOLING SYSTEM

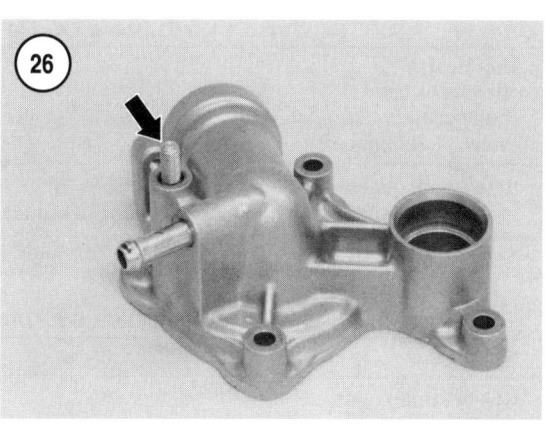

14. Install the water pump by reversing these steps. Note the following:
    a. Lubricate a new O-ring with engine oil and install it against the pump shoulder (A, **Figure 25**).
    b. If the cover was removed, lubricate a new O-ring with coolant and install into the housing groove (B, **Figure 24**).
    c. Install the water pump by aligning the slot in the end of the water pump shaft (B, **Figure 25**) with the shoulder on the end of the oil pump shaft (C). If installing the pump in two parts, turn the impeller to align the shaft ends. If installing an assembled pump, turn the impeller using a finger through the hose opening to align the shaft ends.
    d. Tighten the pump cover and mounting bolts to 13 N•m (115 in.-lb.). Install a new washer on the coolant drain bolt (A, **Figure 23**).
    e. Lubricate new O-rings with coolant and install them against the shoulders on both water pipes (**Figure 22**).
    f. Install the shift arm (B, **Figure 19**) by aligning its groove with the punch mark on the shift shaft. Install the pinch bolt (A, **Figure 19**) and tighten to 12 N•m (106 in.-lb.).
    g. Fill and bleed the cooling system as described in Chapter Three.

Inspection

1. Replace the water pump if there is engine oil in the pump. This indicates that the seal mounted over the pump shaft is damaged.
2. Check the impeller blades for corrosion or damage. If the corrosion buildup on the blades is minor, clean the blades. If the corrosion is severe or if the blades are cracked or broken, replace the water pump assembly.
3. Turn the impeller shaft and check the pump bearing for excessive noise or roughness. If the bearing operation is rough or abnormal, replace the water pump assembly.
4. If the water pump cover stud (**Figure 26**) is loose or was removed, reinstall it so the exposed stud distance measures 10.5-12.5 mm (0.41-0.49 in.).

Table 1 COOLING SYSTEM SPECIFICATIONS

Coolant	
Standard concentration	50:50 mixture coolant and purified water
Type	Honda HP coolant or an equivalent*
Coolant capacity	
Radiator and engine	2.70 L (2.9 qt.)
Reserve tank	0.95 L (1.0 qt.)
Radiator cap relief pressure	108-137 kPa (16-20 psi)
(continued)	

Table 1 COOLING SYSTEM SPECIFICATIONS (continued)

Thermostat	
Begins to open	80-84° C (176-183° F)
Fully open	95° C (203° F)
Valve lift (minimum)	8 mm (0.31 in.)

*Use a high quality ethylene coolant that does not contain silicate inhibitors as they can cause premature wear to the water pump seals and block radiator passages.

Table 2 COOLING SYSTEM TORQUE SPECIFICATIONS

	N•m	in.-lb.	ft.-lb.
Coolant drain bolt*	13	115	–
Cooling fan blade nut*	2.7	24	–
Fan assembly bolt			
2003-2006 models	8.3	73.5	–
2007-on models	8.4	74.3	–
Fan nut	5.1	45	–
Horn mounting bolt	21	–	15
Shift arm pinch bolt	12	106	–
Water pump cover/mounting bolts	13	115	–
Water pump stud bolt	Refer to text		

*Refer to text for additional information.

CHAPTER ELEVEN

WHEELS AND TIRES

This chapter describes repair and maintenance for the front and rear wheels, hubs and tires. Maintenance procedures for these components are in Chapter Three.

Tables 1-4 are at the end of this chapter.

MOTORCYCLE LIFT

WARNING
Regardless of the type of jack or stand used to lift the motorcycle, make sure the motorcycle is properly supported before walking away from it.

Many procedures in this chapter require lifting either the front or rear wheel off the ground. Because the motorcycle is not equipped with a centerstand, a separate jack or chain hoist will be required. The K&L MC450 Center Jack (**Figure 1**) is used in this chapter by placing it under the motorcycle to lift either the front or rear wheel. When using a center jack or scissors jack, have an assistant sit on the motorcycle and center it upright. Place a block of wood across the jack and position the jack underneath the front or rear part of the frame, depending on which wheel will be raised. Operate the jack and lift the motorcycle until the front or rear wheel just clears the ground. When using a chain hoist, cover or remove the fuel tank (Chapter Eight), then install the chain around the motorcycle's steering neck. Slowly operate the hoist, making sure the motorcycle remains centered.

FRONT WHEEL

Removal

1. Support the motorcycle securely with the front wheel off the ground. Note the following:
    a. If a chain hoist is used, lift the motorcycle so the front wheel is 30 cm (12 in.) or more off the ground.
    b. If the motorcycle is supported with a center jack or similar tool, lift the motorcycle until the front wheel just clears the ground.
2. Remove front brake caliper as described in Chapter Fourteen.

NOTE
Do not operate the front brake lever while the front wheel/brake disc is removed from the motorcycle. Insert a spacer block between the pads until the front wheel/brake disc is reinstalled. This will prevent the caliper pistons from extending if the lever is operated.

3. Loosen the right side axle pinch bolts (A, **Figure 2**).
4. Remove the axle bolt (B, **Figure 2**).
5. Loosen the left side axle pinch bolts (A, **Figure 3**).

6. Remove the axle (B, **Figure 3**) and the front wheel.
7. Remove the left (**Figure 4**) and right (**Figure 5**) axle spacers.
8. Inspect the front wheel as described in this section.

Installation

1. Clean the front axle, spacers and axle bolt.
2. Check the axle bearing surfaces on both fork tubes and the axle for burrs and nicks. Smooth with a file.
3. Apply a light coat of grease to the axle and both spacers. Do not lubricate the axle threads. These threads must be free of oil and grease when the axle bolt is tightened.
4. Install the left (**Figure 4**) and right (**Figure 5**) axle spacers.
5. Center the front wheel between the fork sliders.

> *CAUTION*
> *The front axle and pinch bolt tightening sequence in Steps 6-14 correctly seats the front axle so that both sliders are positioned parallel with each other. Fork misalignment can cause premature fork seal and bushing wear, increase the wear against the slider, reduce fork performance and may cause steering problems.*

6. Install the front axle (B, **Figure 3**) from the left side and align the index groove on the axle with the slider's axle bore edge as shown in **Figure 6**. Then tighten the left axle pinch bolts (A, **Figure 3**) to 22 N•m (16 ft.-lb.).
7. Install the axle bolt (B, **Figure 2**) and tighten to 59 N•m (44 ft.-lb.).
8. Tighten the right axle pinch bolt (A, **Figure 2**) to 22 N•m (16 ft.-lb.).
9. Install the front brake caliper as described in Chapter Fourteen.
10. Apply the front brake lever several times to seat the brake pads against the brake disc.
11. Release the brake lever and brake pedal and spin the front wheel. The wheel should turn freely and without any brake drag.
12. Remove the motorcycle from the stand so the front wheel is on the ground. Apply the front and rear brakes, then compress and release the front suspension several times to center the axle in the slider axle bores. Compress the forks as far as possible. Check that the fork legs are parallel.
13. Loosen the left axle pinch bolts (A, **Figure 3**).
14. Apply the front brake lever and pump the front forks several times.

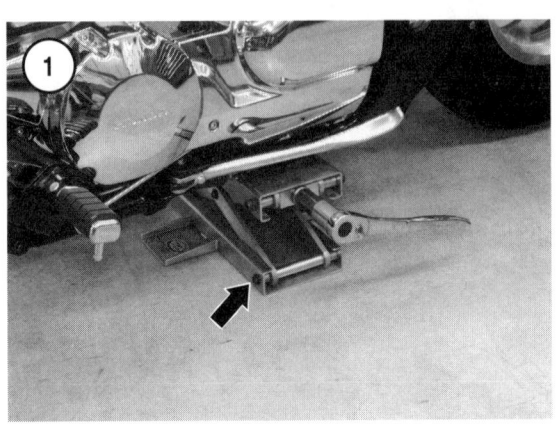

WHEELS AND TIRES

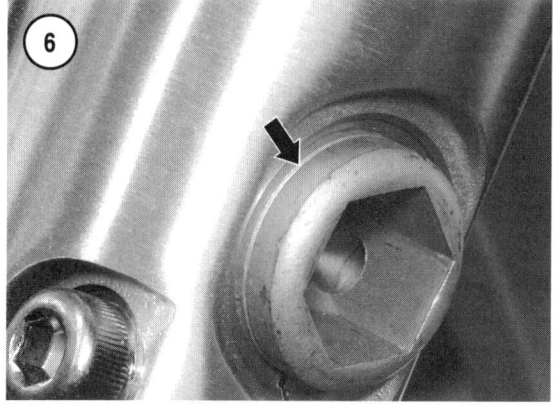

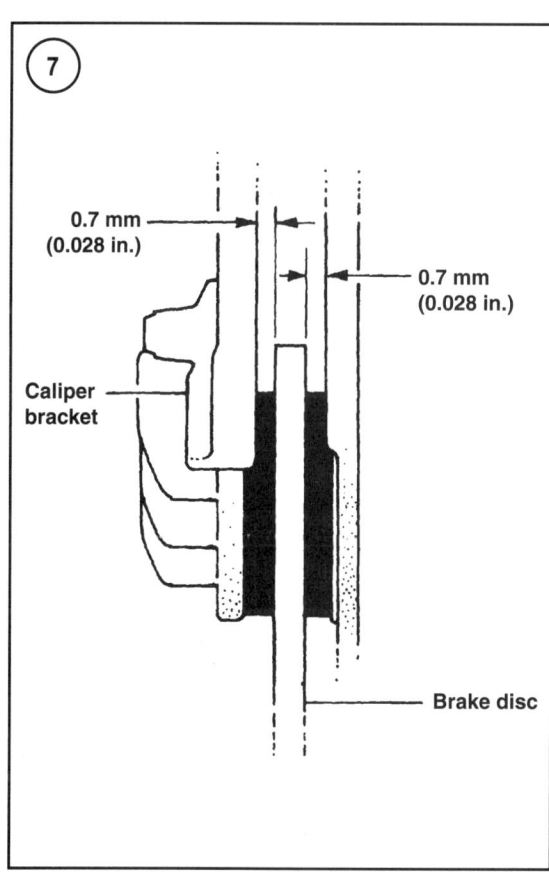

15. Tighten the left axle pinch bolts to 22 N•m (16 ft.-lb.).

WARNING
Step 16 determines if there is adequate brake disc to caliper clearance. Failure to provide adequate clearance may cause brake disc damage and reduced braking efficiency. Both conditions can cause brake failure.

16. Check that the brake disc is centered between the caliper bracket and caliper (not the pads) as shown in **Figure 7**. If the clearance is incorrect, loosen the left axle pinch bolts and move the left slider until the clearance is correct, then tighten the pinch bolts to 22 N•m (16 ft.-lb.). Turn the front wheel and apply the front and rear brakes several times, then recheck the clearance.

WARNING
If the correct clearance cannot be obtained, check the brake disc for loose mounting bolts, excessive runout or damage (Chapter Fourteen). Do not ride the motorcycle until the brake disc clearance is correct.

17. Apply the front brake several times to make sure proper brake pressure is felt at the brake lever.

Inspection

1. Inspect the seals (A, **Figure 8**) for wear, hardness, cracks or other damage. If necessary, replace the seals as described in *Front and Rear Hubs* in this chapter.
2. Inspect the bearings on both sides of the wheel as follows:
   a. Turn each bearing inner race (B, **Figure 8**) by hand and check for smooth, quiet operation.
   b. Try to push the bearing in and out to check for lateral play (**Figure 9**). Slight play is normal.

Try to push the bearing up and down to check for radial play (**Figure 9**). Any radial play should be difficult to feel. If play is easily felt, the bearing is worn out. Always replace bearings as a set. Refer to *Front and Rear Hubs* in this chapter.

3. Check the axle for straightness with a set of V-blocks and dial indicator. Refer to **Table 2** for maximum axle runout. Actual runout will be one-half of the gauge reading. Do not straighten a bent axle.
4. Check the brake disc bolts for tightness. To service the brake disc, refer to Chapter Fourteen.
5. Refer to *Wheel Service* in this chapter for additional information.

REAR WHEEL

Removal

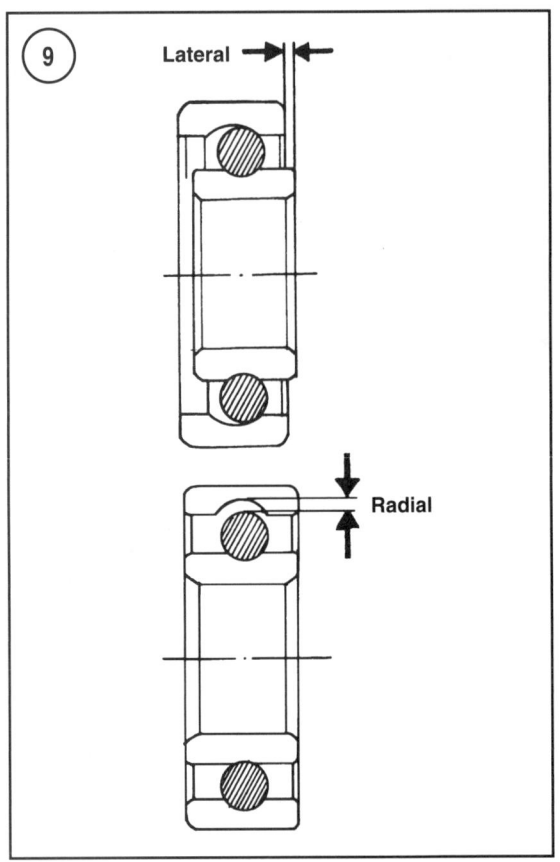

NOTE
The rear of the motorcycle must be raised considerably to provide clearance for removing and installing the rear wheel. Before beginning this procedure, make sure the lift can support the motorcycle at the required height. An alternative is to lift the motorcycle with a hoist or remove the rear fender as described in Chapter Fifteen.

1. Support the motorcycle on its sidestand. Remove the license plate holder to provide additional clearance when removing the wheel.
2. Loosen the axle nut (A, **Figure 10**) and the brake caliper stopper pin bolt (B). If necessary, use a torque adapter (Motion Pro part No. 08-0134) and breaker bar for increased leverage on the stopper pin bolt as shown in **Figure 11**.
3. Support the motorcycle so the rear wheel is approximately 30 cm (12 in.) off the ground.
4. Remove the brake hose clamp bolt (C, **Figure 10**).
5. Loosen the caliper stopper pin bolt (B, **Figure 10**) until it is free from the swing arm, then slide it out of the brake caliper bracket. The exhaust system will prevent complete removal of the caliper stopper pin bolt.
6. On 2003-2007 VTX1300R/S models, remove the two muffler mounting nuts, washers and bolts (**Figure 12**, typical).
7. Remove the axle nut and rear axle.

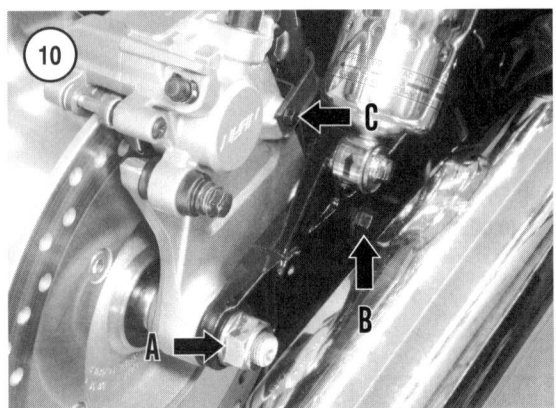

NOTE
Do not operate the rear brake pedal while the rear wheel is removed. If necessary, insert a wooden block between the brake pads. This will prevent the caliper piston from extending if the pedal is operated.

WHEELS AND TIRES

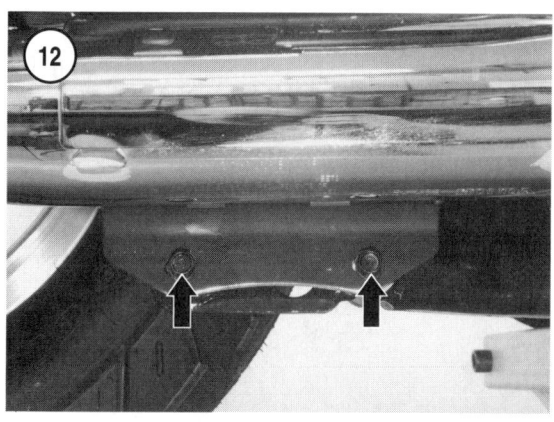

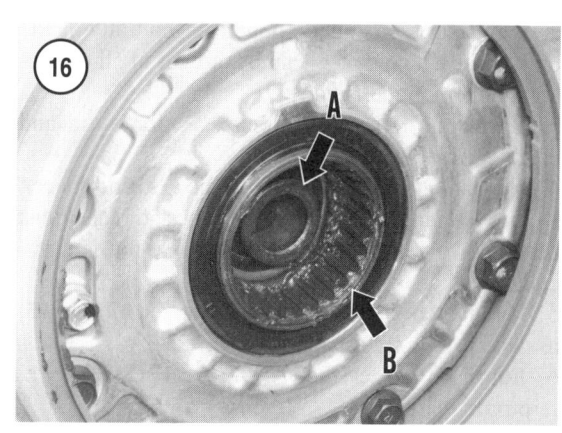

8. Remove the brake caliper and its bracket (**Figure 13**) from the brake disc.
9. Remove the axle spacer (**Figure 14**) from the right side of the wheel.
10. On 2003-2007 VTX1300R/S models, wedge a wooden block between the muffler mounting bracket and swing arm to move and support the muffler outward to provide room for rear wheel removal.

CAUTION
Check the exhaust system for any exposed bolts that could possible contact the brake disc when removing the wheel. If possible, remove these bolts to prevent them from scratching the brake disc.

11. Move the rear wheel toward the right side to free the driven flange (**Figure 15**) from the final drive ring gear.
12. If the spacer (A, **Figure 16**) fell out of the final drive, install it with its shoulder side facing out.
13. If necessary, remove and service the driven flange (**Figure 15**) as described in this chapter.
14. Inspect the rear wheel as described in this section.

Installation

1. Clean the rear axle, spacer and axle nut.

WARNING
The manufacturer recommends installing a new caliper stopper pin bolt and a new brake hose clamp bolt, both of which come with threadlocking compound preapplied. If reusing the original bolts, clean as described in Step 2. Installing a new rear caliper stopper pin bolt may require removal of the exhaust system (Chapter Fifteen).

2. If reusing the caliper stopper pin bolt and/or the brake hose clamp bolt, clean the threads of all threadlocking compound residue.
3. Check the axle bearing surfaces for burrs and nicks. Smooth with a file.
4. Apply a light coat of grease to the axle and spacer. Do not lubricate the axle threads. These threads must be free of oil and grease when the axle nut is tightened.
5. If removed, install the driven flange (**Figure 15**) as described in this chapter.
6. Lubricate the seal lip (A, **Figure 17**) with a waterproof grease.
7. Lubricate the driven flange (**Figure 15**) and ring gear (B, **Figure 16**) splines with Pro Honda Moly 60 Paste or an equivalent molybdenum disulfide paste that contains more than 40% molybdenum disulfide.
8. Install the spacer (A, **Figure 16**) with its shoulder facing out into the final drive, if removed.
9. Lift the rear wheel and mesh the driven flange and ring gear splines.
10. Install the spacer (**Figure 14**) into the seal.
11. Install the rear axle partway through the final drive unit and rear wheel.
12. Install the rear brake caliper over the brake disc, then install the rear axle all the way making sure it passes through the rear brake caliper mounting bracket.
13. If reusing the caliper stopper pin bolt, apply a medium strength threadlocking compound onto the bolt threads.
14. Install the caliper stopper pin bolt (B, **Figure 10**) through the slot in the rear brake caliper bracket and tighten hand-tight.
15. If reusing the brake hose clamp bolt, apply a medium strength threadlocking compound onto the bolt threads.
16. Install the brake hose clamp bolt and tighten hand-tight.
17. If the final drive unit was removed, perform the following:
   a. Tighten the final drive housing mounting nuts (A, **Figure 18**) to 64 N•m (47 ft.-lb.).
   b. Tighten the lower shock absorber mounting bolt (B, **Figure 18**) to 26 N•m (19 ft.-lb.).
18. Install the axle nut (A, **Figure 10**) and tighten to 110 N•m (81 ft.-lb.).
19. Tighten the caliper stopper pin bolt (B, **Figure 10**) to 69 N•m (51 ft.-lb.).
20. Tighten the brake hose clamp bolt (C, **Figure 10**) to 12 N•m (106 in.-lb.).
21. On 2003-2007 VTX1300R/S models, remove the wooden block and install the muffler mounting bolts, washers and nuts and tighten to 34 N•m (25 ft.-lb.).
22. Apply the rear brake several times to seat the caliper piston against the disc and to make sure proper brake pressure is felt at the brake pedal.

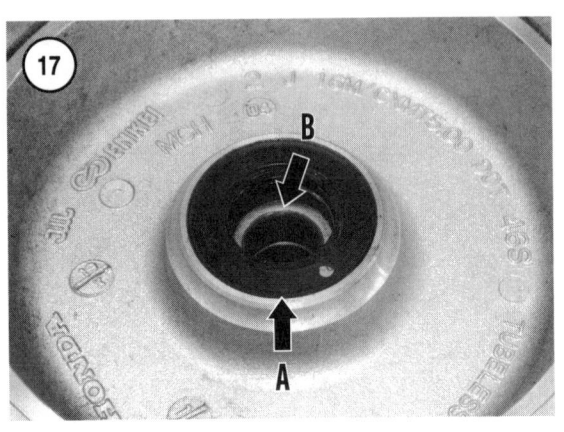

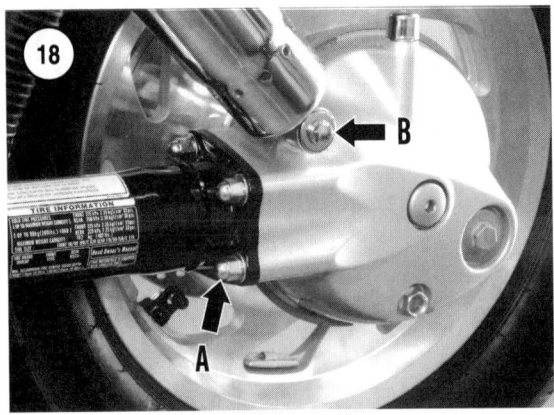

23. Rotate the rear wheel several times to make sure it rotates freely.

Inspection

1. Remove and inspect the driven flange as described in this chapter.
2. Inspect the seal (A, **Figure 17**) for wear, hardness, cracks or other damage. If necessary, replace the seal as described in *Front and Rear Hubs* in this chapter.
3. Inspect the bearings on both sides of the wheel:
   a. Turn each bearing inner race (B, **Figure 17**) by hand and check for smooth, quiet operation.
   b. Try to push the bearing in and out to check for lateral play (**Figure 9**). Slight play is normal. Try to push the bearing up and down to check for radial play (**Figure 9**). Any radial play should be difficult to feel. If play is easily felt, the bearing is worn out. Always replace bearings as a set. Refer to *Front and Rear Hubs* in this chapter.
4. Check the axle for straightness with a set of V-blocks and dial indicator. Refer to **Table 2** for maximum axle runout. Actual runout will be one-half of the gauge reading. Do not straighten a bent axle.
5. Reinstall the driven flange as described in this chapter.

WHEELS AND TIRES

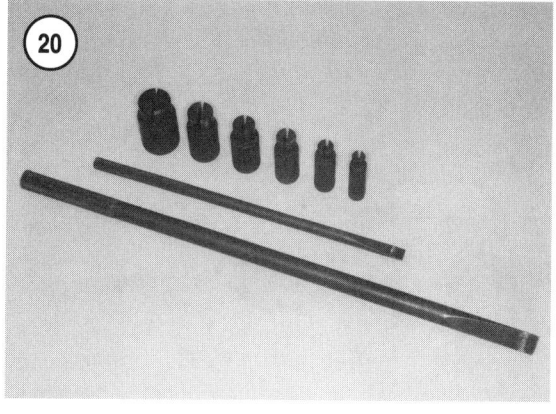

FRONT AND REAR HUBS

Each hub contains two wheel bearings and a distance collar. Seals are also installed in both sides of the front hub and in the rear hub's right side. Refer to Chapter Fourteen to service the brake discs. To service the bearings installed in the driven flange, refer to *Driven Flange* in this chapter.

Procedures for servicing the front and rear hubs are essentially the same. Where differences occur, they will be described in the procedure.

Refer to *Service Methods* in Chapter One for typical bearing procedures and information.

Wheel Bearing Inspection

Initially inspect the bearings with the wheels installed on the motorcycle where leverage can be applied to the bearings to detect wear. In addition, the wheels can be spun to listen for roughness in the bearings. Use the following procedure to check the bearings while the wheels are installed. If the wheels must be removed for further bearing inspection, refer to *Front Wheel* or *Rear Wheel* in this chapter.

1. Support the motorcycle with the wheel off the ground. Verify that the wheel is tightened to specification as described in this chapter.

2. Grasp the wheel with both hands, 180° apart. Rock the wheel up and down, and side to side, to check for radial and lateral bearing play (**Figure 9**). Have an assistant apply the brake while the test is repeated. If the bearings are severely worn, play will be detected even though the wheel is locked.
3. Spin the wheel and listen for bearing noise. A grinding or catching noise indicates worn bearings.
4. If damage is evident, replace the bearings as a set. Always install new hub seals.

Wheel Bearing Seal Removal/Installation

Seals protect the bearings from dirt and moisture contamination. Always install new seals when replacing bearings.

> *CAUTION*
> *In the following procedure, do not allow the wheel to rest on the brake disc. Support the wheel on wooden blocks.*

1. Pry the seal(s) out of the hub with a seal puller, tire iron or wide-blade screwdriver (**Figure 19**). Place a shop cloth under the tool to protect the hub from damage.

> *NOTE*
> *If necessary, replace the bearings before installing the seals.*

2. Clean the seal bore.
3. Inspect unshielded bearings for proper lubrication. If necessary, clean and repack the bearings while installed in the hub.
4. Pack grease into the lip of the new seal.
5. Place the seal in the bore with the closed side of the seal facing out. The seal must be square in the bore.

> *CAUTION*
> *Make sure the edge of the seal driver fits the perimeter of the seal. If the seal driver's outside diameter is significantly smaller than that of the seal, the driver will damage the seal.*

6. Use a seal driver or socket to install the seal in the bore. Install the seal until it is flush with the top of the hub bore surface. Refer to A, **Figure 17**, typical.

Tools

The wheel bearings are installed with a slight press fit and can be removed with or without special tools.
1. Remover sets (**Figure 20**) use a remover head (split collet) that can be wedged against the inner bearing race. A 20-mm remover head is required for

this procedure. The bearing can then be driven from the hub using a driver rod (**Figure 21**). The Motion Pro set shown in **Figure 20** includes remover heads and two driver rods. The remover heads and driver rods are also available separately.

2. Removing the wheel bearings with common shop tools requires a propane torch, drift and hammer.

Wheel Bearing Removal

This section describes removal of the wheel bearings from the front and rear hubs. If the bearings are intact, either of the removal methods described in this section may be used. To remove a bearing where the inner race assembly has fallen out, refer to Step 4.

> *CAUTION*
> *In the following procedure, do not allow the wheel to rest on its brake disc. Support the wheel with wooden blocks placed on the tire.*

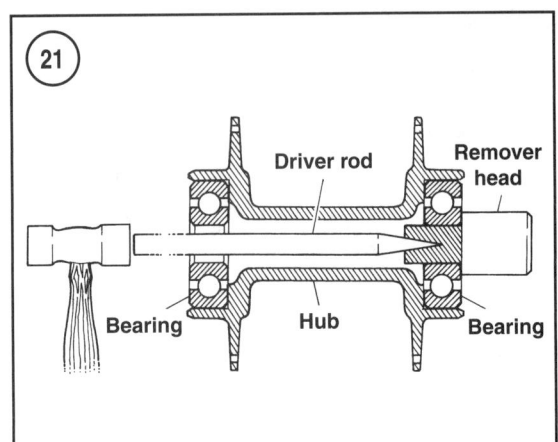

1. Remove the seals as described in this section.
2. Examine the wheel bearings for excessive damage, especially the inner race. If the inner race of one bearing is damaged, remove the other bearing first. If both bearings are damaged, select the bearing with the least amount of damage and remove it first. On severely damaged bearings, the inner race can fall out, leaving the outer race in the hub. Refer to Step 4 to remove the damaged bearing

> *WARNING*
> *Wear safety glasses when removing the bearings.*

> *CAUTION*
> *When using a propane torch to heat the hub, work in a well-ventilated area away from combustible materials. Wear eye protection and insulated gloves.*

3A. Remove the wheel bearings with a remover set (**Figure 20**) as follows:
   a. Select the correct size remover head tool (**Figure 22**) and insert it into one of the hub bearings.
   b. From the opposite side of the hub, insert the driver into the slot in the backside of the remover head. Position the hub with the remover head tool resting against a solid surface and strike the driver to wedge it firmly in the remover head (**Figure 21**).
   c. Position the hub so the remover head is free to move and the driver can be struck again.
   d. Strike the driver (**Figure 23**) to force the bearing (**Figure 24**) from the hub. Then release the driver from the remover head and remove the

first bearing and distance collar. If the bearing will not move, heat the hub area around the bearing with a propane torch as described in Step 3B.
   e. Repeat the procedure to remove the opposite bearing.

3B. Remove the wheel bearings with a hammer, drift and propane torch as follows:
   a. Clean all lubricants from the hub.
   b. Heat the hub around the bearing to be removed. Work the torch in a circular motion around the hub, taking care not to hold the torch in one

WHEELS AND TIRES

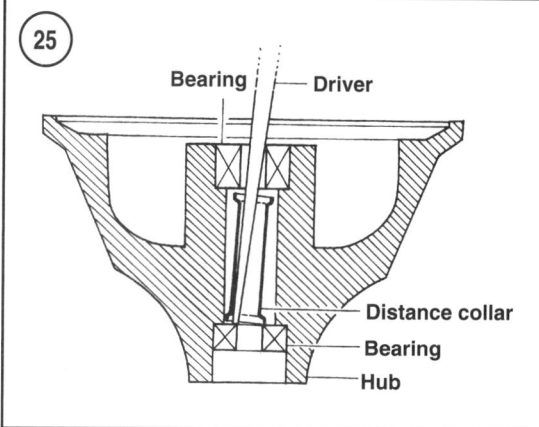

g. Drive out the opposite bearing using a large socket or bearing driver placed on the bearing's race.

h. Inspect the distance collar for burrs created during removal. Remove burrs with a file.

4. On severely damaged bearings, the inner race can break apart, leaving the outer race pressed in the hub. Removal is difficult because only a small part of the race is accessible above the hub's shoulder, leaving little material to drive against. To remove a bearing's outer race under these conditions, first heat the hub evenly with a propane torch. Drive out the outer race with a drift and hammer. It may be necessary to grind a clearance tip on the end of the drift, to avoid damaging the hub bore. Check before heating the hub. Remove the race evenly by applying force at different points around the race. Do not allow the race to bind in its bore. After removing the race, inspect the hub mounting bore for cracks or other damage.

Inspection

1. Clean and dry the interior of the hub.
2. Check the hub bearing bore for cracks or other damage. If a bearing fits loosely in the hub bore (no longer a press fit), replace the hub.

NOTE
The distance collar operates against both wheel bearing inner races to prevent them from moving inward when the axle is tightened. If a distance collar is too short, or if it is not installed, the inner bearing races will move inward and bind on the axle when the axle nut is tightened. This can damage the bearings and the bearing bores in the hub.

3. Inspect the distance collar for corrosion and damage. Clean the bore of all corrosion and other debris. Check the ends for cracks or other damage. Do not try to repair the distance collar by cutting or grinding its end surfaces as this will shorten the distance collar. Replace the distance collar if one or both ends are damaged.

Wheel Bearing Installation

1. Before installing the new bearings and seals, note the following:
   a. Install both bearings with their closed side facing out. If a bearing is sealed on both sides, install the bearing with its manufacturer's marks facing out. If a shield is installed on one side of the bearing, the shield faces out.

area. Turn the wheel over to remove the bearing.

c. Tilt the distance collar away from one side of the bearing with a long driver (**Figure 25**).

CAUTION
The bearing must be removed evenly to prevent it from binding and damaging the hub bearing bore. Reheat the hub as required.

CAUTION
Do not damage the distance collar when removing the bearing. If there is not enough room to tilt the distance collar away from the bearing, grind a clearance groove in the driver to allow it to contact the bearing while clearing the distance collar.

d. Tap around the inner bearing race to remove the bearing. Make several passes until the bearing is removed evenly from the hub. Do not allow the bearing to bind in the bore.

e. Remove the distance collar from the hub.

f. Turn the hub over and heat the opposite side.

b. Apply waterproof grease to bearings that are not lubricated by the manufacturer or that are not sealed on both sides. Work the grease into the cavities between the balls and races.

c. Always support the bottom side of the hub, near the bore, when installing bearings.

2. Heat the hub around the bearing bore with a propane torch.
3. Place the first bearing squarely against the bore opening with its closed side facing out.
4. Place a driver or socket over the bearing (**Figure 26**). The driver should seat against the bearing's outer race. Drive the bearing into the hub until it bottoms.
5. Turn the hub over and install the distance collar.
6. Position the opposite bearing squarely against the bore opening and drive the bearing partway into the bearing bore. Make sure the distance collar is centered in the hub. If not, install the axle through the hub to align the distance collar with the bearing. Then remove the axle and continue installing the bearing until it bottoms.
7. Insert the axle though the hub and turn it by hand. If the axle does not go in, the distance collar is not aligned correctly with one of the bearings. Check for any roughness or binding, indicating bearing damage.
8. Install the seals as described in this section.

DRIVEN FLANGE

Refer to **Figure 27**.

The driven flange connects the rear wheel to the final drive. The driven flange housing is equipped with two bearings and a collar. Wedge-shaped rubber shock dampers installed in the driven flange absorb some of the shock that results from torque changes during acceleration and braking.

Removal

1. Remove the rear wheel as described in this chapter.
2. Remove the O-ring (A, **Figure 28**) and discard if damaged.
3. Remove the nuts (B, **Figure 28**) and the driven flange (C).
4. Remove the snap ring (A, **Figure 29**) and the inner flange (B).
5. Remove the O-ring (A, **Figure 30**) and discard if damaged.
6. Remove the rubber dampers (B, **Figure 30**).
7. Inspect the driven flange assembly as described in this section.

Installation

CAUTION
Do not lubricate the rubber dampers or their flanges in the rear hub.

NOTE
Use Pro Honda Moly 60 Paste or an equivalent molybdenum disulfide paste that contains more than 40% molybdenum disulfide to lubricate the parts specified in this section.

1. Install the rubber dampers (B, **Figure 30**).
2. Lubricate the O-ring and install in the hub groove (A, **Figure 30**).
3. Install the inner flange (B, **Figure 29**) and secure with the snap ring (A). Make sure the snap ring seats in the hub groove completely.
4. Lubricate the driven flange bore (A, **Figure 31**) and the hub mating surface (B).
5. Install the driven flange (C, **Figure 28**) and tighten the nuts (B) to 88 N•m (65 ft.-lb.).
6. Lubricate the O-ring and install into the driven flange groove (A, **Figure 28**). Lubricate the driven flange splines.
7. Install the rear wheel as described in this chapter.

Inspection

Replace parts that show excessive wear or damage.
1. Inspect the rubber dampers (B, **Figure 30**) for damage or deterioration. Replace the dampers as a set.
2. Inspect the inner flange (7, **Figure 27**) and rear hub damper brackets for cracks or other damage.
3. Inspect the studs on the inner flange (7, **Figure 27**) for damage. If necessary, replace the studs as described in *Service Methods* in Chapter One. Install the inner flange (with rubber dampers) into the rear hub and use the rear hub as a holding fixture when replacing the studs.

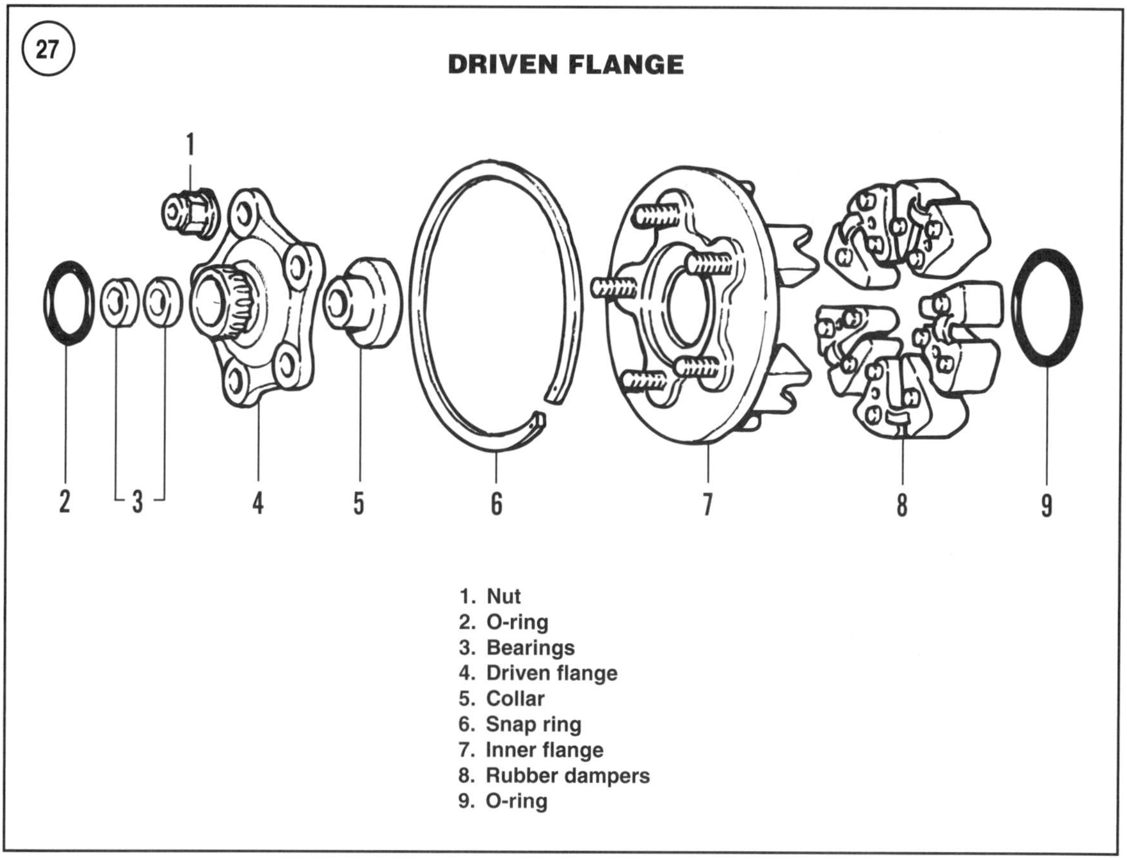

27
DRIVEN FLANGE
1
2
3
4
5
6
7
8
9
1. Nut
2. O-ring
3. Bearings
4. Driven flange
5. Collar
6. Snap ring
7. Inner flange
8. Rubber dampers
9. O-ring

28
A
B
C

30
A
B

29
A
B

31
A
B

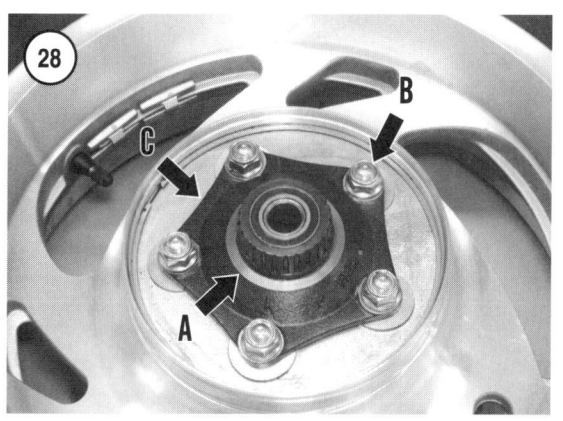

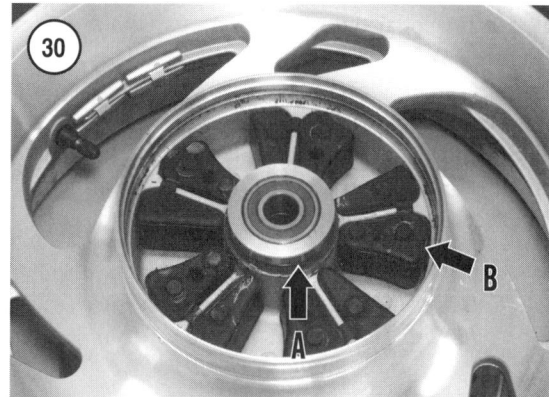

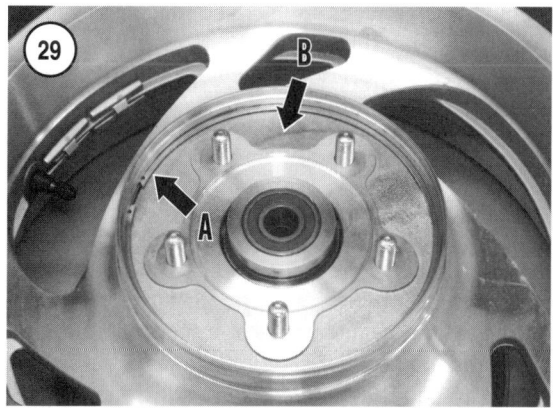

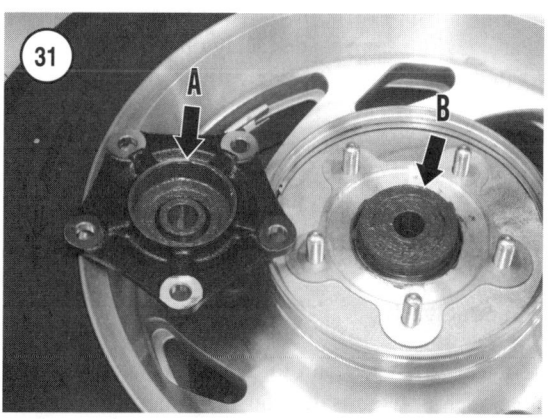

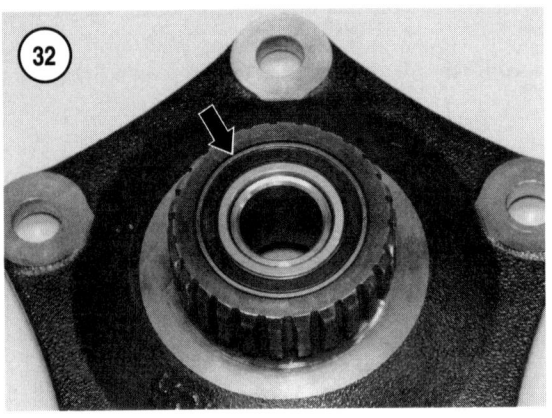

4. Check the outer bearing (**Figure 32**) for damage.
5. Turn the collar (**Figure 33**) by hand. The bearing inner races should turn smoothly with no roughness, binding or excessive noise. There should be no excessive lateral play or radial play (**Figure 9**). Replace the bearings if there is excessive play or visible damage as described in this section.
6. Check that the bearings fit tightly in the mounting bore. If the bearings are loose, replace the driven flange.

Bearing Removal/Installation

Refer to **Figure 27**.
1. Tap the collar out of the bearings with a socket (**Figure 34**).
2. Inspect the collar (**Figure 35**) for damage. Replace if necessary.
3. Support the driven flange in a press and remove both bearings (**Figure 36**). Discard both bearings.
4. Clean and inspect the bearing bore.

> **NOTE**
> The driven flange bearings (**Figure 36**) are shielded on one side. Install the bearings so the open side on each bearing faces each other.

5. Support the driven flange and press in the inner bearing with its open side facing up (A, **Figure 37**).
6. Press in the outer bearing with its closed side facing up (B, **Figure 37**).
7. Tap the collar (**Figure 33**) into the bearings from inside the driven flange.

WHEEL SERVICE (CAST WHEELS)

Runout Check

1. Clean the wheel rim to remove all road grit and other debris. Debris left on the rim can affect its runout. This includes any surface roughness caused by peeled or uneven paint and corrosion.
2. Inspect the wheel rim for dents, bending or cracks. Check the rim and rim sealing surface for scratches that could cause the tire to leak air.

> **NOTE**
> The runout check can be performed with the tire mounted on the rim.

3. Mount the wheel on a truing stand. Refer to **Figure 38** for the dial indicator inspection points.
4. Spin the wheel slowly by hand and measure the radial (up-and-down) runout with a dial indicator as

WHEELS AND TIRES

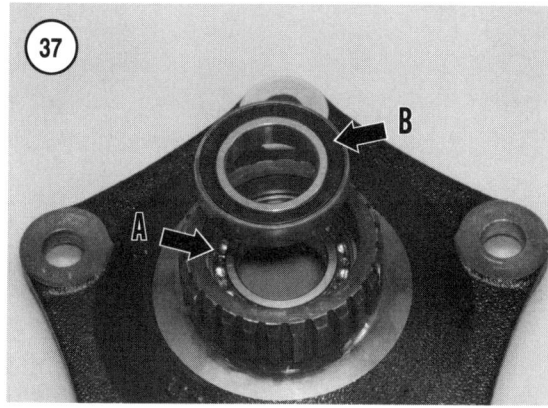

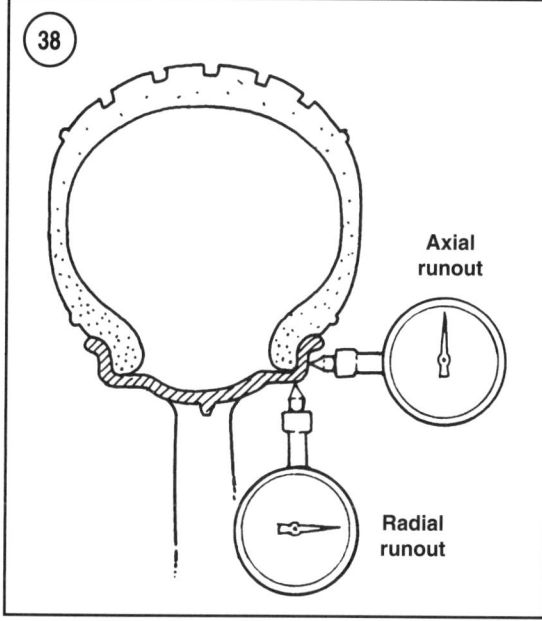

shown in **Figure 38**. If the runout exceeds 2.0 mm (0.08 in.), go to Step 6.

5. Spin the wheel slowly by hand and measure the lateral (side-to-side) runout with a dial indicator as shown in **Figure 38**. If the runout exceeds 2.0 mm (0.08 in.), go to Step 6.

6. If the runout is excessive, remove the wheel from the truing stand and turn each bearing inner race by hand. If necessary, remove the seal as described in *Front and Rear Hubs* in this chapter to check the bearings closely. Each bearing must turn smoothly and be a tight fit in its mounting bore. Some lateral play, or end play, is normal, but radial play, or side play, must be negligible (**Figure 9**). Then check the bearing for visual damage. If a bearing turns roughly, replace both bearings as a set. If a bearing is loose in its mounting bore, the hub is probably damaged. Remove the bearings and check the mounting bore for any cracks, gouges or other damage. Refer to *Front and Rear Hubs* in this chapter. If the wheel bearings and hub are in good condition but the runout is out of specification, have the wheel inspected by a dealership.

WHEEL SERVICE (LACED WHEELS)

Inspection

Inspect the wheels regularly for lateral (side-to-side) and radial (up-and-down) runout, spoke tension and visible rim damage. When a wheel has a noticeable wobble, it is out of true. This is usually caused by loose spokes, but it can be caused by a damaged hub or rim.

Truing a wheel corrects the lateral and radial runout to bring the wheel back into specification. The condition of the individual wheel components will affect the ability to successfully true the wheel. Note the following:

1. Do not attempt to true a wheel with bent or damaged spokes. Doing so places an excessive amount of tension on the spokes, hub and rim. Overtightening the spoke may damage the spoke nipple hole in the hub or rim. It can also cause the spokes to be drawn through the rim and possibly puncture the tube. Inspect for and replace damaged spokes.

2. When truing the wheels the nipples must turn freely on the spoke. However, corroded and rusted spoke threads are common and difficult to adjust. Spray a penetrating liquid onto the nipple and allow sufficient time for it to penetrate before trying to turn the nipples. Turn the spoke wrench in both directions and continue to apply penetrating liquid. If the spoke wrench rounds off the nipple, it will be necessary to remove the tire from the rim and cut the spoke(s) out of the wheel.

3. Minor rim runout can be corrected by truing the wheel. However, do not attempt to correct rim damage by overtightening the spokes. Inspect the rims for cracks, flat spots or dents. Check the spoke holes for cracks or elongation. Replace damaged rims and hubs.

Tightening Loose Spokes

This section describes steps for checking and tightening loose spokes without affecting the wheel runout. When many spokes are loose and the wheel is running out of true, refer to *Wheel Truing* in this section.

1. Support the wheel so that it can turn freely.
2. Spokes can be checked for looseness by one of three ways:
   a. If using a spoke torque wrench, the correct torque specification is 4.2 N•m (37 in.-lb.).
   b. Hand check by grasping and squeezing two spokes where they cross. Loose spokes can be flexed by hand. Tight spokes feel stiff with little noticeable movement. Tighten the spokes until the tension between the different spoke groups feels the same.
   c. Listen to the spoke tone by tapping a spoke. Loose and tight spokes produce different sounds or tones. A tight spoke will ring. A loose spoke has a soft or dull ring. Tap each spoke with a spoke wrench or screwdriver to identify loose spokes.
3. Check the spokes using one of the methods described in Step 2. If there are loose spokes, spin the wheel and note the following:
   a. If the wheel is running true, continue with Step 4 to tighten the loose spokes.
   b. If the wheel is running out of true, go to *Wheel Truing* in this section to measure runout and true the wheel.
4. Use tape and divide the rim into four equally spaced sections. Number the sections as shown in **Figure 39**.
5. Start by tightening the loose spokes in Section 1, then in sections 2, 3 and 4. Do not turn each spoke more than 1/4 to 1/2 turn at a time as this will overtighten the spokes and bring the wheel out of true. Work slowly while checking spoke tightness. Continue until all of the spokes are tightened evenly.

NOTE
If the spokes are hard to turn, spray penetrating oil into the top of the nipple. Wipe excess oil from the rim and tire.

6. When all of the spokes are tightened evenly, spin the wheel. If there is any noticeable runout, true the wheel as described in this section.

Wheel Truing

Preliminaries

Before checking the runout and truing the wheel, note the following:

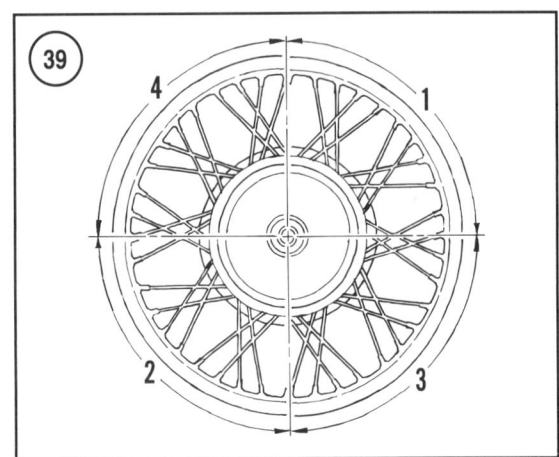

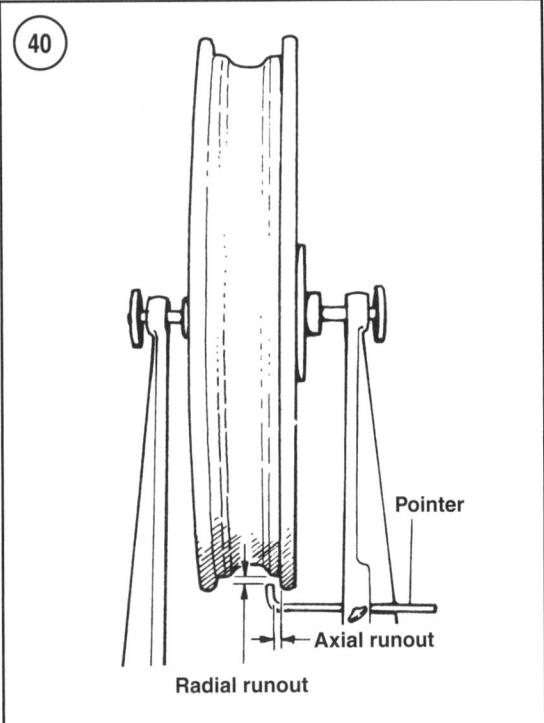

1. Make sure the wheel bearings are in good condition.
2. Check each spoke hole on both sides of the hub for cracks.
3. Check runout by mounting a pointer against the fork or swing arm and slowly rotating the wheel. A truing stand can also be used.
4. Use the correct size spoke wrench. Using the wrong type of tool or incorrect size spoke wrench may round off the spoke nipples, making adjustment difficult.

Procedure

Refer to **Table 3** for specifications.

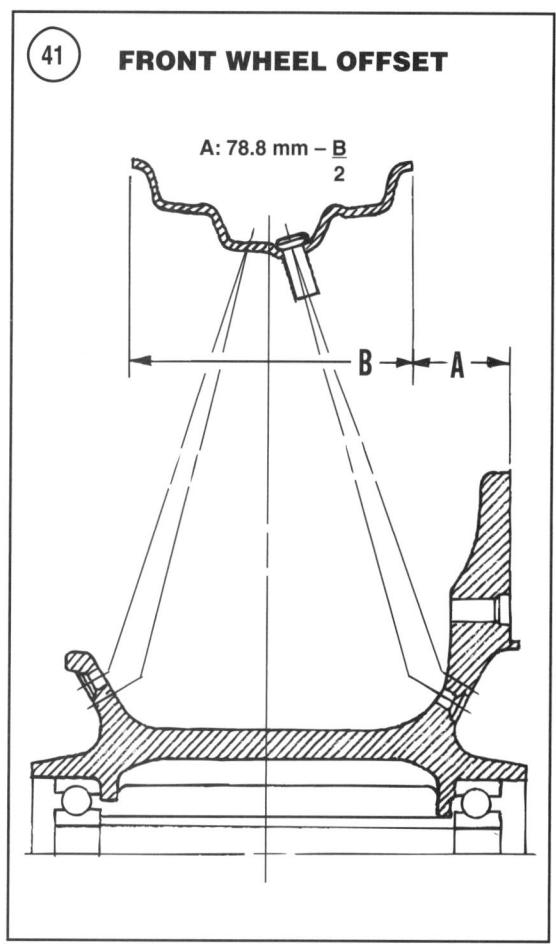

Figure 41 — FRONT WHEEL OFFSET

A: 78.8 mm − $\frac{B}{2}$

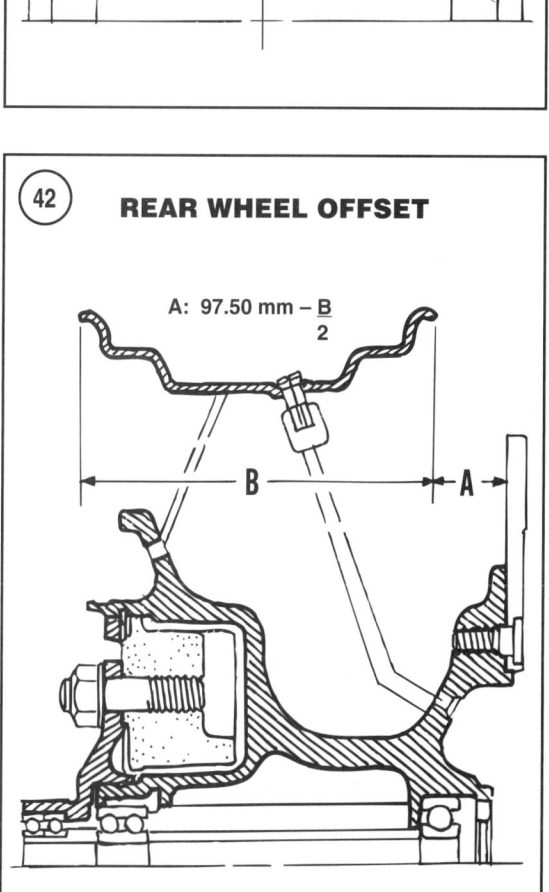

Figure 42 — REAR WHEEL OFFSET

A: 97.50 mm − $\frac{B}{2}$

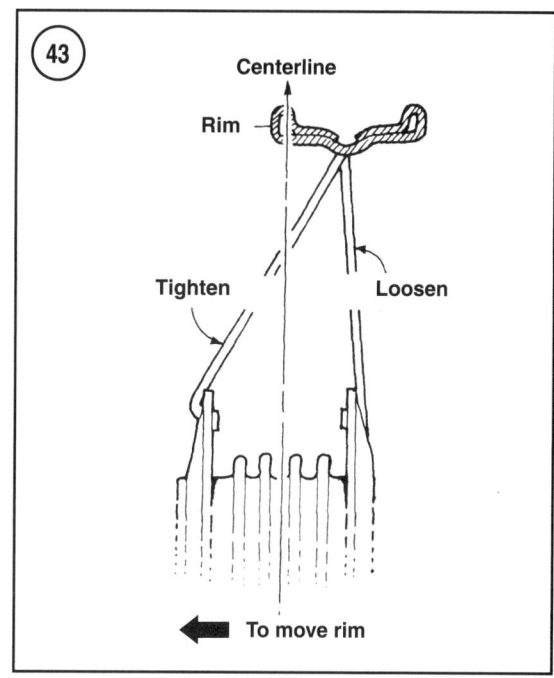

Figure 43

1. Clean the rim, spokes and nipples.
2. Position a pointer against the rim as shown in **Figure 40**. If the tire is mounted on the rim, position the pointer as shown in **Figure 38**.
3. Spin the wheel slowly and check the lateral and radial runout. If the rim is out of adjustment, continue with Step 4.

NOTE
It is normal for the rim to jump at the point where the rim is welded together. Also small cuts and dings in the rim will affect the runout reading, especially when using a dial indicator.

4. Spray penetrating oil into the top of each nipple. Wipe excess oil from the rim and tire.

NOTE
If the runout is minimal, the tire can be left on the rim. However, if the runout is excessive, or if the rim must be centered with the hub (Step 5), remove the tire from the rim as described in this chapter.

5. If there are a large number of loose spokes, or if some or all of the spokes were replaced, check the hub to rim offset as shown in **Figure 41** (front) or **Figure 42** (rear). If necessary, reposition the hub when truing the wheel.
6. Axial runout adjustment: If the side-to-side runout is out of specification, adjust the wheel. For example, to pull the rim to the left side (**Figure 43**), tighten the spokes on the left side of the hub (at the runout point)

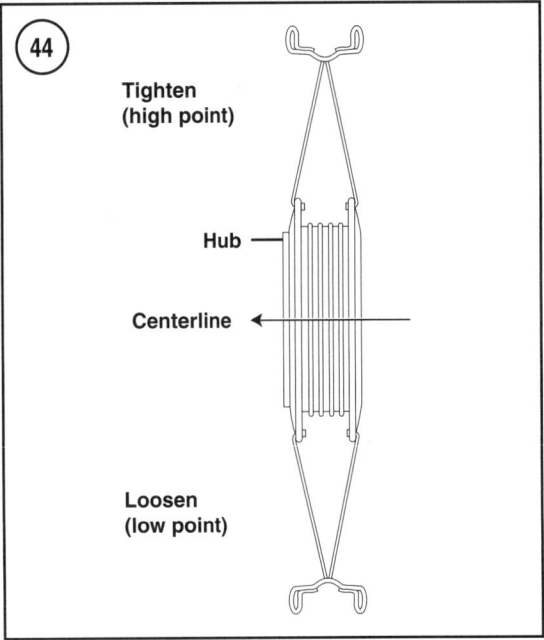

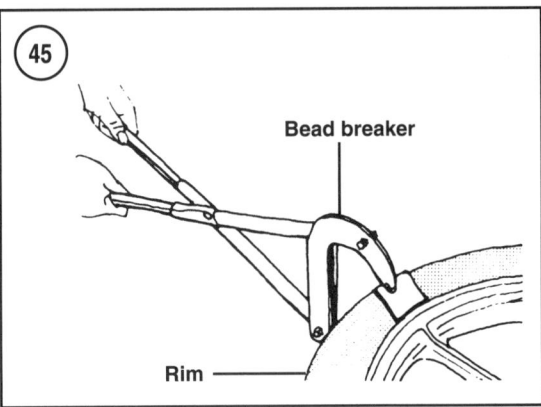

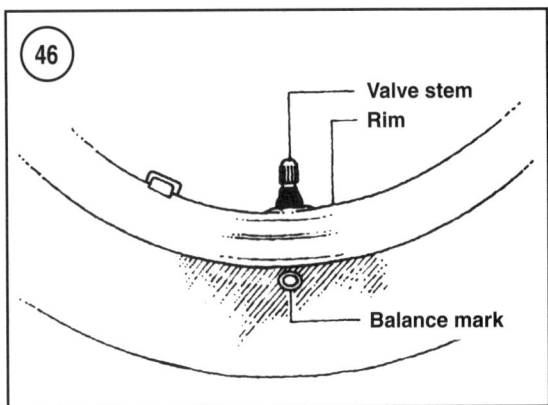

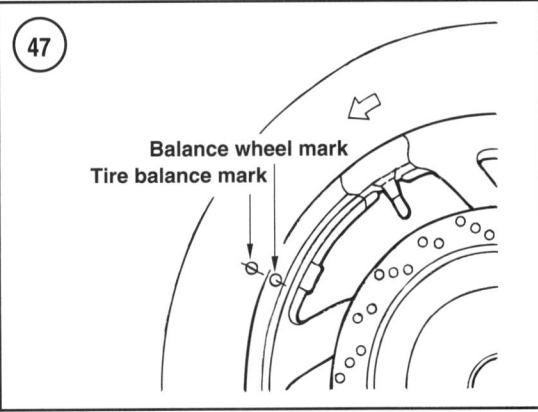

and loosen the adjacent spokes on the right side of the hub. Always loosen and tighten the spokes in equal number of turns.

NOTE
Determining the number of spokes to loosen and tighten will depend on how far the runout is out of adjustment. Loosen two or three spokes, then tighten the opposite two or three spokes. If the runout is excessive and affects a greater area along the rim, loosen and tighten a greater number of spokes.

7. Radial runout adjustment: If the up and down runout is out of specification, the hub is not centered in the rim. Draw the high point of the rim toward the centerline of the wheel by tightening the spokes in the area of the high point, and loosening the spokes on the side opposite the high point (**Figure 44**). Tighten the spokes in equal amounts to prevent distortion.

NOTE
Alternate between checking and adjusting lateral and radial runout. Remember, changing spoke tension on one side of the rim affects the tension on the other side of the rim.

8. After truing the wheel, seat each spoke in the hub by tapping it with a flat nose punch and hammer. Then recheck the spoke tension and wheel runout. Readjust if necessary as described in *Tightening Loose Spokes* in this section.
9. Check the ends of the spokes where they are threaded in the nipples. Grind off any ends that protrude through the nipples to prevent them from puncturing the tube.

TIRES

WARNING
New tires do not have the same adhesion ability and must not be subjected to hard corning, hard acceleration or hard braking for the first 100 miles (160 km). If possible, find a large, de-

WHEELS AND TIRES

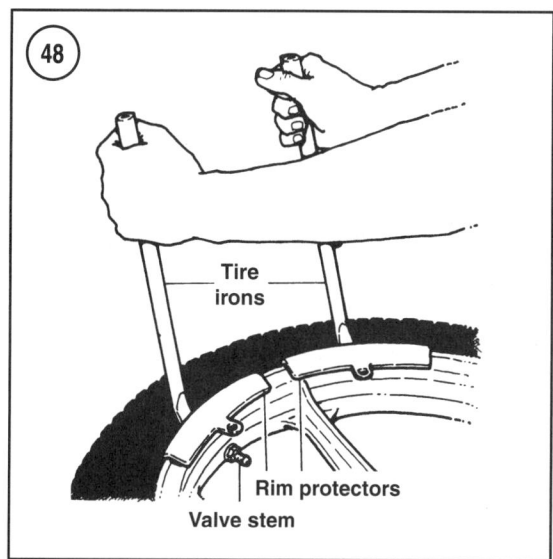

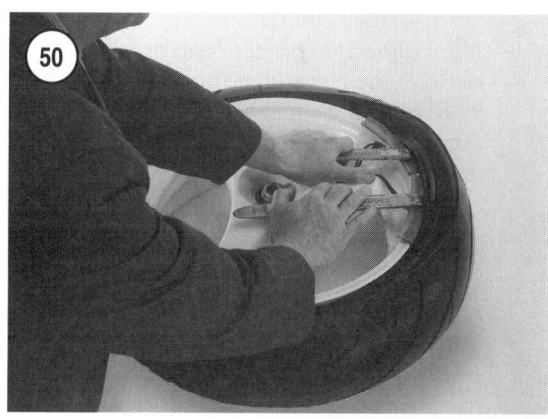

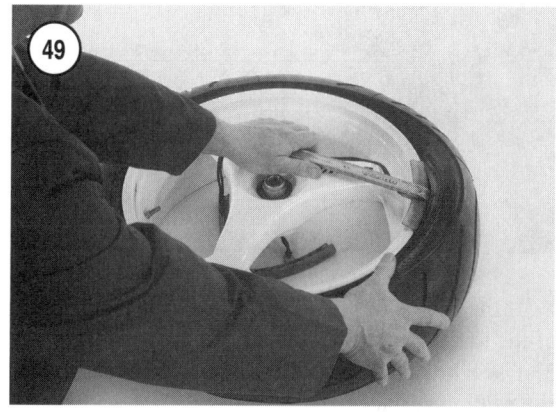

serted parking area and break in new tires without having to ride in traffic.

CAUTION
Wheels, especially cast types, are easily damaged during tire service. Use care when changing a tire to avoid scratches and gouges to the rim surface. This surface is a sealing surface on tubeless tires. Insert rim protectors or scraps of leather between the tire iron and the rim.

CAUTION
Support the tire/wheel assembly during tire removal to prevent brake disc damage.

Tubeless tire removal can be difficult because of the tight tire bead-to-rim seal. Breaking the bead seal may require a bead breaker (**Figure 45**). If unable to break the seal loose, take the wheel to a dealership with a tire-changing machine.

It is easier to change tires when the wheel is mounted on some type of raised platform. A popular item used by many home mechanics is a metal drum. Before placing the wheel on a drum, cover the drum edge with a length of garden hose, split lengthwise and secured in place with plastic ties.

Warming the tire will make it softer and more pliable. Place the tire and wheel assembly in the sun or in a completely closed automobile. Place the new tire in the same location.

Removal

1. If the tire will be remounted, confirm that the tire balance mark (a paint mark on the tire) is positioned as follows:
    a. On S models, the tire balance mark must align with the valve stem (**Figure 46**).
    b. On all other models, the tire balance mark must align with a mark on the left side of the wheel (**Figure 47**).
2. Remove the valve core and deflate the tire.
3. Press the entire bead on both sides of the tire into the center of the rim. Check that the beads are free on both sides of the rim.
4. Lubricate the beads on both sides of the tire with a tire lubricant or soapy water.
5. Insert the first tire iron under the bead on the opposite side of the valve stem. Use rim protectors or insert scraps of leather between the tire iron and the rim to protect the rim from damage (**Figure 48**). Force the bead into the center of the rim, then pry the bead over the rim with the tire iron (**Figure 49**).
6. Insert a second tire iron next to the first to hold the bead over the rim (**Figure 50**). While holding the tire with one tire iron, work around the tire with the second tire iron, prying the tire over the rim and working in small bites of one to two inches at a time. On laced wheels, be careful not to pinch the inner tube with the tire irons.

NOTE
If it is difficult to pry the bead over the rim with the second tire iron, stop and make sure the bottom bead was broken from the rim. Excessive force will split and tear the tire bead.

NOTE
On laced wheels, if the tube is being removed to fix a flat, identify the tube's installed position in the tire immediately after removing it to help locate the object in the tire.

7. On laced wheels when the upper bead is free of the rim, remove the inner tube from the tire (**Figure 51**).
8. Stand the tire upright and pry the second tire bead (**Figure 52**) over the rim. Then peel the tire off the rim. If necessary, use a second tire iron.

Inspection

WARNING
Carefully inspect tires. If there is any doubt about tire condition, replace the tire. Do not chance tire failure.

1. On laced wheels, if the tube was leaking air, pump air into the tube to locate the leak. Then place the tube on top of the tire, facing in its original position, to help locate the object in the tire. Remove the object and check the tire for damage.

NOTE
Cracks in the inner tire liner can pinch and damage the tube. If the tube is leaking air, but there are no foreign objects in the tire, spread the tire and check the inner liner for cracks.

2. Run a rag through the inside of the tire to locate any protruding objects. Do not use your bare hands.
3. Inspect the tire. If any one of the following is observed, replace the tire:
   a. A puncture or split.
   b. A deep scratch or split on the sidewall or along the inner liner.
   c. Any type of ply separation.
   d. Tread separation or abnormal wear pattern.
   e. Tread depth of less than the minimum value specified in **Table 2**.
   f. Scratches on either sealing bead.
   g. The cord is cut in any place.
   h. Flat spots in the tread.
   i. Any abnormality in the inner liner.

4. If the tire can be reused, clean and dry the inside of the tire with compressed air.
5. Use a brush to clean dirt, rust and rubber from the rim sealing surfaces.
6. On laced wheels, perform the following:
   a. Remove the rim strap from the center of the rim. Replace if damaged.
   b. Inspect the spokes for rust and corrosion. Then check for any spoke ends that protrude above the nipple head and into the center of the rim. Grind or file the exposed part of the spoke flush with the nipple.
   c. Check the valve stem hole in the rim for any roughness or cuts that could damage the valve stem. Remove any roughness with a file
   d. Mount the wheel onto a truing stand and check runout as described in *Wheel Service* in this chapter before mounting the tire.
   e. If possible, install a new tube. If not, inflate the original tube to make sure it was not punctured during tire removal. Discard the tube if it has been previously patched, or if it appears balancing liquids were introduced into the tube. Check the inner nut on the valve stem to make sure it is tightened to 2.7 N•m (24 in.-lb.). Check the area around the valve stem for cracks and other weak spots.

WHEELS AND TIRES

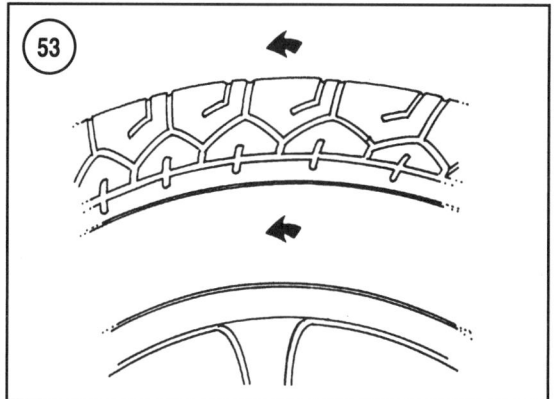

7. On cast wheels, remove the old valve stem and discard it. Inspect the valve stem hole in the rim. Remove any dirt or corrosion from the hole and wipe it dry. Install and properly seat a new valve stem.

Installation

1. On laced wheels, install the rim band around the rim by aligning the hole in the band with the hole in the rim.
2. When installing the tire on the rim, make sure the correct tire, either front or rear, is installed on the correct wheel. Also, install the tire with the direction arrow facing the normal direction of wheel rotation (**Figure 53**).

> *CAUTION*
> *Use a tire lubricant when installing the tire over the rim and when seating the tire beads. Plain or soapy water can also be used. Do not a use a petroleum-based aerosol spray lubricant as a tire lubricant. These lubricants will stay on the tire beads without drying out and can cause the tire to slip on the rim and damage the valve stem on laced wheels. Some chemicals will also damage the tire rubber.*

3. On laced wheels, perform the following:
   a. Sprinkle the tube with talcum powder and install it into the tire (**Figure 54**). The powder minimizes tube chafing and helps the tube distribute itself when inflated.

> *NOTE*
> *If installing the rear tube, make sure the valve stem is correctly angled with the hole in the rim.*

   b. Inflate the tube to shape it against the tire. Then bleed most of the air from the tube. Too much air will make tire installation difficult and too little air will increase the chance of pinching the tube.
4. Most tires are marked with a colored spot near the bead that indicates a lighter point on the tire. Align this spot as follows:
   a. On S models, align the tire balance mark with the valve stem (**Figure 46**).
   b. On all other models, align the tire balance mark with the balance mark on the left side of the wheel (**Figure 47**).
5A. On laced wheels, perform the following:
   a. Lubricate the lower bead. Then start pushing the lower bead over the rim while inserting the air valve through the hole in the rim (**Figure 55**). Install the nut onto the valve stem to prevent the stem from sliding back into the tire.
   b. Continue to push the lower bead over the rim by hand-fitting it as much as possible. The last part of the bead will be the toughest to install. If necessary, grasp the spokes to steady the wheel and push the front part of the tire toward the inside of the rim with your knees. This may provide additional room at the back of the bead to help with its installation. If it is necessary to use a tire lever, use it carefully to avoid pinching the tube or tearing the tire bead.
   c. When the lower bead is installed over the rim, turn the wheel over and check that the tube is

not pinched between the bead and rim. If so, carefully push the tube back into the center of the tire by hand.
d. Turn the wheel back over and lift the upper bead to check the tube. Make sure the tube is placed evenly around the tire. If necessary, inflate the tube to remove any wrinkles, and then bleed most of the air from the tube.
e. Turn the tire so the air valve is aligned with the rim. Also, check that the tire weight mark identified in Step 4 is correctly aligned.

CAUTION
Do not use excessive force when using the tire irons to install the upper tire bead. Instead, use your knees to push the front part of the tire (the part closest to you) toward the inside of the rim and to keep the lower bead positioned in the center of the rim. Forcing the tire irons between the upper bead and rim because the lower bead is not properly positioned can damage the rim, cut the tire bead and pinch the tube.

f. Lubricate the upper tire bead, then start installation opposite the valve stem by hand (**Figure 56**). If necessary, relubricate the bead. Use the tire irons to pry the remaining section of bead over the rim (**Figure 57**). Remember to keep the lower bead positioned in the center of the rim when installing the upper bead.

5B. On cast wheels, perform the following:
a. Place the backside of the tire into the center of the rim. The lower bead should go into the center of the rim and the upper bead outside. Use both hands to push the backside of the tire into the rim (**Figure 58**) as far as possible. Use tire irons when it becomes difficult to install the tire by hand.
b. Press the upper bead into the rim opposite the valve. Pry the bead into the rim on both sides of the initial point with a tire tool, working around the rim to the valve stem (**Figure 59**). If the tire wants to pull up on one side, use another tire iron or a knee to hold the tire in place. The last few inches are the toughest to install. If possible, continue to push the tire into the rim by hand. Relubricate the bead if necessary. If the tire bead wants to pull out from under the rim, use both knees to hold the tire in place. If necessary, use a tire iron for the last few inches (**Figure 60**).
c. Check the bead on both sides of the tire for an even fit around the rim. Align the tire weight mark with the valve stem or wheel as described in Step 4.

WHEELS AND TIRES

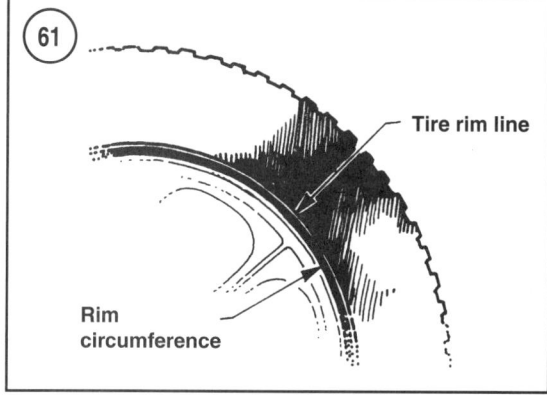

WARNING
Wear safety glasses and never stand directly over a tire while inflating it. If possible, use a clamp-on air chuck and a remote air gauge/inflator. Never exceed 300 kPa (43.5 psi) inflation pressure as the tire could burst, causing injury. If the tire does not seat at the recommended pressure, do not continue by overinflating the tire. Deflate the tire and repeat the procedure.

6. Lubricate both beads. Inflate the tire to seat the beads on the rim.

7. After inflating the tire, check to see that the beads are fully seated and that the rim lines are the same distance from the rim all the way around the tire (**Figure 61**). If not, deflate the tire and repeat the procedure.

8A. On laced wheels, when the beads are correctly seated, deflate the tire (but do not break the tire beads). Then inflate the tire again to help stretch the tube and seat it fully against the tire. Set the tire to the required tire pressure listed in **Table 2**. Tighten the outer valve stem nut and the valve stem cap.

8B. On cast wheels, install and tighten the valve stem cap.

9. Balance the tire and wheel assembly as described in this chapter.

WHEEL BALANCE

Motorcycle wheels can be checked for balance either statically with a balance stand or dynamically with a computerized wheel balancer. This section describes how to static balance the wheels. If necessary, take both wheels to a dealership and have them balanced with a dynamic balancer.

Balance weights are used to balance the wheel and are attached to the spokes (**Figure 62**) on laced wheels and to the rim (**Figure 63**) on cast wheels. Weight kits are available from motorcycle dealerships.

The wheel must be able to rotate freely when checking wheel balance. Because excessively worn or damaged wheel bearings affect the accuracy of this procedure, check the wheel bearings as described in *Front and Rear Hubs* in this chapter.

1. Remove the wheel as described in this chapter.
2. Confirm that the tire balance mark (a paint mark on the tire) is positioned as follows:
   a. On S models, the tire balance mark must align with the valve stem (**Figure 46**).
   b. On all other models, the tire balance mark must align with the balancer mark on the left side of the wheel (**Figure 47**).

NOTE
Leave the brake disc mounted on the wheel when checking and adjusting wheel balance.

3. Remove the weights from the spokes or rim. To check the original balance of the wheel, leave the weights attached to the spokes or rim.
4. Clean the tire, rim, and spokes. Remove any stones or pebbles stuck in the tire tread.
5. Remove the wheel as described in this chapter.
6. Clean the seals and inspect the wheel bearings as described in *Front and Rear Hubs* in this chapter.
7. Mount the wheel with the brake disc attached on a balance stand (**Figure 64**).
8. Spin the wheel by hand and let it coast to a stop. Mark the tire at its bottom point with chalk.
9. Spin the wheel several more times. If the same spot on the tire stops at the bottom each time, the wheel is out of balance. This is the heaviest part of the tire. When an unbalanced wheel is spun, it always comes to rest with the heaviest spot at the bottom.
10A. On cast wheels, tape a test weight to the upper or light side of the wheel.
10B. On laced wheels, attach a test weight to the spoke at the upper or light side of the wheel.
11. Experiment with different weights until the wheel comes to a stop at a different position each time it is spun. When a wheel is correctly balanced, the weight of the tire and wheel assembly is distributed equally.

NOTE
*Do not exceed the maximum wheel balance weight limit specified in **Table 1**. If a wheel requires an excessive amount*

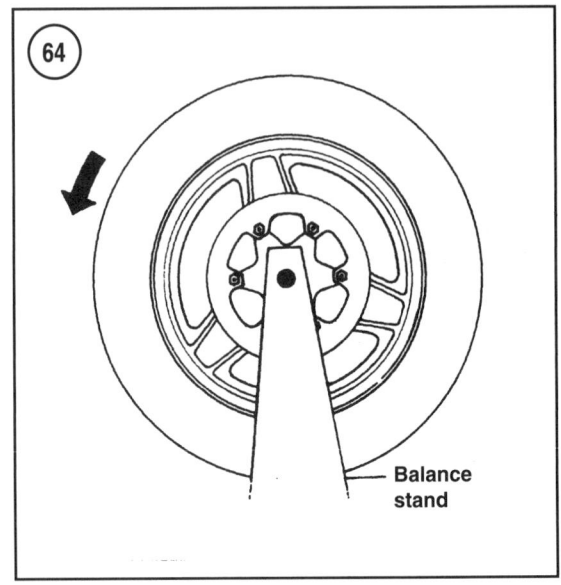

of weight, make sure the tire balance mark on the tire is properly aligned.

12. Remove the test weight and install the correct size weight or weights to the rim. Crimp the weight tightly against the spoke and nipple (**Figure 62**) or against the center joint on the rim (**Figure 63**). If the weight must be placed beside a large spoke or arm on a cast wheel, use a stick-on wheel weight on each side of the rim.
13. Record the amount of weight and its position used on the wheel in the maintenance log at the end of this manual. In the future, if the motorcycle experiences a handling or vibration problem you can refer to the log while inspecting for missing weights.
14. Install the wheel as described in this chapter.

Table 1 TIRE AND WHEEL SPECIFICATIONS*

Tire size	
Front	
VTX1300C models	110/90-19 M/C 62H
VTX1300R/S/T models	140/80-17 M/C 69H
Rear	170/80-15 M/C 77H
Tire brand	
Front	
VTX1300C models	Dunlop F24G
VTX1300R/S/T models	Dunlop D404F
Rear	Dunlop K555J
Maximum wheel balance weight	
Front	60 g (2.1 oz.)
Rear	70 g (2.5 oz.)

*Specifications are for original equipment tires. Aftermarket tires may have different specifications.

Table 2 TIRE INFLATION PRESSURE AND TREAD DEPTH*

	Front kPa (psi)	Rear kPa (psi)
Tire pressure		
Up to 90 kg (200 lb.) load	225 (33)	225 (33)
Maximum weight capacity	225 (33)	250 (36)
Tread depth (minimum)	1.5 mm (0.06 in.)	2.0 mm (0.08 in.)

*Specifications are for original equipment tires. Aftermarket tires may have different specifications.

Table 3 WHEEL AND AXLE SERVICE SPECIFICATIONS

	Service Limit mm (in.)
Axle runout	0.20 (0.008)
Wheel runout	
Lateral (side-to-side)	2.0 (0.08)
Radial (up-and-down)	2.0 (0.08)

Table 4 WHEEL TORQUE SPECIFICATIONS

	N•m	in.-lb.	ft.-lb.
Caliper stopper pin bolt*	69	–	51
Driven flange nut	88	–	65
Final drive housing mounting nut	64	–	47
Front axle bolt	59	–	44
Front axle pinch bolt	22	–	16
Lower shock absorber bolt	26	–	19
Muffler mounting nuts	34	–	25
Rear axle nut	110	–	81
Rear brake hose clamp bolt*	12	106	–
Tire air valve locknut	2.7	24	–
Spoke nipples	4.2	37	–

*Refer to text for additional information.

CHAPTER TWELVE

FRONT SUSPENSION AND STEERING

This chapter describes procedures for the repair and maintenance of the handlebar, front fork and steering components. Refer to Chapter Eleven for front wheel and tire service.

Tables 1-3 are at the end of the chapter.

WARNING
Many of the procedures in this chapter, if improperly performed, may affect the ability to control the motorcycle. Make sure the motorcycle control functions, including the brakes, work before operating the motorcycle.

WARNING
*Replace all fasteners used on the front suspension and steering components with parts of the same type. Do not use a replacement part of lesser quality or substitute design; this may affect the performance of the system or result in failure of the part that leads to loss of control of the motorcycle. Refer to the torque specifications in **Table 3** to ensure proper component retention. If a torque specification is not given, refer to the general torque recommendations table in Chapter One.*

HANDLEBAR

Removal

NOTE
*Depending on the service required, it is possible to remove the handlebar without removing the throttle assembly, clutch and brake master cylinder. Support the handlebar on two stands connected with a length of PVC pipe (**Figure 1**).*

1. Cover the fuel tank with a thick blanket to prevent damage.
2. Note the wiring harness, cable and brake hose routing.
3. Remove both rearview mirrors.
4. Disconnect the clamps securing the cables and wiring harnesses to both sides of the handlebar.
5. Remove the clutch cable mounting bracket:
    a. Disconnect the clutch switch electrical connectors (A, **Figure 2**).
    b. Remove the bolts (B, **Figure 2**), clamp (C) and bracket (D).
6. Remove the left side handlebar switch housing screws and separate the switch housing from around the handlebar (A, **Figure 3**).

FRONT SUSPENSION AND STEERING

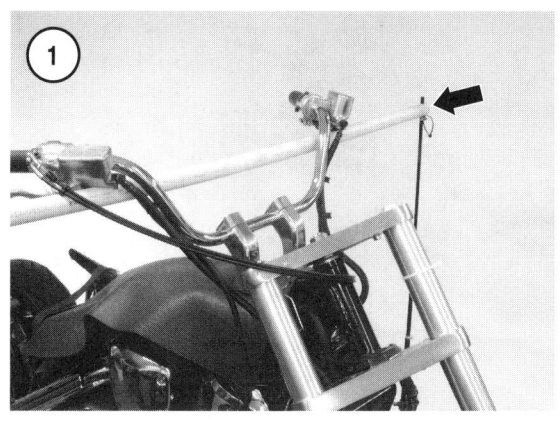

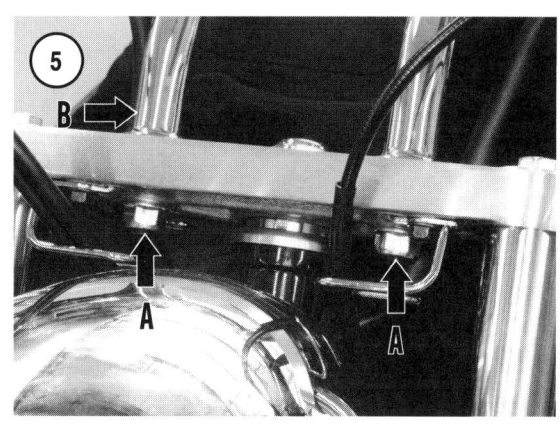

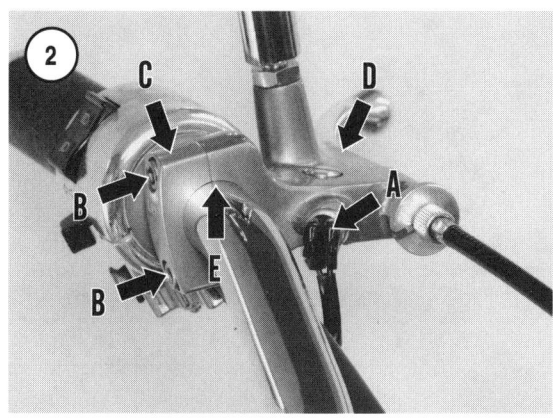

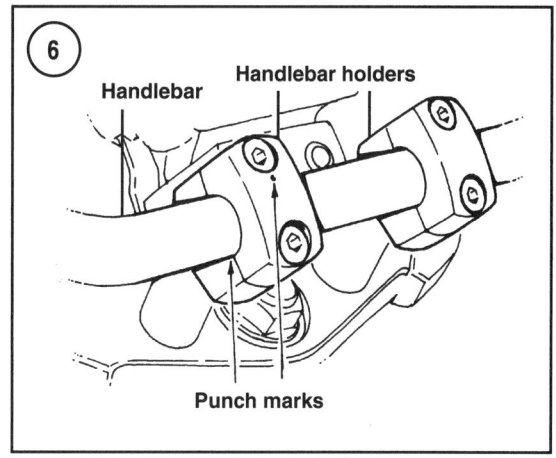

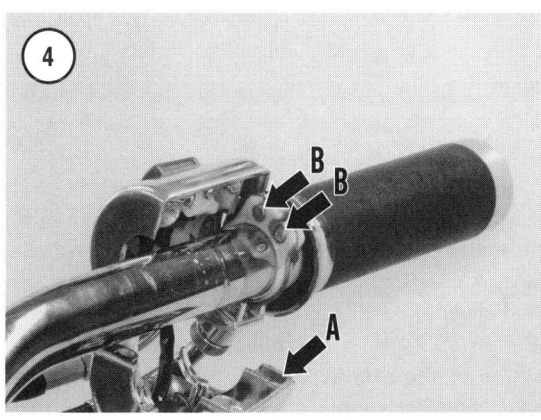

NOTE
Position the brake master cylinder upright to prevent air from entering the hydraulic system.

7. Remove the brake master cylinder from the handlebar as described in Chapter Fourteen. It is not necessary to disconnect the hydraulic brake line.
8. Remove the two right side handlebar switch housing screws and separate the switch housing (A, **Figure 4**) from around the handlebar.
9. Disconnect the throttle cables (B, **Figure 4**) from the throttle grip and slide the throttle grip off the handlebar. If the throttle cables are tight at the throttle grip and cannot be disconnected, wait and slide the throttle grip off the handlebar as it is being removed.
10A. On VTX1300C models, remove the two nuts (A, **Figure 5**), washers and handlebar (B).
10B. On all other models, perform the following (**Figure 6**):
    a. Note the orientation of the punch marks.
    b. Remove the Allen bolt caps.
    c. Remove the Allen bolts, handlebar holders and handlebar.
11. Perform the *Inspection* in this section.

Installation

1. Clean the inside of the throttle grip and both sides of the handlebar of all old grease. Then relubricate lightly with grease. Lubricate the holes for the throttle cables (B, **Figure 4**) in the throttle grip with grease.
2. Reconnect the two throttle cables (B, **Figure 4**) to the throttle grip. Then slide the throttle tube onto the right side of the handlebar. Make sure the throttle cable routing is correct.
3A. On VTX1300C models, install the handlebar (B, **Figure 5**) into the upper bridge and secure with the washers and nuts. Tighten the nuts (A, **Figure 5**) to 64 N•m (47 ft.-lb.).
3B. On all other models, install the handlebar as follows (**Figure 6**):
   a. Center the handlebar into the lower holders.
   b. Install the upper holders with their punch marks facing forward.
   c. Install the handlebar holder mounting bolts and tighten finger-tight.
   d. Position the handlebar so the punch mark on the handlebar aligns with the gap between the holders at the point indicated in **Figure 6**.
   e. Tighten the front handlebar holder Allen bolts first, then the rear bolts to 27 N•m (20 ft.-lb.). Check that there is not a gap at the front end of the holders. The gap must be at the rear end.
   f. Install the Allen bolt caps.
4. Install the right side handlebar switch/throttle housing as follows:
   a. Align the switch housing locating pin (**Figure 7**) with the hole in the handlebar and close the switch halves around the handlebar and throttle tube.
   b. Install the front and rear switch housing screws. Tighten the front screw first, then the rear screw.
   c. Operate the throttle, making sure it snaps back when released.
5. Install the brake master cylinder (Chapter Fourteen).
6. Install the left side handlebar switch housing as follows:
   a. Align the switch housing locating pin (A, **Figure 3**) with the hole in the handlebar and close the switch halves around the handlebar.
   b. Slide the end adapter (B, **Figure 3**) into the switch recess.
   c. Install the front and rear switch housing screw. Securely tighten the front screw first, then the rear screw.
7. Install the clutch cable mounting bracket:
   a. Install the clutch cable mounting bracket onto the handlebar by aligning the edge of the

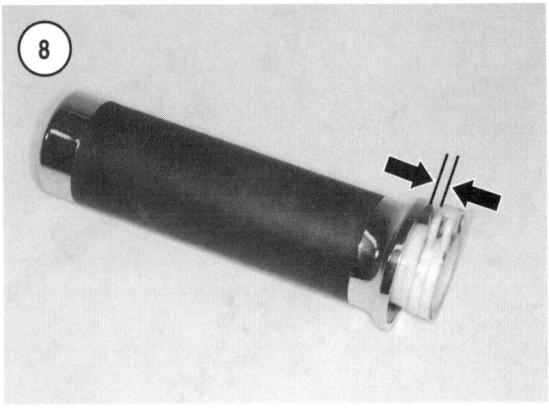

bracket with the punch mark on the handlebar (E, **Figure 2**).
   b. Install the clamp (C, **Figure 2**) with its UP mark facing up and secure with the mounting bolts (B). Securely tighten the upper bolt first, then the lower bolt.
   c. Reconnect the clutch switch electrical connectors (A, **Figure 2**).
8. Secure the wire clamps onto the handlebar.
9. Install and adjust the mirrors.
10. Adjust the throttle cables as described in Chapter Three.
11. If air entered the front master cylinder, bleed the system as described in Chapter Fourteen.
12. After all assemblies are installed, test each one to make sure it operates correctly. Correct any problem at this time.

Inspection

1A. On VTX1300C models, check the threaded studs at the bottom of the handlebar for stripped threads and other damage. If damaged, replace the handlebar.
1B. On VTX1300R/S/T models, clean the knurled section of the handlebar with a wire brush and remove any aluminum debris in the knurling. Clean

FRONT SUSPENSION AND STEERING

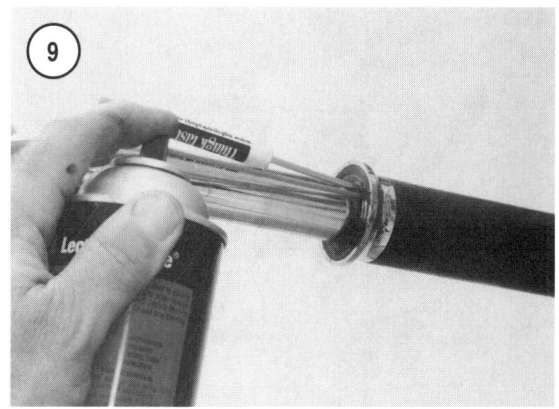

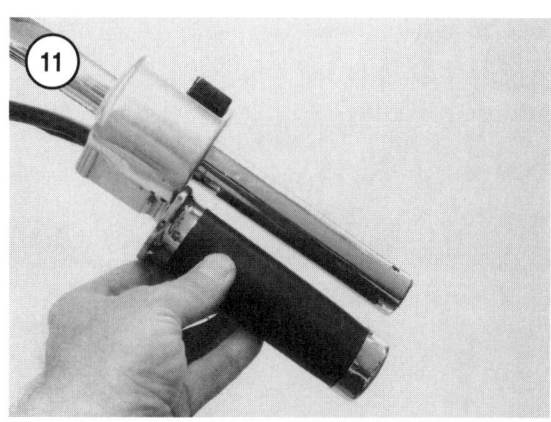

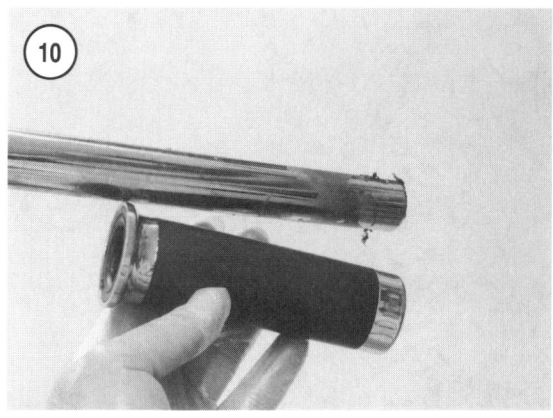

the holder surfaces thoroughly of all residue before installing the handlebar.

2. Check the handlebar for cracks, bends and other damage. Replace the handlebar if bent or damaged. Do not attempt to repair it.

HANDLEBAR GRIPS

WARNING
The handlebar grips must be secured tightly to the left handlebar and to the throttle tube (right side). Replace cut or damaged grips as water may enter between the grip and its mounting surface and cause the grip to slip. This could cause a loss of steering control.

Removal/Installation

1A. On the left hand grip, remove the left handlebar switch as described in *Handlebar* in this chapter.
1B. On the right hand grip, remove the throttle grip as described in *Handlebar* in this chapter.
2. Measure the distance from the inside of the right grip to the cable flange on the throttle tube (**Figure 8**). This gap must be maintained to prevent the grip from contacting the switch housing.

CAUTION
If reusing the hand grips, remove them carefully to avoid damage.

3. Insert a thin blade screwdriver between the grip and handlebar or throttle tube and spray electrical contact cleaner into the open gap (**Figure 9**). Quickly turn the grip to break the cement bond and slide it off (**Figure 10**).
4. If reusing the grips, use an electrical contact cleaner to remove all cement residue from inside the grips.
5. Remove all cement residue from the handlebar or throttle tube.
6. Install the left handlebar switch (**Figure 11**) before installing the grip. This positions the grip and prevents it from being installed too far on the handlebar.

NOTE
When using a grip cement (Honda Grip Cement, ThreeBond Griplock or an equivalent) in the next step, follow the manufacturer's instructions for application and drying time.

7. Apply grip cement onto the left side of the handlebar or onto the outside of the throttle tube. Install the grips as follows:
   a. Install the grip with the chrome end cap installed on the grip.
   b. Rotate the grip during installation to allow the grip cement to evenly coat all contact surfaces.
   c. Install the left side grip until it almost contacts the left switch housing. When the grip is positioned correctly, remove the left switch housing and clean excess cement from the end of the grip, handlebar and left switch housing.

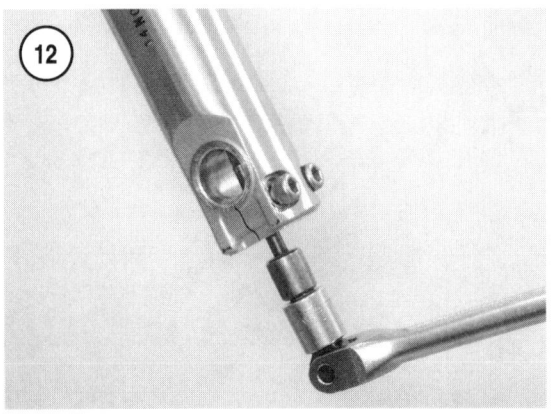

d. Install the right side grip onto the throttle tube to the dimension recorded in Step 2. Wipe off all excess cement.

FRONT FORK

Service Precautions

To prevent damaging the fork when servicing it, note the following:
1. To avoid rounding off the shoulders on the fork caps, use a six-point socket when loosening and tightening the fork caps.
2. Do not overtighten the fork tube pinch bolts, as this can damage the fork bridge threads and fork tubes. Always tighten to the specifications in **Table 3**.
3. The fork tubes and sliders are easily scratched. Handle them carefully during all service procedures.

Removal

1. On models so equipped, remove the windshield (Chapter Fifteen).
2. Note the brake hose, cable and wiring harness routing prior to fork removal.
3. Remove the front wheel (Chapter Eleven).
4. If the fork leg is going to be disassembled, loosen the Allen bolt in the bottom of the slider (**Figure 12**). Do not remove the Allen bolt.
5. Remove the fender bolt securing the brake hose mounting bracket to the fork tube (A, **Figure 13**).
6. Remove the two brake caliper mounting bolts (B, **Figure 13**) and support the brake caliper with a stiff piece of wire. Do not let the caliper hang by the brake hose.
7A. On VTX1300C models, remove the remaining front fender mounting bolts, then slide the front fender down between the fork legs and remove it.
7B. On VTX1300R/S/T models, remove the front fender mounting bolts mounted into the front fork being removed. Allow the front fender to remain

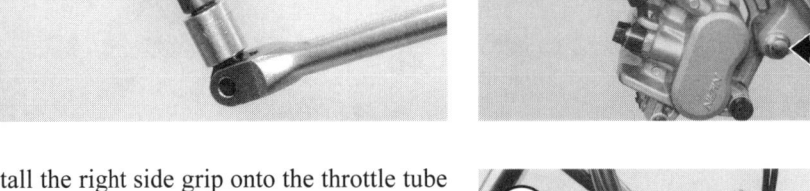

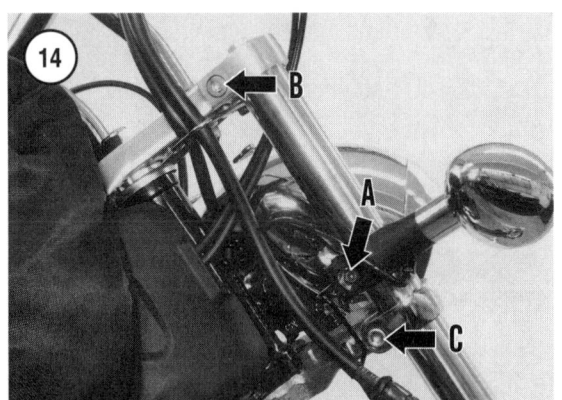

fastened to the other fork tube. The fender will be removed after the first fork tube is removed.
8. On VTX1300C models, note the turn signal wiring harness routing, then remove the wiring harness from the clamp and loosen the turn signal pinch bolt (A, **Figure 14**).
9. Loosen the top fork tube pinch bolt (B, **Figure 14**).
10. If the fork leg is going to be disassembled, loosen the fork cap (**Figure 15**). Do not remove the fork cap.
11. Support the fork leg, then loosen the lower fork tube pinch bolts (C, **Figure 14**) and remove the fork leg.

FRONT SUSPENSION AND STEERING

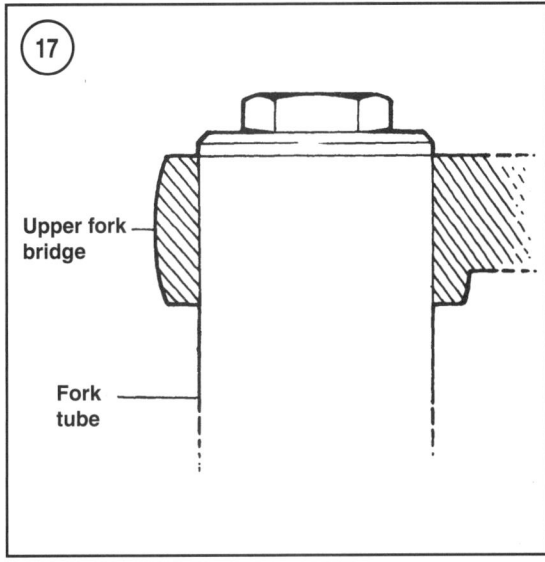

12. On VTX1300R/S/T models, remove the O-ring from inside the fork cover.

CAUTION
Rust and corrosion built up around the fork leg and steering stem clamp surfaces can lock the fork leg in place. Support the fork leg and spray the top area of each clamp with penetrating oil.

13. In VTX1300R/S/T models, remove the remaining front fender mounting bolts and the front fender.
14. Remove the other fork leg.

Installation

WARNING
Refer to the notes made during removal and make sure the brake hose, cables and wiring harnesses are routed correctly around the fork legs.

WARNING
When installation is complete, operate the front brake lever to reposition the caliper pistons. If the brake lever feels spongy, bleed the front brake as described in Chapter Fourteen.

NOTE
The right fork assembly has the brake caliper mounting bosses. If both fork assemblies are removed, be sure to install the fork assembly on the correct side of the motorcycle.

1. Clean the fork tube pinch bolts, fork bridge threads and fork leg bores.
2A. On VTX1300C models, install the front fork as follows:
   a. If disassembled, assemble the bolt and index nut on the front turn signal (**Figure 16**).
   b. Slide the fork leg through the lower fork bridge, front turn signal assembly and upper fork bridge.
   c. Push the fork leg up until it is flush with the top surface of the upper fork bridge (**Figure 17**). Tighten the lower fork tube pinch bolt (C, **Figure 14**) to 49 N•m (36 ft.-lb.).
   d. If loose, tighten the fork cap (**Figure 15**) to 22 N•m (16 ft.-lb.).
   e. Tighten the upper fork tube pinch bolt (B, **Figure 14**) to 22 N•m (16 ft.-lb.).
   f. Lower the front turn signal and insert the arm on the end of the index nut (**Figure 18**) into the slot in the fork bridge. Securely tighten the pinch bolt to secure the turn signal assembly to the fork tube.
   g. Route the wiring harness correctly and secure it with the clamp (**Figure 19**).
2B. On VTX1300R/S/T models, install the fork leg as follows:

NOTE
If both fork tubes were removed, install the right side fork tube first.

a. Loosen the fork cover bolts on the lower fork bridge.
b. Install a new O-ring into the top of the fork cover.
c. Lubricate the fork tube with soapy water to help it slide through the damper and O-ring installed in the fork covers.
d. Slide the fork tube through the lower and upper fork bridges. Position the fork so the top of the fork tube is flush with the top bridge surface (**Figure 17**). Tighten the bottom fork tube pinch bolt (C, **Figure 14**) to 49 N•m (36 ft.-lb.).
e. If loose, tighten the fork cap (**Figure 15**) to 22 N•m (16 ft.-lb.).
f. Tighten the upper fork tube pinch bolt (B, **Figure 14**) to 22 N•m (16 ft.-lb.).
g. Check that its rubber seat is positioned flush against the lower fork bridge.

NOTE
When installing the front fender in substep h, do not install the mounting bolt used to secure the brake hose mounting bracket. This bolt will be installed later.

h. Install the front fender onto the fork leg. Tighten the bolts finger-tight.

3. Perform Step 2A or 2B to install the second fork leg.
4A. On VTX1300C models, install the front fender and tighten the bolts finger-tight.
4B. On VTX1300R/S/T models, install the front fender mounting bolt to the fork leg just installed and tighten finger-tight.
5. Install the front brake caliper with two new mounting bolts (B, **Figure 13**) and tighten to 31 N•m (23 ft.-lb.).
6. Install the front brake hose mounting bracket and the remaining fender mounting bolt (A, **Figure 13**). Make sure the brake hose is properly routed as recorded prior to removal.
7. Tighten the front fender mounting bolts securely.
8. On VTX1300R/S/T models, tighten the fork cover bolts to 12 N•m (106 in.-lb.).
9. Slide the front axle (**Figure 20**) through both sliders, then grab it in the middle and try to turn it by hand. The axle should slide through and turn with minor effort. If the axle is tight and difficult to install or turn, loosen the front fender mounting bolts and then slide the axle into place. Tighten the fender mounting bolts in a crossing pattern until the axle

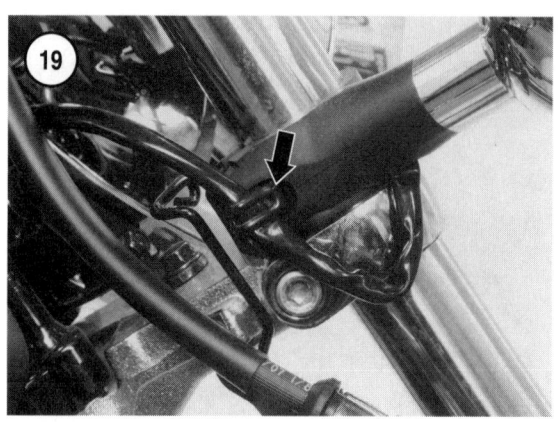

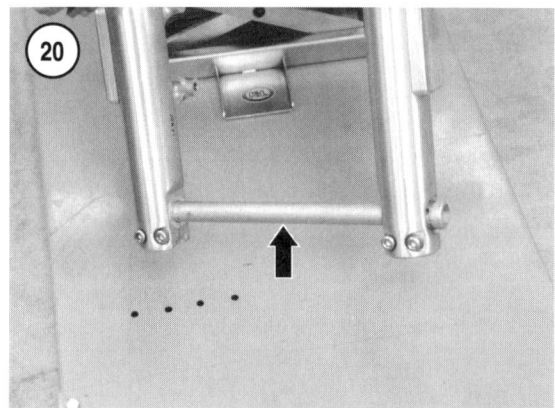

can be turned and removed by hand. If loosening the fender mounting bolts does not change the tension against the axle, check that both fork legs are installed to the same height (**Figure 17**).
10. Install the front wheel (Chapter Eleven).
11. On models so equipped, reinstall the windshield (Chapter Fifteen).

Disassembly

Refer to **Figure 21**.

If only changing the fork oil and/or setting the oil level, follow the required steps. To help secure the fork leg during service, bolt a flat metal plate across the back of the slider as shown in **Figure 22**.

1. If the Allen bolt was not loosened during fork removal, loosen it with an Allen wrench and breaker bar (**Figure 23**) before removing the fork cap and spring. Do not remove the Allen bolt.

CAUTION
The fork cap is under spring pressure. It is easier to control fork cap removal and installation when the fork leg is mounted in the steering stem.

2. Loosen and remove the fork cap and spacer as follows:

FRONT SUSPENSION AND STEERING

FRONT FORK

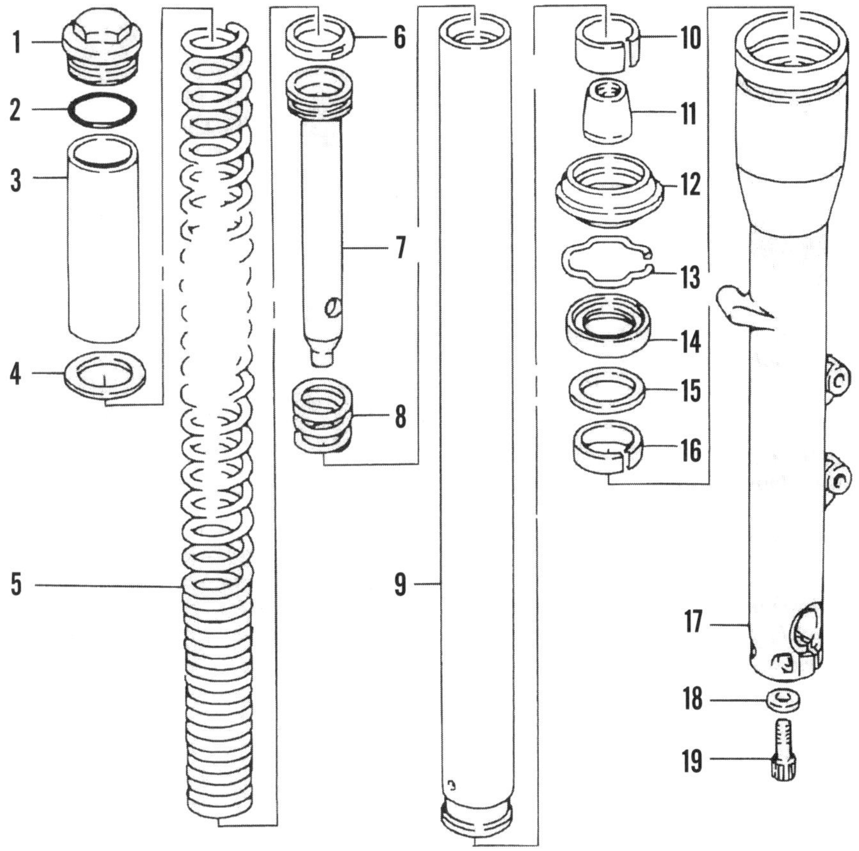

1. Fork cap
2. O-ring
3. Spacer
4. Spring seat
5. Fork spring
6. Piston ring
7. Damper rod
8. Rebound spring
9. Fork tube
10. Fork tube bushing
11. Oil lock piece
12. Dust seal
13. Stopper ring
14. Oil seal
15. Backup ring
16. Slider bushing
17. Slider
18. Washer
19. Allen bolt

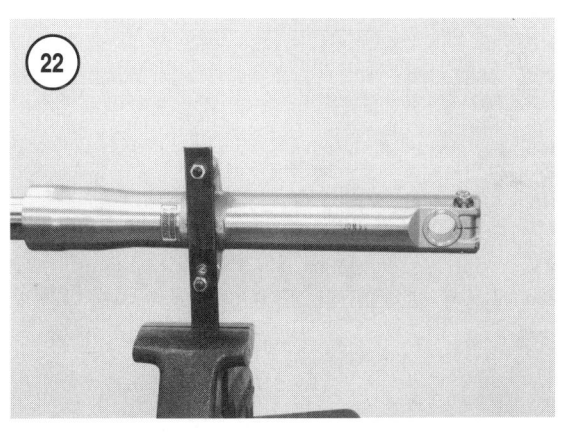

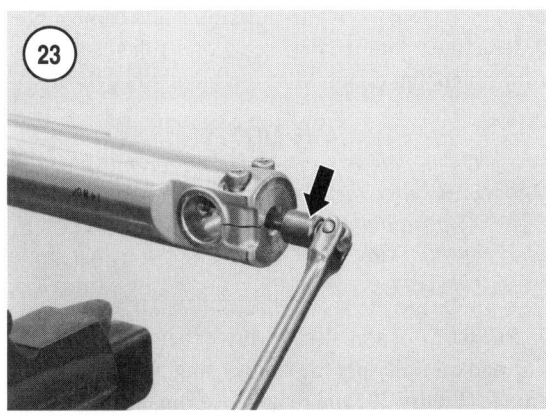

a. Place a blanket across the fuel tank.
b. Mount the fork leg into the steering assembly with the fork cap positioned above the upper fork bridge (**Figure 24**), and tighten the upper and lower fork tube pinch bolts hand-tight. On models with fork covers, it may be necessary to lubricate the fork tube with soapy water to help slide the fork tube up through the covers.
c. Loosen the fork cap (**Figure 24**) with a socket or wrench, but do not remove it.
d. Use a socket and speed handle (A, **Figure 25**) and continue loosening the fork cap until it is free of the fork tube. Make sure to maintain pressure on the fork cap with the socket and speed handle after it is released from the fork tube.
e. Remove the fork cap (B, **Figure 25**) and spacer (C).
f. Remove the fork leg from the steering stem.

3. Lower the fork tube and remove the spring seat (4, **Figure 21**).

4. Place a plastic tie on the top of the fork spring to identify its upper end and remove the fork spring (5, **Figure 21**).

5. Turn the fork leg over a drain pan and pour out the fork oil by operating the fork leg several times.

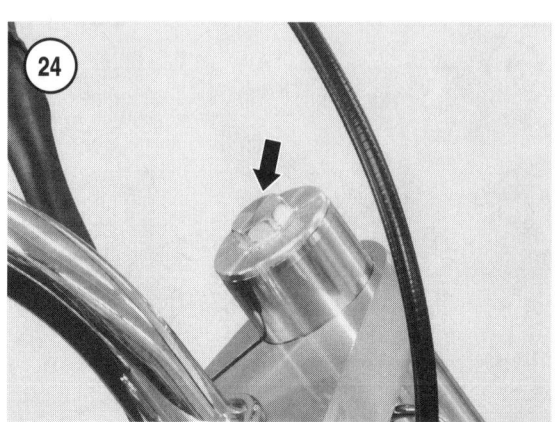

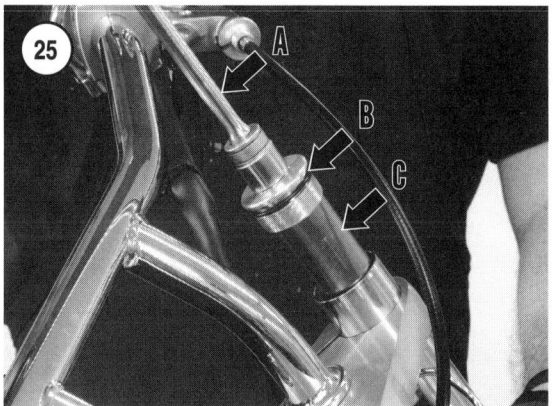

NOTE
*If only changing the fork oil and/or setting the oil level, refer to **Fork Oil Adjustment** in this section. If disassembling the fork leg, continue with Step 6.*

6. Remove the Allen bolt (A, **Figure 26**), previously loosened, and washer from the base of the slider. Discard the washer (B, **Figure 26**).

7. Turn the fork leg over and slide out the damper rod (A, **Figure 27**) and rebound spring (B).

CAUTION
Do not use excessive force when removing the dust seal in Step 8.

8. Pry the dust seal (A, **Figure 28**) out of the slider with a suitable tool. Move the tool around the seal in small increments. It is easy to scratch and damage the slider at the top of the dust seal bore. When selecting a starting point, choose the side facing the wheel.

CAUTION
*On models so equipped, do not remove or damage the cushion ring (B, **Figure 28**) installed in the top of the slider. The cushion ring is not available as a separate part.*

9. Slip the tip of a small screwdriver behind the stopper ring and carefully pry the stopper ring out of the slider groove (**Figure 29**) and remove it from the slider.

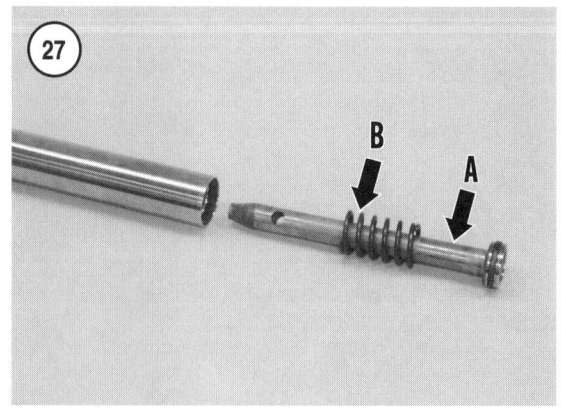

FRONT SUSPENSION AND STEERING

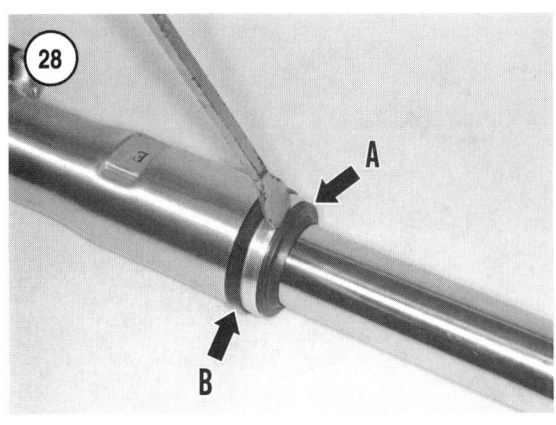

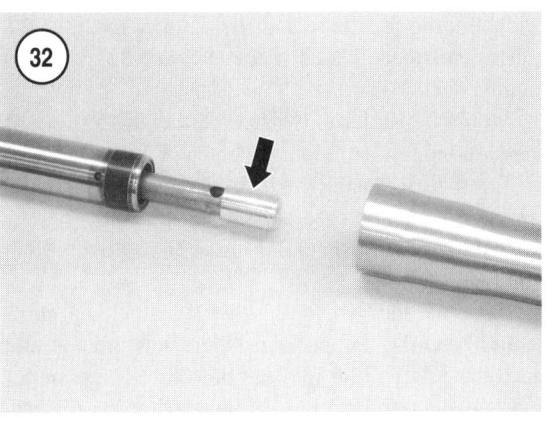

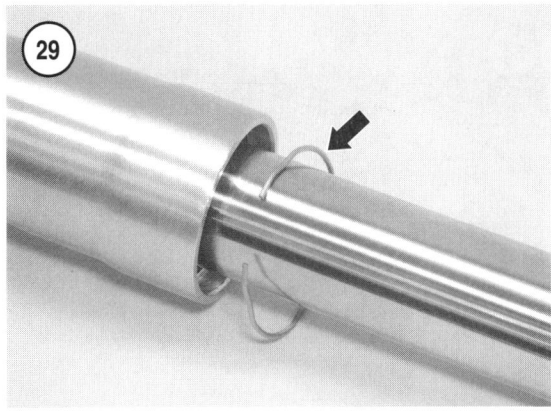

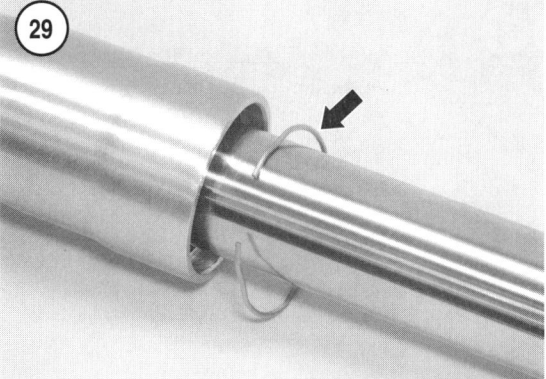

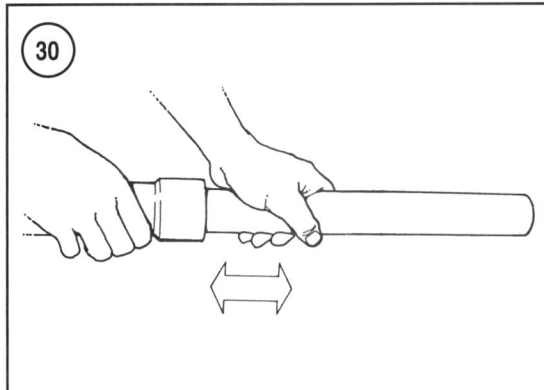

NOTE
A pressed-in bushing in the slider and a bushing on the fork tube keep the slider and fork tube from separating. To remove the fork tube from the slider, use these parts as a slide hammer as described in Step 10.

10. Hold the fork tube and pull hard on the slider, using quick in-and-out strokes (**Figure 30**). Doing so withdraws the oil seal (A, **Figure 31**), backup ring (B) and guide bushing (C) from the slider.
11. Remove the slider and pour any remaining oil in the oil pan.
12. Remove the oil lock piece (11, **Figure 21** and **Figure 32**) from the slider if it did not come out in Step 11.
13. Slide off the oil seal (A, **Figure 31**), backup ring (B) and slider bushing (C) from the fork tube. Discard the dust seal and oil seal.

NOTE
Do not remove the fork tube bushing (D, Figure 31) unless it is going to be replaced. Inspect it as described in this section.

14. Clean and inspect the parts as described in *Inspection* in this section.

Assembly

1. Before assembling the parts, make sure there is no solvent left in the slider or on any part.
2. Coat all parts, except the Allen bolt and damper rod threads, with new fork oil before installation.
3. Install the rebound spring (B, **Figure 27**) onto the damper rod (A) and slide the damper rod assembly through the fork tube.
4. Install the oil lock piece onto the end of the damper rod (**Figure 32**).

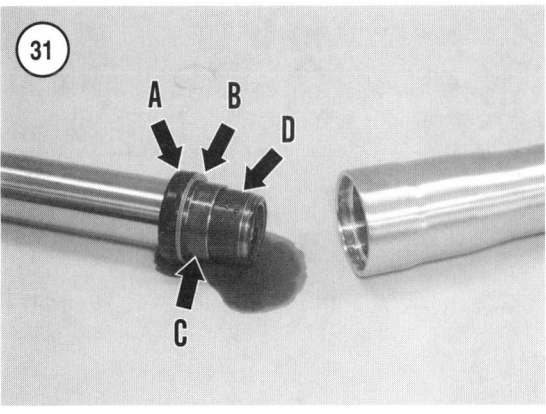

5. Install the fork tube and the damper rod into the slider until the oil lock piece (**Figure 32**) bottoms against the slider.
6. Mount the slider in a vise by attaching a piece of metal to the fender mounting holes (**Figure 22**).
7. Temporarily install the fork spring (5, **Figure 21**), spring seat (4) and spacer (3).
8. Install a new washer (B, **Figure 26**) onto the Allen bolt (A).
9. Install a medium strength threadlocking compound onto the damper rod Allen bolt threads and thread the Allen bolt into the bottom of the damper rod and tighten until the damper rod starts to turn. Then compress the fork tube and tighten the Allen bolt (**Figure 33**) to 20 N•m (15 ft.-lb.).
10. Remove the spacer (3, **Figure 21**), spring seat (4) and fork spring (5).
11. Using the same piece of metal (**Figure 22**) to hold the fork leg, position the slider in the vise with the fork tube facing up.
12. **Figure 34** shows the alignment of the bushing and seal assembly.
13. Install the fork slider bushing and backup ring as follows:
    a. Slide the bushing (A, **Figure 35**) and backup ring (B) down the fork tube. Install the backup ring with its chamfered side facing down and set it on top of the bushing.
    b. Use a fork oil seal driver (**Figure 36**) to drive the bushing into the fork slider until the backup ring bottoms against the slider. The knocking sound made by the driver changes when the backup ring bottoms out.

CAUTION
To avoid damaging the fork seal and dust seal when installing them over the top of the fork tube, first place a plastic bag over the fork tube and coat it with fork oil.

14. Install a new fork seal as follows:
    a. Lubricate the seal lips with fork oil.
    b. Install the seal (**Figure 37**) over the fork tube with its manufacturer's name and size code facing up. Slide it down the fork tube and center it into the top of the slider until its outer surface is flush with the slider's outer bore surface.
    c. Drive the oil seal into the slider with the same tool (**Figure 36**) used in Step 13 until the groove in the slider can be seen above the top surface of the seal.
15. Slide the stopper ring (**Figure 38**) over the fork tube and install it into the groove in the slider. Make sure that the stopper ring is completely seated in the slider groove.

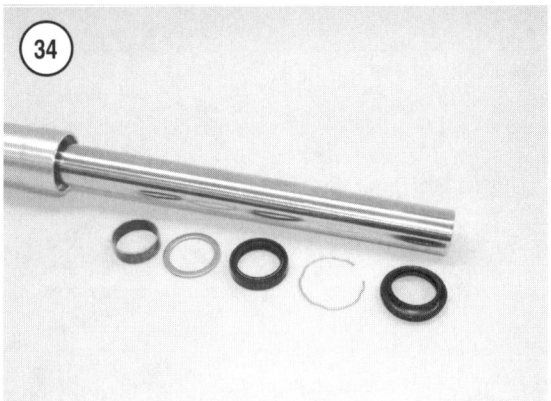
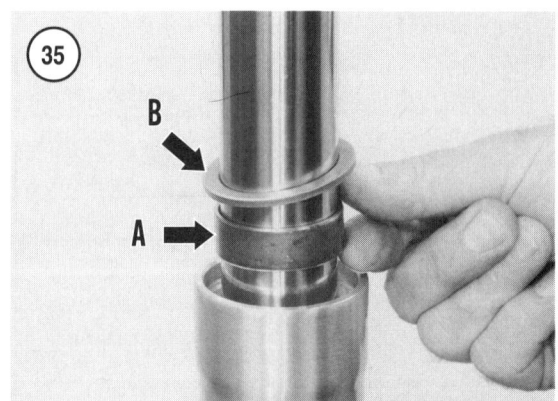
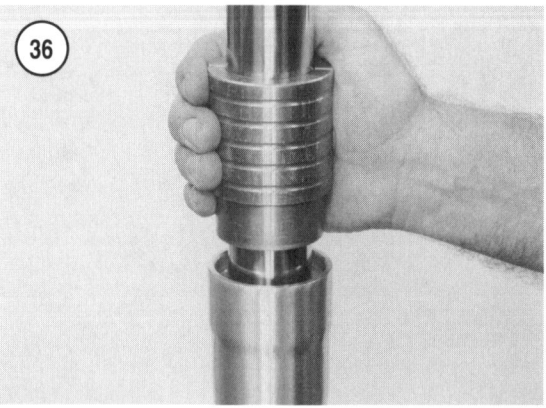

FRONT SUSPENSION AND STEERING

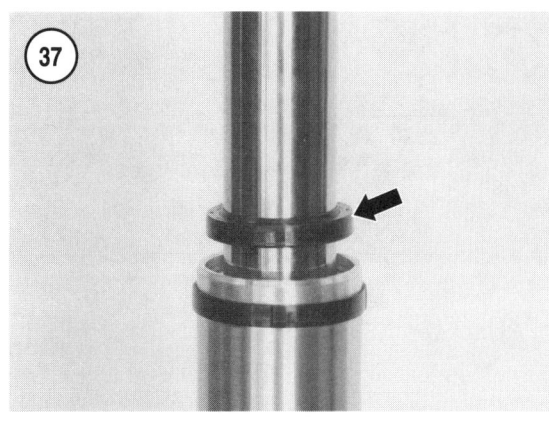

37

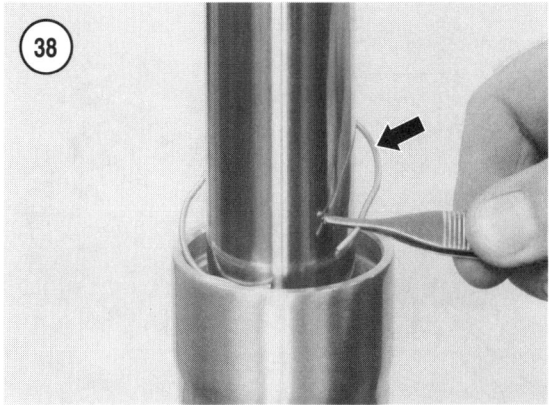

38

39

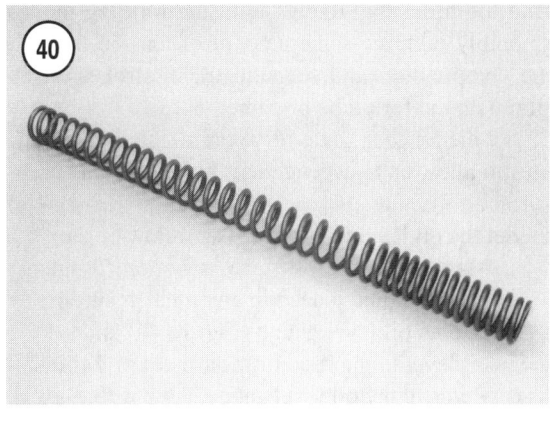

40

NOTE
If the stopper ring cannot seat completely into the slider groove, the seal is not installed far enough into the slider.

16. Slide the dust seal down the fork tube and seat it into the slider (**Figure 39**).
17. Fill the fork with oil and set the oil level as described in *Fork Oil Adjustment* in this section.
18. Install the fork spring with its closer wound spring end (**Figure 40**) facing down.
19. Install the spring seat (4, **Figure 21**) and seat it on top of the fork spring.
20. Install the spacer and fork cap as follows:
    a. Place a blanket across the fuel tank.
    b. Mount the fork leg into the steering assembly so the top of the fork tube is positioned above the upper fork bridge (**Figure 24**), and tighten the upper and lower fork tube pinch bolts hand-tight. On models with fork covers, it may be necessary to lubricate the fork tube with soapy water to help slide the fork tube up through the covers.
    c. Install the spacer (C, **Figure 25**) and seat it on top of the spring seat.
    d. Install a new O-ring onto the fork cap, if needed. Then lubricate the fork cap O-ring with fork oil.
    e. Place the fork cap (B, **Figure 25**) on top of the spacer, then push the fork cap down with a speed handle and socket (A) to compress the spring and carefully thread the fork cap into the fork tube. Continue until the fork cap bottoms (**Figure 24**), then tighten it to 22 N•m (16 ft.-lb.).
    f. Remove the fork leg from the steering assembly.
21. Repeat this procedure for the other fork leg.
22. Install the fork legs as described in this section.

Inspection

Refer to **Table 2**. Replace worn or damaged parts as described in this section.
1. Thoroughly clean all parts in solvent and dry them. Remove all threadlocking compound from the damper rod and Allen bolt threads.
2. Check the fork tube for severe wear or scratches. Check the chrome for flaking or other damage that could damage the oil seal.
3. Check the fork tube for straightness. Place the fork tube on V-blocks and measure runout with a dial indicator. If the runout exceeds specification (**Table 2**), replace the fork tube.
4. Check the slider for dents or exterior damage. Check the stopper ring groove for cracks or damage.

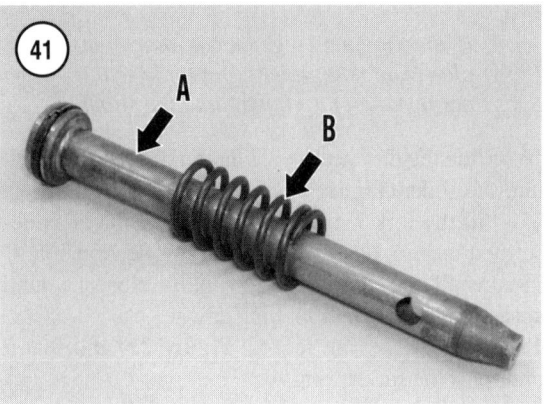

Check the oil seal mounting bore for dents or other damage.

5. Inspect the damper rod (A, **Figure 41**) for straightness, damage or roughness. Check for galling, deep scores or excessive wear. Check the threads for damage.
6. Inspect the rebound spring (B, **Figure 41**) on the damper rod (A) for cracks or other damage.
7. Inspect the piston ring (**Figure 42**) on the end of the damper rod for wear or damage. Replace if necessary.
8. Inspect the oil lock assembly (**Figure 32**) for damage.
9. Measure the free length of the fork spring with a tape measure. Replace the spring if it is too short (**Table 2**). Replace the springs as a set if they are unequal in length.
10. Inspect the slider and fork tube bushings for scoring, excessive wear or damage. Check for discoloration and material coating damage. If the coating is worn off so that the base material is showing on approximately 3/4 of the total surface, the bushing is severely worn. Replace both bushings (**Figure 43**) as a set.
11. To replace the fork tube bushing, pry its slot open with a screwdriver (**Figure 44**) and slide it off the fork tube. Clean the groove on the bottom of the fork tube, then slide the new bushing onto the fork tube until it seats fully in the groove.
12. Replace the fork cap O-ring if damaged or leaking.

Fork Oil Adjustment

This section describes steps on filling the fork with oil and setting the oil level.
Refer to **Table 2**.
1. Remove the fork spring and drain the fork leg as described in *Disassembly* in this section.
2. Push the fork tube down and bottom out against the slider. Support the slider so it cannot tip over.
3. Slowly pour the recommended type of fork oil (**Table 2**) into the fork.

NOTE
As oil replaces air during the bleeding procedure, the oil level in the fork drops. Continue to add oil to maintain a high oil level in the fork. When bleeding the fork leg, do not be concerned with maintaining or achieving the proper oil capacity. Setting the oil level determines the actual amount of oil to use in each fork leg.

4. Hold the slider with one hand and slowly extend the fork tube. Repeat until the fork leg moves smoothly with the same amount of tension through the compression and rebound travel strokes. Then stop with the fork tube bottomed out.
5. Set the fork leg aside for approximately five minutes to allow any suspended air bubbles in the oil to surface.
6. Set the oil level (**Figure 45**) as follows:
   a. Make sure the fork tube is bottomed against the slider and placed in a vertical position.
   b. Use an oil level gauge (**Figure 46**) and set the oil level to the specification listed in **Table 2**.
   c. Remove the oil level gauge.

FRONT SUSPENSION AND STEERING

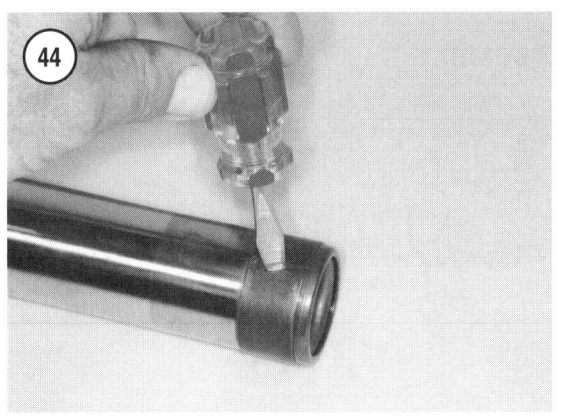

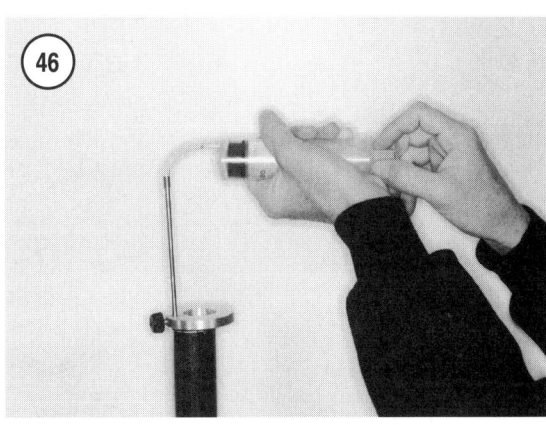

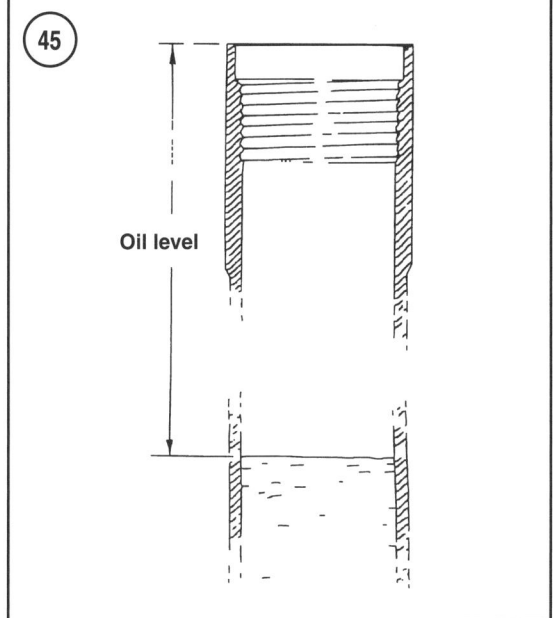

7. Complete fork assembly as described in *Assembly* in this section.

STEERING HEAD AND STEM

Refer to **Figure 47**.

The steering head uses retainer-type steel bearings. Each bearing consists of the inner race, outer race and bearing. The bearings can be lifted out of their operating positions after removing the steering stem. Do not remove the lower inner race (pressed onto the steering stem) or the outer bearing races (pressed into the frame) unless they are to be replaced.

Regular maintenance consists of steering inspection, bearing lubrication and adjustment. When the steering cannot be adjusted correctly, the bearings may require replacement. To determine bearing condition, the steering assembly must be removed and inspected. Check the steering adjustment and lubricate the bearings per the maintenance schedule in Chapter Three.

This section describes service and adjustment procedures for the steering head assembly.

Tools

The steering stem socket (part No. 07916-3710100 or equivalent) and a spring scale are required to adjust the steering stem/bearing assembly. These tools are shown in the appropriate procedure.

Refer to *Steering Head Bearing Race* and *Steering Stem Bearing* in this chapter for service procedures and tools.

Troubleshooting

Before removing the steering assembly to troubleshoot a steering complaint, refer to *Front Suspension and Steering* in Chapter Two. Refer to the condition that most identifies the problem and check the items listed as possible causes.

Removal/Disassembly

Refer to **Figure 47**.
1. On models so equipped, remove the windshield (Chapter Fifteen).
2. Remove the handlebar as described in this chapter.
3. On VTX1300R/S/T models, remove the nuts and the lower handlebar holders if necessary.
4. Remove the headlight housing (Chapter Nine).
5. Remove the turn signal assembly (Chapter Nine).
6. If necessary, remove the bolts and the cable guides from underneath the upper bracket. On VTX1300T models, the upper windshield mounting bracket is removed with the cable guides.
7. Remove the bolt securing the front brake hose mounting bracket (**Figure 48**) to the lower fork bridge.

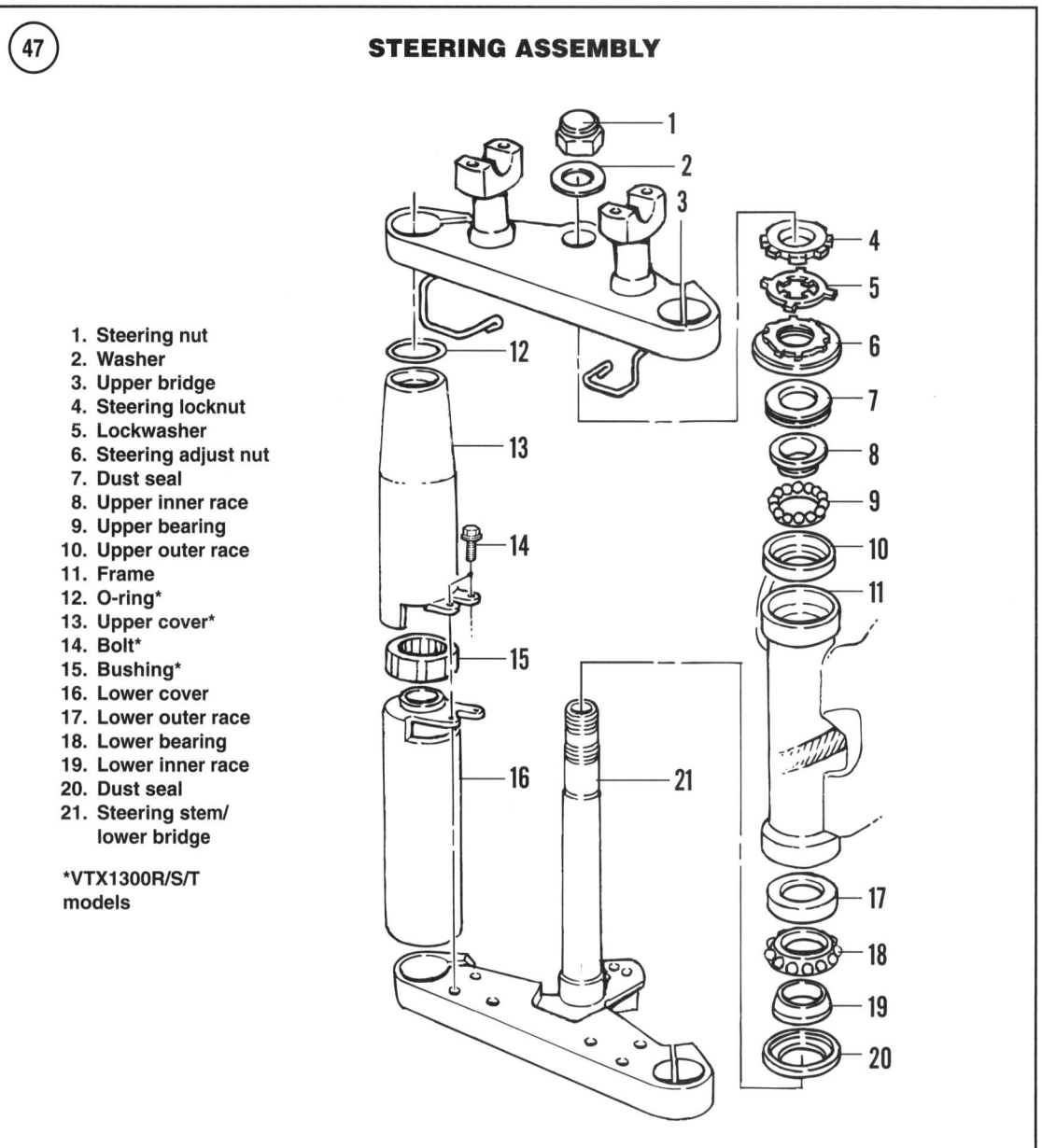

STEERING ASSEMBLY

1. Steering nut
2. Washer
3. Upper bridge
4. Steering locknut
5. Lockwasher
6. Steering adjust nut
7. Dust seal
8. Upper inner race
9. Upper bearing
10. Upper outer race
11. Frame
12. O-ring*
13. Upper cover*
14. Bolt*
15. Bushing*
16. Lower cover
17. Lower outer race
18. Lower bearing
19. Lower inner race
20. Dust seal
21. Steering stem/ lower bridge

*VTX1300R/S/T models

8. Note the routing and then remove the cables and wiring harnesses from the cable guides mounted on the upper bridge.

NOTE
At this point there should be no cable, hose or wiring harness interfering with the movement of the steering stem. Check by turning the steering stem. If so, reposition the item so the steering stem can move with no interference.

9. Before loosening the steering stem nut, check the steering adjustment as described in *Steering Bearing Preload Check* in this chapter.

10. Remove the front wheel (Chapter Eleven).
11. Loosen the steering nut (A, **Figure 49**).
12. Remove the fork legs as described in this chapter.
13. Remove the steering nut (A, **Figure 49**) and washer and the upper bridge (B).
14. On VTX1300R/S/T models, remove the bolts and the upper (13, **Figure 47**) and lower (16, **Figure 49**) fork covers.
15. Pry the lockwasher tabs (A, **Figure 50**) away from the steering locknut grooves. Then remove the steering locknut (B, **Figure 50**) and lockwasher (A). Install a new lockwasher during reassembly.
16. Loosen the steering adjust nut with a steering stem socket (part No. 07916-3710100 [**Figure 51**]) or a spanner wrench.

FRONT SUSPENSION AND STEERING

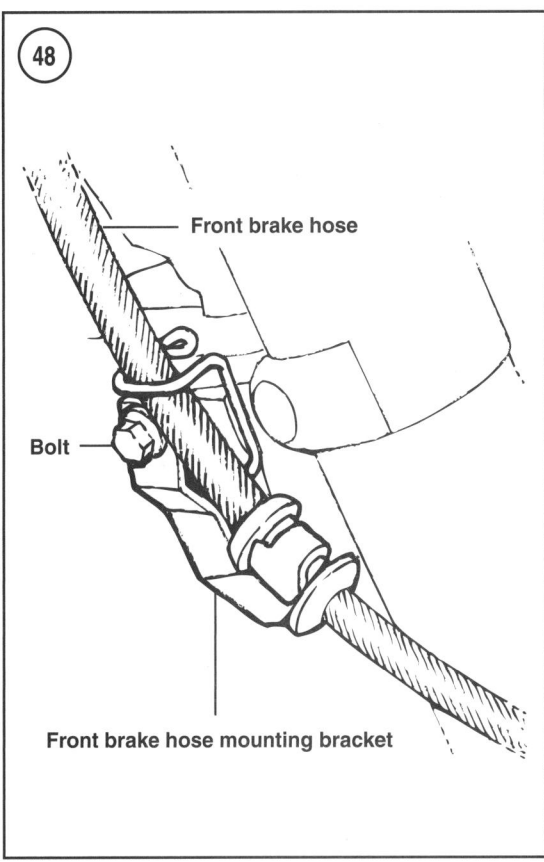

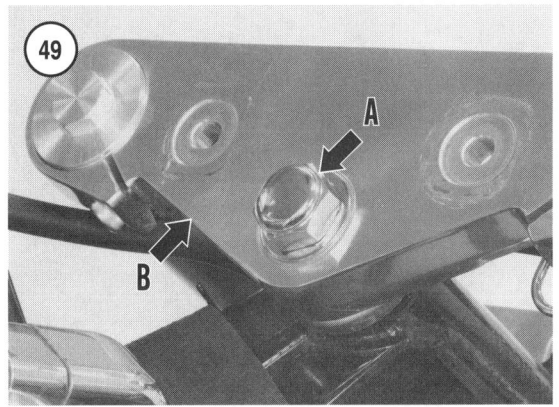

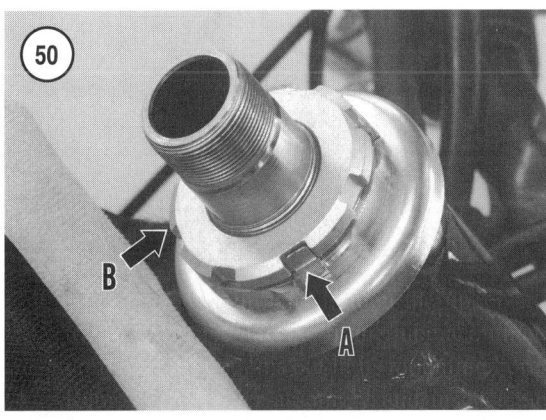

CAUTION
Support the weight of the steering stem assembly while removing the steering adjust nut, or it will drop out of the steering head.

17. Support the steering stem and remove the following:
    a. Steering adjust nut (**Figure 52**).
    b. Dust seal (**Figure 53**).
    c. Lower the steering stem and remove it and the lower bearing assembly (**Figure 54**) from the steering head.

d. Upper inner race and bearing assembly (**Figure 55**).

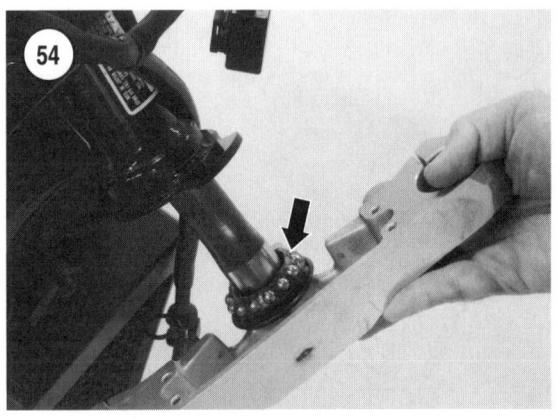

> **NOTE**
> *The upper outer race, lower outer race and lower inner race are installed with a press fit. Only remove these parts when replacing the bearing assembly.*

18. Inspect the steering assembly as described in this section.

Assembly/Adjustment/Installation

1. Make sure the upper and lower outer bearing races are properly seated in the steering head. Then lubricate each bearing race with grease.
2. Thoroughly lubricate each bearing (**Figure 56**) with grease.
3. Lubricate the upper dust seal bottom side with grease and set aside until installation.
4. Lower bearing:
    a. Lubricate the lower outer bearing race and dust seal lip (**Figure 57**) with grease.
    b. Install the lower bearing onto the lower inner race (**Figure 58**).
5. Upper bearing:
    a. Lubricate the upper inner bearing race with grease.
    b. Install the upper inner race into its bearing (**Figure 59**).
    c. Install the upper bearing and its inner race into the outer race in the steering head (**Figure 55**).
6. Install the steering stem (**Figure 54**) into the steering head and through the upper bearing race and hold in place. Make sure the lower bearing is centered inside the lower outer race.
7. Install the upper dust seal (**Figure 53**) and seat it over the bearing assembly with the seal side facing down.

> **NOTE**
> *The steering stem, steering nut and steering adjust nut threads must be clean for accurate tightening of these fasteners. Any dirt, grease and other residue on the threads can affect the steering stem tightening torque and bearing preload adjustment.*

8. Lubricate the steering adjust nut (**Figure 52**) threads with oil and thread it onto the steering stem. Tighten finger-tight.
9. Tighten the steering adjust nut (**Figure 52**) as follows:

FRONT SUSPENSION AND STEERING

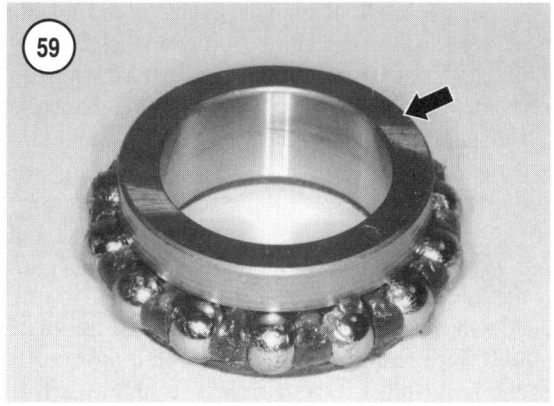

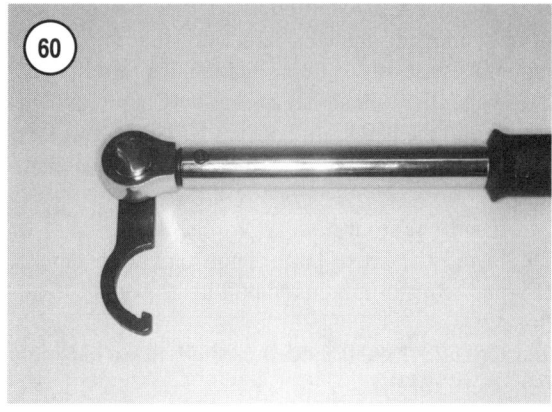

a. Use the steering stem socket or equivalent (**Figure 51**) to seat the bearings in the following steps.

NOTE
*If the steering stem socket is not available, use a spanner wrench and torque wrench (**Figure 60**) to seat the bearings. Refer to **Torque Adapters** in **Tools** in Chapter One for information.*

b. Tighten the steering adjust nut to 21 N•m (15.5 ft.-lb.).
c. Turn the steering stem from lock-to-lock five times to seat the bearings. The steering stem must pivot smoothly.
d. Loosen the steering adjust nut until it is finger-tight.
e. Retighten the steering adjust nut to 21 N•m (15.5 ft.-lb.). Then turn the steering stem from lock-to-lock five times to seat the bearings.
f. Repeat substep d and substep e several times.

NOTE
If the steering stem does not pivot smoothly, one or both bearing assemblies may be damaged. Remove the steering stem and inspect the bearings and races.

NOTE
Do not continue with Step 10 until the steering stem turns correctly. If there is excessive play or roughness, recheck the steering adjustment.

10. Align the tabs of a *new* lockwasher with the grooves in the steering adjust nut and install the lockwasher (**Figure 61**). The two outer tabs are bent into the locknut grooves after completing the adjustment.

WARNING
Never reinstall a used lockwasher, as the tabs may break off, making the lockwasher ineffective.

11. Install and tighten the steering locknut as follows:
    a. Install the steering locknut (B, **Figure 50**) and tighten finger-tight.
    b. Hold the steering adjust nut to keep it from turning and turn the steering locknut approximately 1/4 turn (90°) to align its grooves with the outer lockwasher tabs.
    c. Bend the outer lockwasher tabs (A, **Figure 50**) up into the locknut grooves.

12. Install the upper bridge (B, **Figure 49**), washer and steering nut (A).
13. Install the fork legs through both fork bridges and tighten the pinch bolts temporarily to hold the fork legs in place.
14. Tighten the steering nut (A, **Figure 49**) to 103 N•m (76 ft.-lb.).
15. Turn the steering stem lock-to-lock. Make sure it moves smoothly. There must be no play or binding. Note the following:
    a. If the steering stem turns correctly, continue with Step 16.
    b. If the steering stem is too loose or tight, remove the steering stem nut, washer and upper bridge. Then readjust the steering adjust nut. Repeat until the steering play feels correct. Damaged bearings and races can also cause tightness.

WARNING
If the steering adjustment is too loose, the steering becomes unstable and causes front wheel wobble. If the steering adjustment is too tight, the bearings eventually score or notch the races. The steering will then become sluggish as the damaged bearings and races operate against each other. Both conditions hamper steering performance.

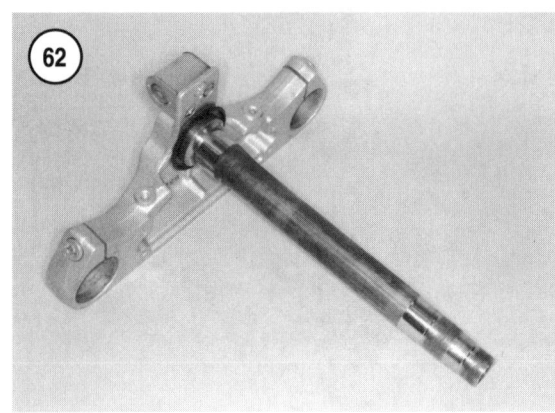

NOTE
Arriving at the proper steering adjustment usually comes down to the steering effort required to turn the handlebar. The number of attempts required to arrive at the correct steering adjustment (feel) can vary.

16. When the steering adjustment is correct, remove the fork legs. With the fork legs removed, check that the steering stem moves smoothly with no excessive play or roughness.

NOTE
When continuing with the following steps, make sure to correctly route the cables and wiring harnesses.

17. On VTX1300R/S/T models, install the lower and upper fork covers. Tighten the bolts to 12 N•m (106 in.-lb.).
18. Install the fork legs as described in this chapter.
19. On VTX1300R/S/T models, if the lower handlebar holders were removed, perform the following:
    a. Install the lower handlebar holders onto the upper bracket and secure with the washers and nuts. Partially tighten the nuts until the holders are snug but can still be turned by hand.
    b. Temporarily install the handlebar as described in this chapter. Make sure the handlebar seats squarely against the upper and lower holders.
    c. Tighten the lower handlebar holder nuts to 64 N•m (47 ft.-lb.). Make sure the handlebar and handlebar holders feel tight and secure.
    d. Remove the handlebar.
20A. On VTX1300C, R and S models, if the cable guides were removed, install them onto the bottom of the upper bracket using new bolts and tighten to 21 N•m (15.5 ft.-lb.).
20B. On VTX1300T models, if the cables guides were removed, install them and the windshield mounting brackets as described in Chapter Fifteen.
21. Install the turn signal assembly (Chapter Nine).
22. Install the headlight housing (Chapter Nine).
23. Install the handlebar as described in this chapter.
24. Install the front wheel (Chapter Ten).
25. Install the brake hose clamp mounting bracket (**Figure 48**) and tighten the bolt to 12 N•m (106 in.-lb.).
26. On VTX1300T models, install the windshield (Chapter Fifteen).
27. Perform the *Steering Bearing Preload Check* in this chapter.

WARNING
Do not ride the motorcycle until all of the controls and brakes work properly.

Inspection

Replace parts that show excessive wear or damage.

WARNING
The improper repair of damaged frame and steering components can cause

FRONT SUSPENSION AND STEERING

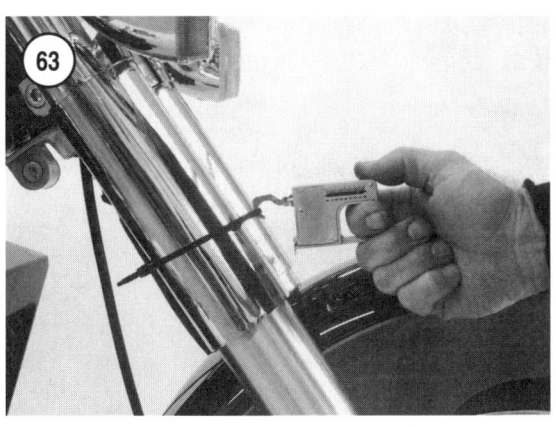

the loss of steering control. If there is apparent frame, steering stem or fork bridge damage, consult with a dealership or qualified frame shop for professional inspection and possible repair.

1. Clean and dry all parts. Make certain the cleaning solution is compatible with the rubber dust seals.
2. Check the frame for cracks and fractures.
3. Inspect the steering stem nut, locknut, and steering adjust nut for excessive wear or damage.
4. Inspect the upper dust seal for tearing, deterioration or other damage.
5. Check the steering stem (**Figure 62**) for:
   a. Cracked or bent stem.
   b. Damaged lower bridge.
   c. Damaged threads.
6. Check the upper bridge for cracks or other damage. Replace if necessary.
7. Inspect the bearing assemblies as follows:
   a. Inspect the bearing races for severe wear, pitting, cracks or other damage. To replace the outer bearing races, refer to *Steering Head Bearing Race* in this chapter. To replace the lower inner race, refer to *Steering Stem Bearing Race* in this chapter.
   b. Inspect the upper and lower bearings (**Figure 56**) for dents, pitting, excessive wear, corrosion, retainer damage or discoloration.
   c. Replace the upper and lower bearing assemblies at the same time.
8. When reusing bearings, clean them thoroughly with a bearing degreaser and dry thoroughly. Repack each bearing with grease.

STEERING BEARING PRELOAD CHECK

Proper steering bearing preload controls bearing play and steering control. If the preload is too loose, excessive play in the steering allows the wheel to wobble, which causes side-to-side movement or oscillation of the handlebar. A wobble may occur at all speeds or start and then stop at certain speeds. The condition can be difficult to troubleshoot. If the preload is too tight, the bearings and races suffer unnecessary wear and cause stiff and uneven steering, requiring the rider to make a greater steering effort when turning the handlebars. Dry or damaged bearings can cause similar conditions.

Check the steering head for looseness at the intervals specified in Chapter Three or whenever the following symptoms or conditions exist:
1. The handlebars vibrate more than normal.
2. The front fork makes a clicking or clunking noise when the front brake is applied.
3. The steering feels tight or slow.
4. The motorcycle does not steer straight on level road surfaces.

Inspection

When installing the steering stem assembly, the steering bearings are preloaded (bearing placed under pressure) by tightening the steering adjust nut and the steering nut. To check bearing preload, the manufacturer specifies the use of a spring scale attached to one of the fork legs. This method measures the amount of weight required to move the steering stem with the front end assembled and the front wheel off the ground. When measuring bearing preload with a spring scale, the steering stem must be free to turn without interference from any cable, hose or wiring harness.

NOTE
This procedure must be performed with the front fork legs and front wheel mounted on the motorcycle.

1. Support the motorcycle so it is sitting level with the front wheel off the ground. The motorcycle must be secure to prevent any false movements.
2. Turn the steering stem side-to-side. There should be no interference or drag from a cable, wire harness or the front brake hose when the steering stem is rotated. If there is interference, reposition or remove the affecting part as required.
3. Attach a plastic zip tie onto one of the fork tubes between the fork bridges. Then attach a spring scale onto the zip tie (**Figure 63**).
4. Center the wheel. Position the spring scale at a 90° angle with the steering stem (**Figure 64**). Pull the spring scale and note the reading on the scale when the steering stem begins to turn. This reading is steering bearing preload. Refer to **Table 1** for the correct steering preload reading.

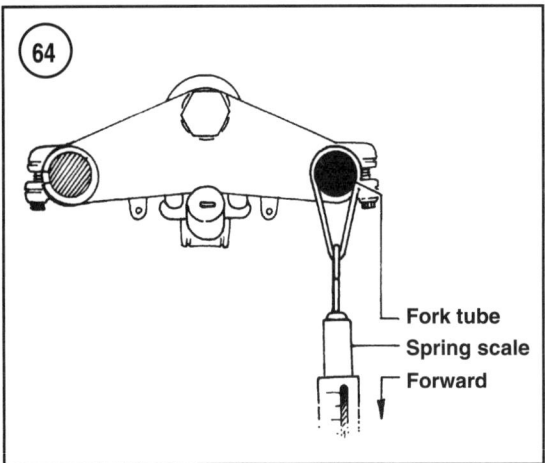

5. If the preload reading is incorrect, adjust the steering assembly as described in *Assembly/Adjustment/Installation* in S*teering Head and Stem* in this chapter. Perform the adjustment with the front forks and front wheel mounted on the motorcycle.

STEERING HEAD BEARING RACE

The steering head bearing races (**Figure 65** and **Figure 66**) are pressed into the frame's steering head. The bearing races should only be removed when new races will be installed.

A threaded rod and disc tool (**Figure 67**) will be used to install the races. When properly used, this tool exerts even pressure around the race. One disc is sized to fit the outer diameter of the races, while the other disc is slightly larger than the diameter of the steering head. This tool is shown in the following procedure.

Replace both bearing races and bearings at the same time.

Removal/Installation

1. Chill the new bearing races in a freezer for a few hours to shrink the outer diameter of the race as much as possible.
2. Insert a drift into the steering head and position it on the edge of the lower race (**Figure 68**). Drive out the race. To prevent binding, make several passes around the perimeter of the race. Repeat the procedure to remove the upper race.
3. Clean the race bores in the frame and check for damage.
4. To install the upper race, do the following:
   a. Place the new upper race (**Figure 69**) squarely into the mounting bore opening with its bearing side facing out.

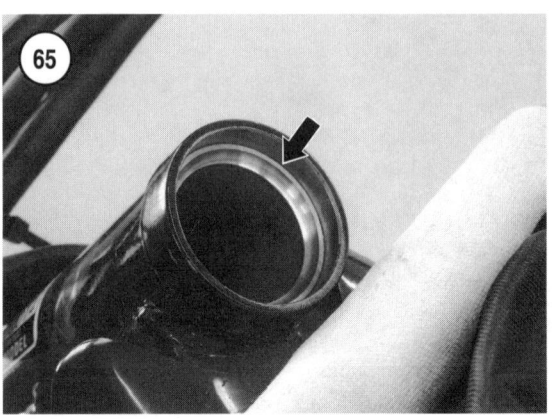

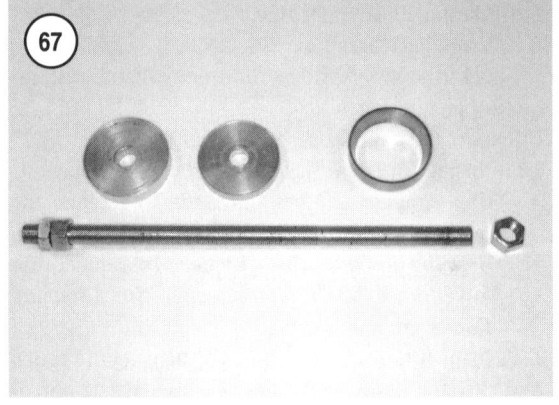

   b. Assemble the threaded rod tool as shown in **Figure 70**.

CAUTION
If there is any binding when installing the bearing races in the following steps, stop and release all tension from the bearing race. Check the tool alignment to make sure the bearing race is moving evenly in its mounting bore. Otherwise, the bearing race may gouge the frame mounting bore and cause permanent damage.

FRONT SUSPENSION AND STEERING

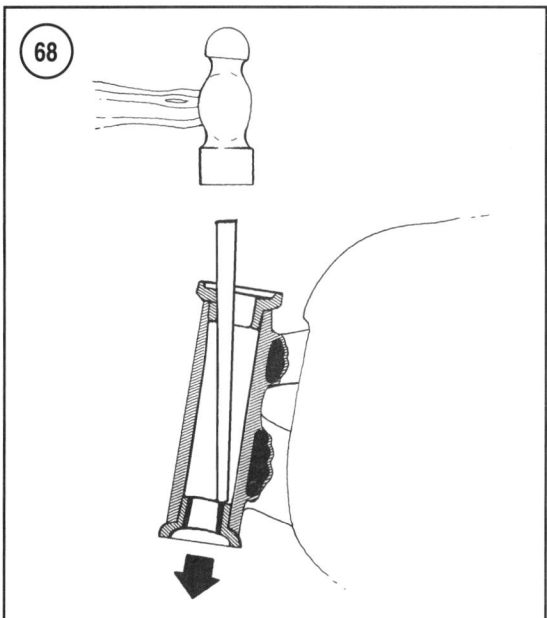

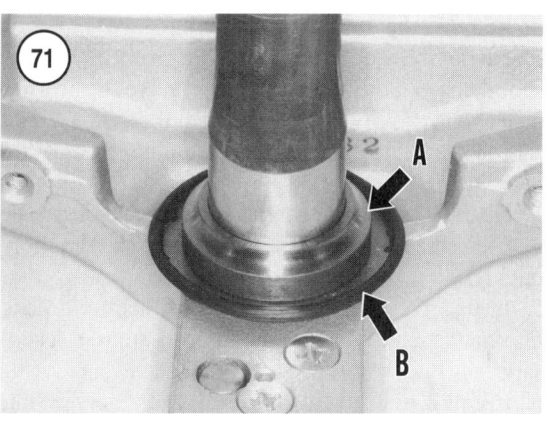

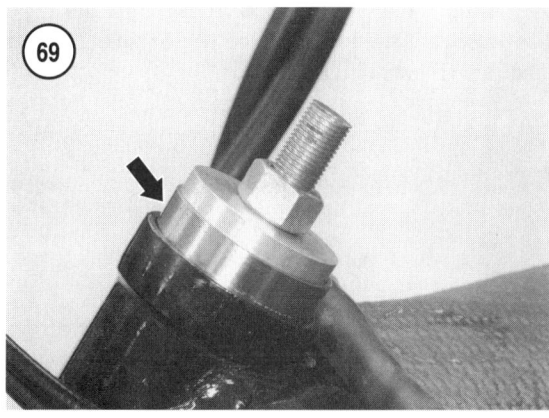

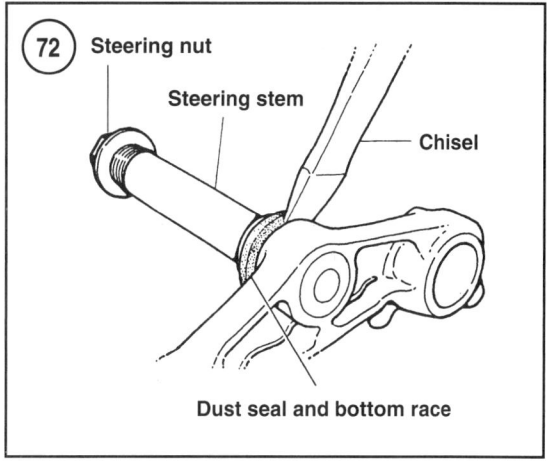

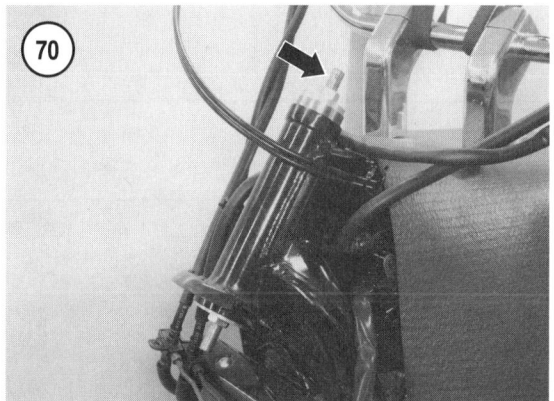

c. Hold the lower nut and tighten the upper nut to draw the race into the frame tube. Continue until the race bottoms out in its mounting bore. Remove the puller assembly and inspect the bearing race. It must seat fully and squarely in the frame tube (**Figure 65**).

CAUTION
Do not allow the installer shaft to contact the bearing race.

5. Reverse the tool and repeat Step 3 to install the lower race (**Figure 66**). Insert the threaded rod tool carefully through the frame to avoid scratching the upper bearing race.
6. Lubricate the upper and lower bearing races with grease.

STEERING STEM BEARING RACE

The lower inner race (A, **Figure 71**) is a press fit on the steering stem. Replace the lower dust seal (B, **Figure 71**) when replacing the lower inner race.

Removal/Installation

1. Thread the steering nut onto the steering stem (**Figure 72**) to help avoid damaging the steering stem threads.

WARNING
Wear safety glasses in Step 2 to prevent eye injury.

2. Remove the lower inner bearing race and dust seal with a chisel as shown in **Figure 72**. To prevent damaging the steering stem, remove the bearing race evenly. Apply pressure against the bearing race a little at a time and at different points around the bearing.
3. Discard the lower inner bearing race and dust seal.
4. Clean the steering stem with solvent and dry thoroughly.
5. Inspect the steering stem race surface for cracks or other damage. Replace the steering stem if necessary.
6. Install a new lower dust seal over the steering stem.
7. Slide the new lower inner bearing race with the bearing surface facing up onto the steering stem until it stops.
8. Install the steering stem in a press. Support the bottom of the steering stem with a bearing driver or piece of round metal. Then install a bearing driver (**Figure 73**) over the steering stem and seat it against the inner bearing race inside shoulder. Do not allow the bearing driver to contact the bearing race surface.

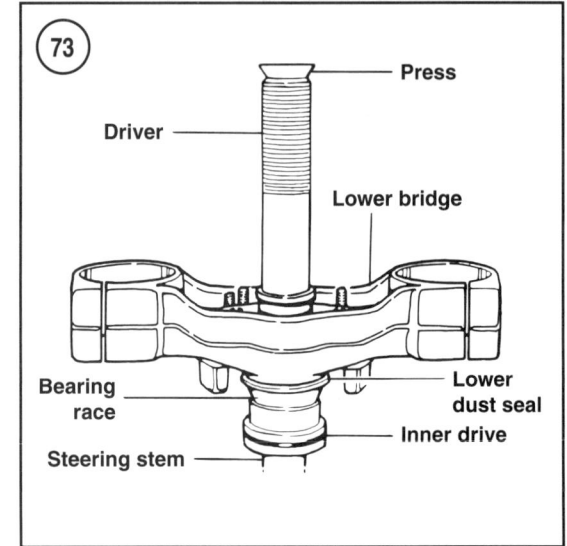

9. Press the lower inner race onto the steering stem until it bottoms.
10. Remove the steering stem from the press.
11. Lubricate the bearing race (A, **Figure 71**) and dust seal (B) with grease.

Table 1 FRONT SUSPENSION AND STEERING SPECIFICATIONS

Front axle travel	110 mm (4.3 in.)
Handlebar outside diameter	25.4 mm (1 in.)
Steering	
Caster angle	32°
Trail length	
VTX1300C models	149 mm (5.9 in.)
VTX1300 R/S/T models	144 mm (5.7 in.)
Steering bearing preload	0.8-1.2 kg (1.8-2.6 lbs.)

Table 2 FRONT FORK SERVICE SPECIFICATIONS

Fork tube runout limit	0.20 mm (0.008 in.)
Fork oil capacity	
VTX1300C models	454.5-459.5 ml (15.4-15.5 oz.)
VTX1300R/S/T models	456.5-461.5 ml (15.4-15.6 oz.)
Fork oil level	
VTX1300C models	125 mm (4.9 in.)
VTX1300R/S/T models	135 mm (5.3 in.)
Fork oil type	Pro Honda Suspension Fluid SS-8 or equivalent 10 wt. fork oil
Spring free length	
VTX1300C models	
New	461.7 mm (18.18 in.)
Service limit	452.5 mm (17.81 in.)
VTX1300R/S/T models	
New	493.8 mm (19.44 in.)
Service limit	483.9 mm (19.05 in.)

Table 3 FRONT SUSPENSION AND STEERING TORQUE SPECIFICATIONS

	N•m	in.-lb.	ft.-lb.
Brake hose clamp bolt	12	106	–
Cable guide bolt*	21	–	15.5
Damper rod Allen bolt*	20	–	15
Fork cap	22	–	16
Fork cover bolt			
VTX1300R/S/T models	12	106	–
Fork tube pinch bolt			
Lower	49	–	36
Upper	22	–	16
Front brake caliper mounting bolt*	31	–	23
Front master cylinder clamp bolt	12	106	–
Handlebar mounting nut			
VTX1300C models	64	–	47
Handlebar holders			
VTX1300R/S/T models			
Upper Allen bolts	27	–	20
Lower nuts	64	–	47
Steering adjust nut*	21	–	15.5
Steering locknut	Refer to text		
Steering nut	103	–	76

*Refer to text for additional information.

CHAPTER THIRTEEN

REAR SUSPENSION

This chapter covers the rear suspension, drive shaft and final drive components. **Tables 1-5** are at the end of this chapter.

Rear wheel, hub and tire service are covered in Chapter Eleven.

SHOCK ABSORBER

The shocks are sealed units. Do not attempt to replace the shock spring or disassemble the shock in anyway. Service is limited to shock adjustment and replacing the shock mount dampers installed in each end of the shock absorber.

Adjustment

WARNING
Both shock absorbers must be adjusted to the same preload number or an unstable riding condition may result.

Each shock absorber can be adjusted to any of 5 spring preload settings. The softest setting is No. 1 and the stiffest setting is No. 5. The standard factory setting is No. 2. Adjust the shock absorbers to best suit different load and riding conditions.

1. Remove the tool kit and assemble the spanner wrench and its extension bar.

CAUTION
Adjust the shock absorber in single increments. For example, if the shock is in position No. 2 and it is necessary to adjust the spring to position No. 5, turn the adjuster to the No. 3, No. 4 and then to position No. 5. Do not turn the adjuster directly from the No. 2 to the No. 5 position without stopping at the other adjustment numbers or the adjuster may be damaged.

2. Using the spanner wrench, adjust the shock absorber to the desired adjustment position (**Figure 1**).
3. Adjust the other shock to the same setting.

Removal/Installation

Remove and install the shocks one at a time. The remaining unit will support the rear of the motorcycle and maintain the correct relationship between the top and bottom mounts.

1. Support the motorcycle so the rear wheel clears the ground.

REAR SUSPENSION

1

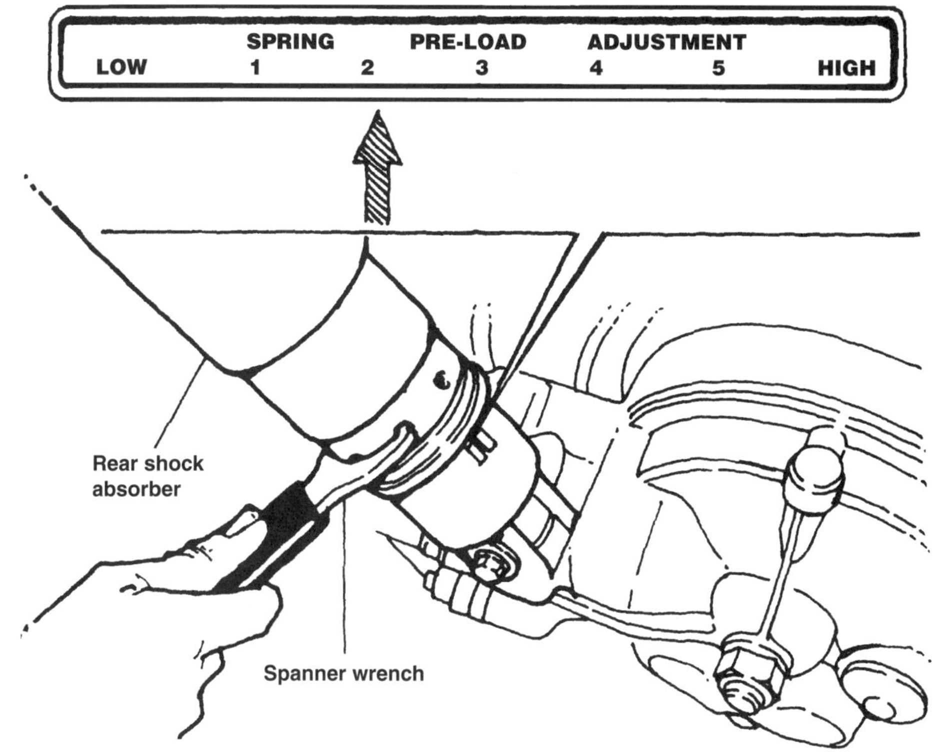

REAR SHOCK ADJUSTMENT

| LOW | SPRING 1 2 | PRE-LOAD 3 | ADJUSTMENT 4 5 | HIGH |

Rear shock absorber

Spanner wrench

2. If the exhaust system interferes with the right shock absorber's lower mounting bolts, loosen the muffler fasteners to provide clearance for removing the lower mounting bolt. Refer to Chapter Fifteen.

3. Remove the upper and lower shock mounting bolts (**Figure 2**) and outer washers and remove the shock absorber. When removing the left shock absorber, remove the inner washer installed on the lower mounting bolt (**Figure 3**).

4. Inspect the shock absorber as described in this section.

5. Installation is the reverse of removal. Note the following:
   a. Install the shock absorber with its adjustment decal facing toward the rear of the motorcycle.
   b. The upper mounting bolts are longer than the lower mounting bolts.
   c. Install the inner washer (**Figure 3**) between the lower left shock mount and the final drive housing.
   d. Tighten the shock absorber mounting bolts (**Figure 2**) to 26 N•m (19 ft.-lb.).
   e. If the muffler fasteners were loosened, identify and tighten them as described in Chapter Fifteen.

Inspection

1. Inspect the shock absorber (A, **Figure 4**) for oil leaks or other damage. Replace the shock absorber if it is leaking.
2. Inspect the upper and lower shock dampers (B, **Figure 4**) for severe wear, age deterioration, hardness or other damage. If necessary, replace the dampers as describe in Step 3.
3. To replace the shock dampers, perform the following:
   a. Assemble a socket, driver and threaded rod with two nuts and install through one of the shock dampers as shown in **Figure 5**. The deep socket must be large enough to accept the damper as it is pressed out.
   b. Hold the nut placed against the socket and turn the other nut to press the damper out of the shock damper bore.
   c. Clean the shock damper bore.
   d. Assemble the threaded rod so the damper is placed against one side of the shock damper bore and the driver is placed against the shock damper. A thick metal plate can be used in place of the socket used during removal. Hold the nut on the opposite side of the damper and turn the other nut to press the damper into the shock damper bore. Refer to **Figure 6**.
   e. Remove the tools and inspect the damper for proper installation.
   f. Repeat to replace the other damper.

SWING ARM

Tools

The following tools are required to remove and install the swing arm:
1. Pivot adjust wrench (part No. 07908-4690003 [A, **Figure 7**]). This wrench is used as a torque adapter when loosening and tightening the right swing arm pivot bolt locknut.
2. 17-mm hex socket (B, **Figure 7**).

Removal

1. Remove the exhaust system (Chapter Fifteen) if it interferes with removal of the right swing arm pivot bolt.
2. Remove the left crankcase rear cover (Chapter Fifteen).
3. Remove the rear wheel (Chapter Eleven).
4. Remove the rear shock absorbers as described in this chapter.
5. Remove the final drive unit and drive shaft as described in this chapter.

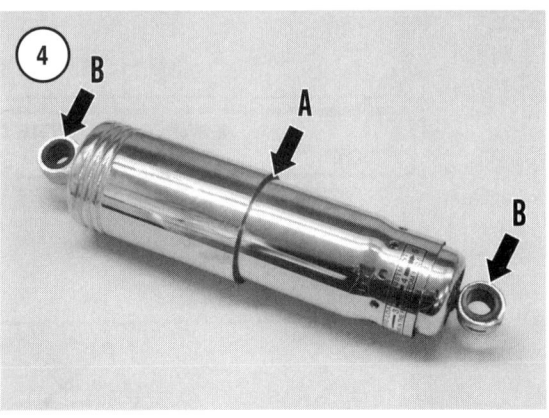
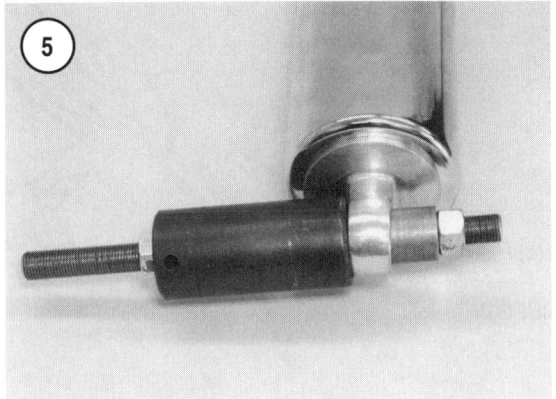
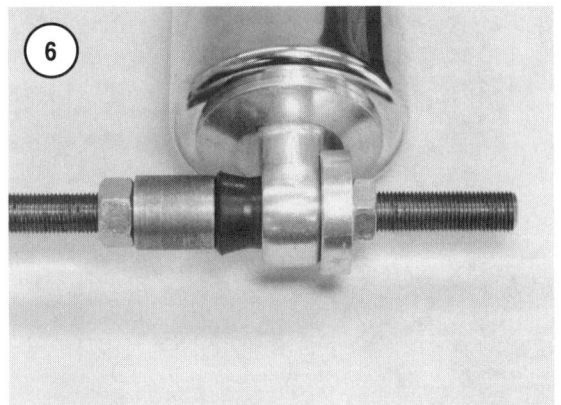
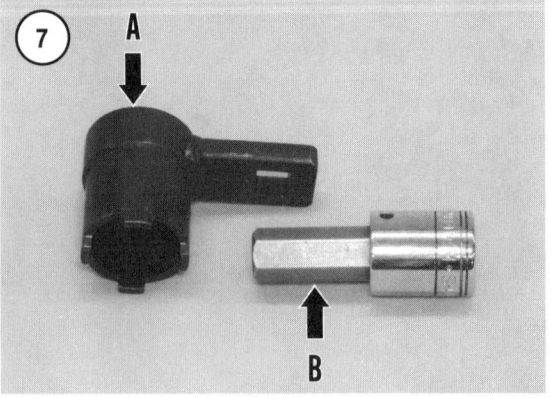

REAR SUSPENSION

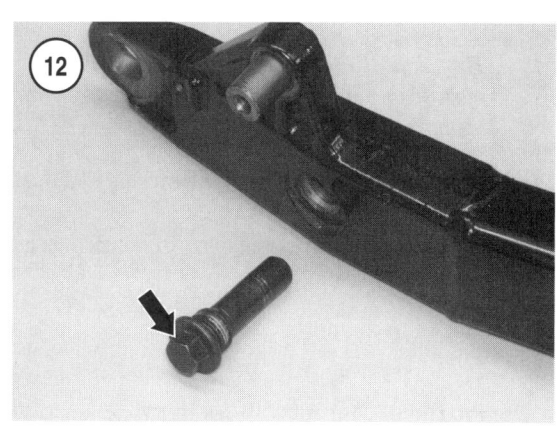

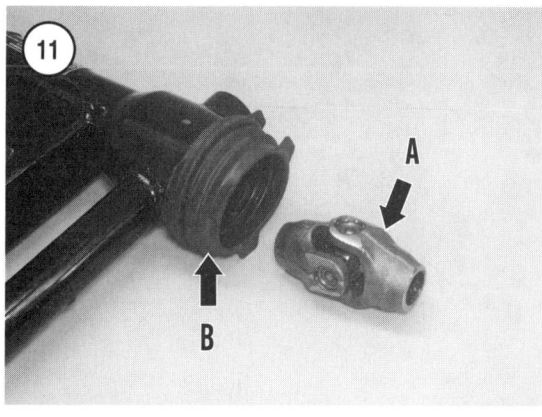

6A. On 2003-2006 models, remove the brake hose clamp bolts from the right side of the swing arm. Then slip the brake hose out of the guide clamps welded onto the swing arm.

6B. On 2007-on models, remove the brake hose clamp bolt. Then slide the brake hose out of the guide clamps welded onto the swing arm.

NOTE
Have an assistant steady the motorcycle when performing Step 7.

7. Grasp the rear end of the swing arm and try to move it from side to side in a horizontal arc. There must be no noticeable side play. Then grasp the rear of the swing arm and pivot it up and down through its full travel. The swing arm must pivot smoothly. If excessive play or binding is evident and the pivot bolts are tightened correctly, inspect the swing arm bearings as described in this section for severe wear or damage.

8. Remove the left and right side swing arm pivot caps.

9. Use the pivot adjust wrench (A, **Figure 8**) to loosen and remove the right pivot bolt locknut (A, **Figure 9**).

10. Use the 17-mm hex socket (B, **Figure 7**) to loosen (B, **Figure 8**) and remove the right pivot bolt (B, **Figure 9**).

11. Loosen and remove the left pivot bolt (A, **Figure 10**) and swing arm.

12. Remove the universal joint (A, **Figure 11**) and boot (B) from the swing arm.

13. Remove the caliper stopper pin bolt (**Figure 12**) from the swing arm if it was not removed earlier. A new bolt must be installed if the bolt is removed.

NOTE
Identify the bearings if they are going to be reused.

NOTE
*The seals (**Figure 13**) are an integral part of the bearings. Do not separate them from the bearings.*

14. Remove the left and right side bearings and dust seals (A, **Figure 14**).
15. Clean and inspect the swing arm and bearings as described in this section.

Installation

Use Pro Honda Moly 60 Paste or molybdenum disulfide grease when grease is called for in the following steps, unless otherwise specified.

1. Install the boot (B, **Figure 11**) by sliding its large outside diameter end onto the swing arm.
2. Lubricate the bearings (A, **Figure 14**) and races (B) with grease.
3. Install the left and right side bearings and dust seals into the swing arm (**Figure 13**).
4. Install the caliper stopper pin bolt (**Figure 12**) into the swing arm. Refer to *Installation* in *Rear Wheel* in Chapter Eleven for caliper stopper pin bolt tightening procedures.
5. Clean the splines on the output driven gear shaft (**Figure 15**) and lubricate with grease.
6. Lubricate the splines in both ends of the universal joint (A, **Figure 16**) with grease.
7. Remove the drive shaft from the final drive unit and install it into the swing arm (A, **Figure 17**). Then install the universal joint (B, **Figure 17**) onto the end of the drive shaft. Slide the universal joint and drive shaft back into the swing arm until the front end of the universal joint is even with the end of the boot.

NOTE
An assistant will be required to hold the swing arm in place in Step 8 until the pivot bolts are installed in Step 9.

8. Install the swing arm into the frame and hold it in place, then use the end of the drive shaft to install the universal joint onto the output shaft. Continue to hold the swing arm in place.
9. Install the pivot bolts as follows:
   a. Lubricate the machined end (A, **Figure 18**) on both pivot bolts with lithium grease. Do not lubricate the pivot bolt or frame threads.
   b. Align the left swing arm pivot flange with the frame hole, then install the left pivot bolt (B, **Figure 18**).
   c. Install the right swing arm pivot bolt (C, **Figure 18**).
   d. Hand-tighten each pivot bolt, then pivot the swing arm to make sure both pivot bolts are

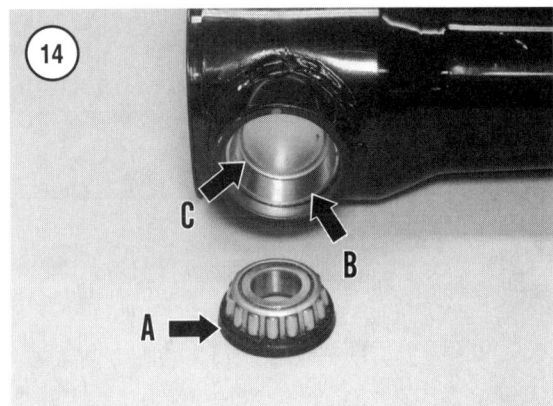

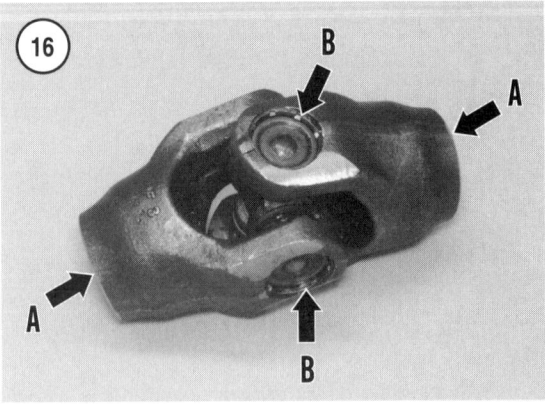

REAR SUSPENSION

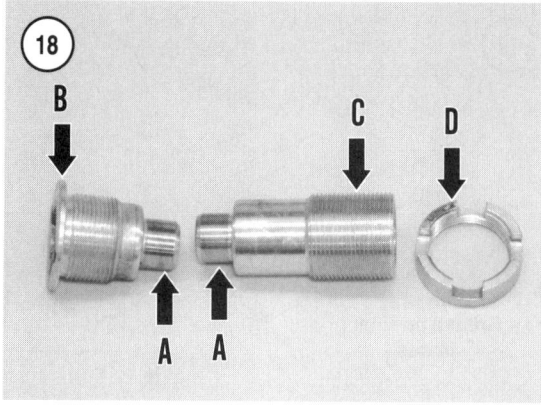

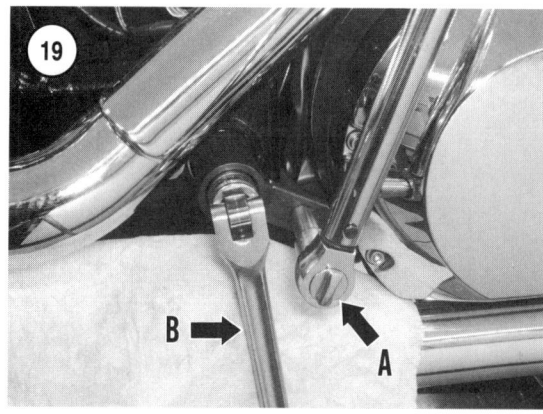

properly installed inside the swing arm bearings.

10. Tighten the left swing arm pivot bolt (A, **Figure 10**) to 103 N•m (76 ft.-lb.).
11. Tighten the right swing arm pivot bolt (B, **Figure 9**) to 14 N•m (10 ft.-lb.).
12. Pivot the swing arm several times to help seat the pivot bearings and to check for roughness and binding.

NOTE
Mount the torque wrench onto the pivot adjust wrench at a right angle as shown

in A, Figure 19. If the torque wrench is mounted so it lengthens the wrench, the torque applied to the locknut will be incorrect (too high). Refer to Torque Adapters in Tools in Chapter One for more information.

13. Install the right pivot bolt locknut (A, **Figure 9**). Hold the right pivot bolt with a 17 mm hex socket (B, **Figure 19**) and tighten the right pivot bolt locknut with the pivot adjust wrench (A) to 113 N•m (83 ft.-lb.).
14. Pivot the swing arm several times. There must be no binding or roughness.
15. Install the left and right side swing arm pivot caps.
16. Install the drive shaft and final drive unit as described in this chapter.
17. Install the boot (B, **Figure 10**) over the output gearcase.
18A. On 2003-2006 models, install the brake hose onto the swing arm guide clamp. Install new brake hose clamp bolts and tighten to 12 N•m (106 in.-lb.).
18B. On 2007-on models, install the brake hose onto the swing arm guide clamps. Install a new brake hose clamp bolt and tighten to 12 N•m (106 in.-lb.).
19. Install the rear shock absorbers as described in this chapter.
20. Install the left crankcase cover (Chapter Fifteen).
21. If removed, install the exhaust system as described in Chapter Fifteen.

Inspection

Swing arm

1. Clean and dry the parts.
2. Clean the frame threads.
3. Inspect the swing arm for cracks and other damage.
4. Inspect each bearing (A, **Figure 14**) and race (B) for severe wear, pitting or other damage. If necessary, replace the bearing races and grease retainer plates (C) as described in this section.
5. Check that each grease retainer plate (C, **Figure 14**) fits tightly in the swing arm.
6. Inspect the pivot bolts (B and C, **Figure 18**) for severe wear, thread damage or corrosion. Make sure the machined end (A, **Figure 18**) on each pivot bolt is smooth. Replace if necessary.
7. Replace the locknut (D, **Figure 18**) if damaged.
8. Replace the boot (B, **Figure 11**) if damaged.

Universal joint

1. Make sure the universal joint pivots smoothly (B, **Figure 16**) with no binding or roughness.

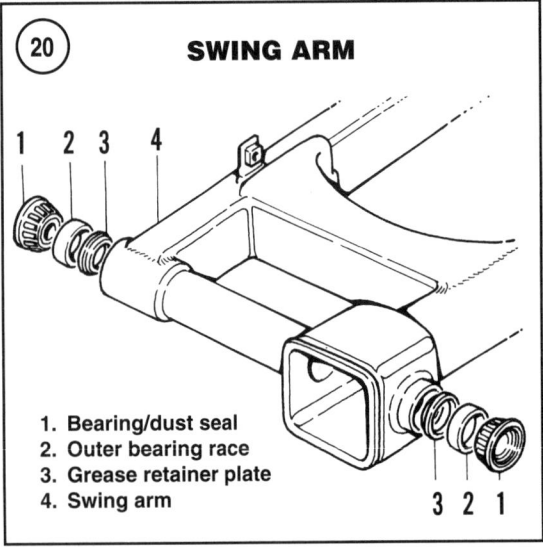

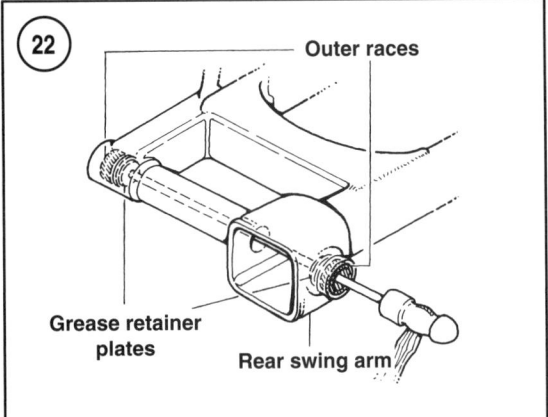

1. Bearing/dust seal
2. Outer bearing race
3. Grease retainer plate
4. Swing arm

2. Inspect both universal joint spline ends (A, **Figure 16**) for damage. If these splines are damaged, inspect the mating drive shaft splines for damage.
3. The universal joint cannot be rebuilt. Replace it if it is damaged.

Grease Retainer and Bearing Race Removal/Installation

Replace the left and right side bearings and races (**Figure 20**) at the same time.
1. Drill a suitable size hole through one of the grease retainer plates (**Figure 21**).
2. Insert a drift through this hole (**Figure 22**) and drive out the opposite bearing race and grease retainer plate.
3. Repeat Step 2 to remove the opposite bearing race and grease retainer plate.
4. Clean the bearing race seating areas in the swing arm.
5. Use a bearing driver (**Figure 23**) to drive a new grease retainer (C, **Figure 14**) and bearing race (B, **Figure 14**) into each side of the swing arm.
6. Lubricate each bearing race with lithium grease.

FINAL DRIVE UNIT AND DRIVE SHAFT

Removal

Refer to **Figure 24**.
1. Drain the final drive oil (Chapter Three).
2. Remove the rear wheel (Chapter Eleven).
3. Remove the bolt (A, **Figure 25**), inner and outer washers and disconnect the shock absorber at the final drive unit.
4. Remove the nuts (B, **Figure 25**) and the final drive unit with drive shaft attached (C).

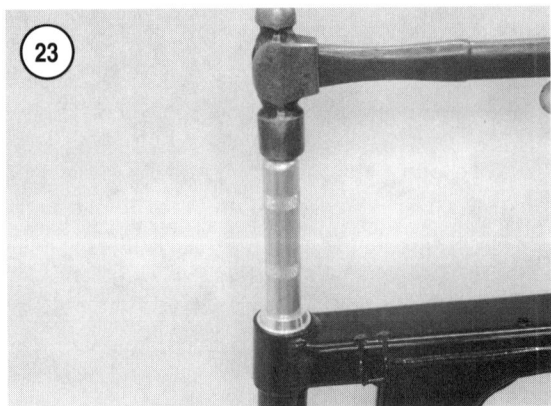

5. Hold the final drive unit, then turn and pull the drive shaft out (A, **Figure 26**).
6. Remove the spring (A, **Figure 27**), stopper ring (B) and seal (C). Discard the stopper ring and seal.
7. Inspect and service the final drive unit and drive shaft as described in this chapter.

Installation

Use Pro Honda Moly 60 Paste or molybdenum disulfide grease when grease is called for in the following steps.

REAR SUSPENSION

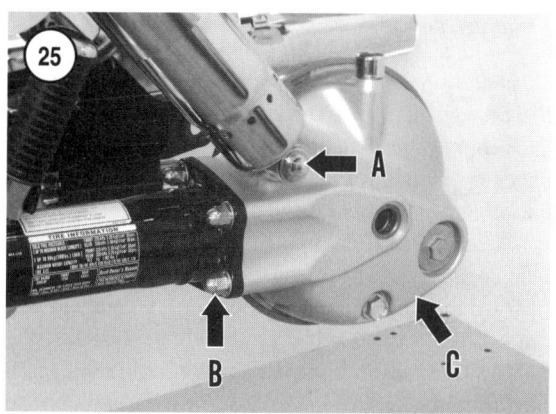

DRIVE SHAFT

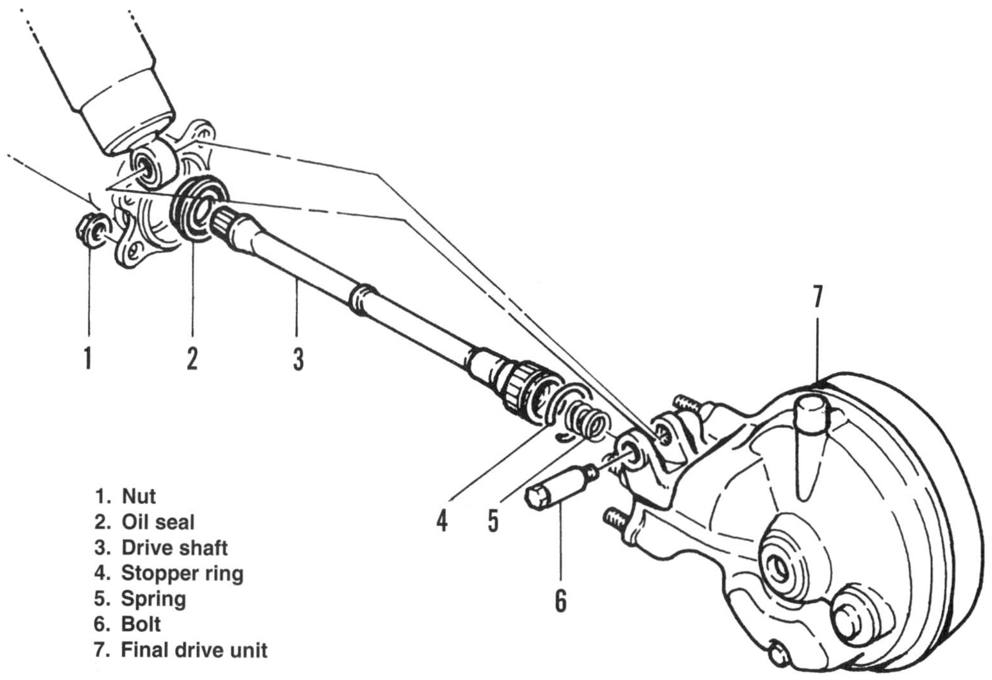

1. Nut
2. Oil seal
3. Drive shaft
4. Stopper ring
5. Spring
6. Bolt
7. Final drive unit

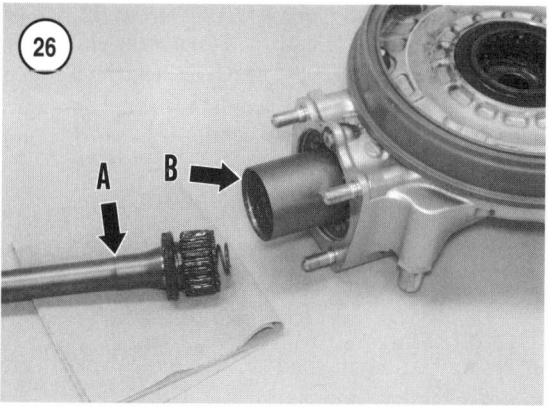

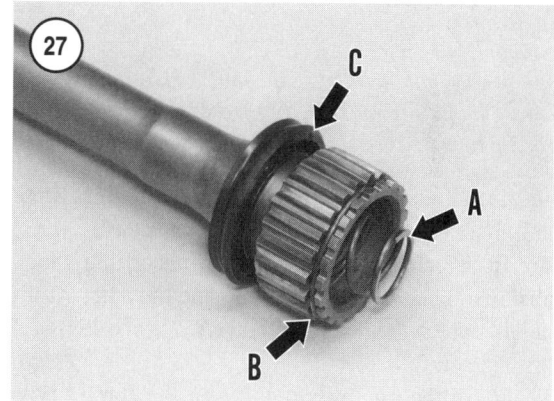

1. Install a new stopper ring (B, **Figure 27**) into the drive shaft groove. The stopper ring is a loose fit as it is designed to close around the drive shaft groove when installed inside the pinion joint.
2. Pack the lips of a new oil seal (C, **Figure 27**) with grease and install with the closed side facing away from the stopper ring.
3. Install the spring (A, **Figure 27**) into the end of the drive shaft.
4. Pack 2 g (0.08 oz) of grease into the pinion joint spline (B, **Figure 26**).
5. Align the drive shaft splines with the pinion joint splines and install the drive shaft until the stopper

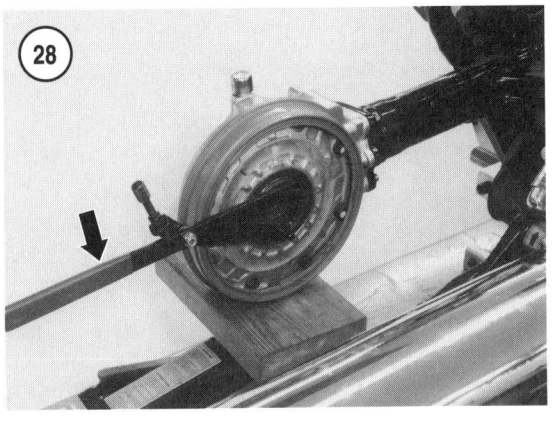

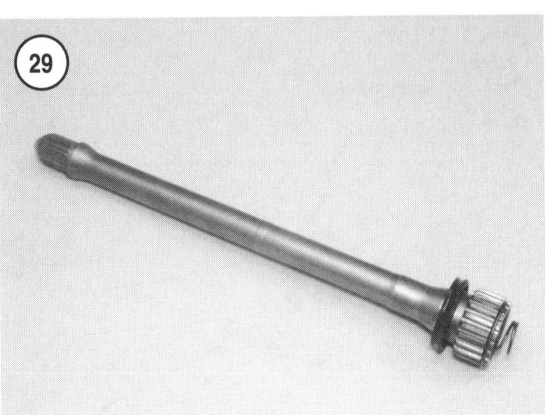

ring seats into the pinion joint spline groove. Lightly pull back on the drive shaft to make sure the stopper ring is properly seated in the groove.

6. Tap the oil seal into the pinion joint.
7. Pack 1 g (0.04 oz) of grease into the drive shaft splines.
8. Shift the transmission into gear. Insert the drive shaft through the swing arm and engage with universal joint splines. If necessary, use a flywheel holder (or similar tool) to turn the ring gear (**Figure 28**) to align the drive shaft and universal joint splines.
9. Push the final drive unit (C, **Figure 25**) studs through the holes in the swing arm and install the nuts finger-tight.

NOTE
*Do not tighten the final drive unit mounting nuts (B, **Figure 25**) until the rear wheel is installed.*

10. Install the rear wheel and tighten the final drive unit mounting nuts as described in Chapter Eleven.
11. Install the inner washer, then install the shock absorber onto the final drive unit and the outer washer and tighten the mounting bolt (A, **Figure 25**) to 26 N•m (19 ft.-lb.).
12. Refill the final drive unit with the correct type and quantity of gear oil (Chapter Three).

Inspection

Drive shaft

1. Clean and dry the drive shaft and spring.
2. Check the drive shaft (**Figure 29**) for damage.

NOTE
To inspect and service the universal joint, remove the swing arm as described in this chapter.

3. Replace the spring (A, **Figure 27**) if damaged.

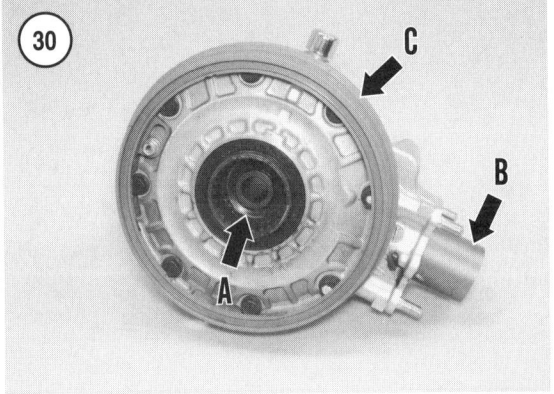

Final drive unit

If additional service or inspection is required, refer to *Final Drive Unit Overhaul* in this chapter.

1. Remove the distance collar (A, **Figure 30**) and check both ends for damage. Reinstall the machined end first into the final drive unit.
2. Check for oil leaks at the pinion shaft and ring gear seals. If either seal is leaking, the corresponding bearing may be worn and allowing the shaft to run out of true.
3. Turn the pinion joint (B, **Figure 30**). If the gears turn roughly, first remove the oil fill cap and check the ring gear for damage. If necessary, disassemble the unit and check for wear and damage.
4. Check for loose or damaged final drive unit studs. Replace damaged studs as described in *Service Methods* in Chapter One. Apply a medium strength threadlocking compound onto the stud threads and install to the dimension shown in **Figure 31**.

FINAL DRIVE UNIT OVERHAUL

Tools

Before beginning final drive overhaul, have the following tools available:

REAR SUSPENSION

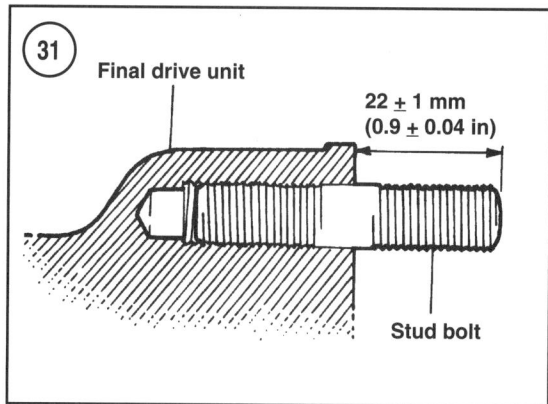

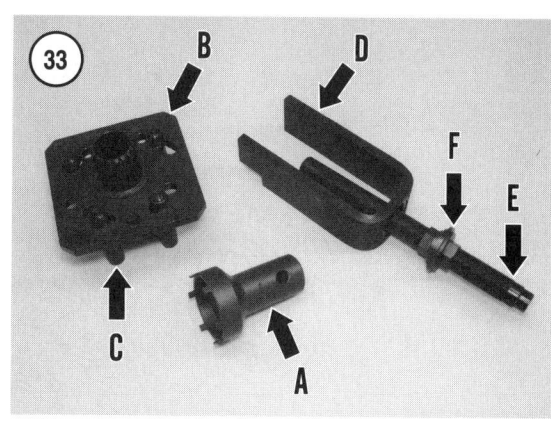

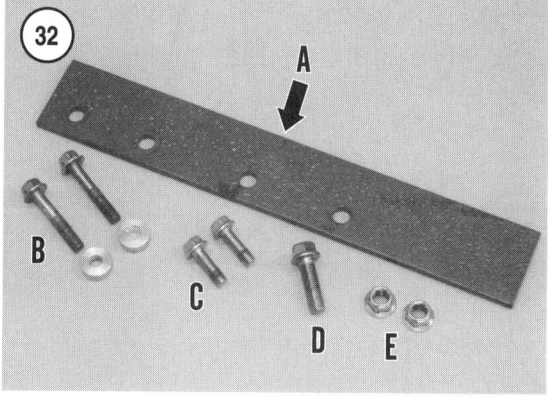

1. A holding fixture is recommended for final drive overhaul. A holding fixture can be made by drilling holes in a flat steel plate (A, **Figure 32**) and using the appropriate metric fasteners as follows:
   a. Flat steel plate (1/4 in. thick × 12 in. × 2 in.).
   b. Two 8–1.25 × 45 mm bolts and spacers approximately 8 mm thick (B, **Figure 32**).
   c. Two 8–1.25 × 25 mm bolts (C, **Figure 32**).
   d. One 10–1.25 × 32 mm bolt (D, **Figure 32**).
   e. Two 10–1.25 mm nuts (E, **Figure 32**).
2. A sturdy vise is recommended to support the holding fixture/final drive unit during use.
3. A heat gun is required when replacing some of the bearings pressed into the housing. Make sure the heat gun can supply and maintain the heat specified in the text. Monitor temperature with heat sticks or an infrared thermometer.
4. A retainer wrench (A, **Figure 33** [part No. 07910-4630100]) is required to loosen and tighten the pinion retainer.
5. A pinion holder plate (B, **Figure 33** [part No. 07924-ME40010]) and collar set (C [part No. 07924-ME40020]) is required to hold the pinion joint when loosening and tightening the pinion joint nut.
6. A pinion puller set (puller base, puller shaft and special nut) is required to remove the pinion gear assembly from the housing:
   a. Puller base (D, **Figure 33** [part No. 07HMC-MM8011A]).
   b. Puller shaft (E, **Figure 33** [part No. 07931-ME4010B]).
   c. Special nut (F, **Figure 33** [part No. 07931-HB3020A]).
7. Bearing removers, drivers and splitters are required. Many of these tools can be rented from tool rental outlets. A hydraulic press is recommended for bearing replacement.

Service Notes

Before servicing the final drive unit, note the following:
1. Refer to *Final Drive* in Chapter Two to troubleshoot the final drive unit. A new or rough sounding noise from the final drive unit is usually the first indication of a problem with the unit.
2. Ring gear removal also requires removal of the ring gear bearing. If the bearing is in good condition, it can be reused.
3. The pinion gear bearing pressed onto the pinion gear shaft can also be reused if in good condition.
4. When checking bearings, they should turn freely and without any sign of roughness, catching or excessive noise. Always replace questionable bearings.
5. Refer to *Bearings* in *Service Methods* in Chapter One for bearing removal and installation techniques. Refer to *Interference fit* and *Heating Components* in *Service Methods* in Chapter One when it is necessary to use heat for the removal and installation of bearings in the housing and housing cover.
6. Use a heat gun when necessary to heat the parts. Do not use a welding torch as this heats the parts unevenly and may cause the component to warp. When heating parts, monitor heat with heat sticks available from a welding supply store or use an infrared thermometer. The text will list the temperature required to remove and install parts.
7. Inspect the ring gear by supporting the motorcycle with the rear wheel off the ground. Remove the

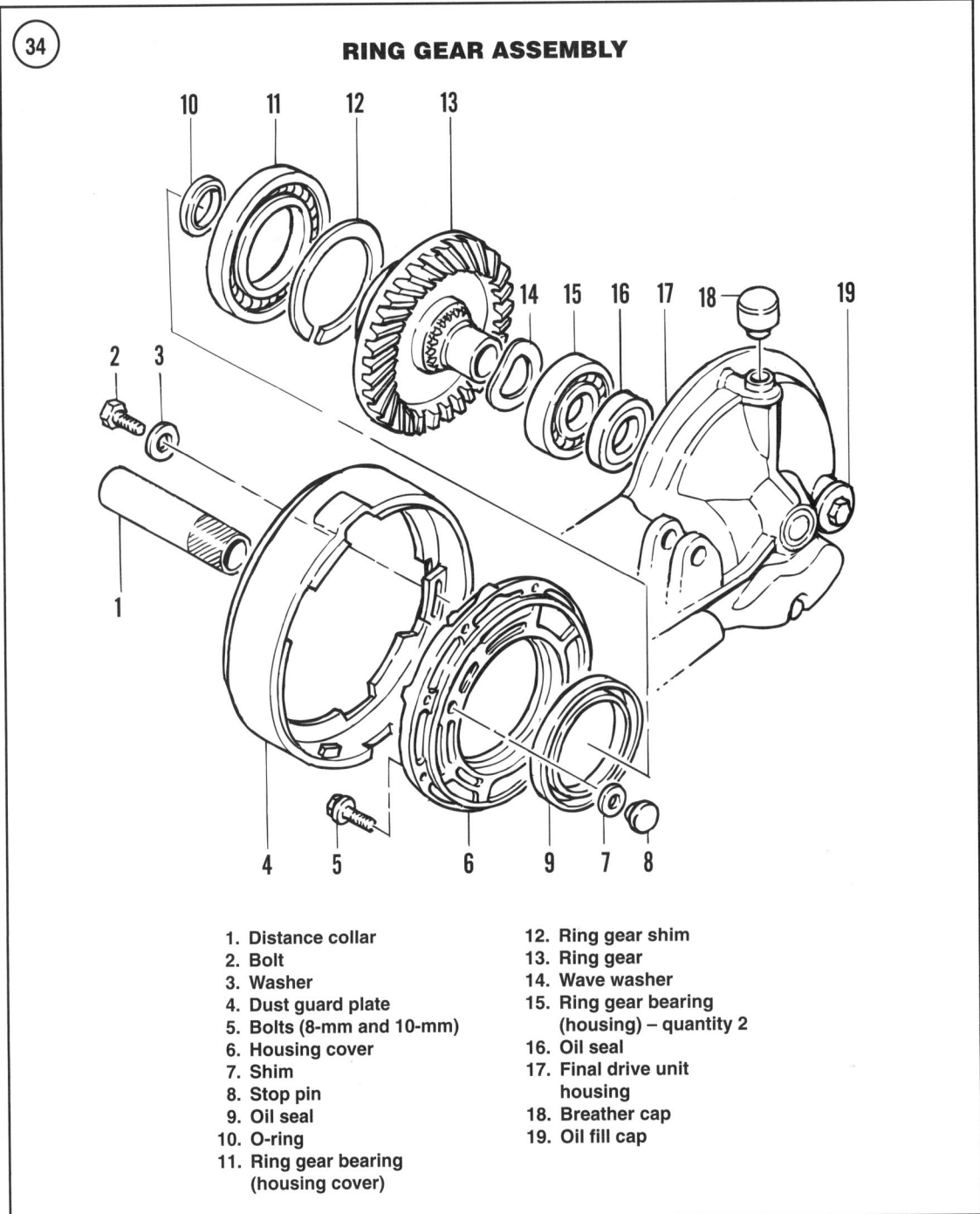

34 RING GEAR ASSEMBLY

1. Distance collar
2. Bolt
3. Washer
4. Dust guard plate
5. Bolts (8-mm and 10-mm)
6. Housing cover
7. Shim
8. Stop pin
9. Oil seal
10. O-ring
11. Ring gear bearing (housing cover)
12. Ring gear shim
13. Ring gear
14. Wave washer
15. Ring gear bearing (housing) – quantity 2
16. Oil seal
17. Final drive unit housing
18. Breather cap
19. Oil fill cap

oil fill cap and turn the rear wheel to inspect the gear through the filler hole. If wear or damage is apparent, drain the oil (Chapter Three) and inspect the oil and the magnet on the oil drain bolt for metal fragments.
8. Do not remove and discard used seals until all of the service and measurement procedures have been competed. Install new seals during final assembly.
9. Use HondaBond 4, ThreeBond 1104 or Yamabond No. 4 gasket sealer to seal the housing cover during assembly.

Ring Gear and Housing Cover

The housing cover, seal ring gear and ring gear bearings can be serviced without removing the pinion shaft assembly.

Removal

Refer to **Figure 34**.
1. Review *Service Notes* in this section.

REAR SUSPENSION

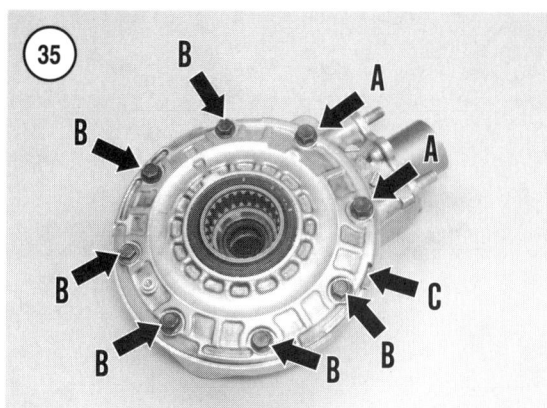

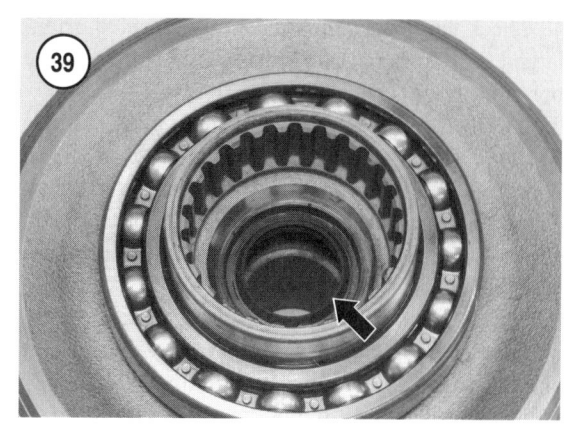

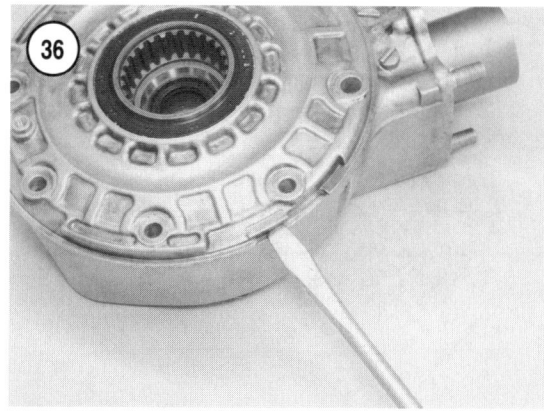

2. Remove the distance collar (A, **Figure 30**).
3. Remove the bolt, washer and dust guard plate (C, **Figure 30**).
4. Perform the backlash measurement described in *Ring and Pinion Gear Measurements* in this chapter.
5. Remove the housing cover 10 mm (A, **Figure 35**) and 8 mm (B) bolts in a crossing pattern.
6. Pry the housing cover (C, **Figure 35**) off the housing with a wide-blade screwdriver at the two pry points (**Figure 36**).
7A. If the ring gear (A, **Figure 37**) remained in the housing cover, locate and remove the wave washer (B). Then support the housing cover in a press with the ring gear facing down (**Figure 38**). Press the ring gear and bearing out of the housing cover. Make sure to catch the ring gear once it is free from the housing.
7B. If the ring gear remained in the housing, remove the ring gear and wave washer from the housing.
8. Pry the seal (**Figure 39**) from inside the ring gear and discard.

Inspection

With the housing cover and ring gear removed from the housing, the ring and pinion gears can be inspected. Replace worn or damaged parts as described in this section.
1. Clean the ring gear in solvent and dry with compressed air.
2. Inspect the ring gear (A, **Figure 40**) for broken, chipped or worn teeth.
3. Inspect the ring gear bearing (B, **Figure 40**) for pitting, galling or cracks. Hold the ring gear and turn the bearing by hand. There should be no roughness, binding or catching.

NOTE
If the ring gear housing cover seal leaks, it may indicate a damaged ring gear bearing.

4. Check the housing cover for an elongated or enlarged bearing bore (C, **Figure 40**). Then check the bore for pitting, cracks and other damage.

5. Inspect the ring gear housing bearings (A, **Figure 41**) for pitting, galling, cracks or a loose fit in the bore. Hold the housing and turn the bearings by hand. There should be no roughness, binding or catching. If necessary, replace both bearings and seal as described in this section.

6. Check the pinion gear (B, **Figure 41**) for broken, chipped or worn teeth. Then rotate the pinion shaft and check for any roughness, grinding or catching, indicating a damaged pinion gear bearing. Refer to *Pinion Gear* in this section to service the pinion gear and its bearing assembly.

7. Check for an oil leak at the front of the housing (C, **Figure 41**). If necessary, replace the pinion shaft seal as described in *Pinion Gear* in this section.

Housing cover oil seal removal/installation

The ring gear oil seal (9, **Figure 34**) is installed in the housing cover (6).

1. Clean and dry the housing cover.
2. Remove the seal with a seal puller as shown in **Figure 42**. Use caution to avoid damaging the housing cover or the seal bore. If a seal puller is not available, pad a tire iron with a rag and pry the seal out. When using a tire iron, do not let the tip of the tire iron contact the seal bore surface. Move the tool around the seal, taking small bites, to avoid damaging the cover. Discard the seal.
3. Check the seal bore for cracks, gouges and other damage, then reclean the housing cover.
4. Support the cover on a wooden surface or rubber mat. Align the new seal with the top of the housing cover with its closed side facing out. Install the seal with a large driver that fits the outer circumference of the seal. The driver should clear the lip part of the seal to avoid damaging it. Install the seal until it rests flush with the top of the housing cover (**Figure 43**). Make sure the garter spring remains in the seal lip.
5. Check the oil seal operating area on the ring gear (A, **Figure 44**) for scoring and other damage that could damage the new seal lip. Smooth any surface roughness with a fine-cut file or 400-600 grade sandpaper.

Ring gear bearing and shim removal/installation

It is only necessary to remove the ring gear bearing (B, **Figure 44**) to replace a damaged part or to replace the ring gear shim installed between the ring gear and ring gear bearing. If the bearing is in good

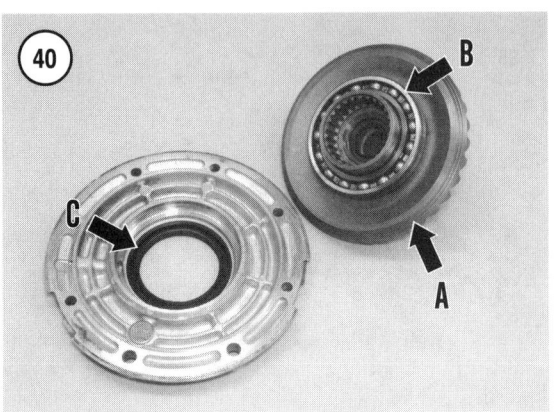

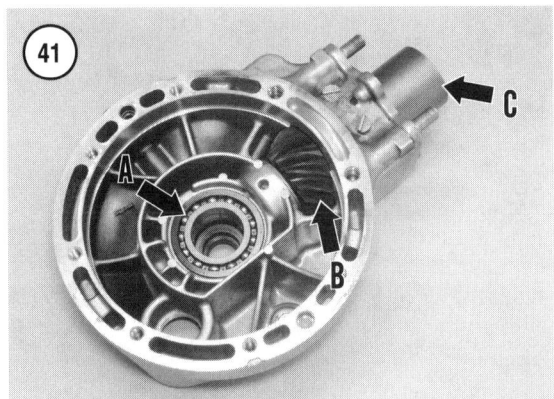

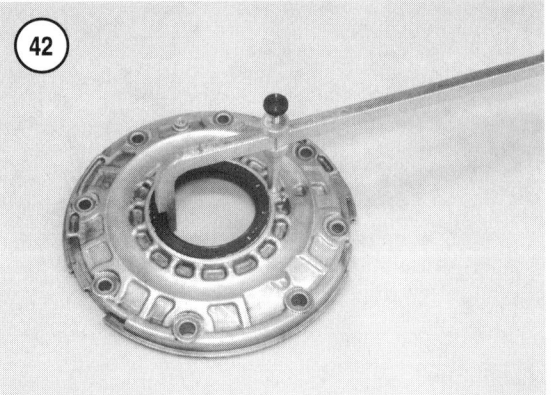

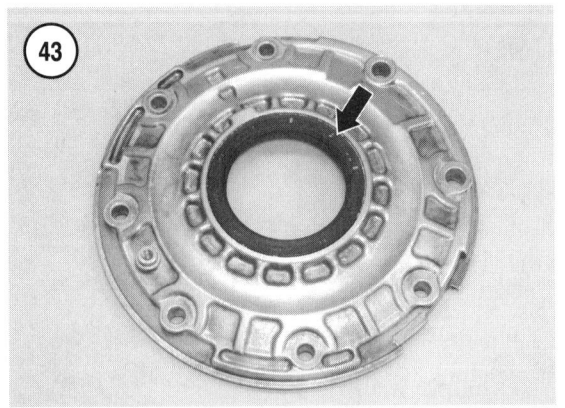

REAR SUSPENSION

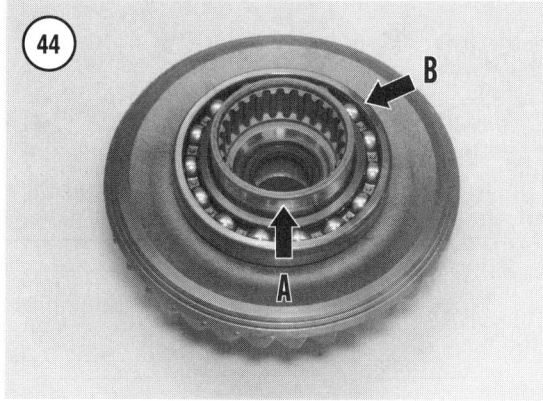

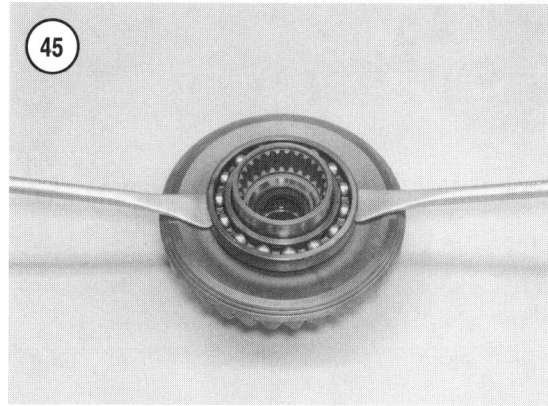

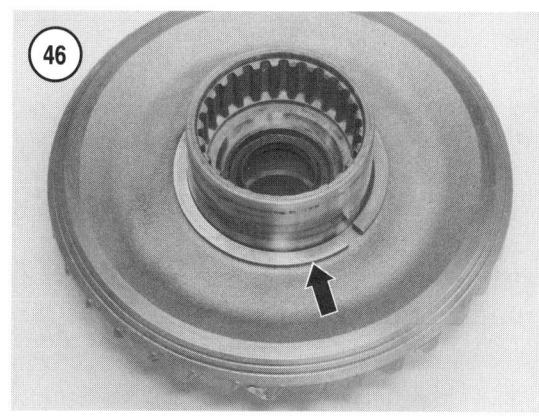

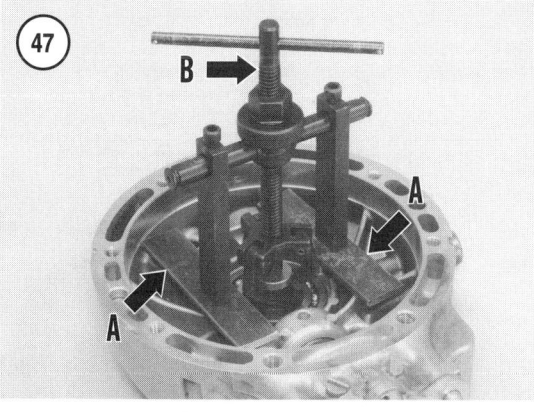

condition and not damaged during its removal, it may be reused.

1. Remove the ring gear by prying it evenly with two tire irons (**Figure 45**). Make sure the ends of the tire irons contact the bearing's outer race and not the bearing balls. If the bearing is tight, remove it with a 2-jaw puller.
2. Remove the ring gear shim (**Figure 46**).
3. Clean and dry the parts.
4. If reusing the original bearing, hold the bearing's outer race and turn the inner race by hand. There should be no roughness, binding or catching. Then check the bearing for other damage. Replace the bearing if necessary.
5. Install the correct size ring gear shim (**Figure 46**) as follows:
   a. If the housing was disassembled to correct the backlash measurement, install the correct size shim determined during the procedure. Refer to *Backlash Measurements* in *Ring and Pinion Gear Measurements* in this chapter.
   b. If the ring and pinion gears, ring gear bearing, pinion bearing, housing cover or housing are being replaced, install a 2.00 mm (0.079 in.) thick shim as a starting point. Then repeat the backlash measurement procedure.
6. Place the ring gear shim (**Figure 46**) onto the ring gear and press the bearing onto the ring gear until it bottoms against the shim.

Ring gear housing bearings and seal removal/installation

The ring gear housing bearings (A, **Figure 41**) are only accessible from one side of the housing and require a bridge type bearing puller (K&L part No. 35-2231 or equivalent) for removal and a hydraulic press for installation. While these bearings rarely require replacement, they must be replaced when removed to replace a damaged seal (16, **Figure 34**).

1. Heat the housing to 80° C (176° F).
2. Use two metal plates (A, **Figure 47**) for support and mount the puller onto the housing as shown in B, **Figure 47**. Adjust the puller so the arms engage the lower bearing's inner race. Tension the puller arms and check they are centered and positioned correctly.
3. Operate the puller and remove the bearings. If the puller arms slip, they may ride up and engage the inner bearing and remove it first. Then repeat to remove the outer bearing. Refer to **Figure 48**.
4. Pry the seal (**Figure 49**) out of the housing with a tire iron or seal removal tool and discard.
5. Clean the housing in clean solvent. Dry with compressed air.
6. Inspect the bearing and seal bores for damage.

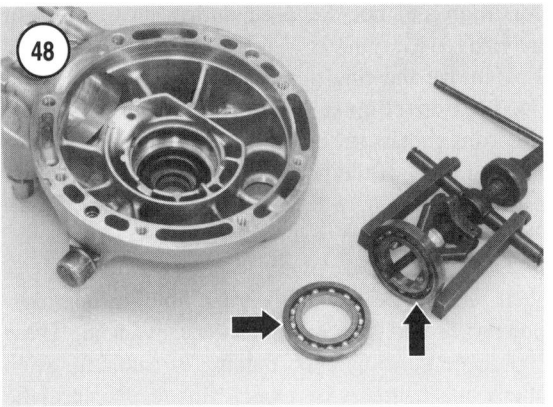

7. Drive a new seal into the housing with its open side (**Figure 49**) facing toward the inside of the housing. Make sure the seal bottoms in its housing bore. Apply grease to the seal lips.

CAUTION
Heat the housing carefully to avoid damaging the seal.

8. Reheat the housing to 80° C (176° F).

CAUTION
These bearings are narrow and difficult to center in the bearing bore. Check the bearings carefully to make sure they start and move squarely into the bore.

9. Support the housing in a press and press the outer bearing into the housing bore until it bottoms. Then press the inner bearing into the housing bore until it bottoms against the other bearing (**Figure 50**). Check the bearings for damage.

Ring gear stop pin side clearance check/adjustment

1. Install the ring gear into the housing cover as described in *Installation* in this section.
2. Measure the clearance between the ring gear and the stop pin with a feeler gauge (**Figure 51**). Refer to **Table 2** for the recommended clearance. The shim (7, **Figure 34**) installed under the stop pin (8) adjusts the clearance.

CAUTION
Heat the housing cover evenly to prevent warp. Do not concentrate the heat in one spot or area for any length of time.

3. To adjust the clearance, remove the ring gear from the housing cover. Heat the housing cover to 80° C (176° F) with a heat gun. When the specified

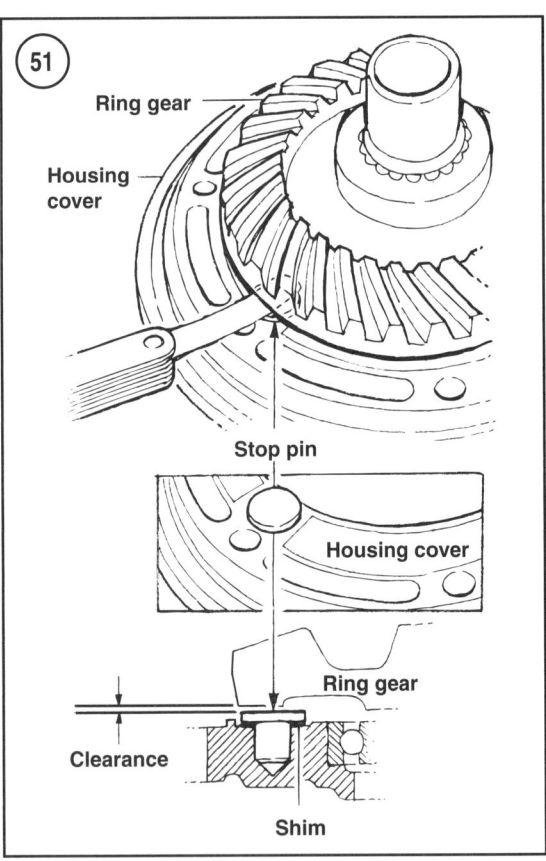

REAR SUSPENSION

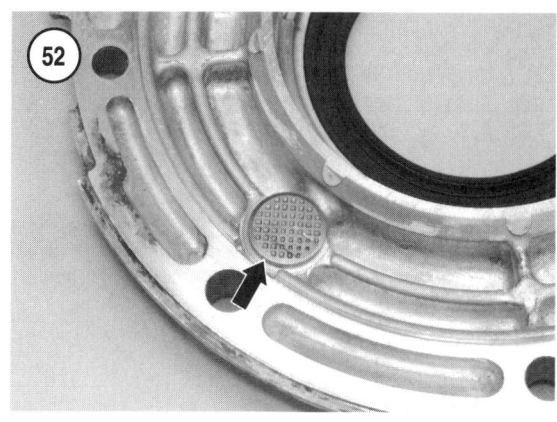

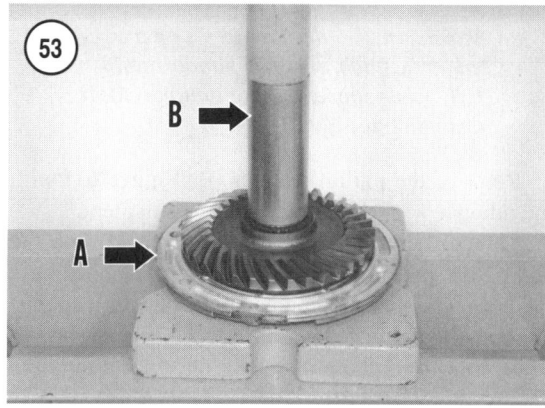

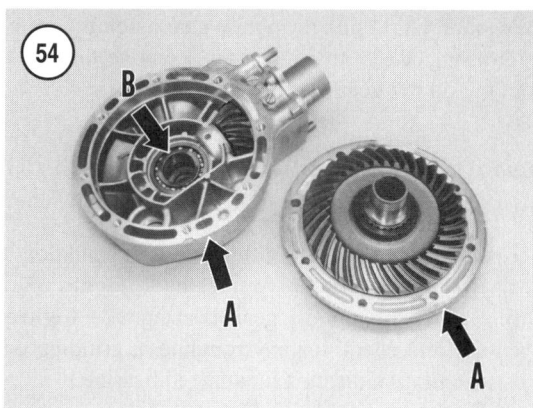

temperature is reached, tap the cover with a plastic mallet to remove the stop pin (**Figure 52**).

4. Install either a 0.10 mm (0.004 in.) or 0.15 mm (0.006 in.) stop pin shim onto the stop pin to obtain the desired clearance. Reheat the housing cover and drive the stop pin (**Figure 52**) with the shim into the housing cover and recheck the clearance. Repeat until the ring gear-to-stop pin clearance is within specifications (**Table 2**).

Installation

This section covers installation of the ring gear assembly, housing cover and final assembly of the final drive unit. If the unit is being assembled to check gear mesh and then disassembled, do not install the new seal (Step 2) or apply sealer to the housing cover and housing mating surfaces (Step 7).

1. If the pinion gear was removed, reinstall it as described in *Pinion Gear* in this section. When the pinion gear is properly installed and the pinion retainer and pinion joint are properly installed and tightened, continue with Step 2.
2. On final assembly of the final drive, apply grease to the lip of a new seal and install it into the ring gear with its open side facing out (toward bearing) as shown in **Figure 39**.
3. Clean the breather passage as follows:
   a. Twist and pull the breather cap (18, **Figure 34**) from the housing.
   b. Clean the breather passages in the gear case cover and housing with compressed air.
   c. Reinstall the breather cap.
4. Install a new housing cover oil seal (9, **Figure 34**) into the housing cover as described in this section.
5. Install the ring gear/bearing assembly into the housing cover as follows:
   a. Place the housing cover (A, **Figure 53**) into a press bed with its bearing bore side facing up.
   b. Align the ring gear bearing with the bearing bore. Press the bearing into the housing cover with a driver (B, **Figure 53**) placed against the ring gear. Press until the bearing bottoms in its bore.
6. Clean and dry the housing cover and housing mating surfaces.
7. Apply HondaBond No. 4, ThreeBond 1104 or Yamabond No. 4 to the housing cover and housing mating surfaces (A, **Figure 54**). Do not apply sealer around the dowel pin/breather holes (**Figure 55**).
8. Lubricate the wave washer with gear oil and center against the bearing's inner race (B, **Figure 54**).
9. Install the housing cover/ring gear assembly by aligning the two 10 mm bolt holes (A, **Figure 56**). It is normal if there is a gap between the housing cover and housing gasket surfaces.

10. Install the 10-mm (A, **Figure 56**) and 8-mm (B) bolts finger-tight.

11. Hand-tighten the housing cover bolts in a crossing pattern and in several steps until the housing cover evenly contacts the housing.

12. Tighten the 8-mm bolts (B, **Figure 56**) in a crossing pattern and in several steps to 25 N•m (19 ft.-lb.).

13. Remove the 10-mm bolts (A, **Figure 56**) and apply a medium strength threadlocking compound onto their threads. Reinstall the bolts and tighten to 62 N•m (46 ft.-lb.).

14. Use the holding fixture and support the final drive housing in a vise. Turn the pinion shaft with a beam type torque wrench and a 22-mm socket and measure the final drive gear assembly preload. The correct preload reading is 0.2-0.4 N•m (1.8-3.5 in.-lb.). If the preload reading is incorrect, disassemble the final drive and check the bearings for damage and proper installation.

15. Install the dust guard plate (C, **Figure 30**) by aligning the tabs on the plate with the grooves in the housing cover, then turn the plate counterclockwise to lock it. Install the bolt and washer and tighten to 10 N•m (88 in.-lb.).

Pinion Gear

Pinion gear assembly removal

Refer to **Figure 57**.

1. Review *Service Notes* in this section.
2. Review *Tools* in this section to identify the tools used in this procedure.
3. Remove the housing cover and ring gear as described in this section.
4. Remove the pinion joint nut (3, **Figure 57**) as follows:
   a. Mount the holding fixture across the housing using two 8–1.25 × 25 mm bolts and then secure the holding fixture in a vise as shown in **Figure 58**.
   b. Install a 22 mm socket inside the pinion joint and engage it with the pinion joint nut.
   c. Install the pinion holder plate (A, **Figure 59**) and collar set C (B) as shown. The pinion holder plate fits inside the pinion joint to prevent it from turning. The collars fit over the studs on the final drive housing and are secured to the pinion holder plate.
   d. Loosen the pinion joint nut.
   e. Remove the tools from the housing.
   f. Remove the pinion joint nut (A, **Figure 60**) and pinion joint (B).
5. Remove the bolt and the retainer lock tab (A, **Figure 61**).

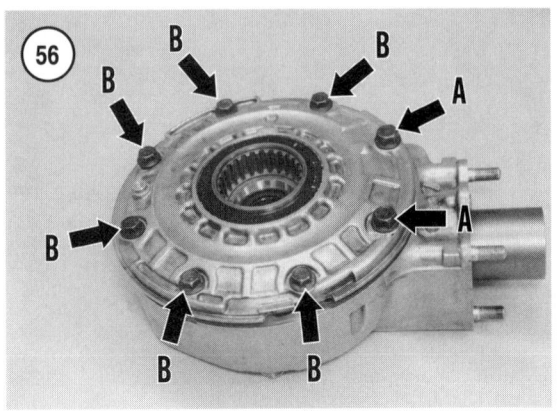

NOTE
Make sure the all of the arms on the retainer wrench grip the pinion retainer fully when loosening the pinion retainer in Step 6.

6. Remove the pinion retainer (B, **Figure 61**) with the retainer wrench (**Figure 62**) or equivalent.

7. Thread the puller shaft (A, **Figure 63**) onto the end of the pinion gear shaft. Install the puller base (B, **Figure 63**) over the puller shaft and seat it against the housing surface. Then thread the special nut (C, **Figure 63**) over the puller shaft and seat it into and against the puller base.

8. Hold the special nut (C, **Figure 63**) and turn the puller shaft (A) to pull the pinion gear assembly from the housing. Refer to **Figure 64**. Remove the tools from the pinion gear assembly.

Pinion gear assembly inspection

1. Clean and dry the pinion gear assembly.
2. Check the pinion gear for the following conditions:
   a. Broken, chipped or worn teeth (A, **Figure 65**).
   b. Rotate the pinion gear bearing (B, **Figure 65**) and check for any roughness, grinding or catching, indicating a damaged bearing.
   c. Damaged threads (C, **Figure 65**).
   d. Damaged pinion joint splines (D, **Figure 65**).
   e. Worn or damaged needle bearing shoulder (E, **Figure 65**). If this shoulder is damaged, the pinion gear needle bearing is also damaged.
3. Inspect the pinion gear needle bearing in the housing (**Figure 66**). The rollers should be smooth and polished with no flat spots, burrs or other damage. Inspect the bearing cage for cracks or other damage. This bearing is pressed deep into the housing and difficult to inspect. If necessary, remove the pinion bearing from the pinion gear and install the pinion gear into the bearing. Turn the pinion gear to check the bearing. If the bearing is damaged, replace as described in this section.

REAR SUSPENSION

57 **PINION GEAR ASSEMBLY**

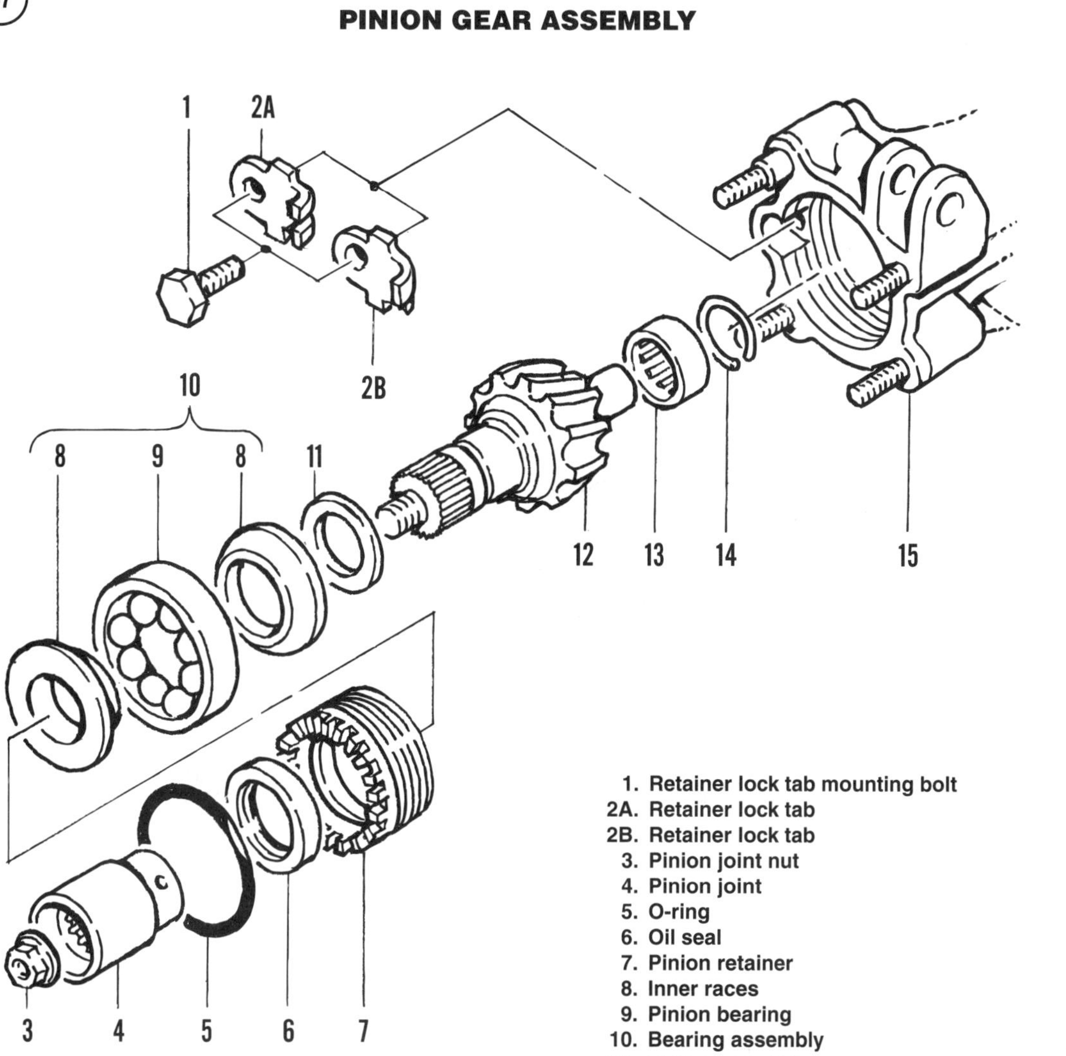

1. Retainer lock tab mounting bolt
2A. Retainer lock tab
2B. Retainer lock tab
3. Pinion joint nut
4. Pinion joint
5. O-ring
6. Oil seal
7. Pinion retainer
8. Inner races
9. Pinion bearing
10. Bearing assembly
11. Pinion gear shim
12. Pinion gear
13. Needle bearing
14. Stopper ring
15. Final drive unit housing

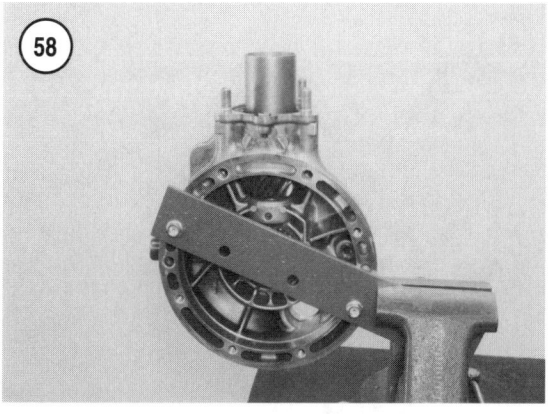

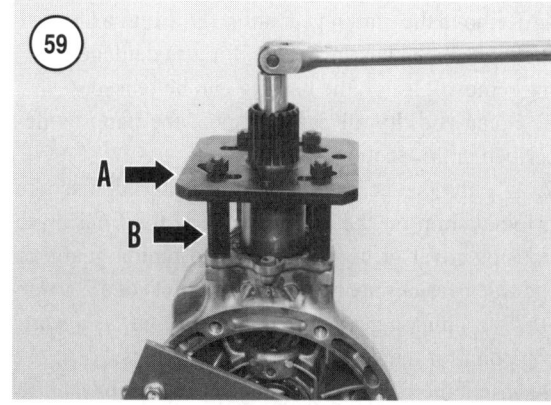

CHAPTER THIRTEEN

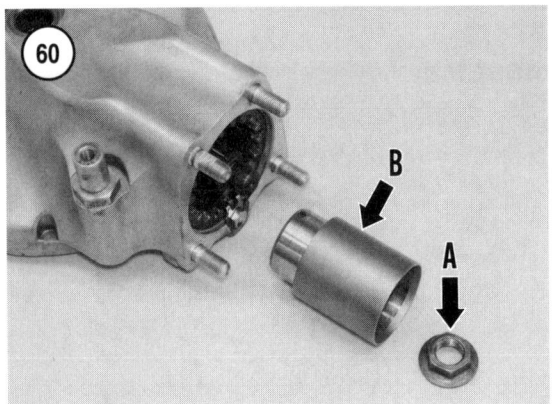

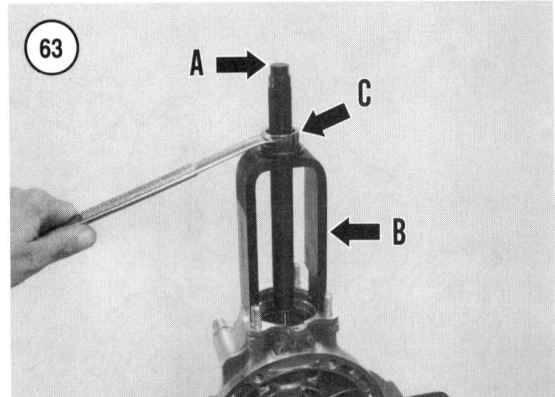

Pinion gear assembly disassembly/reassembly

This section covers the bearing assembly and pinion gear shim installed on the pinion gear. The bearing assembly consists of three separate parts. During removal, the outer bearing race and bearing are removed at the same time. The inner bearing race is removed separately.

1. Support the bearing assembly (**Figure 67**) with a bearing splitter in a press.
2. Operate the press to remove the outer bearing race (A, **Figure 68**) and the bearing (B).
3. Support the inner bearing race (C, **Figure 68**) and press it off the shaft.
4. Remove the pinion gear shim (D, **Figure 68**).
5. Recheck the bearing to see if it was damaged during removal. If not, the bearing can be reused.
6. Clean and dry all parts. Inspect the parts as described in this section.
7. If only the bearing is being replaced, use the original shim on the pinion shaft. If the final drive housing cover or housing, ring and pinion gears, or the side bearings are being replaced, install a 2.0 mm (0.79 in.) pinion gear shim (D, **Figure 68**) as a starting point for the gear position adjustments.
8. Install the pinion gear shim (D, **Figure 68**).

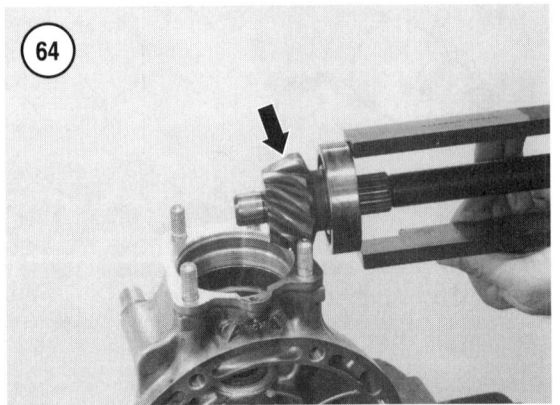

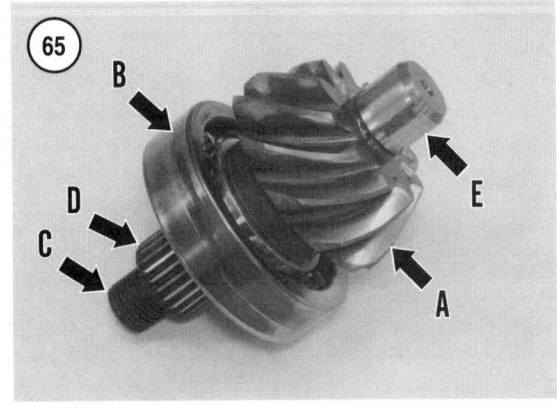

REAR SUSPENSION

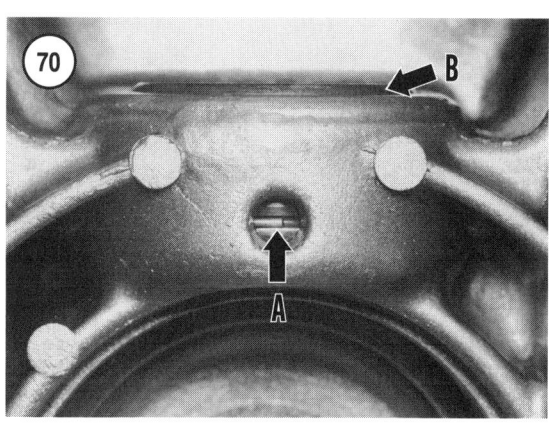

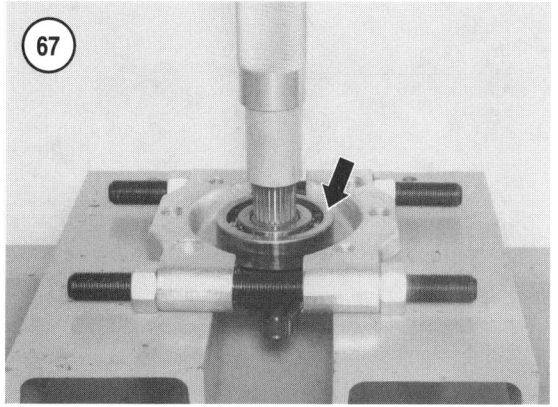

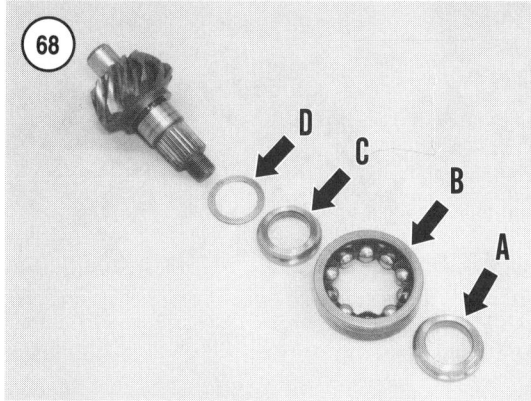

9. Press the inner bearing race (C, **Figure 68**) onto the shaft until it bottoms against the pinion gear shim.
10. Install the bearing (B, **Figure 68**) and seat it against the inner bearing race.
11. Press the outer bearing race (A, **Figure 68**) until it seats against the bearing.
12. Install the pinion gear as described in this section.
13. Perform the *Gear Mesh Pattern Check* described in *Ring and Pinion Gear Measurements* in this chapter.

Pinion gear needle bearing removal/installation

The pinion gear needle bearing (**Figure 66**) is pressed into the housing and equipped with a stopper ring that seats in a groove in the bearing bore (**Figure 69**). The stopper ring ensures that the pinion gear is positioned at its correct depth and cannot float or move during operation. This would change the ring and pinion gear engagement position.

The pinion gear needle bearing is only accessible from one side of the housing and requires a knock puller with a 20-mm collet (Motion Pro part No. 08-0292 or equivalent) for removal and a bearing driver for installation.

NOTE
*The stopper ring (A, **Figure 70**) must be removed before the bearing (B) can be removed from the housing.*

1. Remove the stopper ring through the access hole as follows:
   a. Working through the access hole, rotate the stopper ring until its end gap is visible (**Figure 70**).
   b. Use a small tool and pry one end of the stopper ring up until it can be grabbed with a pair of needle-nose pliers. Then pull and remove the stopper ring through the access hole (**Figure 71**).
2. Mount the holding fixture across the front of the housing and secure the holding fixture in a vise so the

needle bearing is horizontal with the floor (**Figure 72**).

NOTE
Before a 20-mm bearing collet can be installed through the bearing, the bearing's cage and bearing rollers must be removed first.

3. Position the tip of a small round awl between the bearing's race and cage (**Figure 73**). Drive the awl with a hammer to bend the cage inward and weaken it. Repeat at different areas around the cage until it collapses (**Figure 74**). Remove the cage and all of the bearing rollers with a magnet.
4. Heat the housing to 80° C (176° F).
5. Install a 20-mm bearing collet through the bearing, then expand the collet to grip the back-side of the bearing. Operate the puller and remove the bearing (**Figure 75**) from the housing.
6. Remove the holding fixture and housing from the vise and separate them.
7. Clean and dry the bearing bore. Then inspect the bearing bore for damage.
8. Place a new stopper ring into the groove on the new bearing (**Figure 76**) and place the bearing in a freezer for several hours.
9. Mount the holding fixture (A, **Figure 77**) across the side of the housing and secure the holding fixture in a vise so the bearing bore is facing up.
10. Heat the housing to 80° C (176° F).
11. Remove the needle bearing from the freezer and quickly align it with the housing so the stopper ring end is facing down (toward housing). Drive the bearing (B, **Figure 77**) squarely into the housing until the stopper ring seats into the housing groove (**Figure 69**).
12. Check the new bearing for damage.

Pinion retainer seal and O-ring removal/installation

1. Remove the oil seal (A, **Figure 78**) and O-ring (B) and discard them.

REAR SUSPENSION

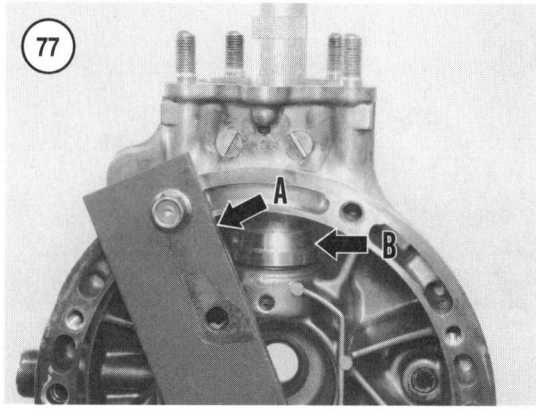

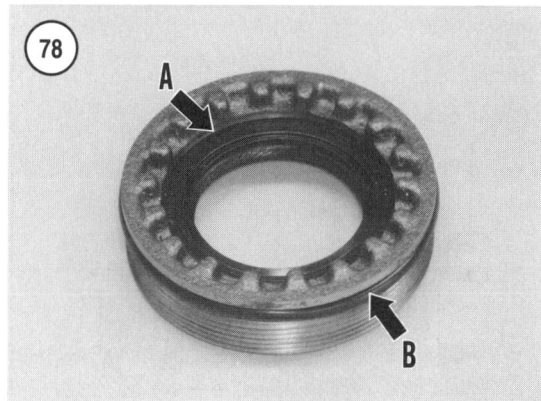

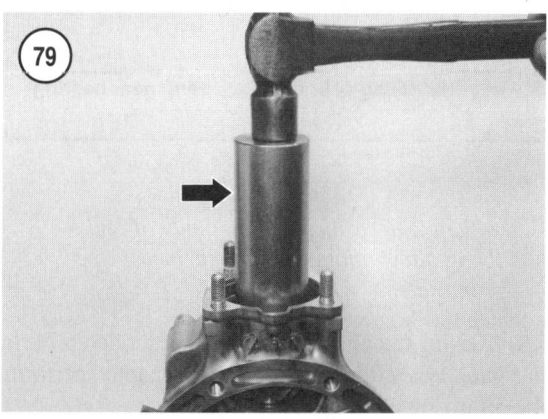

2. Clean and dry the pinion retainer. Check the threads and the seal bore for damage.

3. Install a new seal with its closed side facing toward the top of the retainer. Lubricate the seal's lip with grease.

4. Lubricate a new O-ring with grease and install it in the pinion retainer groove (B, **Figure 78**).

Pinion gear assembly installation

1. Assemble the pinion gear assembly as described in this section.

2. Clean and dry the housing and pinion gear assembly. Make sure the threads on the pinion gear, pinion retainer and inside the housing are clean and dry.

3. Lubricate the pinion gear bearing and the needle bearing in the housing with gear oil.

4. Mount the holding fixture across the housing using two 8–1.25 × 25 mm bolts and then secure the holding fixture in a vise as shown in **Figure 58**.

5. Place the pinion gear into the housing by aligning the end of the pinion gear shaft with the needle bearing. Drive the pinion gear into the housing with a bearing driver (**Figure 79**) until there are enough housing threads visible (**Figure 80**) above the pinion gear to allow installation of the pinion retainer.

6. Thread the pinion retainer (**Figure 78**) into the housing until it seats against the pinion gear bearing. Use the retainer wrench (**Figure 81**) and tighten the pinion retainer to 147 N•m (108 ft.-lb.).

7. Align the pinion retainer lock tab with the notches on the pinion retainer (**Figure 82**). Install the pinion retainer lock tab bolt and tighten to 10 N•m (88 in.-lb.).

NOTE
*Two lock tab designs (2A and 2B, **Figure 57**) are available from the manufacturer. If the original lock tab will not align properly, use the other lock tab.*

8. Install the pinion joint onto the pinion gear shaft.

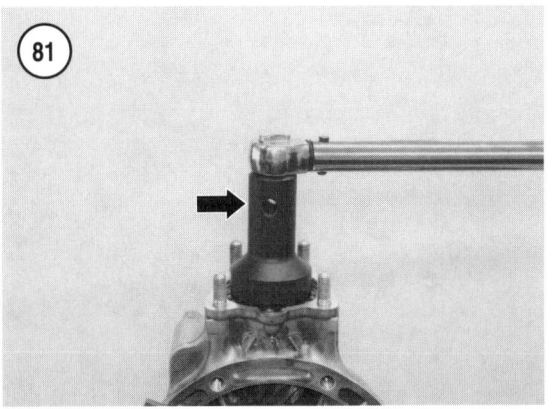
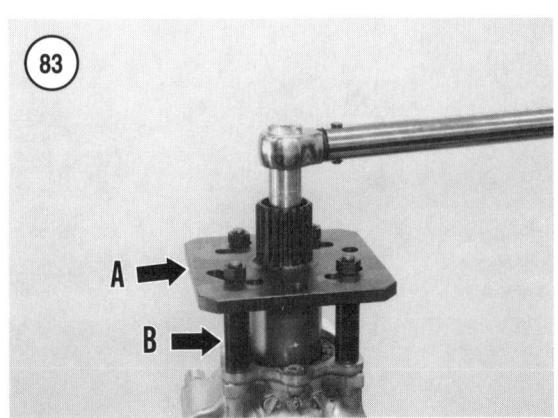

9. Apply a medium strength threadlocking compound onto the pinion joint nut and install it finger-tight.

10. Secure the pinion joint with the pinion holder plate (A, **Figure 83**) and collar set (B) and tighten the pinion joint nut to 108 N•m (80 ft.-lb.). Remove the tools.

RING AND PINION GEAR MEASUREMENTS

Whenever the ring and pinion gear set (**Figure 84**), bearing(s), housing or housing cover are replaced, check and adjust the ring gear backlash and the gear tooth contact pattern.

Backlash Measurement

This procedure covers how to check the backlash between the ring gear and pinion gear to determine gear wear and if the ring gear is running true. Measuring gear backlash is also necessary after a general overhaul. **Figure 85** shows ring and pinion gear engagement and the position of their adjustment shims.

1. Remove the final drive unit as described in this chapter.

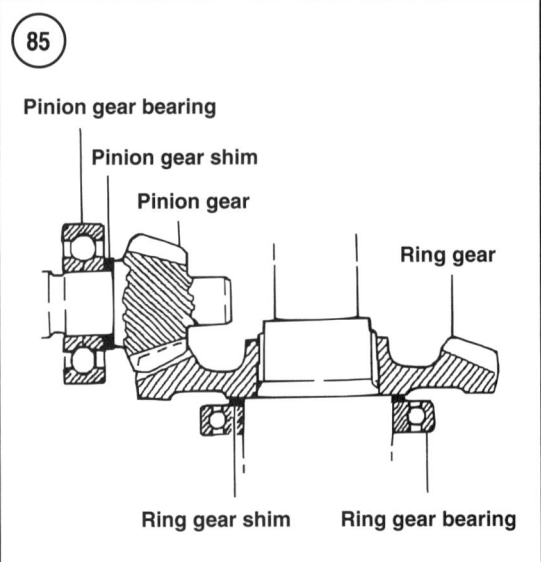

NOTE
Step 2 describes two methods of locking the pinion gear when measuring backlash.

2A. If using the pinion holder tool described n *Tools* in *Final Drive Unit Overhaul* in this chapter, perform the following:

REAR SUSPENSION

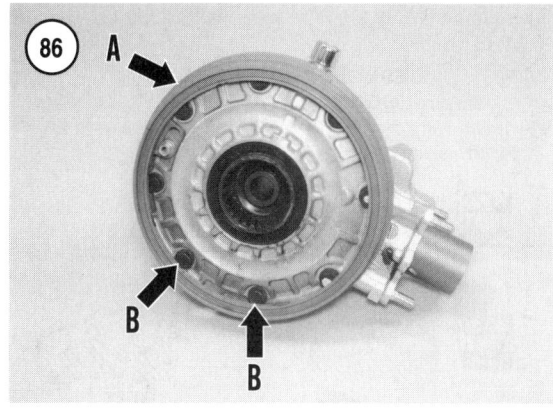

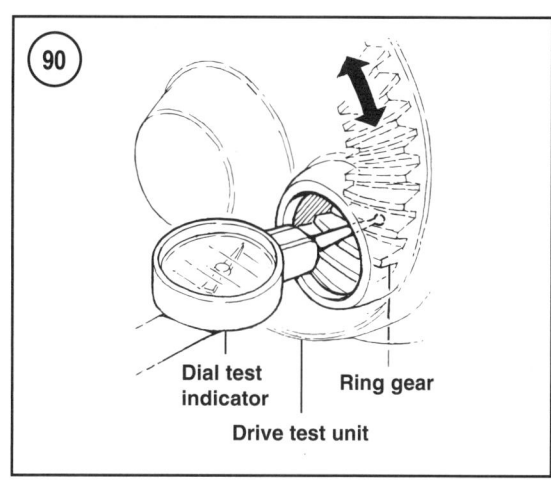

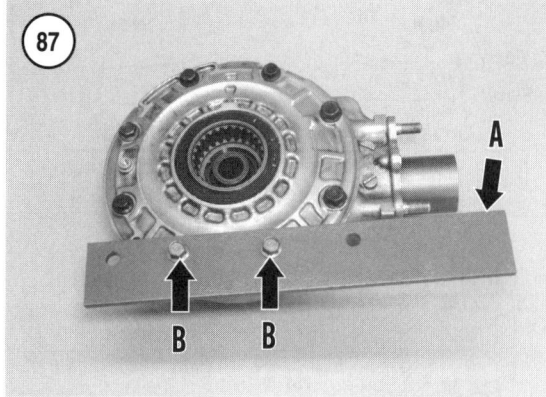

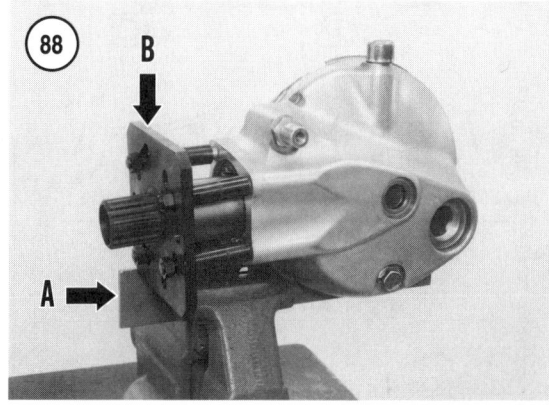

a. Remove the bolt, washer and dust guard plate (A, **Figure 86**).
b. Remove the two rear cover mounting bolts identified in B, **Figure 86**.
c. Mount the holding fixture (A, **Figure 87**) across the final drive using two 8–1.25 × 45 mm bolts (B, **Figure 87**) and 8-mm spacers. The spacers position the holding fixture away from the curved ribs on the housing cover.
d. Secure the holding fixture (A, **Figure 88**) in a vise.
e. Mount the pinion holder plate and collar set as shown in B, **Figure 88**. The pinion holder plate engages the splines inside the pinion joint to prevent the pinion gear from turning.

2B. To lock the pinion joint/pinion gear without the use of special tools, perform the following:
  a. Mount the holding fixture across the final drive using two 10–1.25 nuts and then mount the holding fixture in a vise (A, **Figure 89**).
  b. Drill a 10-mm hole through a small angle bracket and mount it onto the final drive stud as shown in B, **Figure 89**. Secure the angle bracket to the pinion joint with a hose clamp (C, **Figure 89**). This arrangement locks the pinion joint in place to prevent the pinion gear from turning.

3. Remove the oil fill cap.
4. Measure backlash with a dial test indicator mounted on a magnetic stand. Position the indicator so its stem is parallel to the ring gear shaft and its tip contacts the side of one gear tooth as shown in **Figure 90**.
5. Move the ring gear back and forth by hand (**Figure 90**) to determine initial final drive gear backlash. Refer to **Table 2** for the specified backlash. Record the reading.
6. Remove the dial test indicator, then rotate the ring gear and take two additional backlash readings 120° from the original measuring point.

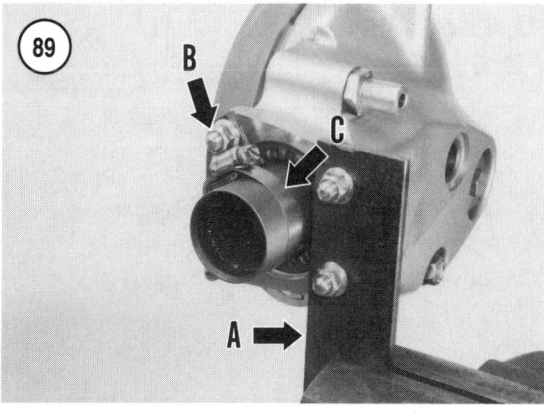

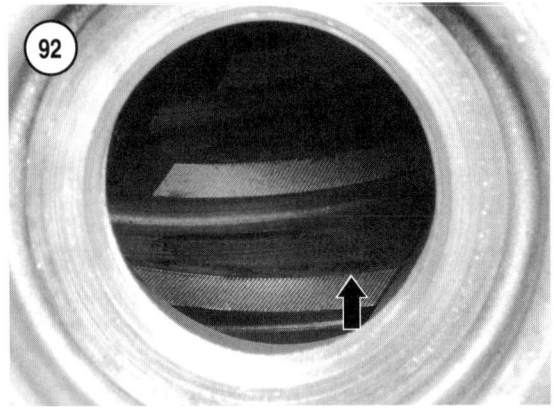

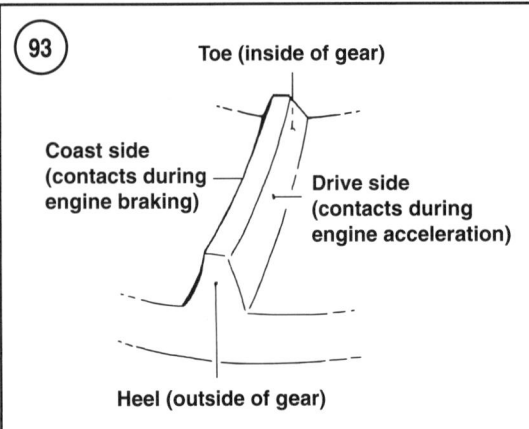

a. If the difference between any two readings exceeds 0.10 mm (0.004 in.), the ring gear is running out of true. This can be caused a damaged bearing or the bearing bore may be damaged.
b. If the backlash measurement is being performed after reassembling the final drive unit, the ring gear bearings may not have been installed correctly.
c. If the backlash reading is out of specification, but the ring gear is running true, go to Step 7.
d. If the backlash reading indicates that the ring gear is running out of true, remove the ring

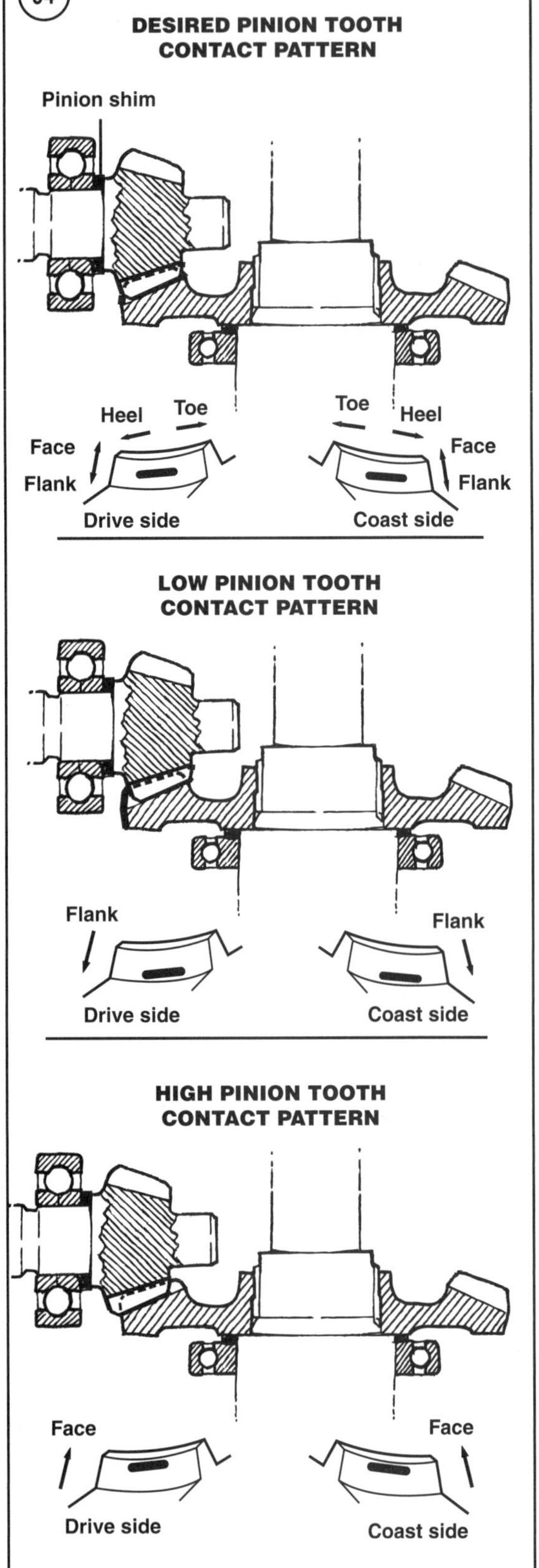

gear and inspect the parts and housing for damage as described in this chapter.
7. To correct backlash, remove the ring gear as described in this chapter. A new ring gear shim (**Figure 85**) must be installed. Note the following:
   a. If gear backlash is too small, replace the ring gear shim with a thinner one.
   b. If gear backlash to too large, replace the ring gear shim with a thicker one.
   c. Refer to **Table 3** for ring gear shim sizes.
   d. Remove the ring gear and press off its bearings to install the correct size shim as described in this chapter.
8. Reverse Steps 1-3. Note the following;
   a. Tighten the housing cover 8-mm mounting bolts (B, **Figure 86**) to 25 N•m (18 ft.-lb.).
   b. If removed, install the dust guard plate (A, **Figure 86**) by aligning the tabs on the plate with the grooves in the housing cover, then turn the plate counterclockwise to lock it. Install the bolt and washer and tighten to 10 N•m (88 in.-lb.).

Gear Mesh Pattern Check

1. Remove the ring gear and wave washer from the housing as described in this chapter.
2. Clean and dry the ring gear and pinion gear teeth.
3. Using an acid brush, apply Prussian blue or an equivalent non-drying gear marking compound to both sides of the pinion gear teeth (**Figure 91**).
4. Install the wave washer, ring gear and housing cover as described in this chapter.
5. Remove the oil fill cap.
6. Rotate the pinion joint several rotations to turn the ring gear in its normal operating direction so a pattern becomes evident on the ring gear teeth (**Figure 92**).
7. Examine the wear pattern on the drive side of the ring gear teeth as follows:
   a. Refer to **Figure 93** to identify the parts of the gear teeth.
   b. The desired gear tooth wear pattern in **Figure 94** shows the pattern positioned approximately in the center of each tooth and slightly toward the flank side of the tooth.
   c. If the pinion contact pattern is low, install a thinner pinion shim (**Figure 94**).
   d. If the pinion contact pattern is high, install a thicker pinion shim.
   e. The pinion gear bearing must be removed to replace the shim. Refer to *Pinion Gear* in this chapter.
   f. Changing shim thickness 0.1 mm (0.004 in.) moves the contact pattern approximately 1.5-2.0 mm (0.06-0.08 in.). Refer to **Table 4** for pinion gear shim sizes.
8. Reinstall the pinion gear and bearing, if they were removed, as described in this chapter. After obtaining a satisfactory pinion gear contact pattern, check the ring gear backlash as described under *Backlash Measurement* in this section.
9. Remove the housing cover and ring gear assembly. Refer to *Ring Gear and Housing Cover* in *Final Drive Unit Overhaul* in this chapter to continue with the final assembly procedure.

Table 1 REAR SUSPENSION SPECIFICATIONS

Rear axle travel	
VTX1300C models	92 mm (3.6 in.)
VTX1300R/S/T models	95 mm (3.7 in.)
Shock absorber standard preload adjuster setting	Second position

Table 2 FINAL DRIVE UNIT SERVICE SPECIFICATIONS

	New mm (in.)	Service limit mm (in.)
Final drive gear backlash		
Standard	0.05-0.15 (0.002-0.006)	0.30 (0.012)
Maximum difference in backlash measurements	–	0.10 (0.004)
Final drive gear assembly preload	0.2-0.4 N•m (1.8-3.5 in.-lb.)	–
Ring gear-to-stop pin clearance	0.30-0.60 (0.012-0.024)	–

Table 3 RING GEAR SHIM SIZES

Ring gear shim	Thickness mm (in.)
A	1.82 (0.072)
B	1.88 (0.074)
C	1.94 (0.076)
D (standard shim)	2.00 (0.079)
E	2.06 (0.081)
F	2.12 (0.083)
G	2.18 (0.086)
H	2.24 (0.088)
I	2.30 (0.091)

Table 4 PINION GEAR SHIM SIZES

Pinion gear shim	Thickness mm (in.)
A	1.82 (0.072)
B	1.88 (0.074)
C	1.94 (0.076)
D	2.00 (0.079)
E	2.06 (0.081)
F	2.12 (0.083)
G	2.18 (0.086)

Table 5 REAR SUSPENSION AND FINAL DRIVE TORQUE SPECIFICATIONS

	N•m	in.-lb.	ft.-lb.
Brake hose clamp bolt* (at swing arm)	12	106	–
Dust guard plate bolt	10	88	–
Final drive housing cover bolts*			
8 mm	25	–	18
10 mm	62	–	46
Final drive housing mounting nut	64	–	47
Final drive oil drain bolt	20	–	15
Final drive oil fill cap	12	106	–
Muffler mounting bolt	34	–	25
Pinion joint nut*	108	–	80
Pinion retainer lock tab bolt	10	88	–
Pinion retainer	147	–	108
Rear brake caliper stopper pin bolt*	69	–	51
Rear brake disc bolt*	42	–	31
Rear shock absorber mounting bolt	26	–	19
Right pivot bolt locknut	113	–	83
Swing arm pivot bolts			
Left	103	–	76
Right	14	–	10

*Refer to text for additional information.

CHAPTER FOURTEEN

BRAKES

Tables 1-3 are at the end of this chapter.

Brake maintenance intervals and routine inspection and adjustment procedures are in Chapter Three.

BRAKE SERVICE

WARNING
Do not ride the motorcycle unless the front and rear brakes are operating correctly.

WARNING
The motorcycles in this manual use DOT 4 brake fluid. Do not use DOT 5 brake fluid. This silicone-based brake fluid is not compatible with glycol-based DOT 3, DOT 4 or DOT 5.1. Do not intermix two different types of brake fluid as it can cause brake component damage and lead to brake system failure.

WARNING
Never reuse brake fluid expelled during brake bleeding. Contaminated brake fluid can cause brake failure. Dispose of brake fluid properly.

WARNING
*Whenever working on the brake system, do **not** inhale brake dust. Do **not** use compressed air to blow off brake parts. It may contain asbestos, which can cause lung injury and cancer. Wear a face mask that meets OHSA requirements for trapping asbestos particles, and wash hands and forearms thoroughly after completing the work. Before working on the brake system, spray the components with brake cleaner. Secure and dispose of all brake dust and cleaning materials properly.*

CAUTION
Cover all parts that could become contaminated by the accidental spilling of brake fluid. Wash any spilled brake fluid from any surface immediately, as it damages the finish. Use soapy water and rinse completely.

When adding brake fluid, use DOT 4 brake fluid from a sealed container. DOT 4 brake fluid is glycol-based and draws moisture, which greatly reduces its ability to perform correctly. It is a good idea to purchase brake fluid in small containers and discard any leftover quantities. Do not store a container of brake fluid with less than 1/4 of the fluid remaining.

The brake system transmits hydraulic pressure from the master cylinder to the brake calipers. This pressure is transmitted from the calipers to the brake pads, which grip both sides of the brake discs and slows the motorcycle. As the pads wear, the pistons move out of the caliper bores to automatically compensate for wear. As this occurs, the fluid level in the master cylinder reservoir goes down. This must be compensated for by occasionally adding fluid.

The proper operation of the system depends on routine inspection, a supply of clean DOT 4 brake fluid and a clean work environment when any service is performed. Any debris that enters the system or contaminates the pads or brake discs can damage the components and cause poor brake performance.

Perform brake service procedures carefully. Do not use any sharp tools inside the master cylinders, calipers or on the pistons. Damage to these components could cause a loss of system hydraulic pressure. If there is any doubt about your ability to correctly and safely service the brake system, have a professional technician perform the task.

Consider the following when servicing the brake system:
1. Do not allow disc brake fluid to contact any plastic parts or painted surfaces; damage will result.
2. Always keep the master cylinder reservoir and spare cans of brake fluid closed to prevent dust or moisture from entering. This contaminates the brake fluid and can cause brake failure.
3. Clean parts with DOT 4 brake fluid, isopropyl alcohol or an aerosol brake parts cleaner. Never use petroleum-based solvents on internal brake system components or any rubber part. These solvents cause seals to swell and distort.
4. Do not allow any grease or oil to contact the brake pads.
5. When cleaning the brake components, wear rubber gloves to keep brake fluid off skin.

NOTE
Removing the reservoir cover(s) does not allow air to enter the hydraulic system unless the fluid level drops to low and exposes the brake fluid passage holes in the reservoir.

6. If the hydraulic system has been opened, bleed the system to remove air from the system. Refer to *Brake Bleeding* in this chapter.

BRAKE BLEEDING

Bleeding the brakes removes air from the brake system. Air in the brake system increases brake lever

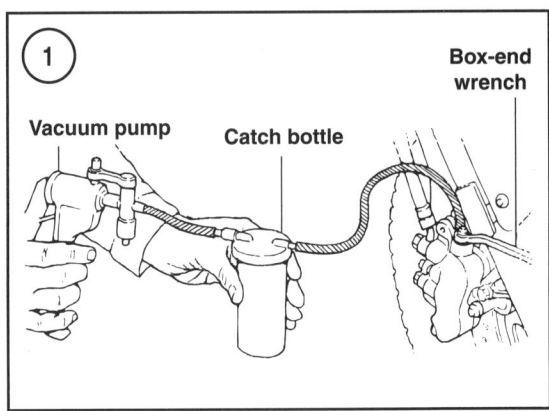

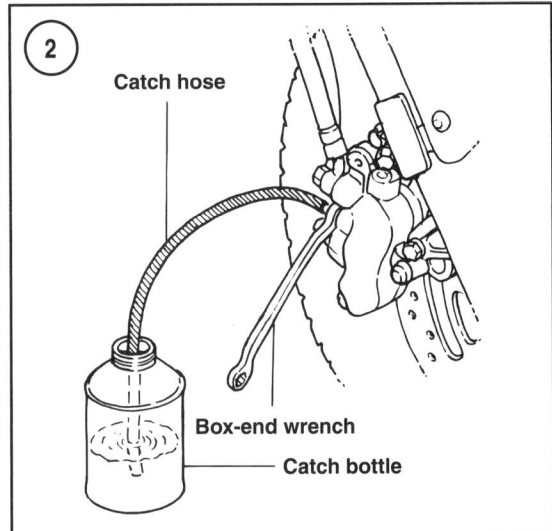

or pedal travel while causing it to feel spongy and less responsive. Under extreme braking (heat) conditions, it can cause complete loss of brake pressure.

Read *Brake Service* in this chapter.

Bleeding Tips

Before bleeding the brakes, note the following:
1. Clean the bleed valves and the area around the valves of all dirt and debris. Make sure the passageway in the end of the valve is open and clear.
2. Use a box-end wrench to open and close the bleed valves. This prevents damage to the hex-head.
3. Replace bleed valves with damaged hex-heads. These are difficult to loosen and cannot be tightened fully.
4. Install the box-end wrench on the bleed valve before installing the catch hose. This allows operation of the wrench without having to disconnect the hose.
5. Use a clear catch hose to allow visual inspection of the brake fluid as it leaves the caliper or brake unit. Air bubbles visible in the catch hose indicate that there still may be air trapped in the brake system.

refill the master cylinder reservoirs without having to disconnect the catch hose.

3. Operate the vacuum pump to create a vacuum in the catch hose connected to the bleed valve. Then open the bleed valve with a wrench to allow brake fluid to be drawn through the master cylinder, brake hoses and lines. Close the bleed valve before the brake fluid stops flowing from the system (no more vacuum in line) or before the master cylinder reservoir runs empty.

4. Repeat Step 3 until the brake fluid running through the vacuum hose is a clear and solid stream without air bubbles.

6. Depending on the play of the bleed valve when it is loosened, it is possible to see air exiting through the catch hose even through there is no air in the brake system. A loose or damaged catch hose also causes air leaks. In both cases, air is being introduced into the bleed system at the bleed valve threads and catch hose connection, and not from within the brake system itself. This condition can be misleading and cause excessive brake bleeding when there is no air in the system.

7. Open the bleed valve just enough to allow fluid to pass through the valve and into the catch bottle. The farther the bleed valve is opened, the looser the valve becomes. This allows air to be drawn into the system from around the valve threads.

8. If the system is difficult to bleed, tap the banjo bolt on the master cylinder a few times to remove air bubbles trapped in the hose connection where the brake fluid exits the master cylinder. Also tap the bolt and line connection points at the calipers and other brake units.

9. When bleeding the brakes, check the fluid level in the front and rear master cylinders frequently to prevent them from running dry, especially when using a vacuum pump. If the fluid level drops too low, air can enter the system and it must be bled again.

Pressure Bleeding

NOTE
When using a vacuum pump, adjust the brake fluid in the reservoir frequently as it will drop quite rapidly.

This procedure uses a vacuum pump with a hydraulic brake bleeding kit (**Figure 1**).

1. Connect the catch hose between the bleed valve and catch bottle. Connect the other hose between the catch bottle and vacuum pump. If necessary, refer to the tool manufacturer's instructions for additional information.

2. Secure the vacuum pump to the motorcycle with a length of stiff wire so it will be possible to check and

Manual Bleeding

This procedure describes how to bleed the brake system with an empty bottle, length of clear hose that fits tightly onto the bleed valve, and a wrench. Refer to **Figure 2**.

1. Connect the catch hose to the bleed valve on the brake caliper. Submerge the other end of the hose into the bottle partially filled with DOT 4 brake fluid. This prevents air from being drawn into the catch hose and back into the brake system.

2. Apply the front brake lever or rear brake pedal until it stops and holds in this position.

3. Open the bleed valve with a wrench and let the lever or pedal move to the limit of its travel, then close the bleed valve. Make sure to close the bleed valve before releasing the brake lever or pedal to prevent air from being drawn back into the system on the lever's or pedal's return stroke.

4. Release the lever or pedal slowly, then repeat Step 2 and Step 3 until the brake fluid running through the hose is a clear and solid stream without air bubbles.

Filling/Bleeding the Front Brake

Refer to *Bleeding Tips* in this section.

1. Turn the handlebars to level the front master cylinder and remove the screws, reservoir cover, diaphragm plate and diaphragm. The float can remain in the reservoir. Fill the reservoir to the level line (**Figure 3**).

NOTE
If the front brake was drained of all brake fluid, initially perform Step 2 to fill the brake line with brake fluid. Do not be concerned about the air bubbles exiting the system at this time. When the brake line is full of fluid, repeat Step 2 to bleed air from the lines.

2. Connect a brake bleeder to the bleed valve (**Figure 4**) on the front caliper. Open the bleed valve and op-

erate the brake bleeder to bleed the brake line as described in *Manual Bleeding* or *Pressure Bleeding* in this section. Repeat until the brake fluid exiting the catch hose is clear and free of air.

3. Repeat Step 2 as necessary until the front brake lever feels firm when applied and there are no air bubbles in the catch hose.

4. After bleeding the front brake, test the feel of the brake lever. It should be firm and should offer the same resistance each time it is operated. If the brake lever feels spongy, air is trapped in the system and the bleeding procedure must be continued.

5. Tighten the bleed valve (**Figure 4**) to 5.5 N•m (49 in.-lb.). Then operate the front brake lever and hold in position. Check the bleed valve for leaks.

6. If necessary, add fresh DOT 4 brake fluid and fill the reservoir to the level mark inside the reservoir (**Figure 3**).

7. Install the diaphragm, diaphragm plate and cover and tighten the screws securely.

8. Test ride the motorcycle slowly at first to make sure that the brakes are operating correctly.

Filling/Bleeding the Rear Brake

Refer to *Bleeding Tips* in this section.

1. Support the motorcycle so the rear reservoir is level.

2. Remove the rear brake reservoir mounting bolt (A, **Figure 5**) and the reservoir cover (B). Reinstall the mounting bolt to hold the reservoir in position. Place a paper towel underneath the reservoir.

3. Remove the rear reservoir cap, diaphragm plate and diaphragm. The float can remain in the reservoir. Fill the reservoir with DOT 4 brake fluid.

4. Operate the rear brake pedal several times to bleed air from the master cylinder.

> *NOTE*
> *If the rear brake system was drained of all brake fluid, initially perform Step 5 to fill the brake line with brake fluid. Do not be concerned about the air bubbles exiting the system at this time. When the brake line is full of fluid, repeat Step 5 to bleed air from the line.*

5. Connect a brake bleeder to the bleed valve (**Figure 6**) on the rear caliper. Open the bleed valve and operate the brake bleeder to bleed the brake line as described in *Manual Bleeding* or *Pressure Bleeding* in this section. Repeat until the brake fluid exiting the catch hose is clear and free of air.

6. Repeat Step 5 as necessary until the rear brake pedal feels firm when applied and there are no air bubbles in the catch hose.

7. After bleeding the rear brake, test the feel of the brake pedal. It should be firm and should offer the

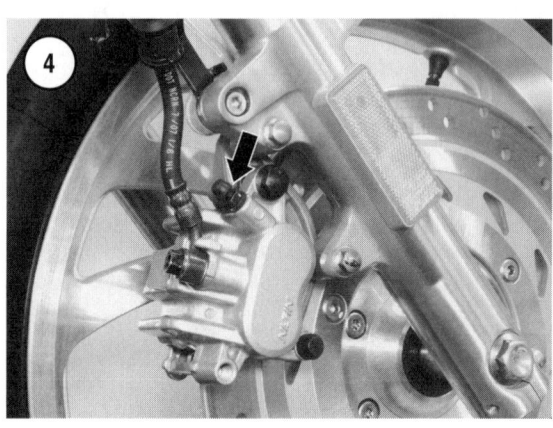

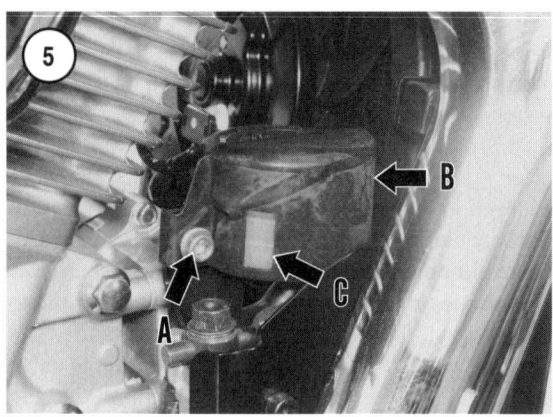

same resistance each time it is operated. If the brake pedal feels spongy, air is trapped in the system and the bleeding procedure must be continued.

8. Tighten the bleed valve (**Figure 6**) to 5.5 N•m (49 in.-lb.). Then operate the rear brake pedal and hold in position and check the bleed valve for leaks.

9. If necessary, add DOT 4 brake fluid to correct the level in the master cylinder reservoir. It must be above the level line (C, **Figure 5**).

10. Install the diaphragm, diaphragm plate and cap.

11. Install the reservoir cover (B, **Figure 5**) and tighten the rear brake reservoir mounting bolt (A) to 10 N•m (88 in.-lb.).

12. Test ride the motorcycle slowly at first to make sure that the brakes are operating correctly.

BRAKE FLUID DRAINING AND FLUSHING

Before disconnecting a hose from the brake system, drain either the front or rear brake system as described in this section.

When flushing the brake system, use *only* DOT 4 brake fluid as a flushing fluid. Flushing consists of pulling enough new brake fluid through the system until all of the old fluid is removed, and the fluid exiting the bleed valve appears clean and without any

BRAKES

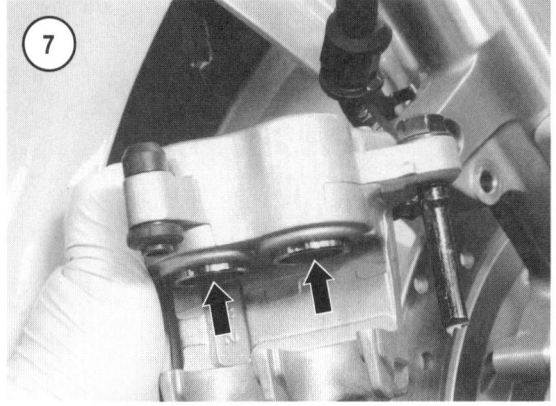

bubbles. To flush the brake system, use one of the bleeding procedures described in this chapter.

1. Read *Brake Service* and *Brake Bleeding* in this chapter.

2A. To service the front brake line, support the motorcycle on its sidestand and turn the handlebar to level the front brake master cylinder reservoir.

2B. To service the rear brake line, support the motorcycle on a workstand to level the rear brake cylinder.

3. Remove the reservoir cover (front) or cap (rear), diaphragm plate and diaphragm. The float can remain in the reservoir unless it requires cleaning.

4. Connect a brake bleeder to the brake caliper as described in this chapter. Operate the bleeder tool to remove as much brake fluid from the system as possible.

5. Close the bleed valve and disconnect the brake bleeder tool.

6. Service the brake components as described in this chapter.

BRAKE PADS

The pistons in the brake calipers are self-adjusting to compensate for brake pad wear. When the brake is applied, hydraulic pressure against the pistons causes the piston seals to stretch and deflect slightly. This allows the pistons to move out where they contact the brake pads and push them against the brake disc. When the brake is released, pressure against the piston seals is reduced and allows them to retract and return to their original shape. This action draws the pistons away from the brake pads and disengages the brake. As the brake pads wear, the pistons will travel farther through the seals in order to contact the brake pads.

There is no recommended mileage interval for changing the brake pads. Pad wear depends greatly on riding habits and the condition of the brake system. As the brake pads wear, the brake fluid level drops.

Refer to *Brakes* in Chapter Three to inspect the brake pad wear.

The following sections describe how to replace the front and rear brake pads with the calipers mounted on the motorcycle. However, a more thorough job of pad replacement is accomplished by removing the brake calipers (without disconnecting the hose). This allows the exposed parts of the caliper pistons to be cleaned before they are pushed back into their bores, preventing dust and dirt on the pistons from damaging the caliper seals. The caliper bracket can also be removed so the fixed shafts can be cleaned, lubricated and the rubber boots replaced if damaged.

Removal/Installation

Front brake pad

Always replace the front brake pads in pairs. Never use one new brake pad with a used brake pad in the caliper.

1. Read *Brake Service* in this chapter.

> *NOTE*
> *Before repositioning the caliper pistons, visually check the exposed parts of the caliper pistons. If the pistons are contaminated, pitted or have a rough appearance, remove the brake caliper (do not disconnect the brake hose) and clean the pistons (**Figure 7**) with a soft brush and cleaner that will not damage or swell the caliper seals. At the same time, clean and relubricate the caliper and mounting bracket fixed shafts and rubber boots. Refer to **Brake Caliper** in this chapter.*

2. Remove the front master cylinder cover, diaphragm plate and diaphragm. Use a large syringe to remove and discard about 50 percent of the fluid from the reservoir. This prevents the master cylinder from overflowing when the caliper pistons are compressed for reinstallation. Do *not* drain the entire reservoir or air will enter the system. Reinstall the diaphragm, diaphragm plate and cover.

CAUTION
Do not allow the master cylinder reservoir to overflow when performing Step 3. Brake fluid damages most surfaces it contacts.

3. Push against the side of the brake caliper so the brake pads push the caliper pistons into their bores to make room for the new brake pads. If the caliper pistons do not move properly, remove and service the caliper as described in this chapter.
4. Remove the pad pin plug (A, **Figure 8**).
5. Remove the pad pin (B, **Figure 8**) and both brake pads (**Figure 9**).

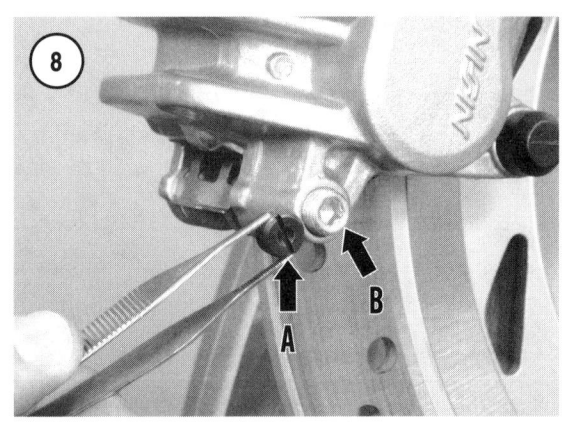

NOTE
***Figure 10** shows the pad spring with the caliper removed for clarity. The pad spring can be serviced with the caliper mounted on the front fork.*

6. Make sure the pad spring (**Figure 10**) is in good condition and installed inside the caliper. Replace the pad spring if damaged.
7. Inspect the pad pin (A, **Figure 11**) for excessive wear, corrosion or damage. Remove corrosion and dirt from the pad pin surface. A dirty or damaged pad pin prevents the brake pads from sliding properly and results in brake drag and overheating of the brake disc.
8. Inspect the brake pads (B, **Figure 11**) as follows:
    a. Inspect the friction material for light surface dirt, grease and oil contamination. Remove light contamination with sandpaper. If the contamination has penetrated the surface, replace the brake pads.
    b. Inspect the brake pads for excessive wear or damage. Replace the brake pads when the friction material is worn to the wear limit groove (**Figure 12**).
    c. Inspect the brake pads for uneven wear. If one pad has worn more than the other, it may be binding on its pad pin, fixed shaft or the caliper is not sliding properly. Inspect the caliper as described in this chapter.
    d. Inspect the shim (C, **Figure 11**) on the inner pad for corrosion, looseness and damage.

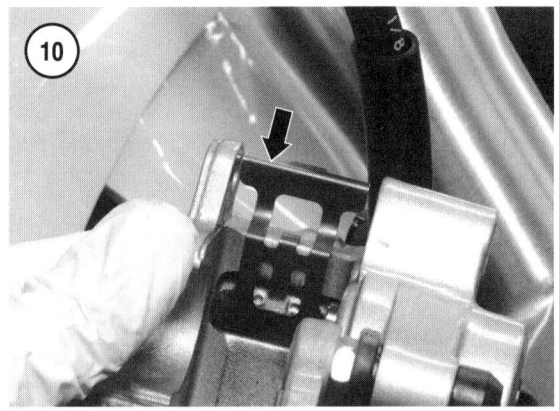

NOTE
If brake fluid is leaking from around the pistons, overhaul the brake caliper as described in this chapter.

9. Service the brake disc as follows:
    a. Use brake cleaner and a fine-grade emery cloth to remove road debris and brake pad residue from the brake disc. Clean both sides of the disc.

NOTE
Cleaning the brake disc is especially important if changing brake pad com-

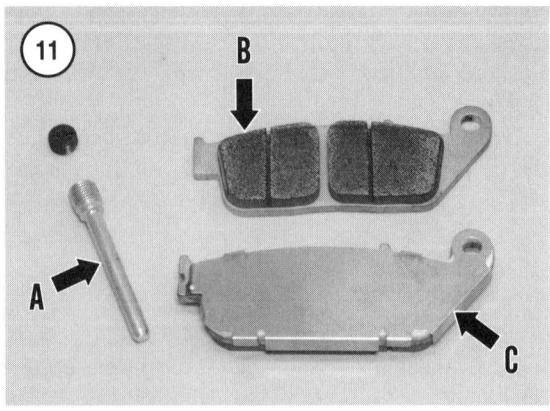

BRAKES

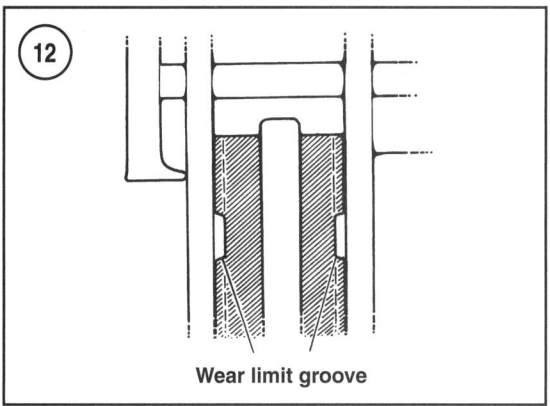

Wear limit groove

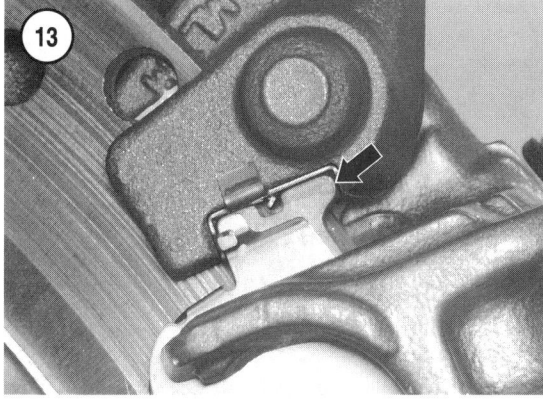

12. Tighten the pad pin (B, **Figure 9**) to 18 N•m (13 ft.-lb.).
13. Tighten the pad pin plug (A, **Figure 9**) to 2.5 N•m (22 in.-lb.).
14. Operate the front brake lever to seat the pads against the disc, then check the brake fluid level in the reservoir. If necessary, add new DOT 4 brake fluid. Refer to Chapter Three.

WARNING
Do not ride the motorcycle until both brakes and the rear brake light work properly.

15. While riding in a safe area, break in the pads gradually following the manufacturer's instructions. Immediate hard application glazes the new pads and reduces their effectiveness.

Rear brake pad

Always replace the rear brake pads in pairs. Never use one new brake pad with a used brake pad in the caliper.
1. Read *Brake Service* in this chapter.
2. Remove the mounting bolt (A, **Figure 5**) and the reservoir cover (B). Reinstall the mounting bolt to hold the reservoir in position. Place a paper towel underneath the reservoir.
3. Remove the rear reservoir cap, diaphragm plate and diaphragm. Use a large syringe to remove and discard about 50 percent of the fluid from the reservoir. This prevents the master cylinder from overflowing when the caliper piston is compressed for reinstallation. Do *not* drain the entire reservoir or air will enter the system. Reinstall the diaphragm, diaphragm plate and cap.

CAUTION
Do not allow the master cylinder reservoir to overflow when performing Step 4. Brake fluid damages most surfaces it contacts.

NOTE
*Before repositioning the caliper piston, check its exposed surface (**Figure 14**) for contamination, pitting and roughness. Because the rear caliper is partially removed when replacing the brake pads, the piston can be cleaned at the same time and then repositioned to make room for the new pads. The caliper bracket can also be removed so that the bracket pin bolt and fixed shaft can be cleaned, lubricated and the rubber boots replaced if damaged; refer to* **Brake Caliper** *in this chapter.*

pounds. Many compounds are not compatible with each other.

  b. Check the brake disc for wear as described in this chapter.
10. Install the brake pads (**Figure 9**) into the caliper so the friction material on both brake pads faces toward the brake disc while inserting the extended arm on the upper end of each pad against the pad retainer in the caliper bracket (**Figure 13**).
11. Push both brake pads up against the pad spring and install the pad pin (B, **Figure 8**) through the brake caliper and brake pads and tighten finger-tight.

4. Push against the side of the brake caliper so the brake pads push in the caliper piston to make room for the new brake pads. If the piston does not move properly, remove and service the caliper as described in this chapter.

5. Remove the pad pin plug (A, **Figure 15**) and loosen the pad pin (B). Do not remove the pad pin.

6. Remove the rear brake caliper bracket pin bolt (C, **Figure 15**) and pivot the caliper away from the brake disc. The caliper will pivot on the caliper bracket's fixed shaft.

7. Remove the pad pin (A, **Figure 16**) and both brake pads (B).

8. Make sure the pad spring (A, **Figure 17**) is in good condition and installed inside the caliper. Replace the pad spring if it appears weak or damaged.

9. Inspect the pad pin (A, **Figure 18**) for excessive wear, corrosion or damage. Remove corrosion and dirt from the pad pin surface. A dirty or damaged pad pin prevents the brake pads from sliding properly and results in brake drag and overheating of the brake disc.

10. Inspect the brake pads (B, **Figure 18**) as follows:

   a. Inspect the friction material for light surface dirt, grease and oil contamination. Remove light contamination with sandpaper. If the contamination has penetrated the surface, replace the brake pads.

   b. Inspect the brake pads for excessive wear or damage. Replace the brake pads when the friction material is worn to the wear limit groove (**Figure 12**).

   c. Inspect the brake pads for uneven wear. If one pad has worn more than the other, it may be binding on its bracket pin bolt or fixed shaft, or the caliper is not sliding properly. Inspect the caliper as described in this chapter.

   d. Inspect the shim (C, **Figure 18**) on the backside of each pad for corrosion, tightness and damage.

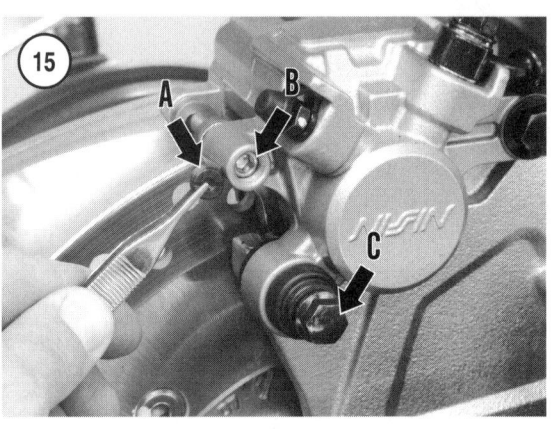

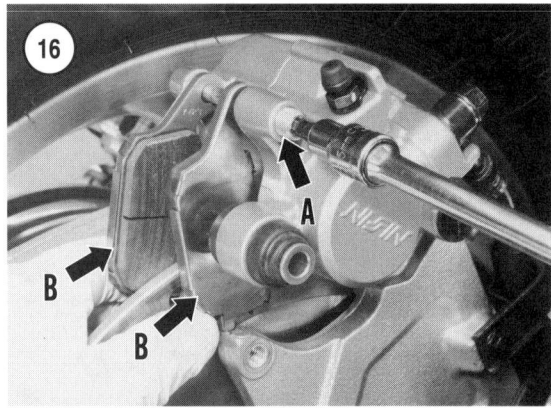

NOTE
If brake fluid is leaking from around the piston, overhaul the brake caliper as described in this chapter.

11. Service the brake disc as follows:

   a. Use brake cleaner and a fine-grade emery cloth to remove road debris and brake pad residue from the brake disc. Clean both sides of the disc.

NOTE
Cleaning the brake disc is especially important if changing brake pad compounds. Many compounds are not compatible with each other.

   b. Check the brake disc for wear as described in this chapter.

12. If necessary, clean the exposed areas on the piston with a cleaner that will not damage the caliper seals. Allow to dry.

13. If the piston was not repositioned, install a brake pad against the piston and use it to move the piston into its caliper bore. Remove the brake pad.

14. Install the brake pads (A, **Figure 19**) against the caliper bracket so the friction material on both brake

BRAKES

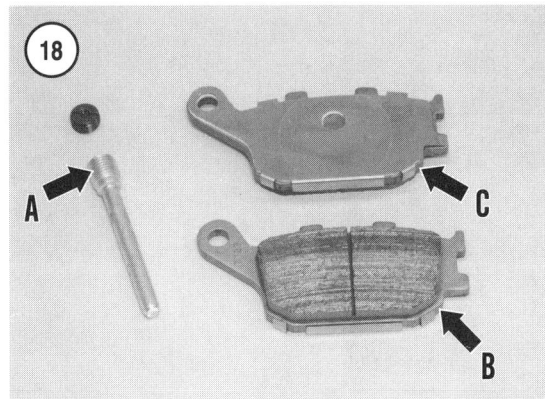

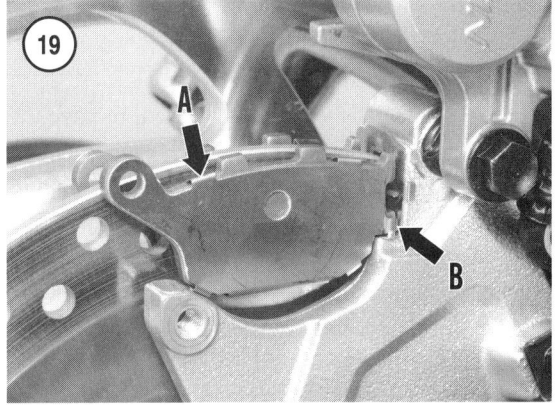

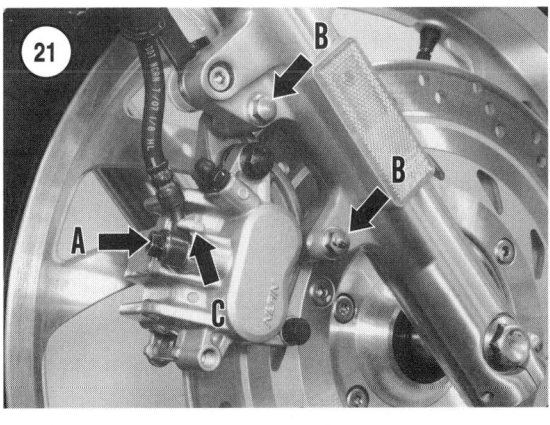

pads faces against the brake disc while inserting the extended arm on the front end of each pad against the pad retainer in the caliper bracket (B).

15. Lower the brake caliper over the brake pads. Push the caliper slightly to compress the pad spring against the brake pads and install the pad pin (B, **Figure 15**). Tighten the pad pin finger-tight while making sure the extended arm on the end of each brake pad is still engaged against the pad retainer (**Figure 20**).

16. Tighten the rear brake caliper bracket pin bolt (C, **Figure 15**) to 23 N•m (17 ft.-lb.).

17. Tighten the pad pin (B, **Figure 15**) to 18 N•m (13 ft.-lb.).

18. Install the pad pin plug (A, **Figure 15**) and tighten to 2.5 N•m (22 in.-lb.).

19. Operate the rear brake pedal to seat the pads against the disc, then check the brake fluid level in the reservoir. If necessary, add new DOT 4 brake fluid. Refer to Chapter Three.

> **WARNING**
> *Do not ride the motorcycle until both brakes and the rear brake light work properly.*

20. While riding in a safe area, break in the pads gradually following the manufacturer's instructions. Immediate hard application glazes the new pads and reduces their effectiveness.

BRAKE CALIPER

Removal/Installation

Read *Brake Service* in this chapter.

Front brake caliper

1. Support the motorcycle on its sidestand and turn the front wheel to access the caliper.

2. If the caliper is going to be removed from the motorcycle:
   a. Remove the brake pads as described in *Brake Pads* in this chapter.
   b. Drain the brake fluid from the front brake line as described in this chapter.
   c. Remove the brake hose banjo bolt (A, **Figure 21**) and washers at the caliper. There should be sealing washers on each side of the brake hose.
   d. Place the loose end of the brake hose in a plastic bag to prevent brake fluid from leaking onto the wheel or fork.

3. Remove the brake caliper mounting bolts (B, **Figure 21**) and remove the brake caliper.

4. If the brake hoses were not disconnected at the caliper, insert a spacer block between the brake pads

and support the caliper with a wire hook. Do not let the caliper hang from the brake hose.

NOTE
The spacer block prevents the pistons from being forced out of the caliper if the front brakes are applied while the brake caliper is removed from the brake disc.

5. If necessary lubricate and service the fixed shafts and boots as described in this section.
6. If necessary, service the brake caliper as described in this section.
7. Installation is the reverse of these steps. Note the following:
   a. Install the caliper assembly over the brake disc. If the pads are installed in the caliper, be careful not to damage their leading edge. Install two new brake caliper mounting bolts (B, **Figure 21**) and tighten to 31 N•m (23 ft.-lb.).

   NOTE
   If reusing the original brake caliper mounting bolts, remove all threadlocking compound residue from the bolt threads and reinstall with a medium strength threadlocking comopound applied to the bolt threads. The threads on new bolts have a threadlocking compound preapplied.

   b. Place a new sealing washer on each side of the brake hose and install the banjo bolt (A, **Figure 21**). Position the hose against the stopper (C, **Figure 21**) on the caliper and tighten the banjo bolt to 34 N•m (25 ft.-lb.).
   c. If removed, install the brake pads as described in this chapter.
   d. Bleed the front brake line as described in this chapter.
   e. Operate the front brake lever to seat the pads against the brake disc.

Rear brake caliper

1. Support the motorcycle on a workstand.
2. If the caliper is going to be removed from the motorcycle:
   a. Remove the brake pads as described in this chapter.
   b. Drain the brake fluid from the rear master cylinder as described in this chapter.
   c. Remove the brake hose banjo bolt (A, **Figure 22**) and washers at the caliper. There should be sealing washers on each side of the brake hose.

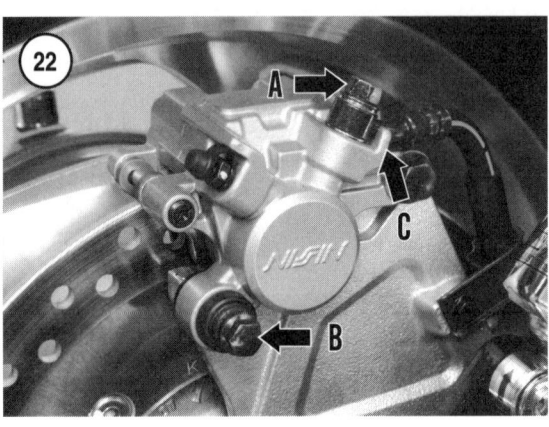

   d. Place the loose end of the brake hose in a plastic bag to prevent brake fluid from leaking onto the swing arm and exhaust pipe.
3. If the brake pads were not removed, remove the rear brake caliper bracket pin bolt (B, **Figure 22**).
4. Pivot the brake caliper upward, then slide it out of the caliper bracket.
5. If the brake hose was not disconnected at the caliper, insert a spacer block between the brake pads and support the caliper with a wire hook. Do not let the caliper hang from the brake hose.

NOTE
The spacer block prevents the piston from being forced out of the caliper if the rear brake pedal is applied while the brake caliper is removed from the brake disc.

6. If necessary lubricate and service the fixed shaft and boots as described in this section.
7. If necessary, service the brake caliper as described in this section.
8. Installation is the reverse of these steps. Note the following:
   a. If removed, install the brake pads as described in this chapter.
   b. Tighten the rear brake caliper bracket pin bolt (B, **Figure 22**) to 23 N•m (17 ft.-lb.).
   c. Place a new sealing washer on each side of the brake hose and install the banjo bolt (A, **Figure 22**). Position the hose against the stopper (C, **Figure 22**) on the caliper and tighten the banjo bolt to 34 N•m (25 ft.-lb.).
   d. Bleed the rear brake line as described in this chapter.
   e. Operate the rear brake pedal to seat the pads against the brake disc.

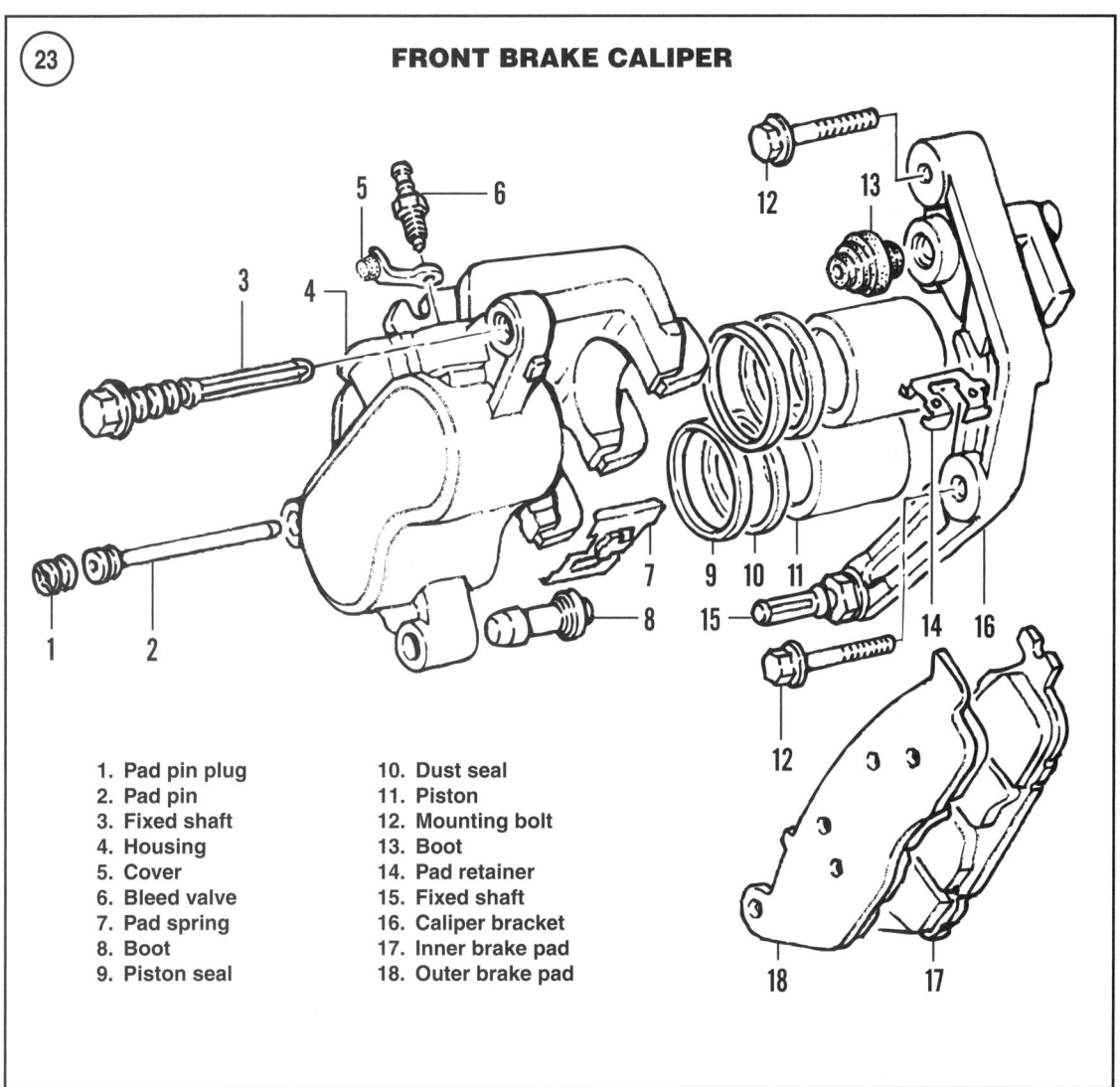

㉓ FRONT BRAKE CALIPER

1. Pad pin plug
2. Pad pin
3. Fixed shaft
4. Housing
5. Cover
6. Bleed valve
7. Pad spring
8. Boot
9. Piston seal
10. Dust seal
11. Piston
12. Mounting bolt
13. Boot
14. Pad retainer
15. Fixed shaft
16. Caliper bracket
17. Inner brake pad
18. Outer brake pad

Overhaul

These procedures apply to the front (**Figure 23**) and rear (**Figure 24**) brake calipers.

Read *Brake Service* in this chapter.

Fixed shafts and boots inspection/removal/installation/lubrication

The brake calipers are a floating design. Fixed shafts mounted on the caliper housing and caliper bracket allow the brake caliper to slide or float during piston movement. The rubber boots installed over each shaft prevent dirt from entering and causing shaft wear. A grooved or damaged shaft may bind and prevent caliper movement. If a caliper is not free to float, it causes the brake pads to drag on the brake disc. This will cause unnecessary pad wear and may overheat the disc and brake fluid.

The fixed shafts and boots can be serviced with the brake calipers mounted on the motorcycle.

1. Remove the brake pads as described in this chapter.
2A. Remove the front brake caliper boots as follows:
   a. Remove the brake caliper as described in this section.
   b. Slide the caliper bracket (**Figure 25**) out of the caliper.
   c. Pinch the caliper boot (A, **Figure 26**) on its open side and remove it from the caliper.
   d. Remove the caliper bracket boot (A, **Figure 27**).
2B. Remove the rear brake caliper boots as follows:
   a. Slide the caliper (B, **Figure 17**) off the caliper bracket.
   b. Remove the caliper bracket boot (A, **Figure 28**).
   c. Remove the caliper boot and collar (B, **Figure 28**).

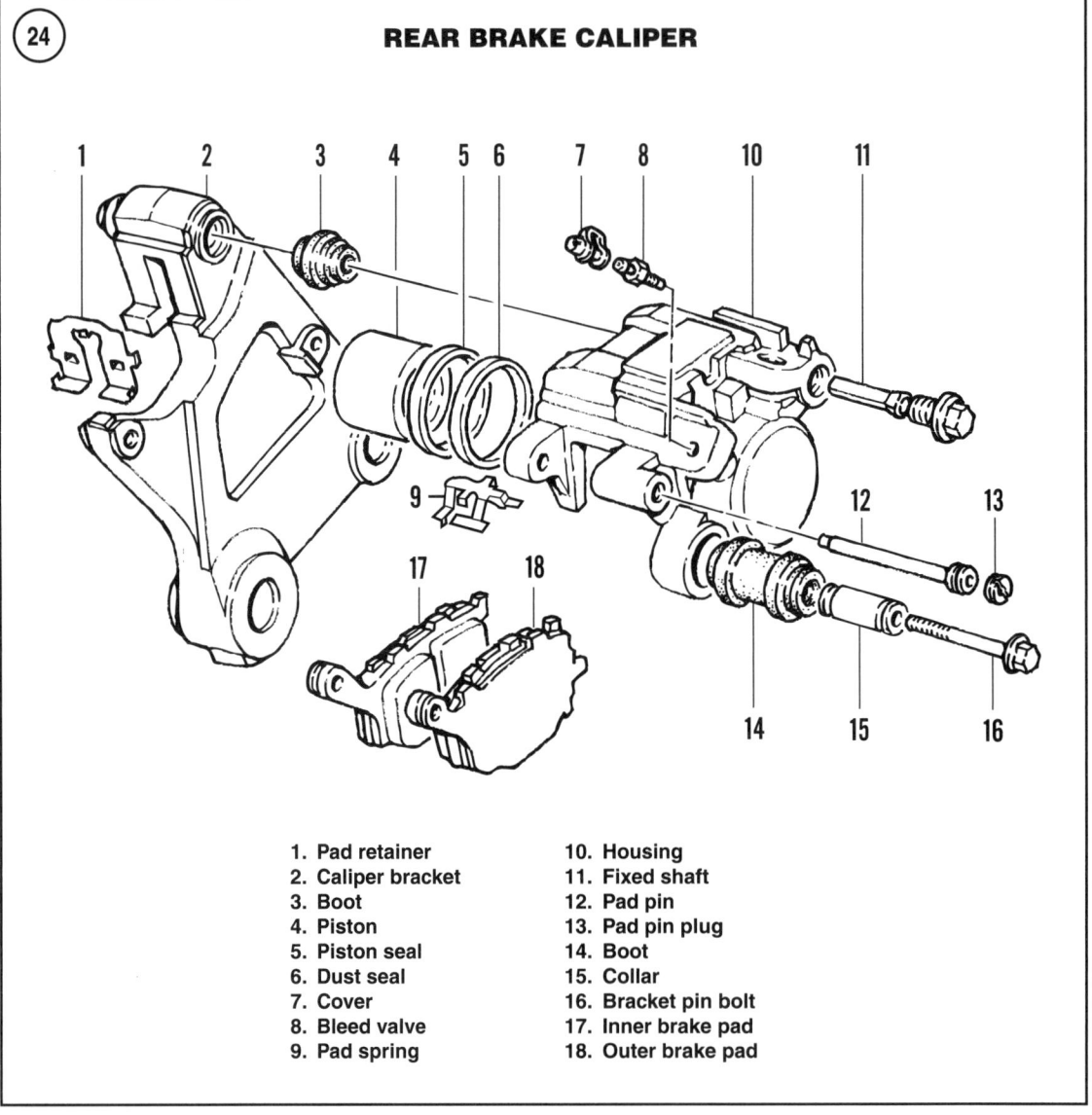

REAR BRAKE CALIPER

1. Pad retainer
2. Caliper bracket
3. Boot
4. Piston
5. Piston seal
6. Dust seal
7. Cover
8. Bleed valve
9. Pad spring
10. Housing
11. Fixed shaft
12. Pad pin
13. Pad pin plug
14. Boot
15. Collar
16. Bracket pin bolt
17. Inner brake pad
18. Outer brake pad

3. Inspect the fixed shaft and boot assembly as follows:
   a. Inspect the rubber boots for hardness, age deterioration and damage.
   b. Check the rear caliper collar (15, **Figure 24**) for damage.
   c. Inspect the caliper housing and caliper bracket fixed shafts for excessive wear, uneven wear, steps and other damage. Replace damaged fixed shafts as required.
4. When reinstalling or replacing a damaged fixed shaft, apply a medium strength threadlocking compound onto the shaft threads and tighten as follows:
   a. Front caliper fixed shaft (B, **Figure 26**): 27 N•m (20 ft.-lb.).
   b. Front caliper bracket fixed shaft (B, **Figure 27**): 13 N•m (115 in.-lb.). This shaft cannot be replaced separately. If damaged, replace the caliper bracket assembly.
   c. Rear caliper fixed shaft (C, **Figure 28**): 27 N•m (20 ft.-lb.).
5. Replace the pad retainer mounted on the front (C, **Figure 27**) and rear (D, **Figure 28**) caliper brackets if weak or damaged. Make sure each pad retainer is clamped onto its caliper bracket.
6. Installation is the reverse of these steps. Note the following:
   a. Partially pack the boots with silicone brake grease and install the boots facing in their original direction. Refer to A, **Figure 26**, A, **Figure 27**, A, **Figure 28** and **Figure 29**.
   b. On the rear caliper, install the collar and center it in its bore (**Figure 29**).
   c. Lightly lubricate the fixed shafts with silicone brake grease.

BRAKES

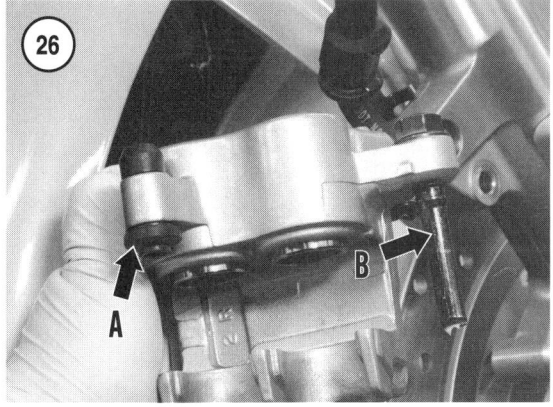

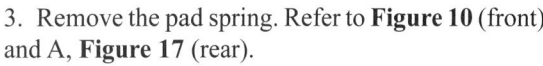

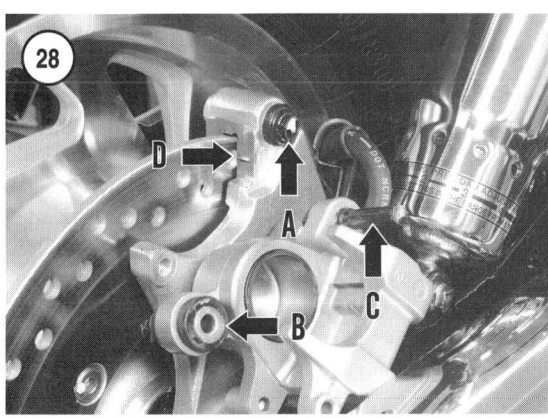

Disassembly

1. Remove the brake pads as described in this chapter. Remove the brake caliper as described in this section.

2. If servicing the front caliper, remove the caliper bracket as described in this section.

> **NOTE**
> *The rear caliper bracket can be serviced with the bracket mounted on the motorcycle. To remove the rear caliper bracket, remove the rear wheel (Chapter Eleven).*

3. Remove the pad spring. Refer to **Figure 10** (front) and A, **Figure 17** (rear).

4. Remove the rubber fixed shaft boot from the caliper as described in this section.

5. Close the bleed valve so air cannot escape.

> **WARNING**
> *Wear eye protection when using compressed air to remove the pistons and keep your fingers away from the pistons.*

> **CAUTION**
> *Do not try to pry the piston(s) out. This may damage the piston and caliper bore.*

6A. On the front caliper, cushion the caliper piston with a shop rag and position the caliper with the piston bores facing down. Be sure to keep hands away from the pistons and apply compressed air through the brake hose port (**Figure 30**) to pop the pistons out. If only one piston came out, block its bore opening with a piece of thick rubber (old inner tube), wooden block and clamp as shown in **Figure 31**. Apply compressed air again and remove the remaining piston.

6B. On the rear caliper, cushion the caliper piston with a shop rag and position the caliper with the piston bore facing down. Be sure to keep hands away from the piston and apply compressed air through the brake hose port to pop the piston out.

CAUTION
Do not damage the caliper bore grooves when removing the seals in Step 7.

7. Remove the dust and piston seals (**Figure 32**) from the caliper bore grooves and discard them.
8. Remove the bleed valve and its cover from the caliper.
9. Clean and inspect the brake caliper assembly as described in this section.

Assembly

Use new DOT 4 brake fluid when lubricating the parts in the following steps.
1. Install the bleed valve and cover into the caliper and tighten finger-tight.
2. Soak the new piston and dust seals in brake fluid.
3. Lubricate the piston(s) with brake fluid.

NOTE
*The piston seals are thicker than the dust seals (**Figure 32**).*

4. Install a new piston seal (**Figure 32**) into the cylinder bore's rear groove. Repeat on the front caliper.
5. Install a new dust seal (**Figure 32**) into the cylinder bore's front groove. Repeat on the front caliper.

NOTE
Check that each seal fits squarely in its groove.

6. Install the piston into its caliper bore with its open side facing out. To prevent the piston from damaging the seals, turn it into the bore by hand until it bottoms out. Repeat on the other caliper.
7. Install the pad spring. Refer to **Figure 10** (front) and A, **Figure 17** (rear).
8. Lubricate and install the rubber boot into the caliper as described in this section.
9. If necessary, service the rubber fixed shaft boot installed in the caliper bracket as described in this section.
10. On the front caliper, install the caliper bracket as described in this section.
11. Install the brake caliper as described in this section. Install the brake pads as described in this chapter.

Inspection

Refer to the specifications in **Table 1** (front caliper) or **Table 2** (rear caliper). Replace worn or damaged parts as described in this section.

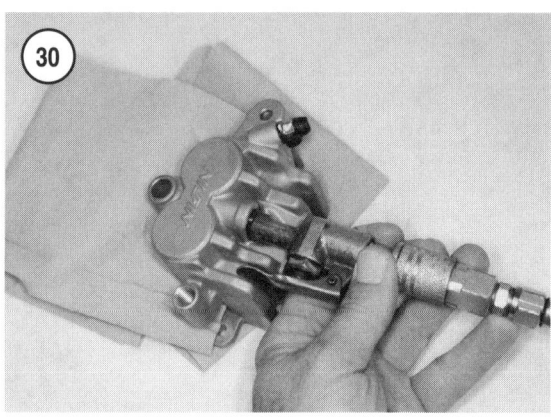

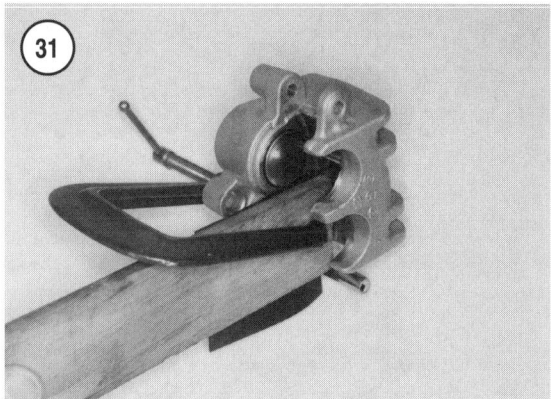

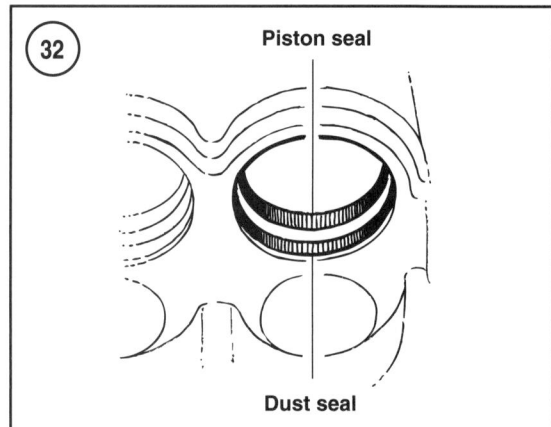

1. Clean and dry the caliper assembly as follows:
   a. Handle the brake components carefully when servicing them.
   b. Use only DOT 4 brake fluid or isopropyl alcohol to wash rubber parts in the brake system. Never allow any petroleum-based cleaner to contact the rubber parts. These chemicals cause the rubber to swell, requiring their replacement.
   c. Clean the dust and piston seal grooves carefully to avoid damaging the caliper bore. Use a small pick or brush to clean the grooves.

BRAKES

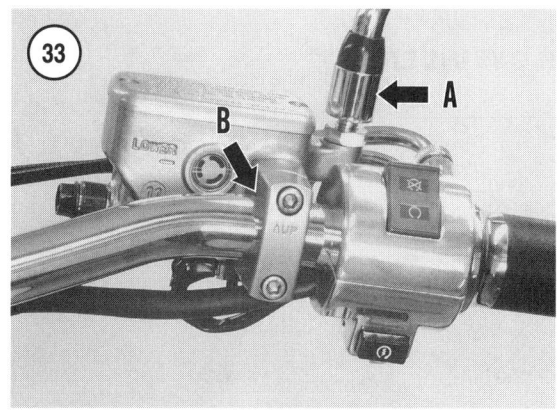

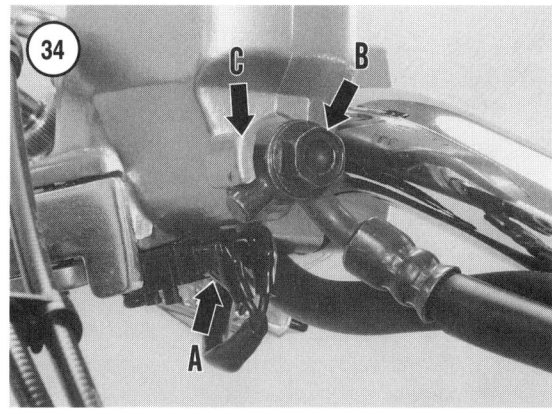

If a hard varnish residue has built up in the grooves, soak the caliper housing in solvent to help soften the residue. Then wash the caliper in soapy water and rinse completely.

   d. If alcohol or solvent was used to clean the caliper, blow dry with compressed air.
   e. Check the fluid passages to make sure they are clean and dry.
   f. After cleaning the parts, place them on a clean lint-free cloth until reassembly.

CAUTION
Do not get any oil or grease onto any of the brake caliper components. These chemicals cause the rubber parts in the brake system to swell, permanently damaging them.

2. Check each cylinder bore for corrosion, deep scratches and other wear marks. Do not hone the cylinder bores.
3. Measure each caliper cylinder bore inside diameter with a bore gauge or use a telescoping gauge and micrometer.
4. Inspect the pistons for pitting, corrosion, cracks or other damage.
5. Measure each piston outside diameter with a micrometer.

6. Clean the bleed valve with compressed air. Check the valve threads for damage. Replace the dust cap if missing or damaged.
7. Clean the banjo bolt with compressed air.
8. Inspect the fixed shafts and rubber boots as described in this section.

FRONT MASTER CYLINDER

Read *Brake Service* in this chapter.

Removal

1. Support the motorcycle on its sidestand and turn the handlebar to level the master cylinder.
2. Cover the fuel tank and other components to prevent contact from brake fluid.
3. Remove the rearview mirror (A, **Figure 33**).
4. Disconnect the front brake light switch connectors (A, **Figure 34**).
5. Drain the front master cylinder as described in this chapter.
6. Remove the banjo bolt (B, **Figure 34**) and washers securing the brake hose to the master cylinder. Cover the brake hose to prevent leaks and contamination.
7. Plug the master cylinder opening.
8. Remove the bolts, clamp (B, **Figure 33**) and master cylinder.
9. If necessary, service the master cylinder as described in this section.
10. Clean the handlebar, master cylinder and clamp mating surfaces.

Installation

1. Mount the master cylinder onto the handlebar and align the master cylinder and clamp mating surfaces with the punch mark on the handlebar.
2. Install the clamp (B, **Figure 33**) with its UP mark facing up. Tighten the upper mounting bolt, then the lower mounting bolt to 12 N•m (106 in.-lb.).
3. Connect the brake hose onto the master cylinder with the banjo bolt (B, **Figure 34**) while installing a new sealing washer on each side of the hose. Position the hose against the stopper (C, **Figure 34**) on the master cylinder and tighten the banjo bolt (B) to 34 N•m (25 ft.-lb.).
4. Reconnect the front brake light switch (A, **Figure 34**) connectors.
5. Refill the master cylinder reservoir and bleed the front brakes as described in this chapter.
6. Reinstall and adjust the rearview mirror (A, **Figure 33**).

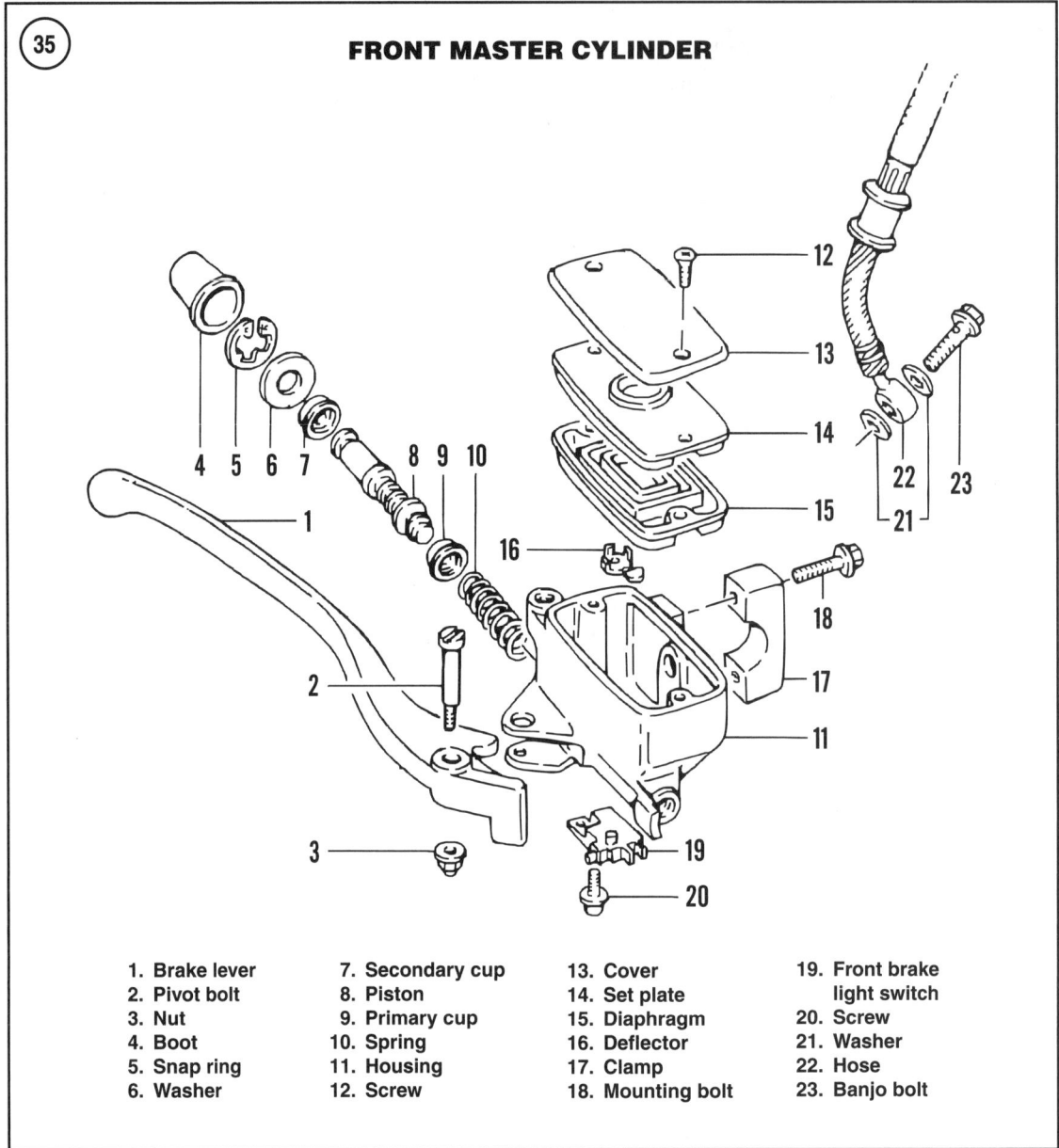

35 FRONT MASTER CYLINDER

1. Brake lever
2. Pivot bolt
3. Nut
4. Boot
5. Snap ring
6. Washer
7. Secondary cup
8. Piston
9. Primary cup
10. Spring
11. Housing
12. Screw
13. Cover
14. Set plate
15. Diaphragm
16. Deflector
17. Clamp
18. Mounting bolt
19. Front brake light switch
20. Screw
21. Washer
22. Hose
23. Banjo bolt

7. Turn the ignition switch on and make sure the rear brake light comes on when operating the front brake lever.

Disassembly

Refer to **Figure 35**.
1. Remove the master cylinder as described in this section.
2. Remove the screw (A, **Figure 36**) and front brake light switch (B).
3. Remove the nut (C, **Figure 36**), pivot bolt and brake lever.
4. Remove the deflector (**Figure 37**) from the reservoir.

WARNING
Inspect the relief port located inside the reservoir for any foreign matter or a swollen primary cup. If this port remains closed after the brake lever is released, pressure will build in the system and cause brake drag. The relief port is the smaller of the two ports.

5. Remove the dust boot (**Figure 38**) from the master cylinder.

NOTE
If brake fluid is leaking from the piston bore, the piston cups are worn or damaged. Replace the piston assembly.

BRAKES

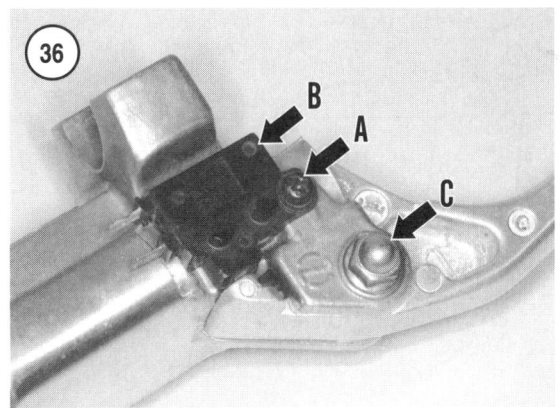

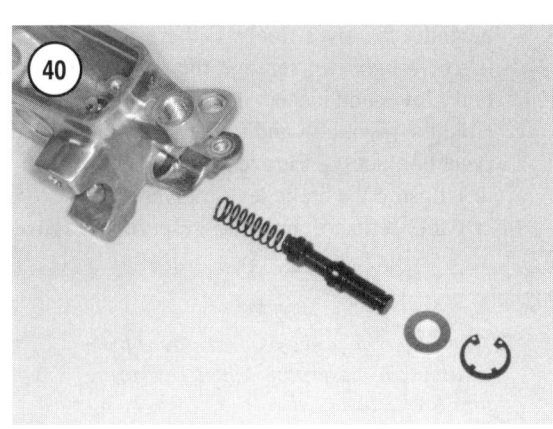

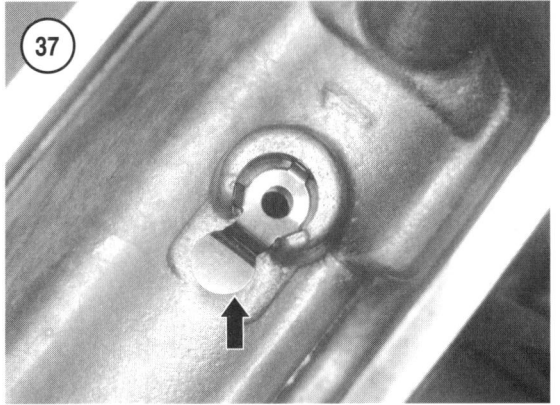

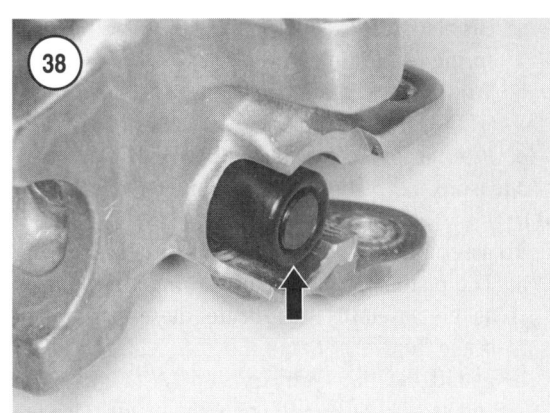

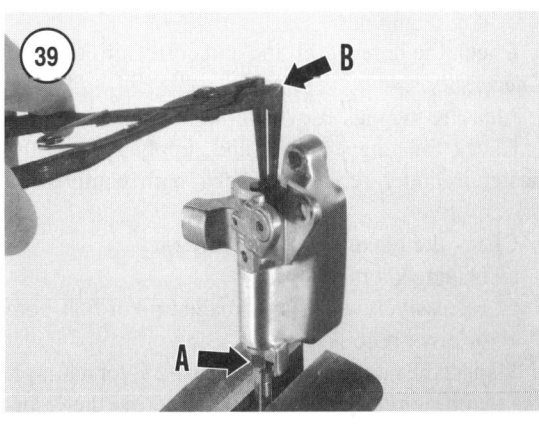

6. Thread a bolt and nut into the brake hose port, and secure the bolt in a vise (A, **Figure 39**). Use the nut to lock the master cylinder in place.
7. Compress the piston and remove the snap ring (5, **Figure 35**) with snap ring pliers (B, **Figure 39**) and the washer if used. Remove the piston assembly from the master cylinder bore (**Figure 40**). Do not remove the cups from the piston.
8. Clean and inspect the master cylinder assembly as described in this section.

Assembly

1. If installing a new piston assembly, assemble it as described in Step 4 of *Inspection* in this section.
2. Lubricate the piston assembly and cylinder bore with DOT 4 brake fluid.

> *CAUTION*
> *Do not allow the piston cups to tear or turn inside out when installing them into the master cylinder bore. Both cups are larger than the bore.*

3. Insert the piston assembly (spring end first) into the master cylinder bore (**Figure 40**). Install the washer (6, **Figure 35**) if used.
4. Compress the piston assembly and install a new snap ring with its flat side facing out. Make sure the snap ring seats in the groove completely. Push and release the piston a few times to make sure it moves smoothly and that the snap ring is secure.
5. Install the boot over the piston with its open side facing the piston's round end (**Figure 38**). Seat the outer end of the boot into the piston groove.
6. Lubricate the end of the piston with silicone brake grease.
7. Install the brake lever assembly:
   a. Lubricate the pivot bolt with silicone brake grease. Do not lubricate the bolt threads.
   b. Install the brake lever and tighten the brake lever pivot bolt to 1 N•m (8.8 in.-lb.). Ensure the

brake lever moves freely. If there is any binding or roughness, remove the pivot bolt and brake lever and inspect the parts.

c. Hold the pivot bolt and tighten the brake lever pivot bolt nut (C, **Figure 36**) to 6 N•m (53 in.-lb.). Ensure the brake lever moves freely.

8. Install the deflector into the reservoir (**Figure 37**).

NOTE
The deflector prevents brake fluid from exiting the reservoir when operating the brake lever when the cover is removed during brake bleeding.

9. Install the front brake light switch (B, **Figure 36**) and screw (B). Tighten the screw securely.
10. Install the master cylinder as described in this section.

Inspection

Refer to the specifications in **Table 1**. Replace worn or damaged parts as described in this section.

1. Clean and dry the master cylinder assembly as follows:
   a. Handle the brake components carefully when servicing them.

WARNING
Never use petroleum-based solvents to clean brake components, or allow solvent to contact rubber parts. Petroleum-based chemicals cause the rubber parts to swell, requiring their replacement.

   b. Use only DOT 4 brake fluid or isopropyl alcohol to wash rubber parts in the brake system.
   c. Clean the master cylinder snap ring groove carefully. Use a small pick or brush to clean the groove. If a hard varnish residue has built up in the groove, soak the master cylinder in solvent to help soften the residue. Then wash in soapy water and rinse completely.
   d. Blow the master cylinder dry with compressed air.
   e. Place cleaned parts on a clean lint-free cloth until reassembly.

CAUTION
Do not remove the cups from the piston.

2. Inspect the piston assembly. If any of these parts are worn or damaged, replace the piston and seals as an assembly. Check for:

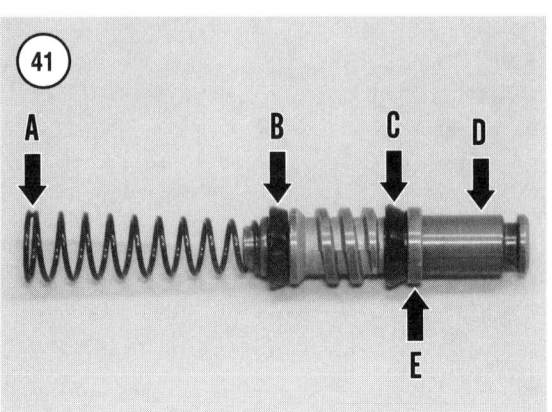

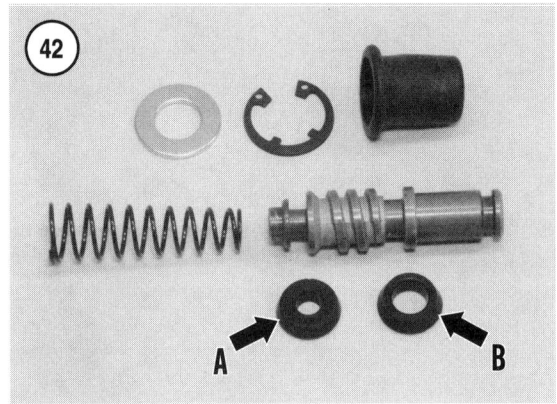

   a. Broken, distorted or collapsed piston return spring (A, **Figure 41**).
   b. Worn, cracked, damaged or swollen primary (B, **Figure 41**) and secondary cups (C).
   c. Worn or pitted piston (D, **Figure 41**).

3. Measure the piston outside diameter (E, **Figure 41**).
4. To assemble a new piston assembly (**Figure 42**):
   a. The piston, both cups and spring are replaced as an assembly. Lubricate these parts with brake fluid.
   b. Install the new primary cup (A, **Figure 42**) and secondary cup (B) onto the piston. Use the original piston (**Figure 41**) as a reference for cup alignment.
5. Check the bore for pitting and corrosion. Discard if necessary.
6. Measure the master cylinder bore inside diameter.
7. Check for plugged relief and supply ports in the master cylinder reservoir. Clean with compressed air.
8. Check the brake lever assembly for:
   a. Damaged brake lever.
   b. Excessively worn or damaged pivot bolt bore or pivot bolt.
9. Inspect the diaphragm (15, **Figure 35**) for damage. The diaphragm prevents air from entering the reser-

43 REAR MASTER CYLINDER / BRAKE PEDAL TYPE 1 (VTX1300R/S/T MODELS)

1. Rear brake pedal pivot bolt
2. Footrest bracket
3. Pivot collar
4. Seal
5. Rear brake pedal
6. Return spring
7. Rear brake pedal pivot bolt nut
8. Rear master cylinder
9. Cotter pin
10. Clevis pin
11. Cover
12. Bolt

voir and is folded so that it can move with changes in the brake fluid level. A damaged diaphragm will allow moisture to enter the reservoir.

10. Inspect the reservoir cover (13, **Figure 35**) for damage. Check the small vent notches in the sealing surface for contamination. These must be clear to vent the reservoir to the atmosphere.

REAR MASTER CYLINDER AND BRAKE PEDAL

Read *Brake Service* in this chapter.

The rear master cylinder and brake pedal assemblies are mounted onto the right side footrest mounting bracket. The footrest mounting brackets are removed with these assemblies attached. Two different footrest mounting brackets have been used and are identified in the text as follows:

1. Type I: VTX1300R/S/T models (**Figure 43**).
2. Type II: VTX1300C models (**Figure 44**).

Removal

1. Support the motorcycle on a workstand.

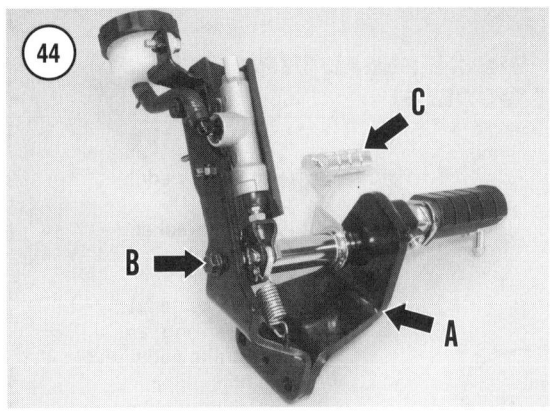

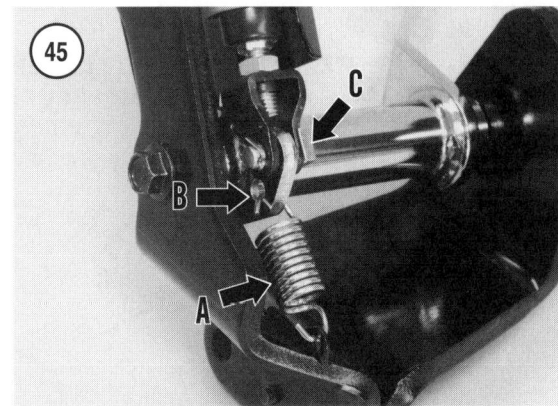

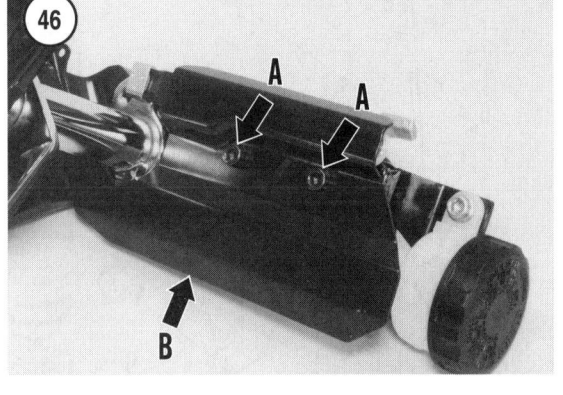

2. On Type I models, remove the footrest board as described in Chapter Fifteen.

CAUTION
Wipe up any spilled brake fluid immediately, as it damages the finish of most plastic and metal surfaces. Use soapy water and rinse thoroughly.

NOTE
The Type II footrest assembly is shown in the following photographs. The Type I assembly (Figure 43) is similar.

3. Remove the right footrest mounting bracket (2, **Figure 43** [Type I] or A, **Figure 44** [Type II]) with the rear master cylinder and reservoir attached as described in Chapter Fifteen. Refer to **Figure 43** (Type I) or **Figure 44** (Type II).
4. Disconnect the rear brake pedal return spring (A, **Figure 45**).
5. Remove the cotter pin (B, **Figure 45**) and clevis pin (C) securing the rear brake pedal to the master cylinder.

NOTE
If it is only necessary to remove the rear brake pedal, continue with Step 9.

6. Remove the two bolts (A, **Figure 46**) and cover (B). On Type II models, remove the two spacers (**Figure 47**).
7. Note the reservoir hose routing, then remove the rear master cylinder (A, **Figure 48**) with the hose (B) and reservoir (C) attached. Refer to 8, **Figure 43** (Type I) or **Figure 48** (Type II).
8. If necessary, service the master cylinder as described in this section.
9A. On Type I models, remove the nut (7, **Figure 43**), pivot bolt (1) and rear brake pedal (5).
9B. On Type II models, remove the pivot bolt (B, **Figure 44**) and rear brake pedal (C).

10. If necessary, remove the pivot collar and seals (**Figure 49**) from the brake pedal bore.

Installation

1. If the rear brake pedal was removed, perform the following:
   a. Clean and dry the rear brake pedal, pivot collar, pivot bolt, nut (Type I) and bracket threads (Type II).
   b. Clean the seals and check for tearing, cracks and other damage. Replace if necessary.
   c. Lubricate the seal lips with grease and install into the brake pedal bores with their open side (**Figure 49**) facing out.
   d. Lubricate the grooves on the pivot collar with grease and install into the brake pedal bore, making sure not to damage the seal lips.
   e. Lubricate the pivot bolt shoulder with grease. Do not lubricate the threads.
2A. On Type I models, install the rear brake pedal (5, **Figure 43**), pivot bolt (1) and nut (7). Hold the pivot bolt and tighten the nut to 27 N•m (20 ft.-lb.).
2B. On Type II models, install the rear brake pedal (C, **Figure 44**) and pivot bolt (B) and tighten to 27 N•m (20 ft.-lb.).

BRAKES

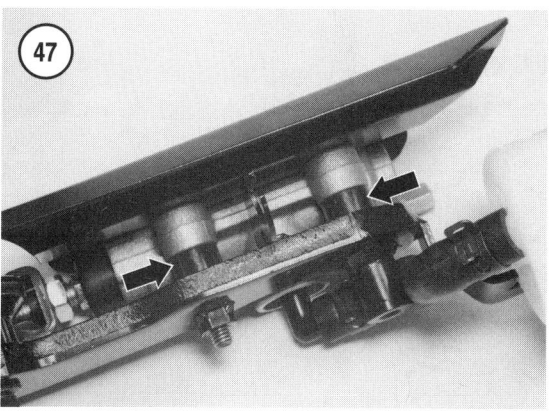

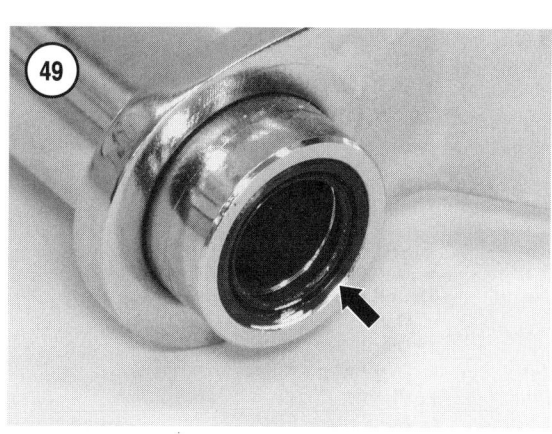

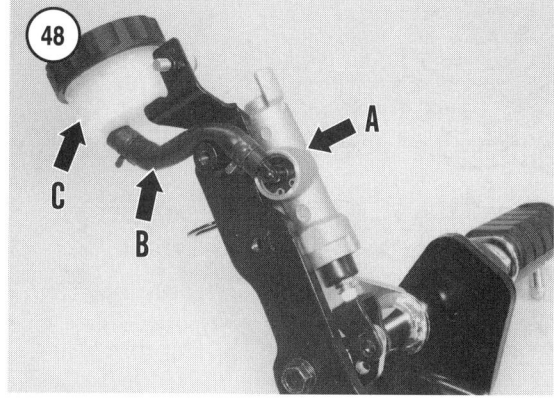

3. Install the master cylinder assembly onto the footrest mounting bracket by routing the reservoir hose along its original path. Refer to 8, **Figure 43** (Type I) or **Figure 48** (Type II).
4. Install the spacers (**Figure 47** [Type II]), cover and mounting bolts. Refer to 11, **Figure 43** (Type I) or B, **Figure 46** (Type II). Install the cover and mounting bolts. Tighten to 12 N•m (106 in.-lb.).
5. Connect the master cylinder to the rear brake pedal and secure with the clevis pin (C, **Figure 45**) installed from the outside of the brake pedal. Install a *new* cotter pin (B, **Figure 45**) and bend its arms over to lock it.
6. Reconnect the brake return spring with the spring ends facing toward the inside of the footrest mounting bracket assembly. Refer to A, **Figure 45**.
7. Install the right footrest mounting bracket with the rear master cylinder and reservoir attached as described in Chapter Fifteen. Refer to **Figure 43** (Type I) or **Figure 44** (Type II).
8. Bleed the rear brake line as described in this chapter.
9. On Type I models, install the footrest board as described in Chapter Fifteen.

Disassembly

Refer to **Figure 50**.

1. Remove the master cylinder as described in this section.
2. Remove the snap ring (A, **Figure 51**) and hose joint (B) from the master cylinder.
3. Remove and discard the O-ring (16, **Figure 50**).
4. Loosen the locknut (A, **Figure 52**) and remove the clevis (B), locknut and boot (C).

NOTE
If brake fluid is leaking from the piston bore, the piston cups are worn or damaged. Inspect and replace the piston assembly as described in this section.

5. Thread a bolt and nut into the brake hose port, and secure the bolt in a vise. Use the nut to lock the master cylinder in place.
6. Compress the piston and remove the snap ring with snap ring pliers. Remove the piston assembly (**Figure 53**) from the master cylinder bore. Do not remove the cups from the piston.
7. Clean and inspect the master cylinder assembly as described in this section.

Assembly

1. If installing a new piston assembly, assemble it as described in *Inspection* in this section.
2. Install the spring, small end first, onto the piston as shown in A, **Figure 54**. It should fit tightly on the piston shoulder.
3. Lubricate the piston assembly and cylinder bore with new DOT 4 brake fluid.

CAUTION
Do not allow the piston cups to tear or turn inside out when installing them into the master cylinder bore. Both cups are larger than the bore.

4. Insert the piston assembly (**Figure 53**), spring end first, by turning and pushing it into the master cylinder bore.

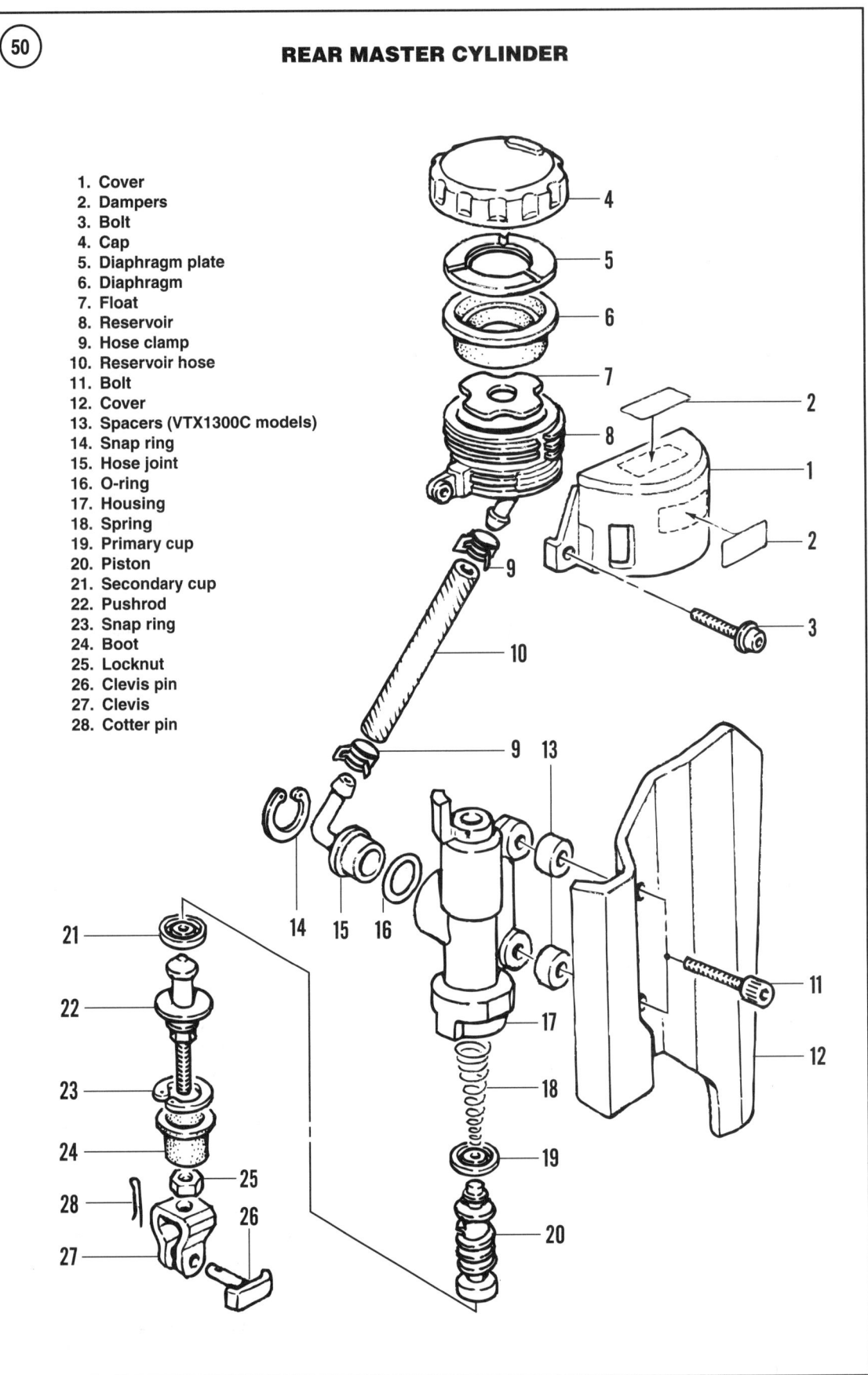

BRAKES

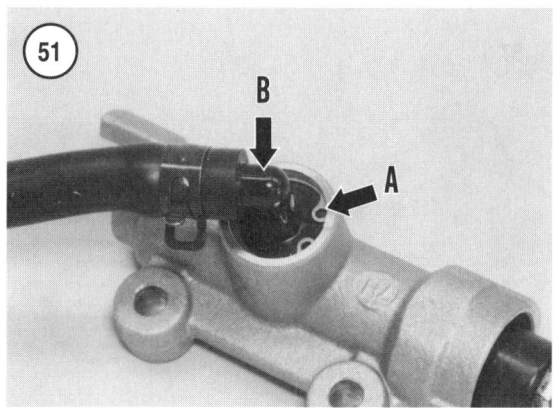

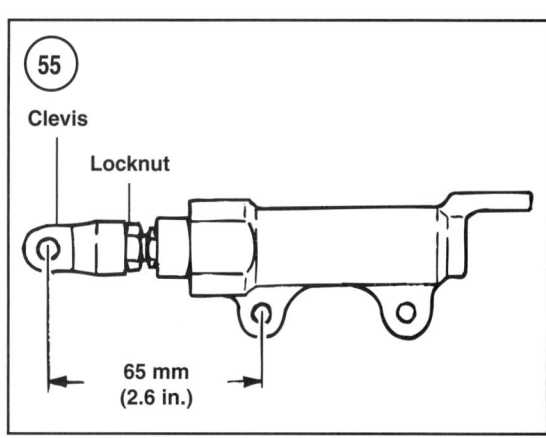

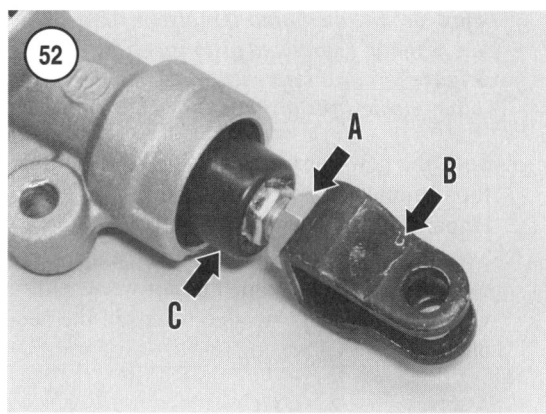

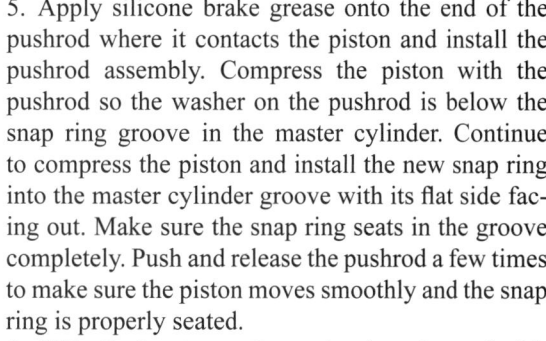

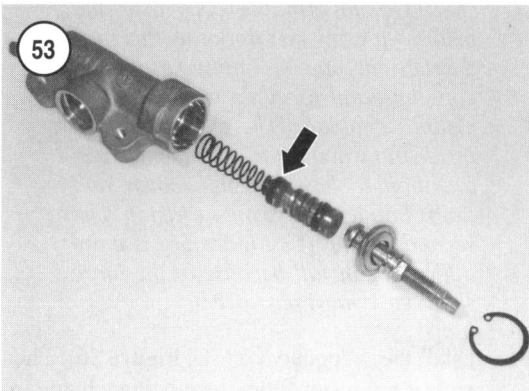

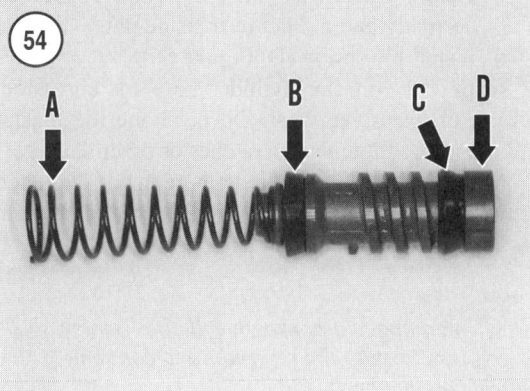

5. Apply silicone brake grease onto the end of the pushrod where it contacts the piston and install the pushrod assembly. Compress the piston with the pushrod so the washer on the pushrod is below the snap ring groove in the master cylinder. Continue to compress the piston and install the new snap ring into the master cylinder groove with its flat side facing out. Make sure the snap ring seats in the groove completely. Push and release the pushrod a few times to make sure the piston moves smoothly and the snap ring is properly seated.

6. Slide the boot over the pushrod as shown in 24, **Figure 50**. Seat the boot's (C, **Figure 52**) large end against the snap ring and install its small end into the pushrod groove. Push and release the pushrod a few times to make sure the dust cover's small end stays in the pushrod groove and is not twisted or folded.

7. Loosely install the locknut (A, **Figure 52**) and clevis (B) onto the pushrod.

8. Measure the pushrod length from the center of the master cylinder's lower mounting bolt hole to the center of the clevis hole as shown in **Figure 55**. The correct distance is 65 mm (2.6 in.). To adjust, turn the clevis as required. Hold the clevis and tighten the locknut to 18 N•m (13 ft.-lb.) and remeasure.

9. Lubricate a new O-ring (16, **Figure 50**) with DOT 4 brake fluid and install it over the hose joint.

10. Install the hose joint (B, **Figure 51**) into the master cylinder and secure with the snap ring (A). Make sure the snap ring seats in the groove completely.

11. Install the master cylinder as described in this section.

Inspection

Refer to the specifications in **Table 2**. Replace worn or damaged parts as described in this section.

1. Clean and dry the master cylinder assembly as follows:
   a. Handle the brake components carefully when servicing them.

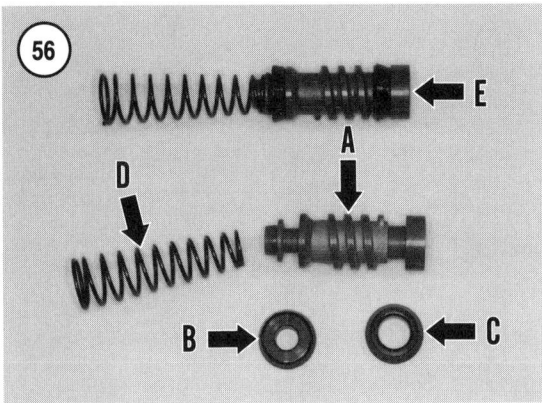

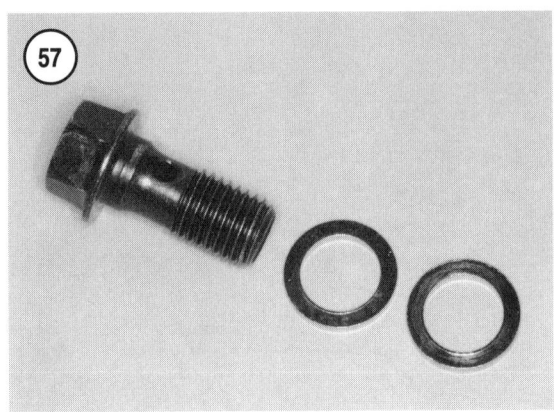

WARNING
Never use petroleum-based solvents to clean brake components, or allow solvent to contact rubber parts. Petroleum-based chemicals cause the rubber parts to swell, requiring their replacement.

b. Use only DOT 4 brake fluid or isopropyl alcohol to wash rubber parts in the brake system.
c. Clean the master cylinder snap ring groove carefully. Use a small pick or brush to clean the groove. If a hard varnish residue has built up in the groove, soak the master cylinder in solvent to help soften the residue. Then wash in soapy water and rinse completely.
d. Blow the master cylinder dry with compressed air.
e. Place cleaned parts on a clean lint-free cloth until reassembly.

CAUTION
Do not remove the cups from the piston assembly.

2. Inspect the piston assembly. If any of these parts are worn or damaged, replace the piston and seals as an assembly. Check for:
   a. Broken, distorted or collapsed piston return spring (A, **Figure 54**).
   b. Worn, cracked, damaged or swollen primary (B, **Figure 54**) and secondary (C) cups.
   c. Worn or pitted piston (D, **Figure 54**).
3. Measure the piston outside diameter (D, **Figure 54**).
4. To assemble a new piston assembly (**Figure 56**), perform the following:

NOTE
A new piston assembly consists of the piston (A, Figure 56), primary cup (B), secondary cup (C) and spring (D). Because these parts come unassembled, the new primary and secondary cups must be installed onto the piston. Use the original piston and pistons cups (E, Figure 56) as a reference when assembling the new piston assembly.

   a. Soak the new cups in new DOT 4 brake fluid for 15 minutes to soften them and ease installation. Clean the new piston in brake fluid.
   b. Secure the front end of the piston in a tap wrench and then mount the tap wrench in a vise so both hands are free to install the secondary cup.

CAUTION
The piston cups can be difficult to install. Do not pry the cups over the piston with any metal tool as this may damage the cup. Carefully stretch the cups by hand to guide them over the piston's shoulder. The cups may turn inside out when installing them, so pay attention to how the cup moves and drops into its groove on the piston. The secondary cup (C, Figure 56) is more difficult to install because of the large shoulder it must pass over.

   c. Install the secondary cup (C, **Figure 56**). Then remove the piston from the tap wrench and install the primary cup (B, **Figure 56**) onto the piston. Check that both cups are positioned correctly and did not turn inside out.
   d. Install the spring (D, **Figure 56**).
5. Inspect the master cylinder bore for corrosion, pitting or excessive wear. Do not hone the master cylinder bore to remove scratches or other damage.
6. Measure the master cylinder bore inside diameter.
7. Inspect the master cylinder reservoir diaphragm for tearing, cracks or other damage.

NOTE
A damaged diaphragm will allow moisture to enter the reservoir and contaminate the brake fluid.

BRAKES

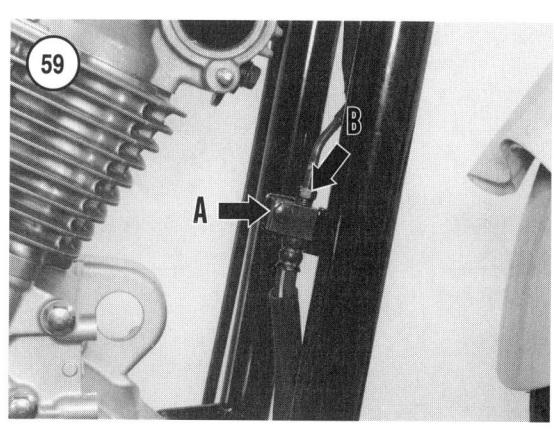

BRAKE HOSE AND BRAKE PIPE

Check the rubber brake hoses and the rear metal brake line at the brake inspection intervals listed in Chapter Three. Replace the brake hoses if they show signs of wear or damage, or if they have bulges or signs of chafing. Replace the rear brake pipe if it is cracked or leaking.

Removal/Installation

To replace a brake hose or the rear brake line, perform the following:
1. Drain the brake system as described in this chapter.
2. Use a plastic drop cloth to cover areas that could be damaged by spilled brake fluid.
3. When removing a brake hose or the rear brake line, note the following:
   a. Record the hose or line routing on a piece of paper or with photographs.
   b. Remove parts as required to access the brake hose or rear brake line.
   c. Remove any bolts or brackets securing the brake hose or brake line to the frame or suspension component. Note the location of any removed.
   d. Before removing the banjo bolts, note how the end of the brake hose is installed or indexed against the part it is threaded into. The hoses must be installed facing in their original position.
4. Replace damaged banjo bolts.
5. Reverse these steps to install the new brake hoses. Note the following:
   a. Compare the new and old hoses to make sure they are the same.
   b. Clean the new washers, banjo bolts and hose ends to remove any contamination.
   c. Referring to the notes made during removal, route the brake hose along its original path.
   d. Install a new banjo bolt washer (**Figure 57**) on each side of the brake hose.
   e. Tighten the banjo bolts to 34 N•m (25 ft.-lb.).
6. Reverse these steps to install a new rear brake line (**Figure 58**). Note the following:
   a. The rear steel brake line is available from the manufacturer and comes equipped with joint bolts and preflared ends.
   b. Blow the new brake line out with compressed air before installing it.
   c. Wipe the brake line ends and joint bolts to remove any contamination.
   d. Do not bend the brake line or try to force it into position during installation. This creases the metal and may cause leaks.
   e. If there is any chance of the tubing ends becoming contaminated with grease during installation, cover the ends with a small plastic bag.
   f. Install the brake line following its original mounting path as noted during removal.
   g. Brake lines can be damaged from vibration and heat. Install the brake in its original position while using the original mounting fasteners and locations.
   h. When the brake pipe was disconnected from both ends, initially thread both brake line joint bolts into their mating joints a few turns only. Do not tighten one nut fully before attempting to install and tighten the other bolt. Also make sure there is no stress on the brake line.
   i. Lubricate the brake pipe joint bolt with DOT 4 brake fluid before reconnecting them.
   j. Tighten the 2-way joint mounting bolt (A, **Figure 59**) to 12 N•m (106 in.-lb.).
   k. Tighten the brake pipe joint bolt (B, **Figure 59**) to 14 N•m (10 ft.-lb.).
7. After installing new hoses around the steering and front fork area, turn the handlebars from side to side to make sure the hose does not rub against any part or pull away from its brake unit.
8. Bleed the brake system as described in this chapter.

BRAKE DISC

Inspection

The front and rear brake discs can be inspected while installed on the motorcycle. Small marks on the disc are not important, but deep scratches or other marks may reduce braking effectiveness and increase brake pad wear. If these grooves are evident and the brake pads are wearing rapidly, replace the brake disc.

Refer to **Table 1** and **Table 2**.

1. Support the motorcycle with the wheel (front or rear) off the ground.
2. Measure the disc thickness at several locations around the disc (**Figure 60**). Replace the disc if its thickness at any point is less than the minimum allowable specification stamped on the disc or less than the service limit.
3. Position a dial indicator stem against the brake disc (**Figure 61**). Zero the dial gauge and slowly turn the wheel and measure runout. If the disc runout is excessive:
   a. Check for loose or missing fasteners.
   b. Remove the wheel and check the wheel bearings as described in Chapter Eleven.
   c. Remove the disc as described in this section and check for disc warp. Replace if warped.
4. Clean the disc of any rust or corrosion and wipe clean with brake cleaner. Never use an oil-based solvent that may leave an oil residue on the disc.

Removal/Installation

1. Remove the front or rear wheel (Chapter Eleven).
2. Remove the bolts securing the brake disc to the wheel and remove the disc. Refer to **Figure 62** (front) or **Figure 63** (rear).
3. Perform any necessary service to the hub (wheel bearing or tire replacement) before installing the brake disc(s).
4. Clean the brake disc threaded holes in the hub.
5. Clean the brake disc mounting surface.
6. Install the brake disc with its directional arrow facing toward the wheel's normal rotating direction.
7. Install new brake disc mounting bolts and tighten to 42 N•m (31 ft.-lb.).
8. Clean the disc of any rust or corrosion and spray clean with brake cleaner. Never use an oil-based solvent that may leave an oil residue on the disc.
9. Install the front or rear wheel (Chapter Eleven).

BRAKES

Table 1 FRONT BRAKE SERVICE SPECIFICATIONS

	New mm (in.)	Service limit mm (in.)
Brake caliper bore inside diameter		
2003-2004 VTX1300R/S/T models	27.000-27.050 (1.0630-1.0650)	27.06 (1.065)
2005-on VTX1300R/S/T and all VTX1300C models	25.400-25.450 (1.0000-1.0020)	25.460 (1.0024)
Brake caliper piston outside diameter		
2003-2004 VTX1300R/S/T models	26.935-26.968 (1.0604-1.0617)	26.92 (1.060)
2005-on VTX1300R/S/T and all VTX1300C models	25.318-25.368 (0.9968-0.9987)	25.31 (0.996)
Master cylinder bore inside diameter		
2003-2004 VTX1300R/S/T models	12.700-12.743 (0.5000-0.5017)	12.755 (0.5022)
2005-on VTX1300R/S/T and all VTX1300C models	11.000-11.043 (0.4331-0.4348)	11.055 (0.4352)
Master cylinder piston outside diameter		
2003-2004 VTX1300R/S/T models	12.657-12.684 (0.4983-0.4994)	12.645 (0.4978)
2005-on VTX1300R/S/T and all VTX1300C models	10.957-10.984 (0.4314-0.4324)	10.945 (0.4309)
Brake disc runout	–	0.30 (0.012)
Brake disc thickness	5.8-6.2 (0.23-0.24)	5.0 (0.20)

Table 2 REAR BRAKE SERVICE SPECIFICATIONS

	New mm (in.)	Service limit mm (in.)
Brake caliper bore inside diameter	38.18-38.23 (1.503-1.505)	38.24 (1.506)
Brake caliper piston outside diameter	38.115-38.148 (1.5006-1.5019)	38.09 (1.500)
Master cylinder bore inside diameter	12.700-12.743 (0.5000-0.5017)	12.755 (0.5022)
Master cylinder piston outside diameter	12.657-12.684 (0.4983-0.4994)	12.645 (0.4978)
Brake disc runout	–	0.30 (0.012)
Brake disc thickness	5.8-6.2 (0.23-0.24)	5.0 (0.20)

Table 3 BRAKE TORQUE SPECIFICATIONS

	N•m	in.-lb.	ft.-lb.
Banjo bolt*	34	–	25
Brake caliper bleed valve	5.5	49	–
Brake disc mounting bolts*	42	–	31
Brake hose 2-way joint mounting bolt	12	106	–
Brake pipe joint bolt	14	–	10
Front brake caliper bracket fixed shaft*	13	115	–
Front brake caliper fixed shaft*	27	–	20
Front brake caliper mounting bolt*	31	–	23
Front brake lever pivot bolt	1	8.8	–
Front brake lever pivot bolt nut	6	53	–
Front master cylinder clamp bolt*	12	106	–
Pad pin	18	–	13
Pad pin plug	2.5	22	–
(continued)			

Table 3 BRAKE TORQUE SPECIFICATIONS (continued)

	N•m	in.-lb.	ft.-lb.
Rear brake caliper bracket pin bolt	23	–	17
Rear brake caliper fixed shaft*	27	–	20
Rear brake pedal pivot nut or bolt	27	–	20
Rear brake reservoir mounting bolt	10	88	–
Rear master cylinder mounting bolt	12	106	–
Rear master cylinder pushrod locknut	18	–	13

*Refer to text for additional information.

CHAPTER FIFTEEN

BODY AND EXHAUST SYSTEM

Table 1 is at the end of the chapter.

SEAT

Removal/Installation

> *WARNING*
> *Make sure the seat is correctly installed and locked in place by pulling up on it firmly and moving it from side to side.*

VTX1300C models

> *NOTE*
> *Take care not to scratch the rear fender when removing the seat.*

1. Place a wide strip of non-permanent tape across the rear fender behind the seat's mounting bracket to protect the fender when removing the seat assembly.
2. Remove the nut (A, **Figure 1**) securing the seat to the rear fender.
3. Remove the Allen bolt (B, **Figure 1**) from each side of the seat.
4. Lift the seat off the stud and slide it back to remove it.
5. Remove the washer from the stud.
6. Installation is the reverse of removal. Note the following:
   a. Insert the hook on the front part of the seat under the frame cross member.
   b. Tighten the bolts and nut securely.

VTX1300R/S/T models

Refer to **Figure 2**.
1. Place a wide strip of non-permanent tape across the rear fender behind the pillion seat to protect the fender when removing the seat assembly.
2. Remove the bolts, collars and seat band.
3. Remove the cap, Allen bolt and pillion seat.
4. Remove the bolts, washers (2007-on models) and rider seat.
5. Installation is the reverse of removal. Note the following:
   a. Insert the hook on the rider seat under the frame cross member, then push the seat forward.
   b. Tighten the fasteners securely.

SIDE COVERS

Removal/Installation

1. Pull the rear of the side cover (**Figure 3**) out to release its mounting boss from the frame mounted grommet, then slide the cover forward to release it from the two frame grommets and remove the cover.
2. Replace any missing or damaged grommets (**Figure 4**).
3. Installation is the reverse of removal.

CYLINDER HEAD SHROUD

Removal/Installation

1. Raise and pull the cylinder head shroud (**Figure 5**) out to release its pins from the grommets on the cylinder head fins.
2. Reverse to install the cylinder head shroud. Note the following:
    a. Replace missing or damaged grommets.
    b. Identify the cylinder head shrouds by the marks cast on their inside surface. Left side: FR-L and RR-L. Right side: FR-R and RR-R.

CYLINDER HEAD FIN COVER

Removal/Installation

1. Remove the cylinder head shroud as described in this chapter.
2. Disconnect the spark plug lead (A, **Figure 6**) at the spark plug.
3. Remove the two bolts and the cylinder head fin cover (B, **Figure 6**). Do not lose the two grommets installed at the bottom of the air fin cover.
4. Installation is the reverse of removal. Tighten the bolts securely.

LEFT CRANKCASE REAR COVER

Removal/Installation

1. Support the motorcycle on its sidestand or on a workstand.
2. Remove the bolts and the left crankcase rear cover (**Figure 7**).
3. Remove the bolts and the upper (A, **Figure 8**) and lower (B) mounting brackets.
4. Installation is the reverse of removal. Tighten the mounting bracket bolts to 10 N•m (88 in.-lb.).

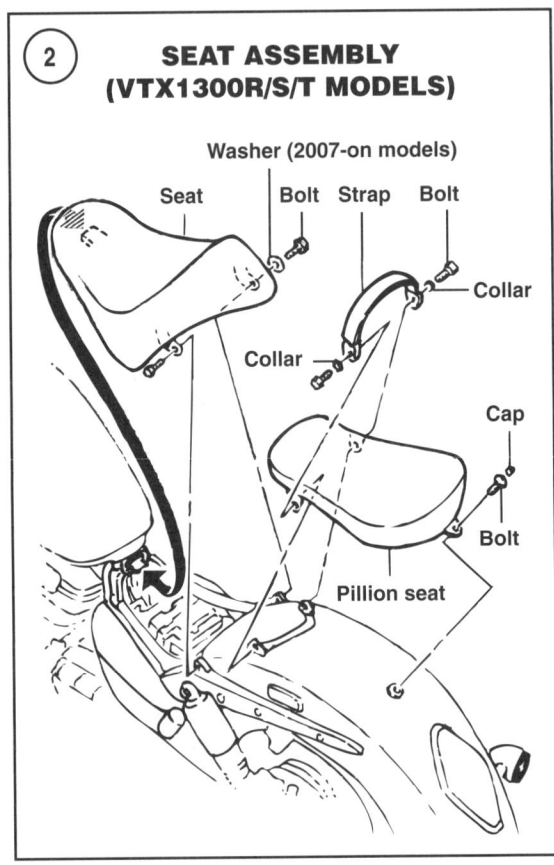

BODY AND EXHAUST SYSTEM

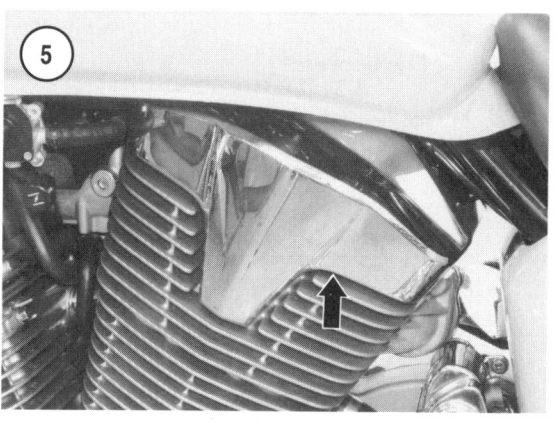

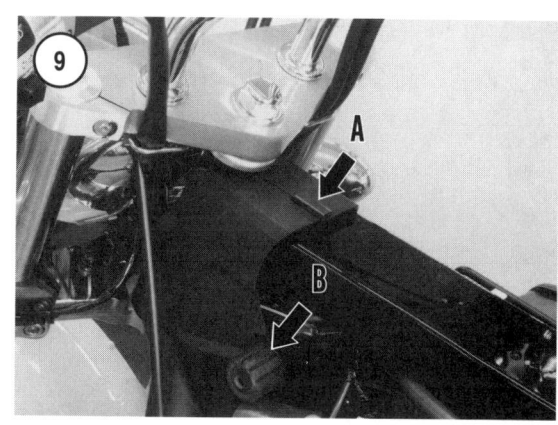

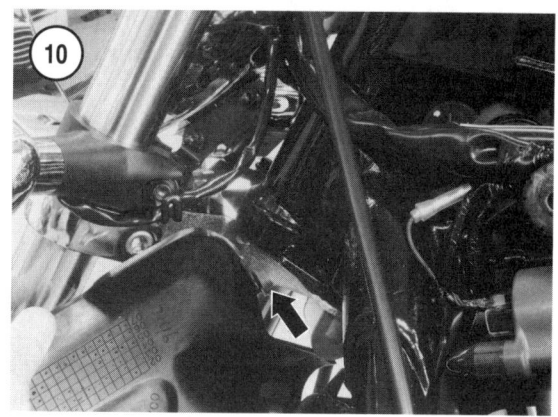

STEERING SIDE COVER

Removal/Installation

1. Remove the fuel tank (Chapter Eight).
2. Note the brake hose, clutch cable, throttle cable and wiring harness routing around and behind the steering side covers.
3. Slide the retaining clip (A, **Figure 9**) back and off the steering side covers.

NOTE
The grommet installed on the bottom of the side cover may fall during cover removal.

4. Release the steering side cover from the fuel tank support (B, **Figure 9**), then lift and remove the steering side cover. Locate the grommet (**Figure 10**) installed on the bottom of the cover.
5. Installation is the reverse of these steps, plus the following:
   a. Insert the grommet (**Figure 10**) into the hole in the frame.
   b. Refer to your disassembly notes on the correct brake hose, clutch cable, throttle cable and wiring harness routing around and behind the steering side covers.

CHAPTER FIFTEEN

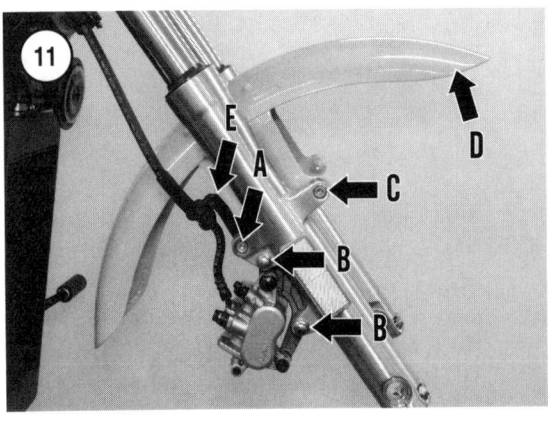

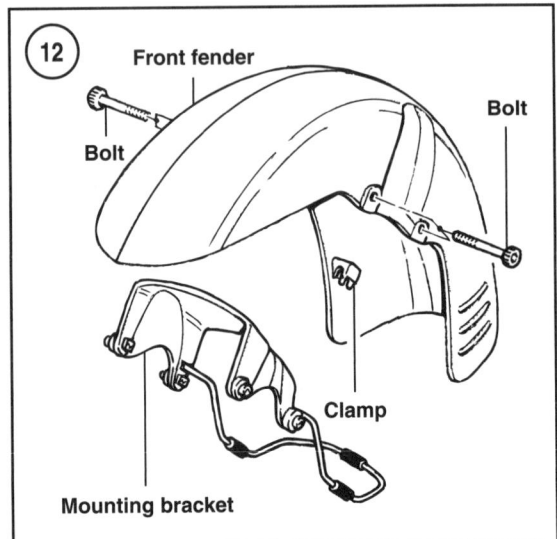

c. Support the motorcycle with the front wheel off the ground and check the steering operation.

FRONT FENDER

Removal/Installation

VTX1300C models

1. Support the motorcycle on a workstand.
2. Remove the front wheel (Chapter Eleven).
3. Mask off the fender edges and the area between the fork tubes with non-permanent tape or newspaper taped in place.
4. Remove the fender bolt (A, **Figure 11**) securing the brake hose mounting bracket to the slider.
5. Remove the brake caliper mounting bolts (B, **Figure 11**) and hang the caliper away from the front fender. Support the caliper with a piece of wire. Do not let the caliper hang by the brake hose.
6. With an assistant holding the front fender, loosen and remove the remaining front fender mounting bolts (C, **Figure 11**).
7. Lower the front fender (D, **Figure 11**) and remove it from between the fork tubes.
8. Installation is the reverse of these steps. Note the following:
   a. Tighten the front fender mounting bolts securely. Make sure the brake hose mounting bracket (E, **Figure 11**) is correctly positioned against the slider.
   b. Install new brake caliper mounting bolts (B, **Figure 11**) and tighten to 31 N•m (23 ft.-lb.).

VTX1300R/S/T models

CAUTION
The front fender is difficult to remove without scratching it.

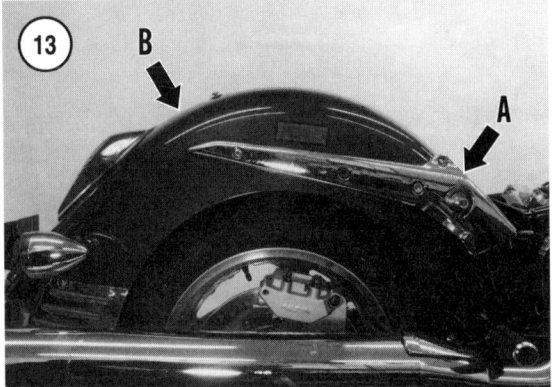

If the front fork will also be removed, remove the front fender as described in *Front Fork* in Chapter Twelve. If it is only necessary to remove the front fender, perform the following:

1. Support the motorcycle on a workstand.
2. Remove the front wheel (Chapter Eleven).
3. Mask off the fender edges and the area between the fork tubes with non-permanent tape or strips of newspaper taped in place.
4. Remove the fender bolt (A, **Figure 11**, typical) securing the brake hose mounting bracket to the slider.
5. Remove the brake caliper mounting bolts (B, **Figure 11**, typical) and hang the caliper away from the front fender. Support the caliper with a piece of wire. Do not let the caliper hang by the brake hose.
6. With an assistant holding the front fender, loosen and remove the remaining front fender mounting bolts (C, **Figure 11**, typical) and remove the mounting bracket (**Figure 12**) from inside the front fender.
7. Squeeze the front fender in its center and carefully lower it from between the fork tubes.
8. Installation is the reverse of these steps. Note the following:

BODY AND EXHAUST SYSTEM

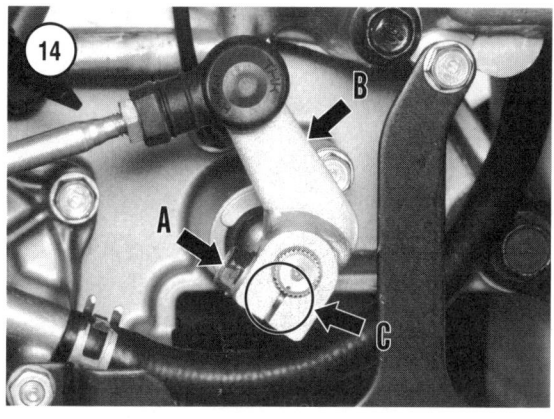

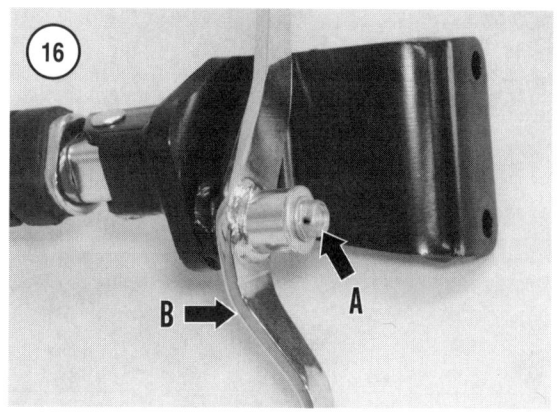

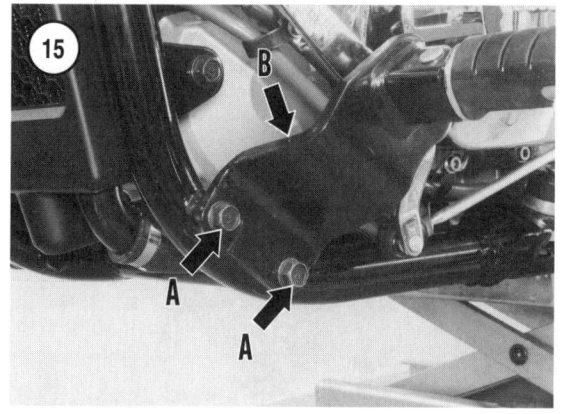

a. Tighten the front fender mounting bolts securely. Make sure the brake hose mounting bracket (E, **Figure 11**, typical) is correctly positioned against the slider.
b. Install new brake caliper mounting bolts (B, **Figure 11**, typical) and tighten to 31 N•m (23 ft.-lb.).

REAR FENDER

Removal/Installation

1. On VTX1300T models, remove the backrest, saddlebags and mounting brackets as described in this chapter.
2. Remove the seat and both side covers as described in this chapter.
3. Remove the shock absorbers (Chapter Thirteen).
4. Disconnect the taillight and brake light electrical connectors located on the right side of the rear fender. Position the fender wiring harness connector ends so they will not catch on the frame when the fender is removed.

CAUTION
The rear fender is heavy and difficult to remove by one person. To avoid scratching and damaging the rear fender, have one or more assistants help with its removal.

5. Remove the shock absorber upper pivot bolts.
6. Remove the bolts and washers (2007-on models) securing the grab rails (A, **Figure 13**) to the fender and frame. Remove both grab rails and the rear fender (B, **Figure 13**).
7. Installation is the reverse of removal. After reconnecting the taillight and brake light connectors, turn the ignition switch on and check the operation of each light.

RIDER FOOTRESTS

Footrest Mounting Bracket Removal/Installation

Left side

1. Support the motorcycle on a workstand.
2. Remove the left crankcase rear cover as described in this chapter.
3. Remove the pinch bolt (A, **Figure 14**). Before removing the shift boss (B, **Figure 14**), make sure the alignment punch mark is visible on the shift shaft. If not visible, make a mark to ensure proper shift boss alignment on the shift shaft.
4. Remove the two mounting bolts (A, **Figure 15**) and remove the footrest mounting bracket assembly. Refer to B, **Figure 15**.
5. To service the shift pedal:
   a. Remove the pivot bolt (A, **Figure 16**), washer and shift pedal (B).
   b. Remove the two seals from the shift pedal and replace if damaged.
   c. Clean and dry all parts.
   d. Lubricate the seal lips with grease and install into the shift pedal.
   e. Lubricate the pivot bolt with grease. Reinstall the shift pedal and secure with the pivot bolt and washer.

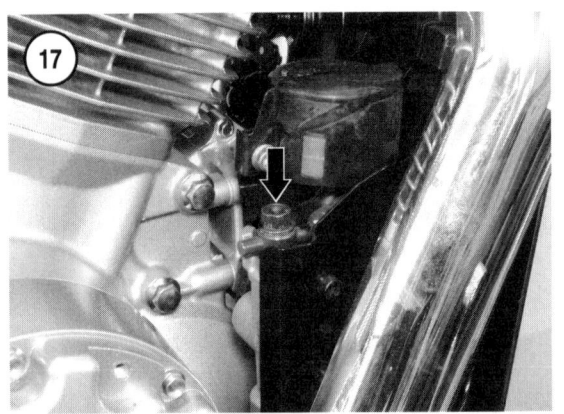

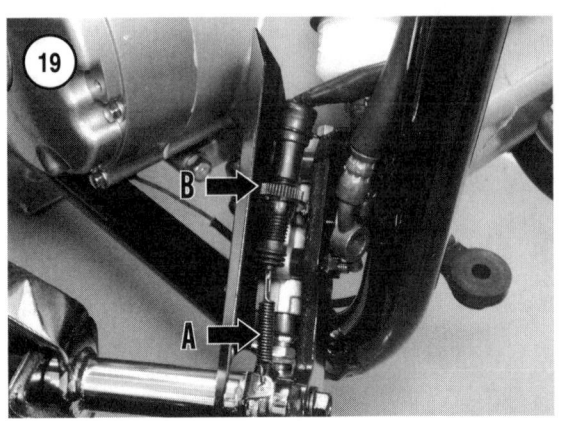

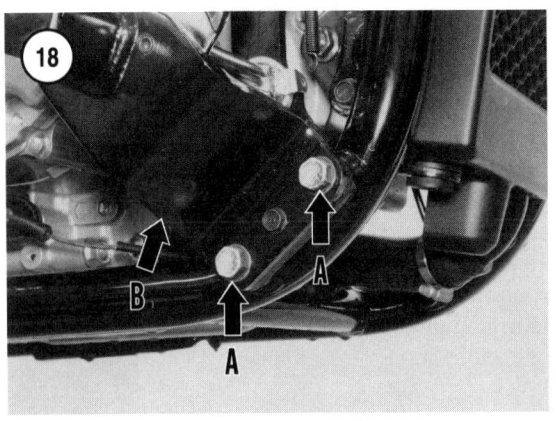

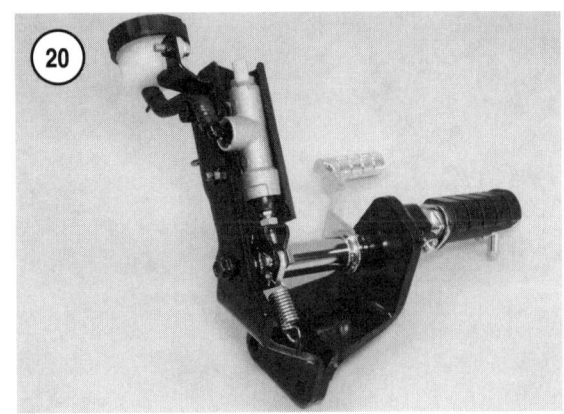

  f. Tighten the bolt securely and check that the pedal pivots smoothly.
6. Installation is the reverse of removal. Note the following:
  a. Tighten the footrest mounting bracket bolts (A, **Figure 15**) to 39 N•m (29 ft.-lb.).
  b. Align the slot in the shift boss with the punch mark (C, **Figure 14**) on the end of the shift shaft. Tighten the pinch bolt to 12 N•m (106 in.-lb.).

Right side

1. Support the motorcycle on its sidestand.
2. Drain the brake fluid from the rear brake system (Chapter Fourteen). Reinstall the diaphragm and reservoir cap.
3. Refer to *Brake Service* in Chapter Fourteen. Remove the banjo bolt (**Figure 17**) and washers from the top of the rear master cylinder. Cover the end of the hose with a plastic bag to prevent brake fluid from dripping onto the exhaust system or frame. Discard the washers.
4. Remove the two footrest mounting bracket bolts (A, **Figure 18**) and position the mounting bracket (B) to expose the rear brake light switch.

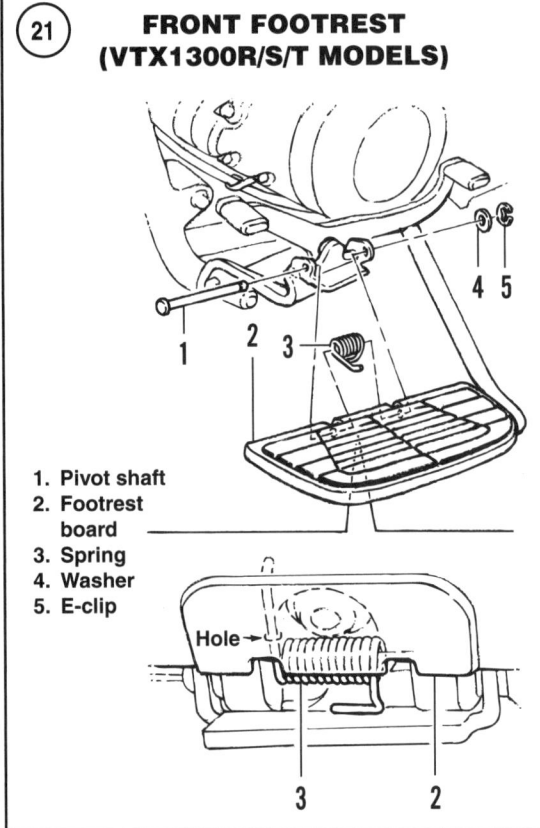

FRONT FOOTREST (VTX1300R/S/T MODELS)
1. Pivot shaft
2. Footrest board
3. Spring
4. Washer
5. E-clip

BODY AND EXHAUST SYSTEM

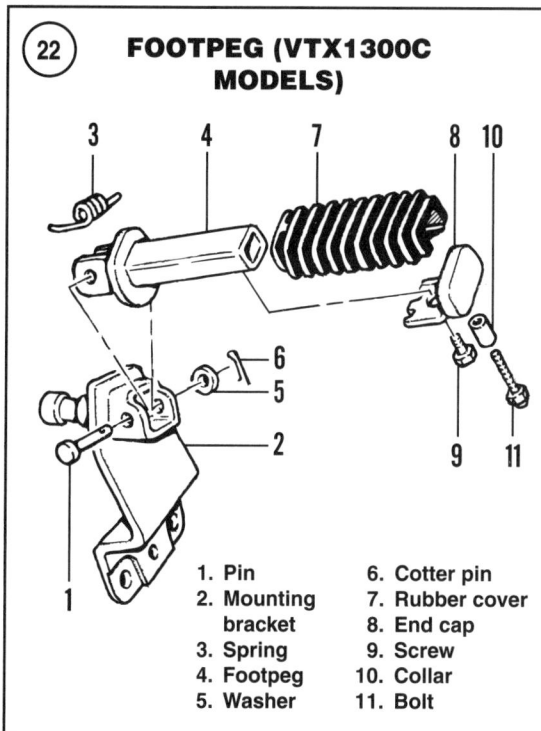

FOOTPEG (VTX1300C MODELS)

1. Pin
2. Mounting bracket
3. Spring
4. Footpeg
5. Washer
6. Cotter pin
7. Rubber cover
8. End cap
9. Screw
10. Collar
11. Bolt

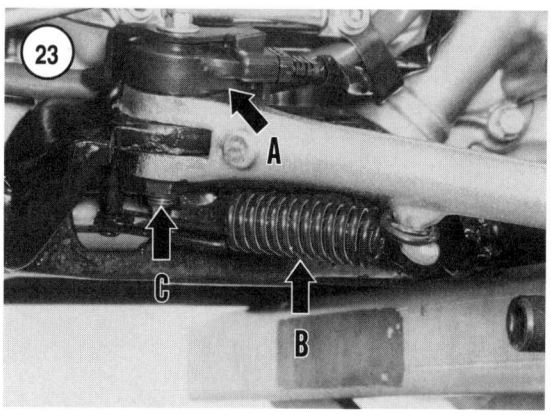

5. Disconnect the brake light switch spring (A, **Figure 19**) and remove the switch (B) from the mounting bracket.
6. Remove the footrest mounting bracket assembly with the rear master cylinder and its reservoir attached. Refer to **Figure 20**, typical.
7. To service the rear master cylinder, refer to *Rear Master Cylinder and Brake Pedal* in Chapter Fifteen.
8. Installation is the reverse of these steps, plus the following:
   a. Tighten the footrest mounting bracket bolts (A, **Figure 18**) to 39 N•m (29 ft.-lb.).
   b. Install the banjo bolt (**Figure 17**) with two new washers and tighten to 34 N•m (25 ft.-lb.).
   c. Fill and bleed the rear brake system (Chapter Fourteen).
   d. Adjust the rear brake light switch (Chapter Three).

Footrest Board Removal/Installation (VTX1300R/S/T Models)

Refer to **Figure 21**.
To remove only the footrest board, perform the following:
1. Remove the E-clip and washer from the pivot shaft.
2. Hold the footrest board and remove the pivot shaft, then remove the footrest board and spring.
3. Clean the pivot shaft, spring and all pivot contact surfaces.

4. Inspect and replace damaged components. Check the spring for damaged coils. Check the pivot shaft for grooves and other wear or damaged areas.
5. Lubricate the pivot surfaces with grease.
6. Insert the spring into the hole in the footrest board.
7. Position the footrest board on the mounting bracket, then hold the exposed spring end with a screwdriver and install the pivot shaft through the mounting bracket, footrest board and spring.
8. Secure the pivot shaft with the washer and E-clip. Replace the E-clip if it is bent or loose.
9. Pivot the footrest board, making sure it pivots under spring tension and returns to its rest position.

Footpeg Removal/Installation (VTX1300C Models)

Refer to **Figure 22**. Install a new cotter pin during installation. Then pivot the footpeg, making sure it pivots under spring tension and returns to its rest position.

SIDESTAND

WARNING
Do not ride the motorcycle until the sidestand and sidestand switch operates correctly. Riding the motorcycle with the sidestand down could cause loss of control.

Removal/Installation

To replace just the sidestand switch, refer to *Sidestand Switch* in Chapter Nine.
1. Support the motorcycle on a workstand.
2. Move the sidestand up to the raised position. This will place the springs in their relaxed position.
3. Remove the sidestand switch (A, **Figure 23**) as described in Chapter Nine. Do not disconnect the sidestand switch connector unless necessary.

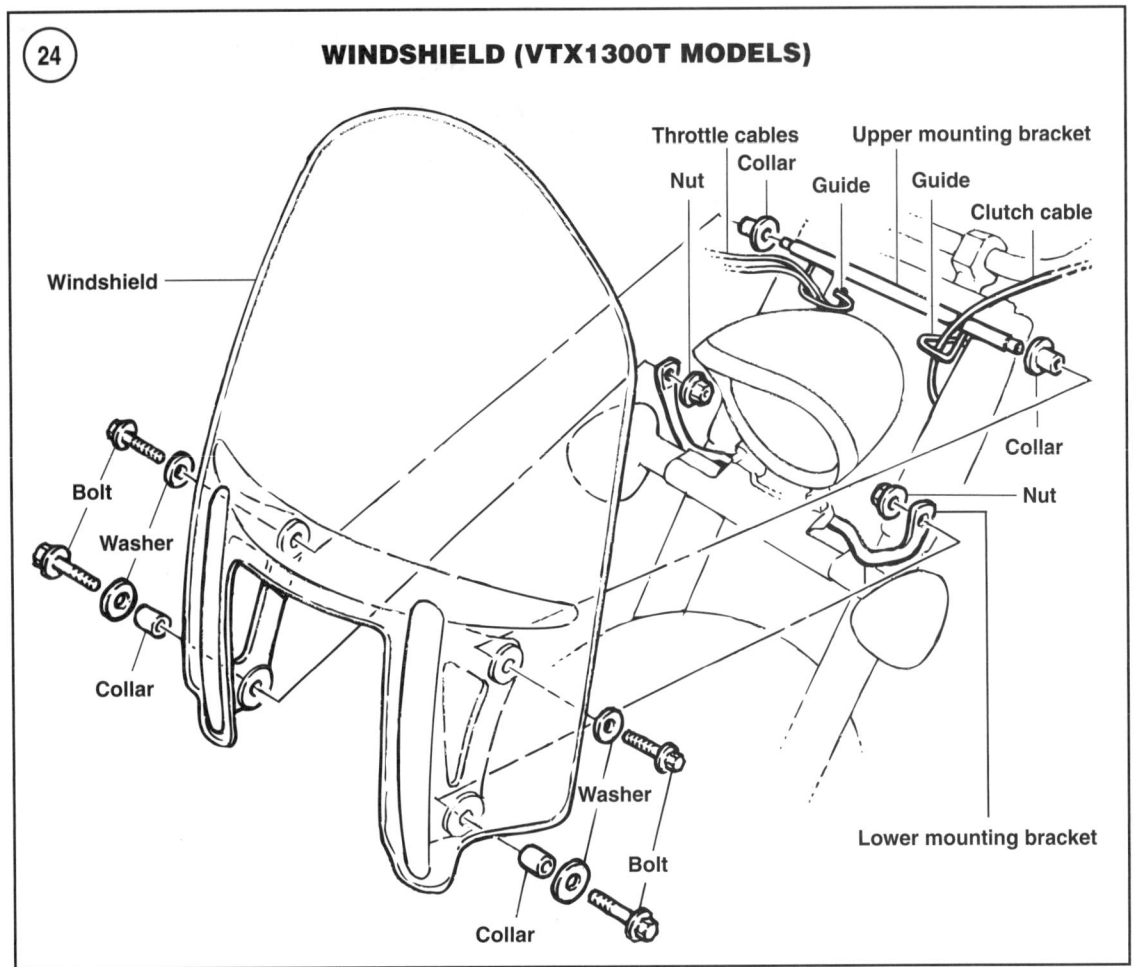

4. Using a suitable tool, disconnect the two return springs (B, **Figure 23**) from the pin on the frame and sidestand.
5. Hold the pivot bolt and remove the locknut (C, **Figure 23**).
6. Remove the pivot bolt and the sidestand.
7. Clean and dry all parts except the sidestand switch.
8. Inspect and replace worn or damaged parts. Replace the locknut if it turns easily on the pivot bolt shaft. This is a U-nut design and must be replaced with an original part.
9. Installation is the reverse of these steps. Note the following:
   a. Lubricate the pivot bolt shoulder (not the threads) with grease.
   b. Tighten the pivot bolt to 10 N•m (88 in.-lb.).
   c. Hold the pivot bolt and tighten the locknut (C, **Figure 23**) to 30 N•m (22 ft.-lb.). Then pivot the sidestand, making sure it pivots smoothly. If there is any binding, remove and inspect the parts for damage.
   d. Install the sidestand switch as described in Chapter Nine.
   e. Operate the sidestand from its raised to lowered positions several times. Check that the sidestand locks in both positions and the springs remain firmly attached to the frame and sidestand pins.
   f. Remove the motorcycle from the stand. Shift the transmission into neutral and start the engine. Shift the transmission into first gear and lower the sidestand. The engine should turn off.

WINDSHIELD (VTX1300T MODELS)

Removal/Installation

Windshield

Refer to **Figure 24**.
1. Remove the bolts, washers and collars securing the windshield to the upper and lower mounting brackets.
2. Remove the windshield from the mounting brackets and around the headlight housing.
3. Installation is the reverse of these steps.

BODY AND EXHAUST SYSTEM

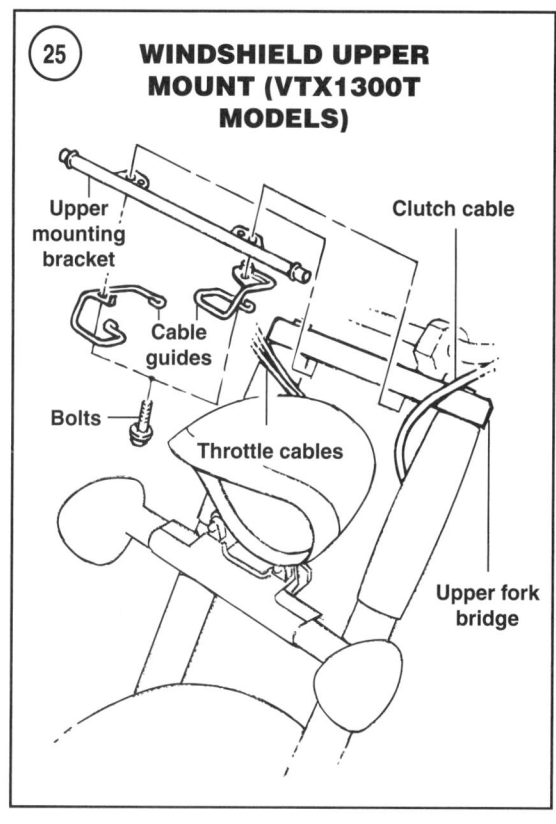

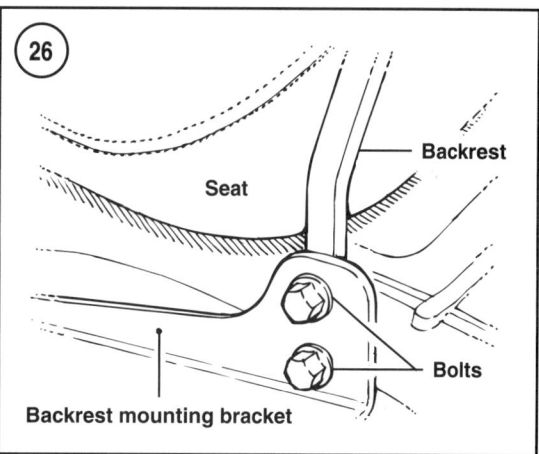

2. Open the saddlebag and remove the bolts and collars securing the saddlebag to the mounting bracket (**Figure 27**).
3. To remove the mounting brackets, remove the bolts, spacers, saddlebag mounting bracket, backrest mounting bracket and spacers (**Figure 28**).
4. Repeat for the opposite side if necessary.
5. Installation is the reverse of these steps. Make sure all spacers are in the correct locations and the bolts are tightened securely.

Mounting brackets

1. Remove the windshield as described in this section.
2. Note the brake hose, clutch cable and throttle cable routing.
3. To remove the lower mounting bracket (**Figure 24**), remove the nuts and bolts securing the lower mounting bracket/headlight housing to the lower fork bridge.
4. To remove the upper mounting bracket (**Figure 25**), remove the bolts, cable guides and upper mounting bracket from the upper fork bridge. Discard the bolts.
5. Installation is the reverse of these steps. Note the following:
   a. Install new upper mounting bracket bolts and tighten to 21 N•m (15 ft.-lb.).
   b. Check the brake hose, throttle cable and clutch cable routing.

BACKREST AND SADDLEBAGS (VTX1300T MODELS)

Removal/Installation

1. Remove the bolts securing the backrest assembly to the mounting brackets and remove the backrest (**Figure 26**).

EXHAUST SYSTEM

Troubleshooting

Periodically inspect the exhaust system for loose or missing fasteners and damage. Note the following:
1. A loose exhaust pipe connection at the cylinder head can cause engine backfiring or afterburn if cold air enters the exhaust system. Periodically check the tightness of the flange nuts.
2. Loose or damaged muffler baffles can restrict the exhaust system and cause low power. Tap the muffler with a rubber or plastic hammer. If the muffler rattles, replace the muffler.
3. Check the exhaust pipes and mufflers for rust, holes and other damage.

Service Notes

1. Before removing the exhaust system, spray fasteners with penetrating oil when the exhaust system is cold.
2. Because exhaust components are often replaced with aftermarket parts, nonstandard fasteners may be used. Check the length of nonstandard fasteners to make sure they are not too short or long.
3. Install new exhaust pipe gaskets during installation.
4. Clean fasteners of all rust and corrosion.

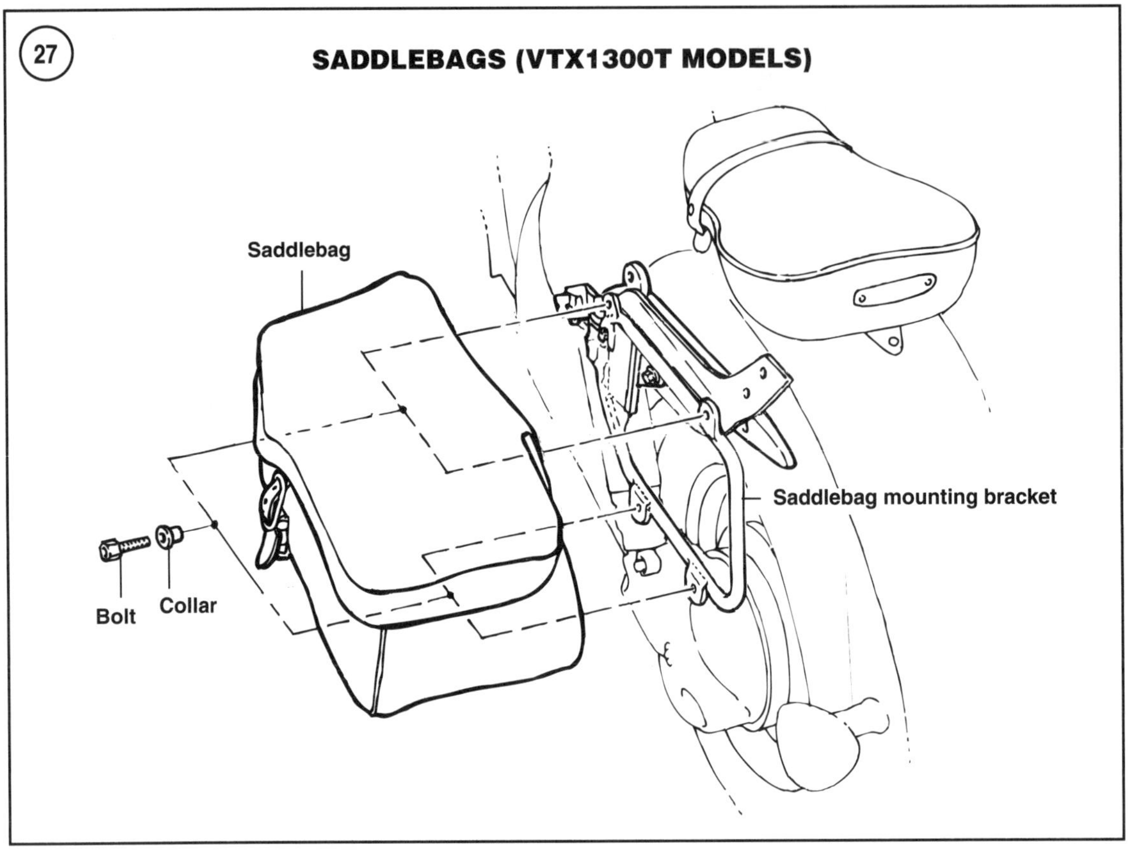

SADDLEBAGS (VTX1300T MODELS)

(27)

- Saddlebag
- Bolt
- Collar
- Saddlebag mounting bracket

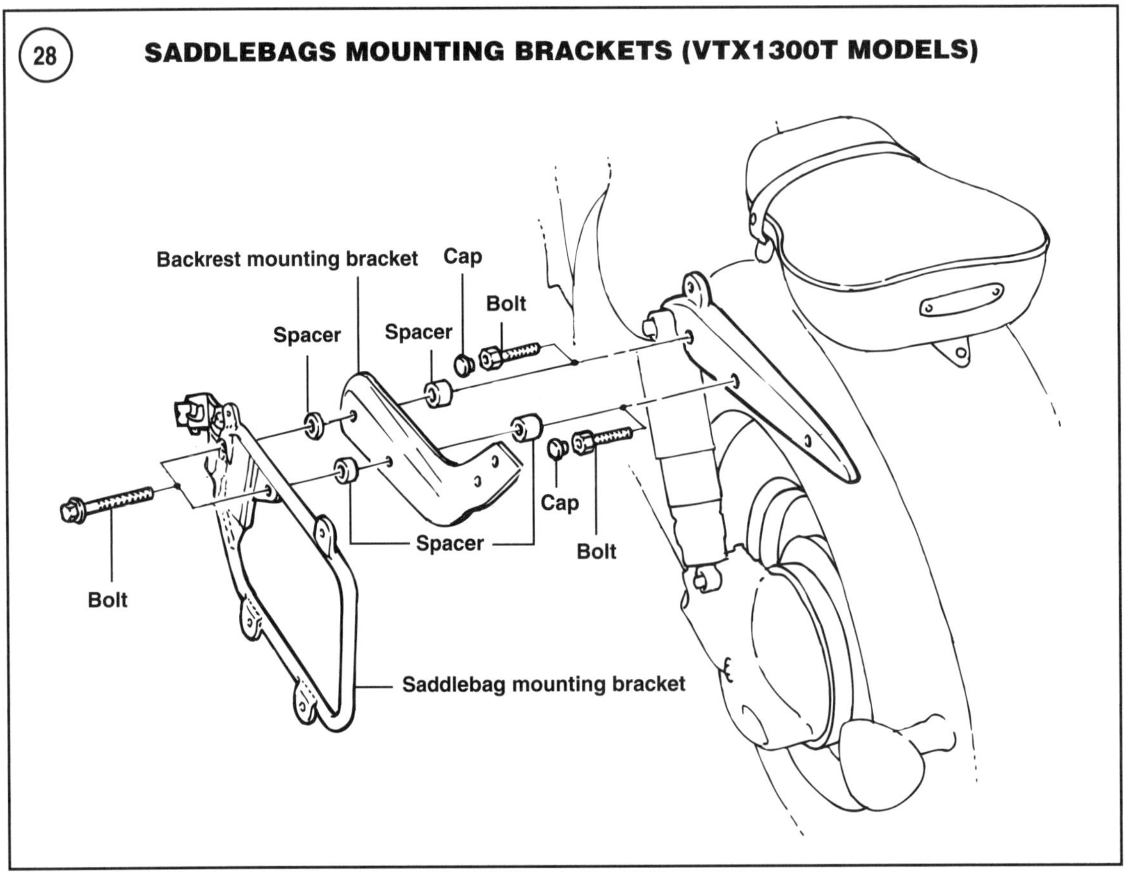

SADDLEBAGS MOUNTING BRACKETS (VTX1300T MODELS)

(28)

- Backrest mounting bracket
- Cap
- Spacer
- Spacer
- Bolt
- Bolt
- Cap
- Spacer
- Bolt
- Saddlebag mounting bracket

BODY AND EXHAUST SYSTEM

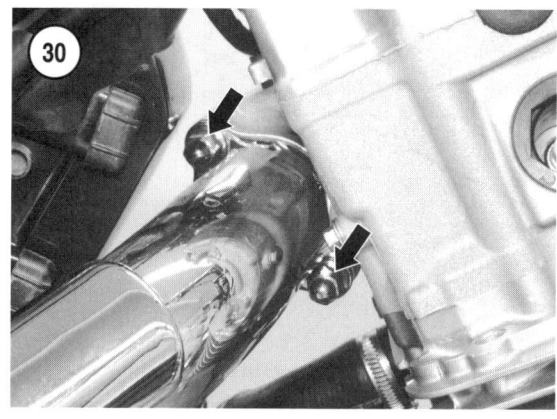

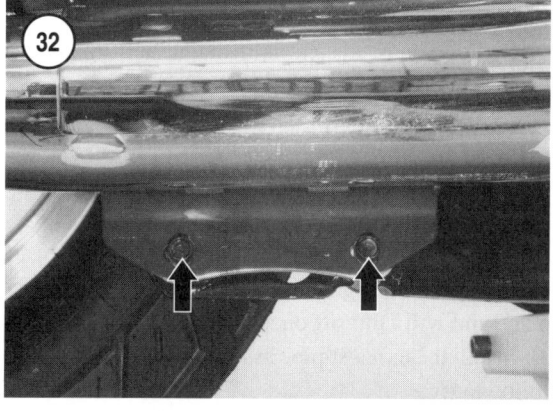

5. The exhaust pipe flanges on some aftermarket exhaust pipes may not be as thick as the flanges used on stock exhaust systems. If original equipment flange nuts (**Figure 29** and **Figure 30**) are used, they may bottom out before they are fully tightened, causing an air leak at the exhaust pipe connection at the cylinder head. When servicing an aftermarket exhaust system, measure the thickness of each flange, and if it is thinner than stock, use washers under the flange nuts to make sure they are tightened fully.

Exhaust System Removal

The exhaust pipes and mufflers are removed as a complete assembly.

1. Remove the right front cylinder head shroud as described in this chapter.
2. Remove the right side cover as described in this chapter.
3. On VTX1300T models, remove the right saddlebag as described in this chapter.
4. Apply a wide strip of non-permanent tape (**Figure 31**) across the section of exhaust pipe directly behind the rear brake pedal assembly.
5. Loosen and remove the front (**Figure 29**) and rear (**Figure 30**) exhaust pipe flange nuts.
6. Remove the nuts, washers and bolts (**Figure 32**) securing the muffler assembly to the exhaust pipe mounting bracket and remove the exhaust system.
7. Remove and discard the gasket installed in each exhaust port.
8. Clean the exhaust port mating surfaces of all carbon and oil residue.
9. Refer to **Figure 33** (2003-2007 models) or **Figure 34** (2008-on models) to service the exhaust pipe/muffler assembly. Note the following:
   a. To remove the exhaust pipe covers, release the retainer tab, then remove the bolts and retainer tab.
   b. Replace the exhaust pipe gaskets identified in **Figure 33** or **Figure 34** if leaking or damaged.

Exhaust Pipe Studs

If the exhaust pipe studs (A, **Figure 35**) are loose or replaced, reinstall them to the specified height of 37.5-38.5 mm (1.48-1.52 in.) measured from the top of the stud to the cylinder head gasket surface. If the studs are not installed correctly, the flange nut may bottom on the stud before it is tightened correctly, thus preventing the exhaust pipe gasket from being compressed properly. This will cause an air leak and backfiring.

CHAPTER FIFTEEN

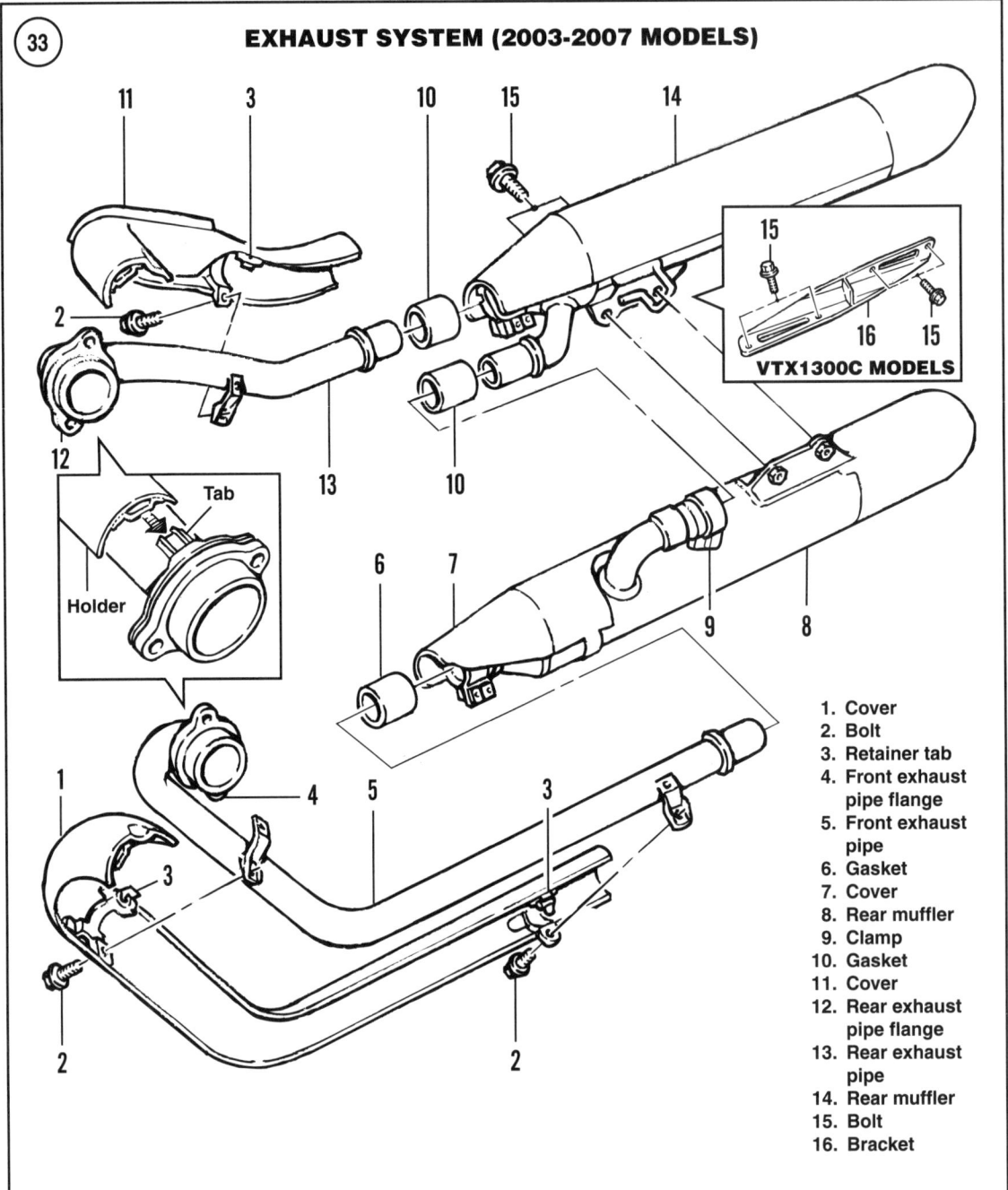

33. EXHAUST SYSTEM (2003-2007 MODELS)

1. Cover
2. Bolt
3. Retainer tab
4. Front exhaust pipe flange
5. Front exhaust pipe
6. Gasket
7. Cover
8. Rear muffler
9. Clamp
10. Gasket
11. Cover
12. Rear exhaust pipe flange
13. Rear exhaust pipe
14. Rear muffler
15. Bolt
16. Bracket

Exhaust System Installation

Refer to the exhaust pipe tightening sequence in **Figures 36-38**.

1. If the exhaust pipe assembly was disassembled, note the following:
   a. Refer to **Figure 33** or **Figure 34** when assembling the exhaust assembly.
   b. If removed, install the exhaust pipe covers onto the exhaust pipes before installing the exhaust pipe assembly onto the motorcycle while leaving the cover mounting bolts loose. After the exhaust system is installed and tightened, tighten the cover bolts securely.
   c. Align the holder on the covers with the tabs on the flange retainers. Refer to **Figure 33** or **Figure 34**.

2. Lightly grease new exhaust pipe gaskets (B, **Figure 35**) and install them into the cylinder head exhaust ports. The grease helps to hold the gaskets in place and will burn off once the engine is started.

3. Install the exhaust pipe assembly while noting the following:

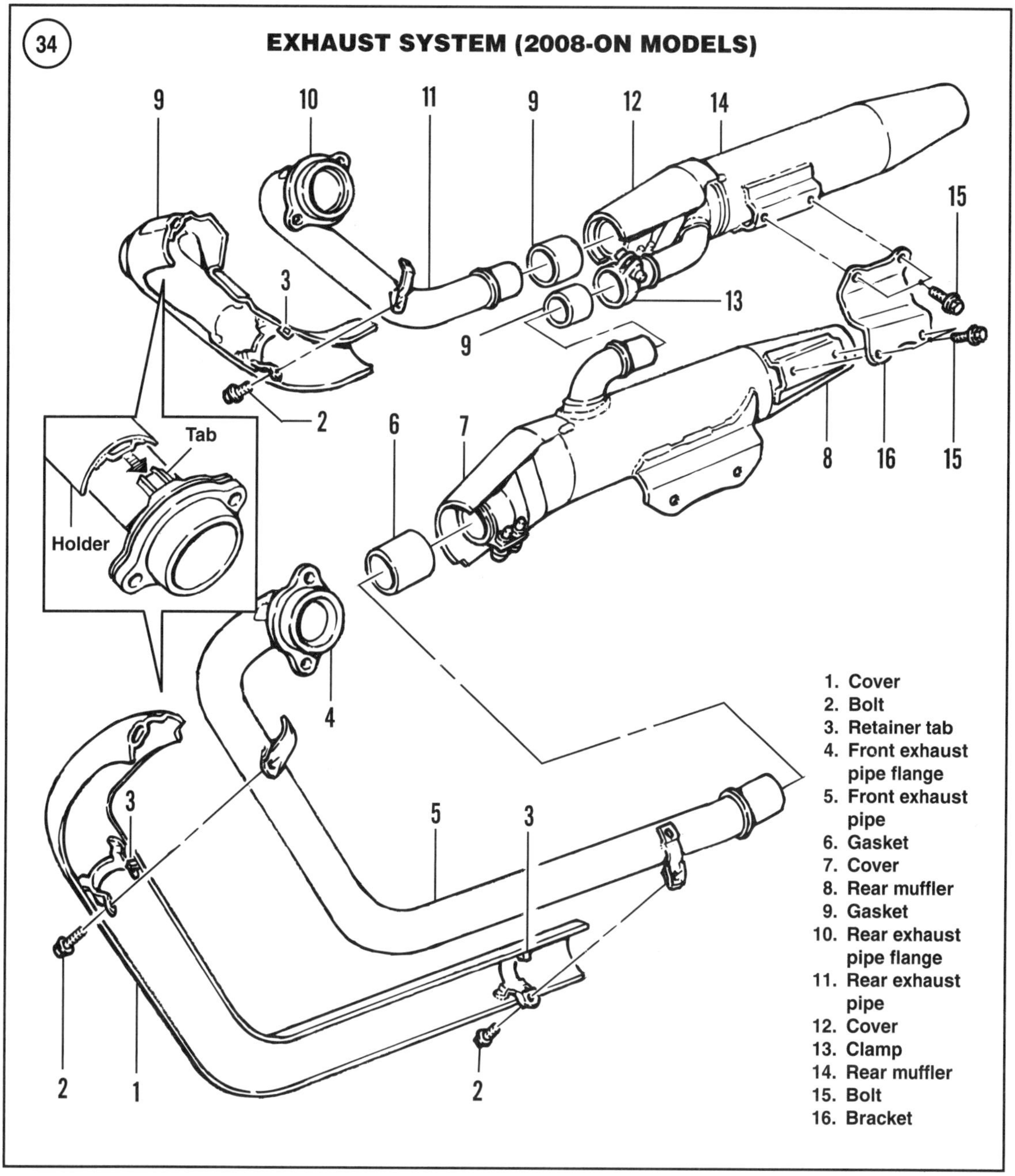

BODY AND EXHAUST SYSTEM

EXHAUST SYSTEM (2008-ON MODELS)

34.

1. Cover
2. Bolt
3. Retainer tab
4. Front exhaust pipe flange
5. Front exhaust pipe
6. Gasket
7. Cover
8. Rear muffler
9. Gasket
10. Rear exhaust pipe flange
11. Rear exhaust pipe
12. Cover
13. Clamp
14. Rear muffler
15. Bolt
16. Bracket

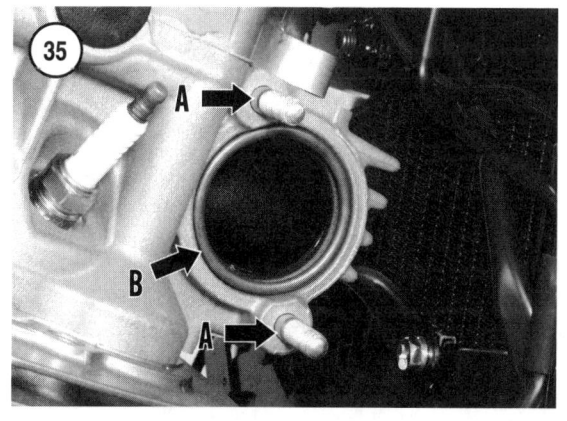

35.

a. Make sure the gaskets did not fall out.
b. The exhaust pipe flanges are marked with FR UP (front cylinder) and RR UP (rear cylinder) alignment designations (**Figure 39**, typical). Position each flange with the correct mark (front and rear cylinder) facing up.
c. Install the exhaust pipe flange nuts and tighten finger-tight. Check that the exhaust pipe gasket is positioned correctly in the port when tightening the flange nuts.

4. Install the muffler mounting bolts, washers and nuts and tighten finger-tight.

CHAPTER FIFTEEN

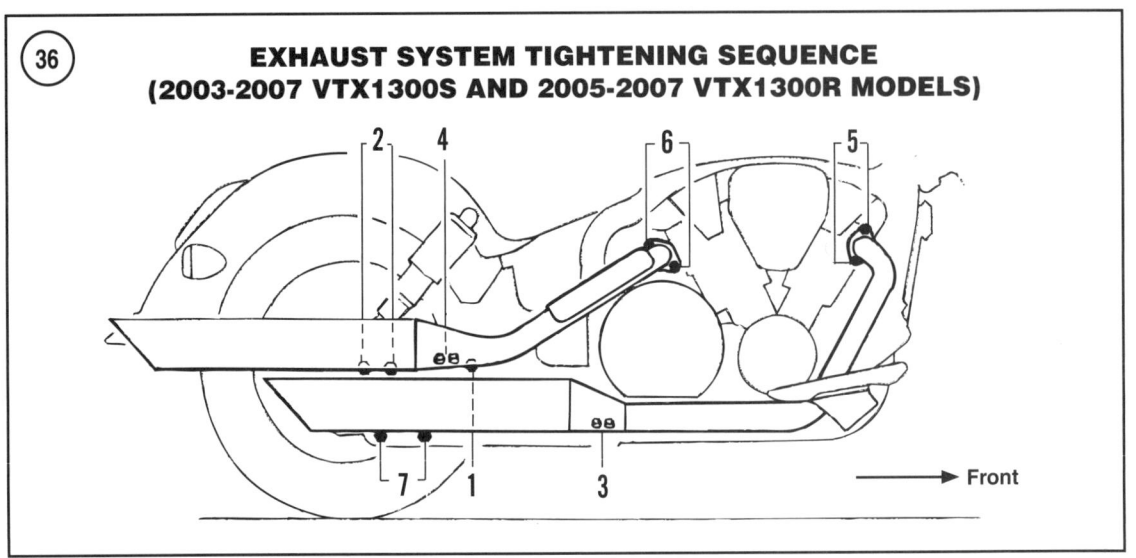

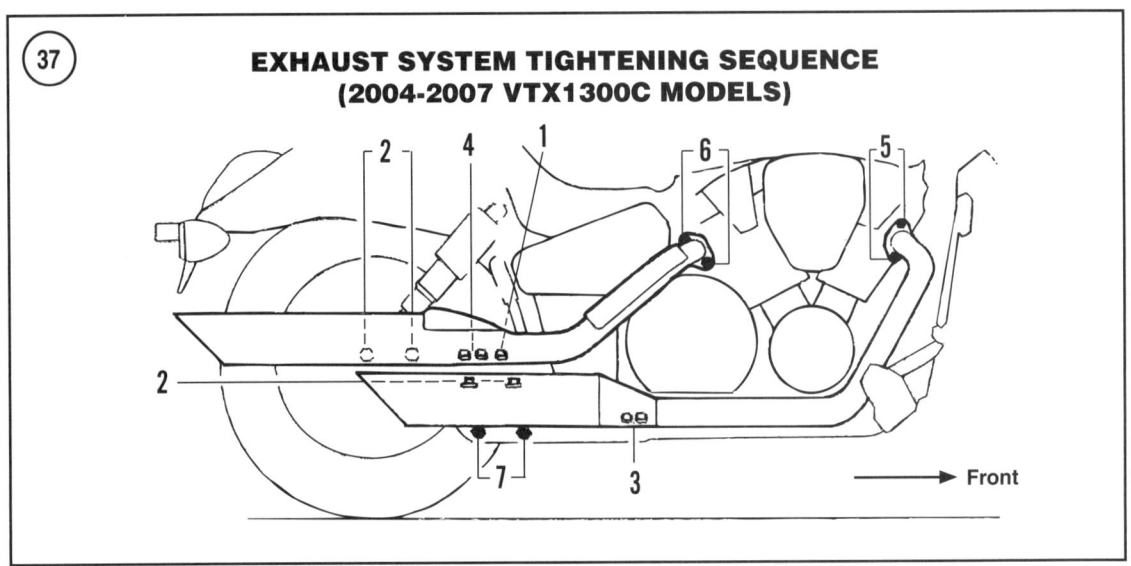

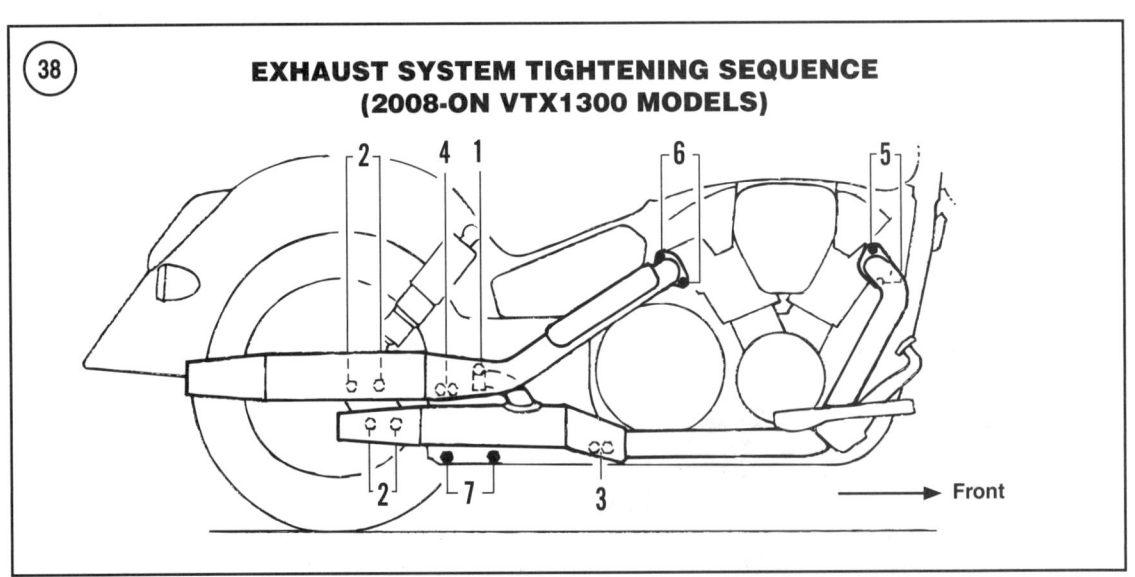

BODY AND EXHAUST SYSTEM

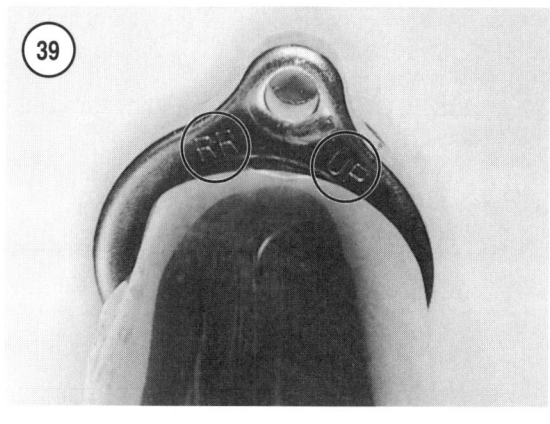

5. Tighten the exhaust pipe fasteners in the following order:
   a. Muffler clamp bolt (1, **Figure 36-38**) to 17 N•m (12 ft.-lb.).
   b. Muffler joint bolt (2, **Figure 36-38**) to 26 N•m (19 ft.-lb.).
   c. Muffler clamp bolts (3 and 4, **Figure 36-38**) to 17 N•m (12 ft.-lb.).
   d. Tighten each pair of exhaust pipe joint nuts (5 and 6, **Figure 36-38**) in a crossing pattern to 23 N•m (17 ft.-lb.).
   e. Muffler mounting nuts (7, **Figure 36-38**) to 34 N•m (25 ft.-lb.).
6. If loose, tighten the exhaust pipe cover mounting bolts.
7. If applied, remove the tape from the exhaust pipe.
8. On VTX1300T models, install the right saddlebag as described in this chapter.
9. Install the right side cover as described in this chapter.
10. Install the right front cylinder head shroud as described in this chapter.
11. Start the engine and check for exhaust leaks. If grease was applied to the exhaust pipe gaskets, allow the engine to run long enough for the grease to burn off.

Table 1 BODY TORQUE SPECIFICATIONS

	N•m	in.-lb.	ft.-lb.
Brake hose banjo bolt	34	–	25
Exhaust pipe joint bolt	23	–	17
Exhaust pipe stud	Refer to text		
Footrest mounting bracket bolt	39	–	29
Front brake caliper mounting bolt*	31	–	23
Upper mounting bracket bolt*			
VTX1300T models	21	–	15
Left crankcase rear cover mounting			
bracket bolt	10	88	–
Muffler clamp bolt	17	–	13
Muffler joint bolt	26	–	19
Muffler mounting nut	34	–	25
Shift boss pinch bolt	12	106	–
Sidestand			
Locknut*	30	–	22
Pivot bolt*	10	88	–
Windshield upper mounting bracket bolts*	21	–	15

*Refer to text for additional information.

INDEX

A

Air filter 50-51
  housing 181
Alternator specifications 263
Axle and wheels service specifications 297

B

Backrest 385
Balancer shaft 140-141
Battery 69, 211-215
  box 215
  charging 214
  load test 213-214
  maintenance-free voltage readings 262
  specifications 262
Body
  backrest and saddlebags 385
  crankcase cover, left rear 378
  cylinder head
    fin cover 378
    shroud 378
  exhaust system 385-391
  fender
    front 380-381
    rear 381
  rider footrests 381-383
  seat 377
  side covers 377
  sidestand 383-384
  specifications, torque 391
  steering side cover 379-380
  windshield 384-385
Brakes 72-74
  bleeding 350-352
  caliper
    overhaul 359-363
    removal/installation 357-358
  disc 374
  fluid draining and flushing 352-353
  hose and pipe 373
  light switch
    front 257
    rear 257-258
  master cylinder
    front 363-367
    rear 367-372
  pads 353-357
  pedal 367-372
  service 349-350
  specifications
    front 375
    rear 375
  system troubleshooting 47-49
  torque specifications 375-376
Bulbs, specifications 263

C

Cam chain 91-93
  tensioner 91-93
Camshafts 84-91
Carburetor 182-194
  specifications 209-210

INDEX

Charging system. 215-218
  specifications 263
Choke cable 199-200
Clutch .149-157
  cable
    and lever 63-64
    replacement 165-166
  diode .241-242
  release assembly 157-159
  specifications 166
    torque. 167
  switch 256-257
  troubleshooting 41
Connecting rods 137-140
  bearing
    selection 146
    thickness 146
    weight selection 146
Coolant
  capacity 77
  reserve tank 269
  temperature indicator 250-252
Cooling system 67-69, 265-267
  coolant reserve tank 269
  fan 268-269
  radiator. 267-268
  pressure test 266-267
  specifications 273-274
    torque. 274
  thermostat 269-270
    housing. 270-271
  water pump 271-273
Countershaft service specifications 175
Crankcase 123-135
  breather
    inspection 51
    system 203
  cover
    left 218-221
      rear. 378
    right 148-149
  seal and bearing 135-136
Crankshaft. 136-137
Current draw test 216-217
Cylinder 102-105
  head 93-95
    and valve service specifications 113-114
    covers and rocker arms. 79-84
    fin cover 378
    shroud 378
    leakdown test troubleshooting. 40-41
    stud 112

E

Electrical system
  alternator specifications 263

battery 211-215
  box 215
  maintenance free voltage readings. 262
  specifications. 262
bulbs, specifications 263
charging system 215-218
  specifications. 263
clutch diode 241-242
component replacement 211
connectors 211
coolant temperature indicator 250-252
crankcase cover, left 218-221
engine coolant temperature (ECT)
  sensor. 250-252
flywheel 221-225
fuel cutoff relay 260
fundamentals. 18
fuses 261-262, 264
horn 261
ignition
  coils 230-231
    peak voltage test. 227-228
  control module (ICM) 231
  pulse generator. 218-221, 231
    peak voltage test. 228-230
  system
    specifications 263
    testing 225-230
    timing 56-57
lighting. 242-247
maintenance-free battery voltage readings . . 262
meter assembly 247-250
oil pressure indicator
  and switch 253-254
sensor test specifications. 263
starter 234-240
  clutch. 221-225
    specifications 263
  drive gears 221-225
  relay switch 240-241
  system troubleshooting. 232-234
starting system specifications 263
stator coil 218-221
switches
  clutch. 256-257
  continuity test 259-260
  fan 252-253
  front brake light 257
  handlebar. 258-259
  ignition 258
  neutral 254-255
  oil pressure 253-254
  rear brake light 257-258
  sidestand 255-256
  starter relay 240-241
throttle position sensor (TPS) 231-232

INDEX

Electrical system (continued)
  torque specifications. 264
  troubleshooting 42-46
  turn signal relay 260
  vehicle speed sensor (VSS) 250
Engine
  break-in 146
  compression test 51-52
  coolant temperature (ECT) sensor. 250-252
  installation 122-123
  lower end 116-123
    balancer shafts 140-141
    break-in 146
    connecting rods 137-140
    crankcase 123-135
      seal and bearing 135-136
    crankshaft 136-137
    oil pump 141-145
    output gear 145
    servicing engine in frame 116
    specifications 146
      connecting rods
        bearing selection 146
        bearing thickness 146
        weight selection 146
      oil pump 147
      torque 147
  lubrication 40
  oil
    and filter 64-66
    capacity 77
    pressure check 66-67
  removal 117-122
  rotation 50
  top end
    cam chain 91-93
      tensioner 91-93
    camshafts 84-91
    cylinder 102-105
      head 93-95
        covers and rocker arms 79-84
        and valve service specifications . . . 113-114
        stud replacement 112
    piston and piston rings 106-112
    specifications 113
      cylinder head and valve service 113-114
      general 113
      piston, rings and bore 114
      torque 114-115, 147
    valves and valve components 95-102
  torque
    lower end 147
    top end 114-115
  troubleshooting 38-40
    lubrication 40
    poor performance 34-36

  starting 30-32
  will not start 32-34
Evaporative emission control system 69
  California models only 205-209
Exhaust system 385-391
External shift mechanism 162-165

F

Fan switch 252-253
Fasteners 4-6
  inspection 75
Fender
  front 380-381
  rear 381
Final drive
  and rear suspension torque specifications . . . 348
  oil 69-70
    capacity 77
    change 69-70
  troubleshooting 46-47
  unit
    and drive shaft 328-330
    overhaul 330-344
    service specifications 347
Flywheel 221-225
Fork, front 302-310
  oil change 75
Fuel system
  carburetor 182-194
    specifications 209-210
  choke cable 199-200
  crankcase breather system 203
  cutoff relay 260
  differences 177
  filter 61
  fuel and lubricants, recommendations 77
  high altitude adjustment 198
  hose inspection 60-61
  intake manifold 194-196
  pilot screw adjustment 196-198
  pulse secondary air supply system 203-205
  pump
    and filter 200-206
    specifications 210
  specifications
    pump 210
    torque 210
  tank 177-178
  throttle cable 199
  troubleshooting 36-38
  valve 178-181
Fuses 261-262, 264

G

Gearshift linkage troubleshooting 42

INDEX

General information
  conversion formulas 27
  dimensions. 25
  electrical system fundamentals 18
  fasteners 4-6
  metric tap and drill sizes. 28
  metric, inch and fractional equivalents 29
  serial numbers and information labels. 3
  service methods 18-24
  shop supplies 6-9
  specifications
    engine 113
    torque. 26
    weight 26
  storage 24-25
  technical abbreviations 27-28
  tools 9-14
    measuring 14-18

H

Handlebar .298-301
  grips 301-302
  switch 258-259
Headlight adjustment 243-244
High altitude adjustment 198
Horn 261

I

Idle speed adjustment 60
Ignition
  coils 230-231
    peak voltage test 227-228
  control module (ICM) 231
  cut-off switch and sidestand 75
  pulse generator. 218-221, 231
    peak voltage test 228-230
  switch 258
  system
    spark test 33
    specifications. 263
    testing 225-230
    timing 56-57
Information labels and serial numbers 3
Intake manifold 194-196
Internal shift mechanism 173-174

L

Lighting system 242-247
Lubrication
  and maintenance schedule. 75-76
  coolant capacity 77
  engine oil
    and filter 64-66
    capacity 77
    pressure check 66-67
  final drive oil 69-70
    capacity 77
    change 69-70
  front fork oil change
  lubricants and fuel, recommendations. 77

M

Mainshaft service specifications 175
Maintenance
  air filter 50-51
  and lubrication schedule. 75-76
  battery 69
  brakes 72-74
  clutch cable and lever 63-64
  coolant capacity 77
  cooling system. 67-69
  crankcase breather inspection 51
  engine
    compression test 51-52
    oil
      and filter 64-66
      capacity 77
      pressure check 66-67
    rotation 50
  evaporative emission control system 69
  fasteners inspection
  final drive oil 69-70
    capacity 77
  front fork oil change
  fuel
    filter 61
    hose inspection. 60-61
  headlight. 74
  idle speed adjustment 60
  ignition timing. 56-57
  lubricants and fuel, recommendations. 77
  secondary air supply system. 69
  service specifications 175
  sidestand and ignition cut-off switch test 75
  spark plugs. 52-56
  steering bearings. 71
  suspension check
    front 71
    rear. 71
  throttle cable. 61-63
  tires
    and wheels 70-71
    inflation pressure and tread depth 78
  torque specifications. 78
  valve clearance 57-60
Master cylinder
  front .363-367
  rear. .367-372
Meter assembly 247-250
Motorcycle lift 275

N

Neutral switch 254-255

O

Oil
  change
    engine 65-66
    final drive 69-70
    fork 75
  capacity
    engine 77
    final drive 77
    fork 320
  pressure switch and indicator 253-254
  pump 141-145
    chain and sprockets 159-162
    specifications 147
Output gear 145

P

Pilot screw adjustment 196-198
Pinion gear
  and ring measurements 344-347
  shim sizes 348
Piston
  and piston rings 106-112
  rings and bore specifications 114
Primary drive and driven gears 159-162
Pulse secondary air supply system 203-205

R

Radiator 267-268
Rider footrests 381-383
Ring
  and pinion gear measurements 344-347
  gear shim sizes 348

S

Saddlebags 385
Seat 377
Secondary air supply system 69
Sensor test specifications 263
Serial numbers and information labels 3
Service
  brakes 349-350
  methods 18-24
  specifications
    brakes
      front 375
      rear 375
    countershaft 175
    cylinder head and valve 113-114
    final drive unit 347
    front fork 320
    mainshaft 175
    shift fork and shift shaft 175-176
    wheel and axle 297
Shift fork and shift shaft
  service specifications 175-176
Shock absorber 322-324
Shop supplies 6-9
Side covers 377
  steering 379-380
Sidestand 383-384
  and ignition cut-off switch test 75
  switch 255-256
Spark plugs 52-56
Spark test 33
Specifications
  alternator and charging system 263
  battery 262
  body torque 391
  brakes
    service
      front 375
      rear 375
    torque 375-376
  bulbs 263
  carburetor 209-210
  clutch 166
    torque 167
  connecting rod
    bearing
      selection 146
      thickness 146
    weight selection 146
  conversion formulas 26-27
  coolant capacity 77
  cooling system 273-274
    torque 274
  countershaft service 175
  cylinder head and valve service 113-114
  electrical system torque 264
  engine
    lower end 146
      torque 147
    oil capacity 77
    top end torque 114-115
  final drive
    unit service 347
    oil capacity 77
  front fork service 320
  front suspension and steering 320
    torque 321
  fuel
    pump 210
    system torque 210
  fuses 264
  general
    dimensions 25

INDEX

engine 113
ignition system 263
lubricants and fuel, recommendations 77
mainshaft service 175
maintenance
   and lubrication schedule 75-76
   torque 78
maintenance-free battery voltage readings . . 262
metric tap and drill sizes 28
metric, inch and fractional equivalents 29
oil pump 147
pinion gear shim sizes 348
piston, rings and bore 114
ring gear shim sizes 348
sensor test 263
shift fork and shift shaft service 175-176
starter clutch 263
starting system 263
   torque 321
suspension
   front
      and steering 320
      torque 321
   rear 347
      and final drive torque 348
technical abbreviations 27-28
tires
   and wheels 296
   inflation pressure and tread depth 78, 297
torque recommendations 26
transmission 174
tune-up 77
weight 26
wheels
   and axle service 297
   and tires 296
   torque 297
Starter 234-240
   clutch 221-225
      specifications 263
   drive gears 221-225
   relay switch 240-241
   system troubleshooting 232-234
Starting
   system specifications 263
   the engine troubleshooting 30-32
Stator coil 218-221
Steering
   bearings 71
      preload check 317-318
      race removal/installation
         head 318-319
         stem 319-320
   head and stem 311-317
   side cover 379-380
   torque specifications 321
   troubleshooting 47

Storage 24-25
Suspension
   final drive 328-330
      drive shaft 328-330
      overhaul 330-344
      pinion gear 338-344
         measurements 344-347
         shim sizes 348
      ring gear 332-338
         measurements 344-347
         shim sizes 348
   fork, front 302-310
      service specifications 320
   handlebar 298-301
      grips 301-302
   maintenance, inspection 71-72
   shock absorber 322-324
   specifications
      front 320
         torque 321
      rear 347
         torque 348
   troubleshooting 47
Swing arm 324-328
Switches
   brakes
      light
         front 257
         rear 257-258
   clutch 256-257
   continuity test 259-260
   handlebar 258-259
   ignition 258
   neutral 254-255
   oil pressure 253-254
   sidestand 255-256

T

Thermostat 269-270
   housing 270-271
Throttle
   cable 61-63
      removal/installation 198-199
   position sensor (TPS) 231-232
Tires
   and wheels 70-71
      specifications 296
   changing 290-295
   inflation pressure and tread depth 297
Tools 9-14
   measuring 14-18
Torque specifications
   body and exhaust 391
   brakes 375-376
   clutch 167

Torque specifications (continued)
  cooling system 274
  general recommendations 29
  electrical system 264
  engine
    lower end 147
    top end 114-115
  front suspension and steering 321
  fuel system 210
  maintenance 78
  rear suspension 348
  wheel 297
Transmission 168-173
  specifications 174
  troubleshooting 42
Troubleshooting
  brakes system 47-49
  clutch 41
  cylinder leakdown test 40-41
  electrical testing 42-46
  engine 38-40
    lubrication 40
    poor performance 34-36
    starting 30-32
    will not start 32-34
  final drive 46-47
  fuel system 36-38
  gearshift linkage 42
  spark test 33
  suspension and steering 47
  transmission 42
Tune-up 50
  air filter 50-51
  battery 69
  brakes 72-74
  clutch cable and lever 63-64
  cooling system 67-69
  crankcase breather inspection 51
  engine
    compression test 51-52
    oil
      and filter 64-66
      capacity 77
      pressure check 66-67
    rotation 50
  evaporative emission control system 69
  fasteners 75
  final drive oil 69-70

  front fork oil change 75
  fuel
    filter removal/installation 61
    hose inspection 60-61
  headlight 75
  idle speed adjustment 60
  ignition timing 56-57
  secondary air supply system 69
  sidestand and ignition cut-off switch test . . . 75
  specifications 77
  steering bearings 71
  suspension check
    front 71
    rear 72
  throttle cable 61-63
  tires
    inflation pressure and tread depth 78
  valve clearance 57-60
  wheels 70-71
Turn signal relay 260

V

Valves
  and valve components 95-102
  clearance 57-60
  specifications 113-114
Vehicle speed sensor (VSS) 250

W

Water pump 271-273
Wheels
  and axle service specifications 297
  and tires 70-71
    specifications 296
  balance 295-296
  driven flange 284-286
  front 275-278
  hub
    front 281-284
    rear 281-284
  rear 278-281
  service
    cast wheels 286-287
    laced wheels 287-290
  torque specifications 297
Windshield 384-385
Wiring diagrams 262, 399-411

WIRING DIAGRAMS

2003 VTX1300S MODELS

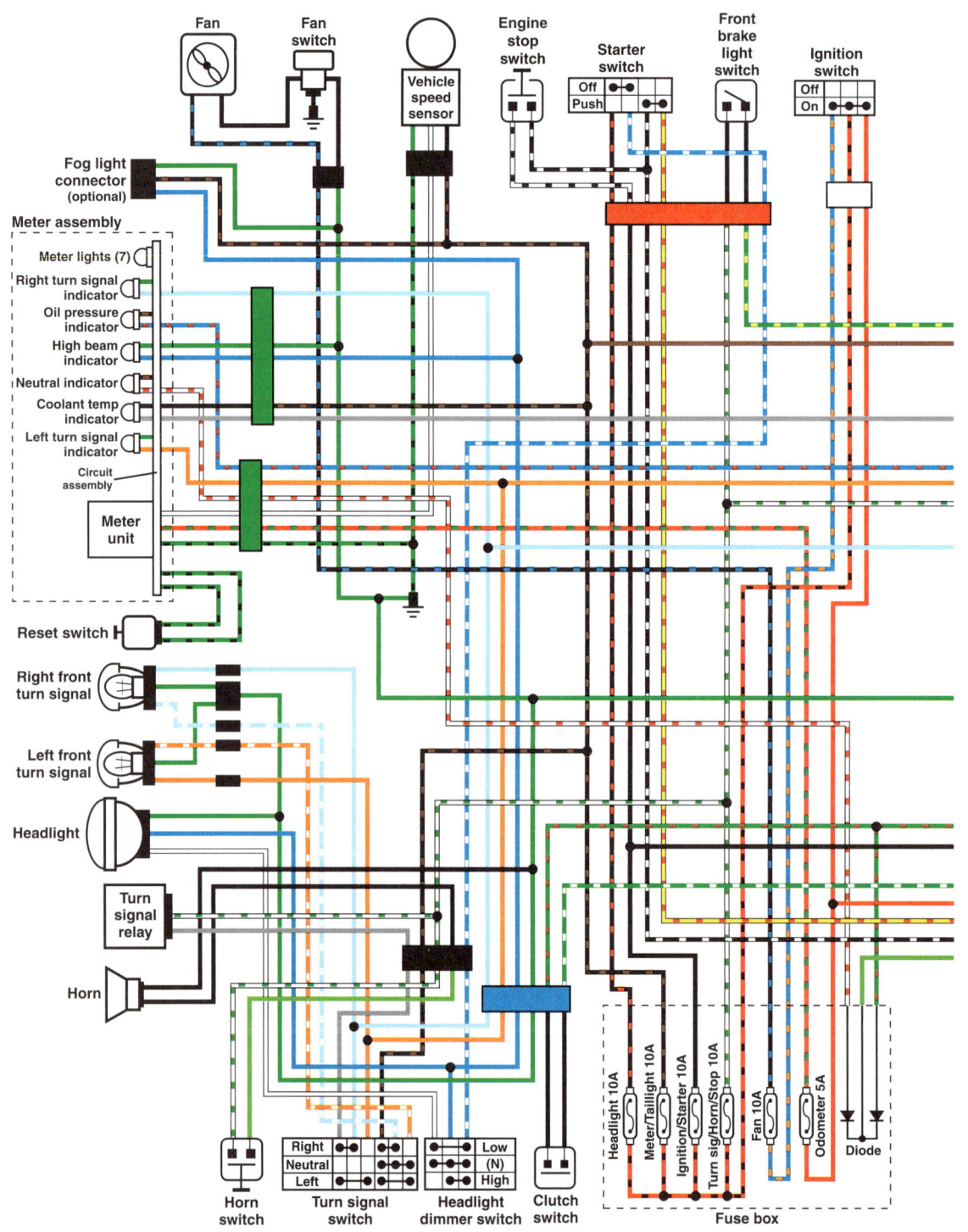

WIRING DIAGRAMS

401

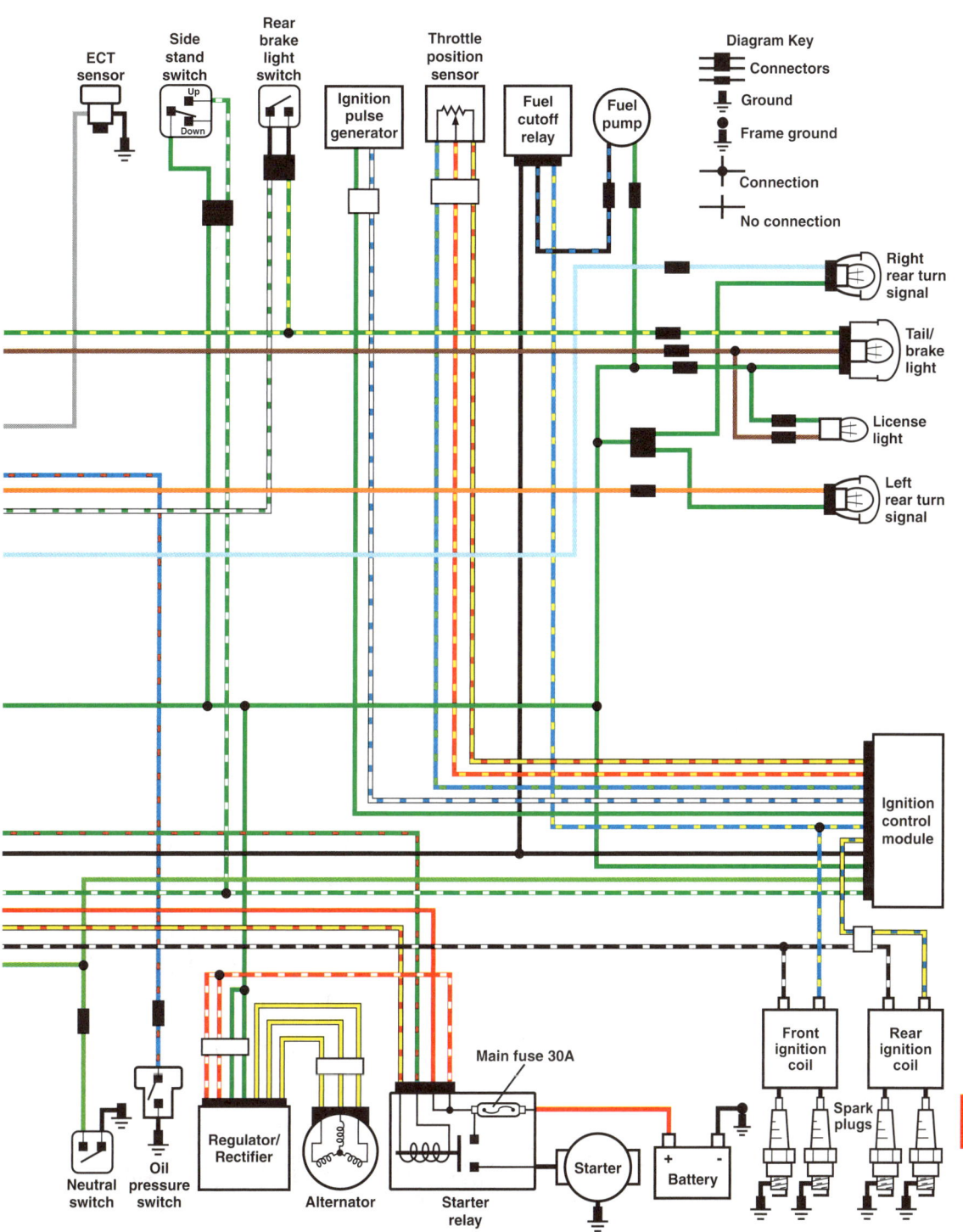

17

2004-2005 VTX1300S/C AND 2005 VTX1300R MODELS

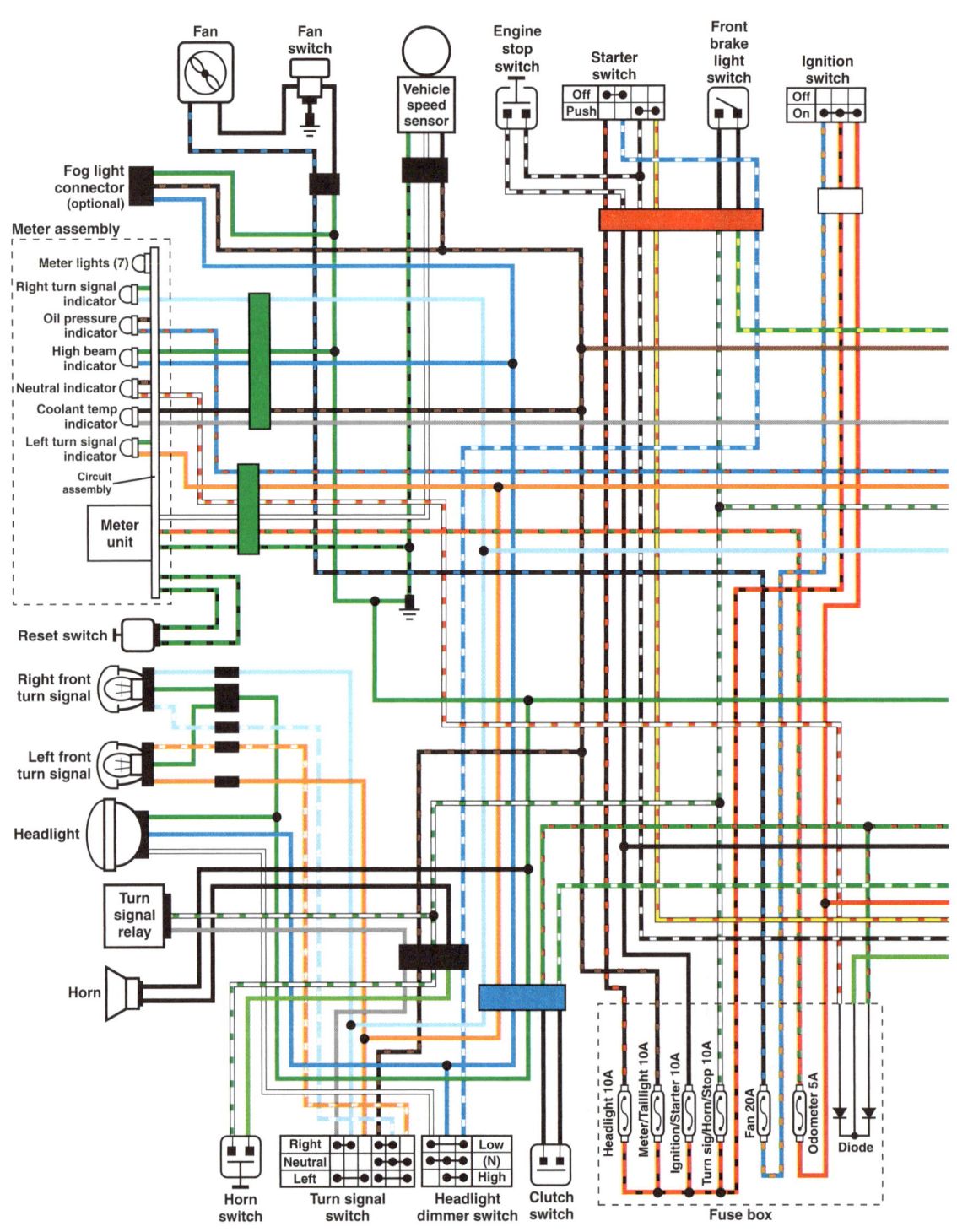

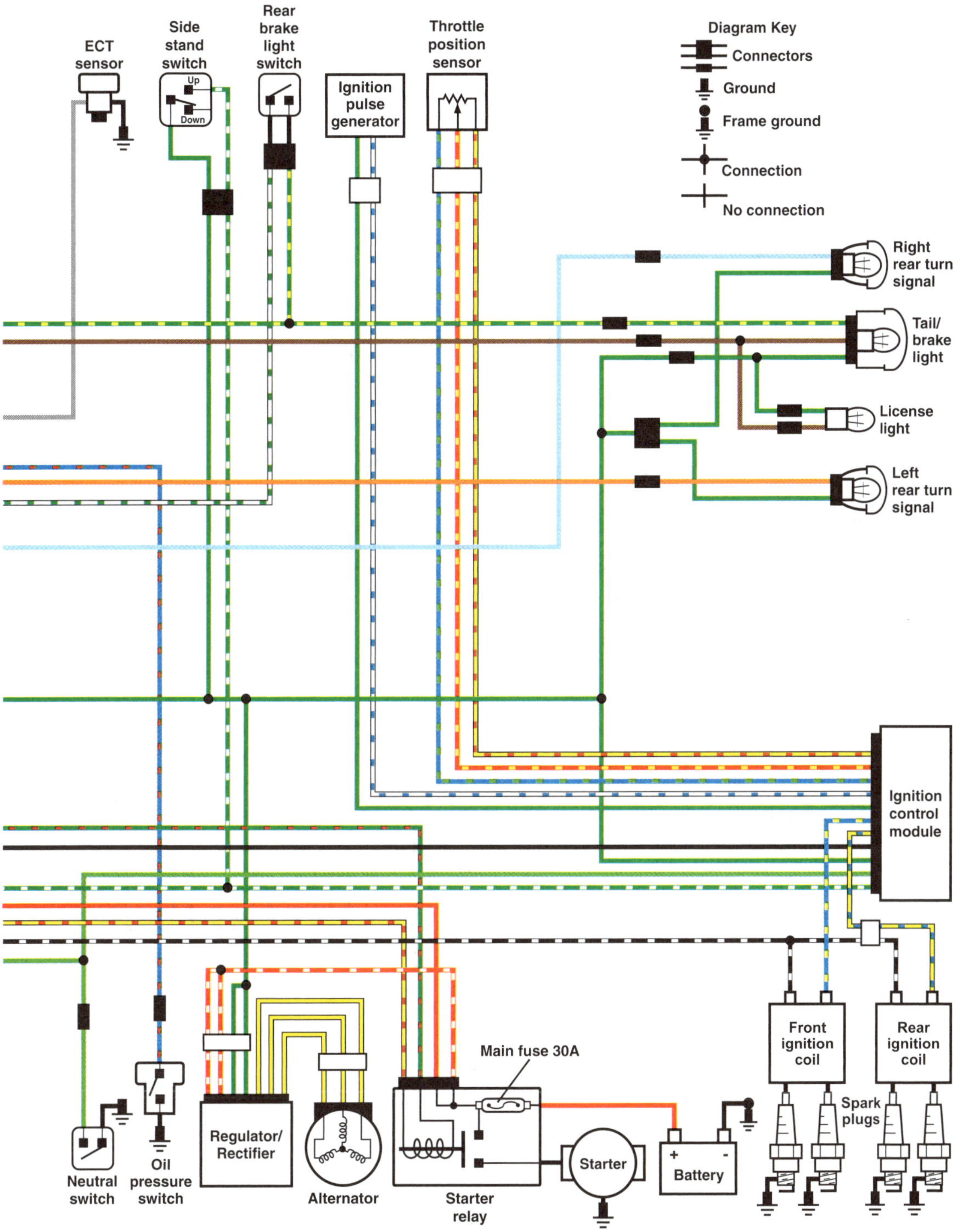

WIRING DIAGRAMS

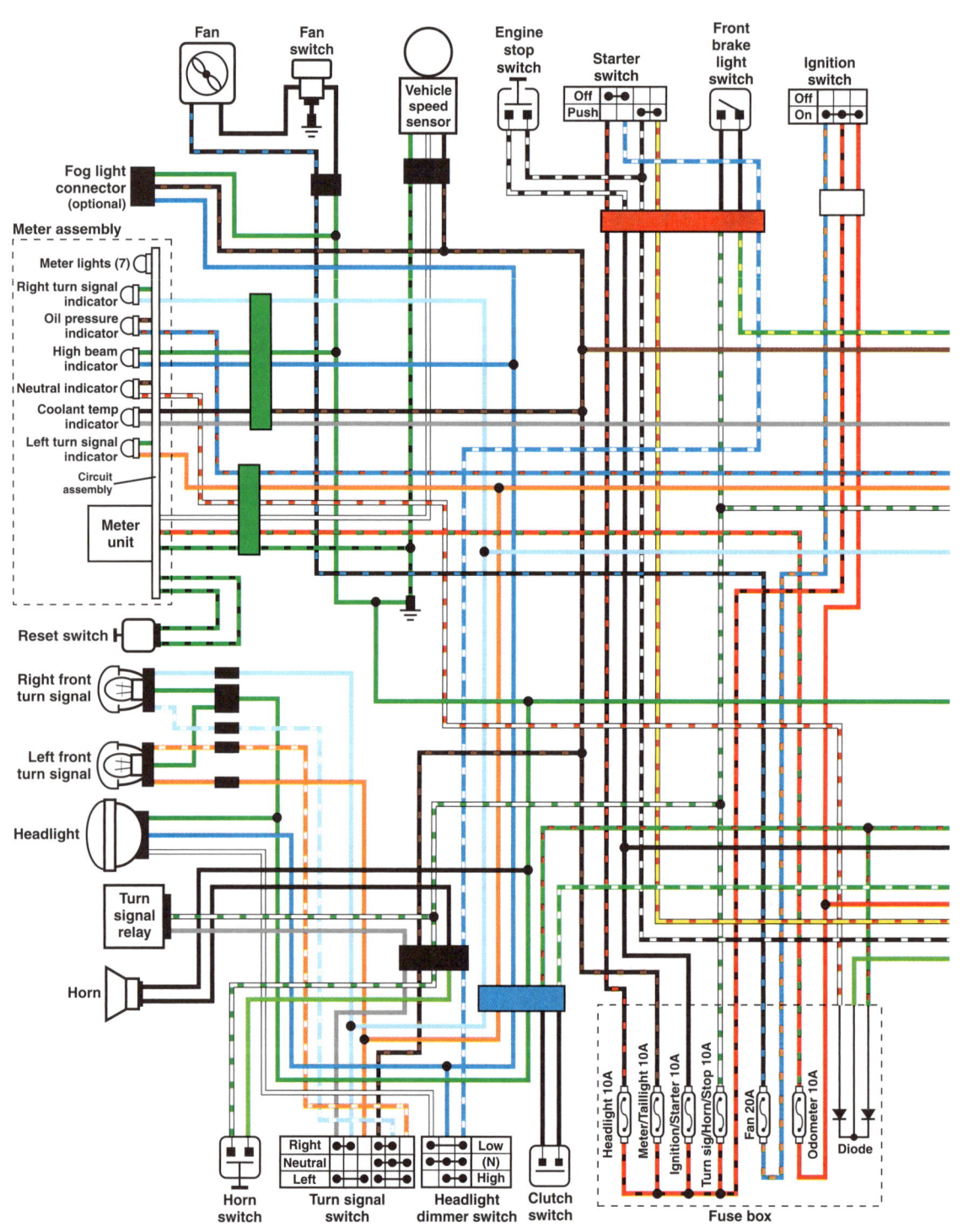

2006 VTX1300C/R/S MODELS

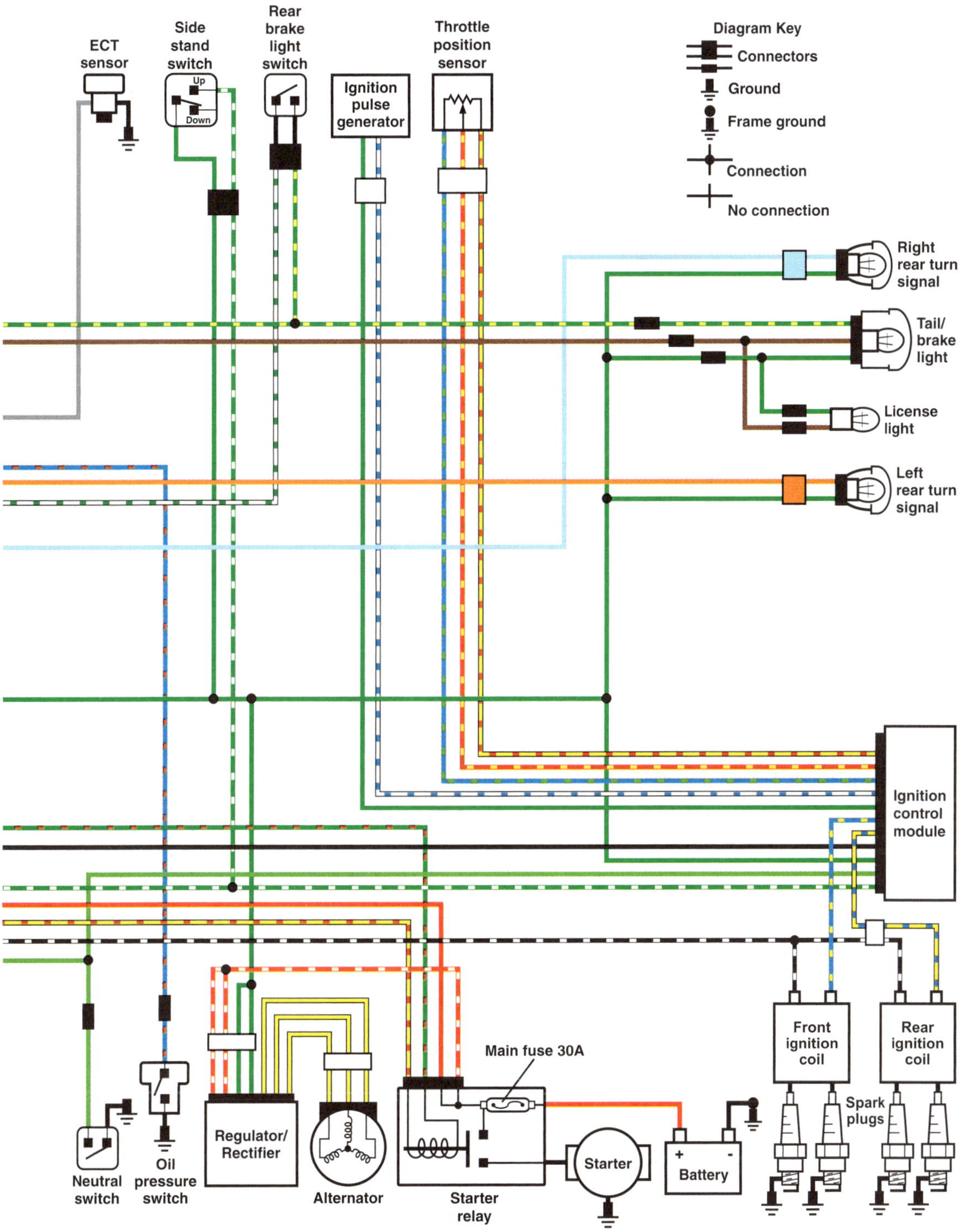

WIRING DIAGRAMS

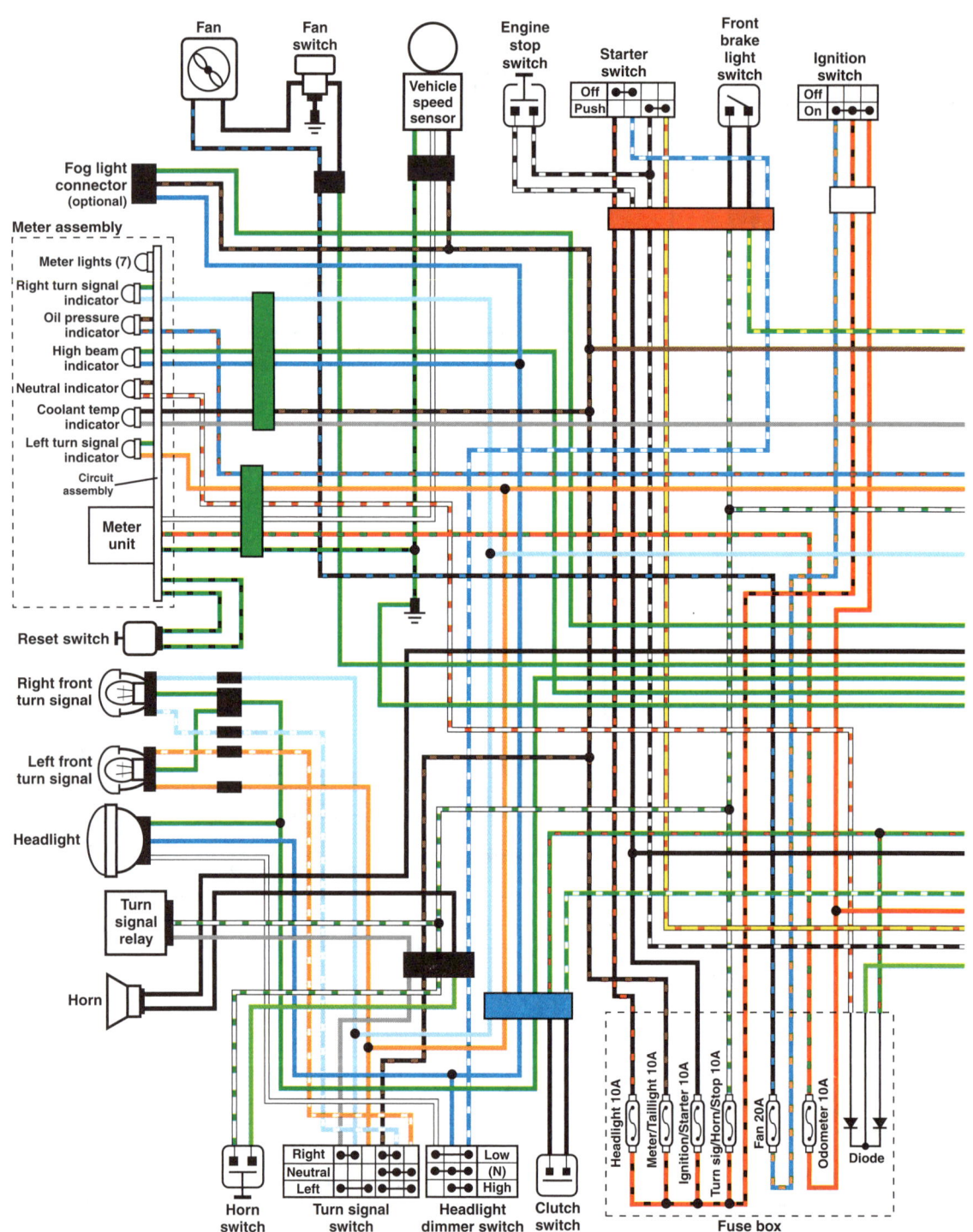

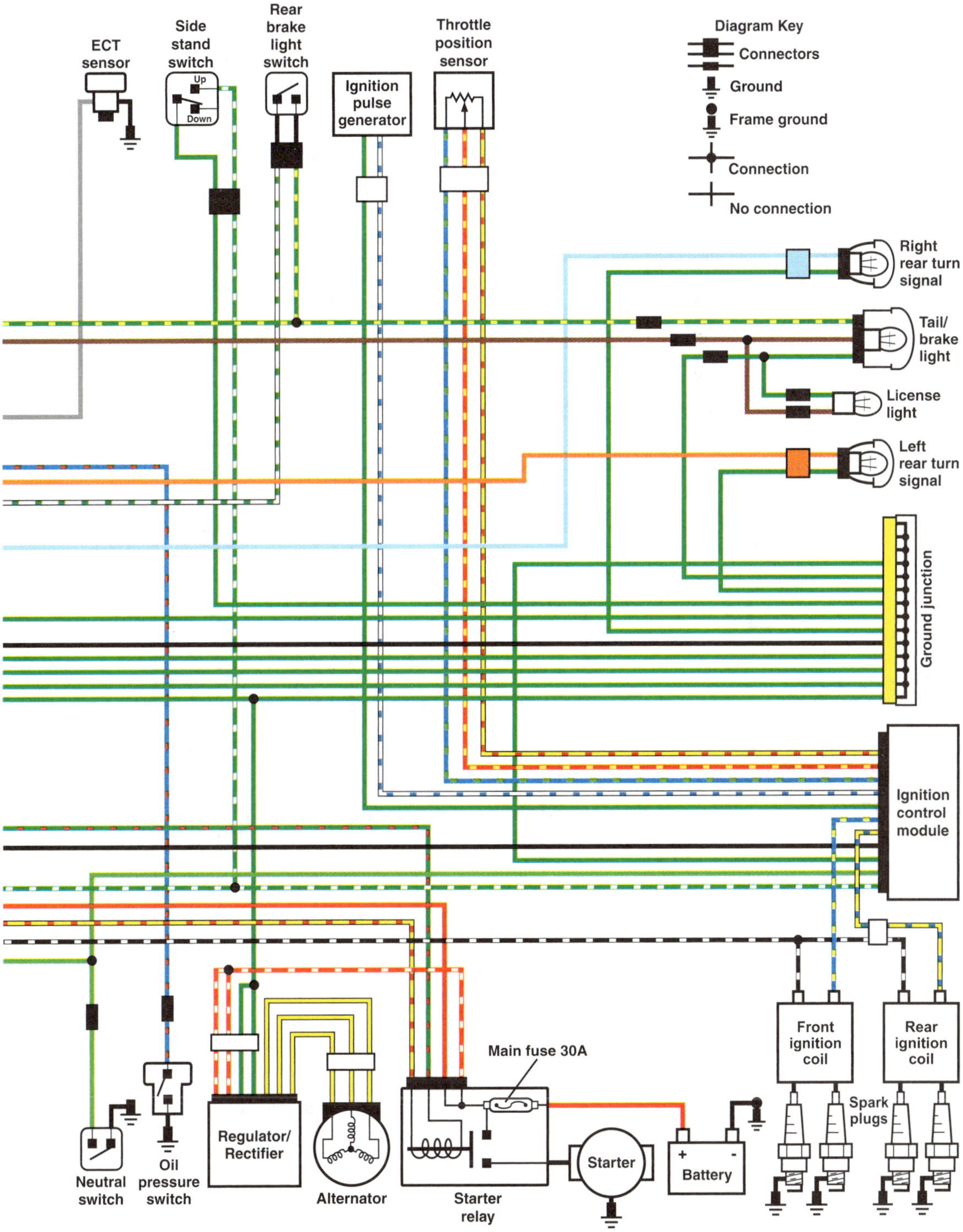

WIRING DIAGRAMS

WIRING DIAGRAMS

2008-2009 VTX1300C/R/T 49 STATES/CANADA MODELS

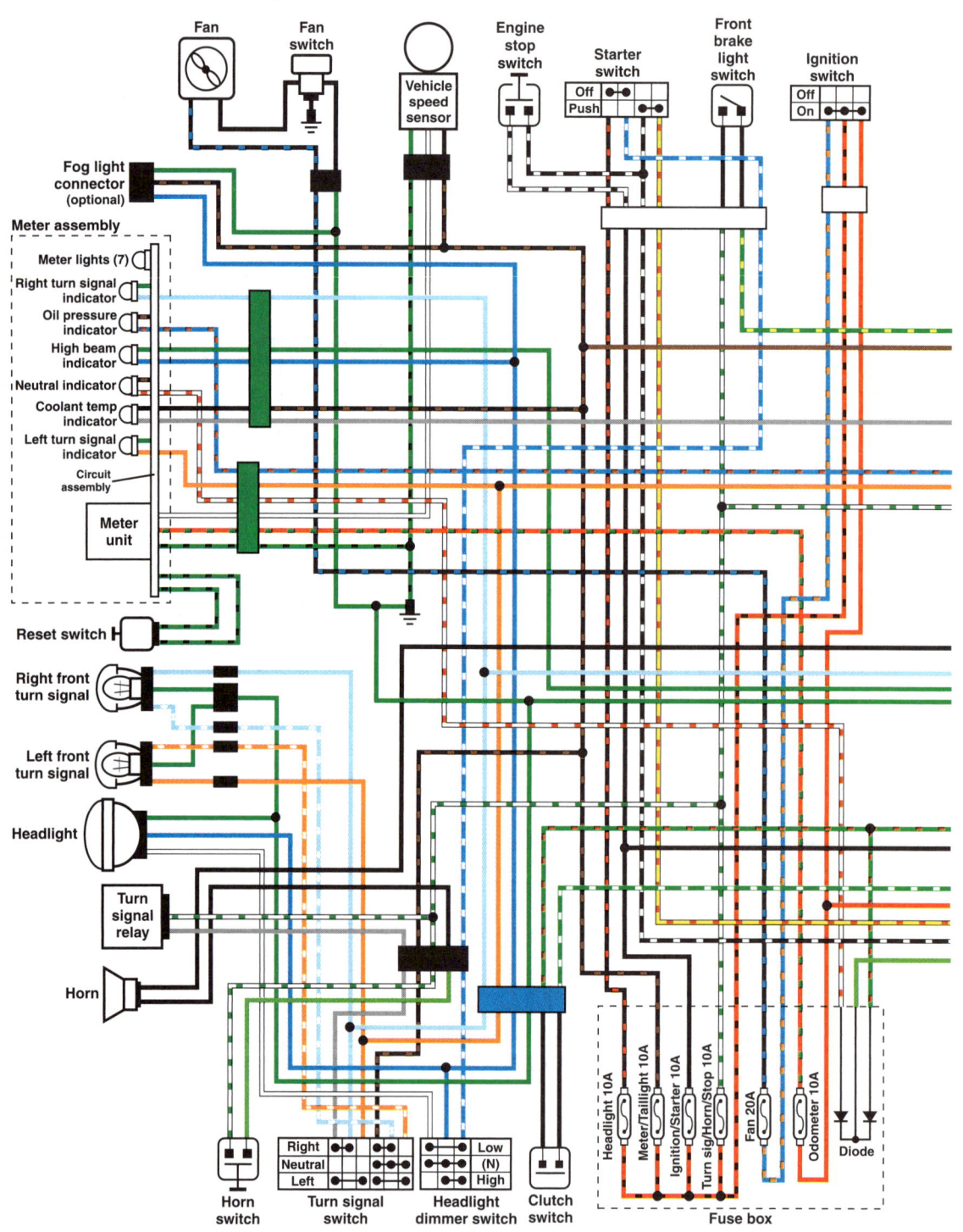

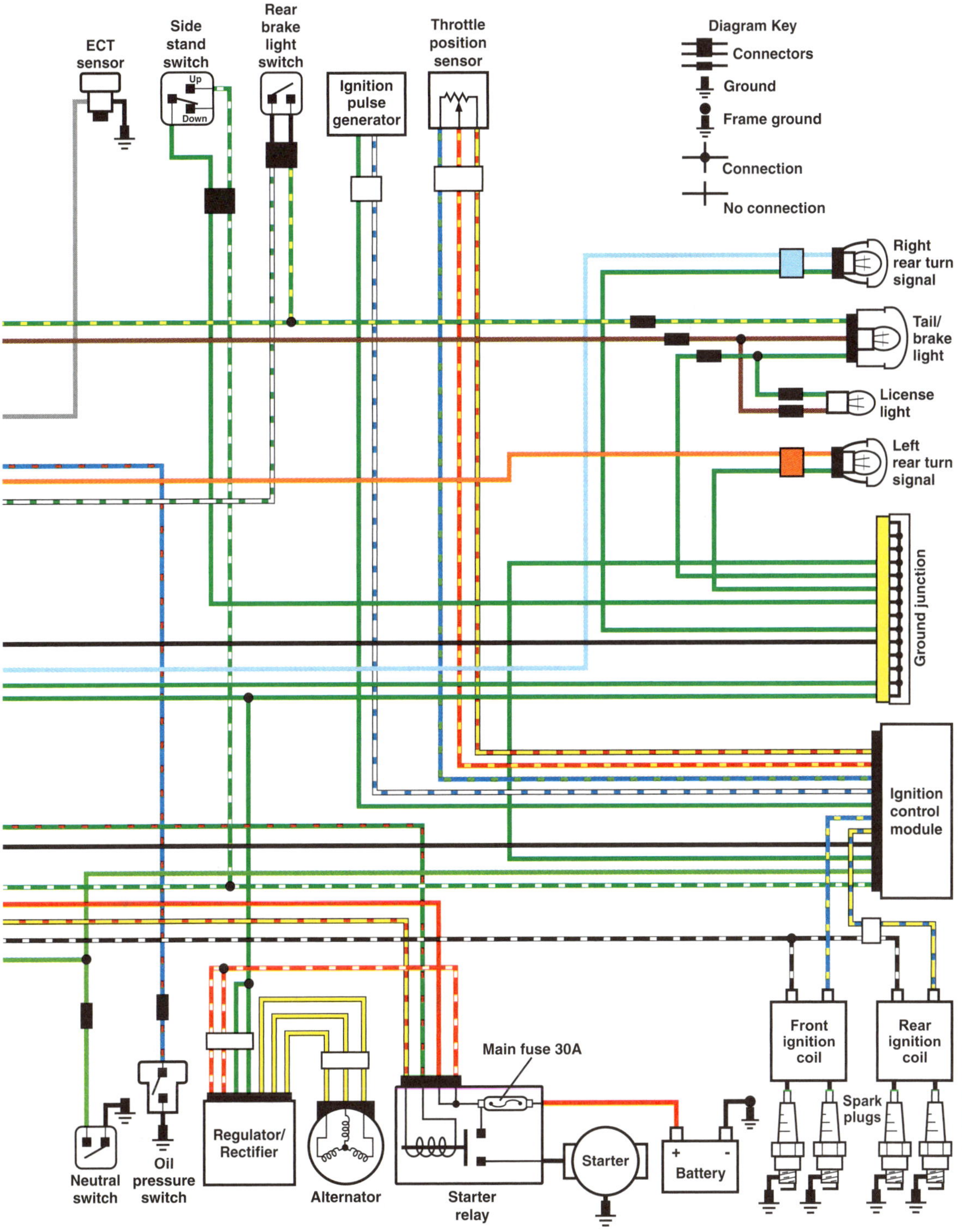

WIRING DIAGRAMS

WIRING DIAGRAMS

2008-2009 VTX1300C/R/T CALIFORNIA MODELS

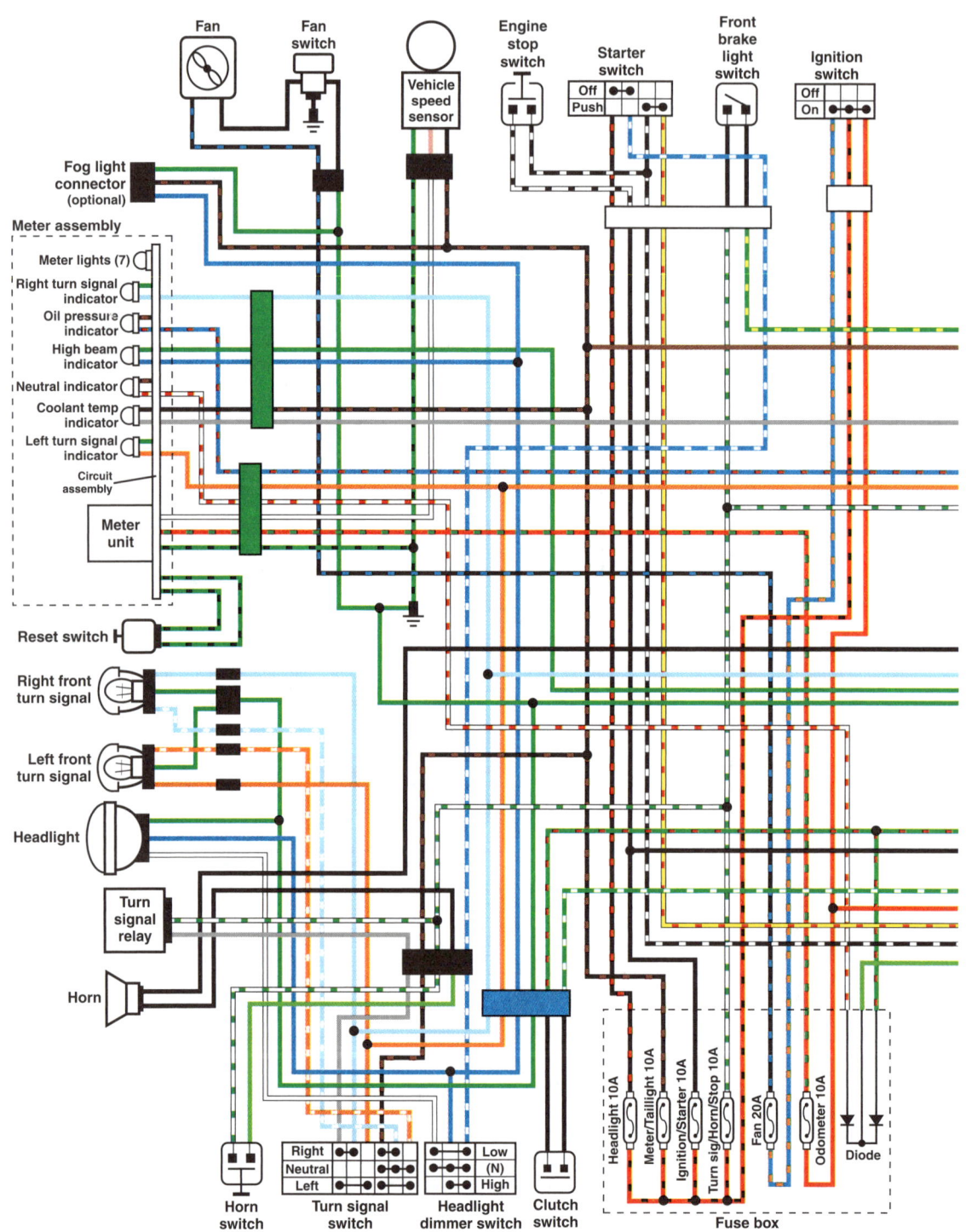

WIRING DIAGRAMS

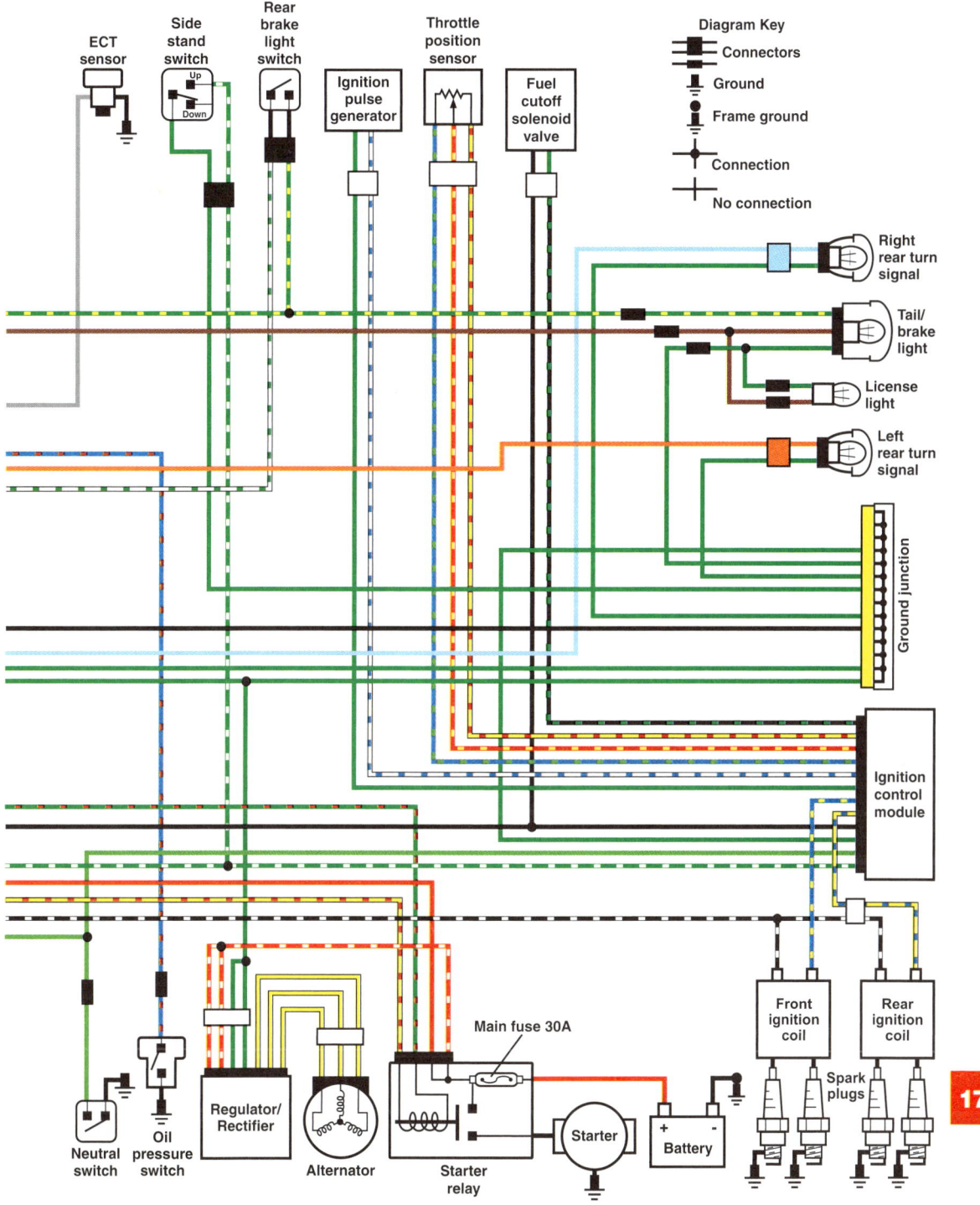

NOTES

MAINTENANCE LOG

Date	Miles	Type of Service

Check out *clymer.com* for our full line of powersport repair manuals.

BMW
M308	500 & 600cc Twins, 55-69
M502-3	BMW R50/5-R100GS PD, 70-96
M500-3	BMW K-Series, 85-97
M501-3	K1200RS, GT & LT, 98-10
M503-3	R850, R1100, R1150 & R1200C, 93-05
M309	F650, 1994-2000

HARLEY-DAVIDSON
M419	Sportsters, 59-85
M429-5	XL/XLH Sportster, 86-03
M427-4	XL Sportster, 04-13
M418	Panheads, 48-65
M420	Shovelheads, 66-84
M421-3	FLS/FXS Evolution, 84-99
M423-2	FLS/FXS Twin Cam, 00-05
M250	FLS/FXS/FXC Softail, 06-09
M422-3	FLH/FLT/FXR Evolution, 84-98
M430-4	FLH/FLT Twin Cam, 99-05
M252	FLH/FLT, 06-09
M426	VRSC Series, 02-07
M424-3	FXD Evolution, 91-98
M425-3	FXD Twin Cam, 99-05
M254	Dyna Series, 06-11

HONDA
ATVs
M316	Odyssey FL250, 77-84
M311	ATC, TRX & Fourtrax 70-125, 70-87
M433	Fourtrax 90, 93-00
M326	ATC185 & 200, 80-86
M347	ATC200X & Fourtrax 200SX, 86-88
M455	ATC250 & Fourtrax 200/250, 84-87
M342	ATC250R, 81-84
M348	TRX250R/Fourtrax 250R & ATC250R, 85-89
M456-4	TRX250X 87-92; TRX300EX 93-06
M446-3	TRX250 Recon & Recon ES, 97-07
M215-2	TTRX250EX Sportrax and TRX250X, 01-12
M346-3	TRX300/Fourtrax 300 & TRX300FW/Fourtrax 4x4, 88-00
M200-2	TRX350 Rancher, 00-06
M459-3	TRX400 Foreman 95-03
M454-5	TRX400EX Fourtrax & Sportrax 99-13
M201	TRX450R & TRX450ER, 04-09
M205	TRX450 Foreman, 98-04
M210	TRX500 Rubicon, 01-04
M206	TRX500 Foreman, 05-11

Singles
M310-13	50-110cc OHC Singles, 65-99
M315	100-350cc OHC, 69-82
M317	125-250cc Elsinore, 73-80
M442	CR60-125R Pro-Link, 81-88
M431-2	CR80R, 89-95, CR125R, 89-91
M435	CR80R & CR80RB, 96-02
M457-2	CR125R, 92-97; CR250R, 92-96
M464	CR125R, 1998-2002
M443	CR250R-500R Pro-Link, 81-87
M432-3	CR250R, 88-91 & CR500R, 88-01
M437	CR250R, 97-01
M352	CRF250R, CRF250X, CRF450R & CRF450X, 02-05
M319-3	XR50R, CRF50F, XR70R & CRF70F, 97-09
M312-14	XL/XR75-100, 75-91
M222	XR80R, CRF80F, XR100R, & CRF100F, 92-09
M318-4	XL/XR/TLR 125-200, 79-03
M328-4	XL/XR250, 78-00; XL/XR350R 83-85; XR200R, 84-85; XR250L, 91-96
M320-2	XR400R, 96-04
M221	XR600R, 91-07; XR650L, 93-07
M339-8	XL/XR 500-600, 79-90
M225	XR650R, 00-07

Twins
M321	125-200cc Twins, 65-78
M322	250-350cc Twins, 64-74
M323	250-360cc Twins, 74-77
M324-5	Twinstar, Rebel 250 & Nighthawk 250, 78-03
M334	400-450cc Twins, 78-87
M333	450 & 500cc Twins, 65-76
M335	CX & GL500/650, 78-83
M344	VT500, 83-88
M313	VT700 & 750, 83-87
M314-3	VT750 Shadow Chain Drive, 98-06
M440	VT1100C Shadow, 85-96
M460-4	VT1100 Series, 95-07
M230	VTX1800 Series, 02-08
M231	VTX1300 Series, 03-09

Fours
M332	CB350-550, SOHC, 71-78
M345	CB550 & 650, 83-85
M336	CB650, 79-82
M341	CB750 SOHC, 69-78
M337	CB750 DOHC, 79-82
M436	CB750 Nighthawk, 91-93 & 95-99
M325	CB900, 1000 & 1100, 80-83
M439	600 Hurricane, 87-90
M441-2	CBR600F2 & F3, 91-98
M445-2	CBR600F4, 99-06
M220	CBR600RR, 03-06
M434-2	CBR900RR Fireblade, 93-99
M329	500cc V-Fours, 84-86
M349	700-1000cc Interceptor, 83-85
M458-2	VFR700F-750F, 86-97
M438	VFR800FI Interceptor, 98-00
M327	700-1100cc V-Fours, 82-88
M508	ST1100/Pan European, 90-02
M340	GL1000 & 1100, 75-83
M504	GL1200, 84-87

Sixes
M505	GL1500 Gold Wing, 88-92
M506-2	GL1500 Gold Wing, 93-00
M507-3	GL1800 Gold Wing, 01-10
M462-2	GL1500C Valkyrie, 97-03

KAWASAKI
ATVs
M465-3	Bayou KLF220 & KLF250, 88-10
M466-4	Bayou KLF300, 86-04
M467	Bayou KLF400, 93-99
M470	Lakota KEF300, 95-99
M385-2	Mojave KSF250, 87-04

Singles
M350-9	80-350cc Rotary Valve, 66-01
M444-2	KX60, 83-02; KX80 83-90
M448-2	KX80, 91-00; KX85, 01-10 & KX100, 89-09
M351	KDX200, 83-88
M447-3	KX125 & KX250, 82-91; KX500, 83-04
M472-2	KX125, 92-00
M473-2	KX250, 92-00
M474-3	KLR650, 87-07
M240-2	KLR650, 08-12

Twins
M355	KZ400, KZ/Z440, EN450 & EN500, 74-95
M241	Ninja 250R (EX250), 88-12
M360-3	EX500, GPZ500S, & Ninja 500R, 87-02
M356-5	Vulcan 700 & 750, 85-06
M354-3	Vulcan 800, 95-05
M246	Vulcan 900, 06-12
M357-2	Vulcan 1500, 87-99
M471-3	Vulcan 1500 Series, 96-08
M245	Vulcan 1600 Series, 03-08

Fours
M449	KZ500/550 & ZX550, 79-85
M450	KZ, Z & ZX750, 80-85
M358	KZ650, 77-83
M359-3	Z & KZ 900-1000cc, 73-81
M451-3	KZ, ZX & ZN 1000 & 1100cc, 81-02
M452-3	ZX500 & Ninja ZX600, 85-97
M468-2	Ninja ZX-6, 90-04
M469	Ninja ZX-7, ZX7R & ZX7RR, 91-98
M453-3	Ninja ZX900, ZX1000 & ZX1100, 84-01
M409-2	Concours, 86-06

POLARIS
ATVs
M496	3-, 4- and 6-Wheel Models w/250-425cc Engines, 85-95
M362-2	Magnum & Big Boss, 96-99
M363	Scrambler 500 4X4, 97-00
M365-5	Sportsman/Xplorer, 96-13
M366	Sportsman 600/700/800 Twins, 02-10
M367	Predator 500, 03-07

SUZUKI
ATVs
M381	ALT/LT 125 & 185, 83-87
M475	LT230 & LT250, 85-90
M380-2	LT250R Quad Racer, 85-92
M483-2	LT-4WD, LT-F4WDX & LT-F250, 87-98
M270-2	LT-Z400, 03-08
M343-2	LT-F500F Quadrunner, 98-02

Singles
M369	125-400cc, 64-81
M371	RM50-400 Twin Shock, 75-81
M379	RM125-500 Single Shock, 81-88
M386	RM80-250, 89-95
M400	RM125, 96-00
M401	RM250, 96-02
M476	DR250-350, 90-94
M477-4	DR-Z400E, S & SM, 00-12
M272	DR650, 96-12
M384-5	LS650 Savage/S40, 86-12

Twins
M372	GS400-450 Chain Drive, 77-87
M484-3	GS500E Twins, 89-02
M361	SV650, 1999-2002
M481-6	VS700-800 Intruder/S50, 85-09
M261-2	1500 Intruder/C90, 98-09
M260-3	Volusia/Boulevard C50, 01-11
M482-3	VS1400 Intruder/S83, 87-07

Triple
M368	GT380, 550 & 750, 72-77

Fours
M373	GS550, 77-86
M364	GS650, 81-83
M370	GS750, 77-82
M376	GS850-1100 Shaft Drive, 79-84
M378	GS1100 Chain Drive, 80-81
M383-3	Katana 600, 88-96 GSX-R750-1100, 86-87
M331	GSX-R600, 97-00
M264	GSX-R600, 01-05
M478-2	GSX-R750, 88-92; GSX750F Katana, 89-96
M485	GSX-R750, 96-99
M377	GSX-R1000, 01-04
M266	GSX-R1000, 05-06
M265	GSX1300R Hayabusa, 99-07
M338	Bandit 600, 95-00
M353	GSF1200 Bandit, 96-03

YAMAHA
ATVs
M499-2	YFM80 Moto-4, Badger & Raptor, 85-08
M394	YTM200, 225 & YFM200, 83-86
M488-5	Blaster, 88-05
M489-2	Timberwolf, 89-00
M487-5	Warrior, 87-04
M486-6	Banshee, 87-06
M490-3	Moto-4 & Big Bear, 87-04
M493	Kodiak, 93-98
M287-2	YFZ450, 04-13
M285-2	Grizzly 660, 02-08
M280-2	Raptor 660R, 01-05
M290	Raptor 700R, 06-09
M291	Rhino 700, 2008-2012

Singles
M492-2	PW50 & 80 Y-Zinger & BW80 Big Wheel 80, 81-02
M410	80-175 Piston Port, 68-76
M415	250-400 Piston Port, 68-76
M412	DT & MX Series, 77-83
M414	IT125-490, 76-86
M393	YZ50-80 Monoshock, 78-90
M413	YZ100-490 Monoshock, 76-84
M390	YZ125-250, 85-87 YZ490, 85-90
M391	YZ125-250, 88-93 & WR250Z, 91-93
M497-2	YZ125, 94-01
M498	YZ250, 94-98; WR250Z, 94-97
M406	YZ250F & WR250F, 01-03
M491-2	YZ400F, 98-99 & 426F, 00-02; WR400F, 98-00 & 426F, 00-01
M417	XT125-250, 80-84
M480-3	XT350, 85-00; TT350, 86-87
M405	XT/TT 500, 76-81
M416	XT/TT 600, 83-89

Twins
M403	650cc Twins, 70-82
M395-10	XV535-1100 Virago, 81-03
M495-7	V-Star 650, 98-11
M284	V-Star 950, 09-12
M281-4	V-Star 1100, 99-09
M283	V-Star 1300, 07-10
M282-2	Road Star, 99-07

Triple
M404	XS750 & XS850, 77-81

Fours
M387	XJ550, XJ600 & FJ600, 81-92
M494	XJ600 Seca II/Diversion, 92-98
M388	YX600 Radian & FZ600, 86-90
M396	FZR600, 89-93
M392	FZ700-750 & Fazer, 85-87
M411	XS1100, 78-81
M461	YZF-R6, 99-04
M398	YZF-R1, 98-03
M399	FZ1, 01-05
M397	FJ1100 & 1200, 84-93
M375-2	V-Max, 85-07
M374-2	Royal Star, 96-10

VINTAGE MOTORCYCLES
Clymer® Collection Series
M330	Vintage British Street Bikes, BSA 500–650cc Unit Twins; Norton 750 & 850cc Commandos; Triumph 500-750cc Twins
M300	Vintage Dirt Bikes, V. 1 Bultaco, 125-370cc Singles; Montesa, 123-360cc Singles; Ossa, 125-250cc Singles
M305	Vintage Japanese Street Bikes Honda, 250 & 305cc Twins; Kawasaki, 250-750cc Triples; Kawasaki, 900 & 1000cc Fours